VISUAL QUICKSTART GUIDE

Photoshop CS2

FOR WINDOWS AND MACINTOSH

Elaine Weinmann
Peter Lourekas

Peachpit Press

Visual QuickStart Guide
Photoshop CS2 for Windows and Macintosh
Elaine Weinmann and Peter Lourekas

Peachpit Press
1249 Eighth Street
Berkeley, CA 94710
510/524-2178
800/283-9444
510/524-2221 (fax)

Find us on the World Wide Web at: www.peachpit.com

Visual QuickStart Guide is a trademark of Peachpit Press, a division of Pearson Education

Cover design: Peachpit Press
Interior design: Elaine Weinmann
Production: Elaine Weinmann and Peter Lourekas
Illustrations: Elaine Weinmann and Peter Lourekas, except as noted

Colophon

This book was created with QuarkXPress 6.5 on two Power Macintosh G5s. The primary fonts used were New Baskerville and Myriad from Adobe Systems Inc.

ISBN 0-321-33655-0
9 8 7 6 5 4

Printed and bound in the United States of America

In loving memory of our mothers,
Bert Weinmann and Theodora Lourekas

Introduction

As the first edition of this book was published over a decade ago, we felt it was time to do some remodeling. But we didn't just give the book a facelift—we rebuilt it from the ground up!

New technology, new priorities

Digital cameras, desktop printers, and other technological advancements have inspired many innovations in Photoshop. As a result, some of the older program features are less relevant than they used to be, or have been surpassed by newer and better ones (such as the photo correction commands and retouching tools, which you'll read about in this edition). To reflect these changes, we created new chapters, sorted existing instructions into different chapters, threw some outdated instructions into the trash bin, and expanded or streamlined others.

Some Photoshop commands are indispensable to us, others we use occasionally, and still others, to be frank, we could happily toss into a "donate" pile. About all of the above, we speak our minds. To open files, for example, we use Bridge, not the Open command. To make tonal corrections, we sing the praises of the Levels and Shadow/Highlight commands and steer you clear of Brightness/Contrast (it just doesn't cut it any more).

New techniques

Over the course of numerous program upgrades, feature upon feature has been added to Photoshop—the new piled on the old. It's so crammed with options that you have numerous ways of performing a given task. Like most people, we like to get things done with as little sweat as possible, so we direct you to the most efficient route, and maybe one alternative—but not so many ways that you'll sit there scratching your head. Case in point: if you can get to a command via the menu bar, a context menu, and a palette menu, we list the context menu method first and maybe the palette menu as an alternate choice for a rainy day.

New ways to stay relaxed

Whether you're a beginner or long-time user of Photoshop, you'll enjoy its ever-increasing flexibility. You can edit (and delete) layers, type, masks, animation frames, layer comps, color swatches, paths, etc. You can reverse your editing steps via the History palette. You can apply colors, patterns, and gradients via editable and removable fill layers, apply a dozen adjustment commands via adjustment layers, and apply editable and removable layer effects. You can even retouch areas of an image by hand and send the results to a separate layer. Needless to say, if a task can be accomplished without commitment or making permanent changes to a file, we show you the way.

New look

For this edition, we created countless new images to illuminate the text. Who doesn't love a good makeover?

What's the same?

We're still dedicated to writing clear, easy-to-follow, heavily illustrated, and methodically tested instructions, and to explaining not just how features work but how they can be of service to you. Sadly, the improvements to this book have come at a cost: The garage is still a mess!

The story behind the book

Sometime in the mid-'80s, a smart guy in Berkeley, California, by the name of Ted Nace got a brainstorm. He decided to start up a computer book publishing company, which he called Peachpit Press (how he came up with the name is another story). The books he published were innovative and user-friendly and offered a fresh approach to learning computer graphics.

I (Elaine) found myself teaching a course in QuarkXPress not long thereafter, and I yearned for a book that would offer steps, like a recipe book, for learning various techniques. If nothing else, I thought, it would make my job easier. Then I got a brainstorm of my own. "What the heck, I have nothing to lose," I said to Peter, and made a cold call to Ted. I'd never written anything longer than a shopping list before, but I had an art background, teaching and practical experience under my belt, and enthusiasm in abundance, and Ted, bless him, let me take the plunge.

Ted supported innovation, not just in content, but also in production. He figured since many of his authors were experienced desktop publishers, why not let them typeset and illustrate their own books (what is known in the trade as "book packaging")? Although the rabbit logo was already on the cover of Peachpit's Visual QuickStart Guide series, the thumb tabs, tips, numbered steps, and other design features that you see in our books were my innovations, fine-tuned with Ted's feedback. I invited my husband, Peter, to come on board for the second book *(Photoshop 2.5: Visual QuickStart Guide)*, and our 24/7 partnership continues today.

Who does what

What started out as a serendipitous idea turned into a career. We write, rewrite, design, typeset, illustrate, and test all of our books, and when we're done sweating over all the nitpicky details and are ready to up the prescription on our reading glasses, we hand the electronic files off to the production folks at Peachpit Press for a final "preflight" check.

The first book *(QuarkXPress 3.1: Visual QuickStart Guide)*, nicknamed by Peter "the little book that could," was 200 pages long. As features are added to the software, revised editions of the books swell accordingly. Some things are easier now than in the old days, such as storing files and sending them hither and thither, but we still rely on other people to help us get the job done.

In 1996, Ted Nace handed the baton to his hand-picked successor, Nancy Aldrich-Ruenzel, who took the baton and ran with it. Under her energetic leadership, Peachpit Press continues to be a thriving and dynamic company.

And then there's Cary Norsworthy, our editor at Peachpit Press, who is always there when we need her. Victor Gavenda, our technical editor at Peachpit, tests the book in Windows and is an indispensable member of our team. Production Editor Lisa Brazieal spearheads the prepress production and then sends the files off to Malloy Lithographing. Peachpit Press is also lucky to have Editor-in-Chief Nancy Davis, Senior Executive Editor Marjorie Baer, Promotions Manager Gary-Paul Prince, and Associate Publisher Keasley Jones on staff, as well as other terrific people who now number too many to mention.

In our writing, testing, and book packaging "department," Nathan Olsen and Jeff Seaver helped us revise some chapters, Rebecca Pepper did the copy editing, Leona Benten did the final proofreading, and Steve Rath generated the index.

Thanks also to Carol Johnson and John Nack and other members of the Photoshop CS2 beta team for their efforts, and to the artists listed on the next page for letting us reprint their beautiful work.

On the home front, we'd like to thank our wonderful family of friends (you know who you are) for helping to give our lives whatever semblance of balance it has. And the biggest thanks of all go to our kids, simply for being there (you make it all worthwhile).

Elaine Weinmann and Peter Lourekas

History and Acknowledgements

Photo credits

We gratefully acknowledge the following companies and individuals for allowing us to use their images:

Photospin (photospin.com), pages 24, 87, 112, 165, 168, 171, 242, 243, 254, 257, 266, 267, 270, 276, 280, 364, 409, 420. All rights reserved.

PhotoDisc (Getty Images) (gettyimages.com), vii, 2, 10, 30, 36, 53, 56, 68, 69, 77, 99, 101, 103, 119, 124, 125, 127, 129, 136, 138, 141, 145, 147, 152, 162, 163, 171, 178, 179, 187, 191, 202, 207, 217, 219, 221, 222, 238, 241, 247, 248, 249, 261, 262, 263, 269, 278, 318, 319, 340, 341, 347, 361, 370, 408, 410, 412, 418, 419, 421, 475, 500, 502, 516, 524, 525, 539.

Corel Professional Photos, pages 295, 299.

Nolan Hester, page 273; **Nadine Markova** (Mexico City), pages 33, 169; **Paul Petroff** (Seattle, WA), pages 123, 127, 174, 177, 281; **Cara Wood** (Poughkeepsie, NY), page 253.

Ultimate Symbol (ultimatesymbol.com), vector path, page 321.

All other images © Elaine Weinmann or Peter Lourekas.

Directory of artists

Clifford Alejandro
voice 201-451-0441
www.oldtin.com
(color section)

Marty Blake
Box 266
2043 Jamesville Terrace
Jamesville, NY 13078
voice 315-492-1332
fax 315-469-5907
mblake01@twcny.rr.com
www.martyblakedesign.com
(color section)

Nina Fuller
www.ninafuller.net
(page 153)

Wendy Grossman
www.rosebudstudios.com
(page 84)

John Kachik
7540 Main St., Suite 11C
Sykesville, MD 21784
voice 410-552-1900
fax 410-552-6645
kachik@adelphia.net
www.johnkachik.com
(color section)

William Low
voice/fax 631-421-5859
info@williamlow.com
www.williamlow.com
(color section)

Paul Mirocha
425 East 17th St.
Tucson, AZ 85701
voice/fax 520-623-1515
paul@paulmirocha.com
www.paulmirocha.com
(color section)

Bert Monroy
bert@bertmonroy.com
www.bertmonroy.com
(color section)

Keri Smith
voice 519-924-3535
info@kerismith.com
www.kerismith.com
(color section)

Mick Wiggins
Mick Wiggins Illustration
www.mickwiggins.com
(color section)

©Elaine Weinmann

TABLE OF CONTENTS

AT A GLANCE

At a Glance

THE WHOLE ENCHILADA

Note: New or changed features are identified by this symbol: ✔

Table of Contents

xv

Table of Contents

Table of Contents

Table of Contents

PHOTOSHOP INTERFACE 1

Too hearty a welcome?

When you launch Photoshop, a welcome screen pops up, offering you access to a list of new features, an online tutorial, etc. If you get tired of seeing it, uncheck **Show this dialog at startup.**

1 *In Windows, click* ***Adobe Photoshop CS2.***

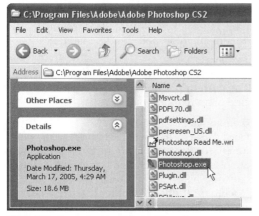

2 *In Windows, double-click the Photoshop* ***application*** *icon.*

Adobe Photoshop CS2

3 *In Mac, click the* ***Adobe Photoshop CS2*** *icon in the Dock.*

Welcome to Photoshop CS2!

In this chapter (which is more of a read than a do), you'll learn how to launch Photoshop and get acquainted with the Photoshop interface—menus, tools, palettes, lingo, and whatnot. You can use this chapter as a reference guide as you work. The next chapter, which is an introduction to color in Photoshop, is more theory than technique, too—but from Chapter 3 onward it's non-stop action.

To launch Photoshop in Windows:

In Windows 2000 or XP, click the Start button on the taskbar, choose All Programs, then click Adobe Photoshop CS2 **1**.

or

Open the C:\Program Files\Adobe\Adobe Photoshop CS2 folder in My Computer, then double-click the Photoshop application icon **2**.

or

Double-click a Photoshop file icon.

To launch Photoshop in Macintosh:

In Mac, click the Photoshop icon in the Dock **3**. (If you don't have an icon there yet, open the Adobe Photoshop CS2 folder in the Applications folder, then drag the Adobe Photoshop CS2 application icon into the Dock.)

or

Open the Adobe Photoshop CS2 folder in the Applications folder, then double-click the Adobe Photoshop CS2 application icon.

or

Double-click any Photoshop file icon.

The Photoshop screen in Macintosh

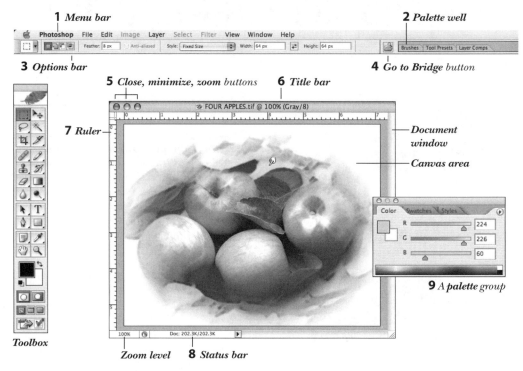

1 *Menu bar*

2 *Palette well*

3 *Options bar*

4 *Go to Bridge button*

5 *Close, minimize, zoom buttons*

6 *Title bar*

7 *Ruler*

Document window

Canvas area

9 *A palette group*

Toolbox

Zoom level

8 *Status bar*

Key to the Photoshop screen: Macintosh and Windows features

1 *Menu bar*
Press any menu heading to access dialog boxes, submenus, and commands. Palettes also have menus. Many commands can also be chosen via context menus.

2 *Palette well*
Use to dock (store) and open palettes.

3 *Options bar*
Use to choose settings for the current tool.

4 *Go to Bridge*
Click this button to go to Bridge, a separate application used for opening and sorting files.

5 *Close, minimize, and zoom buttons (Mac only)*
Click the close (red) button to close a file or a palette. Click the minimize (yellow) button to stow a file in the Dock. Click the zoom (green) button to enlarge a window to its maximum size, or on a palette to show/hide extra options.

6 *Title bar*
Displays, in order, a tiny thumbnail of the image (Mac only), the document title, zoom

level, current layer (or the Background), document color mode, and bit depth.

7 *Rulers*
Choose View > Rulers to show/hide the rulers. The current position of the pointer is indicated by a marker on each ruler.

8 *Status bar*
Click the arrowhead at the bottom of the document window, and from the Show submenu, choose which information you want the status bar to display: Version Cue, Document Sizes, Document Profile, Document Dimensions, Scratch Sizes, Efficiency (the percentage of time Photoshop is processing edits, as opposed to writing to the scratch disk), Timing, Current Tool, or 32-bit Exposure. (To reset the timer, choose Timing with Alt/Option held down.)

9 *Palettes*
There are 19 movable palettes. Most palettes are used for image editing; a few, such as Info and Histogram, provide information only.

Photoshop Screen

The Photoshop screen in Windows

1 *Application Control menu*

Menu bar

Options bar

4 *Application close button*

3 *Application maximize button*

2 *Application minimize button*

Go to Bridge button

Document Control menu

Title bar

Document minimize button

Document close button

Palette well

Document maximize button

Document window

Palette group

Toolbox

Palette group

Status bar

A minimized window, showing the restore button

Photoshop Screen

Key to the Photoshop screen: Windows-only features
(for other Windows features, see the previous page)

1 *Application (or document) Control menu*
The application Control menu commands are Restore, Move, Size, Minimize, Maximize, and Close. The document Control menu commands are Restore, Move, Size, Minimize, Maximize, Close, and Next.

2 *Application (or document) minimize button*
Click the application minimize button to shrink the document to an icon in the taskbar. Click the icon on the taskbar to restore the application window to its previous size.

Click the document minimize button to shrink the document to an icon at the lower left corner of the application window. Click the restore button to restore the document window to its previous size.

3 *Application (or document) maximize/restore button*
Click the application or document maximize button to enlarge a window to its largest possible size. Click the restore button to restore a window to its previous size. When a window is at the restored size, the restore button turns into a maximize button.

4 *Application (or document) close button*
Closes the application (or document).

The menus

Photoshop	
About Photoshop...	
About Plug-In	▶
Preferences	▶
Services	▶
Hide Photoshop	^⌘H
Hide Others	⌥⌘H
Show All	
Quit Photoshop	⌘Q

File	
New...	⌘N
Open...	⌘O
Browse...	⌥⌘O
Open Recent	▶
Edit in ImageReady	⇧⌘M
Close	⌘W
Close All	⌥⌘W
Close and Go To Bridge...	⇧⌘W
Save	⌘S
Save As...	⇧⌘S
Save a Version...	
Save for Web...	⌥⇧⌘S
Revert	F12
Place...	
Import	▶
Export	▶
Automate	▶
Scripts	▶
File Info...	⌥⇧⌘I
Page Setup...	⇧⌘P
Print with Preview...	⌥⌘P
Print...	⌘P
Print One Copy	⌥⇧⌘P
Print Online...	
Jump To	▶

*In Windows, **Open As** and **Exit** are on the File menu.*

Edit	
Undo Crystallize	⌘Z
Step Forward	⇧⌘Z
Step Backward	⌥⌘Z
Fade Crystallize...	⇧⌘F
Cut	⌘X
Copy	⌘C
Copy Merged	⇧⌘C
Paste	⌘V
Paste Into	⇧⌘V
Clear	
Check Spelling...	
Find and Replace Text...	
Fill...	⇧F5
Stroke...	
Free Transform	⌘T
Transform	▶
Define Brush Preset...	
Define Pattern...	
Define Custom Shape...	
Purge	▶
Adobe PDF Presets...	
Preset Manager...	
Color Settings...	⇧⌘K
Assign Profile...	
Convert to Profile...	
Keyboard Shortcuts...	⌥⇧⌘K
Menus...	⌥⇧⌘M

*In Windows, **Preferences** is on the Edit menu.*

Image	
Mode	▶
Adjustments	▶
Duplicate...	
Apply Image...	
Calculations...	
Image Size...	⌥⌘I
Canvas Size...	⌥⌘C
Pixel Aspect Ratio	▶
Rotate Canvas	▶
Crop	
Trim...	
Reveal All	
Variables	▶
Apply Data Set...	
Trap...	

Layer	
New	▶
Duplicate Layer...	
Delete	▶
Layer Properties...	
Layer Style	▶
New Fill Layer	▶
New Adjustment Layer	▶
Change Layer Content	▶
Layer Content Options...	
Layer Mask	▶
Vector Mask	▶
Create Clipping Mask	⌥⌘G
Smart Objects	▶
Type	▶
Rasterize	▶
New Layer Based Slice	
Group Layers	⌘G
Ungroup Layers	⇧⌘G
Hide Layers	
Arrange	▶
Align	▶
Distribute	▶
Lock All Layers in Group...	
Link Layers	
Select Linked Layers	
Merge Down	⌘E
Merge Visible	⇧⌘E
Flatten Image	
Matting	▶

Select

All	⌘A
Deselect	⌘D
Reselect	⇧⌘D
Inverse	⇧⌘I
All Layers	⌥⌘A
Deselect Layers	
Similar Layers	
Color Range...	
Feather...	⌥⌘D
Modify	▶
Grow	
Similar	
Transform Selection	
Load Selection...	
Save Selection...	

Filter

Last Filter	⌘F
Extract...	⌥⌘X
Filter Gallery...	
Liquify...	⇧⌘X
Pattern Maker...	⌥⇧⌘X
Vanishing Point...	⌥⌘V
Artistic	▶
Blur	▶
Brush Strokes	▶
Distort	▶
Noise	▶
Pixelate	▶
Render	▶
Sharpen	▶
Sketch	▶
Stylize	▶
Texture	▶
Video	▶
Other	▶
Digimarc	▶

View

Proof Setup	▶
Proof Colors	⌘Y
Gamut Warning	⇧⌘Y
Pixel Aspect Ratio Correction	
32-bit Preview Options...	
Zoom In	⌘+
Zoom Out	⌘-
Fit on Screen	⌘0
Actual Pixels	⌥⌘0
Print Size	
Screen Mode	▶
✓ Extras	⌘H
Show	▶
✓ Rulers	⌘R
✓ Snap	⇧⌘;
Snap To	▶
Lock Guides	⌥⌘;
Clear Guides	
New Guide...	
Lock Slices	
Clear Slices	

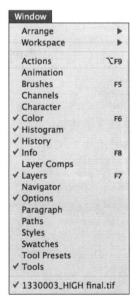

Window

Arrange	▶
Workspace	▶
Actions	⌥F9
Animation	
Brushes	F5
Channels	
Character	
✓ Color	F6
✓ Histogram	
✓ History	
✓ Info	F8
Layer Comps	
✓ Layers	F7
Navigator	
✓ Options	
Paragraph	
Paths	
Styles	
Swatches	
Tool Presets	
✓ Tools	
✓ 1330003_HIGH final.tif	

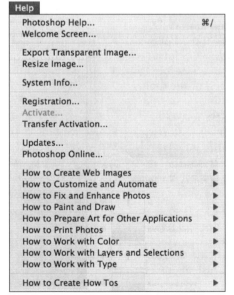

Help

Photoshop Help...	⌘/
Welcome Screen...	
Export Transparent Image...	
Resize Image...	
System Info...	
Registration...	
Activate...	
Transfer Activation...	
Updates...	
Photoshop Online...	
How to Create Web Images	▶
How to Customize and Automate	▶
How to Fix and Enhance Photos	▶
How to Paint and Draw	▶
How to Prepare Art for Other Applications	▶
How to Print Photos	▶
How to Work with Color	▶
How to Work with Layers and Selections	▶
How to Work with Type	▶
How to Create How Tos	▶

In Windows, **About Photoshop** *and* **About Plug-In** *are on the Help menu.*

Menus

The Toolbox

Using the Toolbox

The tools in the Toolbox are used for object creation and editing. If the Toolbox is hidden, choose Window > **Tools** to display it.

To **choose** a tool whose icon is already visible, click once on its icon. Click the tiny arrowhead next to a tool icon to choose a related tool from a pop-out menu. Or even better, choose a tool using its shortcut. Tool shortcuts are listed as boldface letters on the next four pages, and in onscreen tool tips ■. See also "Toolbox shortcuts" at right.

 To learn about a tool's function as you're using it, look at the bottom of the **Info** palette (see page 21). (If no tool information is listed, choose Palette Options from the Info palette menu, then check Show Tool Hints.) Tool tips and helpful usage information are also available for tools in some dialog boxes, such as Extract and Pattern Maker.

Attributes (e.g., brush preset, blending mode, opacity percentage) are chosen for each tool from the **options bar** at the top of your screen (see page 11) ■. (If the options bar is hidden, choose Window > Options.) Options bar settings remain in effect for each tool until they're changed or the tool is reset. You can save tool settings as presets via the **Tool Presets** palette (see page 28).

To reset the default settings for a tool, right-click/Control-click the tool thumbnail on the options bar, then choose **Reset Tool** from the context menu ■. To reset all tools, choose **Reset All Tools** from the same menu.

In Preferences (Ctrl-K/Cmd-K) > Display & Cursors, you can choose to have tool **pointers** look like their Toolbox icon or a crosshair or, for some tools, a circle the size, or half the size, of the current brush diameter.

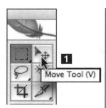

Tool tips

If **Show Tool Tips** is checked in Preferences > General and you rest the pointer on a tool icon without clicking the mouse button, the tool name and shortcut will pop up onscreen ■. Use the same method to learn the function of palette, options bar ■, or dialog box features.

Toolbox shortcuts

Cycle through hidden, related **tools** on the same pop-out menu	Shift plus shortcut key* or Alt-click/Option-click the currently visible tool
Cycle through blending **modes** for the current editing tool or layer	Shift-+ (plus) or Shift - - (minus)
Hide/show the **Toolbox** and all open **palettes**	Tab

__Use Shift Key for Tool Switch__ must be checked in Preferences > General.

■ *Right-click/Control-click the current tool thumbnail on the options bar to access these commands.*

■ *Choose options for the current tool from the **options bar** at the top of your screen.*

Using the Toolbox

Tools on the Toolbox

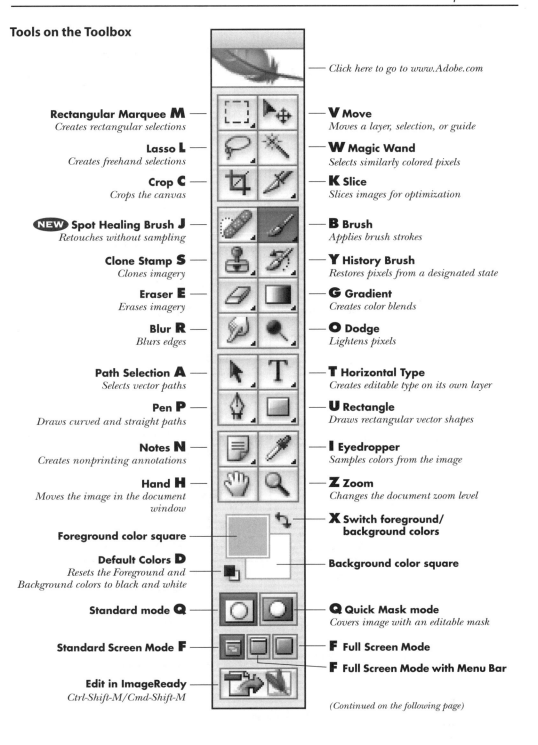

Click here to go to www.Adobe.com

Rectangular Marquee M
Creates rectangular selections

V Move
Moves a layer, selection, or guide

Lasso L
Creates freehand selections

W Magic Wand
Selects similarly colored pixels

Crop C
Crops the canvas

K Slice
Slices images for optimization

NEW Spot Healing Brush J
Retouches without sampling

B Brush
Applies brush strokes

Clone Stamp S
Clones imagery

Y History Brush
Restores pixels from a designated state

Eraser E
Erases imagery

G Gradient
Creates color blends

Blur R
Blurs edges

O Dodge
Lightens pixels

Path Selection A
Selects vector paths

T Horizontal Type
Creates editable type on its own layer

Pen P
Draws curved and straight paths

U Rectangle
Draws rectangular vector shapes

Notes N
Creates nonprinting annotations

I Eyedropper
Samples colors from the image

Hand H
Moves the image in the document window

Z Zoom
Changes the document zoom level

Foreground color square

X Switch foreground/ background colors

Default Colors D
Resets the Foreground and Background colors to black and white

Background color square

Standard mode Q

Q Quick Mask mode
Covers image with an editable mask

Standard Screen Mode F

F Full Screen Mode

F Full Screen Mode with Menu Bar

Edit in ImageReady
Ctrl-Shift-M/Cmd-Shift-M

Toolbox

(Continued on the following page)

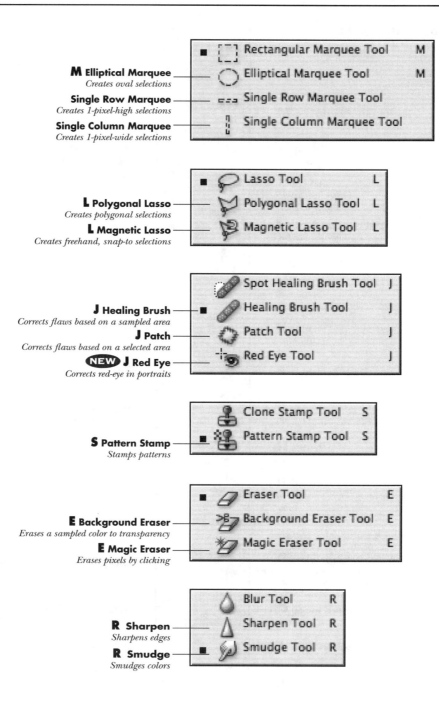

M Elliptical Marquee
Creates oval selections

Single Row Marquee
Creates 1-pixel-high selections

Single Column Marquee
Creates 1-pixel-wide selections

- Rectangular Marquee Tool   M
- Elliptical Marquee Tool   M
- Single Row Marquee Tool
- Single Column Marquee Tool

L Polygonal Lasso
Creates polygonal selections

L Magnetic Lasso
Creates freehand, snap-to selections

- Lasso Tool   L
- Polygonal Lasso Tool   L
- Magnetic Lasso Tool   L

J Healing Brush
Corrects flaws based on a sampled area

J Patch
Corrects flaws based on a selected area

NEW J Red Eye
Corrects red-eye in portraits

- Spot Healing Brush Tool   J
- Healing Brush Tool   J
- Patch Tool   J
- Red Eye Tool   J

S Pattern Stamp
Stamps patterns

- Clone Stamp Tool   S
- Pattern Stamp Tool   S

E Background Eraser
Erases a sampled color to transparency

E Magic Eraser
Erases pixels by clicking

- Eraser Tool   E
- Background Eraser Tool   E
- Magic Eraser Tool   E

R Sharpen
Sharpens edges

R Smudge
Smudges colors

- Blur Tool   R
- Sharpen Tool   R
- Smudge Tool   R

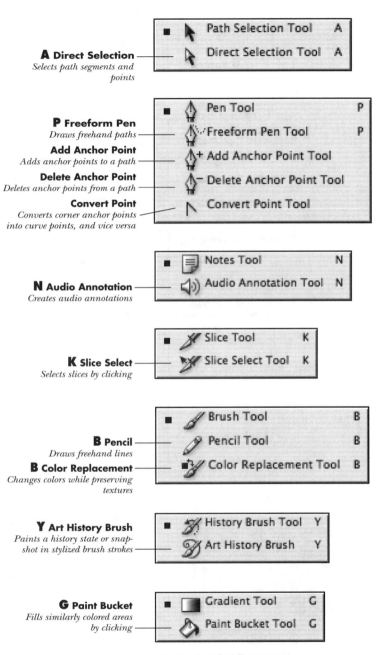

A Direct Selection
Selects path segments and points

- Path Selection Tool   A
- Direct Selection Tool   A

P Freeform Pen
Draws freehand paths

Add Anchor Point
Adds anchor points to a path

Delete Anchor Point
Deletes anchor points from a path

Convert Point
Converts corner anchor points into curve points, and vice versa

- Pen Tool   P
- Freeform Pen Tool   P
- Add Anchor Point Tool
- Delete Anchor Point Tool
- Convert Point Tool

N Audio Annotation
Creates audio annotations

- Notes Tool   N
- Audio Annotation Tool   N

K Slice Select
Selects slices by clicking

- Slice Tool   K
- Slice Select Tool   K

B Pencil
Draws freehand lines

B Color Replacement
Changes colors while preserving textures

- Brush Tool   B
- Pencil Tool   B
- Color Replacement Tool   B

Y Art History Brush
Paints a history state or snapshot in stylized brush strokes

- History Brush Tool   Y
- Art History Brush   Y

G Paint Bucket
Fills similarly colored areas by clicking

- Gradient Tool   G
- Paint Bucket Tool   G

(Continued on the following page)

Tool Pop-Out Menus

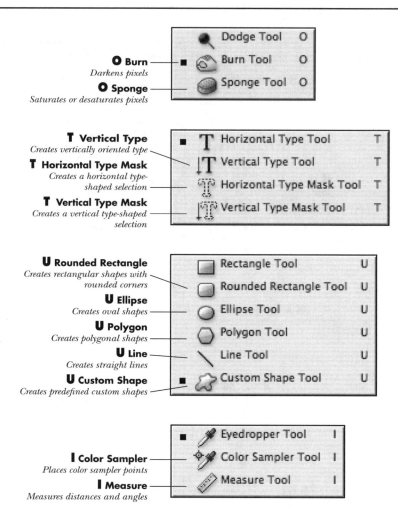

O Burn
Darkens pixels

O Sponge
Saturates or desaturates pixels

Dodge Tool   O
Burn Tool   O
Sponge Tool   O

T Vertical Type
Creates vertically oriented type

T Horizontal Type Mask
Creates a horizontal type-shaped selection

T Vertical Type Mask
Creates a vertical type-shaped selection

Horizontal Type Tool   T
Vertical Type Tool   T
Horizontal Type Mask Tool   T
Vertical Type Mask Tool   T

U Rounded Rectangle
Creates rectangular shapes with rounded corners

U Ellipse
Creates oval shapes

U Polygon
Creates polygonal shapes

U Line
Creates straight lines

U Custom Shape
Creates predefined custom shapes

Rectangle Tool   U
Rounded Rectangle Tool   U
Ellipse Tool   U
Polygon Tool   U
Line Tool   U
Custom Shape Tool   U

I Color Sampler
Places color sampler points

I Measure
Measures distances and angles

Eyedropper Tool   I
Color Sampler Tool   I
Measure Tool   I

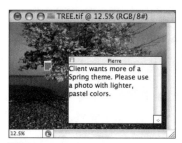

1 *An **annotation** created with the **Notes** tool*

Annotate

The **Notes** tool creates nonprinting Acrobat-compatible notes, which can be used for communicating with a client, output service, etc. **1** When you click a note icon, a note window containing the message opens. The **Audio Annotation** tool creates audio notes.

Change your values

For most options that have a field for entering numerical values, you can also change the value simply by **dragging** slightly to the left or right over the option name, such as Width and Height in dialog boxes, Opacity and Fill on the Layers palette, Input and Output levels in the Levels dialog box, Fuzziness in the Color Range dialog box, and many options bar settings.

To use a **pop-up slider** ▮, click the arrowhead, then drag the slider. To close a slider, click anywhere outside it or press Enter/Return. If you click the arrowhead to open a slider, pressing Esc will restore the last setting.

Options bar

You'll use the options bar to choose settings (e.g., opacity, flow, blending mode) for each tool **2**–**6**. Features on the bar change depending on which tool is being used, and your choices remain in effect until you change them. Like the palettes, the options bar can be dragged to a different part of your screen. Double-click the left edge of the options bar to collapse/expand it. The palette well on the options bar is discussed on the next page.

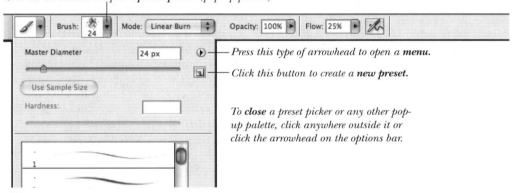

▮ *A pop-up slider on the options bar*

Click the arrowhead to open a ***preset picker*** *(pop-up palette).*

Press this type of arrowhead to open a ***menu***.

Click this button to create a ***new preset***.

To ***close*** *a preset picker or any other pop-up palette, click anywhere outside it or click the arrowhead on the options bar.*

2 *The options bar for the* ***Brush*** *tool*

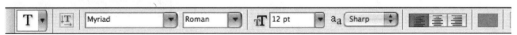

3 *The options bar for the* ***Rectangular Marquee*** *tool*

4 *The options bar for the* ***Gradient*** *tool*

5 *The options bar for the* ***Pen*** *tool*

6 *The options bar for the* ***Type*** *tool*

Options Bar

The palettes

Using the palettes

Many Photoshop operations are triggered by choosing commands on movable palettes. To save screen space, the palettes are joined into default **groups,** such as History/Actions and Color/Swatches/Styles.

You can **dock** (store) palettes in the **palette well** on the right side of the options bar either by dragging the palette into the well **1** or by choosing Dock to Palette Well from the palette menu.

To **open** a palette, choose its name from the Window menu, or click its tab in the palette well, or press its assigned shortcut. The palette will appear in front within its group. A palette that is open but obscured by another palette will have a "–" by its name on the Window menu.

For some tools, you can click the **Toggle palette** button 📄 on the options bar to show/hide a palette that's normally used by that tool (e.g., the Brushes palette is used by the Pencil tool, the Character palette is

used by the type tools). To display a hidden palette in a group, click its tab. To create workspaces that remember which palettes are open, see pages 91–92.

To reset the palettes to their default locations, choose Window > Workspace > **Reset Palette Locations.**

To **show/hide** all open palettes, including the Toolbox, press Tab. To show/hide all open palettes except the Toolbox, press Shift-Tab.

To **separate** a palette from its group, drag its tab out of the group **2–3**; to **add** a palette to a group, drag the tab into the group. You can widen most palettes to make additional tabs visible by dragging the palette **resize** box in the lower right corner.

To **shrink/expand** a palette, double-click its tab. In Windows, you can also click the palette minimize/maximize button. If the palette isn't at its default size, click the minimize box/zoom (green) button once to restore its default size, then click it again to shrink the palette.

TIP Click in any field in a palette or dialog box, then press the up or down arrow to change the value incrementally.

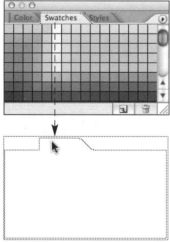

2 *To **separate** a palette from its group, drag the tab (palette name) away from the group.*

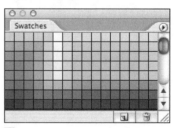

3 *The Swatches palette is now on its own.*

Actions palette

You can automate repetitive editing steps and tasks by recording a series of commands in an action and then replaying your action on one image or on a batch of images. The Actions palette is used for recording, storing, editing, replaying, deleting, and loading actions.

The game plan

The palettes are illustrated in alphabetical order beginning on this page, except for the indispensable Toolbox, which is illustrated on pages 7–10, and the options bar, which is illustrated on page 11.

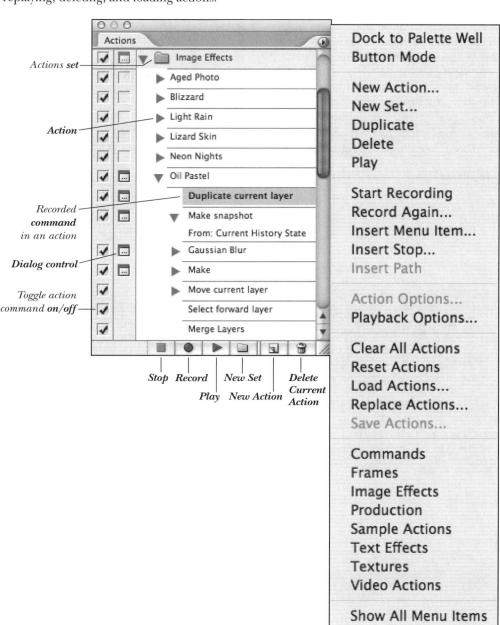

Actions set

Action

Recorded command in an action

Dialog control

Toggle action command on/off

Stop   Record   New Set   Delete Current Action

Play   New Action

Dock to Palette Well
Button Mode

New Action...
New Set...
Duplicate
Delete
Play

Start Recording
Record Again...
Insert Menu Item...
Insert Stop...
Insert Path

Action Options...
Playback Options...

Clear All Actions
Reset Actions
Load Actions...
Replace Actions...
Save Actions...

Commands
Frames
Image Effects
Production
Sample Actions
Text Effects
Textures
Video Actions

Show All Menu Items

Actions Palette

Animation palette

The Animation palette lets you create GIF animations by "recording" the current state of layers on the Layers palette. First, imagery is placed onto separate layers on the Layers palette. The first animation frame on the Animation palette is created automatically, and reflects the original condition of the layers. For each additional animation frame that's created, modifications are made to a layer (e.g., a change in position, opacity, or effects). In-between ("tween") frames are also added to smooth the transitions between layer states.

In Photoshop CS, the Animation palette was available only in ImageReady; now it's available in both Photoshop CS2 and ImageReady.

Animation palette menu

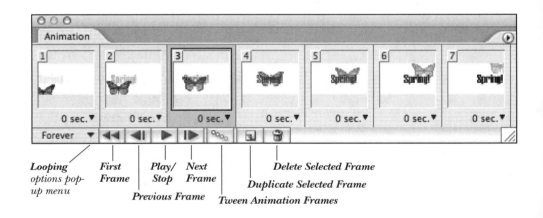

Brushes palette

The Brushes palette is used for choosing and customizing brush tips for the Brush, Pencil, Clone Stamp, Pattern Stamp, History Brush, Art History Brush, Eraser, Blur, Sharpen, Smudge, Dodge, Burn, and Sponge tools. You can also use this palette to choose options for a stylus. Click a category on the left side of the palette to display that panel.

TIP The numeral below a brush tip icon is the diameter of the tip, in pixels.

1 *Click either spot to open the* **Brush Preset picker***.*

Picker or palette?

Brush tips for the painting and editing tools can be chosen from either the **Brushes palette** (shown below) or the **Brush Preset picker,** a pop-up palette that opens from the options bar **1**. To store the Brushes palette for easy retrieval, dock it in the palette well on the options bar; to redisplay it, click the palette tab in the well. To close the Brush Preset picker, click outside it or click the Brush arrowhead again.

Commands for **loading, appending,** and **saving** brushes and brush libraries can be chosen from the Brushes palette menu or the Brush Preset picker menu (click the palette menu button ⊙ on the right side).

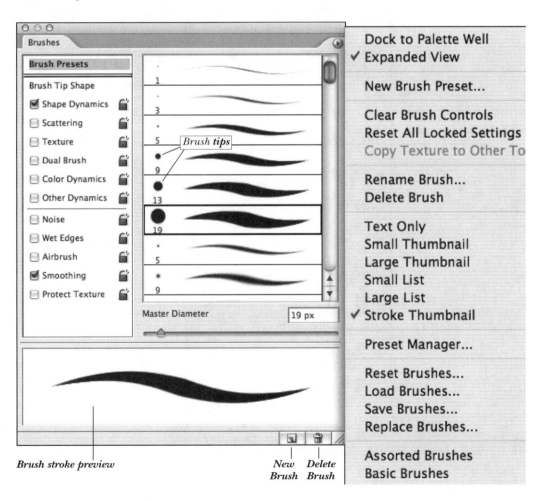

Brush stroke preview

New Brush *Delete Brush*

Brushes Palette

Channels palette

The Channels palette lists the color channels that make up an image. To display one of the channels by itself in the document window, click its name or press the keystroke listed on the palette. To redisplay the composite channel (e.g., RGB or CMYK), click the topmost channel on the palette, or press Ctrl-~/Cmd-~ (tilde).

This palette is also used for creating and displaying alpha channels, which are saved selections, as well as spot color channels, which are used for producing individual spot color plates.

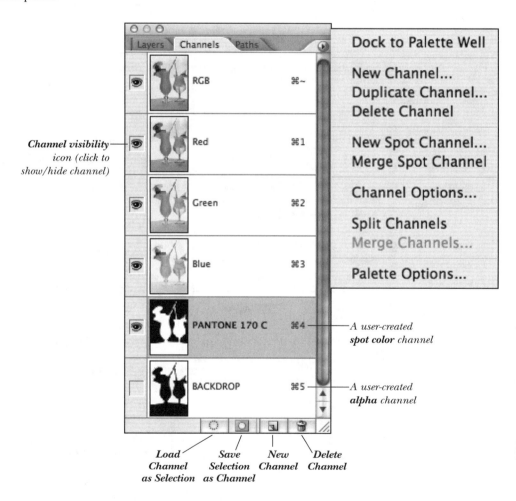

Channel visibility icon (click to show/hide channel)

A user-created **spot color** *channel*

A user-created **alpha** *channel*

Load Channel as Selection   *Save Selection as Channel*   *New Channel*   *Delete Channel*

Dock to Palette Well

New Channel...
Duplicate Channel...
Delete Channel

New Spot Channel...
Merge Spot Channel

Channel Options...

Split Channels
Merge Channels...

Palette Options...

Channels Palette

Character palette

Type attributes can be chosen for a type tool via the Character palette, illustrated below, or from the options bar.

You can open the Character palette from the Window menu or by clicking the 🔳 button on the options bar when a type tool is selected.

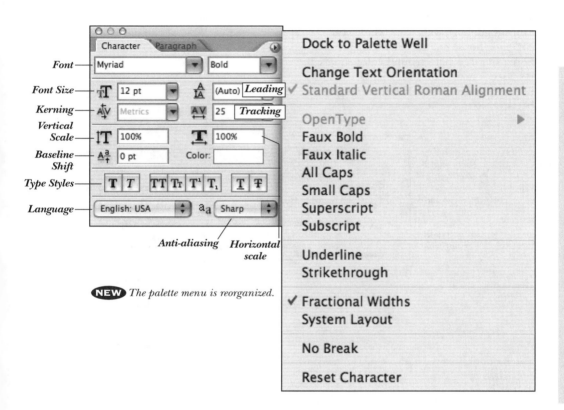

Font

Font Size

Kerning

Vertical Scale

Baseline Shift

Type Styles

Language

Anti-aliasing   Horizontal scale

NEW *The palette menu is reorganized.*

Color palette

The Color palette is used for mixing and choosing colors. Colors are applied via painting and editing tools and via commands such as Fill or Canvas Size. Choose a color model for the sliders or color bar from the palette menu. Mix a color using the sliders, or quick-select a color by clicking the color bar.

To open the Color Picker (or Color Libraries dialog box), from which you can also choose colors, click once on the Foreground or Background color square if it's already active, or double-click the square if it's not active. The active square has a black border.

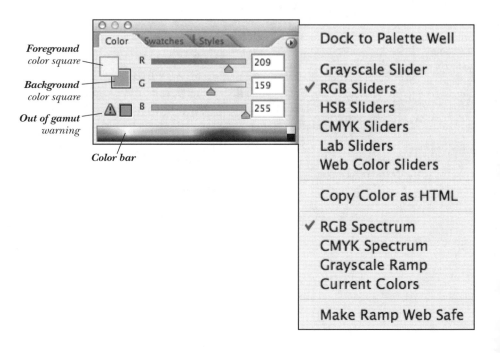

Foreground color square

Background color square

Out of gamut warning

Color bar

Dock to Palette Well

Grayscale Slider
✓ RGB Sliders
HSB Sliders
CMYK Sliders
Lab Sliders
Web Color Sliders

Copy Color as HTML

✓ RGB Spectrum
CMYK Spectrum
Grayscale Ramp
Current Colors

Make Ramp Web Safe

Histogram palette

The Histogram palette diagrams either just
the current light and dark values of an
image, or its current and modified light and
dark values as it's being edited or while an
adjustment dialog box is open. It's used only
for reference.

Via the Channel pop-up menu, you can
choose to have the palette display information about the composite channel (combined channels) or about just one channel.
You can also expand the palette to display
histograms for every channel.

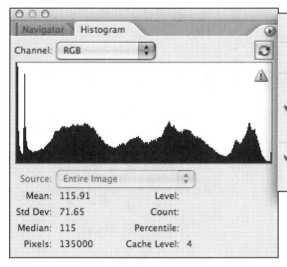

History palette

You can use the History palette to reverse editing steps in a work session. Each brush stroke, filter application, or other image-editing command is listed as a separate state on the palette, with the bottommost state being the most recent. Clicking a prior state restores the document to that stage of the editing process. What happens to the document when you click a prior state depends on whether the palette is in linear or nonlinear mode.

In linear mode, if you click an earlier state and resume image editing from that state, or delete the state, all subsequent (dimmed) states are discarded. In nonlinear mode, you can click an earlier edit state or delete a state without losing subsequent states. To put the palette in nonlinear mode, choose History Options from the palette menu, then check Allow Non-Linear History in the History Options dialog box; for linear mode, uncheck the box. You can switch between these modes at any time during an editing session.

The New Snapshot command creates a state that stays on the palette until the image is closed.

The History Brush tool restores an area of an image to a designated prior state where it's dragged in the document window. The Art History Brush does the same thing, but in stylized strokes.

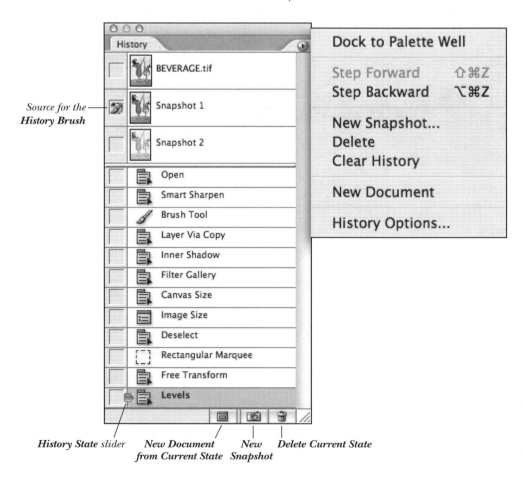

Source for the ***History Brush***

History State slider   ***New Document from Current State***   ***New Snapshot***   ***Delete Current State***

Info palette

The Info palette displays a color breakdown of the pixel currently under the pointer in the document window. While a color adjustment dialog box is open, the palette displays before and after color readouts. The Info palette also lists the *x/y* location of the pointer on the image.

Other information may display on the palette depending on which tool is being used, such as the distance between points when a selection is moved, a shape is drawn, or the Measure tool is used; the dimensions of a selection or crop marquee; or the width (W), height (H), angle (A), and horizontal skew (H) or vertical skew (V) of a layer, selection, or vector object as it's being transformed. The palette will also show readouts for up to four color samplers, if they're placed on the image.

Press one of the tiny arrowheads to choose a color model for that readout (it can differ from the current document color mode). Or to do this via a dialog box, choose Palette Options from the palette menu, then change the mode for the First Color Readout and Second Color Readout **1**.

In the Info Palette Options dialog box, you can also change the Ruler Units for the palette (Mouse Coordinates); check what **NEW** Status Information you want displayed in the lower part of the palette; and check Show Tool Hints to allow interactive information about the current tool or edit to display.

You can click the arrowhead for the X/Y readout to choose a different unit of measurement for the palette and rulers.

Color breakdown for the pixel currently under the pointer

Click the arrowhead to choose a different color model for that readout.

Width and Height of the current selection

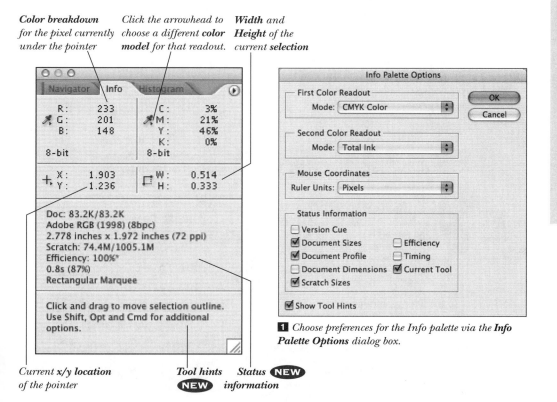

Current x/y location of the pointer

Tool hints **NEW**

Status **NEW** *information*

1 *Choose preferences for the Info palette via the Info Palette Options dialog box.*

Layer Comps palette

A layer comp (short for "composition") is a set of layer characteristics, including visibility (whether the layer is showing or hidden), position, and appearance (any applied layer styles, including the layer blending mode).

The Layer Comps palette provides a convenient palette mechanism for displaying multiple versions of the same image. This comes in handy when you need to decide between several versions, or when you need to present design variations to a client. For example, let's say you were creating a book cover for a client, and they wanted to see it with or without letttering, or with the lettering or background image in two different colors. You could make each version into a layer comp, and in a meeting with your client, instead of having to open and close separate files, you could display one version after another simply by clicking the Apply Layer Comp icon on or off in the left column on the palette.

Layer comps save with the document in which they're created. Whereas histories affect all editing done to an image but can't be saved, layer comps can be saved but let you display only specific layer options and settings.

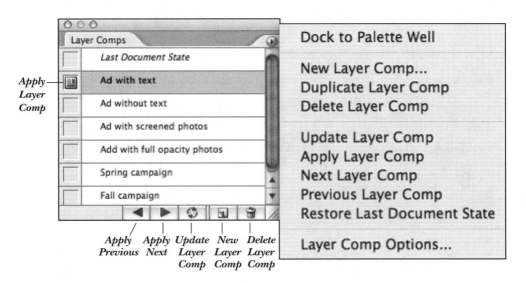

Layers palette

Every new image starts out with either a solid-color Background or a transparent layer (see pages 61–62), on top of which you can add more layers. Using the Layers palette, you can show/hide, duplicate, group, link, delete, or restack layers, as well as change their blending mode, layer opacity, and fill opacity. You'll use this workhorse palette all the time!

In addition to image layers, you can also create other kinds of layers: fill and adjustment layers, which are used for applying temporary color or tonal adjustments to underlying layers; editable type layers, which are created automatically when the Horizontal Type or Vertical Type tool is used; and shape layers, which contain vector shapes.

A smart object layer is generated when you bring an Illustrator vector file, another Photoshop file, or a digital Raw file into a Photoshop document via File > Place. If you double-click a smart object layer, the object reopens in its original application for editing; when you save and close it, the object updates in the Photoshop file.

You can also attach a mask to any layer, or apply layer effects (e.g., Drop Shadow) to, or choose blending options for, any layer.

Only the current (or "active") layer can be edited. To activate a layer, click its thumbnail or next to its name.

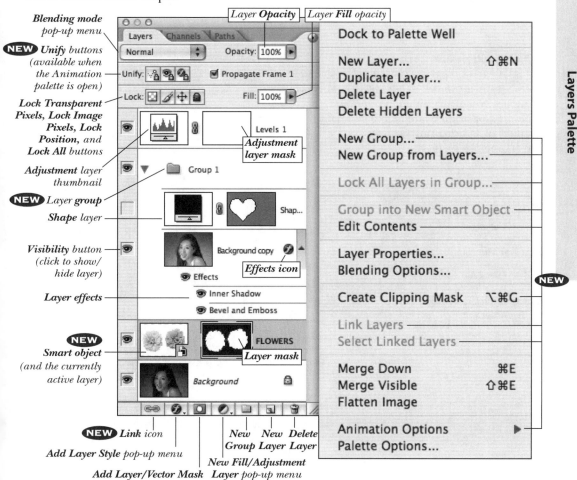

Navigator palette

The Navigator palette is used for moving an image in the document window and for changing the document zoom level.

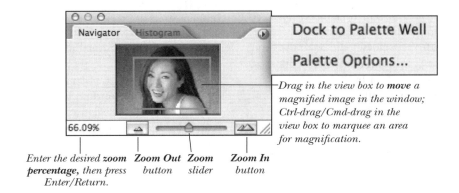

Dock to Palette Well

Palette Options...

Drag in the view box to **move** a
magnified image in the window;
Ctrl-drag/Cmd-drag in the
view box to marquee an area
for magnification.

*Enter the desired **zoom** **Zoom Out** **Zoom** **Zoom In**
percentage,* then press   button   slider   button
Enter/Return.*

Paragraph palette

The Paragraph palette is used for applying paragraph attributes to editable type, including horizontal alignment, indentation, space before, space after, and auto hyphenation. Other type formatting features are accesssed from the palette menu.

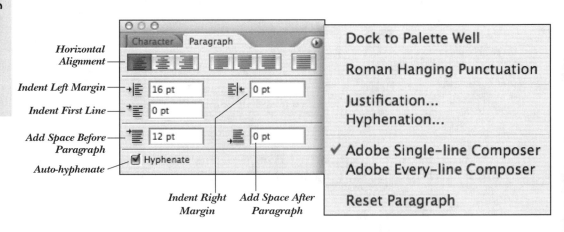

*Horizontal
Alignment*

Indent Left Margin

Indent First Line

*Add Space Before
Paragraph*

Auto-hyphenate

*Indent Right
Margin*

*Add Space After
Paragraph*

Dock to Palette Well

Roman Hanging Punctuation

Justification...

Hyphenation...

✓ Adobe Single-line Composer

Adobe Every-line Composer

Reset Paragraph

Navigator, Paragraph Palettes

Paths palette

In addition to the bitmap image that serves as the foundation of your Photoshop document, you can also draw vector shapes, called paths, which consist of curved and straight line segments connected by anchor points. You can use the Paths palette to save, activate, duplicate, apply a fill or stroke to, and delete paths, and to load paths as selections.

Paths can be drawn directly with a shape tool or the Pen tool, or by creating a selection and then converting the selection into a path. Conversely, to create a precisely drawn selection, you can draw a path and then convert it into a selection.

Once a path is drawn, you can apply a color to its fill or stroke, and you can reshape it by using the Pen tool or any of its relatives: the Add Anchor Point, Delete Anchor Point, and Convert Point tools.

When you click a shape layer or an image layer containing a vector mask, the path for that layer or vector mask is listed on the Paths palette.

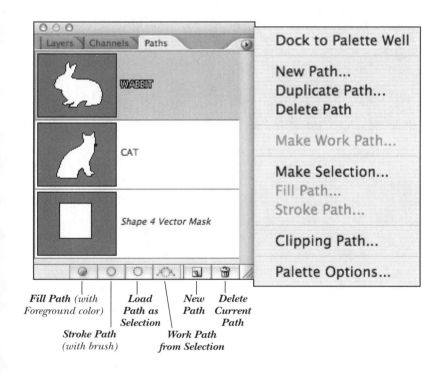

Fill Path (*with Foreground color*)

Stroke Path (*with brush*)

Load Path as Selection

Work Path from Selection

New Path

Delete Current Path

Styles palette

Layer effects (e.g., Drop Shadow, Inner Glow) are applied via the Layers palette; the Styles palette is used for storing and applying single or multiple layer effects. Custom style libraries can be loaded, appended, and saved using commands on the Styles palette menu.

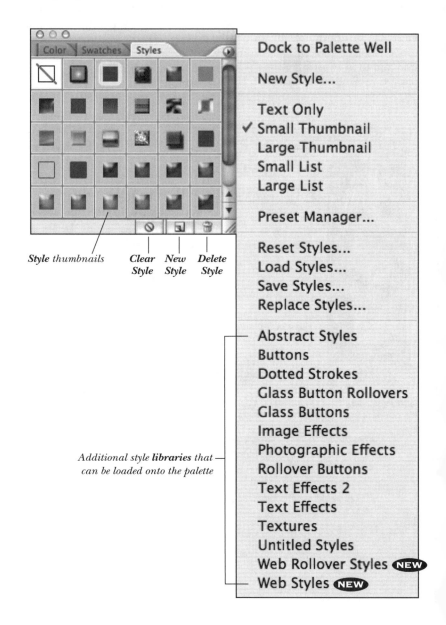

Style thumbnails   *Clear Style*   *New Style*   *Delete Style*

*Additional style **libraries** that can be loaded onto the palette*

Swatches palette

The Swatches palette is used for saving and choosing colors. Custom swatch libraries (e.g., PANTONE) can also be saved, loaded, and appended via commands on the Swatches palette menu.

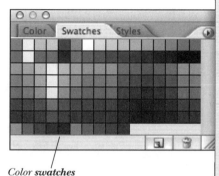

*Color **swatches***

NEW *New to CS2 are the Large Thumbnail, Large List, Save Swatches for Exchange, the HKS E, K, N, and Z Process colors, PANTONE solid to process EURO, Photo Filter Colors, TOYO Color Finder, and TOYO Process Color Finder.*

*Swatch **libraries** that can be loaded onto the palette*

Dock to Palette Well

New Swatch...

✓ Small Thumbnail
Large Thumbnail
Small List
Large List

Preset Manager...

Reset Swatches...
Load Swatches...
Save Swatches...
Save Swatches for Exchange...
Replace Swatches...

ANPA Colors
DIC Color Guide
FOCOLTONE Colors
HKS E Process
HKS E
HKS K Process
HKS K
HKS N Process
HKS N
HKS Z Process
HKS Z
Mac OS
PANTONE metallic coated
PANTONE pastel coated
PANTONE pastel uncoated
PANTONE process coated
PANTONE process uncoated
PANTONE solid coated
PANTONE solid matte
PANTONE solid to process EURO
PANTONE solid to process
PANTONE solid uncoated
Photo Filter Colors
TOYO Color Finder
TRUMATCH Colors
VisiBone
VisiBone2
Web Hues
Web Safe Colors
Web Spectrum
Windows

Swatches Palette

Tool Presets palette

You can save and reuse tool settings, just as you can any other type of preset. Say, for example, you frequently resize and crop images to a particular set of dimensions using the Crop tool. If you save a preset for the tool with those width, height, and resolution parameters, the next time you use the tool, instead of having to type in the numbers, all you have to do is click your Crop tool preset on either the Tool Presets palette or the Tool Preset picker **1**.

The Tool Presets palette is used for saving, storing, loading, sorting, renaming, resetting, and deleting tool presets. To have the palette list the presets for the current tool only, check Current Tool Only; uncheck this option to display all the presets.

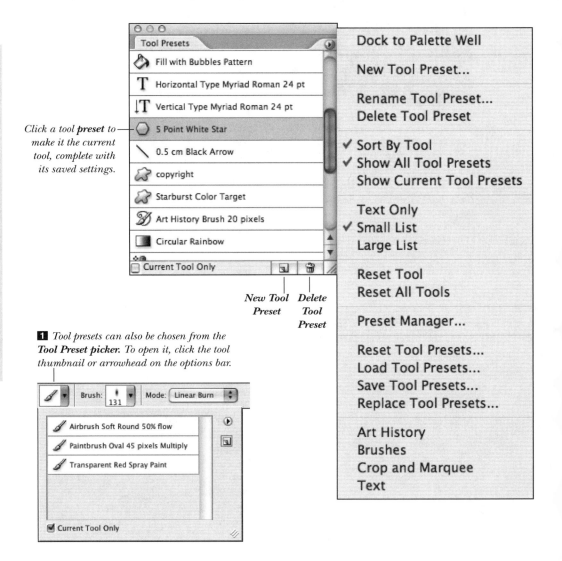

*Click a tool **preset** to make it the current tool, complete with its saved settings.*

New Tool Preset *Delete Tool Preset*

1 *Tool presets can also be chosen from the **Tool Preset picker**. To open it, click the tool thumbnail or arrowhead on the options bar.*

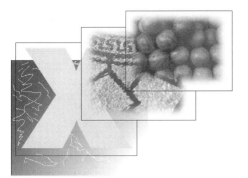

1 *Layers can contain opaque and transparent pixels.*

2 *Curves is but one of many commands that can be applied via adjustment layers.*

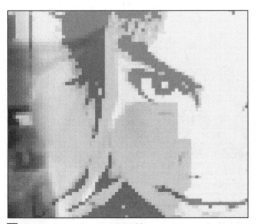

3 *At this zoom level of 500%, you can see individual pixels.*

Mini-glossary

Layer

An image can have just a Background (no layers), or it can have multiple layers **1**. Only the currently active layer can be edited. Individual layers can contain layer effects; they can be restacked and moved; you can choose blending options for them; and you can apply masks to them.

Adjustment and fill layers

Unlike standard layers, adjustment and fill layers don't alter actual pixels until they're merged with underlying layers **2**. You can use them to try out color and tonal adjustments without commitment.

Pixels

Pixels are dots that are used to display a bitmapped image in a grid onscreen **3**.

Vector

In addition to pixel imagery, you can also create mathematically defined vector paths, shapes, and editable type in Photoshop **4**. Vector elements print at the printer resolution, not the file resolution.

Smart objects

A smart object layer is created when you place an Illustrator vector file, another Photoshop file, or a Camera Raw file into a Photoshop document. You can double-click a smart object layer to edit its contents in the original application; when you save and close it, the object updates automatically in the Photoshop file.

(Continued on the following page)

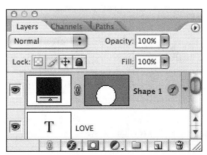

4 *Two types of vector layers: a shape layer and an editable type layer*

Mini-Glossary

Selection

A selection is an area of an image that's isolated via a "marching ants" marquee; the unselected area is protected from editing 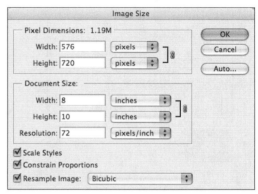. A selection can be created by using a selection tool (e.g., Lasso), by using a command (e.g., Color Range), by converting a path into a selection, or by loading an alpha channel mask as a selection. Another way to protect part of an image is by using a vector mask or Quick Mask.

Preset

A saved swatch, type, brush, gradient, pattern, shape, contour, or style, or tool settings.

History

Every change that's made to an image is listed on the History palette as a separate state. While an image is still open, it can be restored to any prior state on the list.

Layer effects

Effects (e.g., Drop Shadow, Outer Glow, Gradient Overlay) that can be applied to any layer and are fully editable and removable. A style is an effect or combination of effects that's saved to and applied via the Styles palette.

Pixel dimensions, resolution

The Pixel Dimensions value is the number of pixels an image contains. The resolution is the density of pixels per unit of measure (usually per inch) **2**.

Brightness, hue, saturation

Brightness is a color's relative lightness **3**; its hue is the wavelength of light that gives it its name, such as red or blue; and saturation is its purity (how much gray it contains).

Optimization

Optimization, the preparation of an image for Web output, involves choosing file format, color, and size parameters. By using slices, you can apply differing optimization settings to different sections of an image.

Rollover

A rollover is a change on a Web page (e.g., the temporary appearance of hidden text or a picture) that occurs when the user mouses over or clicks on a designated area.

1 *A **selected** area of an image*

2 *The **Image Size** dialog box is used for changing an image's pixel dimensions and/or resolution.*

Hue slider

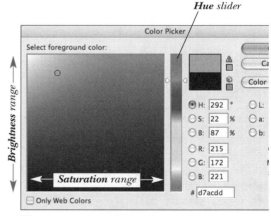

3 *The Photoshop **Color Picker***

Build your image using layers

You can work on one layer at a time without disturbing other layers **1**, and discard any layers you don't need. (To conserve memory when working on a large image, merge layer pairs together periodically.)

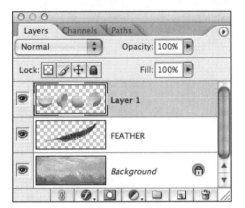

1 *Layers allow for flexibility in editing.*

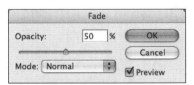

2 *Use the **Fade** command to lessen the impact of the latest edit without having to undo and redo.*

Use available info

Not sure what an icon means or a palette or dialog box option does? Rest the pointer on it, and a helpful **tool tip** will pop up onscreen.

Keep an eye on the **Info** palette for color breakdowns, document info, and tool hints.

Use the **Histogram** palette to monitor tonal ranges in an image as you apply color and tonal corrections.

Take a spin through Photoshop **Help** (but it's no substitute for this book!) :0)

Working smart

Add these techniques to your repertoire gradually as you become familiar with them:

Undo

➤ To undo the last modification, choose Edit > **Undo** (Ctrl-Z/Cmd-Z) (Some commands can't be undone.) To undo multiple steps, click a prior state on the **History** palette or use the **History Brush** tool to restore selective areas. Click the **New Snapshot** button at the bottom of the History palette periodically; click a snapshot thumbnail at any time to revert to that version of the image.

➤ Use Edit > **Fade** (Ctrl-Shift-F/Cmd-Shift-F) to lessen the impact of the last applied filter, adjustment command, or tool edit **2**.

Save time

➤ Use **Bridge** to search for, sort, open, place, move, rename, and delete files, and to activate Automate commands.

➤ Create and save theme-oriented **workspaces,** complete with color-coded menu labels.

➤ **Dock** palettes in the well for quick and easy access.

➤ Memorize the **keyboard shortcuts** for frequently used commands and tools. To learn the shortcuts for tools, use onscreen tool tips or refer to pages 7–10. Shortcuts are listed in most of our instructions.

➤ **Drag** to the left or right across names of options that have a value field (e.g., "Fill" or "Opacity" on the Layers palette) to change values without having to enter them. Some values can also be changed by pressing an arrow key.

➤ **Stop** the screen from fully redrawing after executing a command or applying a filter by choosing a different tool or command.

➤ Save repetitive editing sequences into **actions** so they can be applied quickly and easily to multiple images.

➤ Import Camera Raw images or objects from Illustrator as **smart objects** for easy re-editing.

(Continued on the following page)

Working Smart

Working Smart

Try out

➤ Use **adjustment layers** and **fill** layers to try out tonal and color adjustments.

➤ Apply editable and removable **layer effects.**

➤ Use **layer comps** to show off variations of the same document to clients instead of opening and closing separate files.

Reuse

➤ Save layer effect combos to the **Styles** palette to use in any file.

➤ Create and save **presets** for brushes, swatches, gradients, type, patterns, shapes, contours, styles, and tools.

➤ Save custom color swatches, shapes, brushes, etc. in **libraries** for safekeeping and easy access.

Save selections

➤ Save a selection to an **alpha** (grayscale) **channel,** then load it as a selection when needed. Or even better, save it as a **path,** which occupies far less storage space and can also be converted into a selection.

➤ Use **Quick Mask** mode to turn a selection into a mask, modify the mask contour using a painting tool, then go back to Standard mode to convert the mask into a selection.

Save memory

➤ CMYK files process more slowly than RGB files, so for print output, work in RGB Color mode, use View > Proof Setup > **Working CMYK** to simulate CMYK Color mode, and convert a copy of the file to true CMYK Color mode when it's done.

➤ Choose the Edit > **Purge** submenu commands periodically to regain RAM used for the Clipboard, the Undo command, the History palette, or All (of the above).

➤ Choose the **minimum** resolution and dimensions for your document, given your output requirements. Remember that vector layers, such as editable type, shapes, and vector masks, output at the printer resolution, not the file resolution.

Use the context menus!

A list of commands pops up onscreen when you right-click/Control-click a palette thumbnail, name, or feature **1**. Other commands appear when you right-click/Control-click in the document window, depending on where you click and which tool is selected **2**–**3**. We don't even list the menu bar as a choice in many of our instructions because context menus are so much faster and more fun to use.

1 *You can choose some palette commands via context menus.*

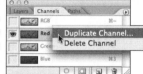

2 *Right-click/ Control-click with a type tool to choose type commands.*

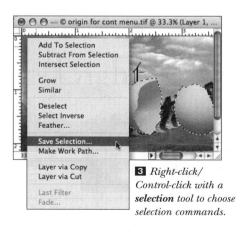

3 *Right-click/ Control-click with a selection tool to choose selection commands.*

PHOTOSHOP COLOR 2

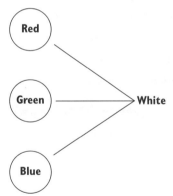

1 *A close-up of an image, showing individual **pixels***

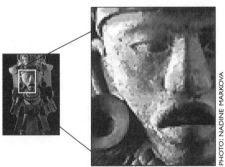

2 *The **additive primaries** on a computer monitor*

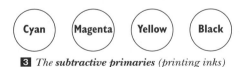

3 *The **subtractive primaries** (printing inks)*

THIS CHAPTER CONSISTS OF AN introduction to Photoshop's document color modes, and also to the program's color management features, an essential first step before image editing.

Color basics

Pixels

Onscreen, your Photoshop image is a **bitmap** —a geometric arrangement (mapping) of a layer of dots of different shades or colors on a rectangular grid. Each dot, or pixel, represents a color or shade. If you drag with a painting tool across an area of a layer, pixels under the pointer are recolored. By magnifying an area of an image, you can edit pixels individually **1**. Images can originate from digital or scanned photos, from files saved in other applications, or entirely within Photoshop, using painting tools and editing commands. Bitmap programs like Photoshop are ideal for producing painterly, photographic, or photorealistic images that contain subtle gradations of color (continuous tones). (Don't confuse Bitmap mode with the term "bitmap.")

RGB vs. CMYK color

Red, green, and **blue** (RGB) **lights** are used for displaying color images on a monitor. When these additive primaries in their purest form are combined, they produce white light **2**. The primary **inks** used in four-color process printing are **cyan** (C), **magenta** (M), **yellow** (Y), and **black** (K) **3**.

The display of color on a computer monitor is highly variable and subject to the whims of ambient lighting, monitor temperature, and room color. What's more, many colors that are seen in nature can't be printed, some

(Continued on the following page)

colors that can be displayed onscreen can't be printed, and some printable colors can't be displayed onscreen. All monitors display colors using the RGB model, whereas CMYK colors, used for printing, can only be simulated onscreen. If your image is going to be output online or to a film recorder, keep it in RGB Color mode.

An exclamation point will appear on the Color palette if you choose a nonprintable (out-of-gamut) color **1**. Exclamation points will also display on the Info palette if the color currently under the pointer is out of gamut **2**. Using Photoshop's Gamut Warning command, you can display nonprintable colors in your image in gray.

You can use the grayscale, **RGB** (red-green-blue), **HSB** (hue-saturation-brightness), **CMYK** (cyan-magenta-yellow-black), or **Lab** (lightness, a-component, and b-component) color model when you choose colors in Photoshop via the Color Picker or Color palette.

Channels

Every Photoshop image is a composite of one or more semitransparent overlays of colored light, called **channels.** For example, an image in RGB Color mode has three channels: red, green, and blue. To illustrate, open a color image, then click Red, Green, or Blue on the Channels palette to display only that channel. Click RGB (Ctrl-~/ Cmd-~) to restore the composite display.

Color adjustments can be made to an individual channel, but normally modifications are made and displayed in the multichannel, composite image (the topmost channel name on the Channels palette), and affect all of the channels in an image at once. Special grayscale channels that are used for saving selections as masks, called alpha channels, can be added to an image; you can also add channels for individual spot colors (**1**, next page) Only the currently highlighted channels can be edited.

Web graphics

When creating images for the Web, use the RGB color model. Bear in mind that RGB colors—or colors from any other color model, for that matter—may not match the color palette of your viewer's Web browser. For dependable results, load a Web or Visibone palette onto the Swatches palette and choose **Web Color Sliders** and **Make Ramp Web Safe** from the Color palette menu.

Default channels, per image mode

One	Three	Four
Bitmap	RGB	CMYK
Grayscale	Lab	
Duotone	Multichannel	Multichannel
Indexed Color		

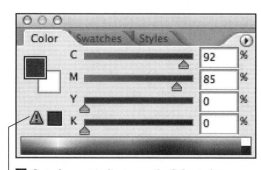

1 *Out-of-gamut* indicator on the **Color** palette

2 *Out-of-gamut* indicator on the **Info** palette

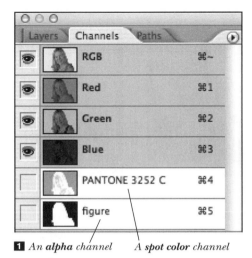

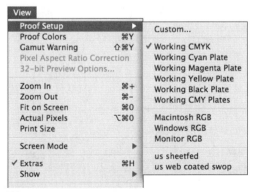

1 *An* **alpha** *channel*   *A* **spot color** *channel*

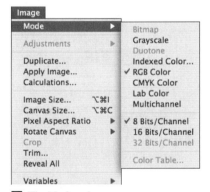

2 *The* **Mode** *submenu*

3 *The* **Proof Setup** *submenu*

The more channels a document contains, the larger its file storage size. The storage size of a document in RGB Color mode, which has three channels (Red, Green, and Blue), will be three times larger than the same document in Grayscale mode, which has only one channel. The same document in CMYK Color mode will have four channels (Cyan, Magenta, Yellow, and Black), and will be even larger.

Document color modes

A document can be converted to, displayed in, and edited in any one of eight color modes: **Bitmap, Grayscale, Duotone, Indexed Color, RGB Color, CMYK Color, Lab Color,** or **Multichannel.** To convert a document, choose a mode from the Image > Mode submenu **2**. To access a mode that's unavailable (dimmed), you must first convert your document to a different mode as an intermediate step. For example, to convert a document to Indexed Color mode, it must be in RGB Color or Grayscale mode.

Some mode conversions cause noticeable color shifts. For example, dramatic changes may occur if a document is converted from RGB Color mode to CMYK Color mode, as printable colors will be substituted for luminous RGB colors. Color accuracy may diminish if a document is converted back and forth between RGB and CMYK Color modes too many times.

Digital cameras and medium- to low-end scanners produce RGB images. If you're creating an image that's going to be printed, for faster editing and to access all the filters, edit it in RGB Color mode and then convert it to CMYK Color mode when you're ready to output it. You can use View > **Proof Setup** **3** in conjunction with View > **Proof Colors** (Ctrl-Y/Cmd-Y) to preview ("soft proof") an image in CMYK Color mode without actually changing its mode. You can preview your image in CMYK in one window and, in a second window, display the same image in its actual mode.

(Continued on the following page)

Document Color Modes

Some conversions cause layers to be flattened, such as a conversion to Indexed Color, Multichannel, or Bitmap mode. For other conversions, you'll have the option to click Don't Flatten to preserve layers.

Images that are saved by high-end scanners in CMYK Color mode should be kept in that mode to preserve their color data. Photoshop CS2 can handle large scans, even those saved with a pixel depth of 16 bits or 32 bits per channel. You can't do much to a 32-bit image in Photoshop, though.

The availability of some commands and tool options in Photoshop may also vary depending on an image's current mode. Some output devices require that an image be saved in a particular image mode. The following is a brief description of the **image modes** that you can convert an image to in Photoshop:

In **Bitmap** mode 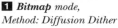, pixels are 100% black or 100% white only, and layers, filters, and adjustment commands aren't available. An image must be in Grayscale mode before it can be converted to Bitmap mode.

In **Grayscale** mode , pixels are black, white, or up to 254 shades of gray (for a total of 256). If an image is converted from a color mode to Grayscale mode and then saved and closed, its luminosity (light and dark) values will remain intact, but its color information will be deleted and can't be restored.

Duotone is a commercial printing method in which two or more extra plates are used to add richness and tonal depth to a grayscale image.

Images in **Indexed Color** mode have one channel and a color table that contains a maximum of 256 colors or shades (8-bit color). It's often helpful to reduce images to 8-bit color for use in multimedia applications. An image that's been reduced to 8-bit color for Web output should be optimized in the GIF format (see page 506).

1 *Bitmap* mode, *Method: Diffusion Dither* **2** *Grayscale* mode

The **Channels** *palette for an image in various modes*

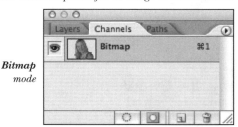
Bitmap mode

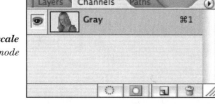
Grayscale mode

Duotone mode

Indexed Color mode

*The **Channels** palette for an image in various modes*

RGB Color mode

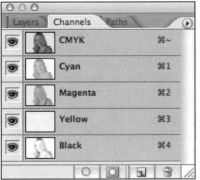

CMYK Color mode

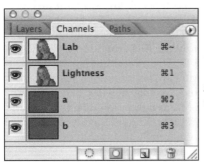

Lab Color mode

Multichannel mode

RGB Color is the most versatile of all. Not only is it used by digital cameras, it's also the only mode in which all of Photoshop's tool options and filters are accessible, and the mode used for online output and export to video and multimedia applications.

TIP For most desktop inkjet printers, especially those that use six or more ink colors, you'll achieve the best results by leaving the file in RGB Color mode and letting the printer driver perform the conversion to its own color space.

One of Photoshop's strengths is that it lets you display and edit images in **CMYK Color** mode. You can also edit your document in RGB Color mode, then convert it to CMYK Color mode when you're ready to color-separate it, export it to a page layout application, or output it on a composite color printer.

Lab Color is a three-channel mode that was developed for the purpose of achieving consistency among various devices, such as printers and monitors. The channels represent lightness, the colors green to red, and the colors blue to yellow. PhotoCD images can be converted to Lab Color (or RGB Color) mode in Photoshop. In Lab Color mode, the luminosity and color values in an image can be edited independently of one another.

Multichannel images are composed of multiple 256-level grayscale channels. This mode is used for some grayscale printing situations. It can also be used for assembling individual channels from several images as an intermediary step; the composite image can then be converted to another color mode. If you convert an image from RGB Color to Multichannel mode, its Red, Green, and Blue channels will be converted to Cyan, Magenta, and Yellow. As a result, the image may become lighter and its contrast may be diminished. This mode preserves spot color and alpha channels.

Document Color Modes

Color management

Problems with color can creep up on you when various hardware devices and software packages you use treat color differently. If you open an image in several different **imaging** programs and in a **Web** browser, the colors in the image might look completely different in each case, and thus may not match the color of the picture you originally shot with your digital camera or digitized via a scanner. **Print** the image, and you will probably find that your results are different yet again. In some cases, you might find these differences to be slight and unobjectionable, but in other cases, such color changes can wreak havoc with your design and turn a project into a disaster!

A **color management** system can solve most of these problems by acting as a color interpreter. Such a system knows how each device and program understands color, and adjusts colors so your images look the same as you move them from one program or device to another. It does this by using **color profiles,** which are mathematical descriptions of the color space of each device. The applications in the Adobe Creative Suite 2 use the standardized ICC (International Color Consortium) profiles to tell your color management system how specific devices use color.

You can find most of Photoshop's color management controls in the **Color Settings** dialog box (Edit menu). This dialog box gives you access to predefined management settings for various publishing situations, including prepress output and Web output.

Photoshop also supports color management policies for RGB and CMYK color files, for files that use spot colors, and for grayscale files. These color management policies govern how Photoshop deals with color when opening images that do or don't have an attached color profile.

Color management is especially important when you use the same image for multiple purposes, such as for the Web and for print. It's essential that you consult with your prepress service provider, if you're using one, about color management to ensure that your color management workflows work smoothly with theirs.

Monitor basics

Computer monitors come in two basic types: CRT (wide depth) and LCD (flat panel). **CRT**s fluctuate in display performance due to their analog technology, and because their display phosphors (which produce the glowing dots on the screen) fade over time. Also, they must be calibrated at least once a month using their built-in brightness and contrast controls. The average lifespan of a CRT monitor, as far as calibration is concerned, is only about 3 years; after that they can't be reliably calibrated.

LCDs use a grid of fixed-sized liquid crystals that individually filter color coming from a back-light source. Although you can adjust only the brightness on an LCD (not the contrast), LCD digital technology achieves more reliable and consistent color output than a CRT, without the flickering that is characteristic of CRTs. The newest models provide good viewing angles, accurately display a neutral color and 6500K white balance, and are produced to tighter manufacturing standards than CRTs. The profile provided by the factory is usually accurate at describing monitor characteristics.

Calibration basics

Calibrating a monitor involves adjusting three basic monitor characteristics: setting the **contrast** to the maximum, setting the **brightness** to a consistent working standard, and making sure that the **neutral gray** (gray balance) displays as a true gray. The basic monitor profile produced by calibration contains data that describes the white point, black point, and gamma.

White point data enables the monitor to display a pure white that matches an industry-standard color temperature. Photographers generally use a D65/6500K temperature setting for the white point.

Black point data specifies the darkest black a monitor can display. All other dark shades will be lighter than darkest black, thus ensuring the proper display of shadow details.

Gamma defines the onscreen brightness of the midtones exactly midway between pure black and pure white. This setting, in turn, determines how the rest of the midtone shades are distributed; it doesn't affect the lightest or darkest shades. Professional photographers recommend using a gamma of 2.2 for both PCs and Macs.

Caveat: What we're outlining in this section is a basic calibration method. Professional-level calibration requires more precise monitor measurement using expensive hardware devices, such as colorimeters and spectrophotometers (what?).

Color Management

The first step toward achieving color consistency is to **calibrate** your **display** (monitor) by adjusting the contrast, brightness, gamma, color balance, and white point. In Windows, the Adobe Gamma utility is installed with Photoshop CS2; in Macintosh, you'll use the operating system's display calibration utility in System Preferences > Displays.

Both the Adobe Gamma and Displays control panels generate an ICC profile that Photoshop can use as its working RGB space in order to display the colors in your document accurately. You have to calibrate your display and save the settings as an ICC profile only once; thereafter, the profile will be available to all applications.

To calibrate your display in Macintosh:

1. If you have a CRT display, let it warm up for 30 minutes to allow the display to stabilize, and for either monitor type, establish a level of room lighting that you can count on remaining constant (paint your windows black, ha-ha). Also, make the desktop pattern light gray.

2. Choose Apple > **System Preferences,** click **Displays,** click the **Color** tab, then click **Calibrate.** The Display Calibrator Assistant appears onscreen ▇.

Optional: Check Expert Mode to access advanced options.

Note: Some options discussed in the following steps may not be available for LCD (flat-panel) displays.

3. Click Continue to advance to the next options panel.

4. CRTs only: In **Display Adjustment,** leave your display's contrast at the maximum setting, but adjust the brightness until the light gray oval is barely visible and the background looks like solid black ▇. Click Continue.

5. In the **Determine your display's native gamma** screen (Expert Mode only), the gray square represents a combined

Finding the calibration utility

In Windows, choose Start menu > Control Panel > **Adobe Gamma,** or run the **Adobe Gamma.cpl** utility from C:\Program Files\Common Files\Adobe\ Calibration.

In Mac, choose Apple > System Preferences, click **Displays,** then click the **Color** tab in the Displays panel.

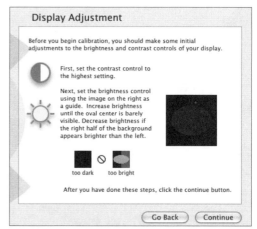

▇ *This screen in the **Display Calibrator Assistant** is the starting point for calibrating your monitor in Mac.*

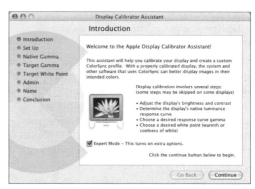

▇ *The first step in calibrating a **CRT** monitor is to set the **contrast** and **brightness** to the proper values.*

Calibrate Macintosh Display

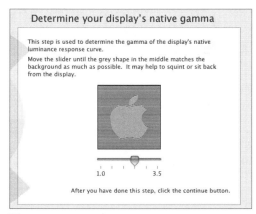

Determine your display's native gamma

This step is used to determine the gamma of the display's native luminance response curve.

Move the slider until the grey shape in the middle matches the background as much as possible. It may help to squint or sit back from the display.

1.0   3.5

After you have done this step, click the continue button.

1 *For a CRT display, drag the slider to make the gray apple fade into the background.*

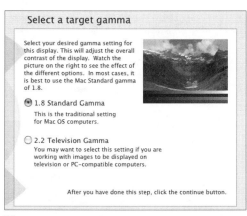

Select a target gamma

Select your desired gamma setting for this display. This will adjust the overall contrast of the display. Watch the picture on the right to see the effect of the different options. In most cases, it is best to use the Mac Standard gamma of 1.8.

⦿ 1.8 Standard Gamma
This is the traditional setting for Mac OS computers.

◯ 2.2 Television Gamma
You may want to select this setting if you are working with images to be displayed on television or PC-compatible computers.

After you have done this step, click the continue button.

2 *For a CRT or LCD display, choose a **gamma** setting (this is non-Expert mode).*

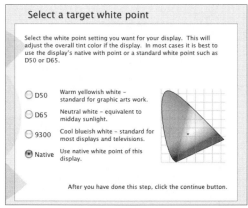

Select a target white point

Select the white point setting you want for your display. This will adjust the overall tint color if the display. In most cases it is best to use the display's native with point or a standard white point such as D50 or D65.

◯ D50   Warm yellowish white – standard for graphic arts work.

◯ D65   Neutral white – equivalent to midday sunlight.

◯ 9300   Cool blueish white – standard for most displays and televisions.

⦿ Native Use native white point of this display.

After you have done this step, click the continue button.

3 *Choose the **target white point** that's appropriate for the type of work you do (this is non-Expert mode).*

grayscale reading of your display **1**. To adjust the gamma, move the slider until the solid gray apple shape matches the surrounding, stripey box (try squinting). If you checked Expert Mode earlier, you'll march through a series of five screens in which you adjust the brightness of the gray shape and remove any hint of color (for both CRT and LCD displays). Click Continue.

6. For **Select a target gamma,** choose which gamma you want your display to use: **1.8 Standard Gamma** for Mac or **2.2 Television Gamma** for Windows **2**. If you chose Expert Mode, you'll be able to choose from a range of gamma settings via a slider here. Click Continue.

7. For **Select a target white point,** choose a target white point based on the kind of work you'll be doing **3**. If you checked Expert Mode, a slider will be available for setting the white point. Click Continue.

8. In the Administrator options screen (Expert mode only), check **Allow other users to use this calibration** to share your new profile with the other users of your machine. Click Continue.

9. Finally, name the profile, click Continue, then click Done. It will be saved in Users/[user name]/Library/ColorSync/Profiles (or if you checked "Allow other users…" it will be stored in Library/ColorSync/Profiles/Displays), and can be accessed via the RGB pop-up menu in the Working Spaces area of the Color Settings dialog box (see pages 44–45).

Calibrate Macintosh Display

To calibrate your display in Windows:

1. If you have a CRT display, allow 30 minutes for it to warm up and for the display to stabilize, and for either monitor type (LCD or CRT), establish a level of room lighting that will remain constant.

2. Make the desktop pattern light gray.

3. Choose Start menu > **Control Panel,** then open the **Adobe Gamma** utility.

4. Click **Step by Step (Wizard),** which will walk you through the process 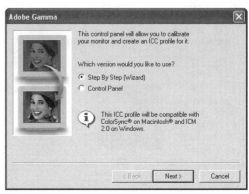. Click Next to advance to the next dialog box.
   or
   Click **Control Panel** to choose settings from a single dialog box without explanations. (If the Adobe Gamma dialog opens directly, you can skip this step.)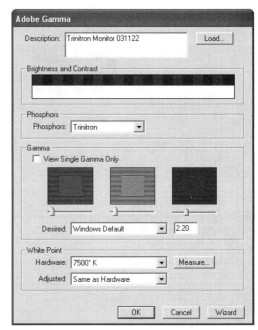

5. Leave the default monitor ICC profile as is.
   or
   Click **Load** and choose a profile that more closely matches your monitor.

6. Turn up your monitor's brightness and contrast settings. Leave the contrast at the maximum, but adjust the brightness until the alternating gray squares in the top bar are very dark, but not black, while keeping the lower bar bright white.

7. For **Phosphors,** choose your monitor type, or choose Custom and enter the Red, Green, and Blue chromaticity coordinates that are specified by your monitor's manufacturer.

8. For **Gamma,** the gray square represents a combined grayscale reading of your monitor. Adjust the gamma using this slider until the smaller, solid-color box matches the outer, stripey box (try squinting). You might find it easier to uncheck View Single Gamma Only and make separate adjustments based on the readings for Red, Green, and Blue.

9. For **Desired,** choose Windows Default (value of 2.2), if available.

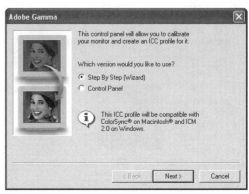

1 *This is the **Adobe Gamma** dialog box, set for the **Step by Step (Wizard)** calibration method.*

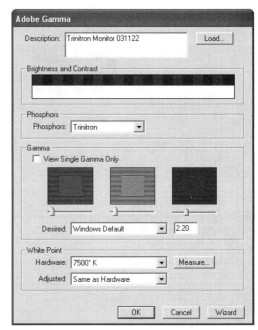

2 *This **Adobe Gamma** dialog box will open if you click **Control Panel** in the Adobe Gamma dialog box (see the previous figure). With the View Single Gamma Only option off, you can make adjustments to the individual Red, Green, and Blue components.*

Calibrate and recalibrate

If you adjust your monitor's brightness and contrast settings or change the room lighting (e.g., open or close your window shades), remember to **recalibrate** your **monitor!**

10. For **White Point: Hardware,** choose the white point the monitor manufacturer specifies, or click Measure and follow the instructions.

11. For **Adjusted,** choose Same as Hardware, or, if you know the color temperature at which your image will ultimately be viewed, you can either choose it from the pop-up menu or choose Custom and enter it there. This option isn't available for all monitors.

12. When you're satisfied with the settings you've chosen, click OK to close the Adobe Gamma dialog box. If you've made changes to the settings, the Save As dialog will appear; give the new profile a name and save it in WindowsXP\system32\spool\drivers\color (the ".icc" suffix will be appended automatically). Photoshop can use this profile as its working RGB space in the Color Settings dialog box (see the next page).

Calibrate Windows Display

Color Settings

To choose predefined color management settings:

1. Choose Edit > **Color Settings** (Ctrl-Shift-K/Cmd-Shift-K). The Color Settings dialog box opens **1**.

2. Choose a configuration option from the **Settings** pop-up menu:

NEW Monitor Color uses the working space defined for your monitor. This works best for graphics intended for video applications, but isn't suitable for work with CMYK documents.

NEW North America General Purpose 2 meets the requirements for screen and print output in the U.S. and Canada. All profile warnings are turned off.

NEW North America Prepress 2 manages color based on common press conditions in the U.S. CMYK values are unchanged when documents are opened.

NEW North America Web/Internet is designed for the preparation of images for the Web. All RGB images are converted to the sRGB working space.

Clicking the **More Options** button adds more configurations (some from older versions of Photoshop) to the menu:

ColorSync Workflow (Mac only) manages color using the ColorSync color management system. Profiles are based on those in the ColorSync control panel (including any monitor profile you may have created using the Apple Display Calibrator utility). This setting is a good choice if you need to keep color consistent between Adobe and non-Adobe applications.

Emulate Acrobat 4 and **Emulate Photoshop 4** produce color content that matches the color handling found in those two applications.

*The **Description** area provides valuable information about whichever dialog box option the pointer is currently over. You can use these tool tips to learn about the various Color Settings features.*

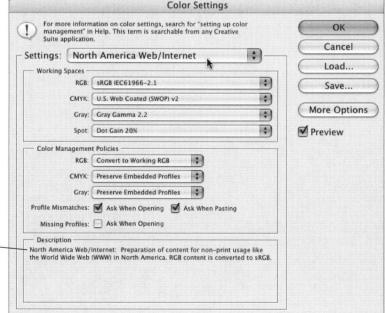

1 *The **Color Settings** dialog box, with **North America Web/Internet** chosen from the **Settings** pop-up menu*

Europe/Japan General Purpose 2, Prepress 2, and **Web/Internet** are equivalent to their American counterparts, but in each case the CMYK working space is changed to a press that's standard for that region.

Japan Color for Newspaper and **Japan Magazine Advertisement Color** use CMYK working spaces appropriate to periodical publishing in that country.

Photoshop 5 Default Spaces uses the same working spaces as the default settings found in Photoshop 5.

At this point you can click OK to accept the predefined settings or proceed with step 3 to choose custom settings.

3. Next, you can choose color **working spaces,** which define how RGB and CMYK colors will be treated in your document. For CMYK settings, you should ask your output service provider which working space to choose. You can also specify a dot gain value or gamma setting for grayscale images and a dot gain value for spot colors.

The following RGB settings are available:

Monitor RGB [current monitor name]: This choice sets the RGB working space to your monitor's profile, and is useful if you know that other applications you'll be using for your project don't support color management. Keep in mind, however, that if you share this configuration with another user, the configuration will use that user's monitor profile as the RGB working space, and color consistency may be undermined.

ColorSync RGB: (Mac only) Use this color space to match Photoshop's RGB space to the space specified in the Apple ColorSync Utility. This can be the profile you created using System Preferences > Displays. If you share this configuration with another user, it will utilize the ColorSync space specified by that user.

Adobe RGB (1998): This color space produces a wide range of colors and is useful when converting RGB images to CMYK images, but it's not a good choice for Web work.

Apple RGB: This space is useful for files that you plan to display on Mac monitors, as it reflects the characteristics of the older standard Apple 13-inch monitors. It's also a good choice for older desktop publishing files, such as Adobe Photoshop 4.0 files.

ColorMatch RGB: This space produces a smaller range of colors than the Adobe RGB (1998) model, but it matches the color space of Radius Pressview monitors and is useful for print production work.

sRGB IEC61966-2.1: This is a good choice for Web work, as it reflects the settings on the average computer monitor. Many hardware and software manufacturers are using it as the default space for scanners, low-end printers, and software. Don't use it for prepress work; use Adobe RGB or ColorMatch RGB instead.

4. Click OK.

Quick color setup for photographers and print designers

If you're using Photoshop primarily to create or enhance photos for print output (as in output by a commercial printer, not from a desktop inkjet printer), choose Edit > **Color Settings,** then choose a preset from the **Settings** pop-up menu that's appropriate for your geographic location.

If you're in the United States, for example, choose North America Prepress 2. This will change the default RGB workspace from the sRGB color space to the Adobe RGB (1998) color space, and will set the color management policies to the safe choice of Preserve Embedded Profiles. The Adobe RGB color space preserves and color-manages a larger range of colors in the CMYK print gamut than RGB does, and it produces better print output.

If the color settings in another Adobe Creative Suite program (e.g., Illustrator CS2) don't match the current settings in Photoshop, an alert will display in the Color Settings dialog box in Photoshop **1**. If you don't own the complete Adobe Creative Suite, you'll have to start up the errant application and fix its color settings by hand. If you are lucky enough to have a copy of the whole suite installed, you can use the **Suite Color Settings** dialog box in Bridge to **synchronize** the color settings of all of the programs in the suite.

To synchronize color settings using Bridge:

1. In Bridge, choose Edit > **Creative Suite Color Settings** (Ctrl-Shift-K/Cmd-Shift-K). The Suite Color Settings dialog box opens **2**, with the same list of settings as the Color Settings dialog box (see page 44), with Fewer Options displaying.

2. Click one of the settings to select it, then click **Apply.** Bridge then changes (synchronizes) the color settings of the other Adobe Creative Suite applications to match.

Note: Checking Show Expanded List of Color Settings Files displays all of your color settings on the list (the same list as in the Color Settings dialog box when More Options are displaying).

Document-specific color

Photoshop supports **document-specific color,** meaning each open document has its own color space and keeps its own profile for controlling how it previews and how its color is managed on output. The current working space is used for creating previews for documents that lack an embedded profile.

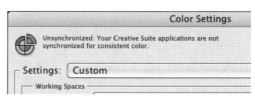

1 *This alert tells us that our color settings aren't uniform across our Creative Suite applications.*

2 *Use the **Suite Color Settings** dialog box to synchronize the color settings of the applications in the Adobe Creative Suite.*

Creative Suite Color Settings (vertical sidebar text)

You can choose a **customized color management** policy that will tell Photoshop how to deal with images that don't match your current color settings.

To customize your color management policies:

1. Choose Edit > **Color Settings** (Ctrl-Shift-K/Cmd-Shift-K).

2. For **Working Spaces,** choose custom settings from the **RGB, CMYK, Gray,** and **Spot** pop-up menus.

3. From the pop-up menus in the **Color Management Policies** area **1**:

If you choose **Off,** Photoshop won't color-manage color files that are imported or opened.

Choose **Preserve Embedded Profiles** if you think you're going to be working with both color-managed and non-color-managed documents. This will tie each color file's profile to the individual file. In Photoshop, each open document can have its own profile.

Choose **Convert to Working…** if you want all your documents to reflect the same color working space. This is usually the best choice for Web work.

For Profile Mismatches, check **Ask When Opening** to have Photoshop display a message if the color profile in a file you're opening doesn't match the current working space. If you choose this option, you can override your color management policy when opening documents.

Check **Ask When Pasting** to have Photoshop display a message when color profile mismatches occur as you paste color data into your document. If you choose this option, you can override your color management policy when pasting.

For files with Missing Profiles, check **Ask When Opening** to have Photoshop display a message offering you the opportunity to assign a profile.

4. Click OK.

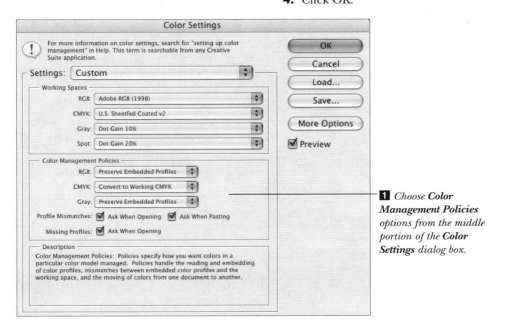

1 *Choose* **Color Management Policies** *options from the middle portion of the* **Color Settings** *dialog box.*

To customize your conversion options:

1. Choose Edit > **Color Settings** (Ctrl-Shift-K/Cmd-Shift-K).

2. Click the **More Options** button. 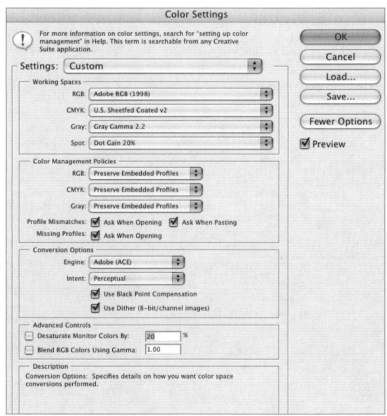.

3. Under **Conversion Options,** choose a color management **Engine** to be used for converting colors between color spaces: **Adobe (ACE)** uses Adobe's color management system and color engine; both **Apple ColorSync** and **Apple CMM** use Apple's color management system; and **Microsoft ICM** uses the system provided in Windows 98 and later systems. Other color engines can be chosen to fit into color workflows that use specific output devices.

4. Choose a rendering **Intent** to determine how colors will be changed as they're moved from one color space to another:

Perceptual changes colors in a way that seems natural to the human eye, although the color values actually do change. It's a good choice for continuous-tone images.

Saturation changes colors with the intent of preserving vivid colors, although it compromises color fidelity. It's a good choice for charts and business graphics.

Absolute Colorimetric keeps colors that are inside the destination color gamut unchanged, but changes the relationships among colors outside this gamut in an attempt to preserve color fidelity.

Relative Colorimetric, the default intent for all predefined settings options, is the same as Absolute Colorimetric, except

1 *When the **More Options** button is clicked in the **Color Settings** dialog box, the **Conversion Options** become available.*

Saving settings

➤ To save your custom settings for later use, click **Save** in the **Color Settings** dialog box. If you want your custom file name to display on the Settings pop-up menu in Windows, save it in the default location: Program Files\Common Files\Adobe\ Color\Settings. To do the same thing in Mac, save the file in User/[User Name]/Library/Application Support/Adobe/Color/Settings.

➤ When you're ready to reuse the saved settings, choose the file name from the **Settings** pop-up menu. To locate a settings file that isn't in the Settings folder (and thus isn't on the Settings menu), click **Load** in the Color Settings dialog box.

➤ In the Save As dialog box, when you save a file in a format that supports embedded profiles, such as Photoshop PSD or Photoshop PDF, you can check **ICC Profile** in Windows or **Embed Color Profile** in the Mac to embed a profile with the document, if one has been assigned.

it compares the white point, or extreme highlight, of the source color space to the destination color space and shifts all colors accordingly. The accuracy of this intent depends on the accuracy of the white point information in an image's profile.

Important note: Differences between rendering intents are visible only on a printout or upon a conversion to a different working space.

Check **Use Black Point Compensation** if you want adjustments to be made for differences in black points between color spaces. When this option is chosen, the full dynamic range of the source color space is mapped into the full dynamic range of the destination color space. If you don't choose this option, your blacks may display or print as grays. We recommend that you check this option for a RGB-to-CMYK conversion, but consult with your print shop before checking it for a CMYK-to-CMYK conversion.

Check **Use Dither (8-bit/channel images)** to let Photoshop dither colors when converting 8-bits-per-channel images between color spaces. Sometimes when an image is converted from one color space to another, colors that don't exist in the target space are lost, resulting in banding or undesirable color artifacts (stray pixels). With this option checked, Photoshop will mix blocks of similar colors to simulate a missing color, thus achieving smoother overall continuous tones. We recommend keeping Use Dither (8-bit/channel images) checked when converting between RGB and CMYK spaces for print, but turning it off for Web graphics. The Save for Web dialog box provides more precise controls for dithering images (see pages 503–504).

5. Click OK.

Conversion Options

You may need to switch color profiles if you change your color management settings or when preparing a document for a specific output device; or you may want to remove a profile altogether. The **Assign Profile** command reinterprets the color data directly in the color space of the new profile (or lack thereof), and may cause visible color shifts. If you use the Convert to Profile command (see the next instructions), the color numbers are recalculated before the new profile is applied, in an effort to preserve the document's appearance. In either case, keep Preview checked so you know what you're getting into!

To change or delete a document's color profile:

1. Choose Edit > **Assign Profile** ■. If the document contains layers, an alert dialog may appear, warning you that the appearance of the layers may change; click OK.

2. Click one of the following:

Don't Color Manage This Document to remove the color profile.

Working [document color mode and the name of the working space you're using] to assign that particular working space to a document that doesn't use a profile or that uses a profile that's different from the current working space.

Profile to reassign a different profile to a color-managed document, and choose a profile from the pop-up menu.

3. Click OK.

The **Convert to Profile** command lets you preview a conversion to an assortment of color modes, output profiles, and intents, and then performs the mode conversion.

To convert a document's color profile:

1. Choose Edit > **Convert to Profile** (■, next page).

2. From the **Destination Space: Profile** pop-up menu, choose the space that you want to convert the document to. It doesn't have to be the current working space. For the Conversion Options, see page 48.

Where you'll see it

In the File > Print with Preview dialog box, if **More Options** is clicked and **Color Management** is chosen from the pop-up menu, the assigned profile will be listed next to Document in the Print area.

If you choose **Document Profile** from the status bar pop-up menu at the bottom of the application/document window, the profile will also appear on the **status** bar.

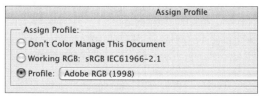

■ *Use the **Assign Profile** dialog box to change or delete a document's **color profile**.*

Assign Profile; Convert to Profile

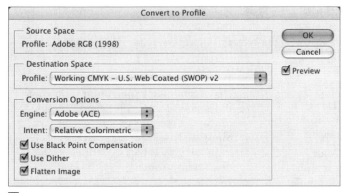

1 *Use the Convert to Profile dialog box to assign a different color profile to your document.*

Specifying a color management setup is all well and good, but you also need to get an idea of how a document is going to look in print or on the Web. You can do this by **soft-proofing** your colors. Although this method is less accurate than actually making a print, getting a proof, or viewing your Web artwork on different monitors, it can give you a general idea of how your work will look in different settings. You can choose either a preset proof setup or custom settings.

To proof colors using preset settings:

1. From the View > **Proof Setup** submenu, choose the output display type that you want Photoshop to simulate:

   Working CMYK to soft-proof colors using the CMYK working space as defined in the Color Settings dialog box.

   Working Cyan Plate, Working Magenta Plate, Working Yellow Plate, Working Black Plate, or **Working CMY Plates** to soft-proof specific ink colors as defined by the current CMYK working space.

   Macintosh RGB or **Windows RGB** to soft-proof colors using a Mac or Windows monitor profile as the proofing space you want to simulate.

   Monitor RGB to soft-proof colors using your monitor profile.

2. View > **Proof Colors** will be checked automatically so the soft proof can be previewed. You can uncheck it at any time to turn off proofing (Ctrl-Y/Cmd-Y).

Proof Setup

To proof colors using custom settings:

1. From the View > **Proof Setup** submenu, choose **Custom.** The Customize Proof Condition dialog box opens, allowing you to choose custom proofing settings for a specific output device 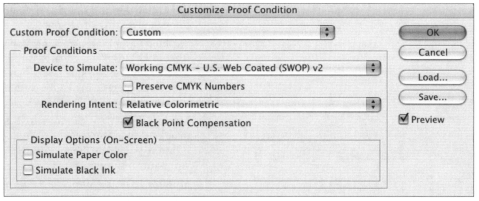.

NEW 2. Check Preview, then from the **Device to Simulate** pop-up menu, choose the color profile for your target output device.

3. Check or uncheck **Preserve [Color Mode] Numbers,** if this option is available. If checked, Photoshop will simulate how the colors will look if they're not converted to the proofing space. If you leave this option off, Photoshop will simulate how the colors will look if they're converted; and you'll need to specify a rendering intent, as described in "To customize your conversion options" on page 48.

   Note: Preserve [Color Mode] Numbers is available only if the color mode of the output device that you chose from the Device to Simulate pop-up menu matches that of the current file (e.g., if the chosen proofing profile and the document color mode are both RGB).

4. For the Rendering Intent options, see page 48–49.

   For the Black Point Compensation option, see page 49.

5. In the **Display Options (On-Screen)** area, check **Simulate Paper Color** to preview the shade of the print paper as defined in the document's profile, or check **Simulate Black Ink** to preview the full range of gray values as defined in the document profile.

6. Click OK. View > Proof Colors will be checked automatically to allow the soft proof to be previewed. Uncheck it at any time to turn off proofing.

TIP To save a custom proof setup, click Save in the Customize Proof Condition dialog box. Saved proof setups are listed at the bottom of the Proof Setup submenu and on the Customize Proof Condition pop-up menu.

TIP The Proof Setup command simulates how colors will display without actually converting colors to the chosen profile. Colors are converted only when you convert the document to a different mode.

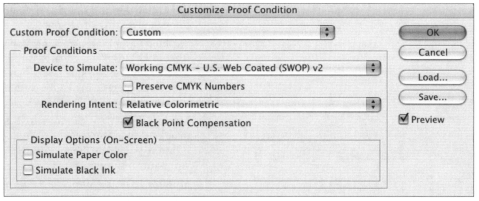

1 *Use the **Customize Proof Condition** dialog box to choose which device you want Photoshop to simulate.*

CREATE AND SAVE FILES 3

Photoshop PDF
✓ Photoshop
BMP
CompuServe GIF
Photoshop EPS
JPEG
Large Document Format
PCX
Photoshop 2.0
Photoshop Raw
PICT File
PICT Resource
Pixar
PNG
Portable Bit Map
Scitex CT
Targa
TIFF
Photoshop DCS 1.0
Photoshop DCS 2.0

1 *Files can be saved in any of these* **formats** *in Mac. In Windows, all of the above formats are available except Photoshop 2.0 and PICT Resource.*

DIGITAL CAMERAS ARE HOT, HOT, HOT, and sales are showing no signs of slowing down—thus we start this chapter off with a few basic pointers on buying a digital camera and shooting digital photographs. You'll also learn how to choose an appropriate resolution, scan images, create new documents, create document presets, save and copy documents, and close up shop. (If you don't know how to launch Photoshop, see page 1!)

Images can be created, opened, edited, and saved in over a dozen different **file formats** in Photoshop **1**. Of this large selection, you'll probably use only a handful on a regular basis, such as TIFF, GIF, JPEG, EPS, Photoshop PDF, and PSD (a native Photoshop file format). There's also a native Large Document format, or PSB (nicknamed "Photoshop Big"), which is designed solely for huge files.

Because Photoshop accepts so many formats, imagery can be gathered from many sources, such as digital cameras, scanners, drawing applications, PhotoCDs, and video captures. Images can also be created entirely within Photoshop using brushes, filters, and commands, or by collaging or assembling imagery from multiple files. In the next chapter, you'll learn how to open existing files.

Using digital cameras NEW

Digital cameras are a relatively new source of imagery for Photoshop users. Pictures are digitized by the camera, eliminating the need for scanning, and then can be upoaded directly to a computer.

Buying a digital camera

The first step is to figure out which camera model suits your output requirements and budget. Camera makers usually list a camera's resolution as width and height dimensions, in pixels (e.g., 3000 pixels x 2000

(Continued on the following page)

pixels). If you multiply those two values, you'll arrive at a number in the millions, which is the camera's **megapixel** value. This value controls how many pixels the camera captures and is one of the key factors to consider when deciding which model to buy. If your camera captures enough pixels, you'll be able to print high-quality closeups and enlargements of your photos.

Compact, inexpensive "point-and-shoot" cameras offer few or no manual controls and have resolutions of 3 to 5 megapixels. They capture enough detail to produce decent quality 4" x 6" prints (not larger) and acceptable online output.

Advanced amateur camera models have resolutions of 5 to 8 megapixels. You can get high-quality 8" x 10" prints from these cameras, and they offer more manual controls.

Professional camera models (such as the digital SLRs) have resolutions of 9 to 11 megapixels or higher and can produce high-quality 11" x 14" prints—or even larger. but these cameras are costly!

The more megapixels an image contains, the larger the image file size and the longer the upload time from camera to computer. (See our comparison of megapixels to print size on page 60.)

NEW **Shooting digital photographs**

You've purchased or borrowed a camera—now you need to know how to use it. In order to get the best-quality photographs, you need to choose your camera settings wisely. Here are a few basic guidelines.

Medium and high-end digital cameras let you choose an **ISO** setting, which controls the sensitivity of the camera's digital sensor to light (comparable to film speed in film-based photography). High ISO settings tend to produce digital noise in low light areas, so try to choose the minimum ISO setting that still lets you get the proper exposure.

Next, you need to decide whether your camera will capture the photos in the **JPEG** or **Raw** file format. If you chose JPEG, you'll need to choose a color space (**sRGB** for

onscreen or online output; **Adobe RGB** for print output).

For JPEGs, you also need to choose a **white balance** setting that's appropriate for the lighting conditions where the photos are being shot; this setting will be used to process the image data inside the camera. If you decide to use the Raw format instead, don't worry about the white balance setting, as the images won't be processed inside the camera.

Whether you choose the JPEG or Raw format, color casts and other imaging problems can be corrected via the Camera Raw dialog box in Photoshop.

If your camera has a **histogram** display, we suggest you read our section on histograms so you'll be able to interpret the correctness of your exposure before snapping the shutter (see pages 172–173).

Regarding the **exposure** setting, don't deliberately over- or underexpose your photos. If you overexpose them, too much detail will be lost in the highlight areas; if you underexpose them (stop down too much), too much detail will be lost in the shadows. Remember, Photoshop can process and adjust only the details that your camera captures!

Images captured by the camera are stored in a **Compact Flash** (CF) memory card. To upload images from your camera to a computer, you'll need to use a **USB** or **Firewire cable,** depending on which connection your camera supports. Of the two, Firewire is faster. If you want to be able to shoot, store, and upload photos without having to tether your camera to a computer, you can remove the Flash card and insert it into a **card reader** device, then upload from the card reader to your computer via a USB cable. In Windows, use Windows Image Acquisition (WIA) to handle uploading; in Mac, we recommend the OS X Image Capture utility. For more information, see Photoshop Help.

To learn about opening Raw photos via the Camera Raw dialog box, see Chapter 15.

What's the bit about 16 bit?

Why is it better to capture **16 bits per channel?** You can't get good-quality output unless you capture a good tonal range at the outset, and also preserve that range as you edit the document. By starting off with a high-resolution scan or a photo from a digital camera that can capture 16 bits per channel, you've got a head start, because the image will probably contain an abundance of pixels in all levels of the tonal spectrum.

Image-editing commands in Photoshop, especially tonal adjustment commands such as Levels or Curves, change the distribution of pixels in the tonal spectrum. For images that contain 8 bits per channel, such changes will be visible on high-end print output, whereas images that contain 16 bits per channel usually contain an ample number of pixels in all parts of the tonal spectrum, and thus are less likely to suffer a noticeable decline in quality.

If your system or storage limitations prevent you from working with 16-bit images, we suggest a two-stage approach: Perform your initial tonal corrections (e.g., Levels and Curves adjustments) on the 16-bits-per-channel image, then convert it to 8 bits per channel for further editing.

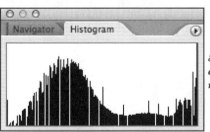

8 bits/ channel mode

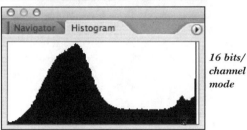

16 bits/ channel mode

1 *As a result of the same Levels command adjustment, the 8-bit image on top shows signs of tonal degradation (spikes and gaps), whereas smooth tonal transitions are preserved in the 16-bit image below.*

16-bits-per-channel mode

Like cameras, scanners range widely in quality. Consumer level scanners can capture 10 bits of accurate data per channel, whereas high-end professional scanners can capture up to 16 bits of accurate data per channel. The wider the dynamic color range and optical density (preferably 3.3 or higher), the finer the subtleties of color and shade the scanner can capture. Shadow areas in particular are notoriously hard to scan well. Starting off with extra pixels can help mitigate the quality reduction caused by editing and resampling commands in Photoshop **1**. (Just for comparison, most advanced amateur and professional digital SLR cameras capture a minimum of 12 bits of accurate data per channel.)

Photoshop can open CMYK or RGB 16-bits-per-channel files. Except for the following restrictions, such images can be successfully edited and adjusted in Photoshop:

➤ Most of the filters on the Blur, Noise, Sharpen, Stylize, and Other submenus on the Filter menu are available, as well as the Distort > Lens Correction filter and the two Render filters, but filters on the other submenus are not.

➤ The Art History brush isn't available (sorry, Van Gogh wannabes).

➤ 16-bits-per-channel files can be saved in only the following formats: Photoshop (.psd), Large Document (.psb), Photoshop PDF (.pdf), Photoshop RAW (.raw), PNG (.png), TIFF (.tif), Portable **NEW** Bit Map (.pbm), JPEG2000 (.jpf), and Cineon (.cin, .sdpx, .dpx, .fido).

And finally, a note about print output: Your output service provider may ask or require you to convert your 16-bit image to 8-bit (Image > Mode > 8 Bits/Channel).

16-Bits/Channel Mode

Resolution for print

Each digital camera model captures a fixed number of pixels. With scanner software, on the other hand, you can control the input resolution.

The print resolution for digitized images (regardless of where they originate from—camera or scanner) is calculated in **pixels per inch** (ppi) **1**–**3**. You want to choose the minimum resolution necessary to obtain the desired output quality from your target output device, but no higher.

High-resolution images contain more pixels, and thus finer detail, but also have larger file sizes, take longer to render onscreen, require more processing time for edits, and take longer to print. Low-resolution images look coarse and jagged and lack detail.

➤ When opening digital photos in the Raw format, you'll set the image resolution in the **Camera Raw** dialog box (see pages 224–227).

➤ When opening digital photos in the JPEG format, you'll set the image resolution in the **Image Size** dialog box (see page 93).

➤ When scanning, you'll use the **scanning software** to set the image resolution.

Before selecting a resolution for print output, ask your print shop what printer or imagesetter resolution and halftone screen frequency they're going to use (the document resolution is different from the output device resolution). As a general rule, for grayscale images, the proper resolution will be in the neighborhood of one-and-a-half times the halftone-screen frequency (lines per inch) of your target output device, and twice the halftone-screen frequency for a color image. These are just general guidelines, though—each printer and print shop is different!

1 *72 ppi*

2 *150 ppi*

3 *300 ppi*

Using scanners

Using a scanning device and scanning software, slides, flat artwork (e.g., drawings), and printed photographs can be digitized (translated into numbers, actually) so they can be read, displayed, edited, and printed by a computer. You can scan images directly into Photoshop, or you can use other scanning software and save the scan in a file format that Photoshop can read.

To produce a high-quality scan for print output, you need to start with a high-quality original. Some scanners will compress an image's dynamic range and increase its contrast, so starting off with a photograph with good tonal range is an important first step. If you're going to scan the photo yourself, take the time to set your scanning parameters carefully.

In addition to the scanning parameters, your scan results will also be limited by the quality of the scanning device itself. If you're going to dramatically transform the image in Photoshop (e.g., by applying filters or performing drastic color adjustments), you can get away with using an inexpensive flatbed scanner. These scanners produce RGB scans. Another option that nets more accurate color and crisper details is to scan a transparency by using a slide scanner.

For professional-quality print output, an even better bet is to pay an output service provider to scan your artwork on either a high-resolution CCD scanner (e.g., a Scitex Smart-Scanner) or a drum scanner. These devices capture wider dynamic ranges of color and shade and can optically distinguish subtle differences in luminosity, even in shadow areas. High-end scanners usually produce CMYK scans, with correspondingly larger file sizes.

Choosing desktop scanner settings

Scanning software usually offers most of the options discussed below, although feature names may vary from one product to another. The quality and file storage size of a resulting scan can be controlled somewhat by several factors under your control, such as the mode, resolution, scale, and crop size.

Preview: Place your artwork in the scanner, then click Preview, PreScan, or an equivalent button.

Scan mode: Choose Black-and-White Line Art (no grays), Grayscale, or Color (choose millions of colors, if available). The file size of an image scanned in Color will be approximately three times larger than if scanned in Grayscale.

Resolution: Choose a resolution value that will allow you to obtain good-quality output from your printer. For grayscale printing on a printer with a 133-line screen, enter 200 ppi as your scan resolution; for color printing, enter 300 ppi; and for line art, enter a high scanning resolution (600 ppi or higher). To calculate the appropriate file size for a scan, see page 60.

Cropping: If you're going to use only part of the original image, you can reduce the scan area by repositioning the handles of the bounding box in the preview area. Cropping can significantly reduce the file size of a scan.

Scale: You can enlarge an image's dimensions by raising the scale percentage above 100%, but doing so may cause it to look blurry. This is because the software uses mathematical guesswork (interpolation) to fill in the missing information.

Scan: Click Scan, and choose a location in which to save the resulting file.

To **scan** into Photoshop, the scanner's plug-in or Twain module must be installed in your system as per the instructions that came with your scanner. If your scanner doesn't have a Photoshop-compatible scanner driver, you can scan your image outside Photoshop instead, save it as a TIFF, and then open it in Photoshop as you would any other image.

To calculate the proper resolution to use when scanning a photo for print or online output, follow the instructions on the next page before performing the following steps.

To scan into Photoshop:

1. Choose File > **Import,** then choose a scanning module or a Twain scanning device.

2. Click Prescan or Preview **1**.

3. Following the guidelines outlined on the previous two pages, choose a scan mode, a resolution value, and other options.

4. *Optional:* Choose a different scaling or magnification percentage and/or manually crop the image preview.

5. Click Scan. The scanned image will appear in a new, untitled document window.

6. Save the document (see pages 65–67). If it needs to be straightened out, see page 104. Also read about the Crop and Straighten Photos command on page 99.

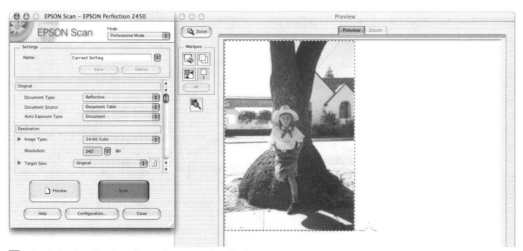

1 *The dialog box for the software in a **scanning** device*

Resolution for Web graphics

When creating an image for Web output, you need to estimate how large your user's browser window is likely to be, and then calculate how much of that window you want your image to cover. Most viewers have their browser window open to around 800 x 600 pixels. Subtract the space taken up by menu bars, scroll bars, and other controls in the browser interface, and you're left with a "live area" of approximately 740 x 460 pixels at most. For most viewers, the browser window doesn't fill the entire screen, so you can count on only about **660 x 420** pixels.

You might find it helpful to create a document preset for the 660 x 420-pixel size, with a resolution of 72 pixels per inch. Document presets appear on the Preset pop-up menu in the New dialog box (see page 61). (Don't pay attention to the inch equivalent for pixels—onscreen imagery is measured in pixels.)

1 *You can use the **Auto Resolution** dialog box to calculate the appropriate resolution for an image based on your chosen print output parameters.*

The **resolution** of Photoshop files, like that of all bitmapped images, is independent of the monitor's resolution and can be customized for particular output devices, with or without modifying their file storage sizes. Nevertheless, it's always best to scan an image at or above the size and resolution required for your target output device.

To calculate the scan resolution for print output:

1. Create a new document (File > New), enter the target Width and Height dimensions, choose Resolution: 72 pixels/inch, choose Color Mode: RGB Color, then click OK. (Stay tuned: The resolution will be readjusted in step 5.)

2. Choose Image > **Image Size.**

3. Click **Auto** on the right side of the dialog box. The Auto Resolution dialog box opens **1**.

4. Enter the **Screen** frequency of your target output device, that is, the lpi, or lines per inch, setting to be used by your desktop or commercial printer.

5. Click **Quality:** Draft (1x screen frequency), Good (1½x screen frequency), or Best (2x screen frequency).

6. Click OK.

7. Jot down the value you see in the **Document Size: Resolution** field. That's the value you'll need to enter in the Camera Raw dialog box for a Raw digital photo, or when scanning your image. *Note:* If you're going to scale the image in Photoshop, multiply the resolution by that scale factor to arrive at the proper resolution for scanning (e.g., if you're going to shrink the image by half, divide the resolution value by 2).

8. Now that you've gotten the information you need, click Cancel.

TIP For output to an inkjet printer, make the document resolution 240 ppi or higher.

File storage sizes

Size (In Inches)	PPI (Resolution)	Black/White 1-Bit	Grayscale 8-Bit	RGB Color 24-Bit
2 x 3	150	17 KB	132 KB	436 KB
	300	67 KB	528 KB	1.66 MB
4 x 5	150	56 KB	440 KB	1.39 MB
	300	221 KB	1.72 MB	5.44 MB
8 x 10	150	220 KB	1.72 MB	5.44 MB
	300	879 KB	6.87 MB	21.64 MB

Note: These file storage sizes are for a one-layer TIFF file with no alpha channels.

Potential gray levels at various output resolutions and screen frequencies (print output)

Output Resolution (dpi)	Screen Frequency (lpi) 60	85	100	133	150
300	26	13			
600	101	51	37	21	
1270	256*	224	162	92	72
2540		256*	256*	256*	256*

Note: Ask your commercial printer what screen frequency (lpi) you will need to specify when imagesetting your file. Also ask your output service provider what resolution (dpi) to use for imagesetting. Some imagesetters can achieve resolutions above 2540 dpi. Note that as the line screen frequency (lpi) goes up at a constant dpi, the number of gray levels goes down.

*PostScript Level 2 printers produce a maximum of 256 gray levels, whereas PostScript Level 3 printers can produce more.

Photo print size versus megapixels NEW

Megapixels (rounded off)	Print Size (in Inches, Rounded Off) 2	3	5	6	8	11
Image resolution of 150 ppi	8 x 10	11 x 14	12 x 16	14 x 20	16 x 20	18 x 24
Image resolution of 300 ppi	4 x 5	5 x 7	6 x 9	7 x 10	8 x 10	10 x 14

Note: The above print sizes are approximations. For a more detailed listing of print sizes, do a Google search on the Web for "translate megapixels to print size."

Creating new, blank documents

In these instructions, you'll create a **new, blank** document. Into this document, you can drag and drop or copy and paste imagery from other files, and of course you can edit it by using all the image-editing features that Photoshop has to offer, such as brushes, shapes, effects, filters, etc.

To create a new, blank document:

1. Choose File > **New** (Ctrl-N/Cmd-N).

2. Enter a name in the **Name** field ▮.

3. Choose a unit of measure from the pop-up menu next to the **Width** field; the same unit will be chosen automatically for the **Height.** Or hold down Shift while choosing a unit to change the value for that dimension only. Next, enter Width and Height values; or position the pointer over the word "Width" and drag to the left or right to choose a value, then do the same for the Height.
   or
   To choose a preset size, choose from the **Preset** pop-up menu. The Default Photoshop Size is illustrated below. The preset sizes are listed in groups in the following order: paper sizes for print, print sizes for photos, monitor sizes (in pixels), European print sizes, and video output sizes. For more about the presets, see page 63.

4. Enter the **Resolution** required for your target output device—whether it's an imagesetter or the Web (resolution issues are discussed on pages 56–57). You can position the pointer over the word "Resolution," then drag to the left or right to choose a value.

5. Choose a document color mode from the **Color Mode** pop-up menu, then, from the adjacent pop-up menu, choose 8 bit or 16 bit for the color depth. You can convert the image to a different mode later (see "Document color modes" on pages 35–37).

(Continued on the following page)

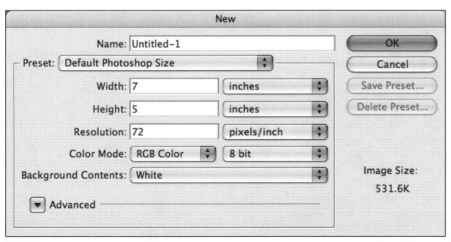

▮ *In the **New** dialog box, enter a Name; choose a Preset size or enter Width, Height, and Resolution values; and choose Color Mode and Background Contents options.*

6. Note the Image Size listed on the right side of the dialog box. If you need to reduce that size, you can choose smaller dimensions, a lower resolution, or a lower bit depth.

7. For the Background of the image, choose **Background Contents: White** or **Background Color.** (To choose a Background color, see pages 182–185); or choose **Transparent** if you want the bottommost tier of the document to be a layer.

8. *Optional:* When you click the Advanced arrowhead, the Color Profile pop-up menu becomes available. You can assign a Color Profile here and now, or you can do it later via Edit > Assign Profile. The profile list will vary depending on which Color Mode you've chosen. To learn more about color profiles, see pages 44–45 and 50.

For Web or print output, choose Square as the Pixel Aspect Ratio, or for video output, choose one of the other options. For more information about these options, see Photoshop Help.

9. Click OK. A new, blank document window will appear onscreen **1**–**2**. To save this new file, see page 65.

TIP To have the New dialog box settings match those of another open document, with the New dialog box open, from the bottom of the Preset pop-up menu, choose the name of the document that has the desired dimensions.

TIP If the current Clipboard contents originated from Photoshop or Illustrator, the New dialog box will automatically display its dimensions. Another way of getting those dimensions to show up in the New dialog box is by choosing Clipboard from the Preset pop-up. If you want to prevent those dimensions from displaying, hold down Alt/Option as you choose File > New; the last-used dimensions will display instead.

Photoshop Big

In Photoshop, you can create and save files as large as 300,000 x 300,000 pixels, or over 2 gigabytes (GB), with up to 56 user-created channels. Your gonzo files can be saved in the **Large Document (PSB)** format, which is designed specifically to handle large documents. Files in this format can be opened and edited only in Photoshop CS or CS2.

So what are we supposed to do with these files, we ask? Well, as Victor, our technical editor, points out, 30,000 x 30,000 pixels is the largest printable file size. So if you have the space to store and work with PSB files, great, but you'll have to drastically lower the resolution in order to output them (duplicate the file first, of course!).

1 *A **new**, untitled document window in Windows*

2 *A **new**, untitled document window in Mac*

Create New, Blank Document

Choose your defaults

In Preferences (Ctrl-K/Cmd-K) > Units & Rulers, for **New Document Presets Resolutions,** you can enter **Print Resolution** and **Screen Resolution** values, which appear in the Resolution field in the File > **New** dialog box when you choose a preset from the Preset pop-up menu. The Print Resolution value (default 300 ppi) is used for the paper and photo print presets; the Screen Resolution value (default 72 ppi) is used for the monitor presets.

Creating document presets

If you tend to use the same document sizes, color modes, or other settings repeatedly, it's worth your while to create **document presets** that contain those settings. This will lessen the time it takes you to create new files.

To create a document preset:

1. Open the **New** dialog box (Choose File > New or press Ctrl-N/Cmd-N).

2. Choose the desired settings in the dialog box, such as width, height, resolution, color mode, bit depth, background contents, and color profile. For any setting that you don't want included in the preset, simply don't choose a value for it; you'll be able to exclude it from the preset in step 5.

3. Click **Save Preset.** The New Document Preset dialog box opens **1**.

4. Enter a name in the **Preset Name** field.

5. In the **Include In Saved Settings** area, uncheck any New dialog box settings that you don't want included in the preset.

6. Click OK. The preset will appear on the Preset pop-up menu in the New dialog box.

TIP To delete a user-created preset, choose it from the Preset pop-up menu, click Delete Preset, then click Yes (this can't be undone).

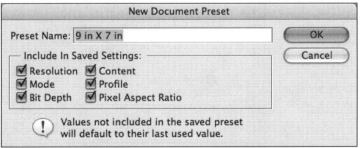

1 *Use the New Document Preset dialog box to control which of the current settings in the New dialog box will be saved in your document preset.*

Create Document Presets

Using the status bar

In Windows and Mac, press the **Status Bar** arrowhead at the bottom of the application/ document window, then from the **Show** 🆕 submenu, choose one of the following:

For **Version Cue,** see your network administrator or Photoshop Help.

Document Sizes to display the file storage size both for the flattened file (the first amount), and for the file with all its layers (the second amount) **1**.

Document Profile to display the embedded color profile; the words "Untagged [RGB or CMYK]" appear when no profile is present.

Document Dimensions to display the dimensions of the image.

Scratch Sizes to display the amount of RAM Photoshop is using for all currently open pictures (on the left) and the amount of RAM currently available to Photoshop (on the right). When the first amount is greater than the second amount, it means Photoshop is currently utilizing virtual memory on the scratch disk.

Efficiency to display the percentage of processing time that's currently being devoted to actual program operations in RAM. A percentage below 100 indicates the scratch disk is being used.

Current Tool to display the name of the currently chosen tool.

Press and hold on the status bar to display the page **preview**—a thumbnail of the image relative to the current paper size (including custom printing marks, if any).

To find out a file's storage size:

In Windows, use Windows Explorer to locate the file you're interested in, and look in the Size column **2**. Or for a more accurate figure, right-click the file icon and choose **Properties.**

In Mac, look at the file information in the Finder. Or for a more accurate figure, click once on the file icon in the Finder, then choose File > **Get Info** (Cmd-I) **3**.

Do this any time

Regardless of which option is chosen from the status bar pop-up menu, you can Alt-press/Option-press the status bar to display the image's **dimensions,** number of **channels, mode, bit depth,** and **resolution.**

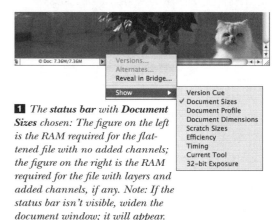

1 The **status bar** with **Document Sizes** chosen: The figure on the left is the RAM required for the flattened file with no added channels; the figure on the right is the RAM required for the file with layers and added channels, if any. Note: If the status bar isn't visible, widen the document window; it will appear.

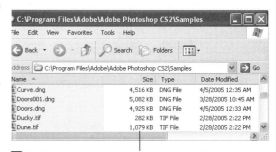

2 In Windows, file sizes are listed in the **Size** column.

3 In Mac, to learn the **storage size** of a file, use **Get Info** (Cmd-I).

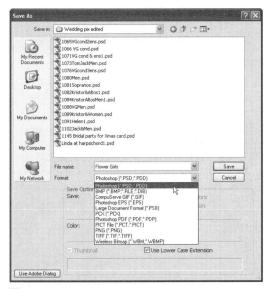

1 *The Save As dialog box in* **Windows**

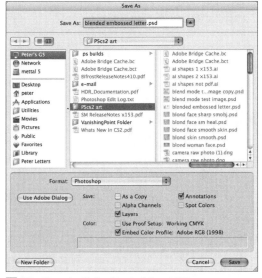

2 *The Save As dialog box in* **Mac OS X**

Use Adobe Dialog?

If you're using Version Cue, click the **Use Adobe Dialog** button in the Save As, Open, or Place dialog box to access the Adobe file management feature (see Photoshop Help). If you're not using Version Cue, stick with the dialog boxes for your operating system.

Saving files

If you're not sure which format to choose when **saving** your file, we recommend the native Photoshop format, PSD. In Chapter 32, you'll learn why and how to save files in the EPS, DCS, PDF, and TIFF formats; in Chapter 33, you'll find information about the GIF, JPEG, and PNG formats.

To save an unsaved document:

1. If the document window isn't completely blank, you can choose File > **Save** (Ctrl-S/Cmd-S); if it's blank, choose File > **Save As.**

2. Type a name in the **File name 1**/ **Save As 2** field.

3. Choose a location for the file.

   In Windows, to locate another folder or drive, use the **Save in** pop-up menu at the top of the dialog box.

   In Mac, click a drive or folder in the **Sidebar** panel on the left side of the window. To locate a recently used folder, use the pop-up menu below the name field.

4. Choose a file format from the **Format** pop-up menu. Only the native Photoshop (PSD), Large Document (PSB), TIFF, and Photoshop PDF formats support layers.

5. If you're not familiar with the features listed in the **Save** area, you can leave the settings as is.

   The As a Copy option is discussed on page 67. If the file contains an embedded profile and the format you're saving to supports embedded profiles, the Color: Embed Color Profile: [ ] option can be checked; read about this feature on page 50.

6. Click Save.

TIP In Mac, to have a three-character file extension appended automatically to your files, in Photoshop > Preferences > File Handling, choose Append File Extension: Always or Ask When Saving. Extensions are required when exporting Mac files to the Windows platform.

Save an Unsaved Document

Saving layers, vectors, and effects

Photoshop (PSD), Large Document (PSB), TIFF, and **Photoshop PDF** are the only formats that preserve the following:

➤ Multiple layers and layer transparency (including shape layers, smart objects, etc.)

➤ Adjustment layers

➤ Editable type layers

➤ Layer effects

➤ Grids and guides

➤ ICC color management profiles (well, actually, the PICT, JPEG, Photoshop DCS, and Photoshop EPS formats preserve these profiles, too)

➤ Lab Color mode (the Photoshop EPS and Photoshop DCS formats also preserve this mode)

Note: An image in Duotone color mode can be saved only in the native Photoshop, Large Document, Photoshop EPS, or Photoshop PDF format.

If you're going to export a file to another application, be sure to save a flattened copy of it in another format, as few applications can read Photoshop's layer transparency.

TIP Flatten a copy of a layered image instead of the original (see the following page). That way, you'll preserve your option to rework the original layers later.

Each time you choose the **Save** command, the prior version of your file is overwritten.

To save a previously saved file:

Choose File > **Save** (Ctrl-S/Cmd-S).

The simple **Revert** command restores your document to its last-saved version, whereas the History palette, which we discuss in Chapter 10, is a full-service multiple undo feature. Its partner, the History Brush tool, can be used to selectively revert a portion of an image. Revert does show up as a state on the History palette, so you can undo a Revert by clicking an earlier history state.

To revert to the last saved version:

Choose File > **Revert.**

PSD file compatibility

If, in Edit (Photoshop, in Mac) > Preferences > File Handling, you choose **Maximize PSD and PSB File Compatibility: Always**, each time you save a file that contains layers, a flattened version is saved along with it. This is helpful when exporting images to applications that don't read layers.

If you prefer to decide on a file-by-file basis whether to save the extra flattened version with your file, choose **Ask** from the pop-up menu instead. Each time you use the Save or Save As command, an alert dialog box will appear, at which point you can decide whether to include the extra image.

What is the Duplicate command?

The Image > **Duplicate** command copies a document and all its layers, layer masks, and channels into currently available memory without saving a permanent copy of the file to disk. You can use this command to try out variations without altering the original file, but be aware that if an application freeze or system crash occurs, whatever is currently in memory will be deleted, including any unsaved duplicates!

1 *The Save As dialog box in Windows*

2 *The Save As dialog box in Mac*

You can use the **Save As** command to save a copy of a document in a different color mode (e.g., save a copy in CMYK Color mode and keep the original version in RGB Color mode) or to spin off design or adjustment variations.

To save a new version of a file:

1. Choose File > **Save As** (Ctrl-Shift-S/ Cmd-Shift-S).

2. Change the name in the **File name 1**/ **Save As 2** field.

3. Choose a location in which to save the new version by using the **Save in** pop-up menu in Windows or the **Sidebar** panel and scroll windows in Mac.

4. *Optional:* Choose a different file format from the Format pop-up menu. Only formats that are available for the document's current color mode and bit depth will appear on the list.

   Beware! If the chosen format doesn't support multiple layers, the Layers option will automatically become dimmed, an alert icon will display, and the saved file will be flattened.

5. Check any available options in the **Save** area, as desired, and also check ICC Profile/Embed Color Profile: [profile name], if available (see page 50).

   Check **As a Copy** to have the copy remain closed and the original stay open; or leave this option unchecked to have the original close and the copy stay open.

6. Click Save. For an EPS file, follow the instructions on pages 489–490. For a TIFF or PDF file, follow the instructions on pages 492–496. For other formats, see Photoshop Help.

TIP If you don't change the file name and you click Save, an alert dialog box will appear. Click Replace to save over the original file, or click Cancel to return to the Save As dialog box.

TIP Explore layer comps, an elegant way of presenting multiple versions of a document in a single file, on pages 292–294.

Ending a work session

To close a document:

Click the **Close** button in the upper right corner of the document window (Win) **1** / upper left corner of the document window (Mac) **2**.

or

Choose File > **Close** (Ctrl-W/Cmd-W).

If you attempt to close a file that was modified since it was last saved, a warning prompt will appear **3**. Click No/Don't Save to close the file without saving it; or click Yes/Save to save the file before closing; or click Cancel to cancel the close operation.

To exit/quit Photoshop:

In Windows, choose File > **Exit** (Ctrl-Q) or click the application window close box.

In the Mac, choose Photoshop > **Quit Photoshop** (Cmd-Q).

All open Photoshop files will close. If any changes were made to any open file since it was last saved, a prompt will appear. Click **No** (N)/**Don't Save** (D) to close the file without saving it; or click **Yes** (Y)/**Save** to save it before exiting/quitting; or click **Cancel** to cancel the exit/quit operation.

1 *In Windows, click the **Close** button.*

2 *In Mac, click the **close** (red) button.*

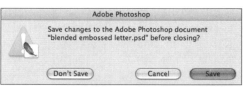
3 *In Mac, if you attempt to **close** a file that contains unsaved changes, this prompt will appear. A similar prompt appears if you exit/quit Photoshop and any open files contain unsaved changes.*

Victor Gavenda's tip

Mac users are familiar with the traffic light buttons in the title bar of every window: Red means close, yellow means minimize (to the Dock), and green means zoom (to full size). One of the more obscure features of OS X is a little **dot** that appears in the close button of an document window if the file has been **modified** since it was **last saved**.

BRIDGE 4

1 *As with Photoshop, you can explore **Bridge** in depth or just use a handful of its key features.*

2 *In Photoshop, click the **Go to Bridge** button on the options bar.*

What's next?

You've calibrated your monitor and opened an image into Photoshop (via Bridge, via the Place or Open command, or via the Camera Raw dialog box). Now what?

If you're going to paint on it or distort it via filters, you can get right to work! Most images need some tonal or color correction, though, which we urge you to apply via **adjustment layers** (see Chapter 11) and monitor via the **Histogram** palette. To correct the color, see Chapter 13; for **exposure** correction, see Chapter 16; and for **refocusing,** see Chapter 17.

BRIDGE IS A STANDALONE APPLICATION, aptly named because it serves as a conduit among all the programs in Adobe Creative Suite 2 (it replaces the File Browser from Photoshop CS). In this chapter, you'll learn how to use Bridge to open files, find files, sort and label file thumbnails, create folders, delete files, rename files, and assign keywords to files. You'll also learn how to customize the Bridge window **1**. To complete the chapter, we'll show you how to open, paste, and place AI (Adobe Illustrator), EPS, and PDF files into Photoshop.

Launching Bridge (NEW)

We like to use **Bridge** to open our files into Photoshop, as it lets us view and open Creative Suite files using thumbnails (easy identification!) instead of just file names. Bridge has a host of other useful features, too. You can use it to locate, read info about, sort, rename, move, rotate, and delete files, apply automate commands, and if you have Adobe Creative Suite 2 installed, synchronize color settings for the whole suite.

Start by learning how to use Bridge to open files (it's easier to use than the Open command!), then learn about its other features when you're ready.

To launch Bridge:

In Photoshop, near the middle of the options bar , click the **Go to Bridge** button (Ctrl-Alt-O/Cmd-Option-O) 🖳 **2**.
or
Double-click the Bridge application icon in Program Files\Adobe\Adobe Bridge in Win; Applications folder in Mac.
or
In Mac, click the Bridge icon 🍂 on the Dock.

The Bridge window opens.

The Bridge window

The panels

On the left side of the Bridge window (**1**, next page) are five panels, each with its own folder tab.

NEW Bridge features can be accessed quickly from the top part of the **Favorites** panel (use Edit [Bridge, in Mac] > Preferences > General to control what appears on the list). Below that, you can select from a user-created list of folders. To add a folder to that list, click the folder in the Browser panel on the right, then choose File > **Add to Favorites.** To remove a selected Favorites folder from the list, choose File > Remove from Favorites.

The **Folders** panel contains a scroll window with a hierarchical listing of the top-level and nested folders on your hard drive.

The **Preview** panel displays a preview or an icon of the file currently selected in the Browser panel, depending on the file type, or a folder thumbnail, if a folder is selected.

Using the **Keywords** panel, you can categorize images by assigning keywords to them, such as by event, name, location, or other criteria. This will enable you to find image thumbnails based on keyword searches (see page 81 and Bridge Help).

The **Metadata** panel contains several sections. The File Properties section lists info about the currently selected file, such as the filename, kind (format), date created, date modified, and file size, and in some cases the dimensions, resolution, bit depth, and color mode.

Further down in the Metadata panel, you can use the IPTC section to attach caption, contact, and copyright info to the currently selected file. (IPTC stands for International Press Telecommunications Council, an organization that has developed an information standard for transferring and publishing text and images.) Click the pencil icon for a listing, enter or modify the file description information, then click the Apply ✔ button. The info also updates in the Description, Origin, or IPTC panels of the File Info

dialog box, and vice versa. To learn about the Camera Data (Exif) and Stock Photos sections of the Metadata panel, see Bridge Help.

Continuing our tour, on the right side of the Bridge window, in the **Browser** panel, you'll see image thumbnails and/or nested folders within the currently selected folder.

TIP To shrink the entire Bridge window, click **NEW** the Compact Mode button 🔲 in the upper right corner. Click it again to restore the window to its previous size.

TIP If the Browser panel is in Thumbnails, **NEW** Filmstrip, or Versions and Alternates view (see page 74), you can rest the pointer over a thumbnail or file name to learn more about that file **1**.

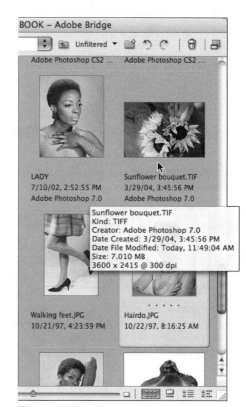

1 *Use **tool tips** to learn about a file.*

Bridge Window

1 *You can use **Bridge** to locate, sort, open, move, rename, and even delete files. In this screen shot, the Browser panel (on the right) is in **Thumbnails** view.*

Opening files

The number of images that can be **open** at a time in Photoshop depends on currently available RAM and scratch disk space.

To open files via Bridge: NEW

1. Use the **Folders** panel to navigate to the file you want to open. Scroll upward or downward, expand or collapse any folder by using the arrowheads or by double-clicking, or open a folder by clicking its icon. You could also choose a Favorites or Recent Folders category from the pop-up menu at the top of the Bridge window.

   To move up one level at a time in the folder hierarchy, click the **Go Up** button ⬆ at the top of the Bridge window.

2. Click an image thumbnail in the **Browser** panel. A light border will appear around it, a preview will appear in the Preview panel (click the Preview tab), and file data will appear in the Metadata panel. *or*
   Ctrl-click/Cmd-click multiple non-consecutive thumbnails **1**. Or click the

---

Refresh yourself

If you move, add, or rename files in the Finder or Windows Explorer, Bridge updates automatically the next time you make it the active window. You can force it to update at any time by choosing **Refresh (F5)** from the Folders panel menu or the View menu.

---

first thumbnail in a series of consecutive thumbnails, then Shift-click the last.

3. Double-click a thumbnail (or one of several selected thumbnails) or press (Ctrl-O/Cmd-O). Photoshop will launch, if it isn't already running, and the image will appear onscreen. Once opened, images can be resaved in other formats via File > Save As.

TIP By default, the Bridge window stays open after you use it to open a file. To minimize/close the Bridge window as you open a file, hold down Alt/Option as you double-click a thumbnail.

TIP If this icon appears ⬚ below a thumbnail, it means the file has been opened and modified in Camera Raw.

Switching documents

In Photoshop, if multiple documents are **open,** you can do any of the following to **switch** among them:

➤ Click in a document window.

➤ Choose a document name from the bottom of the Window menu.

➤ Cycle among open documents by pressing Ctrl-Tab/Control-Tab.

To **reopen** a file that was recently worked on in the same work session and then closed, in Photoshop, choose the file name from the File > **Open Recent** submenu.

1 *Ctrl-click/Cmd-click to select multiple file **thumbnails**.*

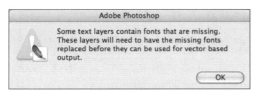

1 *This alert dialog box will appear if you open a file for which a font is missing.*

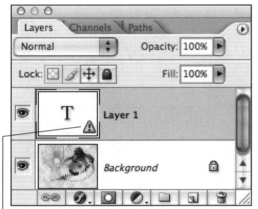

2 *The missing fonts alert icon for an editable type layer on the Layers palette*

3 *This alert dialog box will appear if you try to edit an editable type layer for which a font is missing.*

If you **rotate** a thumbnail, and then open the file, it will open in the new orientation.

To rotate a thumbnail:

Click the thumbnail (or select multiple thumbnails), then click the **Rotate 90° counterclockwise** ↻ or **Rotate 90° clockwise** button ↻ at the top of the Bridge window.

TIP To rotate a document after it's opened, see page 104.

Dealing with the "ifs"

When you open a file in some formats, a dialog box opens automatically; you'll need to choose options and click OK before you can work on the document. For example, if you open a file in the Adobe Illustrator (AI version 9 or later) or PDF format, which requires a conversion from vector to bitmap, the **Import PDF** dialog box appears onscreen. Follow steps 3–4 on pages 82–83.

If a **font** is **missing** (is unavailable or not installed) when you open a Photoshop document that contains editable type, an alert dialog box will appear **1** and an alert triangle will appear in the thumbnail of the offending layer on the Layers palette **2**. If you then try to edit the layer, yet another alert dialog box will appear **3**. You have two choices: Either click OK to have Photoshop change the font to a generic one, or click Cancel, close the Photoshop document, open the required font, then reopen the document.

If the **Embedded Profile Mismatch** alert dialog box appears, it means the file's color profile doesn't match the current working space. See page 47.

If the file you want to open simply won't open, it may be because the required plug-in module for that format (e.g., Scitex CT or PICT Resource) isn't in the **Photoshop Plug-Ins** folder. Install the plug-in, then try opening the file.

Open Files

You can **customize** the **panels** to your liking —a bit more of this, a bit less of that **1**.

To customize the Bridge window: NEW

Do any of the following:

➤ To make a panel **taller** or **shorter,** drag a horizontal bar; the other panels will resize automatically.

➤ To adjust the **width** of all the panels, drag the vertical bar to the left or right.

➤ To **hide** a panel, uncheck its name on the View menu.

➤ Drag any folder tab into another **group.**

➤ To have the thumbnails area fill the entire window, click the **Show/Hide Panels** button in the lower left corner of the window. Click the button again to redisplay the panels.

➤ To change the **size** of the **thumbnails,** move the thumbnail size slider at the bottom of the window; or click the Smallest Thumbnail Size button or the Largest Thumbnail Size button.

➤ To change the thumbnail layout, click one of the four **view** buttons in the lower right corner of the Bridge window. You can also choose a thumbnail view from the View menu.

➤ In Filmstrip view, you can toggle between the vertical and horizontal layouts by clicking the **Switch Filmstrip Orientation** button or scroll through thumbnails by clicking these buttons.

➤ To have images and folders display in the Browser panel, on the View menu, check **Show Folders**; or turn this option off to display image thumbnails but not folders. To reveal the contents of a nested folder, double-click its thumbnail.

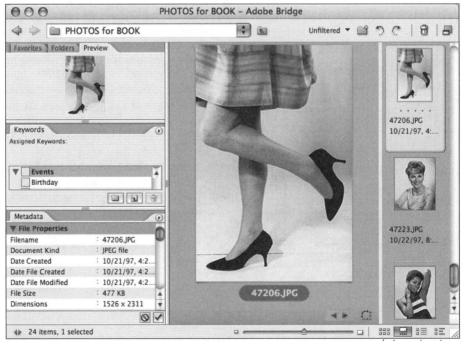

1 *In this* **Bridge** *window, the Browser panel is in* **Filmstrip** *view.*

Thumbnails *view* / **Details** *view* **Versions** **And** **Alternates** *view* / **Filmstrip** *view*

Customize Bridge Window

Window dressing

The Edit (Bridge, in Mac) > **Preferences** dialog box (Ctrl-K/Cmd-K) lets you specify default settings. For example, in the **General** panel, for **Thumbnails,** you can move the **Background** slider to set a gray value for the Browser panel, decide whether to **Show Tooltips,** and choose what types of **data** (called metadata) will display below the thumbnails. Or in the **Favorites Items** area, you can check which default items and folders you want listed in the Favorites panel. For information about Bridge Preferences panels, see pages 460–461 and Bridge > Help.

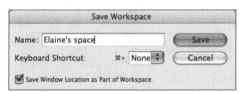

1 *Use the **Save Workspace** dialog box to assign a name and keyboard shortcut to a custom workspace.*

By saving your custom **workspaces** in Bridge, you won't have to set up your window configuration each time you relaunch.

To save a workspace: NEW

1. Choose a size and location of the overall Bridge window, a size (and groupings) for the panels, and a thumbnail view for the Browser panel, then choose Window > Workspace > **Save Workspace.** The Save Workspace dialog box opens **1**.

2. Enter a **Name** for the workspace, choose a **Keyboard Shortcut** (or choose None), check Save Window Location as Part of Workspace (optional), then click **Save.**

3. To choose any saved workspace, use the assigned shortcut or choose the workspace name from the Window > **Workspace** submenu. You can also choose from a list of preset workspaces (e.g., Filmstrip Focus) on this submenu.

The Bridge menus NEW

➤ Use **File** menu commands to open, delete, and access File Info for selected file(s). You can use the Open With command to open a selected file using any Adobe program installed on your system.

➤ Use **Edit** menu commands to copy and paste a file into another folder, to quickly select thumbnails that either do or don't have labels, and to access the Find command to search for files.

➤ Use **Tools** menu commands to purge or export thumbnail cache files and to run automate commands.

➤ Use **Label** menu commands to assign star ratings and color labels to thumbnails.

➤ Use **View** menu commands to choose a thumbnail view, control which panels display, sort thumbnails, control which file formats display, and Refresh (update) the window display.

➤ Use **Window** menu commands to save or delete custom workspaces, restore the default workspace, and choose preset and user-created workspaces.

Save Workspace; Bridge Menus

Searching for files

To find files via Bridge: **NEW**

1. In Bridge, choose Edit > **Find** (Ctrl-F/ Cmd-F). The Find dialog box opens **1**.

2. Choose a folder to search through from the **Look in** pop-up menu. If you need to select a different folder, click Browse, locate the folder, then click Choose.

3. Check **Include All Subfolders** to search all subfolders within the designated folder, or uncheck this option to search through only the Look in folder.

4. From the pop-up menus in the **Criteria** area, choose search criteria (e.g., file name, date created, label, or rating), and enter data in the adjoining field(s). If you need additional criteria fields in which to enter data, click the plus sign. ⊕

5. From the **Match** pop-up menu, choose **If any criteria are met** to find files based on one or more criteria; or choose **If all criteria are met** to narrow the selection to files that meet all the chosen criteria.

6. *Optional:* Check **Show find results in a new browser window** to have the results

of the search appear in a new Bridge window. If you uncheck this option, the results will display in the current window.

7. Click **Find.**

The results of the search will display in Bridge in a temporary folder called **Find Results,** which will remain on the Recent Folders list (accessible from the pop-up menu at the top of the Bridge window) until either another search operation is conducted or you exit/quit Bridge.

To save the find results to a permanent file group, click **Save as Collection,** enter a Name, then click Save. File collections can be viewed by clicking **Collections** in the Favorites panel, then double-clicking the desired collection thumbnail.

> ### The real thing
> To locate an "actual" file in Explorer/Finder, click a thumbnail in Bridge, then choose File > **Reveal in Finder/Reveal in Explorer.** The file's folder will open as a window. In Mac, the file icon will also be highlighted.

1 *Use the **Find** dialog box to search for and locate files by various criteria.*

Find Files

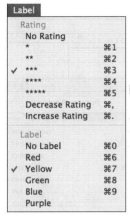

1 *Use the **Label** menu to assign a star **Rating** and/or color **Label** to selected thumbnails.*

Labeling and sorting thumbnails

By labeling thumbnails with a star **rating** or color **label,** you'll be able to display them based on the presence or absence of labels, and find them easily via the Find command.

To label thumbnails: NEW

1. Select one or more thumbnails in the main window. Ctrl-click/Cmd-click multiple nonconsecutive thumbnails, or click the first thumbnail in a series of consecutive thumbnails, then Shift-click the last.

2. From the Label menu **1**, choose a star **Rating** and/or a color **Label,** or press the assigned keyboard shortcut. A file can have both a rating and a label; it will require making two trips to the menu. *or*
Click a thumbnail, then click one, two, three, four, or five of the dots below the thumbnail. A **star** will appear for each dot you click.

   TIP To remove a star, click the star to its left. To remove all the stars from a thumbnail, click to the left of the first star.

3. On the **Unfiltered/Filtered** pop-up menu at the top of the Bridge window **2**, check a rating and/or label category; only thumbnails bearing that label will be displayed. To redisplay all thumbnails regardless of label, check **Show All Items.**

TIP If you get an alert prompt regarding where labels and ratings are stored, click Don't show again, then click OK.

You can **rearrange** and **sort** thumbnails in the Browser panel. This is especially important if you use batch or automate operations, as these commands process files based on the current sequence of thumbnails.

To rearrange thumbnails manually: NEW

Drag a thumbnail (or thumbnails) to any new location. It will remain where you place it unless you perform a sorting operation.

2 *Use the **Unfiltered/Filtered** pop-up menu to control which thumbnails are displayed based on their star rating and/or color labels.*

Choosing a **sorting** order (By Date Created, By Date File Modified, etc.) for your files organizes them and saves you from having to fish through a lot of files to locate them.

To apply a sorting method: **NEW**

From the View > **Sort** submenu, choose a sorting criterion for all the currently displayed thumbnails **1**. You can leave **Ascending Order** checked on this menu; or uncheck this option to sort thumbnails in descending order.

To create a new folder:

1. Via the Folders panel or by choosing from the "Look In" pop-up menu at the top of the Bridge window, navigate to the desired drive or folder that you want the new folder to appear in.

2. Click the **New Folder** button 📁 at the top of the window, type a name in the highlighted field; press Enter/Return.

Deleting files

To delete files: **NEW**

1. Click a thumbnail, then click the **Delete File** 🗑 button at the top of the window (Backspace/Delete). (To delete multiple files, Ctrl-click/Cmd-click multiple thumbnails first; or click the first in a series of thumbnails, then Shift-click the last in the series.)

2. Click Yes. *Note:* You can also delete a whole folder full of files, so be careful! To retrieve a deleted file or folder, double-click the system's Recycle Bin/Trash icon, then drag the item from the Trash window back into the Bridge window.

Renaming files

To rename a file:

1. Click a thumbnail, then click the file name below the thumbnail. The text to the left of the period will become high-lighted automatically.

2. Type a new name **2** (don't try to delete the extension), then press Enter/Return or click outside the name field.

Moving stuff around

You can drag a **file** or **folder** thumbnail from the Browser panel into the Folders panel to move it to another folder (or to the Desktop). Ctrl-drag/Option-drag a thumbnail to add a copy of the file or folder to another folder.

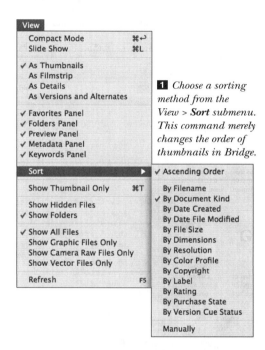

1 *Choose a sorting method from the View > Sort submenu. This command merely changes the order of thumbnails in Bridge.*

2 *Change the filename.*

When you upload digital photos from your camera to your computer, they keep the sequential number labels (e.g., "CRW-0016") that were assigned to them by your camera. To help you identify your photos, you can attach more recognizable **names** to them (e.g., "Dancer" or "Dog"). This can be done quickly via a batch-processing command.

To batch-rename files: NEW

1. In Bridge, click then Shift-click a series of consecutive files, or Ctrl-click/Cmd-click nonconsecutive files, or press Ctrl-A/Cmd-A to select all the files in the window.

2. Choose Tools > **Batch Rename** (Ctrl-Shift-R/Cmd-Shift-R). The Batch Rename dialog box opens **1**.

3. For the **Destination Folder,** choose:

   Rename in same folder to rename the files and leave them in their current location.

   Move to other folder to rename the files and move them to a new location.

   Copy to other folder to leave the original files unchanged and rename the copies in the new location—an easy way to duplicate your photos.

For the Move or Copy option, click Browse, choose a new folder location, then click Choose.

4. For **New Filenames,** do any of the following:

   Choose an option from the pop-up menu. **Text** lets you enter text for the new filenames (probably the best choice); **Current Filename** lets you modify the original name; **Sequence Number** and **Letter** let you include a number or letter that increments from filename to filename (enter a starting number or letter).

   Click the ⊕ button to display another row of criteria fields; click the ⊖ button to remove a row of fields.

   The current and new names will preview at the bottom of the dialog box.

5. For **Options**, check "Preserve current filename in XMP Metadata" to keep the former filename in the file's metadata. This option lets you reinstate that name in a later batch-rename session by choosing Preserved Filename from the pop-up menu. Check **Compatibility** options.

6. Click **Rename.**

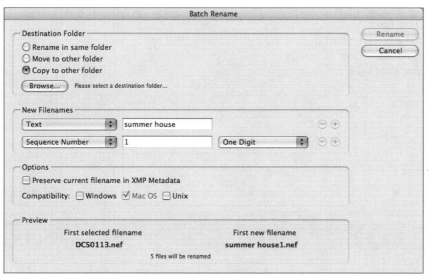

1 *The **Batch Rename** dialog box lets you rename files en masse.*

Exporting the cache

Each time a folder is displayed in the Browser panel, the program automatically creates a **cache** file containing information (e.g., large thumbnail data, ratings, and labeling) about the files in that folder. Having the cache helps speed up the redisplay of image thumbnails.

If you copy files to a removable disk or to a shared folder on a network, you should also copy the cache files. But before you can do so, you have to export the cache files to the currently displayed folder.

NEW **To export the cache for the current folder:**

Choose Tools > Cache > **Export Cache.** Two cache files—named **Adobe Bridge Cache.bc** (metadata cache) and **Adobe Bridge Cache.bct** (thumbnail cache)—will be placed into the currently displayed folder in the Browser panel.

Note: To display the cache files in Bridge, choose View > Show Hidden Files. The cache files will display in the Browser window.

If you suspect the cache may be causing a display problem, you can use a command to purge it. Note that the large thumbnail data that's stored in the cache isn't retrievable!

NEW **To delete the cache files:**

1. To remove the cache files from the current folder, choose Tools > Cache > **Purge Cache for This Folder.**

2. Click OK.

Alas, poor Open command

With Bridge now taking center stage, the Open command is relegated to this puny little sidebar! To use the Open command, in Photoshop, choose File > **Open** (Ctrl-O/Cmd-O). Locate the file you want to open; choose All Formats/All Readable Documents at the top of the dialog box or choose a format from the Files of type/Format drop-down menu; click the desired filename; then click Open.

Another way to open a file is by double-clicking its **file icon** in **Windows Explorer/Finder;** this will also launch Photoshop if it's not already running.

Export, Purge Cache

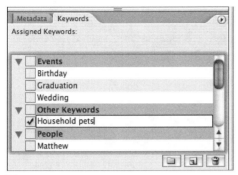

1 *A name is entered for a new **keyword**.*

Assigning keywords

Keywords are used by search utilities to locate files and by file management programs to organize them. In Bridge, you can **create keywords** and assign them to your files.

To assign keywords to files:

In the **Keywords** panel, do any of the following:

To create a **new keyword,** click the New Keyword button ▣ and type a name **1**.

To create a new **keyword set,** click the New Keyword Set button ▢ and type a set name.

To **assign** a keyword to an image, click an image thumbnail (or select multiple thumbnails), then click the box to the left of a keyword category to make a check mark appear.

To **rename** a category, click the category, choose Rename from the Keywords panel menu, then type a name.

To **remove** a category, click the category, click the Delete Keyword button, 🗑 then click OK.

Opening PDF, AI, and EPS files

When you open Adobe Illustrator (version 9 or later), Illustrator EPS, or PDF files in Photoshop, they're rasterized, meaning they're converted from their native vector format into the Photoshop pixel format. Follow these instructions to **open** such files as **new documents,** or follow the instructions on page 84 to place them into existing Photoshop files.

Note: When opened in Photoshop CS2, Illustrator 9 and later files that are saved with the Create PDF Compatible file option open in the Photoshop PDF format, not EPS.

NEW **To open a PDF, Adobe Illustrator, or Illustrator EPS file as a new document:**

1. In Bridge, locate and click the image you want to open, then choose File > Open With > **Adobe Photoshop CS2.** The Import PDF dialog box opens.

2. Choose an option from the **Thumbnail Size** pop-up menu **1**. *Note:* If you're opening a PDF that contains more than one page, click the thumbnail for the page you want to open.

3. For **Page Options,** do the following:

   Choose a **Crop To** option. Bounding Box, Crop Box, and Art Box crop artwork to the artboard or to a user-created crop area. The other options use custom settings, if any, entered into Illustrator's Print dialog box.

   Enter the **Resolution** required for your final output device. Entering the correct final resolution now, before the image is rasterized, produces optimal rendering.

   Choose a document color mode from the **Mode** pop-up menu. (See "Document color modes" on pages 35–37.)

   Choose a **Bit Depth.**

   Check **Anti-aliased** to reduce jaggies and soften edge transitions.

   Leave **Suppress Warnings** unchecked (our recommendation) to allow any

Illustrator into Photoshop **NEW**

You can get Adobe Illustrator files into Photoshop via any of these methods:

Open command	Opens the file as a new document; converts paths into pixels
Place command	Opens the file as a smart object layer in an existing Photoshop document
Drag path from Illustrator into Photoshop document	Appears as a new smart object layer
Copy object in Illustrator, **Paste** into Photoshop document	Via Paste dialog box, choose to paste as a smart object, pixels, path, or shape layer; the latter two options keep the shapes as vector objects

To import type from Illustrator, see the sidebar on page 393. To learn about smart objects, see page 313.

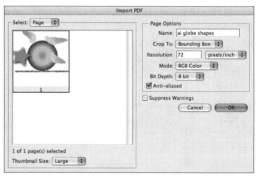

1 *In the **Import PDF** dialog box, choose options for the file you're opening.*

Open PDF, AI, or EPS File

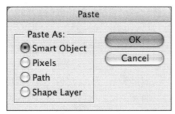

1 *When you paste an object from Illustrator into Photoshop, the Paste dialog box opens.*

color profile management policies you set up in Edit > Color Settings to monitor the presence or absence of profiles.

4. Click OK.

TIP If the PDF contains security settings, before the file can be opened, either those settings must be disabled via Adobe Acrobat or you must enter the document password.

TIP If you didn't check PDF Compatible when you saved your file in Illustrator, the thumbnail in the Import PDF dialog box will display only a repeating text message. Reopen the Illustrator file in Illustrator, choose File > Save As, rename or replace the file, then click Save. In the Illustrator Options dialog box, check Create PDF Compatible File, then click OK. Now open the file in Photoshop.

TIP To create a solid Background, create a new layer, fill it with white, then choose Layer > New > Background From Layer.

Note: In order to have the **Paste** dialog box display when you paste an Adobe Illustrator file, in Illustrator, in the Preferences dialog box, File Handling & Clipboard panel, check the Copy As: PDF and AICB options, and click Preserve Appearance and Overprints.

To paste an Adobe Illustrator object into Photoshop:

1. Edit > **Copy** an object in Illustrator, then in a Photoshop document, choose Edit > **Paste.** The Paste dialog box opens.

2. Click **Paste As: Smart Object, Pixels, Path,** or **Shape Layer 1**. (To learn about **NEW** smart objects, see pages 313–314. To learn about shape layers, see pages 382–388.)

TIP If Resize Image During Paste/Place is **NEW** checked in Preferences (Ctrl-K/Cmd-K) > General, when vector art is pasted into Photoshop, it's scaled automatically to fit the current canvas area.

When you **place** vector art into a Photoshop document, it arrives as vector art on a new smart layer, but is rendered in the resolution of the Photoshop image when you output the file **1**. The higher the resolution of the Photoshop image, the sharper the rendering.

NEW **To place a PDF, Adobe Illustrator, or Illustrator EPS file in a Photoshop image:**

1. Open a Photoshop image.

2. In **Bridge,** locate and click a file, then choose File > Place > **In Photoshop.**
   or
   In **Photoshop,** choose File > **Place,** locate and click a file, then click Place.

   The Place PDF dialog box opens.

3. Choose a **Thumbnail Size;** for a multipage PDF file, also choose a **page;** choose a **Crop To** option (see page 82); then click OK.

4. A box will appear in the Photoshop document, and then the objects will render inside it.

5. *Do any of these optional steps (use the Undo command to undo any of them):*

   To **resize** the placed image, drag a handle on the bounding box. Shift-drag to preserve the proportions as you resize.

   To **move** the placed image, drag inside the bounding box.

   To **rotate** the placed image, position the pointer outside the bounding box (curved pointer ↰), then drag. You can move the center point to rotate the image from a different axis.

6. To accept the placed image, press Enter/Return or double-click inside the bounding box. The placed image will appear on a new smart object layer (see pages 313–314).

TIP To cancel the Place operation before it's been accepted, press Esc. To delete the smart layer, drag it to the trash on the Layers palette.

1 *To produce this image, artist* **Wendy Grossman** *created the musical notes and other objects in Illustrator and then imported them into Photoshop.*

Auto scale **NEW**

If **Resize Image During Paste/Place** is checked in Preferences (Ctrl-K/Cmd-K) > General, when a pixel or vector image is placed into Photoshop, it's scaled automatically to fit the current canvas area.

WORKSPACE 5

New chapter!

*If the image is magnified, you can drag the view box on the thumbnail to **move** the image in its window. Or Ctrl-drag/Cmd-drag across part of the thumbnail (as in this illustration) to marquee an area for **magnification.***

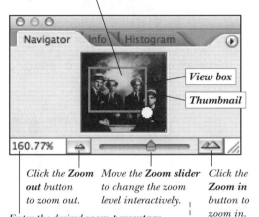

*Click the **Zoom out** button to zoom out.* *Move the **Zoom slider** to change the zoom level interactively.* *Click the **Zoom in** button to zoom in.*

*Enter the desired **zoom percentage** (in Mac, press Return). To zoom to a percentage and keep the field highlighted, press Shift-Enter/Shift-Return.*

*The portion of the image shown in the view box is **magnified.***

NOW THAT YOU'VE LEARNED HOW TO create a document, you're ready to customize your workspace. In this chapter, you'll learn how to change the zoom level of an image; move an image in its window; switch screen display modes; open a second window for an image; hide/show and assign color labels to menu and palette menu commands; and save and delete custom workspaces.

Navigating

In this section you'll learn how to change the zoom level for an image; move an image in its window; switch screen display modes; and display, scroll, or change the zoom level for an image in more than one window.

You can display an entire image in its window or magnify part of an image to work on a small detail. The **zoom level** is indicated as a percentage in three locations: on the document window title bar, in the lower left corner of the application/document window, and in the lower left corner of the Navigator palette. The zoom level of an image has no bearing on its output size.

To change the zoom level using the Navigator palette:

See the illustration at left.

TIP You can also change the zoom level by double-clicking the zoom percentage field in the lower left corner of the application/document window, then typing the desired zoom percentage (press Return in Mac).

TIP Photoshop trivia: To change the outline color of the view box on the Navigator palette, choose Palette Options from the palette menu, then choose a preset color from the Color pop-up menu, or click the color swatch and choose from the Color Picker.

1 *Choose settings for the Zoom tool on the options bar.*

To change the zoom level using the Zoom tool:

1. Choose the **Zoom** tool (Z). 🔍

2. *Optional:* On the Zoom tool options bar **1**, you can check Resize Windows To Fit to allow the document window to resize as you zoom in or out. With this option checked, you can also check Ignore Palettes to allow the document window to enlarge all the way to the right edge of your screen (palettes will be on top).

3. To **zoom in,** click in the document window **2**, or drag a marquee across an area to magnify that area.
   or
   To **zoom out,** Alt-click/Option-click in the document window **3**.
   or
   To view the image at actual pixel size, click **Actual Pixels** on the options bar. *Note:* The zoom level will equal the actual print size only when the display ratio is 100% and the image resolution is the same as the monitor resolution.
   or
   To display the entire image at the largest possible size that can fit on your screen/application window, click **Fit Screen** on the options bar (Ctrl-0/Cmd-0).
   or
   Click **Print Size** on the options bar to display the image at its print size.

TIP Hold down Ctrl-Spacebar/Cmd-Spacebar and click or drag to zoom in when another tool is chosen or when a dialog box with a Preview option is open. Alt-Spacebar-click/Option-Spacebar-click to zoom out.

Zoom shortcuts

	Windows	**Macintosh**
Zoom in*	Ctrl- +	Cmd- + (plus)
Zoom out*	Ctrl- –	Cmd- – (minus)
Actual pixels/ 100% view	Ctrl-Alt-0 (zero)	Cmd-Option-0 (zero)
Fit onscreen	Ctrl-0	Cmd-0

*If Zoom Resizes Windows is checked in Preferences > General, the document window will resize, too. Add Alt/Option to the shortcut to produce the opposite effect from the current preference setting.

2 *Click on the image with the Zoom tool to zoom in (plus sign pointer).*

3 *Alt-click/Option-click on the image with the Zoom tool to zoom out (minus sign pointer).*

1 *Click outside, or drag, the view box on the Navigator palette to move a magnified image...*

2 *...or move an image in the document window using the Hand tool.*

3 *Standard Screen Mode*   **4** *Full Screen Mode with Menu Bar*   **5** *Full Screen Mode*

Keep pressing F to cycle through the screen modes.

6 *Full screen mode with menu bar*

If the zoom level is above 100%, you may need to **move** the **image** in its **window.**

To move a magnified image in its window:

Click outside, or drag, the view box on the **Navigator** palette **1**.

or

Click the up or down scroll arrow on the **document** window. Or to move the image more quickly, drag the horizontal or vertical scroll box.

or

Choose the **Hand** tool (H), then drag in the document window **2**.

TIP Other shortcuts for moving an image in its window are listed on page 551.

To change screen modes:

Click the **Standard Screen Mode** button in the lower left corner of the Toolbox (F) **3** to display the document window, menu bar, options bar, and palettes, with the Desktop visible behind everything. This is the default screen mode.

or

Click the **Full Screen Mode with Menu Bar** (middle) button (F) **4** to display the image on a gray background (obscuring the Desktop), with the menu bar, options bar, and palettes visible **6**.

or

Click the **Full Screen Mode** (rightmost) button (F) **5** to display the image on a black background (trés dramatique), with the palettes and options bar visible, but not the menu bar.

TIP Press Tab to show/hide the Toolbox and any open palettes. Or press Shift-Tab to show/hide just the palettes, leaving the Toolbox open.

TIP You can use the Hand tool (H) to reposition the onscreen image when a full-screen mode is in effect. (Hold down the Spacebar to use a temporary Hand tool while another tool is selected.)

Move Image in Window: Screen Modes

You can display an image in **two windows** simultaneously. "Why?" you ask. Well, you could choose a high zoom level, such as 400%, for one window to edit a small detail, and choose a lower zoom level, such as 100%, for the other in order to view the overall image. Or you could leave the image in RGB Color mode in one window and choose View > Proof Setup > Working CMYK for the image in the second window. That way, you get the best of both worlds (er, windows). Listings on the History palette will be identical for both windows.

To display one image in two windows:

1. With an image open, choose Window > Arrange > **New Window for** [file name]. The same image will appear in a second window ■.

2. *Optional:* Choose Window > Arrange > Tile Vertically; or move either (or both) windows by dragging the title bar; or resize either window by dragging its lower right corner.

This method for **scrolling** or **zooming** is a great time-saver when you have several documents open (tiled) or have created multiple windows for the same document.

To scroll or zoom in multiple windows:

Hold down **Shift** while scrolling with the **Hand** tool or while zooming with the **Zoom** tool to scroll (or zoom) all open Photoshop document windows.

or

Check **Scroll All Windows** on the options bar before using the Hand tool, or check **Zoom All Windows** on the options bar before using the Zoom tool.

TIP If two or more document windows are open, you can choose Window > Arrange > Match Zoom to force all the windows to match the zoom level of the currently active image; or choose Match Location to synchronize the position of all the images in their windows; or choose Match Zoom & Location to perform both functions at once.

■ *This image is displayed in* **two windows**—*one at a low zoom level for previewing, the other at a higher zoom level for editing.*

NEW

Window		
Arrange	▶	
Workspace	▶	Save Workspace...
		Delete Workspace...
Actions	⌥F9	
Animation		Default Workspace
Brushes	F5	
Channels		Reset Palette Locations
Character		Reset Keyboard Shortcuts
✓ Color	F6	Reset Menus
Histogram		
✓ History		Keyboard Shortcuts & Menus...
Info	F8	Automation
Layer Comps		Basic
✓ Layers	F7	Color and Tonal Correction
✓ Navigator		Image Analysis
✓ Options		Painting and Retouching
Paragraph		Printing and Proofing
Paths		Web Design
Styles		What's New in CS2
Swatches		Working with Type
Tool Presets		
✓ Tools		peter
		Special Effects
✓ Untitled–1		Elaine's Workspace
		Vector Art

1 *Choose predefined and user-defined **workspaces** from the bottom of the Window > **Workspace** submenu.*

Customizing menus (NEW)

The sheer number of commands in Photoshop can be daunting, but you can use the **Keyboard Shortcuts and Menus** dialog box to make the interface more user-friendly. You can assign color labels to menu bar or palette menu commands to make it easier to locate them, and you can also hide any commands you don't use.

Just to get a taste of how the labels look and how they might be useful, choose one of the predefined workspaces on the Window > Workspace submenu **1**, such as Color and Tonal Correction, or Painting and Retouching (click OK when the alert dialog box appears), then take a few minutes to browse through the menu bar and a few palette menus. On page 91, you'll learn how to save your menu labels and screen layout (palette locations) as a workspace.

To assign color labels to, or hide/show, menu commands:

1. Choose Edit > **Menus** (Ctrl-Alt-Shift-M/ Cmd-Option-Shift-M).
   or
   Choose Window > Workspace > **Keyboard Shortcuts and Menus,** then click the **Menus** tab.

2. If you've already created a custom menu set or sets, choose from the **Set** pop-up menu (see step 5, below).

3. From the **Menu For** pop-up menu (**1**, next page), choose **Application Menus** or **Palette Menus.**

4. Expand any menu header or palette name by clicking the arrowhead, then:

   To **hide** a command, click the eye icon; click again to redisplay it.

   To assign a **color label** to a command, click in the Color column and choose a color from the pop-up menu. (To remove a color label, choose None.)

5. To create a **new menu set** based on the current settings, click the 💾 button, enter a name (keep the default location), then click Save. Once you've

(Continued on the following page)

created a set or sets, whenever you revisit this dialog box, make a point of choosing the set you want to edit from the Set pop-up menu before making changes.

To **save** your edits to the **current** set, click the 💾 button.

(To delete the current set, click the 🗑 button, then click Yes when the alert dialog box appears.)

6. Click OK. *Note:* The display of color labels is also turned on/off via the Show Menu Colors option in Preferences > General.

To make all the menu commands visible and remove all color labels:

Choose Window > Workspace > **Reset Menus.**

Note: If you didn't click Save in the Keyboard Shortcuts & Menus dialog box before clicking OK, choosing the Reset Menus command will cause an alert dialog box to appear. Click Save, accept the current name, click Save again, then click Replace in the next alert dialog box.

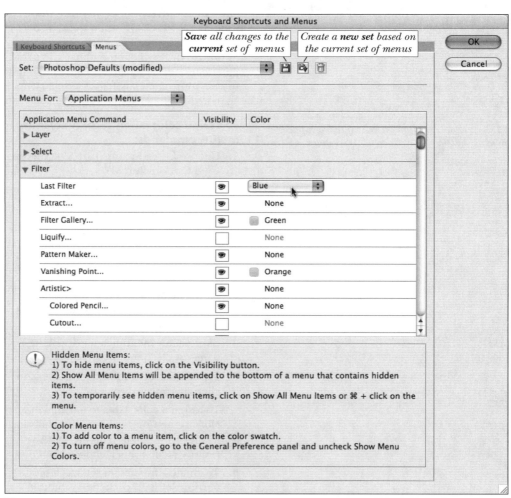

1 *Use the **Menus** panel of the **Keyboard Shortcuts and Menus** dialog box to **hide/show** or assign a **color tint** to menu and palette menu commands.*

Reset Menus

Saving workspaces

If Save Palette Locations is checked in Preferences (Ctrl-K/Cmd-K) > General, palettes that are open when you exit/quit Photoshop will reappear in their same location when you relaunch the program.

To further customize your onscreen working environment, you can **set up** and **save workspaces** for different kinds of tasks. Workspace settings include palette locations, menu visibility and labels settings (menu sets), and custom keyboard shortcuts.

Your custom workspaces should reflect your normal work habits. For example, to set up a text-intensive workspace, you would open the Character and Paragraph palettes and assign color labels to commands that you normally use when creating text. Or to create a painting workspace, you would open the Brushes, Color, and Swatches palettes, assign color labels to the brush preset commands, and maybe even hide some non-related commands.

To create a custom workspace:

1. Do any or all of the following:

Open and **position** all the **palettes** where you want them, including the Toolbox, in the desired palette **groups.** Close the palettes you rarely use. Palettes will reappear where you positioned them.

Resize any of the palettes, including any that open from the palette well.

Choose a **thumbnail** or **swatch size** from any palette menu, including any preset menus that open from the options bar.

Use the **Keyboard Shortcuts and Menus** NEW dialog box to assign custom keyboard shortcuts. (Click the Keyboard Shortcuts tab to access the list of palettes, menus, or tools, then select a command and enter a shortcut.) For menu visibility and color label settings (see pages 89–90).

2. Choose Window > Workspace > **Save Workspace.**

(Continued on the following page)

Save Custom Workspace

3. Enter a descriptive **Name** for the new workspace (or enter your own name) **1**.

4. In the **Capture** area, check which of the custom settings listed you want captured in the workspace.

5. Click Save. Your workspace will be listed on, and can be chosen from, the lower portion of the Window > Workspace submenu.

TIP To restore the default workspace (palette locations, shortcuts, menu visibility and labels—the whole shebang), choose Window > Workspace > Default Workspace. To restore just the palettes to their default groups and locations, choose Window > Workspace > Reset Palette Locations.

TIP On a computer with dual displays, you can distribute your palettes among the displays and save the setup as a workspace.

To delete a custom workspace:

1. Choose Window > Workspace > **Delete Workspace.**

2. Choose the name of the workspace you want to get rid of, or choose All to get rid of 'em all **2**.

3. Click Delete, then click Yes.

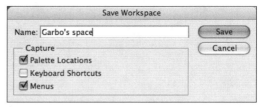

1 *In the **Save Workspace** dialog box, enter a **name** for your workspace, and check which features you want **captured** in the workspace.*

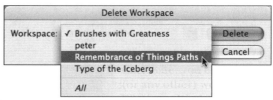

2 *In the **Delete Workspace** dialog box, choose a workspace name or choose All.*

PIXEL BASICS 6

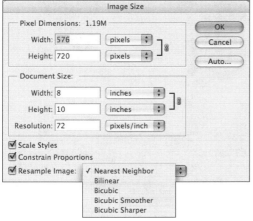

1 The **Image Size** dialog box

BEFORE APPLYING ADJUSTMENT OR image-editing commands, you need to make sure your file has the proper size and orientation. In this chapter you'll learn how to change a document's dimensions and resolution; change the canvas size; and crop, flip, rotate, and straighten an image.

Changing an image's **dimensions** in Photoshop while preserving its current **resolution** (leaving the Resample Image box checked) involves a process known as resampling, which degrades image quality. To minimize resampling, it's best to scan or create an image at or close to the desired output size, and then if you have to resample it, apply a sharpening filter afterward to resharpen (see pages 256–260).

Changing dimensions and resolution

To change an image's pixel dimensions for Web output:

1. Choose Image > **Image Size** (Ctrl-Alt-I/ **NEW** Cmd-Option-I).

2. Make sure **Resample Image** is checked **1**, then choose an interpolation method from the pop-up menu. The Bicubic, Bicubic Smoother, and Bicubic Sharper methods degrade the image the least but also take longer to process.

3. To preserve the image's width-to-height ratio, check **Constrain Proportions.**

4. Set the **Resolution** to 72 pixels/inch (or "ppi" for short).

5. In the **Pixel Dimensions** area, choose pixels from the pop-up menu, then enter exact Width and/or Height values.

6. Check or uncheck **Scale Styles** to control whether applied layer styles in the image will be scaled to fit the new resolution (see page 331).

7. Click OK.

Change Onscreen Dimensions

To change an image's dimensions for print output:

1. Choose Image > **Image Size** (Ctrl-Alt-I/
Cmd-Option-I).

2. To preserve the image's width-to-height
ratio, check **Constrain Proportions;** or
to modify the image's width independently of its height, uncheck Constrain
Proportions.

3. Decide whether you want to preserve
the image resolution. If so, check
Resample Image. If you leave this option
unchecked, the Resolution will change.

If you checked Resample Image, from
the adjacent pop-up menu, choose an
interpolation method: **Nearest Neighbor,
Bilinear, Bicubic, Bicubic Smoother,** or
Bicubic Sharper. The bicubic methods
cause the least degradation in image
quality but also take the longest to
process. If you're enlarging the image,
choose Bicubic Smoother; if you're making the image smaller, choose Bicublic
Sharper.

4. In the **Document Size** area, choose a **unit**
of **measure** from the pop-up menu next
to the Width field; the same unit will be
chosen automatically for the Height.

5. Enter new Document Size: **Width** and/or
Height values corresponding to the
physical dimensions you've chosen for
the printed image.

6. Check or uncheck **Scale Styles** to control
whether applied layer styles in the image
will be scaled.

7. Click OK.

TIP To restore the original Image Size settings while the dialog box is still open,
Alt-click/Option-click Reset.

TIP You can also use File > Print with Preview
to resize or rescale an image's print
dimensions, but this command won't
preserve the image resolution.

Previewing the print

To see an approximation of how the image will fit
the current paper size based on its total pixel count,
choose View > **Print Size.** To see more precisely
how the image fills your chosen paper size, either
press and hold on the status bar at the bottom of
the document window ■, or choose File > **Print
with Preview,** then click Cancel.

1 *To preview the image size relative to the **paper size,**
press and hold on the status bar at the bottom of the
document window.*

Cash in on extra pixels

Each digital photo or scanned image contains a given number of pixels, which can be allocated to either the print size or the print resolution, depending on your output scenario.

Case 1: High resolution, small dimensions
If the file resolution is higher than needed for printing (more than twice the screen frequency), you can uncheck Resample Image to make the width, height, and resolution interdependent, then lower the resolution to twice the screen frequency. The width and height values will increase, and the file storage size and pixel dimensions will remain constant—no pixels will be added to or deleted from the image.

Case 2: Low resolution, large dimensions
If the document dimensions are larger than needed, uncheck Resample Image and then lower the width and height values until the resolution value increases to twice the screen frequency. Here, too, the file storage size and pixel dimension remain constant. This is recommended for large digital photos and PhotoCD images that have a resolution of 72 ppi.

Case 3: Medium resolution, small dimensions
If you don't have enough resolution to allocate to document dimensions, check Resample Image, enter the desired resolution value, then enter the desired Width value. The Height value will change proportionately, and the file storage size and pixel dimensions will increase; the image will be resampled.

If you increase an image's **resolution** with Resample Image checked, pixels will be added to the image, its file storage size will increase, and its sharpness will diminish. If you decrease an image's resolution (downsample), information will be deleted from the file, which can be retrieved only by clicking the original state on the History palette before closing the image. Blurriness caused by resampling may not be evident until the image is printed; it may not be discernible onscreen. Just one more reason to scan or create an image at the proper resolution. Follow the instructions on pages 256–260 to resharpen a resampled image. (See also pages 57 and 59.)

To change an image's resolution:

1. Choose Image > **Image Size** (Ctrl-Alt-I/ Cmd-Option-I).

2. To preserve the image's Document Size (Width and Height), check **Resample Image** 1 and choose an interpolation method from the pop-up menu. The image's pixel count will change.
   or
   To preserve the image's current Pixel Dimensions (pixel count), uncheck Resample Image. The Width and Height dimensions will change in order to preserve the pixel count.

3. Enter a **Resolution** value.

4. Click OK.

TIP The History Brush tool won't work on an image that's been resampled (new dimensions chosen with Resample Image checked). You'll be able to set the source for the History Brush tool from only the current state forward.

1 *Check Resample Image in the Image Size dialog box to allow resampling, or uncheck this option to prevent it.*

Image Size

Pixel Dimensions: 3.36M

Width: 1878 pixels
Height: 1878 pixels

OK
Cancel
Auto...

Document Size:

Width: 6.26 inches
Height: 6.26 inches
Resolution: 300 pixels/inch

☑ Scale Styles
☑ Constrain Proportions
☑ Resample Image: Bicubic

Interpolate the pixel information

The **Fit Image** command has no effect on an image's resolution—it only changes its width and height. Use this command to fit an image to a specific dimension. This command resamples an image (changes its pixel count) as it changes its dimensions in order to keep the resolution constant.

To resize an image to fit a specific width or height:

1. Choose File > Automate > **Fit Image.**

2. Enter the desired Constrain Within: **Width** or **Height** value (not both) in pixels **1**. The other field will change automatically when you exit the dialog box, thus preserving the width-to-height ratio.

Even if you enter a value in both fields, the command will fit the image to the smaller of the two dimensions. For example, let's say you start with a source image of 210 x 237 pixels. You enter 275 in the Height field and 1500 in the Width field. The image will become 275 pixels in height, with its original aspect ratio preserved.

3. Click OK.

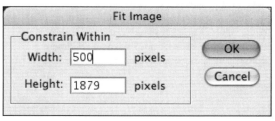

1 *Use the **Fit Image** command to scale an image to a specific **Width** or **Height** dimension while preserving its resolution.*

Fit Image

1 *Click **Print** or **Online**.*

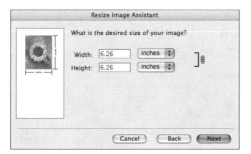

2 *Enter the desired **print size**.*

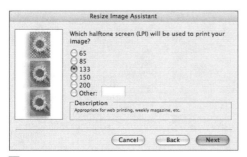

3 *Click or enter the **lpi** that your print shop specifies.*

4 *Move the slider to the desired image **quality**.*

The **Resize Image** command duplicates an image and resizes the duplicate automatically based on the lpi setting to be used by a commercial printer. All you have to do is respond to a sequence of dialog boxes—Photoshop will figure out the math for you. (If you're printing to a desktop inkjet, skip these instructions; they don't apply.)

To resize an image automatically:

1. Choose Help > **Resize Image**. The Resize Image Assistant dialog box opens.

2. Click **Print** or **Online** **1**, then click Next.

3. Enter the desired **output dimensions** **2**, then click Next. If you chose Online in the previous step, click Finish now. For print output, follow the remaining steps.

4. As per instructions from your commercial printer, either click the appropriate **lpi** (lines per inch setting) or click Other and enter the desired lpi **3**, then click Next.

5. Move the **image quality** slider **4**, noting the final image size in the Results area. If a message appears below the Results area, read that as well. If you want to proceed, click Next.

6. Click Finish **5**, and then save the new duplicate, resized image.

TIP To retrace your steps at any time while the Resize Image Assistant is open, click Back.

5 *Click **Finish**.*

Resize Image

Changing the canvas

The **Canvas Size** command enlarges or shrinks the live, editable image area.

Note: If you want to enlarge the canvas area using a marquee, use the Crop tool instead (see page 99). You can also use the Crop command to reduce the canvas area.

To change the canvas size:

1. Choose Image > **Canvas Size** (Ctrl-Alt-C/ **NEW** Cmd-Option-C) –2.

2. *Optional:* Choose a different unit of measure from the Width pop-up menu; the same unit will be chosen automatically for the Height. Or to choose different units, hold down Shift as you choose each one. If you choose "columns," the current Column Size: Width setting in Preferences (Ctrl-K/Cmd-K) > Units & Rulers will be used as the increment.

3. Enter new **Width** and/or **Height** values. The dimensions are independent of one another; changing one won't affect the other.
   or
   Check **Relative,** then in the Width and Height fields enter the amount by which you want to increase or decrease each dimension. Enter a negative value to decrease a dimension.

4. *Optional:* To reposition the image on its new canvas, click an arrow in the **Anchor** diagram. The white (Win)/gray (Mac) square represents the existing image area.

5. From the **Canvas extension color** pop-up menu, choose a color for the added pixels (see page 181). Or to choose a color from the Color Picker, choose Other or click the color square. If the image doesn't have a Background (look for it on the Layers palette), this menu won't be available.

6. Click OK 3. Any added canvas area will automatically be filled with the color you chose in the previous step, unless the bottommost tier of the image is a layer with transparency, in which case the added canvas area will be transparent.

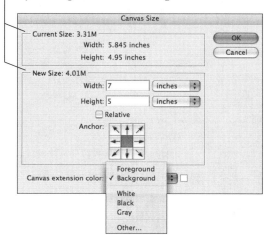

1 *The original image*

2 *Compare the* **Current Size** *to the* **New Size** *as you change the Width and Height values.*

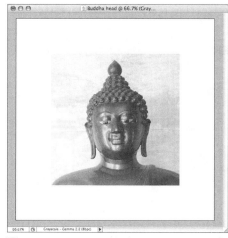

3 *After* **adding canvas** *pixels*

Crop and straighten

The File > Automate > **Crop and Straighten Photos** command is an action that searches for straight edges and rectangular areas in an image, copies each rectangular section that it finds into a new document window, and rotates each image, if necessary, to square it off. You can scan more than one image at a time and let the command sort the images into individual documents.

If you think Crop and Straighten Photos sounds too good to be true, you're partially correct. For one thing, it may take a while to process. And for another, the feature isn't as smart as you are, so it can be fooled. For example, it may mistake a shadow that the scanner detects around the actual photo for the edge of the image. Also, the images may end up being slightly off square. To help the command do its job properly, don't overlap pictures in the scanner or let them hang off the side. And finally, at least in our testing, it didn't work with digital photos.

1 *Marquee the part of the image that you want to keep.*

An entire image can be cropped using the Crop tool, the Crop command, or the Trim command. First, the **Crop tool.**

To crop an image using a marquee:

1. Choose the **Crop** tool (C).
2. Drag a marquee over the portion of the image that you want to keep **1**.
3. On the options bar, do any of the following **2**:

   If you're cropping a layer (not the Background), you can either click **Cropped Area: Delete** to have the cropped-out areas be deleted or click **Hide** to have those areas save with the file but extend outside the visible canvas area. (You can use the Move tool later to move hidden pixels back into view.)

   Check **Shield** if you want the area outside the crop marquee to be darkened by a cropping shield (this helps you see what will remain after cropping). Click the Color swatch if you want to change the shield color; you can also change its Opacity percentage.

   For the Perspective option, see Photoshop Help.

4. Do any of these optional steps:

   To **resize** the marquee, drag any handle (double-arrow pointer). Shift-drag a corner handle to preserve the marquee's proportions. Alt-drag/Option-drag a handle to resize the marquee from its center.

   To **reposition** the marquee, position the pointer inside it, then drag.

   To **rotate** the marquee, position the cursor outside it (curved arrow pointer ↻), then drag in a circular direction. To change the axis point around which the marquee rotates, drag the circle away from the center of the marquee before

   (Continued on the following page)

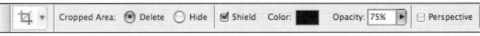

2 *The **Crop** tool options bar **after** drawing a marquee with the tool*

rotating. (This is a quick way to crop and straighten a photo.)

5. Press Enter/Return .
or
Double-click inside the marquee.
or
Right-click/Control-click the image and choose Crop.

If you rotated the marquee, the rotated image will be squared off in the document window, but the image orientation will be changed.

TIP To cancel the crop marquee, press Esc, or click the ⊘ button on the options bar.

To specify dimensions and resolution as you crop an image:

1. Choose the **Crop** tool (C). ⌗

2. On the options bar, enter **Width** and **Height** values for the final image **2**. (You can click the Swap Width and Height button ⇄ to reverse the values.)
or
To crop using the Width, Height, and Resolution values (in pixels) from another image, click in that other image, click **Front Image** on the options bar, then click back in the image to be cropped.

3. *Optional:* Modify the **Resolution.** If, after clicking Front Image, you change the Resolution value, the image will be resampled as it's cropped.

To empty the Width, Height, and Resolution fields at any time, click Clear.

4. Drag a crop marquee on the image. (The values you entered in step 2 were for the final image size, not the marquee size.)

5. To accept the crop, double-click inside the marquee; or press Enter/Return; or right-click/Control-click the image and choose Crop.

TIP To resharpen an image after cropping, apply a sharpening filter (see pages 256–260).

1 *The **cropped** image*

*If you change the Resolution, Width, and Height values on the **Crop** tool options bar and then use the tool to crop the image, the image will be resampled as a result.*

2 *The options bar **prior** to drawing a marquee with the **Crop** tool*

Crop Tool

Crop one image to fit inside another

Open both images, click in the image that you want the imagery to be added to, choose the Crop tool (C), click **Front Image** on the options bar, click in the image that you want to crop, then draw a marquee. After cropping, Shift-drag-and-drop the layer from the Layers palette or copy and paste the layer onto the target image. The newly copied layer will adopt the resolution of the target image.

1 *Drag any of the crop marquee handles **outside** the canvas area into the work canvas.*

2 *Our newly **cropped** image has new proportions. The added pixels filled automatically with black, our chosen Background color.*

Cropping with a marquee that's larger than the image effectively **increases** the image's canvas size. If any of your image layers extend beyond the live canvas area, you can use this technique to reveal them.

To enlarge the canvas area using the Crop tool:

1. Choose a Background color (see Chapter 12).

2. Enlarge the document window so that a large amount of the work canvas (gray area) around the image is showing.

3. Choose the **Crop** tool (C). 🔲

4. Draw a crop marquee within the image.

5. Drag any of the handles of the marquee into the work canvas (outside the live canvas area) **1**–**2**.

6. Double-click inside the marquee.
   or
   Press Enter/Return.
   or
   Right-click/Control-click the image and choose **Crop.**

   If the image has a Background (Layers palette), the added canvas area will be filled with the current Background color. If the image doesn't have a Background, the added canvas area will be filled with transparent pixels.

   Also, any pixels on the layer that were formerly outside the live canvas area may now fall within it, depending on the new canvas size.

The **Crop** command is simple and straight-forward, but it's useful only if you can draw a selection marquee that's the exact size needed for the crop, and you don't need any of the options that the Crop tool provides.

To crop an image using the Crop command:

1. Choose the **Rectangular Marquee** tool (M or Shift-M).

2. Draw a marquee over the part of the image you want to keep.
   or
   To control the size of the marquee, on the Rectangular Marquee tool options bar, choose Style: **Fixed Aspect Ratio** or **Fixed Size,** enter Width and Height values, then click on the image.

3. Choose Image > **Crop,** then deselect (Ctrl-D/Cmd-D).

You can use the **Trim** command to quickly trim away any excess transparent or solid-color areas, such as a frame or border, from around an image.

To crop an image closely using the Trim command:

1. Choose Image > **Trim.**

2. Click a **Based On** option 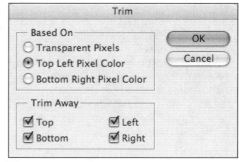:

   Transparent Pixels trims away any extra transparency at the edges of the image, while preserving all image pixels. If the image doesn't contain any transparent pixels, this option won't be available.

   Top Left Pixel Color removes any border areas that match the color of the left uppermost pixel in the image.

   Bottom Right Pixel Color removes any border areas that match the color of the right bottommost pixel in the image.

3. Check which areas of the image you want the command to **Trim Away:** Top, Bottom, Left, and/or Right.

4. Click OK.

1 *The* **Trim** *command removes excess transparent areas or color areas, depending on which* **Based On** *option you click.*

1 *The original image*

The Rotate Canvas > **Flip Canvas Horizontal** and **Flip Canvas Vertical** commands flip all the layers in an image, creating a mirror image. (To flip just one layer at a time, use Edit > Transform > Flip Horizontal or Flip Vertical instead.)

To flip an image:

To flip the image from left to right, choose Image > Rotate Canvas > **Flip Canvas Horizontal** **1**–**2**.

or

To flip the image upside-down, choose Image > Rotate Canvas > **Flip Canvas Vertical** **3**.

Flip Image

2 *The image **flipped horizontally***

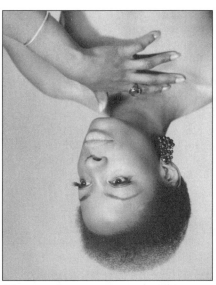

3 *The original image **flipped vertically***

The **Rotate Canvas** commands rotate all the layers in an image. (To rotate one layer at a time, use a rotate command from the Edit > Transform submenu instead.)

To rotate an image by a preset amount:

Choose Image > Rotate Canvas > **180°, 90° CW** (clockwise), or **90° CCW** (counterclockwise).

TIP You can also use Bridge to rotate an image or images (see page 73).

To rotate an image by specifying a number:

1. Choose Image > Rotate Canvas > **Arbitrary.**

2. Enter an **Angle** between −359.99° and 359.99° .

3. Click °**CW** (clockwise) or °**CCW** (counterclockwise).

4. Click OK .

You can use the **Measure** tool to quickly **straighten** out a crooked digital photo or scanned image.

To quickly straighten a crooked image:

1. Choose the **Measure** tool (it's grouped with the Eyedropper tool).

2. Drag along a feature of the image that you want to be perfectly horizontal or vertical. Note the angle (the A: value) on the options bar.

3. Choose Image > Rotate Canvas > **Arbitrary.** The angle you just dragged will appear in the Angle field.

4. Click OK. Your image will be rotated. You can crop it to remove any exposed background color areas that were generated by the rotation.

1 *You can enter a custom angle in the **Rotate Canvas** dialog box.*

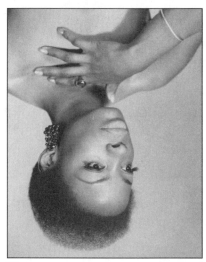

2 *The original image*

3 *The image **rotated 180°** (compare with the flipped images on the previous page)*

Rotate, Straighten Image

*This image has three **layers** and a **Background**.*

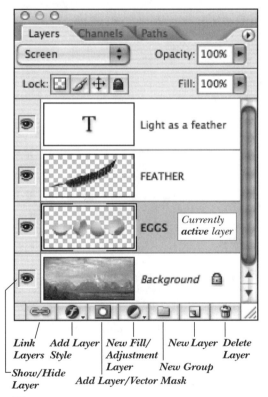

*The **Layers** palette for the image shown above*

Link Layers

Show/Hide Layer

Add Layer Style

New Fill/ Adjustment Layer

Add Layer/Vector Mask

New Layer

New Group

Delete Layer

IF YOU CHOOSE Background Contents: White or Background Color as you create a new document (File > New), the bottommost tier of the image will be the Background, which isn't a layer. If you choose Background Contents: Transparent, the bottommost tier of the image will be a layer. Layers can be added to an image at any time, but a document can contain only one Background.

Creating layers

Unlike the Background, layers are like acetate sheets—opaque where there's imagery 1 and **transparent** where there's none. By default, transparent areas on a layer are represented by a checkerboard. By assigning imagery to different layers, you can easily edit the imagery on one layer while leaving the rest untouched.

Layers are listed on the **Layers palette** 2 from topmost to bottommost; the Background is always at the bottom of the list. To each layer you can assign a different opacity and blending mode to control how it interacts with the layers below it. You can also hide/show, duplicate, or change the stacking order of any layer, and link layers together.

The Layers palette has so many important features and functions that it's the star player in two other chapters and plays an essential supporting role in many others. In this chapter, you'll learn the basics: how to create and duplicate layers, turn a selection or the Background into a layer (and vice versa), activate layers, choose options for layers (e.g., blending mode, opacity, fill percentage), hide/show layers, and create layer groups. But wait, there's more! You'll also learn how to move, restack, and delete, copy, merge, and flatten layers. Let's start by learning how to create layers.

Layers Palette

When you paste a selection, create type, or create a shape, a new layer is created automatically. In this section, you'll learn how to create **new, blank layers.** You can add as many layers to a file as available memory and storage allow.

To create a layer:

1. To create a layer with Opacity and Fill percentages of 100% and Normal mode, click the **New Layer** button ⬚ at the bottom of the Layers palette and skip the remaining steps.

or

To choose options for the new layer as you create it, Alt-click/Option-click the **New Layer** button ⬚ at the bottom of the Layers palette; or press Ctrl-Shift-N/ Cmd-Shift-N; or choose New Layer from the palette menu. The New Layer dialog box opens. Follow the remaining steps.

2. *Do any of the following optional steps:*

Change the layer **Name 1**.

Check **Use Previous Layer to Create Clipping Mask** to make the new layer a part of a clipping mask (see page 305). (Skip this option for now until you get used to creating and using layers.)

Choose a nonprinting **Color** for the area on the Layers palette behind the eye icon.

Choose a different blending **Mode** or **Opacity** (both can easily be changed later).

3. Click OK. The new layer will appear directly above the previously active layer.

Note: Multilayered images are considerably larger than flat ones **2**, so when you're done editing your image, consider using a merge or flatten command to shrink it back down! See pages 116–118 in this chapter.

Preserving or flattening layers

When using File > Save As, the following file formats will save a document with layers intact, provided the **Layers** box is checked: **Photoshop PDF, Photoshop, Large Document Format,** and **TIFF.**

File formats that don't preserve layers flatten them automatically and convert any transparency in the bottommost layer to opaque white.

Also, when switching **document color modes** (e.g., from RGB to CMYK), be sure to click Don't Flatten or Don't Merge if you want layers preserved!

1 *Use the **New Layer** dialog box to rename and choose options for a layer.*

2 *After adding layers to your file, on the status bar pop-up menu, choose **Show > Document Sizes.** The* **NEW** *first value is the current **image size;** the second value is the amount of **RAM** the multilayered file is using. The image pictured in this screenshot contains three layers, which explains why the second value is almost triple the first.*

1 *A detail of the Layers palette, showing the original **Background***

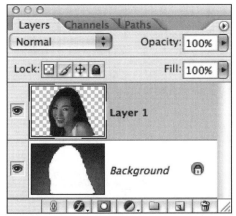

2 *The **Layer Via Cut** command cuts the current selection from the Background and places it onto a new layer.*

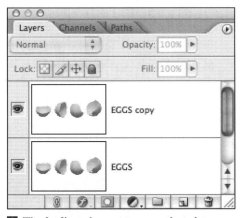

3 *The **duplicate** layer appears on the palette.*

To turn a selection into a layer:

1. On the Layers palette, click a layer or the Background, then create a selection in the document window.

2. To place a copy of the selected pixels on a new layer and leave the original layer intact, right-click/Control-click in the document window and choose **Layer Via Copy** (Ctrl-J/Cmd-J).
   or
   To place the selected pixels on a new layer and remove them from the original layer, right-click/Control-click in the document window and choose **Layer Via Cut** (Ctrl-Shift-J/Cmd-Shift-J) **1**–**2**.

   Either way, a new layer appears on the palette.

Follow these instructions to **duplicate** a **layer** or a **layer group.** To learn about layer groups, see pages 110–111.

To duplicate a layer or layer group:

Drag a layer or layer group over the **New Layer** button at the bottom of the palette. The duplicate will appear above the original.
or
Right-click/Control-click a layer and choose **Duplicate Layer** or **Duplicate Group,** enter NEW a name in the "As" field for the duplicate, if desired, then click OK **3**.

To rename any layer, double-click the name on the palette, then type.

TIP You can also press Ctrl-J/Cmd-J to duplicate a layer.

TIP When you duplicate a layer, any effects and/or layer mask on that layer will also be duplicated.

There are many things that you can do to a layer that you can't do to the Background. For example, you can't move the Background upward in the layer stack, choose a blending mode, opacity percentage, or fill percentage for it, apply layer effects to it, or assign a mask to it. If you **convert** your **Background** into a **layer,** however, it will then function like any other layer.

To convert the Background into a layer:

Alt-double-click/Option-double-click the Background on the Layers palette to turn it into a layer without choosing options.
or
Double-click the **Background** on the Layers palette **1**, type a new Name **2**, choose a Color for the area behind the eye icon on the palette, choose a Mode, choose an Opacity percentage, then click OK **3**.

If you need to **create** a **Background** for a file that doesn't have one, you can convert any existing layer into the Background.

To convert a layer into the Background:

1. Click a layer.
2. Choose Layer > New > **Background From Layer** (at the top of the Layer menu). The new Background will appear at the bottom of the stack on the Layers palette.

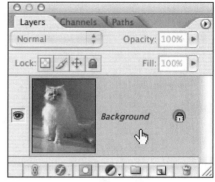

1 *Double-click the **Background.***

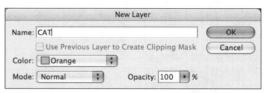

2 *Enter a name and choose options for the layer.*

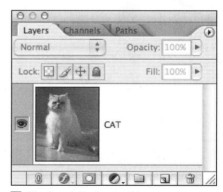

3 *The former Background is now a **layer.***

Background to Layer, Layer to Background

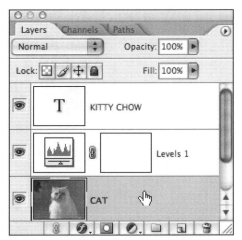

1 *Click a layer to activate it.*

2 *Choosing a layer from a context menu*

Activating layers

Get in the habit of remembering to **activate** the **layer**(s) you want to edit before making changes to your document. The currently active layer or layer group has a blue highlight **1**. The name of the currently active layer or layer group is listed on the title bar of the document window. To create layer groups, see pages 110–111.

To activate layers via the Layers palette:

To activate a **layer** or **layer group,** click the layer thumbnail or the area to the right of the layer or group name.
or
To activate **multiple layers,** click a layer, then Shift-click the last in a series of consecutively listed layers, or Ctrl-click/Cmd-click individual layers (Ctrl-click/Cmd-click to deselect one layer at a time).
or
To activate all the layers in your document, **NEW** choose Select > **All Layers** (Ctrl-Alt-A/Cmd-Option-A).
or
To select all layers of a similar kind, such as all image layers, or all shape layers, or all adjustment layers, right-click/Control-click **NEW** one of the layers you want to activate and choose **Select Similar Layers.**

To activate a layer or layer group with the Move tool:

1. Choose the Move tool (V).

2. **Right-click/Control-click** in the document window and choose a layer or layer group name on the context menu **2**. (Ctrl-right-click/Cmd-Control-click with any other tool selected.) Only layers containing nontransparent pixels under the pointer will be listed on the context menu.
or
Check **Auto Select Layer** on the Move tool options bar, then click any visible pixels in the document window. *Note:* The layer won't become selected if the pixels you click on have an opacity below 50% or if you click an area that another layer is overlapping.

Activate Layers

Restacking layers

To restack layers:

1. Click the layer (or group) you want to restack.

2. Drag the layer name upward or downward on the palette, and release the mouse when a dark horizontal line appears in the desired location **1**–**4**.

TIP To move the Background upward on the list, you must first convert it into a layer (see page 108). You can't stack layers below the Background.

TIP You can also restack an active layer by using the shortcuts listed on page 553, or by choosing a command on the Layer > Arrange submenu.

Using layer groups NEW

Layer groups are to layers what folders are to files: they allow you to collect, label, and organize. By using layer groups, you shorten the list of names on the palette (less scrolling up and down). Groups can be nested inside other groups, up to five levels deep.

But layer groups aren't just handy for tidying up. You can also move, rotate, scale, duplicate, restack, lock/unlock, hide/show, link, and copy grouped layers en masse.

Any adjustment layer, blending mode (except for Pass Through), or opacity percentage that you apply to a group will affect only layers within the group. A layer mask or vector mask, when applied to a layer group, will affect all the layers in the group.

NEW To create a layer group:

Method 1

1. To create a group without choosing settings, click the layer above which you want the group to appear, then click the **New Group** button ▭ at the bottom of the Layers palette.
or
To choose settings for the group as you create it, choose **New Group** from the palette menu, change the Name, Color,

1 *The original image*

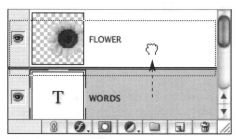

2 *Dragging the WORDS layer **upward***

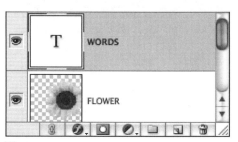

3 *Now the WORDS layer is above the FLOWER layer.*

4 *Here's the result.*

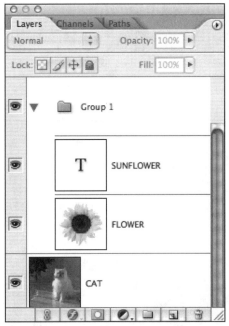

1 *The SUNFLOWER and FLOWER layers were dragged into the* **Group 1** *folder, and the group list was expanded.*

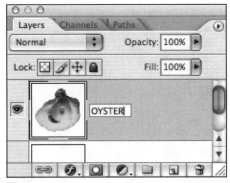

2 *A layer is renamed.*

blending Mode, or Opacity setting for the new group, if desired; then click OK.

2. On the Layers palette, drag layers onto the group folder icon or thumbnail **1**.

Method 2

1. Click a layer, then Shift-click or Ctrl-click/Cmd-click two or more layers.

2. Press **Ctrl-G/Cmd-G.**
or
From the palette menu, choose **New Group From Layers.** The selected layers will be nested inside the new group.

TIP Click the arrow to expand/collapse any group list.

TIP To group layers into a smart object, see pages 313–314.

Follow these instructions to **ungroup** (disband) a layer **group** without deleting the layers it contains.

To ungroup a layer group:

1. Click a layer group. **NEW**

2. Press Ctrl-Shift-G/Cmd-Shift-G.

To rename a layer or layer group:

1. Double-click a layer or layer group name on the Layers palette.

2. Type a new name **2**.

3. Press Enter/Return.

Hiding/showing layers

By **hiding** layers you're not currently working on, you remove them as a visual distraction.

Notes: Only visible layers can be merged with other layers (you'll learn about merging and flattening at the end of this chapter). Be especially careful when using the Flatten Image command, as it discards hidden layers! Also, if you're going to be printing your image, remember that only visible layers will print.

When we say "layers" in the following instructions, we're collectively referring to layers and the Background; the Background has a visibility icon, too.

To hide or show layers:

To hide a **layer** or **layer group,** click the eye icon on the Layers palette **1**–**3**. Click in the eye column again to redisplay the layer or layer group.
or
To hide or show **multiple** layers, drag upward or downward in the eye column.
or
To hide or show **all** layers **except** the **one** you click on, Alt-click/Option-click an eye icon or right-click/Control-click in the eye column and choose **Show/Hide all other layers.**

Deleting layers and groups

To delete a layer:

On the Layers palette, click a layer. Click the **Delete Layer** button, 🗑 then click **Yes;** or to bypass the prompt, Alt-click/Option-click the Delete Layer button.
or
Right-click/Control-click the layer you want to delete, choose **Delete Layer** or **Delete Group** from the context menu, then click Yes.

TIP Change your mind? No problem. Choose Edit > Undo or click a prior state on the History palette.

1 *The original image contains a Background and two layers.*

2 *The **eye** icon is **hidden** for the FLOWER layer.*

3 *The image with the FLOWER layer **hidden***

Photo of woman ©www.photospin.com

1 *The original image*

2 *After moving the type layer with the Move tool*

Move smart NEW

If you turn on View > Show > **Smart Guides,** as you move a layer or layer group, temporary guide lines will appear onscreen. Use them to align the edge of the layer you're moving with the edge or center of other layers in the document.

Flip out

On the Layers palette, click a layer or layer group, then choose Edit > Transform > **Flip Horizontal** or **Flip Vertical.** Any layers that are linked to the active layer(s) will also flip (see page 307).

You can **delete** a **group** and the layers it contains, or merely **disband** the group and keep the layers.

To delete a layer group: NEW

On the Layers palette, click a group. Click the **Delete Layer** button, 🗑 then click **Group Only** or **Group and Contents;** or to bypass the prompt, Alt-click/Option-click the **Delete Layer** button.

or

Right-click/Control-click the group you want to delete, choose **Delete Group** from the context menu, then click **Group Only** or **Group and Contents.**

Moving layer pixels

Follow these instructions to **move** a **layer** or **group** of layers. To move linked layers, see page 307.

To move layer pixels:

1. On the Layers palette, click a layer or group.

2. Choose the **Move** tool (V) ⤴ or hold down Ctrl/Cmd if another tool is chosen (temporary Move tool).

3. Drag in the document window. The entire layer or layer group will move **1**–**2**. If pixels are moved beyond the existing edge of the image, don't worry —they'll be saved with the document, and you can move them back into view at any time.

TIP To move a whole group, click the group layer, choose the Move tool (V), check Auto Select Layer and Auto Select Groups on the options bar, then drag the group in the document window. To move an individual layer in a group, uncheck Auto Select Groups.

TIP To nudge an active layer one pixel at a time, choose the Move tool, then press an arrow key. Press Shift-arrow to move a layer 10 screen pixels at a time. (Don't press Alt-arrow/Option-arrow— that shortcut duplicates the layer!)

Choosing palette options

You can dramatically change the appearance of a layer and the layers below it by changing its **blending mode, opacity** percentage, or **fill** percentage **1**.

Note: As you use painting and editing tools, bear in mind that in addition to the settings you've chosen for your tool from the options bar, the blending mode, opacity, and fill percentage of the currently active layer also contribute to the overall result **2**.

To choose a blending mode, opacity, or fill percentage for a layer or layer group:

1. Click a layer or layer group.

2. Choose a **blending mode** from the pop-up menu, or change the **Opacity** percentage. For a layer (not a layer group), you can also change the **Fill** percentage (for blending modes, see pages 190–194; for the Opacity and Fill options, see page 295).

By default, transparent pixels on a layer are represented by a checkerboard. Use the **Lock Transparent Pixels** button to allow or prevent the editing of transparent pixels.

To lock/unlock transparent pixels:

1. Click a layer.

2. To allow only **nontransparent** pixels on the layer to be edited or recolored, click the **Lock Transparent Pixels** button ▨ **3**. Deactivate this button at any time to edit transparent pixels on the layer.

TIP Press / to toggle the Lock Transparent Pixels option on or off.

TIP Transparent pixels on editable type layers always remain locked, whereas for rasterized type layers Lock Transparent Pixels can be turned on or off.

3 *With the* **Lock Transparent Pixels** *option on, only nontransparent pixels on a layer can be edited.*

Custom checkerboard

To change the **size** or **color** of the checkerboard that represents transparent pixels or to turn off the checkerboard pattern, go to Preferences (Cmd-K/Control-K) > **Transparency & Gamut.**

What about the other buttons?

Button	Icon	Chapter
Link button	🔗	20
Layer Style pop-up menu	🎨	21
Add Layer Mask button	◻	22
Fill/Adjustment layer pop-up menu	◕	11

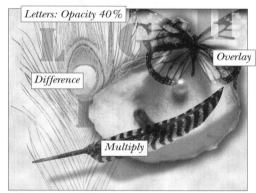

Letters: Opacity 40%

Overlay

Difference

Multiply

1 *Layer* **blending modes** *and* **opacity** *percentages*

2 *If the Pencil* **tool** *opacity is 50% (options bar), and the* **layer** *opacity is 75%, the opacity of the resulting stroke will be 37%.*

Set the master opacity for the layer

COCONUT

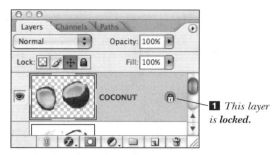

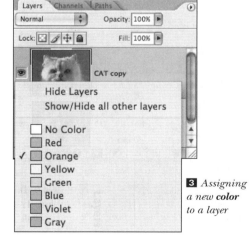

1 *This layer is **locked**.*

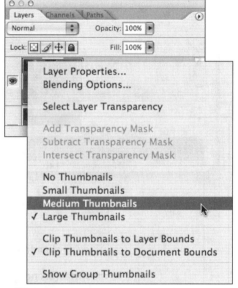

2 *Use the context menu to **customize** the palette.*

3 *Assigning a new **color** to a layer*

Use the **lock** options for layers to prevent inadvertent edits.

To lock a layer or layer group:

1. Click a layer or layer group.

2. Do any of the following:

   Click the **Lock Image Pixels** button 🖌 to prevent layer pixels from being edited. You can still move the layer, as well as choose options for it, such as layer effects, blending mode, fill, etc.

   Click the **Lock Position** button ✛ to lock only the layer's location. The layer pixels can still be edited.

   Click the **Lock All** button 🔒 to prevent the layer from being moved or edited. This button is also available for layer groups (see page 110).

   A lock icon **1** will appear on the palette.

To choose thumbnail options for the ⬤NEW Layers palette:

Right-click/Control-click a layer thumbnail and choose any of the following:

A different thumbnail **size**, or **No Thumbnails** (turning off thumbnails boosts the program's performance but we find it hard to work without them) **2**.

Clip Thumbnails to Layer Bounds to show only the area that encompasses the opaque pixels on the layer in the palette thumbnails; or **Clip Thumbnails to Document Bounds** to include surrounding transparent pixels in the thumbnails.

TIP To specify the above options via a dialog box, choose Palette Options from the Layers palette menu. Via the Use Default Masks on Adjustments check box, you can also specify whether layer masks are included when adjustment layers are created.

TIP To assign a different color to the area behind the eye icon on a layer, click the layer, right-click/Control-click the eye column, and choose a color **3**.

Lock Layer, Group; Layer Thumbnails

Merging layers

Whereas the Flatten Image command (see page 118) is used when a file is complete, you would use the merge commands (**Merge Down, Merge Layers,** and **Merge Visible**) periodically as you edit your document. You can merge two or more layers together on a case-by-case basis while leaving the remaining layers intact. The active layers will be merged into the bottommost active layer.

NEW **To merge layers:**

1. Click the upper layer of two layers you want to merge **1**. The layers can be in a group, single, or a combination thereof.
   or
   Ctrl-click/Cmd-click nonconsecutive layers.
   or
   Click a group. All the layers in the group will be merged.

   Notes: You can merge adjustment layers. To merge a shape layer or editable type layer, make sure it's the topmost of all the selected layers.

2. Right-click/Control-click one of the layers and choose **Merge Down,** or **Merge Layers** if you've selected multiple layers, or **Merge Group** if you've selected a group.
   or
   Press **Ctrl-E/Cmd-E** **2**.

   If the underlying layer contains a layer or vector mask, an alert dialog box will appear **3**; click Preserve or Apply, whichever you prefer.

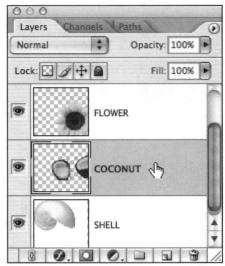

1 *The COCONUT layer is clicked.*

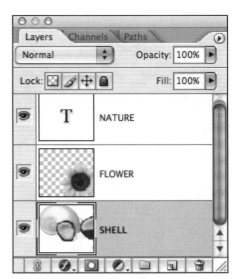

2 *After choosing the **Merge Down** command*

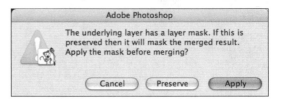

3 *This alert dialog box will appear if the underlying layer being merged contains a layer or vector **mask.***

Merge Layers

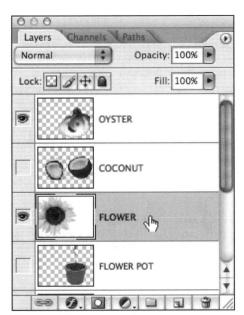

1 *Only two layers are visible; the FLOWER layer is clicked.*

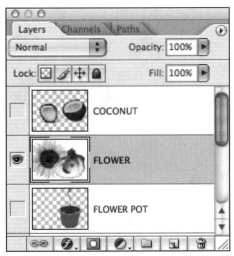

2 *The Merge Visible command merged the OYSTER layer into the FLOWER layer. The other layers remain separate, though still hidden.*

The **Merge Visible** command merges only the currently visible layers into the active layer, but doesn't discard hidden layers.

To merge only visible layers:

1. Make sure only the layers you want to merge are visible (have eye icons) and hide any layers (including the Background) that you don't want to merge.

2. Click any one of the layers or layer groups to be merged **1**. *Note:* If you merge an editable type layer, shape layer, or adjustment layer, it will cease to be editable.

3. Right-click/Control-click one of the layers and choose **Merge Visible;** or press Ctrl-Shift-E/Cmd-Shift-E **2**.

TIP To merge layers in a clipping mask (see page 305), click the layer that has the underlined name, then choose Merge Clipping Mask (Ctrl-E/Cmd-E) from the Layers palette menu. Any hidden layers in the clipping mask will be discarded.

If you're going to test out some filters or transformations on multiple layers, why not do so on layers that have been copied and merged, and leave the originals intact? By using a shortcut, you can **copy** and **merge layers** in one step!

To copy and merge layers: NEW

1. Click the layers you want to merge.

2. Hold down Alt/Option as you choose **Merge Layers** from the palette menu (release the mouse after you see the new layer appear on the palette). The new layer name will contain the word "(merged)" and the latest state on the History palette will be "Stamp Layers." *or* To copy only visible layers, hold down Alt/Option as you choose **Merge Visible** from the palette menu.

Merge Visible Layers; Copy Merged Layers

Flattening layers

Unfortunately, only the Photoshop PDF, Photoshop, Large Document Format, and TIFF file formats support multiple layers. In order to export your file to another application, it may have to be flattened. We think the best way to do this is to save a flattened copy of it, using File > **Save As** with **As a Copy** checked and **Layers** unchecked (the layered version will remain open). This way, the layered version will be preserved so you can overwork it to death some other time.

Or if you're the cocky sort and you're positive your image is totally and completely done, *finis,* you can flatten it down into the Background using the **Flatten Image** command. Actually, because flattened files are smaller than layered files, flattening the stuff you're done with is a good way to free up disk space.

The Flatten Image command merges the currently visible layers into the bottommost visible layer and **discards** hidden layers. Read this paragraph once more before proceeding!

To flatten layers: (NEW)

1. Make sure all the layers and layer groups you want to flatten are visible (have eye icons) **1**. It doesn't matter which layer is active.

2. Right-click/Control-click the palette and choose **Flatten Image.** If the file contains any hidden layers, an alert dialog box will appear; click OK **2**.

   Any transparent areas in the bottommost layer will now be white.

   Note: The image in the first figure at right contains an adjustment layer, a layer style, and a layer mask, all of which the Flatten Image command rasterized, applied to the image, and flattened.

Saving layers

Before saving a file to a format that doesn't support layers, you can save individual layers to separate documents. Right-click/Control-click a layer or group and choose **Duplicate Layer** (or **Duplicate Group**). In the Duplicate dialog box, choose Document: New. In the As: field, enter a name for the layer or group in the new file; for Destination: Name, enter a name for the new file, then click OK. Save the new document that appears onscreen. You also might want to explore File > Scripts > Export Layers To Files.

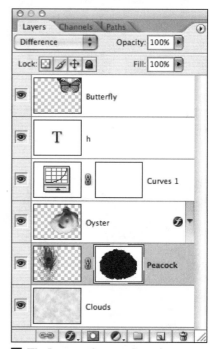

1 *The Layers palette **pre-flattening**…*

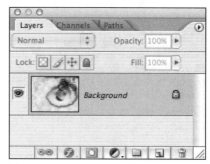

2 *…and **post-flattening***

SELECT 8

You can stay on the Background

If you're not comfortable working with layers, for the instructions in this chapter, instead of choosing a layer, just work with the pixels on the **Background.**

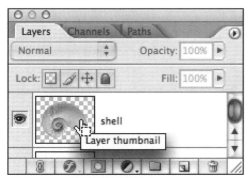

1 *Ctrl-click/Cmd-click a layer thumbnail to select* ***all*** *the opaque pixels on that layer.*

2 *Only* ***opaque pixels***—*not transparent areas*— *are selected on this layer.*

WHEN A LAYER OR PART OF A LAYER is selected, only that area is editable —the rest of the image is protected. Selections have a "marching ants" marquee. In this chapter, you'll learn how to create selections using the Rectangular Marquee, Elliptical Marquee, Single Row Marquee, Single Column Marquee, Lasso, Polygonal Lasso, Magic Wand, and Magnetic Lasso tools, and the Color Range command. You'll also learn how to deselect, reselect, and delete selected pixels; move, smooth, invert, hide, and transform a selection marquee; add to and subtract from a selection; save and load selections; and use the Extract command to "lift" imagery out of a layer.

Creating selections

A **selection** contains pixels from whichever **layer** is currently active. If you move a selection on the Background of an image using the Move tool, the current Background color is applied automatically to the exposed area. If you move a selection on a layer using the Move tool, the exposed area becomes transparent.

TIP A selection can be converted into a path for precise reshaping, then converted back into a selection (see pages 366 and 376). Quick Masks, which are painted on an image and then converted into selections, are covered on pages 339–340.

To select layer pixels:

Click a layer or the Background on the Layers palette, then choose Select > **All** (Ctrl-A/Cmd-A). A marquee will surround the entire layer.
or
To select opaque and semitransparent pixels (not transparent pixels), **Ctrl-click/Cmd-click** a layer thumbnail on the Layers palette **1**–**2**, or right-click/Control-click a layer thumbnail and choose **Select Layer Transparency.**

To create a rectangular or elliptical selection:

1. Click a layer.

2. Choose the **Rectangular Marquee** or **Elliptical Marquee** tool (M or Shift-M) **1**. Or to create the thinnest possible selection, choose the **Single Row Marquee** or **Single Column Marquee** tool.

3. *Optional:* To specify the exact dimensions of the selection, with the Rectangular or Elliptical Marquee tool highlighted choose **Fixed Size** from the Style pop-up menu on the options bar **2**, then enter Width and Height values. Remember, though, you're counting pixels based on the file's resolution, not the monitor's resolution, so the same Fixed Size marquee will appear larger in a low-resolution file than in a high-resolution one.

Or to specify the width-to-height ratio of the selection (e.g., 3-to-1), choose **Fixed Aspect Ratio** from the Style pop-up menu, then enter Width and Height values. Enter the same value in both fields to create a circular or square selection.

4. *Optional:* To soften the edges of the selection, enter a **Feather** value above zero on the options bar. Also, the Anti-alias option can be checked on or off for the Elliptical Marquee tool.

5. If you specified Fixed Size values (or are using the Single Row Marquee or Single Column Marquee tool), click on the image. For any other style, drag diagonally **3**–**4**. A marquee will appear. To create a square or circular selection for the Normal style, start dragging, then finish the marquee with Shift held down.

Hold down the Spacebar to move the marquee while the mouse button is still down. To move the marquee after releasing the mouse, drag inside it.

TIP As you draw the marquee, the dimensions of the selection will be indicated in the W and H areas on the Info palette.

TIP To add to or subtract from a selection, see page 132.

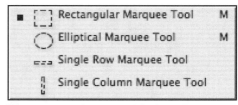

1 *Choose one of the four* **marquee** *tools.*

Swaps the **width** *and* **height** *values*

2 *Instead of drawing a marquee manually, you can choose* **Fixed Size** *from the Style pop-up menu on the options bar and enter exact Width and Height values.*

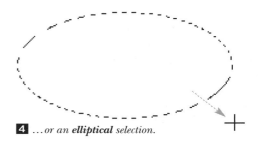

3 *Drag diagonally to create a* **rectangular** *selection…*

4 *…or an* **elliptical** *selection.*

Anti-aliasing

Check **Anti-alias,** if available, on the options bar before using a selection tool to create a selection with a softened edge that fades gradually to transparency, or uncheck Anti-alias to create a crisp, hard-edged selection (see the illustrations below).

 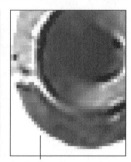

Aliased   *Anti-aliased*

1 *A hand-drawn **Lasso** tool selection*

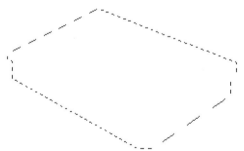

2 *A straight-edged **Polygonal Lasso** tool selection*

TIP As it's difficult to precisely reselect an area (unless you save your selection in an alpha channel or as a path), try to refine your selection before deselecting it.

TIP If the shape you want to select isn't too complex, use the Pen or Freeform Pen tool to trace it (and then convert the path into a selection; see page 376) instead of using the Lasso—you'll get a smoother selection. You can also convert a selection into a path for precise reshaping.

To create a freeform selection:

1. Click a layer.
2. Choose the **Lasso** tool (L or Shift-L).
3. *Optional:* Enter a Feather value above zero on the Lasso tool options bar to soften the edges of the selection.
4. Drag around an area of the layer **1**. When you release the mouse, the open ends of the selection will join automatically.

TIP To create a straight side using the Lasso tool, with the mouse button still down, press Alt/Option, and click to create corners. Drag, then release Alt/Option to resume drawing a freehand selection.

To create a polygonal selection:

1. Click a layer.
2. Choose the **Polygonal Lasso** tool (L or Shift-L).
3. To create straight sides, click to create points **2**. To join the open ends of the selection, click the starting point (a small circle will appear next to the pointer). Or Ctrl-click/Cmd-click or double-click anywhere on the image to have the selection close automatically.

   Alt-drag/Option-drag to draw a curved segment as you create a polygonal selection. Release Alt/Option to resume drawing straight sides.

TIP While creating a selection with the Polygonal Lasso tool, press Backspace/Delete to erase the last-created corner.

Lasso, Polygonal Lasso Selection

If you click a layer pixel with the **Magic Wand** tool, a selection will be created that includes adjacent pixels of a shade, color, or transparency level similar to the one you clicked on. You can then add similarly colored, nonadjacent pixels to the selection by using the Similar command, or add non-similar colors by Shift-clicking.

To select by color using the Magic Wand tool:

1. Click a layer.

2. Choose the **Magic Wand** tool (W).

3. On the Magic Wand tool options bar **1**:

   Check **Anti-alias,** if desired, to allow the tool to pick up semitransparent pixels along the edge of a shape.

   Check **Contiguous** to limit the selection to areas that are connected to the first pixel you click on, or uncheck this option to allow noncontiguous areas to be selected.

   Check **Sample All Layers** to create a selection based on colors in all the currently displayed layers, or uncheck Sample All Layers to sample colors on just the current layer.

4. Click a shade or color in the image.

5. *Do any of these optional steps:*

   To enlarge the selection based on the current Tolerance value on the Magic Wand tool options bar, right-click/Control-click in the document window and choose **Grow** as many times as you like. We recommend using a low Tolerance value.

   To select additional, noncontiguous areas of a similar color or shade based on the current Tolerance value on the options bar, right-click/Control-click

Feather after

To feather a selection after it's created, with the selection active, right-click/Control-click and choose **Feather,** then enter a **Feather Radius** value (.2–250 pixels). The higher the image resolution, the wider you need to make the feather radius. The feathering won't be visible on the selection marquee but will become evident if you modify the selection with a painting tool; copy/paste, move, or fill it; or apply a filter or Image menu command to it. See page 138.

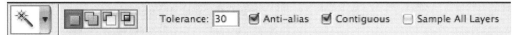

1 *The Magic Wand tool options bar*

1 *A selection created using the **Magic Wand** with a **Tolerance** value of **10***

2 *A selection created using the **Magic Wand** with a **Tolerance** value of **40:** At the higher Tolerance value, more pixels are selected.*

in the document window and choose **Similar.** (This command works the same whether Contiguous is checked on the options bar or not.)

To change the range of shades or colors within which the Magic Wand tool creates a selection, enter a **Tolerance** value (0–255) on the Magic Wand tool options bar, then click in the document window again **1**–**2**. For example, at a Tolerance value of 32, the Magic Wand will select within a range of 16 shades below and 16 shades above the shade it's clicked on. Enter 0 to select only one color or shade.

To gradually expand or narrow the range of shades or colors the Magic Wand tool selects, change the Tolerance value between clicks. The higher the Tolerance value, the broader the range of colors the tool selects.

TIP To deselect a selection or undo a Grow or Similar command, use the History palette.

TIP To grow or shrink a selection by a specified number of pixels, choose Select > Modify > Expand or Contract. Other methods of enlarging and subtracting from selections are discussed on page 132.

TIP To remove a flat background color from around a shape on a layer, choose the Magic Wand tool, uncheck Contiguous on the options bar, click the background area, then press Backspace/Delete.

Magic Wand Selection

1 *The Magnetic Lasso tool options bar*

You can use the **Magnetic Lasso** tool to select irregular shapes. It doesn't do the job perfectly, but it's a useful tool nevertheless. As you drag or move the tool, it snaps to the nearest distinct shade or color that defines the edge of a shape, creating a freeform selection. *Note:* This tool utilizes a lot of processing time and RAM. If you move or drag the mouse quickly on a large image, the tool may not keep pace with you.

To select using the Magnetic Lasso tool:

1. Choose the **Magnetic Lasso** tool (L or Shift-L).

2. Change any of the options bar settings **1** for the tool:

Feather (0–250 pixels) for the softness of the edges of the selection.

Width (1–256 pixels) for the size of the area in pixels under the pointer that the tool considers when it places a selection line **2**. Use a wide Width for a high-contrast image that has strong edges; use a narrow Width for an image with subtle contrast changes or small shapes close together.

Edge Contrast (1–100%) for the degree of contrast needed between shapes for the tool to consider it an edge. Use a low Edge Contrast for a low-contrast image.

TIP If you enter a low or high Width, do the same for the Edge Contrast.

Frequency (0–100) to control how often fastening points are placed as a selection is made. The lower the Frequency, the less frequently points are placed. Use a high Frequency to select a highly irregular contour.

To use tablet pressure to control the Width, click the ✎ button.

Make your life easier

To temporarily heighten the contrast in an image to help the Magnetic Lasso tool work "smarter," choose **Brightness/Contrast** from the New Fill/Adjustment Layer pop-up menu ◑ at the bottom of the Layers palette, move the Contrast slider to the right (and also the Brightness slider, if necessary), then click OK. Delete this adjustment layer when you're done using the Magnetic Lasso.

2 *If **Other Cursors: Precise** is chosen in Preferences (Cmd-K/Control-K) > **Display & Cursors**, the pointer is a circle with a crosshair in the center, with the current Width as its diameter. Or for a temporary Precise pointer, press Caps Lock.*

Scrap it

Press **Esc** to cancel a partial selection line drawn using the Magnetic Lasso tool (then you can start anew).

Press **Backspace/Delete** to erase the last-drawn fastening points in reverse order.

1 *With the **Magnetic Lasso** tool, move the mouse **slowly** around a shape.*

2 *After **closing** the selection*

3. Click on the image to establish a fastening point. Move the mouse, with or without pressing the mouse button, along the edge of the shape that you want to select **1**; the selection line will snap to the edge of the shape. The temporary points that appear will disappear later when you close the selection.

4. If the selection line starts to follow adjacent shapes that you don't want to select, click the edge of the shape that you *do* want to select to add a fastening point manually, then continue to move or drag the mouse.

5. To close the selection line **2**:

   Double-click anywhere over the shape.
   or
   Click the starting point (a small circle will appear next to the Magnetic Lasso tool pointer).
   or
   Press Enter/Return.
   or
   Ctrl-click/Cmd-click.
   or
   Alt-double-click/Option-double-click to close the selection with a straight segment.

TIP To decrease the Width setting by one pixel as you create a selection, press [. To increase the width, press].

TIP Alt-click/Option-click to use the Polygonal Lasso tool temporarily while the Magnetic Lasso tool is selected, or Alt-drag/Option-drag to use a temporary Lasso tool.

TIP To enhance the ability of the Magnetic Lasso to find shape edges, on the Channels palette, click each color channel separately. Pick a channel in which the shape you want to select contrasts well with its surroundings, use the Magnetic Lasso with that channel chosen, and then, on the Layers palette, click the layer you want to edit.

Using the **Color Range** command, you can select areas based on colors in the image or based on a luminosity or hue range.

To use the Color Range command to create a selection:

1. Click a layer. The Color Range command samples colors from all the currently visible layers, but only the current layer will be available for editing. You can limit the selection range by creating a selection first.

2. Choose Select > **Color Range,** or if a selection tool is chosen, right-click/Control-click in the document window and choose Color Range. The Color Range dialog box opens **1**.

3. Choose from the **Select** pop-up menu. You can limit the selection to a preset **color** range (e.g., Reds, Yellows), to a **luminosity** range (Highlights, Midtones, or Shadows), or to **Sampled Colors** (shades or colors you'll click on with the Color Range eyedropper; see step 6). The **Out of Gamut** option will be available only if the image is in Lab Color or RGB Color mode.

4. Choose a **Selection Preview** option for how the selected areas are depicted in the document window.

5. To preview the selection, click the **Selection** button; to redisplay the whole image, click the **Image** button. Or hold down Ctrl/Cmd with either option chosen to toggle between the two. If the image extends beyond the edges of the document window, we recommend using the Image option, so the entire image will be displayed in the preview area.

6. If you chose Sampled Colors in step 3, click the **eyedropper** 🖋 in the dialog box, then click or drag in the preview area or in the document window to sample colors in the image.

To add more colors or shades to the selection, Shift-click in the document window or in the preview area; or Alt-click/Option-click to remove colors or shades from the selection. You could also click the 🖋 or 🖋 eyedropper in the dialog box, then click on the image or in the preview area without holding down Shift or Alt/Option.

Move the **Fuzziness** slider to the right to expand the range of selected colors or shades, or to the left to narrow the range.

7. *Optional:* To swap the selected and nonselected areas, check Invert.

8. Click OK. (If you chose a preset color range and the image contains only light saturations of that color, an alert dialog box will inform you that the selection marquee will be present but invisible.)

TIP Click Save in the Color Range dialog box to save the current settings. Click Load to locate and load previously saved settings.

1 *Use the **Color Range** command to select areas of an image based on their color or luminosity range.*

1 *A* **frame** *selection created using the Rectangular Marquee tool*

2 *After using the Elliptical Marquee tool with a* **Feather** *setting of 10 px to select the women's faces, choosing* **Select Inverse** *to reverse the selected and nonselected areas, then using Image > Adjustments > **Levels** to screen back the selected area*

Border Selection

Width: 15   pixels   OK   Cancel

3 *Enter a* **Width** *in the* **Border Selection** *dialog box.*

In the first set of instructions on this page, you'll create a **border-shaped selection** by dragging with a selection tool. In the second set of instructions, you'll create a border selection by entering a value in a dialog box.

To create a border selection manually:

Method 1

1. Click a layer.

2. Choose the **Rectangular Marquee** or **Elliptical Marquee** tool (M or Shift-M), then drag to create a selection.
or
Choose Select > **All** (Ctrl-A/Cmd-A).

3. Alt-drag/Option-drag a smaller selection inside the first one **1**. (To subtract from a selection by using a different method, see page 132.)

Method 2

1. Click a layer.

2. Choose the **Rectangular Marquee** or **Elliptical Marquee** tool (M or Shift-M), choose a Feather value on the options bar (if desired), then drag to create a selection in the document window.

3. Right-click/Cmd-click in the document window and choose **Select Inverse 2**.

TIP To create a vignette, see pages 277–279.

To create a border selection by using a dialog box:

1. Create a selection of any shape.

2. Choose Select > Modify > **Border.**

3. Enter the desired **Width** (1–200 pixels) for the border **3**.

4. Click OK. The new selection will evenly straddle the edge of the original selection **4**.

4 *A* **border** *selection*

PHOTO: PAUL PETROFF

Working with selections

To deselect a selection:

With any selection tool chosen, right-click/Control-click the image and choose **Deselect.**

or

With any tool chosen, press **Ctrl-D/Cmd-D.**

or

Click **inside** the selection with any selection tool **1**.

TIP Deselect a selection only when you're sure you're done using it, as it's difficult to reselect the same area twice. If you deselect unintentionally, you can use the History palette to reselect. If you think you might want to reuse a selection, save it as a path (see page 366) or in an alpha channel (see page 133).

To reselect the last selection:

With any selection tool chosen except the Magic Wand, right-click/Control-click the image and choose **Reselect.**

or

With any tool chosen, press **Ctrl-Shift-D/Cmd-Shift-D** (or choose Select > Reselect).

or

Click the state on the **History** palette that's named for the tool you used to create the selection.

If you **delete** a selection from a layer, the original selection area will become transparent **2**. If you delete a selection from the Background, the selection area will fill with the current Background color **3**.

To delete selected pixels:

1. On the Layers palette, click a layer or Background. If you click the Background, choose a Background color (see Chapter 12).
2. Press **Backspace/Delete.**

   or

   Choose Edit > **Clear.**

   or

   Choose Edit > **Cut** (Ctrl-X/Cmd-X) to place the selection on the Clipboard.

PHOTO: PAUL PETROFF

1 *Click **inside** a selection to **deselect** it.*

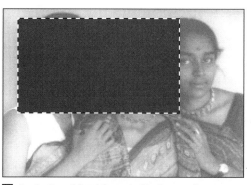

2 *A selection deleted from a **layer***

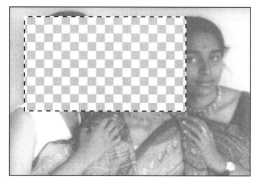

3 *A selection deleted from the **Background***

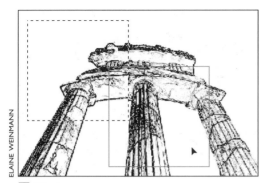

1 *Moving a marquee*

2 *The original Magic Wand tool selection of background areas*

3 *After applying the Smooth command*

Follow these instructions to move only the selection **marquee**—not its contents.

To move a selection marquee:

1. *Optional:* To help you position the marquee, choose View > Show > Grid and turn on View > Snap To > Grid; or drag a guide from the horizontal or vertical ruler and turn on View > Snap To > Guides.

2. Choose a selection tool, then click the **New Selection** button ▣ on the options bar.

3. **Drag** inside an existing selection **1**. Hold down Shift after you start dragging to constrain the mouse to a multiple of 45°.
   or
   Press any **arrow** key to nudge the marquee one pixel at a time.

TIP You can drag a selection marquee from one document window into another with a selection tool.

TIP If you drag a selection on a layer with the Move tool, the selection's pixel contents will be cut from that layer and the empty space will be replaced by transparent pixels. If you move a selection on the Background, the empty space will be filled with the current Background color.

The **Smooth** command adds unselected pixels to, or removes unselected pixels from, a selection within a specified radius. It's a good way to eliminate extraneous selection areas, particularly after using the Magic Wand tool or the Color Range command.

To smooth a selection:

1. With a selection active in the document **2**, choose Select > Modify > **Smooth.**

2. Enter a **Sample Radius** value (1–100 pixels). The higher the Sample Radius, the more extraneous, nonselected areas will be included within the selection. Start with a moderate value, as a high value may cause the selection to be enlarged too much, or may cause large areas to become deselected.

3. Click OK **3**.

ELAINE WEINMANN

Move Selection Marquee; Smooth Selection

To switch the selected and unselected areas:

With any selection tool chosen, right-click/Control-click the image and choose **Select Inverse.**

or

With any tool chosen, press **Ctrl-Shift-I/Cmd-Shift-I** (or choose Select > Inverse) **1**–**2**.

Choose the same command or shortcut again to switch back to the original selection.

TIP Here's an easy way to select a shape on a solid-color background: Choose the Magic Wand tool, enter 10 or less in the Tolerance field on the options bar, click the solid-color background to select it entirely, then right-click/Control-click and choose Select Inverse.

Sometimes selection edges (those "marching ants") can be distracting or downright annoying. If you follow the instructions below to **hide** them, remember that the selection remains active even if you can't see it!

To hide a selection marquee:

Choose View > Show > **Selection Edges** to uncheck the command. The selection will remain active.

To redisplay the selection marquee, choose the command again (it should have a check mark).

The Ctrl-H/Cmd-H shortcut hides/shows whichever options are currently available on the Show submenu. The Show Extras Options dialog box (View > Show > Show Extras Options), in turn, controls which options are listed on the Show submenu.

TIP To verify that a selection is still active, press on the Select menu. When a selection is active, most of the commands on the menu are available.

TIP You can hide or show selection edges while some Image > Adjustments dialog boxes are open (use the shortcut).

1 *The original selection: The angels are selected.*

2 *After **inverting** the selection, now the background is selected.*

1 *Scaling a selection marquee*

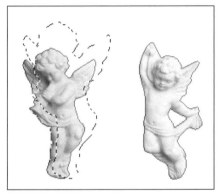

2 *The selection marquee is enlarged, but not its contents.*

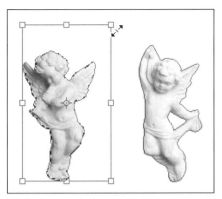

3 *You can use any command on the **Select** > **Modify** submenu to modify a selection.*

The **Transform Selection** command affects only the selection marquee—not its contents. (To transform selected pixels, you can either use a command on the Edit > Transform submenu or manipulate the bounding box of the selection.)

To transform a selection marquee:

1. With any selection tool chosen, right-click/Control-click the image and choose **Transform Selection.**
or
With any tool chosen, choose Select (not Edit!) > **Transform Selection.**

2. Follow steps 4–5 on pages 309–310 to perform a scale, rotate, skew, distort, or perspective transformation **1**–**2**.

To modify a selection marquee via a menu command:

Choose Select > Modify > **Smooth** (see page 129) **3**.
or
Choose Select > Modify > **Expand** or **Contract,** enter a value, then click OK.
or
Choose Select > **Grow** or **Similar.** These two commands use the current Tolerance setting for the Magic Wand tool (see pages 122–123). You can repeat either command to further expand the selection.
or
Choose the **Magic Wand** tool, then right-click/Control-click the image and choose **Grow** or **Similar.**

Transform, Modify Selection Marquee

131

To add to a selection:

Choose any selection tool but the Magic Wand, click the **Add to Selection** button on the options bar **1**, choose other options bar settings for the tool, if desired, then drag across the area to be added **2**–**3**. Or without clicking the Add to Selection button, position the cursor over the selection, then Shift-drag over the area to be added.
or
Choose the Magic Wand tool, click the Add to Selection button on the options bar, then click outside the selection. Or without clicking the Add to Selection button, Shift-click outside the selection.

If the additional selection overlaps the original selection, it will become part of the new, larger selection. If the addition doesn't overlap the original selection, a second, separate selection will be created.

To subtract from a selection:

Choose any selection tool but the Magic Wand, click the **Subtract from Selection** button on the options bar **1**, choose other options bar settings, if desired, then drag around the area to be subtracted. Or without clicking the Subtract from Selection button, Alt-drag/Option-drag around the area to be subtracted.
or
Click the **Magic Wand** tool, click the **Subtract from Selection** button on the options bar, then click inside the selection. Or without clicking the Subtract from Selection button, Alt-click/Option-click inside the selection.

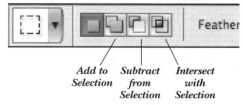

Add to   Subtract   Intersect
Selection   from   with
         Selection   Selection

1 *Use any of these buttons on the options bar to amend a selection, then click the New Selection (first) button to restore the tool's normal function.*

2 *The original selection*

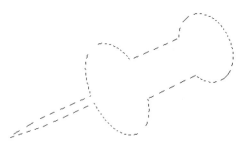

3 *After **adding** a new area to the selection*

1 *A circular selection is drawn over an existing selection with **Alt/Option** and **Shift** held down.*

2 *As a result, only the **intersection** of the two selections remains selected.*

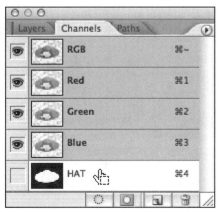

3 *Ctrl-click/Cmd-click the **alpha channel** that you want to load as a **selection**.*

4 *The **alpha channel** appears in the document window as a **selection**.*

To select the intersection of two selections:

1. With a selection present, choose a selection tool.

2. Click the **Intersect with Selection** button on the options bar, then create a new selection that overlaps the current one **1**–**2**. Or without clicking the button, Alt-Shift-drag/Option-Shift-drag.

Saving and loading selections

In Chapter 22, you'll learn all about saving and loading selections in depth. For now, it's reassuring to know that the intricate selection you created with the Magic Wand tool or Color Range command—and then painstakingly reshaped—can be saved for future use.

A **selection** that's saved in an alpha **channel** can be loaded onto any image whenever you need to use it. Note that alpha channels do make your files larger, so just create (and keep) only the ones you need.

To save a selection to a channel:

1. Create a selection.

2. Click the **Save Selection as Channel** (second) button at the bottom of the Channels palette. A new channel will appear on the Channels palette.

TIP To delete an alpha channel, click it, click the Delete Current Channel button, then click Yes.

To load an alpha channel onto an image as a selection:

On the Channels palette, **Ctrl-click/Cmd-click** the alpha channel you want to load **3**. Your selection will reappear in the document window **4**.

TIP To rename an alpha channel for easier reference, double-click the name on the palette, then type.

Extracting imagery

If you've ever torn your hair out trying to select or mask a shape with an irregular edge (e.g., a figure with frizzy or fly-away hair, or an animal or other foreground subject in a landscape), you'll appreciate what the **Extract** command can do. Using masking tools, you'll select an area of a layer on a full-size preview in the dialog box. The nonselected areas on the current layer will be eliminated when you click OK.

To extract imagery from a layer:

1. Click the layer that you want to extract imagery from, then press Ctrl-J/Cmd-J to duplicate it. Hide the original layer.

2. Choose Filter > **Extract** (Ctrl-Alt-X/ Cmd-Option-X). A large, resizable dialog box will appear onscreen **1**.

3. You'll use the Edge Highlighter to mask the object border first, and then click the interior with the Fill tool to define the fill area.

Choose the **Edge Highlighter** tool from the toolbox in the dialog box (B) **2**.
and
In the Tool Options area **3**, enter or choose a **Brush Size** (1–999 pixels) for the highlighter. The sharper the edge of the object you're going to extract, the smaller the brush you can use. Use a large brush if the shape has wide, choppy edges (e.g., hair blowing in the wind).
and
Choose Red, Green, or Blue as the **Highlight** color for the mask. Or choose Other and choose a color from the Color Picker.

4. *Optional:* If you're going to trace a crisp-edged shape (e.g., a geometric shape), check Smart Highlighting. The highlight will be the minimum width necessary to cover the edge of the shape, regardless of the current brush size.

5. Drag a border around the area of the image you want to extract. Complete the

1 *After outlining the chimp with the **Edge Highlighter** tool and filling the interior of the chimp with the **Fill** tool*

Edge
— Highlighter **B**

— Fill **G**

— Eraser **E**

— Eyedropper **I**

— Cleanup **C**

— Edge Touchup **T**

— Zoom **Z**

— Hand **H**

2 *Tools and tool shortcuts in the **Extract** dialog box*

3 *Choose **Tool Options** on the right side of the **Extract** dialog box.*

Channel it

To make the marker highlight conform to the shape of a **selection,** create a selection, choose Select > Modify > **Border** (Width about 12 pixels), then click OK. Inverse the selection, and save it in an alpha channel (see page 133). Choose Filter > **Extract,** then choose that alpha channel from the Extraction: **Channel** pop-up menu. Finally, click with the **Fill** tool (G) inside the highlighted area.

loop to make a closed shape. Drag along the border of the shape so as to catch any frizz or fringe. You don't need to drag along the edge of the canvas area if the imagery extends that far.

6. *Optional:* In the Extraction area, check Textured Image to include texture as a factor determining what is to be extracted. The higher the Smooth value (0–1000), the more extraneous pixels are eliminated.

7. Use the **Eraser** tool (E) from the dialog box if you need to erase any of the edge highlighting. Choose a Brush Size for the Eraser in the Tool Options area of the dialog box. Use the Edge Highlighter again to mark the edge.

   TIP To zoom in on the preview, press Ctrl-+/Cmd-+(plus). To zoom out, press Ctrl--/Cmd--(minus). You could also use the **Zoom** tool from the dialog box (Alt-click/Option-click with the tool to reduce the view).

   TIP If the preview is greater than 100% view, you can use the **Hand** tool from the dialog box (H) to move the preview in the window (press the Spacebar to access the Hand tool temporarily).

8. Choose the **Fill** (second) tool (G) from the toolbox in the dialog box.
   and
   Choose **Red, Green,** or **Blue** as the Fill color for the mask. Or choose Other and choose a color from the Color Picker.
   and
   Click **inside** the area of the image that you want to extract. (Click again to unfill.)

9. Click Preview, then in the Preview area of the dialog box, do any of the following:

   Choose **Show: Extracted** to toggle to the extracted image view; choose **Original** to toggle back to the original image.

   (Continued on the following page)

(Continued on the following page)

Extract Command

Choose **Display:** None to display the background as transparent; choose Black Matte, Gray Matte, or White Matte to display the extracted shape on a background of black, gray, or white, respectively; choose Other to choose a color from the Color Picker; or choose Mask to display the discarded area as black and the protected area as white.

Check **Show Highlight** and/or **Show Fill.**

10. To refine the mask further, do any of the following:

Drag with the **Cleanup** tool (C) to gradually subtract opacity from the extracted imagery. (Alt-drag/Option-drag to restore opacity.)

Use the **Edge Touchup** tool (T) to gradually sharpen edges. Don't use this tool on thin strands (e.g., wispy hair or feathers); you'll lose too much detail.

Change the **Smooth** value, then click Preview again.

11. Click OK. If you want to restore any lost areas, use the History Brush tool, using the "Layer via Copy" state as the source **1**–**2** (see pages 162–163). Or to erase more areas, use the Background Eraser (see pages 220–221).

TIP Press [or] to adjust the brush diameter of the Edge Highlighter tool on the fly.

*The **Extract** command overdid it in these areas.*

1 *After extracting (chimp not in the mist)*

2 *This is after using the **History Brush** tool to restore areas of the chimp's face and arm. The Cleanup tool could have been used instead (see step 10).*

COMPOSITING 9

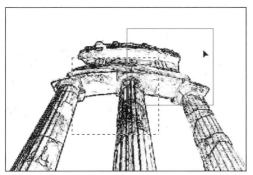

1 *If you click a **layer**, then move a selection,...*

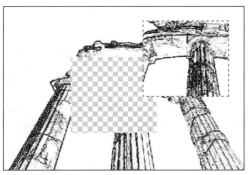

2 *...the exposed area will fill with **transparent** pixels.*

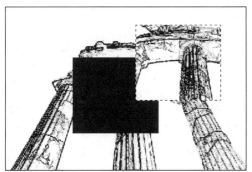

3 *If you click the **Background**, then move a selection, the exposed area will fill with the **Background color**.*

YOU CAN ACHIEVE BEAUTIFUL results by compositing image elements. Techniques covered in this chapter include drag-copy, drag-and-drop, the Clipboard commands (Cut, Copy, Copy Merged, Paste, and Paste Into), pattern stamping, cloning, the Photomerge command, and features that help you position, align, and smooth the seams between image elements.

Moving selection contents
In the instructions on this page and the next, you'll be **moving** actual image **pixels.** (To move just a selection marquee without moving its contents, see page 129.)

To move selection contents:
1. Create a selection. *Optional:* To help you position the selection, choose View > Show > Grid (Ctrl-'/ Cmd-') or display the rulers, then drag a guide from either ruler; also turn on View > Snap To > Guides and Snap To > Grid.

2. On the Layers palette, click the Background, then choose a Background color (see page 182). The area you expose will fill automatically with this color.
   or
   Click a layer. The exposed area will fill automatically with transparent pixels.

3. Choose the **Move** tool (V). (You can use Ctrl/Cmd to access the Move tool when most other tools are chosen.)

4. Position the pointer over the selection (the pointer will have a scissors icon), then drag. Imagery within the selected area will move **1**–**3**.

   Beware! When you deselect a selection, its pixel contents drop back into its original layer (in its new location), regardless of which layer is currently active.

TIP With the Move tool chosen, press an arrow key to nudge a selection marquee by one pixel at a time.

Feathering selections

The **Feather** command fades the edge of a selection by a specified number of pixels inward and outward from the marquee. A feather radius of 5, for example, creates a feather area 10 pixels wide. The feather won't be visible until you copy-and-paste, move, fill, or paint on the selection; or apply a filter or Image menu command to it.

To feather a selection:

1. With a selection active, right-click/ Control-click in the document window and choose **Feather** (or choose Select > Feather).

2. Enter a **Feather Radius** value (.2–250 pixels). The higher the document resolution, the wider you need to make the feather radius.

3. Click OK ■. *Note:* If the feather radius is too wide for the current selection area, an alert message will appear onscreen: "No pixels are more than 50% selected…"

TIP To specify a feather radius before creating a selection, choose any marquee or lasso tool, then enter a Feather value on the options bar.

Duplicating selections

To drag-copy a selection in the same document:

1. Click a layer, and create a selection.

2. Choose the **Move** tool (V), ⬚ then Alt-drag/Option-drag a selection. The copied pixels will remain selected ■–■.
or
Without choosing the Move tool, Ctrl-Alt-drag/Cmd-Option-drag a selection.

TIP Press Alt-arrow/Option-arrow to offset a duplicate of a selection from the original in one-pixel increments, or press Alt-Shift-arrow/Option-Shift-arrow to offset a duplicate in 10-pixel increments.

■ *We created a selection, applied a **Feather** value, inverted the selection, then pressed Delete.*

■ *Alt-drag/ Option-drag…*

■ *…to duplicate a selection.*

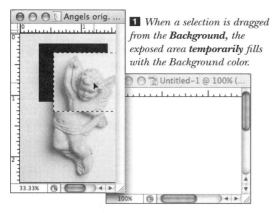

1 *When a selection is dragged from the **Background**, the exposed area **temporarily** fills with the Background color.*

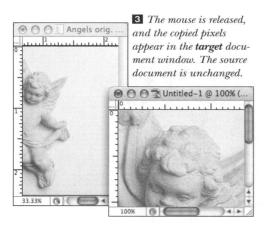

2 *A **dark border** appears in the target document window.*

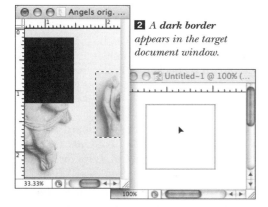

3 *The mouse is released, and the copied pixels appear in the **target** document window. The source document is unchanged.*

When you **drag and drop** selected pixels from one document to another, presto, a duplicate of those selected pixels appears on a new layer in the target document. This method bypasses the Clipboard (see the next page), which makes it less memory-intensive.

To drag and drop a selection between documents:

1. Open the source and target documents, and arrange the windows so they don't completely overlap each other.

2. In the source document, create a selection, then click a layer or the Background.

3. Choose the **Move** tool (V). (You can use Ctrl/Cmd to access the Move tool when most other tools are chosen.) If you're using the Move tool, you can check Show Transform Controls on the (NEW) Move options bar to make the bounding box that surrounds the selection visible.

4. Drag the selection into the target document window, and release the mouse where you want the pixels to be dropped **1**–**3**. If you Shift-drag, the selection will appear in the exact center of the target document. The copied imagery will appear automatically on a new layer. You can reposition it using the Move tool.

   Does the imagery look larger or smaller? See the sidebar on the following page!

> **More ways than two**
>
> As an alternative to using the drag-copy or copy-and-paste commands, you can also get **imagery** onto a **new layer** by doing either of the following:
>
> ➤ To extract imagery from a layer and have it appear on a new layer, use Filter > **Extract** (see pages 134–136).
>
> ➤ To turn a selection into a new layer, right-click/Control-click in the document window and choose **Layer Via Copy** or **Layer Via Cut** (see page 107).

Drag and Drop Selection Between Documents

Using the Clipboard

You can use the Edit > **Cut, Copy,** or **Copy Merged** command to save a selection to a temporary storage area called the Clipboard, and then use Edit > **Paste** or **Paste Into** to paste the Clipboard pixels onto another layer in the same document or in another document . The Cut, Copy, Copy Merged, and Paste Into commands are available only while a selection is active.

If you create a selection and choose Edit > Cut, the selection will be placed on the Clipboard. (The Clear command doesn't use the Clipboard.) If you Cut or Clear a selection from the Background, the exposed area will be filled with the current Background color. If you remove a selection from a layer, the area left behind will be transparent.

TIP For a soft transition between pasted imagery and a layer, check Anti-alias on the options bar for your selection tool before using it.

The Edit > Paste command automatically pastes the Clipboard contents into a new layer. If you paste into a smaller size document, any pasted pixels that extend beyond the canvas area will be preserved and can be moved into view using the Move tool. The pixels outside the canvas area will save with the document.

Who shrank my imagery?!

When you **paste** or **drag-and-drop** a selection between files, it is rendered in the resolution of the **target document.** If the resolution of the target document is higher than that of the source imagery, the source imagery will appear smaller when pasted or dropped. Conversely, if the resolution of the target document is lower than that of the source document, the source imagery will appear larger when pasted or dropped.

To keep the imagery the same size, before copying it or dragging it, make the resolution (and dimensions, if desired) of the source and target documents the same using Image > **Image Size.** To paste into a smaller document, see page 143.

You can paste the same Clipboard contents as many times as you like. If **Export Clipboard** is checked in Preferences > General, the Clipboard contents will be stored in temporary system memory even if you exit/quit Photoshop. Only one selection can be stored on the Clipboard at a time, and the Clipboard contents are replaced each time the Cut, Copy, or Copy Merged command is chosen.

TIP The dimensions in the New dialog box automatically match the dimensions of the current contents of the Clipboard.

1 *A composite image*

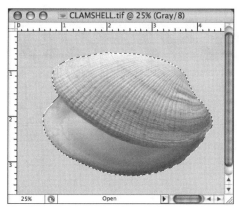

1 *An area is selected, then Edit > **Copy** is chosen.*

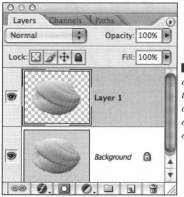

2 *The **Paste** command places the Clipboard contents onto a new layer automatically.*

De-matte or defringe

If the imagery you move or paste was originally on a black or dark background and was selected with the Anti-alias option on, try using Layer > Matting > **Remove Black Matte** to remove unwanted remnants from the black background; or choose Layer > Matting > **Remove White Matte** if the imagery was originally on a white background. You'll notice the change more on feathered selections.

Maybe you did a less than perfect job of selecting an object in a photo, then used Paste or Layer Via Cut to put it onto a new layer? The **Defringe** command recolors the edges of the current layer (where image pixels meet transparency), helping to mask the seams between collaged image elements. Click a layer, choose Layer > Matting > Defringe, and enter a **Width** (try 2 or 3 pixels).

When using the **Clipboard** commands (Cut, Copy, or Copy Merged; then Paste), if the dimensions of the selection being copied are larger than those of the target document, some pixels will paste outside the canvas area and will be hidden from view. You can move the layer with the Move tool to bring pixels back into view.

To copy and paste a selection:

1. Click a layer or the Background, then create a selection. *Optional:* To feather the selection, right-click/Control-click and choose Feather, enter a Feather Radius value, then click OK.

2. Choose one of the following commands:

Edit > **Copy 1** (Ctrl-C/Cmd-C) to copy pixels from the current layer within the selection area.

Edit > **Copy Merged** (Ctrl-Shift-C/Cmd-Shift-C) to copy pixels from all visible layers within the selection area.

Edit > **Cut** to cut the selection out of the layer.

3. Click in any document window.

4. Choose Edit > **Paste** (Ctrl-V/Cmd-V) **2**. The pasted pixels will appear in a new layer. The layer can be restacked using the Layers palette, moved using the Move tool, or defringed (see the sidebar at left).

TIP A large Clipboard selection reduces available program memory. To empty the Clipboard at any time to reclaim memory, choose Edit > Purge > Clipboard, then click OK. This can't be undone.

If you use the **Paste Into** command to paste the Clipboard contents inside a selection, a new layer will be created automatically and the active marquee will become a layer mask. The pasted imagery can then be repositioned within the layer mask, or the mask itself can be reshaped to reveal more or reveal less.

To paste into a selection:

1. Select an area of a layer. *Optional:* Right-click/Control-click and choose Feather, enter a value, then click OK.

2. Choose Edit > **Copy** to copy pixels from the active layer only, or choose Edit > **Copy Merged** (Ctrl-Shift-C/Cmd-Shift-C) to copy pixels within the selection area from all the currently visible layers.

3. Leave the same layer active, or click a different layer, or click a layer in another document.

4. Select the area (or areas) that you want to paste the Clipboard contents into.

5. Choose Edit > **Paste Into** (Ctrl-Shift-V/Cmd-Shift-V). A new layer and layer mask will be created **1**–**3**.

6. *More options:*

   The entire Clipboard contents were pasted onto the layer, but the layer mask is probably hiding some of those pixels. To **move** the layer **mask** relative to the layer, choose the Move tool (V), click the layer mask thumbnail (the thumbnail on the right), then drag in the document window. Or to **move** the layer **contents,** click the layer thumbnail, then drag in the document window.

   Click the layer mask thumbnail, then paint on the layer mask in the document window with white to **expose** more of the image or with black to **hide** more of the image.

   To move the layer and layer mask in **unison,** click between the layer and layer mask thumbnails to link the two layer components together, choose the Move tool, then drag in the document window. Click the link icon 🔗 to unlink.

1 *To create this effect, we selected and copied a music layer in one document, then in another document, Ctrl-clicked/Cmd-clicked a type layer and chose Edit > Paste Into. A new layer resulted.*

2 *The layer contents can be repositioned within the layer mask because the two thumbnails aren't linked together. For this document, the music layer thumbnail was clicked, then the layer contents were moved upward using the Move tool.*

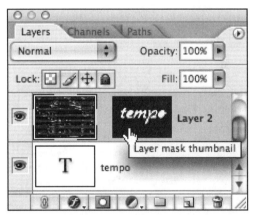

3 *When the **Paste Into** command is chosen, the pasted imagery appears on a new layer, and a layer mask is created for it automatically. In this case, the pasted imagery (the music) is visible only within the white areas in the layer mask (the letter shapes).*

Off the edge

➤ If you apply an image-editing command, such as a filter, to a **layer,** any pixels outside the live canvas area will also be affected.

➤ To **enlarge** the canvas area to include hidden pixels, use Image > **Canvas Size.**

➤ To **select** all nontransparent pixels on a layer, including any pixels **outside** the live canvas area, Ctrl-click/ Cmd-click the layer thumbnail on the Layers palette. (Don't use Select > All.)

➤ To **remove** pixels that extend outside the live canvas area of a layer, click the layer, choose Select > All, then choose Image > **Crop.** Trimming off the extra pixels will reduce the file size.

➤ If a layer that contains pixels outside the live canvas area is **merged** with the Background, the hidden pixels will be **trimmed** away.

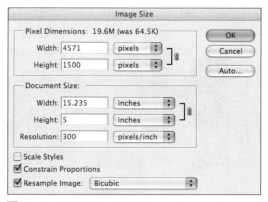

1 *Use the **Image Size** dialog box to change a document's resolution and/or dimensions.*

When collaging imagery, sometimes you need to copy from an image that has larger pixel dimensions than the document you're collaging to. If that's the case, follow these instructions to **scale down** the imagery you're copying.

To paste into a smaller document:

1. Display the **Info** palette, and note the document width, height, and resolution info at the bottom of the palette. (If it's not there, choose Palette Options from the palette menu, then check Document Sizes and Document Dimensions.) **NEW**

2. Click in the source document window, choose Image > **Duplicate,** then click OK.

3. With the duplicate document window active, choose Image > **Image Size** (Ctrl-Alt-I/Cmd-Option-I).

4. Check **Resample Image,** and change the **Resolution** to the same value as that of the target document **1**. In the Document Size: **Width** or **Height** field, enter the smaller of the two dimensions that you noted for step 1 (the width or height), then click OK.

5. In the source document, click the layer you want to copy.

6. Choose Select > **All** (Ctrl-A/Cmd-A) to select the layer, choose Edit > **Copy,** click in the target document, then choose Edit > **Paste.**
   or
   Shift-drag the source layer name into the target document window.

7. Close the duplicate document. Save the original document, if desired.

TIP In lieu of steps 3 and 4 above, you can choose File > Automate > Fit Image and enter the smaller of the two pixel dimensions (the width or height, from step 1). Note that the Fit Image action won't change the document resolution. Instead, the copied or dragged layer will adopt the resolution of the target file.

Paste into Smaller Document

Duplicating layers

If you **drag and drop** a layer, layer group, or multiple selected layers from the Layers palette in one document into another document window, any pixels outside the live canvas area on those layers will be duplicated too.

To drag and drop layers between documents:

1. Open the document that contains the layer(s) that you want to duplicate (the source document) and the document you want to duplicate the layer(s) to (the target document). Make sure the two windows don't completely overlap each other.

2. Click in the **source** document window **1**, then on the Layers palette, click the layer, Background, or layer group that you want to duplicate, or Ctrl-click/ Cmd-click multiple layers **2**. (It doesn't matter which tool is selected.)

3. Drag the layer, layer group, etc. from the Layers palette into the **target** document window, and release the mouse when the dotted border is in the desired location **3**–**4**. The new layer(s) will be stacked above the previously active layer in the target document. If you dragged the Background, it will show up as a layer in the target document.

   Note: If you duplicate a layer between an 8-bits-per-channel document and a 16-bits-per-channel document, a prompt will alert you that the image quality may be diminished due to the difference in pixel depths between the two files. Click Yes to accept the drop, or click No to cancel.

   See also the sidebar on page 95 regarding image resolution.

TIP To trim overhanging areas, see the sidebar on the previous page.

TIP Shift-drag a layer to have the duplicate appear in the center of the target document.

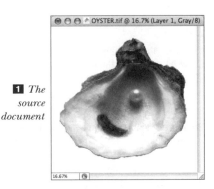

1 *The source document*

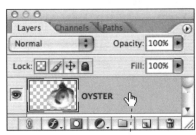

2 *Click a layer in the source document,...*

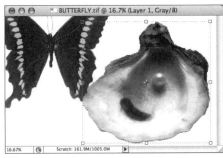

3 *...and drag it into the target window.*

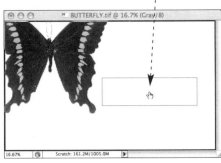

4 *The OYSTER layer appears in the target window.*

Pattern stamping

To use the Pattern Stamp tool:

1. *Optional:* To create a custom pattern, choose the **Rectangular Marquee** tool (M or Shift-M), click in a document window or select an area of a layer **1**, choose Edit > **Define Pattern,** type a Name, click OK, then deselect (Ctrl-D/ Cmd-D).

2. Choose the **Pattern Stamp** tool (S or Shift-S).

3. On the options bar:

   Choose options as per step 3 on the next page. Check **Aligned** to stamp pattern tiles in a perfect grid, regardless of how many separate strokes you use; or uncheck Aligned if you don't want the tiles to align perfectly.

   Click the **Pattern Preset** picker arrowhead or thumbnail, then click a pattern on the picker **2**. If you created a pattern (step 1, above), it will be the last pattern on the picker.

   Optional: Check Impressionist to apply a soft, blurry version of the pattern.

4. In the same document or in another document, click a layer, then click or drag to stamp the pattern in the image **3**. Try also stamping multiple patterns **4**. No source point is required for this tool.

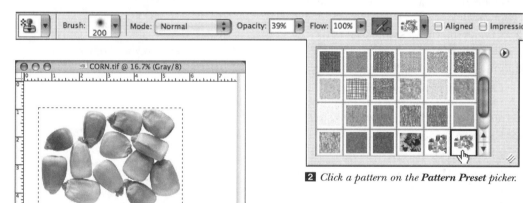

2 *Click a pattern on the* ***Pattern Preset*** *picker.*

1 *Select an area of an image, then choose Edit >* ***Define Pattern.***

3 *You can apply the pattern in any document with various opacities chosen for the* ***Pattern Stamp*** *tool.*

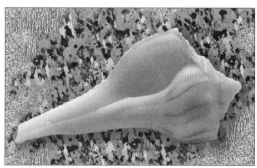

4 *The shell is surrounded by transparent pixels; multiple patterns were stamped on a blank layer below it.*

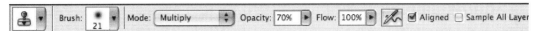

1 *The options bar for the **Clone Stamp** tool*

Cloning

You can use the **Clone Stamp** tool to clone imagery from one layer to another within the same document or from one document to another.

To clone imagery:

1. If you're cloning between two documents, position the two windows side by side. If they're both color files, they must both have the same color mode (e.g., both RGB or both CMYK). You can also clone between a color document and a grayscale document.

2. Choose the **Clone Stamp** tool (S or Shift-S).

3. On the options bar **1**, do the following:

   Click the Brush Preset picker arrowhead, then click a **brush** that has an appropriate size for the area you want to clone.

   Choose a blending **Mode.**

   Choose an **Opacity** percentage.

   Choose a **Flow** percentage to control the rate of application.

   Check **Aligned** to create a single, uninterrupted clone from the same source point, even if you release the mouse or switch modes or brushes between strokes **2**. Or uncheck Aligned to create repetitive clones from the same source point, in which case the crosshair pointer will return to the same source point each time you release the mouse **3**.

   Check **Sample All Layers** to sample pixels from all currently visible layers that you Alt-click/Option-click over; or uncheck Sample All Layers to sample pixels from the current layer only.

2 *Drag the mouse where you want the clone to appear. Here, the **Aligned** option is **on** for the Clone Stamp tool.*

3 *Uncheck the **Aligned** option to create multiple clones from the same source point.*

Sample All **NEW**

With **Sample All Layers** checked on the options bar for the current tool (e.g., Blur, Sharpen, Smudge, Magic Eraser, Healing Brush, Spot Healing Brush, or Clone Stamp), the tool will sample pixels from all the currently visible layers and send the results to the current layer. Whether this option is on or off, pixels can be modified only on the currently active layer!

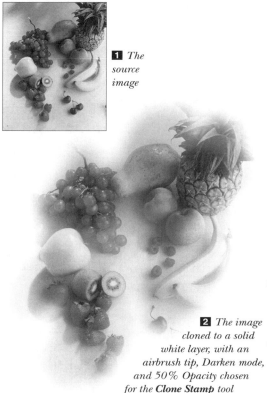

1 *The source image*

2 *The image cloned to a solid white layer, with an airbrush tip, Darken mode, and 50% Opacity chosen for the **Clone Stamp** tool*

3 *50% **Opacity** was chosen for the **Clone Stamp** tool to create this "double-exposure."*

Optional: To apply the cloned imagery in an airbrush style, click the Airbrush button. 🖌

4. If Sample All Layers is unchecked on the options bar, click the layer that you want to clone pixels from.

5. In the source document, Alt-click/Option-click the area you want to clone from to establish a source point (don't click a transparent part of the layer).

6. If you're cloning from one document to another, click in the target (yes, target) document window.

7. Click the layer you want the imagery to appear on, then drag the mouse back and forth to make the clone appear.

Two pointers will appear on the screen: a pointer over the source point and a pointer where you drag the mouse. Imagery from the source point will appear where the mouse is dragged, replacing any underlying pixels.

Note: If Lock Transparent Pixels is enabled on the Layers palette when you use the Clone Stamp tool, the cloned imagery will replace only nontransparent pixels.

8. *Optional:* To establish a new source point to clone from, Alt-click/Option-click a different area or click a different layer in the source document.

TIP To create a brush stroke version of an image (or to montage multiple images), choose a large, soft brush and clone to a solid-color or white background in another file **1**–**2**.

TIP You can change options bar settings for the Clone Stamp tool between strokes.

TIP To create a "double-exposure" effect, choose a low Opacity percentage for the tool so the underlying pixels will partially show through the cloned pixels **3**.

Clone Stamp Tool

Using alignment features

Grids, rulers, and **guides** can help you position objects more precisely than you can do "by eye."

To hide or show rulers:

To show/hide the rulers, choose View > **Rulers** (Ctrl-R/Cmd-R). Rulers will appear (or disappear from) the top and left sides of the document window, and the current position of the pointer will be indicated by a dotted marker on each ruler **1**. Move the pointer, and you'll see what we mean.

TIP To change the ruler units quickly, right-click/Control-click either ruler and choose a unit from the context menu. Or to get to the Units & Rulers panel in the Preferences dialog box quickly, where you can also change the units, double-click either ruler.

The **zero origin** for the rulers is the point from which selection and layer locations are calculated (as shown on the Info palette).

To change the zero origin for the rulers:

1. *Optional:* Choose View > Show > Grid (Ctrl-'/ Cmd-') to help you position the ruler origin.

2. From the intersection of the rulers in the upper left corner of the document window, drag diagonally into the image **2**–**3**. Note the new location of the zeros on the rulers.

TIP To reset the ruler origin, double-click the square in the upper left corner of the document window where the two rulers intersect.

1 *The* **location** *of the* **pointer** *is indicated by a dotted marker on each ruler.*

2 *Dragging the* **ruler origin**

3 *A new location for the* **ruler origin**

Rulers

Show or snap all

You can show or hide Layer Edges, Selection Edges, the Target Path, Grid, (ruler) Guides, Smart Guides, Slices, Annotations, or all of the above via the View > **Show** submenu **1** (or via the View > Show > Show Extras Options dialog box).

The **Extras** command (Ctrl-H/Cmd-H) shows/hides whichever items are currently enabled on the Show submenu.

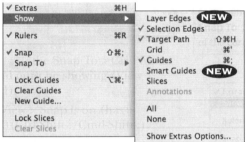

1 *The **Extras** command shows/hides all the currently enabled items on the **Show** submenu.*

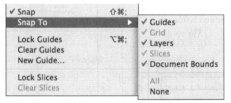

2 *Choose the **Snap** command to activate/ deactivate all the currently enabled commands on the **Snap To** submenu.*

3 *The **grid** displayed*

The **Snap** feature works like an electronic "tug." When View > Snap is on, as you move a selection border, slice, drawing tool pointer, path, or shape, that item will snap to the nearest guide, grid, slice, or document edge, depending on which of those options is chosen on the View > Snap To submenu.

To use the Snap feature:

1. Choose View > **Snap To** > **Guides, Grid,** **NEW** **Layers, Slices, Document Bounds, All** (of the above), or to turn off all of the above, choose **None 2**.

   Note: To turn on the Snap To > Grid function, the grid must be showing (View > Show > Grid).

2. Make sure **View > Snap** is on (has a check mark) (Ctrl-Shift-;/Cmd-Shift-;). This command enables whichever options are currently checked on the Snap To submenu.

The **grid 3** is a nonprinting framework that can be used to align image elements.

To show/hide the grid:

To show/hide the grid, choose View > **Show** > **Grid** (Ctrl-'/Cmd-'). The grid can be turned on or off for individual files. If View > Snap To > Grid is on, a selection or tool pointer will snap to a grid line if it's moved within eight screen pixels of the line.

Smart guides are temporary guide lines that **NEW** appear onscreen as you move layer imagery. You may find them most helpful when moving silhouetted imagery.

To show/hide smart guides:

To show/hide smart guides, choose View > **Show** > **Smart Guides.** The default color for smart guides is magenta.

TIP In the Guides, Grid & Slices panel of the Preferences dialog box, you can change the color used for displaying the grid and smart guides, and also choose other grid options.

You can use nonprinting, user-created ruler **guides** to align selections and layers.

To create and use ruler guides:

Make sure the rulers are showing, then drag from the **horizontal** or **vertical ruler** into the document window 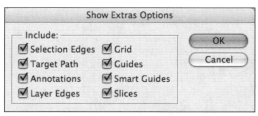.

You can also do any of the following:

Turn on View > Snap, then Shift-drag to snap a guide to a **ruler** increment.

Display the grid and turn on View > Snap To > Grid, then snap a guide to a **grid line.**

Snap a guide to a **selection** marquee.

Turn on View > Snap To > **Guides,** then snap a selection or tool pointer to a guide.

Alt-drag/Option-drag as you create a guide to switch its **orientation** from vertical to horizontal (or vice versa).

To **move** an existing guide, drag it using the Move tool (make sure the guides aren't locked). Guides will keep their relative positions if you resize the document, provided they're not locked.

To lock all guides so they can't be moved with the Move tool, choose View > **Lock Guides** (Ctrl-Alt-;/Cmd-Option-;).

To create a guide at a specific location:

1. Choose View > **New Guide.** The New Guide dialog box opens.

2. Click Orientation: **Horizontal** or **Vertical** , enter a **Position** relative to the 0 (zero) point on that axis, in any measurement unit used in Photoshop, then click OK.

To remove guides:

To remove **one** guide, choose the **Move** tool (V), then drag the guide out of the document window (this works only if guides aren't locked).
or
To remove **all** guides, choose View > **Clear Guides.**

1 *A* **guide** *is dragged downward from the horizontal ruler.*

2 *Use the* **New Guide** *dialog box to create a new guide at a specific location.*

Showing extras

You can use the View > Show > **Show Extras Options** dialog box **3** to control which onscreen features you want the View > **Extras** (Ctrl-H/Cmd-H) command to show and hide.

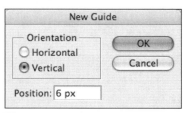

3 *In the* **Show Extras Options** *dialog box, check which onscreen features you want the View > Extras (Ctrl-H/Cmd-H) command to show and hide.*

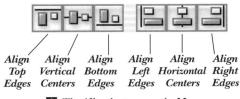

Align Top Edges | Align Vertical Centers | Align Bottom Edges | Align Left Edges | Align Horizontal Centers | Align Right Edges

1 *The Align buttons on the Move tool options bar*

2 *When you drag in the document window with the Measure tool…*

3 *…angle (A) and distance (D) readouts appear on the Info palette.*

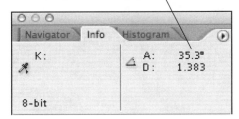

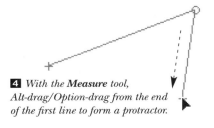

4 *With the Measure tool, Alt-drag/Option-drag from the end of the first line to form a protractor.*

5 *If you create a protractor, its angle (A), as well as the distance (D1 and D2), or length, of each line from the point where they meet will be displayed on the Info palette.*

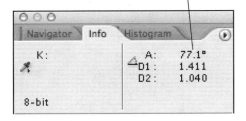

As with objects in a drawing program, you can align layers to one another via the **Align** buttons on the options bar.

To align layers to one another:

1. Choose the **Move** tool (V), then click **Auto Select Layer** on the options bar.

2. Click one image layer, then Ctrl-click/ **(NEW)** Cmd-click another image layer (or layers).

3. Click an **Align** button on the options bar **1**.

To use the Measure tool:

1. Choose the **Measure** tool (I or Shift-I) (on the Eyedropper tool pop-out menu).

2. Show the **Info** palette (F8).

3. Drag in the document window **2**. The angle (A) and length (D) of the measure line will be listed on the Info palette **3**. You can Shift-drag to constrain the angle to a multiple of 45°.

4. *Optional:* After dragging with the Measure tool, Alt-drag/Option-drag from either end of the line to create a protractor **4**. The angle (A) formed by the two lines will display on the Info palette **5**. You can change the angle at any time by dragging either end of the line.

5. Choose another tool when you're done using the Measure tool. If you choose it again, the measure line will redisplay.

   To **remove** a measure line, choose the Measure tool, then click **Clear** on the options bar.

   You can also use the Measure tool to **move** a measure line or protractor to another area of the document (but don't drag an endpoint unless you want to change the angle).

Blurring edges

The **Blur** tool softens edges between shapes by decreasing contrast. In these instructions, you'll send the strokes produced by the tool to a new layer so you don't alter pixels on any existing layers.

To blur edges:

1. Create a new layer.

2. Choose the **Blur** tool (R or Shift-R).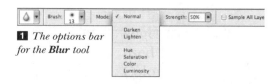

3. On the options bar **1**, do all of the following:

   Click the Brush Preset picker arrowhead, then click a hard-edged or soft-edged **brush**.

   Choose a blending **Mode.** Normal blurs pixels of any shade or color; Darken blurs only pixels that are darker than the Foreground color; and Lighten blurs only pixels that are lighter than the Foreground color (the other modes don't appear to produce any changes).

   Choose a **Strength** percentage. Try a low setting at first (say around 30%).

   Check **Sample All Layers** to pick up pixel colors from all visible layers under the pointer (and send them to the new layer). Hide any layers you don't want to sample from or blur.

4. Drag across an area in the document window to blur pixels **2**–**4**. To intensify the effect, drag again.

TIP To reduce the Blur tool's effect afterward, lower the opacity of the new layer. To remove Blur tool strokes, erase them from the layer.

TIP We don't recommend using the Sharpen tool any more because it creates artifacts. Better to select the area you want to sharpen and apply the Smart Sharpen filter (see page 256).

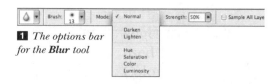

1 *The options bar for the **Blur** tool*

2 *The original image*

3 *After softening the bottom edge of the shell with the **Blur** tool, and sending the results to a new layer*

4 *The **blur** strokes were applied to Layer 2.*

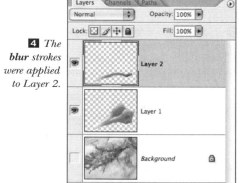

Merging photos

The **Photomerge** feature combines a series of separate photos into one document. You can either have the command blend the photos into one seamless view or leave the arranged documents intact as individual layers for later blending and editing by hand. As an added bonus, you can use this command to apply perspective and then modify the vanishing points.

To merge photos via the Photomerge command:

1. In Bridge, rearrange the images, if necessary, so they're sequential, then multiple-select the files for the panorama **1**.

> **NEW**

The source files must have a bit depth of 8-bits/channel; different file formats (e.g., .psd, .tif, .jpg) can be combined.

2. Choose Tools > Photoshop > **Photomerge.** Sit tight as the Photomerge command opens and duplicates the source files, imports them into the Photomerge dialog box, and makes your lunch.

3. The Photomerge dialog box opens (**1**, next page). Any files that Photoshop wasn't able to merge will be stored in the lightbox at the top of the dialog box. You can drag any image to or from the lightbox into the work area, and you can reposition any image in the work area.

4. In the **Navigator** area on the right side of the dialog box, you'll see a red rectangle, which represents the overall border of the work area. You can drag the red rectangle to reposition the composition within the work area. To change the zoom level of the composition, use the Zoom Out or Zoom In button or slider.

5. Use any of these tools to edit the images:

Drag with the **Select Image** tool (A) to reposition any individual image.

Drag with the **Rotate Image** tool (R) to rotate any individual image.

Click with the **Zoom** tool (Z) to zoom in, or Alt-click/Option-click to zoom out.

Collecting files via Photoshop

Either put a sequence of image files into one folder, or open all the files you want to use, then choose File > Automate > **Photomerge.** A dialog box for choosing source files opens. Choose **Use: Files,** click Browse, multiple-select the files you want to use, then click Open (click Browse again to add more files); or choose Use: **Folder,** click Browse, locate and click the desired folder, then click Choose; or choose Use: **Open Files.** To remove any selected files from the list, click Remove. *Optional:* To have Photomerge try to arrange the documents for you, check Attempt to Automatically Arrange Source Images. Click OK.

Drag with the **Hand** tool (H) to reposition the whole composite image.

6. Click **Settings: Normal** to create a flat collage, or click **Perspective** to apply perspective (as if the image were created using a wide-angle lens, with a fisheye effect at the edges). To change the vanishing point used for the perspective, choose the **Vanishing Point** tool (V), then click in the work area.

(Continued on the following page)

PHOTOS ©NINA FULLER

1 *The six original image files*

7. In the **Composition Settings** area:

For the Perspective setting, click **Cylindrical Mapping** to make the Perspective look as if it's wrapping around the viewer, without wide-angle distortion.

For the Normal or Perspective setting, click **Advanced Blending** to produce the smoothest transitions between images. This option may increase the processing time and will flatten the Photoshop file. (If Keep as Layers is checked, Advanced Blending is disabled.)

Click **Preview** to view the effects of the settings you've chosen; click **Exit Preview** to return to editing mode.

Optional: Click **Snap to Image** to snap the images to a common horizon (not available for the Perspective setting).

Optional: Click **Keep as Layers** to have each image appear on a separate layer in the final file, with no blending between them.

8. Click OK, then twiddle your thumbs as Photomerge creates a seamless image, ready to be edited and saved.
or
To save the current arrangement as a Photomerge (.pmg) file for future editing, click **Save Composition As,** choose a location (preferably the same folder as the source images), click Save, then click OK to exit the Photomerge dialog box. If you choose this option, when you're ready to reopen the Photomerge (.pmg) composition and its component files in Photoshop, close all files, choose File > Automate > Photomerge, click **Open Composition,** locate the desired .pmg file, then click Open. You can't reopen a .pmg file using File > Open or Bridge.

TIP To remove all images from the work area and place them in the lightbox, hold down Alt/Option and click Reset. You can also use Undo to reverse individual changes made within the dialog box.

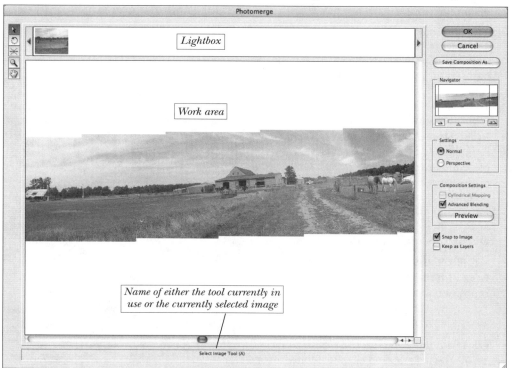

1 *The **Photomerge** dialog box has its own toolbox, lightbox, and work area, and an assortment of controls.*

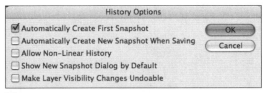

1 *In the* **History Options** *dialog box, choose whether or not to* **Allow Non-Linear History.**

Source for the
History Brush tool   *The current history* **state**

2 *This* **History** *palette is in* **linear** *mode. Note that all the steps below the current state are dimmed. The screen shot on the next page shows the palette in non-linear mode.*

USING THE HISTORY PALETTE, YOU CAN selectively undo up to 1,000 previous stages (called "states") of a work session. In this chapter, you'll learn how to restore, delete, and clear previous states; preserve states by using snapshots; create a new document from a state or snapshot; and restore areas of an image to a prior state by using the History Brush and Art History Brush tools, and by filling a selection with a history state.

Using the History palette

The **History palette** displays a list of the most recent states (edits) that were made to an image, with the bottommost state being the most recent. Clicking a prior state restores the image to that stage of the editing process. What happens to the image when you do this depends on whether the palette is in linear or nonlinear mode, so you need to learn the difference between these two modes.

To toggle between modes, choose History Options from the palette menu, then in the History Options dialog box, check or uncheck **Allow Non-Linear History 1**. You can switch between these two modes at any time during an editing session.

In **linear** mode (Allow Non-Linear History unchecked), if you click back on an earlier state and resume image editing from that state or delete it, all subsequent (dimmed) states will be discarded **2**.

In **nonlinear** mode, if you click back on or delete an earlier state, subsequent states won't be deleted (or dimmed). If you then resume image editing with that earlier state selected, each new edit will show up as the latest state on the palette, and all the states in between will be preserved. The latest state will incorporate the earlier stage of the

(Continued on the following page)

History Palette Modes

image plus your newest edit. If you change your mind, you can click any in-between state whenever you like and resume editing from there. Nonlinear is the more flexible of the two modes **1**.

When would you want to work in nonlinear mode? When you need flexibility. Let's say you apply paint strokes to a layer, try out different blending modes for that layer, and then settle on a blending mode that you like. If you want to reduce the number of states on the palette, you can then delete any of the other blending mode states, whether they're before or after the one you've settled on. You can pick and choose.

When would you want to work in linear mode? If you find nonlinear mode confusing or disorienting, or if you want the option to revert back to an earlier state with a nice, clean break.

The Allow Non-Linear History option also affects what happens when you click a snapshot. (Snapshots are like freeze frames of current states; see pages 159–161.)

To specify the number of states that can be listed on the palette for an editing session, go to Preferences (Ctrl-K/Cmd-K) > General, then enter a **History States** value (1–1000). If the maximum number of history states is exceeded during an editing session, earlier steps will be removed automatically to make room for the new ones. *Note:* The maximum number of states may be limited by various factors, including the image size, the kind of edits that are made to the image, and currently available memory. Each open image keeps its own list of states.

NEW If **Make Layer Visibility Changes Undoable** in the History Options dialog box is checked, the hiding and showing of layers (via the eye icon) on the Layers palette are listed as states on the History palette.

1 *This* **History** *palette is in* **nonlinear** *mode. All of the states are available, even those below the current state.*

History palette contents:
- LADY.tif
- 5:51:58 PM
- 5:52:16 PM
- Open
- Crosshatch
- New Layer
- Levels 1 Layer
- Brush Tool
- New Layer
- Blur Tool
- Canvas Size
- Master Opacity Change

(sidebar) **History States**

1 *After clicking a prior state with the **History** palette in **linear** mode*

2 *After clicking a prior state with the **History** palette in **nonlinear** mode*

Changing states

If the History palette is in **linear** mode (the Allow Non-Linear History option is off) and you click an earlier state, all the states below the one you click on will become dimmed. If you then delete the state you clicked on or continue editing the image with that earlier state selected, all the dimmed states will be deleted. (If you change your mind, you can choose Undo immediately to restore the deleted states.)

In **nonlinear** mode, if you click an earlier state and then perform an edit, the new edit will become the latest state, but the prior states won't be deleted.

To change history states:

Click a **state** on the History palette **1**–**2**.
or
On the left side of the palette, drag the **slider** upward or downward to the desired state.
or
To **Step Forward** one state, press Ctrl-Shift-Z/Cmd-Shift-Z, or to **Step Backward** one state, press Ctrl-Alt-Z/Cmd-Option-Z.

TIP You can Alt-click/Option-click a state to create a duplicate, but it will be listed generically as "Duplicate History State," and thus will be hard to identify.

Change History States

Deleting and clearing states

If Allow Non-Linear History is checked and you **delete** a **state,** only that state will be deleted. If Allow Non-Linear History is unchecked and you delete a state, that state and all subsequent states will be deleted (you can choose Edit > Undo to restore them).

To delete a state:

Right-click/Control-click a state and choose **Delete** from the context menu **1**, then click Yes when the alert dialog box appears **2**.
or
Drag the state that you want to delete over the **Delete Current State** button 🗑 on the History palette.
or
To delete consecutive states from the current state backward, click a state, then Alt-click/Option-click the **Delete Current State** button (and keep clicking). Note that the Undo command can restore only the last deleted state.

TIP When File > Revert is chosen, it becomes a state on the History palette, and as with any state, all the states preceding it are retained. You can restore an image to a state prior to the Revert command being applied, or restore a state selectively with the History Brush tool (see pages 162–163).

To clear the History palette:

To clear all the states (not the snapshots) from the History palette for all currently open documents in order to free up memory, choose Edit > Purge > **Histories,** then click OK. This command can't be undone.

To clear all states from the History palette for just the current document, Right-click/Control-click and choose **Clear History.** This command can be undone.

1 *Right-click/Control-click a state, choose* **Delete** *from the context menu, then click Yes when the alert dialog box appears.*

2 *The Allow Non-Linear History option was* **checked** *when we deleted the "Sharpen Tool" state, so subsequent states weren't deleted.*

Using snapshots

A **snapshot** is like a copy of a history state, with one major difference: unlike a state, a snapshot remains on the palette, even if the state from which it was created is deleted due to the maximum number of history states being reached or the palette being cleared or purged. All snapshots are deleted when a document is closed.

To choose snapshot options:

1. Choose **History Options** from the History palette menu. The History Options dialog box opens **1**.

2. Do any of the following:

   To have a snapshot be created automatically each time a file is opened, check **Automatically Create First Snapshot.** (This option is checked by default.)

   To have a snapshot be created every time a file is saved, check **Automatically Create New Snapshot When Saving.** The time of day that the snapshot was created will be listed next to the thumbnail.

   To have the New Snapshot dialog box appear whenever you click the New Snapshot button, check **Show New Snapshot Dialog by Default.**

3. Click OK. To learn how to create snapshots, follow the instructions on the next page.

Choose Snapshot Options

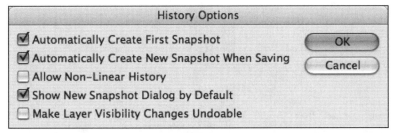

1 *There are three snapshot options to choose from in the* ***History Options*** *dialog box.*

If the Automatically Create New Snapshot When Saving option is off, get in the habit of **creating snapshots** periodically as you work, and before running any actions on your document. If you use the New Snapshot dialog box (the second method below), you'll be able to choose whether the snapshot is made from the full document, from merged layers, or from just the current layer.

To create a snapshot of a state without choosing options:

1. On the History palette, click the state that you want to create a snapshot of.

2. If the Show New Snapshot Dialog by Default option is off in the History Options dialog box, click the **New Snapshot** button. If the dialog option is on, Alt-click/Option-click the New Snapshot button. A new snapshot thumbnail will appear after the last snapshot at the top of the palette.

To choose options as you create a snapshot:

1. To create a snapshot of a layer, click that layer on the Layers palette.

2. Right-click/Control-click a state and choose **New Snapshot** ■.

3. In the New Snapshot dialog box, type a **Name** for the snapshot ■.

4. Choose From: **Full Document** to create a snapshot that preserves all the layers on the Layers palette at that state; or **Merged Layers** to create a snapshot that merges all layers on the Layers palette at that state; or **Current Layer** to make a snapshot of only the currently active layer at that state.

5. Click OK ■.

TIP If the Show New Snapshot Dialog by Default option is on in the History Options dialog box, you can open the New Snapshot dialog box by clicking a state, then clicking the New Snapshot button at the bottom of the palette. Or if the dialog option is off, Alt-click/Option-click the New Snapshot button.

1 *Right-click/Control-click a state and choose **New Snapshot** from the context menu.*

2 *In the **New Snapshot** dialog box, enter a name and choose which part of the image you want the snapshot to be created from.*

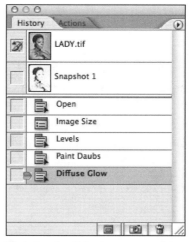

3 *A thumbnail for the new snapshot appears on the History palette.*

Create Snapshot

1 *Right-click/Control-click a snapshot or state and choose* **New Document.**

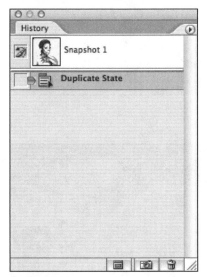

2 *This is the History palette for the new document.*

To make a snapshot become the current state:

Click a **snapshot thumbnail.** If the Allow Non-Linear History option is off and edits were made to the document after that snapshot was taken, the document will revert to the snapshot stage of editing and all the states will be dimmed. If you then resume editing, all dimmed states will be deleted. If Allow Non-Linear History is on, subsequent states will remain on the palette.

or

Regardless of the Allow Non-Linear History option setting, you can Alt-click/Option-click a snapshot thumbnail to have the other states remain available and that snapshot become the latest state. This is a very useful option.

To delete a snapshot:

Click the snapshot, right-click/Control-click and choose **Delete** (or click the Delete Current State button 🗑), then click Yes.

or

To bypass the prompt, drag the snapshot to the **Delete Current State** button. 🗑

Creating new documents

Using the **New Document** command, you can spin off variations of your current document based on a state or snapshot.

To create a new document from a history state or snapshot:

Right-click/Control-click a snapshot or a state, then choose **New Document** from the context menu **1**.

or

Drag a snapshot or a state over the **New Document from Current State** button, 📄 (or click a snapshot or a state, then click the button).

A new document window will appear onscreen, bearing the title of the snapshot or state from which it was created, and "Duplicate State" will be the name of the starting state for the new document **2**. Save this new document!

1 *Choose settings from the **History Brush** tool options bar.*

Restoring areas selectively

You can use any snapshot or state on the History palette as a source of earlier pixel data for the **History Brush** tool. Dragging with the brush restores pixels from that prior state of editing.

Note: The History Brush tool can't be used on an image if you've changed its pixel count since it was opened (e.g., by cropping or by changing the document color mode or canvas size). Furthermore, the tool can't restore deleted or modified layer effects, vector data layers (type or shapes), imagery from a deleted layer, or the effects of an adjustment layer. So keep your layers!

To use the History Brush tool:

1. Choose the **History Brush** tool (Y or Shift-Y).

2. On the options bar **1**:

   Click the Brush Preset picker arrowhead, then click a **brush** on the picker.

   Choose a blending **Mode, Opacity** percentage, and **Flow** percentage. Click the **Airbrush** button to soften the stroke.

3. On the History palette, click in the leftmost column for the state or snapshot that you want to use as a source for the History Brush tool (the history source icon will appear there).

4. On the Layers palette, click the layer that you want to restore pixels on, and turn off Lock Transparent Pixels.

5. Draw strokes on the image. Pixel data from the prior state of that layer will replace the current pixel data where you draw strokes **2**–**3**.

TIP Here's an example of how the History Brush tool could be used to restore an earlier stage of an image. Let's say you add brush strokes to a layer and then

> ## Snapshot as History Brush source
>
> Modify a layer (e.g., apply an adjustment command, sharpen filter, or brush strokes), take a snapshot of the current state, then delete that state. Set the **History Source** icon to the snapshot, then with the History Brush tool, add strokes in areas of the modified layer that you want to restore.

2 *The original image*

3 *After applying the Graphic Pen filter, positioning the **History Source** icon at a prior state, and then painting on parts of the image using the **History Brush** tool at 95% opacity*

1 *The original image*

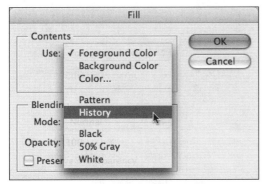

2 *Choose Use: History in the Fill dialog box.*

3 *We applied the Glass filter to a layer, selected the area around the tree, and then filled the selection with an earlier history state via Edit > Fill > Use: **History**. You could try using the Distort > Wave or Ripple filter or an Artistic or Sketch filter instead of the Glass filter.*

decide several editing steps later that you want to remove them. Clicking the state prior to the brush strokes state could cause other edits to be deleted. Instead, click in the box next to any state prior to the state in which the strokes were added to set the source for the History Brush tool, click the layer on the Layers palette to which the brush strokes were added, choose the History Brush tool, then paint out the added strokes.

TIP When restoring from a snapshot, you can choose which layer you want to restore pixels onto if the snapshot you're using as a source was created with the Full Document or Merged Layers option chosen in the New Snapshot dialog box. If the Current Layer option was chosen instead, you can paint only on the layer that was preserved in the snapshot.

The **Fill** command, when used with the History option, fills a layer or selection with pixels from a history state or snapshot. The *Note* on the previous page also applies to this command.

To fill a selection or a layer with a history state or snapshot:

1. Click a layer that contains pixels **1**.
2. *Optional:* Create a selection.
3. On the History palette, click in the left-most column for the state or snapshot you want to use as a fill (the History Source icon will appear where you click).
4. Choose Edit > **Fill** (Shift-Backspace/ Shift-Delete or Shift-F5).
5. Choose Use: **History** **2**.
6. Choose a **Blending Mode** and an **Opacity** percentage.
7. *Optional:* Check Preserve Transparency to replace only existing pixels, or leave this option unchecked to allow pixels to appear anywhere on the layer. This option will be available only if the current layer contains transparent pixels.
8. Click OK **3**.

1 *The **Art History Brush** tool options bar*

Using the **Art History Brush** tool, you can paint a designated history state or snapshot back onto an image in an assortment of different-shaped strokes (actually, in our humble opinion, all the brush choices— Tight Long, Loose Curl, etc.—look like worms). Adjacent colors are blended to produce a painterly effect, and those colors will vary depending on the current Tolerance setting for the Art History Brush tool. If you have a stylus, go ahead and use it.

To use the Art History Brush tool:

1. Perform some edits on a layer, if you haven't already done so, to create states on the History palette.

   TIP If you're working on the Background, before using the Art History Brush tool, fill the layer with white or a solid color to create a clean background for your Art History strokes.

2. On the History palette, click in the leftmost column for the state or snapshot that you want to use as the source for the tool. The **history source** icon ![icon] appears.

3. Choose the **Art History Brush** tool (Y or Shift-Y). ![icon]

4. On the options bar **1**, do the following:

   Click the **Brush Preset** picker arrowhead, then click a small brush in the picker.

   Choose a **Mode** and an **Opacity.**

   Choose a painting style from the **Style** pop-up menu.

   Choose an **Area** (0–500 pixels) for the size of the area the strokes can cover.

   Choose a **Tolerance** value (0–100%). Choose a low Tolerance to allow strokes to appear over most areas of the image; or a high Tolerance to limit strokes to

2 *To this photo, we applied the Artistic > Cutout filter, clicked the leftmost column on the History palette at a prior state, then added brush strokes in the center with the **Art History Brush** tool.*

only areas that differ sharply from colors in the source state.

5. Choose a layer, then draw strokes in the document window **2**. The longer you keep the mouse button down in the same spot, the more the colors in that area will be remixed.

TIP For a more handmade look, try switching stroke shapes and other parameters on the Art History Brush tool options bar between strokes, or choose different source states on the History palette. Or for your brush preset, create variations via the Shape Dynamics, Scattering, Texture, Color Dynamics, or Other Dynamics panels on the Brushes palette.

TONAL ADJUSTMENTS 11

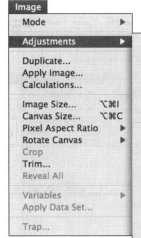

1 *With each Photoshop upgrade, the list of commands on the Image > Adjustments submenu grows longer!*

YOU'RE HAPPY WITH THE composition of a photo, but the exposure is off or it looks a bit dull? Enter the digital darkroom. Photoshop offers so many commands for adjusting images **1**, we couldn't fit them all into one chapter.

First, we'll show you how to use adjustment layers—a highly flexible method for applying adjustment commands. Next, you'll learn how to use a few of the simpler one- and two-step adjustment commands: Auto Contrast, Invert, Threshold, and Posterize. And finally, we'll show you how to use the Histogram palette to gauge the effectiveness of your work as you use the more powerful Levels and Channel Mixer commands, edit an adjustment layer mask, and use a neutral color layer to burn (darken) and dodge (lighten) areas of an image.

Applying adjustment commands

First, a few general pointers:

➤ Although adjustment commands can be applied directly to any layer via the Image > Adjustments submenu, for flexibility in editing, we prefer to apply them via **adjustment layers.** We're so keen on this method, it's the only method we list in the instructions in this chapter!

➤ To restrict the effect of an adjustment command to a specific area, create a **selection** before choosing the command.

➤ To **reset** the settings in a dialog box, hold down Alt/Option and click Reset.

➤ To see how an adjustment will affect your document, check **Preview** in the adjustment dialog box; uncheck Preview to view the unadjusted document.

➤ To reduce the impact of an adjustment command immediately after applying it, choose Edit > **Fade** (Ctrl-Shift-F/Cmd-Shift-F), move the Opacity slider, then click OK.

Applying Adjustment Commands

Using adjustment layers

The commands in an **adjustment layer** affect all the layers below it, but the changes don't become permanent until you decide to merge it with the underlying layer. We like to use adjustment layers because they're editable, meaning you can use them to test out various adjustment commands and settings without commitment, and because they can be applied, hidden, or deleted at any time.

To create an adjustment layer:

1. Click the layer above which you want the adjustment layer to appear (but don't worry, you can restack the adjustment layer later).

2. From the **New Fill/Adjustment Layer** pop-up menu ⊘. at the bottom of the Layers palette, choose an adjustment command **1**.
or
Choose a command from the Layer > **New Adjustment Layer** submenu, then click OK.

3. The dialog box for the chosen command opens. Make the desired adjustments, then click OK **2**. The adjustment layer appears on the Layers palette, with an editable mask.

To change settings for an adjustment layer:

1. On the Layers palette, double-click the adjustment layer thumbnail (the thumbnail on the left).

2. Make the desired changes in the adjustment dialog box, then click OK.

TIP You can change how an adjustment layer affects your document by restacking it above a different layer.

TIP While any adjustment dialog box is open, you can Ctrl-Spacebar-click/ Cmd-Spacebar-click to zoom in or Alt–Spacebar-click/Option-Spacebar-click to zoom out; or hold down Spacebar to move a magnified image in the window.

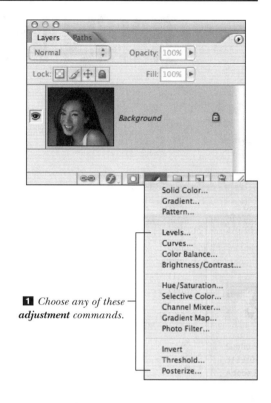

1 *Choose any of these* **adjustment** *commands.*

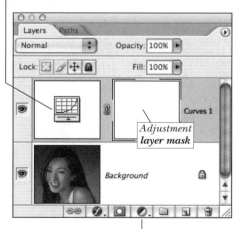

2 *Each command has a unique icon in the* **adjustment layer** *thumbnail.*

New Fill/Adjustment Layer pop-up menu

Create, Edit Adjustment Layer

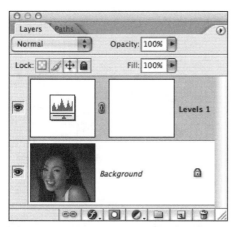

1 *Click an adjustment layer.*

2 *The **Merge Down** command applied the Levels values from the adjustment layer to the layer below it (in this case, to the Background).*

You can keep an adjustment layer right where it is but **change** which adjustment **command** it contains (e.g., change Levels to Curves or change Hue/Saturation to Color Balance).

To choose a different command for an adjustment layer:

1. Click an adjustment layer on the Layers palette.

2. From the Layer > **Change Layer Content** submenu, choose the command you want to switch it to.

3. Make the desired adjustments, then click OK.

TIP To discard an adjustment layer, drag it to the Delete Layer button. 🗑

When you **merge down** an adjustment layer, the adjustments become permanent for the image layer below it. If you change your mind, you can either choose Edit > Undo (right away) or click the prior state on the History palette.

To merge an adjustment layer:

Click the adjustment layer you want to merge downward **1**, then press Ctrl-E/Cmd-E **2**.
or
Right-click/Control-click the adjustment layer and choose **Merge Down.**

TIP Adjustment layers don't contain pixels, so you can't merge them with one another. However, you can merge multiple adjustment layers into an image layer (or layers) by using either the Merge Visible or the Flatten Image command (see pages 116–118).

Change Layer Content; Merge Adjustment Layer

Ways to use adjustment layers

Changing an adjustment layer's blending mode can dramatically change how it affects underlying layers. Click an adjustment layer, then choose a different **blending mode** from the pop-up menu on the Layers palette. Try Saturation mode to heighten saturation, Luminosity mode to lessen saturation, Darken mode to darken the image, or Lighten mode to lighten it.

Try stacking several adjustment layers, then **hide** ▊ or lower the **opacity** of each one to see how it affects the underlying image.

To compare different settings for the same adjustment command, create **multiples** of the same adjustment layer (e.g., Levels), hide all the adjustment layers, and then **show/hide** them one by one.

To limit the area an adjustment layer affects, create a **selection** before you create it. The selection area will be shown in white on the layer mask thumbnail ▊–▊.

Paint or **fill** with black on an adjustment layer to hide the adjustment effect, or with white to reveal the adjustment effect. The strokes will display on the layer mask thumbnail. See page 178.

To **prevent** an underlying layer from being affected by an adjustment layer, restack it so it's above the adjustment layer.

You can also use a **clipping mask** to limit an adjustment layer's effect to a single layer instead of all the visible layers below it (see pages 305–306). If you create your adjustment layer via the Layer > New Adjustment Layer submenu, you can create a clipping mask at the outset by checking Use Previous Layer to Create Clipping Mask in the New Layer dialog box.

And finally, let's say you have a series of photos that were taken under the same lighting conditions, and you've created an adjustment layer to enhance the color in one of them. You can **drag** the **adjustment layer** onto each of the other document windows to quickly apply the same adjustment.

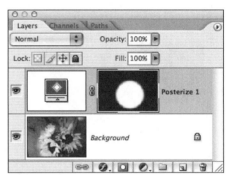

▊ *You can* ***show*** *and* ***hide*** *adjustment layers to compare their effects.*

▊ *We created a round, feathered* ***selection*** *before creating our adjustment layer; the selection shows up as a* ***mask*** *on the adjustment layer.*

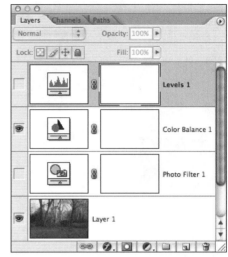

▊ *The* ***Posterize*** *adjustment layer affects only the area within the mask.*

1 *The original image*

2 *After applying **Auto Contrast***

3 *The original image*

4 *The image **inverted***

One- and two-step commands

Next we'll show you how to use a few of the one- or two-step adjustment commands: **Auto Contrast, Invert, Threshold,** and **Posterize.** The latter three commands produce marked stylized changes and, like most of the adjustment commands, can be applied either directly to a layer or indirectly via an adjustment layer. Try applying them to a grayscale image first to learn how they work, then try them out on some color images.

As you explore these commands, view what's happening on the Histogram palette (see pages 172–173). This palette displays before and after diagrams of the light and dark values of an image as it's edited. Some dialog boxes, such as Levels and Threshold, also have a histogram built into them.

The one-step **Auto Contrast** command turns the almost-lightest pixels in an image white and the almost-darkest pixels black, then redistributes the gray levels in between.

To apply the Auto Contrast command:

1. Click a layer or the Background **1**.

2. Choose Image > Adjustments > **Auto Contrast** (Ctrl-Alt-Shift-L/Cmd-Option-Shift-L) **2**.

The **Invert** command makes a layer (or the Background) look like a film negative. Each pixel color is replaced with its opposite in brightness and/or color.

To apply the Invert command:

1. Click a layer or the Background **3**.

2. Choose **Invert 4** from the New Fill/ Adjustment Layer pop-up menu *⬤*. at the bottom of the Layers palette.

Auto Contrast, Invert Commands

The **Threshold** dialog box makes the current layer or the Background high-contrast by converting color or gray pixels into black or white pixels.

To apply the Threshold command:

1. Click a layer or the Background .

2. Choose **Threshold** from the New Fill/Adjustment Layer pop-up menu at the bottom of the Layers palette. The Threshold dialog box opens.

3. Move the slider below the histogram to the right to increase the number of **black** pixels, or to the left to increase the number of **white** pixels.
   or
   Enter a **Threshold Level** value (1–255). Pixels lighter than the value you enter will become white; pixels darker than that value will become black.

4. Click OK.

TIP To have the Threshold command convert midtones into linework, before using it apply Filter > Other > High Pass with a Radius setting of around 5.

1 *The original image*

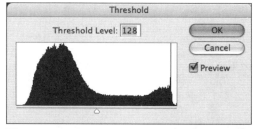

2 *Use the slider in the **Threshold** dialog box to control the cutoff point for black and white values.*

3 *After applying the **Threshold** command*

4 *We applied the **High Pass** filter to this image before applying the **Threshold** command.*

Threshold Command

©www.photospin.com

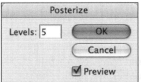

1 *The original image*

2 *A Levels value is entered in the Posterize dialog box.*

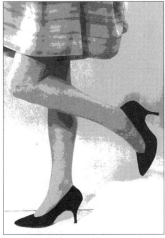

3 *After applying the Posterize command (5 Levels)*

Use the **Posterize** command to reduce the number of color or value levels in an image to a specified number. When applied with a low number of Levels, this command creates the look of a silkscreen. It's also useful for reducing the number of colors in an image before optimizing it in the GIF format (for online output).

To apply the Posterize command:

1. Click a layer or the Background **1**.

2. Choose **Posterize** from the New Fill/ Adjustment Layer pop-up menu 🖊 at the bottom of the Layers palette. The Posterize dialog box opens.

3. Make sure Preview is checked, then enter the desired number of **Levels** (2–255) **2**. To make the layer look like a poster or silkscreen, try a Levels value between 4 and 6.

4. Click OK **3**–**5**.

TIP If you reduce the number of tonal values in a document, whether by the Posterize command or any other command (without using an adjustment layer), then save and close your file, the original tonal information will be discarded permanently.

4 *The original image*

5 *Post-Posterize (6 Levels)*

Posterize Command

Using the Histogram palette

The **Histogram** palette displays a graph of the current light and dark tonal values in an image. The palette and its options are accessible while adjustment and adjustment layer dialog boxes are open, and the graph updates continuously as you edit your document to help you judge the effectiveness or impact of your adjustments and edits.

But before you even start editing your scanned image or digital photo, you can study the histogram to evaluate the distribution of tonal values. The horizontal axis on the palette represents the gray or color levels between 0 and 255; the number of pixels at each level are stacked in bars on the vertical axis. The overall graph shape represents the current tonal range of the image.

The histogram for an image that has been adjusted aggressively and thus has lost tonal details in the shadow, midtone, or highlight areas will have gaps between the vertical lines and noticeable spikes (like teeth on a comb). That doesn't mean the image is a failure, though. Many intentional edits with desirable results, such as applying filters or adding a black or white border, can produce a lousy-looking histogram.

Via the Histogram palette menu, you can choose a view for the palette: **Compact View** (just the histogram) **1**; **Expanded View** (the histogram plus information about the combined channels or individual channels) **2**; or **All Channels View** (all of the above plus a histogram for each channel).

While a large file is being edited, Photoshop maintains the redraw speed of the Histogram palette by reading from the cache data for the histogram—not from the actual data. As this is occurring, the **Cached Data Warning** icon ⚠ appears on the palette. Be sure to keep **updating** the **palette**—even while adjustment dialog boxes are open—so it continues to reflect the current tonal values in the image. You can specify a **Cache Levels** value (1–8) in Preferences > Memory & Image Cache; relaunch Photoshop to activate the new setting.

To update the Histogram palette:

Double-click anywhere on the histogram.
or
Click the **Cached Data Warning** icon. ⚠
or
Click the **Uncached Refresh** button. ⟳

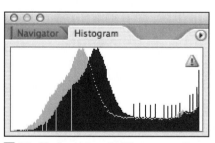

1 *The black areas on the **Histogram** palette represent the tonal and color changes being made to image pixels. The gray areas, which display if you apply an adjustment command to a layer directly (not via an adjustment layer), represent the distribution of pixels prior to adjustment. This figure shows the palette in **Compact View**.*

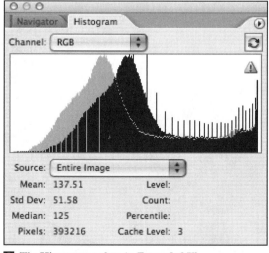

2 *The **Histogram** palette in **Expanded View***

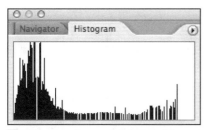

1 *Histogram for an **underexposed** image*

2 *Histogram for an **overexposed** image*

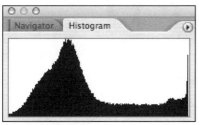

3 *Histogram for an image that has a **good tonal range***

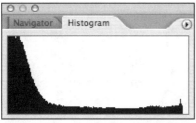

4 *Histogram with **shadow pixels clipped***

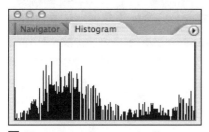

5 *Histogram with **gaps** and **spikes***

Interpreting the histogram

A histogram is a graph of the distribution, or tonal range, of pixels in an image. Shadow pixels are shown on the left, mid-tone pixels in the middle, and highlight pixels on the right. An image with a wide tonal range will have a fairly balanced distribution of pixels in the shadow, midtone, and highlight areas. When an image lacks pixels in any of those areas, the result is a loss of image detail. Learning how to read a histogram as you apply adjustment commands can help you judge their impact.

Images fall loosely into three categories, based on their overall tonal range. For a dark (low-key) image, such as a night scene, pixels will be clustered primarily on the left side of the histogram; for an image with more balanced light and dark areas (average-key), you'll see a more even distribution of pixels across the histogram; and for a light image with little or no shadow areas (high-key)— think polar bear romping in the snow— pixels will be clustered primarily on the right side of the histogram.

If an image is average-key but under-exposed, pixels will be clustered primarily on the left side of the histogram, indicating that the image lacks detail in the highlights **1**. If an image is overexposed, pixels will be clustered mostly on the right side of the histogram, indicating that the image lacks detail in the shadows **2**. An image with a good tonal range will have a mostly solid histogram and a relatively smooth (not spiky) contour **3**.

If an area of pixels rises sharply upward off the left or right edge of the histogram **4**, it means pixels were clipped (details were discarded) from either the extreme shadow areas or the extreme highlight areas.

Small gaps or spikes in a histogram **5** indicate a loss of detail in tonal or color transitions, or possibly posterization. And finally, a comb formation in a histogram indicates that the image is either of poor quality to begin with or has been extensively edited.

Interpret the Histogram

Using the Levels command

The "strong, yet sensitive" **Levels** command lets you make separate adjustments to a layer's highlights, midtones, and shadows, and enhance or diminish contrast—all the while preserving a wide range of tonalities.

Levels is a good command to start with when you first bring a photograph into Photoshop, and may prove to be useful during the editing process as well. In the preproduction stage of your project, you may reach for Levels yet again, to, say, make the shadow and highlight levels conform to the gamut of your chosen output device (online or print).

1 *The original image is dull (lacks contrast).*

To apply the Levels command:

1. Click a layer **1**, then choose **Levels** from the New Fill/Adjustment Layer pop-up menu *○,* at the bottom of the Layers palette. The Levels dialog box opens.

2. Do any of the following **2**:

   To brighten the highlights and enhance the contrast, move the white **Input** highlights slider to the left. To darken the shadows, move the black Input shadows slider to the right. All pixels to the left of the black slider will become the darkest tonal value; all pixels to the right of the white slider will become the lightest tonal value.

   Another way to figure out where to position the highlights and shadows sliders in Grayscale and RGB images is to hold down Alt/Option, then drag the highlights or shadows slider. This activates **Threshold** mode—a high-contrast view of the image. As you drag the highlights slider, release the mouse when just a few areas of white appear **3**; these pixels will become the lightest tonal value. As you drag the shadows slider, release the mouse when just a few areas of black display (**1**, next page); these pixels will become the lowest pixel value.

3. With the shadows and highlights sliders in place, now move the gray **Input** midtones slider to lighten or darken the

2 *In the **Levels** dialog box, we moved the **Shadows** and **Highlights Input** sliders inward, to the ends of the histogram.*

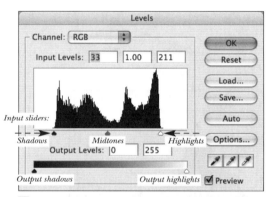

3 *A view of **Threshold** mode while Alt/Option dragging the white highlights slider*

1 *A view of Threshold mode while Alt/Option dragging the black shadows slider*

PHOTO: PAUL PETROFF

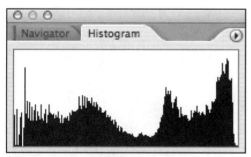

2 *After **Levels** adjustments*

3 *The histogram for the image **after** Levels adjustments. The tonal range was expanded to the edges, producing stronger shadows and highlights, and better contrast.*

midtones separately from the shadows or highlights.

4. If the image is going to be printed, Photoshop will bring the shadows and highlights into the printable range automatically when you convert the file to CMYK mode or when the file is converted to the printer profile for your output device.

If you're outputting to a grayscale printer, however, you can bring shadow and highlight extremes into the printable gamut by doing the following:

Force the darkest shadow areas above 0 (100% black) by moving the black **Output** shadows slider to the right, to a value between 8 and 12 (95% black).

Force the lightest highlights below 255 (0% black) by moving the white Output highlights slider to the left, to a value between 244 and 249 (5% black). Remember: 0% black equals white.

5. *Optional:* To save the current settings, click **Save.** To apply the saved settings to other images (e.g., images taken under similar lighting conditions that require the same adjustments), click **Load.**

6. Click OK **2**–**3**.

TIP To learn about the Options button, see page 204.

TIP The Shadow/Highlights command gives you more options and controls for adjusting lights and darks in an image than Levels. See pages 237–239.

Levels Command

Face-off

Although the **Brightness/Contrast** command is easy to use, it discards a lot of pixel data from an image's entire tonal range. If you want to adjust shadows, midtones, and highlights individually with more precision and control, we recommend using our dear friend the **Levels** command (or even better, the **Shadow/Highlight** command). The Histogram palette screenshots on this page show why the Levels command is superior!

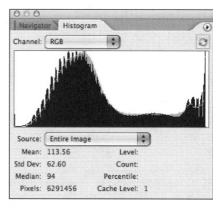

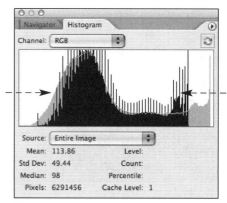

1 *The histogram for the unadjusted image*

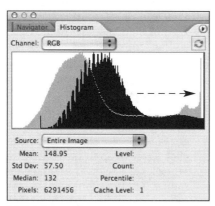

2 *Brightness/Contrast: Moving the Brightness slider to the right shifts all the tonal values to the right, resulting in a loss of highlight detail and a redistribution of all the tonal values.*

3 *Brightness/Contrast: Moving the Contrast slider to the left shifts all the tonal values toward the center, resulting in a loss of tonal values in the shadows and highlights.*

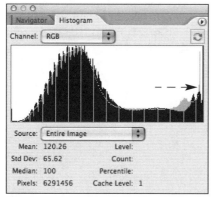

4 *Levels: Moving the Highlights slider shifts tonal values on the right side of the graph further to the right, while preserving shadow and midtone values.*

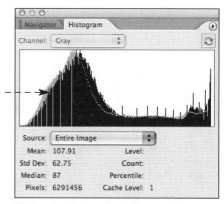

5 *Levels: Moving the Midtones slider to the right shifts only the midtone values while preserving shadow and highlight values.*

1 *The original image*

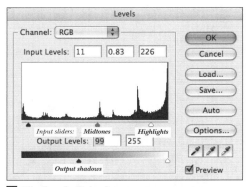

2 *The **Levels** dialog box*

3 *The **screened-back** version*

Screening back imagery is another great use for the **Levels** command.

To screen back a layer:

1. *Optional:* To limit the screened-back effect to a specific area of the image, create a selection.

2. Click a layer or the Background **1**, then choose **Levels** from the New Fill/ Adjustment Layer pop-up menu at the bottom of the Layers palette.

3. To reduce contrast, move the **Input** highlights slider slightly to the left **2** and move the **Output** shadows slider to the right.

4. To lighten the midtones, move the **Input** midtones slider to the left.

5. Click OK **3**–**4**.

4 *To produce this image, a rectangular **selection** was created before the **Levels** adjustment layer was made.*

Masking an adjustment layer

By default, all new adjustment layers have a **layer mask.** You can ignore the mask, or you can use it to control which area of an image the adjustment layer affects. In these instructions, you'll edit the mask either by creating and filling a selection or by applying brush strokes.

To mask an adjustment layer:

1. Click an adjustment layer, then choose black as the Foreground color. The Color palette will reset automatically to Grayscale.

2. To mask the adjustment layer effect:

Create a **selection** using any selection tool (e.g., Rectangular Marquee, Lasso, or Magic Wand), choose Edit > **Fill** (Shift-Backspace/Shift-Delete), choose Use: Foreground Color, then click OK. *or*
Choose the **Brush** tool (B or Shift-B), choose a brush, Mode: Normal, and Opacity 100% on the options bar, then paint on the image **1**. Or to create a partial mask, choose a lower opacity for the Brush tool.

3. *More options:*

To **restore** the adjustment layer effect (that is, remove the mask), paint or fill with white.

To **reveal** just a small area of the adjustment effect, fill the entire layer with black, then paint with white over some areas.

To make the adjustment effect visible again on the **entire** image, fill the whole adjustment layer with white.

TIP To diminish the effect of the adjustment layer across the entire layer by a percentage, lower the opacity of the adjustment layer via the Opacity slider on the Layers palette **2**.

TIP By default, adjustment layer masks are pixel-based. To create a vector mask for an adjustment layer, see page 387.

Layer mask shortcuts

For the following shortcuts, repeat the same command to toggle the feature off:

View the **mask** in the document window	Alt-click/Option-click adjustment layer mask thumbnail
View the mask in a **rubylith** color (red)	Alt-Shift-click/Option-Shift-click adjustment layer mask thumbnail
Deactivate/activate the mask for an adjustment layer	Shift-click adjustment layer mask thumbnail
Convert the **unmasked** area into a **selection**	Ctrl-click/Cmd-click adjustment layer mask thumbnail

1 *We painted with black on the left side of the* **Threshold** *adjustment layer mask. The Threshold effect is visible only in the areas we didn't paint on.*

2 *Here, the adjustment layer* **opacity** *was lowered to 60%, causing the Threshold effect to blend with the original underlying image.*

Mask Adjustment Layer

1 *The original image*

2 *A view of the **neutral gray layer,** showing dark and light strokes that were added (the other layers are hidden)*

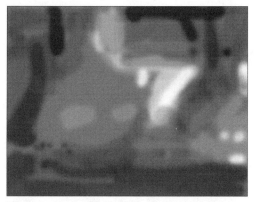

3 *After painting on the **neutral gray layer** to **burn** (darken) the foreground and **dodge** (lighten) the background. The glassware was also lightened/darkened.*

Dodging and burning

If you need to lighten or darken pixels by hand in small areas, the Dodge and Burn tools might seem like an obvious choice. However, these tools permanently alter layer pixels (something we strenuously try to avoid!). In these instructions, you'll **dodge** and **burn** areas of an image with the Brush tool on a special removable, editable neutral color layer.

To dodge and burn colors using a neutral color layer:

1. If the document isn't already in RGB Color mode, choose Image > Mode > RGB Color.

2. Click a layer **1**, then Alt-click/Option-click the **New Layer** button 🔲 on the Layers palette. In the New Layer dialog box, do the following:

   Type a **Name** for the layer.

   Choose **Mode: Overlay.**

   Check **Fill with Overlay-neutral color (50% gray).**

   Click OK.

3. Choose the **Brush** tool (B or Shift-B). ✐ Via the options bar, choose a brush preset (try a large, soft-edged brush) and an Opacity of 20%. Press **D** to reset the default black and white colors.

4. Paint with **black** to darken areas of the image; press **X** to paint with **white** to lighten areas of the image **2**–**3**.

   If you're not happy with the results in a specific area, choose 50% gray via the Color palette, then paint over the area to restore the neutral gray, thus removing the dodge or burn effect.

TIP If painting with white seems to lighten an area too much, via the options bar, either lower the brush opacity or choose Soft Light as the brush mode.

TIP To lessen the overall dodge/burn effect, on the Layers palette, click the neutral gray layer, then lower the Opacity or choose Soft Light as the blending mode.

Making a layer grayscale

If you convert a layer to grayscale by using the **Channel Mixer** command, you can control how much each color channel is used as a source for luminosity levels in the grayscale layer. And after using the command, you can selectively restore color to the layer by painting on the layer mask. (To make a layer grayscale without using a dialog box, see page 201.)

To make a layer grayscale using the Channel Mixer:

1. Click a layer or the Background, then press Ctrl-J/Cmd-J to copy it.

2. Choose **Channel Mixer** from the New Fill/Adjustment Layer pop-up menu ◍, at the bottom of the Layers palette. The Channel Mixer dialog box opens.

3. Check **Monochrome** **1**. The layer will become grayscale and Gray will now be the only choice on the Output Channel pop-up menu.

4. Move any of the **Source Channels** sliders to control how much that color channel is used as a source for the luminosity levels in the grayscale image. Drag a slider to the left to darken the channel, or to the right to lighten it. Try to have the combined three values total somewhere between 100 and 110, and try not to overlighten the highlights.

5. Move the **Constant** slider to the left to add black or to the right to add white.

6. Click OK **2**–**3**. Despite the grayscale appearance of the layer, the image is still in its original color mode.

7. *Optional:* To restore some of the original layer color, lower the opacity of the adjustment layer. Or to selectively restore color from the underlying layer, paint on the layer mask (see page 178).

TIP If you use an adjustment layer in the instructions above, then convert the whole image to Grayscale mode (Image > Mode > Grayscale), click Merge or Flatten in the alert box (don't click OK).

Try one of theirs

To use one of the **preset** Channel Mixer effects (e.g., RGB Rotate Channels or CMYK Swap Cyan & Magenta), first make sure the **Channel Mixer Presets** folder has been copied from the Goodies folder on the Adobe Photoshop CS2 installation CD into the Adobe Photoshop CS2/Presets folder.

To **load** an effect, click Load in the Channel Mixer dialog box, open the Presets > Channel Mixer Presets folder in the application folder, open one of the four folders there, click a mixer name, then click Load. In Windows, the abbreviated names represent Channel Swaps, Grayscale, Special Effects, and YCC Color.

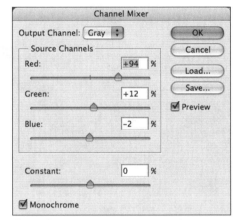

1 *Check* **Monochrome** *in the* **Channel Mixer** *dialog box to make the layer grayscale.*

2 *After using the* **Channel Mixer** *command to add more* **blue** *and lower the green and red*

3 *After using the* **Channel Mixer** *command to add more* **green** *and lower the blue and red*

Channel Mixer Command

CHOOSE COLORS 12

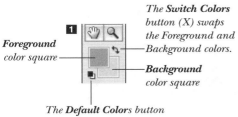

*The **Switch Colors** button (X) swaps the Foreground and Background colors.*

Foreground *color square*

Background *color square*

*The **Default Colors** button (D) makes the Foreground color **black** and the Background color **white**.*

*The currently active square has a black border. This is the **Foreground** color square.*

Background *color square*

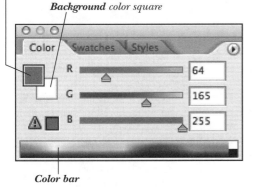

Color bar

2 *The **Color** palette is used for mixing colors.*

IN THIS CHAPTER, YOU'LL LEARN HOW to choose colors via the Color Picker, Color Libraries dialog box, Color palette, Swatches palette, and Eyedropper tool; save colors to the Swatches palette; copy a color as a hexadecimal value; and fill a selection or layer with a solid color. The last part of this chapter is a reference guide to the blending modes. You'll apply colors using tools and commands in other chapters.

Choosing colors

The current **Foreground** color is applied when you use a painting tool or the Stroke command, create type, enlarge the canvas area, etc. The current **Background** color is applied when you use the Eraser tool on the Background or on a layer with Lock Transparent Pixels on, when you apply a transform command to, or move a selection on, the Background with the Move tool, etc.

The Foreground and Background colors are displayed in the Foreground and Background color squares on the Toolbox **1** and on the Color palette **2**. (When written with an uppercase "F" or "B," these terms refer to those two colors, not to the foreground or background areas of a picture.)

The methods for choosing Foreground and Background colors are described on the following pages. In brief, you can:

➤ Enter values in the fields, or click the large color square, in the **Color Picker.**

➤ Choose a premixed color from a matching system by using the **Color Libraries** dialog box.

➤ Enter values in the fields, or move sliders, on the **Color** palette.

➤ Click a swatch on the **Swatches** palette.

➤ Pluck a color from an image by using the **Eyedropper** tool.

Foreground and Background Colors

181

To choose a color using the Color Picker:

1. Click the Foreground or Background color square on the Toolbox.
or
Click the Foreground or Background color square on the Color palette, if it's already active (has a black border).
or
Double-click the Foreground or Background color square on the Color palette, if it's not active.

Note: If the square you click contains a custom color from a matching system, the Color Libraries dialog box will open. Click Picker to get to the Color Picker dialog box.

2. *Optional:* In the Photoshop Color Picker, check Only Web Colors to make only Web-safe colors available.

3. Click a color on the vertical color slider to choose a **hue** 🔳, then click a variation of that hue in the large square 🔳.
or
To choose a specific process color for print output, enter percentages from a printed color matching system swatchbook in the **C, M, Y,** and **K** fields.
or
For onscreen output, enter **R, G,** and **B** values (0–255). If you enter 0 in all three fields, you'll get black; if you enter 255 in all three fields, you'll get white. You could also enter numbers in the **H, S,** and **B** or **L, a,** and **b** fields.

4. Click OK. The color will appear in the Foreground or Background color square on the Toolbox and the Color palette. To save the color to the Swatches palette for future use, see page 185.

TIP To access your system's color picker, in Preferences > General, choose Color Picker: Windows/Apple. Set this menu back to Adobe (the default) to access the Photoshop Color Picker. Only one color picker can be accessed at a time.

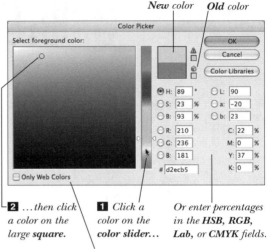

New color   *Old color*

🔳 *...then click a color on the large* **square.**

🔳 *Click a color on the* **color slider...**

Or enter percentages in the **HSB, RGB, Lab,** *or* **CMYK** *fields.*

Check **Only Web Colors** *to make only Web-safe colors available.*

⚠ or 🧊

An **out-of-gamut** icon ⚠ in the Color Picker 🔳 or Color palette signifies that the chosen color can't be printed using inks, and so is outside the printable gamut. If your image is going to be printed, you should change the color to an in-gamut color or click the exclamation point to have Photoshop substitute the closest printable color (shown in the swatch next to or below the exclamation point). Another option is to convert your image to CMYK Color mode, which brings the entire image into the printable gamut. The out-of-gamut range is defined by the CMYK output profile currently chosen in Edit > Color Settings.

The **non-Web-safe** icon 🧊 in the Color Picker signifies that the chosen color isn't Web-safe. Click the swatch below the cube to have Photoshop substitute the closest Web-safe color to yours.

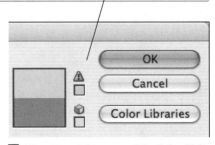

🔳 *The upper right corner of the* **Color Picker**

Color Picker

Choosing a library for print output

ANPA colors are used for newspaper printing.

DIC Color Guide and **TOYO Color Finder** colors are used in Japan.

FOCOLTONE is a process color system developed (in the U.K.) to help prevent registration problems.

HKS process colors and HKS spot colors (no "Process" in the name) are used in Europe.

PANTONE process colors and PANTONE spot colors (no "Process" in the name) are used widely in the U.S.

TRUMATCH is a process color system; colors are organized in a different way from PANTONE colors.

Spot or process?

By default, when **color-separating** an image for printing, Photoshop separates all colors—process and spot colors!—into the four process colors (C, M, Y, and K). If you want to output a spot color to a separate plate from Photoshop, you have to create a **spot color channel** for it (see page 478).

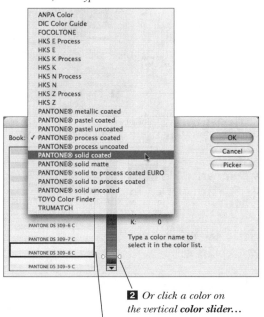

1 *Choose a matching system from the **Book** pop-up menu, then type a **number**.*

2 *Or click a color on the vertical **color slider...***

*...then click a **swatch**.*

The color percentages in custom colors are specified by third-party manufacturers, and are chosen in the **Color Libraries** dialog box.

Note: For print output, because your monitor can't display matching system colors reliably, before choosing custom colors in Photoshop, find out which brand of ink your commercial printer is planning to use, then decide which specific colors you're going to choose in Photoshop by flipping through a printed (yes, printed) PANTONE, TRUMATCH, TOYO, DIC, FOCOLTONE, HKS, or ANPA Color swatch book. For Web publishing, there's no need to refer to a printed book.

To choose a color from a color library:

1. Click the Foreground or Background color square on the Toolbox.
or
Click the Foreground or Background color square on the Color palette, if it's already active (has a black border).
or
Double-click the Foreground or Background color square on the Color palette, if it's not active.

Note: If the color square you click on isn't a custom color, the Color Picker dialog box will open. From there, click Color Libraries to open the Color Libraries dialog box.

2. From the **Book** pop-up menu, choose a matching system **1**.

3. Without clicking anywhere, type the number assigned to the desired color (for print output, refer to your swatch book); the swatch will become selected.
or
Click a color on the vertical color slider, then click a swatch on the left side of the dialog box **2**.

4. Click OK (or click Picker to return to the Color Picker, then click OK).

TIP To load a matching system library onto the Swatches palette, see page 186.

To choose a color using the Color palette:

1. Click the Foreground or Background color square, if the desired square isn't already active **1**.

2. From the Color palette menu, choose a color model for the sliders **2**. For print output, choose **Grayscale Slider** or **CMYK Sliders;** for onscreen output, choose **RGB Sliders, HSB Sliders,** or **Web Color Sliders** (for web-safe colors).

3. Move any of the sliders.
   or
   Click on or drag across the color bar.
   or
   Enter values in the fields.

TIP To choose a different spectrum style for the color bar or to quickly access the Make Ramp Web Safe command, right-click/Control-click the color bar.

TIP Alt-click/Option-click the color bar to choose a color for whichever color square isn't currently selected.

TIP If Dynamic Color Sliders is checked in Preferences (Ctrl-K/Cmd-K) > General, colors in the slider bars will update interactively as you drag the sliders.

TIP When using the RGB model, white (the presence of all colors) is produced when all the sliders are at the far right, black (the absence of all colors) is produced when all the sliders are at the far left, and gray is produced when all the sliders are aligned vertically at any other location.

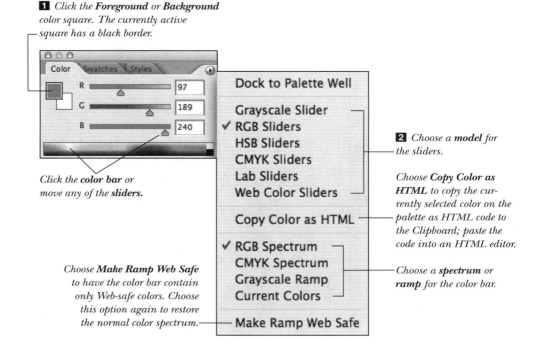

1 *Click the* **Foreground** *or* **Background** *color square. The currently active square has a black border.*

Click the **color bar** *or move any of the* **sliders.**

Choose **Make Ramp Web Safe** *to have the color bar contain only Web-safe colors. Choose this option again to restore the normal color spectrum.*

Dock to Palette Well

Grayscale Slider
✓ RGB Sliders
HSB Sliders
CMYK Sliders
Lab Sliders
Web Color Sliders

Copy Color as HTML

✓ RGB Spectrum
CMYK Spectrum
Grayscale Ramp
Current Colors

Make Ramp Web Safe

2 *Choose a* **model** *for the sliders.*

Choose **Copy Color as HTML** *to copy the currently selected color on the palette as HTML code to the Clipboard; paste the code into an HTML editor.*

Choose a **spectrum** *or* **ramp** *for the color bar.*

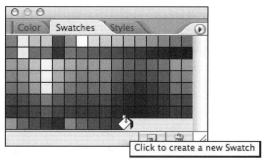

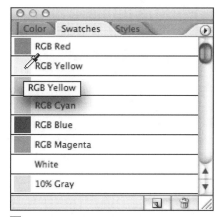

1 *To **add** a color to the palette, click the blank area below the swatches.*

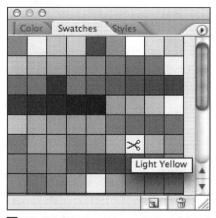

2 *The Swatches palette in **Small List** mode*

3 *Alt-click/Option-click a swatch to **delete** it.*

Using the Swatches palette

Note: We recommend that you detach the Swatches palette from the Color palette group before following these instructions.

To choose a color from the Swatches palette:

To choose a color for the currently active color square, click a color swatch.
or
To choose a color for the square that isn't currently active, Ctrl-click/Cmd-click a color swatch.

TIP To load or append a different set of swatches to the palette, follow the instructions on the next page.

To add a color to the Swatches palette:

1. Mix a Foreground color by using the Color palette or the Color Picker.

2. Show the Swatches palette.

3. Click the blank area below the swatches on the palette (paint bucket pointer) **1** or right-click/Control-click any existing swatch and choose **New Swatch.** Enter a Name, then click OK.
   or
   To create a new swatch without entering a custom name, click the **New Swatch of Foreground Color** button ▣ at the bottom of the Swatches palette.

   Regardless of which method you use, the new swatch will appear as the last swatch on the palette.

TIP To rename a swatch, double-click it, change the name, then click OK. To see the swatch name, choose Small List or Large List **2** from the palette menu, or use the tool tip.

To delete a color from the Swatches palette:

Alt-click/Option-click the swatch to be deleted (scissors pointer) or right-click/ Control-click a swatch and choose **Delete Swatch 3**. This can't be undone.

To save the current swatches as a library:

1. Choose **Save Swatches** from the Swatches palette menu.

2. In the File Name/Save As field, enter a name for the edited library (keep the .aco extension) **1**.

3. Choose a location in which to save the library (for locations, see the sidebar).

4. Click Save.

Onto the Swatches palette, you can **load** any of the preset color swatch libraries that are supplied with Photoshop or any user-created library. You can either replace the existing swatches with the new library or append (add) the additional swatches without deleting the existing ones.

To replace or append a swatches library:

1. Choose a library name from the bottom of the palette menu.

2. Click **Append** to add the new library swatches to the current palette.
   or
   Click **OK** to replace the current palette with the new library swatches, then respond to the prompt, if it appears **2**.

TIP To enlarge the palette to display more swatches, drag the palette border/resize box or click the palette zoom button.

You'll need to follow the instructions below only if the swatches library you want to open isn't in the **default** location listed in the sidebar.

To load a swatches library:

1. Choose **Load Swatches** from the Swatches palette menu.

2. Locate and highlight the swatches library you want to open.

3. Click **Load.** The loaded swatches will appear below the existing swatches on the Swatches palette.

To restore the default swatches:

Choose **Reset Swatches** from the Swatches palette menu, then click OK.

Finding defaults

In Windows, swatches libraries are stored in Program Files\Adobe\Adobe Photoshop CS2\Presets\Color Swatches; in Mac, they're in Applications/Adobe Photoshop CS2/Presets/Color Swatches. In both platforms, some swatch libraries are also stored in the Adobe Photoshop Only folder in the Color Swatches folder.

Creative exchange **NEW**

If you want to use your current swatches in another Creative Suite 2 application, save them via the **Save Swatches for Exchange** command on the Swatches palette menu.

1 *Keep the .aco suffix when saving swatches as a library.*

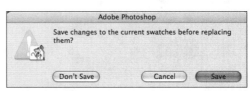

2 *This prompt will appear in Mac if you decide to **replace** your current Swatches palette colors with a new library, and the current swatches haven't yet been saved. In Windows, the buttons are Yes, No, and Cancel.*

Save, Replace, Load, Reset Swatches

1 *Sampling a color from an image with the **Eyedropper** tool*

Choosing a sample size

To change the area within which the Eyedropper tool samples, from the Eyedropper options bar, choose **Sample Size: Point Sample** (the exact pixel that's clicked on), or **3 by 3 Average** or **5 by 5 Average** (an average within a 3-by-3-pixel or 5-by-5-pixel square) **2**. The latter two choices are useful for sampling an area in an image that contains multiple colors, such as skin tones in a portrait photo or the background area of a landscape.

You can also right-click/Control-click in the document window with the Eyedropper tool and choose a sample size from the context menu. (For the Copy Color as HTML option, see the next page.)

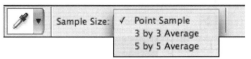

2 *Choose a **Sample Size** for the **Eyedropper** tool from the options bar (or from the context menu).*

Using the Eyedropper tool

To choose a color from an image using the Eyedropper:

1. Decide whether you want to choose a Foreground or Background color, then click that color square on the Color palette if it's not already active.

2. Choose the **Eyedropper** tool (I or Shift-I).

3. Click a color in any open document window **1**.
   or
   Drag in any open document window (the currently active color square will update interactively on the Toolbox and Color palette), and release the mouse when the pointer is over the desired color.

TIP To choose a color based on its color components, note the color percentages on the Info palette as you drag with the Eyedropper tool, or even when the tool is resting on any area of the image.

TIP Alt-click/Option-click or drag in the document window with the Eyedropper tool to choose a Background color when the Foreground color square is active, or to choose a Foreground color when the Background color square is active.

Copying colors as hexadecimals

Colors can be copied as **hexadecimal values** from a file in Photoshop or ImageReady and then pasted into an HTML file for Web output. There are two methods for doing this.

To copy a color as a hexadecimal value:

Method 1

1. Choose the **Eyedropper** tool (I or Shift-I).

2. In Photoshop: Right-click/Control-click a color in the document window, then choose **Copy Color as HTML.**
   or
   In ImageReady: Click the color that you want to copy in the document window (it will become the Foreground color). Then, with the Eyedropper tool still over the image, right-click/Control-click and choose **Copy Foreground Color as HTML.** To learn more about ImageReady, see Chapter 33.

   The selected color will be copied to the Clipboard as a hexadecimal value.

3. To paste the color into an HTML file, display the HTML file in your HTML-editing application, then choose Edit > **Paste** (Ctrl-V/Cmd-V). You can insert the code for any HTML element that allows a color property.

Method 2

1. Choose a Foreground color via the Color palette, Color Picker, or Swatches palette.

2. In Photoshop or ImageReady, from the Color palette menu, choose **Copy Color as HTML.**
   or
   In ImageReady, choose Edit > **Copy Foreground Color as HTML.**

   The Foreground color will be copied to the Clipboard as a hexadecimal value.

3. To paste the color into an HTML file, open the destination application, display the HTML file, then choose Edit > **Paste.**

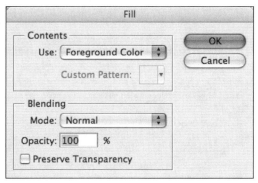

1 *You can use the **Fill** dialog box not only to apply a solid color, but also to apply a pattern or gradient.*

Shortcuts for filling a selection or layer

Windows

Fill with the Foreground color, 100% opacity	Alt-Backspace
Fill with the Background color, 100% opacity	Ctrl-Backspace
Fill only nontransparent pixels with the Foreground color	Alt-Shift-Backspace
Fill only nontransparent pixels with the Background color	Ctrl-Shift-Backspace

Mac

Fill with the Foreground color, 100% opacity	Option-Delete
Fill with the Background color, 100% opacity	Cmd-Delete
Fill only nontransparent pixels with the Foreground color	Option-Shift-Delete
Fill only nontransparent pixels with the Background color	Cmd-Shift-Delete

Filling with a solid color

To fill a selection or a layer with a solid color:

1. Click a layer, or create a new layer. *Optional:* Create a selection on the layer.

   TIP Use the Select > Color Range command to select areas by color or luminosity (see page 126).

2. Choose a Foreground color via the Color or Swatches palette.

3. Choose Edit > **Fill.** The Fill dialog box opens **1**.

4. Choose **Use: Foreground Color.** (You could also choose Color, then choose a color from the Color Picker.)

5. Check **Preserve Transparency** to recolor only existing opaque pixels on the layer, or uncheck it to recolor the whole selection or layer.

6. *Optional:* Choose a Blending Mode or change the Opacity percentage for the color.

7. Click OK.

   TIP A more flexible way to apply a solid color, gradient, or pattern is via the Fill/Adjustment layer pop-up menu on the Layers palette (see page 196).

Fill Command

Choosing blending modes

You can choose from a list of blending modes **1** in many locations in Photoshop, such as the options bar (for most painting and editing tools), the Layers palette, the Layer Style dialog box, and the Fill, Stroke, Fade, and Fill Path dialog boxes. The mode you choose for a tool or a layer affects how that tool or layer modifies underlying pixels.

In the descriptions for the illustrations on the next 4 pages, the color of the underlying pixels is called the **base color,** and the color that's applied via a layer or tool (e.g., the Pencil or Brush tool), and for which the mode is chosen, is called the **blend layer.** As for the images themselves, a dark color was used for the blend layer on the left and a light color was used on the right. Except for Dissolve, the blend layer always had an opacity of 100%.

For most blending modes, Photoshop compares the colors of the two layers (or the layer and the paint being applied by a tool) on a channel-by-channel basis. For example, the lightness of a pixel in the Red channel of the blend layer is compared to the lightness of a corresponding pixel in the Red channel of the base layer.

Opacities add up

When choosing an opacity percentage for a **tool** via the options bar, keep in mind that the tool's impact will also be affected by the opacity of the **layer** that strokes are applied to. For example, strokes applied with the Brush tool at a 50% opacity on a layer opacity of 50% will appear lighter than the same strokes on a layer opacity of 100%.

Cycling through

To cycle through the **blending modes** for the current tool, press **Shift - +** (plus) or **Shift - –** (minus).

Normal	
Dissolve	*Basic*
Darken	
Multiply	
Color Burn	*Darken*
Linear Burn	
Lighten	
Screen	
Color Dodge	*Lighten*
Linear Dodge	
Overlay	
Soft Light	
Hard Light	
Vivid Light	*Contrast*
Linear Light	
Pin Light	
Hard Mix	
Difference	*Comparative*
Exclusion	
Hue	
Saturation	
Color	*HSL*
Luminosity	

1 *The **blending modes** are organized into related groups based on their function.*

Basic *blending modes* **replace** *the base color*

NORMAL

All base colors are modified. *Note:* When an image is in Bitmap or Indexed Color mode, Normal mode is called Threshold.

DISSOLVE

Creates a chalky, dry brush texture with the blend layer color. The higher the pressure or opacity of the tool, or the higher the opacity of the layer, the more solid the color.

Darken *blending modes* **darken** *the base color*

DARKEN

The blend color darkens lighter pixels in the base layer; darker pixels remain unchanged. Contrast is lowered in the blend layer.

MULTIPLY

A dark blend layer color produces a darker base color; a light blend layer color just tints the base color. All base colors are darkened. Good for creating semitransparent shadows.

COLOR BURN

Increases contrast in the base color by making the shadow areas darker and the highlights lighter.

LINEAR BURN

Uses the blend color to darken the base color by decreasing the brightness.

Lighten blending modes **lighten** the base color

LIGHTEN

Base colors that are darker than the blend layer color are modified; base colors that are lighter than the blend layer color are not.

SCREEN

A light blend layer color produces a lighter, bleached base color; a dark blend layer lightens the base color less.

COLOR DODGE

A light blend layer color lightens the base color by decreasing the layer's contrast; a dark blend layer color tints the base color slightly.

LINEAR DODGE

A light blend layer color lightens the base color by increasing the layer's brightness; a dark blend layer color tints the base color slightly.

Contrast blending modes increase or decrease overall **contrast**

OVERLAY

Multiplies (darkens) dark base colors and screens (lightens) light base colors, while preserving luminosity (light and dark) values. Black and white pixels aren't changed, so details are maintained.

SOFT LIGHT

Lowers contrast in the blend layer, producing a softening and fading effect. Preserves luminosity values in the base color.

Blending Modes

Contrast blending modes (continued)

HARD LIGHT

Screens (lightens) the base color if the blend layer color is light; multiplies (darkens) the base color if the blend layer color is dark. Contrast is increased in the blend layer. Good for painting glowing highlights or creating composite effects.

VIVID LIGHT

Burns (darkens) the base colors by increasing contrast if the blend layer color is dark; dodges (lightens) the base color by decreasing contrast if the blend layer color is light.

LINEAR LIGHT

Burns (darkens) the base color by decreasing its brightness if the blend layer color is dark; dodges (lightens) the base color by increasing its brightness if the blend layer color is light.

PIN LIGHT

The blend color replaces the base color, depending on its relative brightness. If the blend color is lighter than 50% gray, only dark base colors are replaced; if the blend color is darker than 50% gray, only light base colors are replaced.

HARD MIX

Posterizes (reduces) the base color down to approximately 5–8 flat colors. A dark blend color will produce more black in the base color; a light blend color will produce more white in the base color.

Comparative *modes* **invert** *the base colors*

DIFFERENCE
Inverts the base and blend colors. The lighter the blend layer color, the more saturated the inverted color.

EXCLUSION
Grays out the base color where the blend layer color is dark; inverts the base color where the blend layer color is light. Lowers contrast.

HSL *modes apply a specific* **color component**

HUE
The blend color's hue is applied. Saturation and luminosity values aren't changed in the base color.

SATURATION
The blend color's saturation is applied. Hue and luminosity values aren't changed in the base color.

COLOR
The blend color's saturation and hue are applied. Light and dark (luminosity) values aren't changed in the base color. Details are preserved, making this a good mode to use for tinting.

LUMINOSITY
The base color's luminosity values are replaced by luminosity values from the blend color, but hue and saturation values in the base color aren't changed.

BEHIND
On a layer for which Lock Transparent Pixels is off, only transparent areas are modified, not existing base color pixels, producing an effect similar to painting on the reverse side of clear acetate. Good for creating shadows. This mode can't be used on the Background.

CLEAR
Makes the base color transparent where strokes are applied (turn off Lock Transparent Pixels). Available only for a multilayer image when using the Paint Bucket tool; the Line tool with the Fill Pixels button clicked; or the Fill, Stroke, or Fill Path command. This mode can't be chosen for a layer or used on the Background.

COLOR ADJUSTMENTS 13

Monitor your progress!
For up-to-the-minute feedback, display the **Info** palette and/or **Histogram** palette and leave either or both palettes open while using the adjustment command dialog boxes.

FROM **PROFESSIONAL-LEVEL** correction to exotic color shifts, Photoshop has a command to suit your needs. First try to figure out which colors need correcting, then decide which command will help you achieve your goal. For straightforward figurative photography, aim for color fidelity; for a montage, just aim for colors that strike the right mood. In this chapter, you'll learn to create fill layers; use the Color Sampler tool to get color readouts; strip color from a layer; and make adjustments using Color Balance, Hue/Saturation, Levels, and Curves adjustment layers. Some adjustment commands (e.g., Color Balance, Levels) are simpler to use than others (e.g., Curves, Hue/Saturation), but when you forego simplicity, you gain more options and control.

Important note: Make sure your monitor is **calibrated** before performing color adjustments! See pages 40–43.

In lieu of choosing adjustment commands directly from the Image > Adjustments submenu, which affect only the currently active layer, whenever possible, we apply these commands via **adjustment layers** 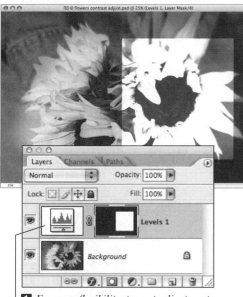. An adjustment layer affects all the currently visible layers below it, but doesn't actually change pixels until you merge it with the layer below (read more about adjustment layers on pages 166–168). Similarly, for added flexibility, you can use a **fill layer** to apply a solid color, gradient, or pattern instead of applying it directly to a layer.

1 *For more flexibility, try out adjustments via* **adjustment layers.**

Most adjustment command dialog boxes have a **Save** button that you can use to save your color adjustment settings. You can then apply those settings to another layer or to another file via the **Load** button in the same dialog box. To share settings even more quickly, you can **drag and drop** an adjustment layer from one document to another.

Creating fill layers

Fill layers function like adjustment layers in that they can be edited, their fill content can be changed at any time, and they can be removed easily. Fill layers can contain a solid color, gradient, or pattern.

To create a fill layer:

1. On the Layers palette, click the layer that you want the fill layer to appear above (you can restack it later). You can also create a selection to limit the fill effect.

2. Choose **Solid Color, Gradient,** or **Pattern** from the New Fill/Adjustment Layer pop-up menu ⬤. at the bottom of the Layers palette.
   or
   To choose options for the fill layer as you create it, choose Layer > **New Fill Layer** > **Solid Color, Gradient,** or **Pattern,** then do any of the following: change the layer Name; check Use Previous Layer to Make Clipping Mask to make the new layer a part of a clipping mask (see page 305); choose a different blending Mode; or change the Opacity percentage. Click OK. All of these options can be changed later.

3. For a **Solid Color** layer, choose a color from the Color Picker (or click Color Libraries to choose a custom color), then click OK.

   For a **Gradient** layer, choose a preset from the Gradient Preset picker, choose a Style, and choose Angle and Scale values, then click OK. (For the Reverse, Dither, or Align with layer options, see page 412).

   For a **Pattern** layer, choose a preset from the Pattern Preset picker and choose a Scale percentage (1–1000) **1**–**3**. *Optional:* Uncheck Link with Layer to keep the pattern stationary if the layer is moved; click Snap to Origin to have the upper left corner of the pattern snap to the current ruler origin (where the zeros on the horizontal and vertical rulers meet). Click OK.

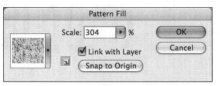

1 *Use the **Pattern Fill** dialog box to choose a pattern and scale. (We created our pattern using a photograph of flowers and the Pattern Maker filter.)*

2 *An image of a plain paper bag with a **Pattern Fill** layer above it (opacity 33%)*

3 *The final image*

Fill Layer

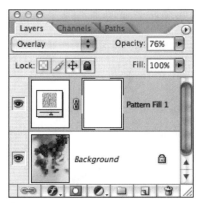

1 For this **pattern fill layer,** we chose **Overlay** mode and an Opacity of 76%.

4. *Do any of the following optional steps:*

Click the fill layer, then adjust the blending mode or opacity of the layer via the Layers palette.

Click the fill layer, then either paint or fill a selection with black in the layer mask to block the fill layer effect, or with white to restore masked areas.

5. Click OK **1**–**3**.

TIP To create a custom pattern, select an area of a layer with the Rectangular Marquee tool (without feathering), choose Edit > Define Pattern, enter a Name, click OK, then Deselect (Ctrl-D/ Cmd-D). The new pattern will appear on the Pattern picker automatically. You can also use the Pattern Maker filter to create custom patterns (see pages 361–363).

TIP You can also apply a Color Overlay, Gradient Overlay, or Pattern Overlay effect via the Layer Style dialog box to apply a color, gradient, or pattern, respectively, to a layer (see pages 326–327).

2 You can use a **pattern fill layer** to add **texture** to a photograph.

3 To produce this image, we created a **pattern fill layer,** duplicated the layer, lowered the opacity of the duplicate to 43%, changed its blending mode to **Multiply,** and offset it from the original.

Fill Layer

Color Sampler Tool

Using color samplers

Instead of using the Eyedropper tool to get a color readout from one spot, you can use the **Color Sampler** tool to place up to four color readout markers, called color samplers, in a document. As you perform color and shade adjustments, before and after color breakdown readouts taken from the sampler locations will display on the Info palette. You can also add color samplers while any adjustment layer dialog box is open by Shift-clicking in the document window. Color samplers save with the file.

To place color samplers in a document:

1. Choose the **Color Sampler** tool (I or Shift-I).

2. Click in up to four locations in the document window—a color sampler will appear for each click **1**. You might want to place a sampler in a highlight area, a midtone area, and a shadow area, and perhaps the fourth sampler on a color that you want to monitor closely.

   Note: If you choose a tool other than the Color Sampler, the Eyedropper, or a painting or editing tool, the samplers will disappear from view. To redisplay them, choose one of the above-mentioned tools or open an adjustment dialog box. To deliberately hide them, choose Color Samplers from the Info palette menu to uncheck that command.

TIP You can also add samplers by Shift-clicking with the Eyedropper tool.

TIP Color samplers gather data from the topmost visible layer that contains pixels in the spot where the sampler is located. If you hide a layer from which a sampler is reading, the sampler will then read from the next layer down that contains visible pixels in that location. The Info palette will update if you hide a layer from which it was reading sampler data.

TIP Samplers will move accordingly if the whole canvas is flipped or rotated.

1 *Click in the document window with the* **Color Sampler** *tool to create up to four samplers.*

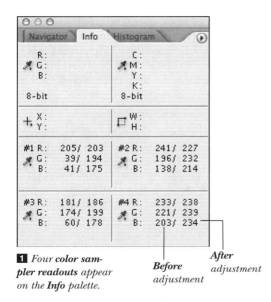

1 *Four color sampler readouts appear on the Info palette.*

Before adjustment

After adjustment

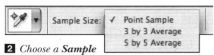

2 *Choose a Sample Size from the Color Sampler tool options bar.*

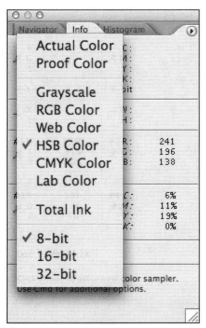

3 *A different color mode can be chosen for each color sampler.*

To move a color sampler:

Choose the **Color Sampler** tool (I or Shift-I), then drag a color sampler.

or

Choose the **Eyedropper** tool (I or Shift-I), then Ctrl-drag/Cmd-drag a color sampler.

Using the Info palette with the Color Sampler tool

The Info palette displays before-adjustment and after-adjustment color breakdowns of the pixel or pixel area under each color sampler **1**. To control the size of the sample area, choose the Color Sampler tool, then pick an option from the **Sample Size** pop-up menu on the options bar **2**: **Point Sample** to sample only the pixel directly under the pointer; or **3 by 3 Average** (our preferred choice) or **5 by 5 Average** to sample an average color from a 3- or 5-pixel-square area. When you change the Sample Size for the Color Sampler tool, the setting also changes for the Eyedropper tool, and vice versa.

To choose a **color mode** (Grayscale, RGB Color, etc.) for a section of the Info palette, click the tiny arrowhead next to a dropper icon on the palette, then choose from the pop-up menu **3**: **Actual Color** is the current document color mode; **Proof Color** is the color profile mode currently chosen in View > Proof Setup; and **Total Ink** is the total percentage of CMYK under the pointer based on the current output settings in the CMYK Working Space (in Edit > Color Settings). The mode you choose for the Info palette doesn't have to match the current document color mode.

To remove a color sampler:

Choose the **Color Sampler** tool, then Alt-click/Option-click a sampler (the pointer will become a scissors icon) or drag the sampler out of the document window. The readout for that sampler will disappear from the Info palette.

or

Choose the **Eyedropper** tool, then Alt-Shift-click/Option-Shift-click a sampler.

Using Color Balance

You can use the **Color Balance** dialog box to apply or correct a warm or cool cast in a layer's highlights, midtones, or shadows. Sometimes we'll use this command to test out preliminary corrections in each color range, just to see the impact of adding more of one color or removing some of another. The color pairing on the sliders helps us conceptualize the color relationships—adding more green reduces magenta, etc. When adjusting broad color ranges doesn't do the trick, we hone in more precisely by using the Curves or Hue/Saturation command (see pages 202–207).

To apply the Color Balance command:

1. Click a layer or the Background, and show the Histogram palette.

2. Choose **Color Balance** from the New Fill/Adjustment Layer pop-up menu , at the bottom of the Layers palette. The Color Balance dialog box opens.

3. At the bottom of the dialog box, click the **Tone Balance** range you want to adjust: **Shadows, Midtones,** or **Highlights** ■.

Optional: Leave Preserve Luminosity checked to preserve lightness values as you make corrections. Unchecking this option will lower the overall height of the histogram—a sign of lowered luminosity.

4. In the **Color Balance** area:

Cool and warm colors are paired opposite each other. Move a slider toward any color you want to add more of, then pause to preview. Move sliders toward related colors to make an image warmer or cooler (e.g., move sliders toward Cyan and Blue to produce a cool cast). Don't move the Shadows sliders in one direction and the Midtones sliders in the opposite direction, though, unless you like odd color shifts.

5. *Optional:* Repeat the previous step with any other Tone Balance button selected.

6. Uncheck and recheck Preview to evaluate your adjustments.

7. Click OK.

TIP Before using Color Balance to apply a color tint to a Grayscale document, convert the document to a color mode.

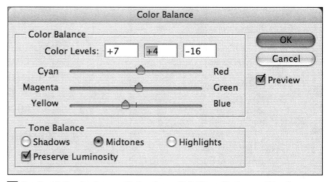

■ *In the **Color Balance** dialog box, click **Tone Balance: Shadows, Midtones,** or **Highlights,** then move any of the sliders.*

Adding color tints

To tint the current layer, in the Hue/Saturation dialog box, check **Colorize.** Move the Hue slider to apply a different tint; move the Saturation slider to reduce or increase the color intensity; or move the Lightness slider to lighten or darken. To tint a grayscale document, convert it to RGB Color or CMYK Color mode first, then follow the same steps. (To produce a duotone, see pages 482–483.)

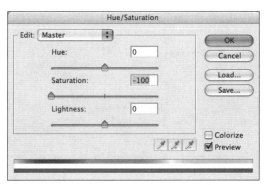

1 *In the **Hue/Saturation** dialog box, move the **Saturation** slider all the way to the left to remove color from a layer.*

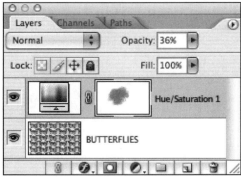

2 *We applied brush strokes to an **adjustment layer** mask.*

Converting layers to grayscale

You can use the **Desaturate** command to strip color from a layer (convert it to grayscale) without having to change the color mode for the whole document.

To convert a layer to grayscale:

1. Click a layer or the Background.
2. Choose Image > Adjustments > **Desaturate** (Ctrl-Shift-U/Cmd-Shift-U).

To convert a color layer to grayscale and selectively restore its color:

1. Click a layer in a color document. Layers below this one will be affected by the adjustment layer you're about to create.
2. Create an adjustment layer by choosing **Hue/Saturation** from the New Fill/ Adjustment Layer pop-up menu ⊘, at the bottom of the Layers palette. The Hue/Saturation dialog box opens.
3. Move the **Saturation** slider all the way to the left (to –100) **1**.
4. Click OK.
5. Set the Foreground color to black.
6. Click the adjustment layer, then paint on the image where you want to restore the **original** colors from underlying layers **2**. Paint with white to restore **grayscale** areas.

   You can also try lowering the **opacity** of the adjustment layer via the Layers palette.

   To prevent a layer from being affected by the adjustment layer, **restack** it above the adjustment layer.

TIP To limit the adjustment layer effect to only the layer directly below it, Alt-click/ Option-click the line between the two. This creates a clipping mask.

TIP To use the Channel Mixer command to make a layer grayscale, see page 180.

Convert to Grayscale, Then Restore Color

Using Hue/Saturation

For making precise hue or saturation corrections, the **Hue/Saturation** command is a better choice than Levels or Curves. It lets you target a specific range of colors, then shift those colors to a different hue, or adjust their saturation or lightness.

To apply the Hue/Saturation command:

1. Click a layer **1**.

2. Choose **Hue/Saturation** from the New Fill/Adjustment Layer pop-up menu ◐. at the bottom of the Layers palette. The Hue/Saturation dialog box opens.

3. From the **Edit** pop-up menu, choose Master to adjust all the document colors at once, or choose a preset range (e.g., Reds or Blues) to adjust colors only in that range **2**.

4. Make sure Preview is checked.

5. Do any of the following:

   Move the **Hue** slider **3** to shift colors to another part of the color bar.

   Move the **Saturation** slider to the left to decrease saturation or to the right to increase it. (For print output, converting the document to CMYK Color mode will desaturate colors and bring them into the printable gamut; you don't have to do it here.)

   Move the **Lightness** slider to the right to lighten the colors, or to the left to darken them. When changing the Lightness, you may need to increase the Saturation to restore lost color intensity.

6. To widen or narrow the range of colors to be adjusted, do the following:

   Choose a color range from the **Edit** pop-up menu. The color selection droppers become available, and the adjustment slider appears above the chosen color range on the color bar **4**.

   Drag either or both of the lighter gray areas on the adjustment slider (not the triangles) to widen or narrow the **color**

1 *The apples in this original image are a dull, brownish red (take our word for it!).*

2 *From the **Edit** pop-up menu, choose Master or choose a preset color range...*

3 *...then move the **Hue, Saturation,** and **Lightness** sliders.*

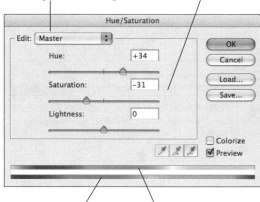

Adjustments display in this color bar.

*The **reference** color bar doesn't change.*

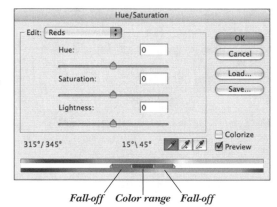

Fall-off   Color range   Fall-off

4 *The **adjustment slider** has three sections.*

Hue/Saturation Command

1 *The lighter gray area is moved to the left to **widen** the range of colors (represented by the darker gray) to be affected by the adjustment.*

2 *The triangle is moved to the right to **widen** the **fall-off**, allowing changes to affect a wider area of adjacent colors, but leaving the inner color range unchanged.*

3 *In this image, when we tried restricting the Blues preset range to only the sky colors, the fall-off areas became too narrow, resulting in posterization. Smoother color transitions were produced by **widening** the **fall-off** areas (moving the triangles outward).*

4 *Increasing the saturation in the red range made the apples a brighter, more appetizing red.*

range. The color range is represented by the darker inner bar **1**.

Drag the outer triangles on the slider to control how many **adjacent** colors will be adjusted (the fall-off range) **2**. Drag outward to widen the fall-off range and soften the effect, or inward to narrow it. Try not to shorten the whole adjustment slider and fall-off areas too much **3**.

To see which image colors are in the chosen range, drag the **Hue** slider to an extreme end. The colors in the chosen range will shift in hue. Adjust the size of the color range and/or fall-offs, if necessary, then drag the Hue slider back to 0.

TIP If the adjustment slider wraps off one edge of the color bar and around to the other, you can Ctrl-drag/Cmd-drag either color bar to bring it back to the middle of the color area. This won't affect your adjustments.

If you move the whole slider or expand the color range for any of the preset ranges, a new listing will appear on the Edit pop-up menu. For example, if you expand the preset Reds color range so it enters the Yellows range, Yellows, and Yellows 2 will be on the menu, but Reds will be removed from the menu because the Yellows range now includes Reds. (To restore the original settings, Alt-click/Option-click Reset.)

Click the **Add to Sample** eyedropper *✦* or **Subtract from Sample** *✦* eyedropper, then click on the image to add to or subtract specific colors from the current color range. The color range (darker) area of the slider readjusts automatically. With the Eyedropper selected, you can hold down Shift to temporarily access the Add to Sample eyedropper, or hold down Alt/Option to access the Subtract from Sample eyedropper.

7. Click OK **4**.

TIP See page 178 to learn how to use the mask on an adjustment layer to remove Hue/Saturation effects from select areas.

Hue/Saturation Command

Using the Levels command

The **Auto Color Correction Options** command adjusts the color, tonal range, and contrast in an image using preset algorithms (formulas) and lets you establish target values for the shadows, midtones, and highlights. We recommend using these auto correction options only as a starting point for further corrections.

To apply auto color correction options:

1. Display the Histogram palette. Click a pixel (nonvector) layer, then choose Image > Adjustments > **Levels.** The Levels dialog box opens.

2. Click the **Options** button. The Auto Color Correction Options dialog box opens. Move it, if necessary, so you can watch the Levels histogram update as you choose options.

3. Click one of the **Algorithms** ∎ (see the sidebar at right).

4. Check Snap Neutral Midtones to have Photoshop adjust colors that are closest to neutral to match the Midtones target color swatch in the dialog box.

5. *Optional:* To change the target values that will be assigned to midtone areas, check Snap Neutral Midtones, then click the Midtones swatch. In the Color Picker, with the "H" button clicked, click a color on the vertical bar, then drag the circle upward or downward in the large square to change midtone brightness, or drag into the square to change the midtone color. Note how the Levels histogram updates. Midtones is the only swatch you really need to bother adjusting; the other two adjust automatically when the document colors are converted to a printer profile.

6. Click OK to close the Color Picker, then the Auto Color Correction Options dialog box, then the Levels dialog box.

TIP To monitor how adjustments are affecting a particular channel, choose that channel on the Histogram palette.

Auto Color Correction algorithms

Enhance Monochromatic Contrast moves the black and white input sliders inward, resulting in lighter highlights and darker shadows. The sliders are moved by the same amount for each channel in order to preserve color relationships among the channels. (The Auto Contrast command uses this algorithm.)

Enhance Per Channel Contrast moves the input sliders inward by a different amount for each channel, resulting in more noticeable color casts and changes in contrast. (The Auto Levels command uses this algorithm.)

Find Dark & Light Colors finds the average darkest and lightest pixels in the document and uses those values to position the black and white input sliders in each channel. The result is increased contrast. Of the three algorithms, this is the one we prefer. (The Auto Color command uses this algorithm, and also is the only "Auto" command that uses the Snap Neutral Midtones option.)

The same Auto Color Correction options can also be accessed by clicking **Options** in the **Curves** dialog box (see page 206). There, the curve for each color channel will be adjusted, but the changes won't be reflected on the curve for the composite channel.

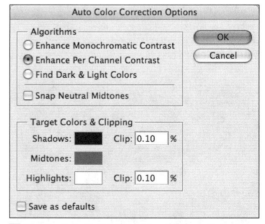

∎ *Use the **Auto Color Correction Options** dialog box to correct an image using preset algorithms.*

Fight oversaturation!

When you increase contrast via a Levels or Curves adjustment layer, you also increase color saturation. To reduce the saturation, choose **Luminosity** as the blend mode for the adjustment layer. To monitor the increase in saturation, set one of the readouts on the Info palette to HSB Color; then, as you increase or decrease the contrast, pass the pointer over the document and see how the S value changes.

Midtones, yes; shadows, no

Each adjustment command has inherent strengths and limitations. For example, the **Levels** command gives you greater control over **midtone** corrections than shadow corrections. For **shadow** corrections, we recommend using the **Curves** command.

1 *Choose an individual* **channel.**

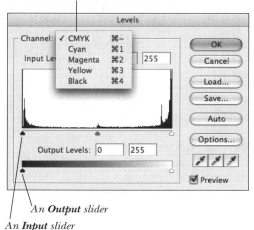

*An **Output** slider*
*An **Input** slider*

When using the **Levels** (or Curves) command to make color or tonal adjustments, we recommend taking this approach: Adjust the tonal values (lights and darks) of the overall document (composite channel) first, then adjust individual color channels, if necessary (say, a tad more cyan, a tad less magenta).

To adjust color channels using the Levels command:

1. Show the **Info** palette.

2. Create an adjustment layer by choosing **Levels** from the New Fill/Adjustment Layer pop-up menu ⊘. at the bottom of the Layers palette. The Levels dialog box opens.

3. Check Preview.

4. To correct an obvious predominance of one color in the image (such as a red or green color cast), choose that color from the **Channel** pop-up menu **1**.

   Follow any of these steps for an RGB Color document (do the opposite for a CMYK Color document!):

   To **decrease** the amount of that color, move the gray Input slider to the right.
   or
   To **increase** the amount of that color, move the gray Input slider to the left.
   or
   To **tint** the document with the chosen channel color, move the black Output slider to the right.

   Repeat step 4 for any other channels that need adjusting, while keeping the relationships among all the colors in mind. For example, reducing Red increases Cyan, reducing Green increases Magenta —as you may have observed in the Color Balance dialog box.

5. Click OK.

TIP With the dialog box still open, hold down Alt/Option and click Reset to restore the last-used settings.

TIP Shift-click in the document window to place Color Sampler points while the Levels dialog box is open.

Using the Curves command

The **Curves** command is powerful because it lets you make adjustments to more narrowly defined tonal ranges (e.g., highlights, quarter tones, midtones, three-quarter tones, shadows) than the Levels command. Precision corrections can be applied to the composite channel, which is all the channels combined, or to individual color channels.

To use the Curves command:

1. Show the Histogram palette, and choose Expanded View from the palette menu.

2. Create an adjustment layer by choosing **Curves** from the New Fill/Adjustment Layer pop-up menu ●, at the bottom of the Layers palette. The Curves dialog box opens.

3. As you move the pointer over the grid, note the default Input and Output readouts **1**, which represent the brightness values for RGB Color mode, or the percentage values for CMYK Color mode. (You can click the gradient bar below the grid to switch the Input and Output readouts; we tend to leave them be.)

4. To adjust the tonal values in the composite RGB or CMYK channel first, leave the **Channel** setting as is, then do any of the following:

To **increase** the **contrast,** drag the points at the extreme end of the curve inward horizontally to force more shadow and highlight levels in the image to become absolute black or white.

To **lessen** the **contrast,** drag the points vertically inward from the corner to reduce absolute black to less than 100% (or greater than 0, for RGB), or absolute white to greater than 0% (or less than 255, for RGB) **2**.

To **lighten** or **darken** the **midtones,** drag the middle of the curve upward or downward. Or click the curve to add two points (as in **1**) so you can adjust the darker midtones separately from the lighter midtones.

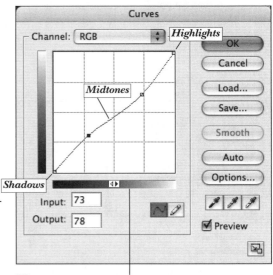

1 *For an RGB document, the **gradient bars** represent brightness values. The horizontal gradient bar represents the values before adjustment; the vertical gradient bar represents the values following adjustment.*

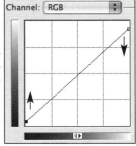

2 *To lessen the contrast, move the endpoints vertically inward.*

Curves Command

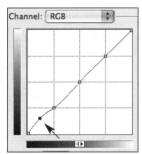

1 *Points were added at the **quarter** tone, **midtone** and **three-quarter** tone segments of the curve, then the **shadows** were lightened.*

2 *The original image lacks contrast.*

3 *After a **Curves** adjustment*

5. *Optional:* Choose an individual color channel to adjust it separately.

6. If your document is in CMYK Color mode, drag the part of the curve you want to adjust upward to darken or downward to lighten that tonal range. For RGB Color mode, drag upward to lighten or downward to darken.
and/or
To narrow the color range to be edited, click on the curve to create additional points (up to 14)—perhaps at the mid-point of the grid (50, 50 for CMYK or 128, 128 for RGB) and at the quarter and three-quarter tone points **1**—then drag the segment between any pair of points to adjust that particular color range. (To remove a point, click it, then press Backspace/Delete; or Ctrl-click/Cmd-click it.)

Once you've added a point, you can enter numbers in the Input and/or Output fields for that point or use the arrow keys to nudge it.

7. Click OK **2**–**3**.

TIP With the composite channel or an individual color channel chosen in the Curves dialog box, you can click in an RGB image to see where the color value you click falls on the curve, or Ctrl-click/Cmd-click the image to make a corresponding point appear on the curve. To do this in a CMYK image, you must choose an individual channel.

TIP Alt-click/Option-click the grid in the Curves dialog box to toggle between a grid spacing of 4 by 4 and 10 by 10.

TIP Shift-click in the document window to place Color Sampler points while the Curves dialog box is open.

TIP Click the button in the lower right corner of the Curves dialog box to toggle between its normal and expanded sizes.

TIP Choose a different opacity percentage for the curve adjustment layer, or paint on the adjustment layer mask to lessen or remove the effect in specific areas.

Curves Command

Other commands to explore

To use the **Photo Filter** command to apply a premixed color, mimicking the tinting effect of a photographic lens filter, see page 240.

To use the **Shadow/Highlight** command to adjust lights and darks in over- or underexposed images, see pages 237–239.

And finally, to use the **Match Color** command to match individual colors in one document with those in another, see pages 262–263.

Further your studies

For in-depth information on scanning, tonal adjustments, color correction, output, and other related topics, we recommend these Peachpit Press titles:

Real World Adobe Photoshop CS2, by David Blatner and Bruce Fraser

Real World Color Management, Second Edition, by Bruce Fraser, Fred Bunting, and Chris Murphy

Photoshop Color Correction, by Michael Kieran

And of course you can also take it straight from the horse's mouth—Photoshop Help.

You won't find these topics in our index!

The **Selective Color** command is used primarily for fine-tuning a CMYK document after a print proof has been done. If a color doesn't look right on the proof, the Selective Color sliders can be used to make corrections to any of the preset color ranges listed in the dialog box (any of the four ink colors that make up the chosen color range). After correcting, you should print another proof and evaluate it.

With the **Sponge** tool, you can drag across color areas on the current layer to increase or reduce saturation. The drawback of the tool is that you can't reverse your edits or control which color range is being edited—with the result being uneven color changes. Besides, the conversion from RGB to CMYK color automatically brings out-of-gamut colors into the designated output gamut anyway. For performing color corrections, the adjustment commands give you way more power and control.

Further Your Studies

Tool shortcuts

These shortcuts work with any tool for which the option or feature is available (e.g., Brush, Paint Bucket, Pencil, Smudge, Dodge, Burn).

Cycle through the **blending modes** on the options bar	Shift- + (plus) or Shift - - (minus)
Decrease/increase the **master diameter** for a brush preset	[or]
Change the **opacity, exposure,** or **strength** percentage* (Shift-press a number to change the flow level**)	0–9 (e.g., 2 = 20%) or quickly type a percentage (e.g. "38")

*If the Airbrush option is on, pressing a number changes the flow percentage and Shift-pressing a number changes the opacity percentage.

**When Shift-pressing in Windows, use the numbers on the main keyboard, not on the keypad.

*Click in either of these two spots to open the **Brush Preset** picker.*

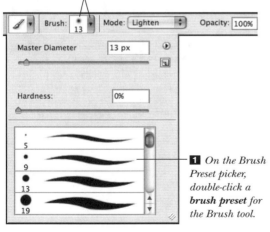

1 On the Brush Preset picker, double-click a **brush preset** for the Brush tool.

IF YOU LIKE TO PAINT, YOU'LL ENJOY this chapter! You'll master the Brush tool; use the Brush Preset picker and Brushes palette to customize brush presets; smudge colors with the Smudge tool; and erase areas of an image with the Eraser, Background Eraser, and Magic Eraser tools.

Using the Brush tool

First, just to get started, let's get acquainted with the **Brush** tool. In these instructions, you'll choose an existing brush preset (brush tip) for the Brush tool, and then choose various options bar settings to customize how the tool applies pigment. In the next section, you'll learn how to customize brush presets by using a wide assortment of options on the Brushes palette.

To use the Brush tool:

1. Click a layer. *Optional:* Create a selection on the layer if you want to restrict your brush strokes to that area.
2. Choose the **Brush** tool (B or Shift-B).
3. Choose a **Foreground** color (see pages 181–184).
4. On the options bar, do the following:

   Click the **Brush Preset** picker arrowhead or thumbnail, then click a preset **1**.

   Choose a blending **Mode** (see pages 190–194).

   Choose an **Opacity** percentage. At 100%, the stroke will completely cover underlying pixels.

   Choose a **Flow** percentage to control how fully and smoothly the paint is applied.

   Click the **Airbrush** button to simulate traditional airbrushing.
5. Drag across any area of the picture. If the Airbrush option is on and you

(Continued on the following page)

Brush Tool

press and hold in the same spot, the paint drop will gradually widen (up to the maximum diameter of the brush) and become more dense and opaque **1**–**2**.

Note: On the Layers palette, click the Lock Transparent Pixels button ▨ for the current layer to have the tool recolor only nontransparent areas.

TIP To draw a straight stroke, click once to begin the stroke, then Shift-click or Shift-drag in a different location to complete the stroke.

TIP Click an image layer, then Alt-click/ Option-click in the document window to sample colors while a painting tool is chosen (this is a temporary Eyedropper).

Choosing temporary settings

Each brush preset has its own built-in **Master Diameter** and **Hardness** settings, but you can make temporary changes to either setting via a context menu or the options bar.

To choose temporary settings for a brush preset:

1. Choose any tool that uses brush presets (e.g., the Brush, Pencil, Dodge, Burn, or Eraser tool).

2. Right-click/Control-click in the document window, then change the **Master Diameter** and/or **Hardness** setting **3**. These settings can also be changed on the Brush Preset picker.

3. Press Enter/Return or click in the document window. This setting will remain in effect only until you choose a different preset.

Airbrushing

The **Airbrush** function can be turned on or off via this button 🖊 on the options bar for many tools, such as the Brush, Clone Stamp, Pattern Stamp, History Brush, Eraser, Dodge, Burn, and Sponge.

1 *A brush stroke created with the **Airbrush** option off*

2 *A brush stroke created with the **Airbrush** option on*

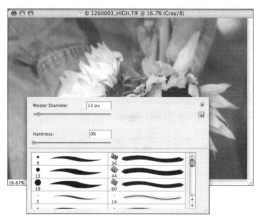

3 *Via the context menu, you can change the **Master Diameter** and **Hardness** for a preset on the fly.*

Docked in the well

By default, the Brushes palette is **docked** in the **palette well** at the right side of the options bar. To open the palette, click the tab; to hide it, click the tab again, or click in the document window or options bar.

If you don't see a Brushes tab in the palette well, you can dock the palette there by dragging the palette tab into the well or by choosing **Dock to Palette Well** from the Brushes palette menu.

To access the **palette menu** when the Brushes palette is docked, click the tab, then click the arrowhead on the tab.

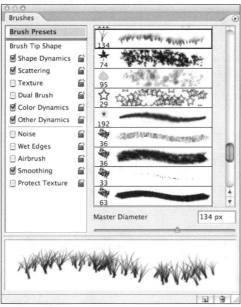

1 *Use the **Brushes** palette to choose and customize brush presets.*

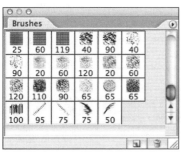

2 *Faux Finish Brushes,* one of many libraries available on the Brushes palette menu

Using the Brushes palette

The **Brushes** palette offers a myriad of options for **customizing** brush **presets** for the Brush, Pencil, History Brush, Art History Brush, Clone Stamp, Pattern Stamp, Eraser, Blur, Sharpen, Smudge, Dodge, Burn, and Sponge tools. The options are organized into categories, such as Shape Dynamics, Scattering, Texture, and Color Dynamics. Settings for a stylus or an airbrush input device can also be chosen.

The first step is to get acquainted with the palette. This is **Brushes Palette 101.**

To use the Brushes palette:

1. Choose any of the tools listed in the introductory paragraph above.

2. To **display** the Brushes palette **1**, click the Toggle palette button in the middle of the options bar or click the Brushes tab in the well.

3. If you don't see a list of categories on the left side of the palette, choose **Expanded View** from the palette menu.

4. To resize the palette, drag the lower right corner.

5. Check the **box** for any of the first six categories to activate the features for that category. If a category is dimmed, it means it's not available for that tool. The categories are discussed in depth in the next set of instructions.

6. To display the panel for a category, click the category **name.** The bottom five categories can only be switched on or off; no settings can be chosen for them.

7. To choose a different **display** option for the palette, from the palette menu, choose Text Only, Small Thumbnail, Large Thumbnail, Small List, Large List, or Stroke Thumbnail. The Small options compact the list; the Large options allow you to see the brush tips more easily.

8. To **save** and **load** alternate brush preset libraries, see pages 462–465 **2**.

Brushes Palette

Customizing brushes

Just a quick glance at the list of categories on the left side of the Brushes palette will give you an inkling of how infinite your choices are for **customizing brush presets.** We've divided the instructions into manageable chunks, though, with the ones we use most often listed separately from the ones we use less often (writing a book isn't fun unless you can reveal your biases!). You can pick and choose among the various options to create your dream brush. And don't forget, when we talk about applying "pigment," with the brush presets, you can use many other tools besides the Brush!

Note: Changes made to a preset remain in effect only until another preset is chosen.

To customize a brush preset (main course):

1. Choose a tool that uses brush presets, and display the **Brushes** palette.

2. Click **Brush Presets** ■ in the upper left corner of the Brushes palette, then click a preset. You can use the scroll arrows or bar to scroll down the list.

3. To change basic shape or size settings for the preset, click **Brush Tip Shape** at the top of the list ■, then keep an eye on the brush preview at the bottom of the palette as you make any of these changes:

   Enter a **Diameter** value (1–2500 pixels) or move the slider to change the brush size.

   Enter a new **Angle** or drag the arrowhead around the circle to alter the brush slant.

   Enter a new **Roundness** value (0–100%) or drag either of the two tiny dark circles inward to make the brush tip more elliptical and less round ■.

   Change the **Hardness** value (0–100%) to feather or sharpen the edge of the brush (not available for all brush tips) ■.

   To control the distance between brush tips within the stroke, check **Spacing,** then enter or choose a value (1–1000%) ■.

Side margin: Customize Brush Preset

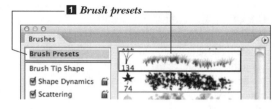

1 *Brush presets*

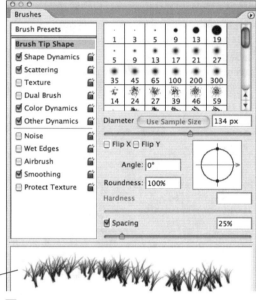

2 *The currently chosen preset **previews** at the bottom of the **Brushes** palette as you change settings.*

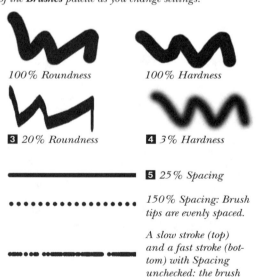

100% Roundness

100% Hardness

3 *20% Roundness*

4 *3% Hardness*

5 *25% Spacing*

150% Spacing: Brush tips are evenly spaced.

A slow stroke (top) and a fast stroke (bottom) with Spacing unchecked: the brush tips are unevenly spaced.

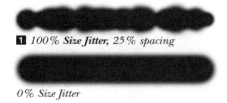

■ *100% Size Jitter, 25% spacing*

0% Size Jitter

■ *0% Scatter, 100% Spacing*

*500% Scatter, **Both Axes** option **checked***

*500% Scatter, **Both Axes** option **unchecked***

■ *0% Count Jitter, 100% Spacing*

*100% **Count Jitter:** The Count varies randomly from 1% to 100% of the Count value.*

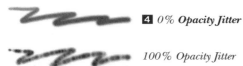

■ *0% Opacity Jitter*

100% Opacity Jitter

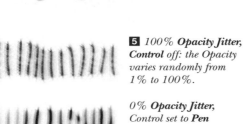

■ *100% **Opacity Jitter**, Control off: the Opacity varies randomly from 1% to 100%.*

*0% **Opacity Jitter**, Control set to **Pen Pressure:** the Opacity is controlled by the amount of pressure exerted on the tablet stylus.*

4. To control how much variation is allowable in the brush tip shape, click **Shape Dynamics** (click the words—the box will become checked automatically), then do any of the following:

Change the **Size Jitter** ■, **Angle Jitter,** and **Roundness Jitter** values to establish variation parameters for those attributes. ("Jitter" is the amount of random variation allowable for that option.)

From the **Control** pop-up menus, choose a stylus feature to directly control that option's variation (see pages 216–217). Variations occur even if Off is chosen.

Change the **Minimum Diameter** value for the brush size variations.

Change the **Minimum Roundness** value.

5. To control the placement of pigment in the stroke, click **Scattering,** then do any of the following:

Check **Both Axes** ■ to allow pigment to be scattered both along and perpendicular to the path. Uncheck Both Axes to have strokes be scattered perpendicular to, but not along, the path. Also choose a Control option, if desired.

Change the **Scatter** value (1–1000%) to control how far pigment can veer off the path drawn by the mouse. The lower the Scatter value, the more solid the stroke.

Change the **Count** value (1–16) to control the stroke's overall density (the amount of pigment).

Change the **Count Jitter** value ■ (0–100%) to control how much the Count (density) can vary.

6. To control how randomly the overall stroke opacity can vary as you paint, click **Other Dynamics,** then do any of the following:

Change the **Opacity Jitter** (0–100%) ■–■ for the amount the opacity can vary. Choose a Control option to control fading.

(Continued on the following page)

Change the **Flow Jitter** (0–100%) to control how smoothly the pigment is applied. A high Flow Jitter makes for a blotchy stroke, but maybe that's what you want. Choose a Control option.

7. And last but not least (you're almost done!), check any or all of these options:

Noise to add random grain to brush strokes to make them look rougher.

Wet Edges to simulate the buildup of pigment at the edges of brush strokes, as in traditional watercoloring **1**–**4**.

Airbrush to allow a stroke to build up for as long as the mouse button is held down in the same spot. You can also click the ✍ button on the options bar.

Smoothing to create smoother curves.

To apply the same texture pattern and scale to other brushes that currently use a texture option, or to which you add a texture option, check **Protect Texture.** This method will create a uniform surface texture on the entire canvas.

8. *Optional:* Click an open lock icon 🔓 next to any category name to make the current settings for that category uneditable, even if you change presets (it will turn into a closed lock icon). The locked settings will be applied, but not saved, to any other preset you choose. Click a closed lock icon 🔒 to make those settings editable again. (To unlock all locked settings, choose Reset All Locked Settings from the palette menu.)

9. To save your custom preset, click the **New Brush** button 🗋 at the bottom of the palette or choose **New Brush Preset** from the palette menu, then click OK when the dialog box opens. To learn more about saving and managing brush presets, see pages 462–465.

Customize Brush Preset

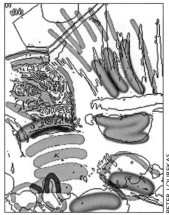

1 *Strokes created with the Brush tool with **Wet Edges** checked*

2 *More **Wet Edges***

3 *Wet Edges **unchecked***

4 *Wet Edges **checked***

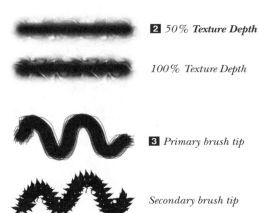

1 *Painting with a **texture** preset with **Pen Pressure** chosen as the Opacity Jitter Control (see the following page)*

2 *50% **Texture Depth***

100% Texture Depth

3 *Primary brush tip*

Secondary brush tip

*Tips combined using **Dual Brush** option with Linear Burn mode*

4 *0% **Foreground/Background Jitter***

100% Foreground/Background Jitter

To customize a brush preset (side dishes):

1. Choose a tool that uses brush presets, and show the **Brushes** palette.

2. To use the texture from a pattern in a brush stroke, on the left side of the palette, click **Texture 1**, then do any of the following:

Click the **Pattern Preset** arrowhead, then click a pattern in the picker.

Check **Invert** to swap the light and dark areas in the pattern.

Change the texture's **Scale** (1–1000%).

Check **Texture Each Tip** to allow the Depth (see below) to vary within each stroke, or uncheck this option to have the Depth value remain constant.

Choose a blending **Mode** to control how the texture mixes with the brush stroke.

Choose a **Depth** value (0–100%) **2** to control how deeply paint sinks into the texture. At a high Depth value, paint will be applied only to the high points in the texture, and the texture will look more prominent.

If you checked Texture Each Tip, you can choose a **Minimum Depth** to keep a texture from appearing too flat. Some brushes reveal texture more than others. Also choose a **Depth Jitter** value to control how much the Depth can vary, and an option from the Control pop-up menu to specify if and how the brush stroke may fade (see page 217).

3. As an added bonus to make the brush preset more interesting, try adding another tip to it. Click **Dual Brush 3**; click a tip; choose a Mode to control how the two tips interact with each other; then choose Diameter, Spacing, Scatter, and Count values.

4. To control how much the color can vary as you use the brush, click **Color Dynamics,** then do any of the following:

Enter a **Foreground/Background Jitter** value **4** for the amount of variation

(Continued on the following page)

Customize Brush Preset

between the Foreground and Background colors. Choose an option from the Control pop-up menu to specify if and how colors can fade.

Enter **Hue Jitter, Saturation Jitter,** and **Brightness Jitter** values to establish variation parameters for those attributes.

Enter a **Purity** value to control how much of the Foreground color can appear in the stroke. The lower the Purity, the grayer the stroke.

TIP To copy the currently chosen texture setting to all the nonpainting tools that have a texture option, check Texture, then choose Copy Texture to Other Tools from the Brushes palette menu.

If you want to make your brush strokes look more painterly or take advantage of the capabilities of a pressure-sensitive tablet, you can specify how the stylus will control such variations as opacity, size, and scatter.

Not all **Control** options work with all types of graphics tablets. For example, some tablet models may not sense the tilt of a stylus (Pen Tilt) or support airbrush devices. The Fade, Initial Direction, and Direction options, on the other hand, work with a mouse or with any other input device.

To customize a brush preset (dessert):

1. Choose a tool that uses brush presets, and show the Brushes palette.

2. To have an attribute vary randomly as you paint with a stylus or other tablet device, choose from the **Control** pop-up menu below any Jitter attribute **1** or below the Scatter attribute. For example, to allow the stylus to control opacity, in the Other Dynamics panel, choose an option from the Control pop-up menu below Opacity Jitter. Not all of these Control options are available for every attribute (read the last tip on the following page):

Off turns off interactive control.

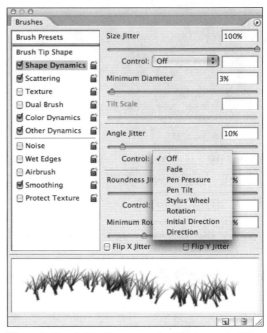

1 In the **Brush Tip Shape** panels, choose a method from the **Control** pop-up menu below any option.

Brush from an image

You can create a brush from existing imagery (be creative!). With the Rectangular Marquee tool, marquee a small area of a picture **1**, preferably a distinct shape on a white background, choose Edit > **Define Brush Preset,** enter a Name, then click OK. The new preset will appear on the Brush Preset picker and the Brushes palette **2**. Adjust any of the settings for the preset via the Brushes palette (e.g., increase the Spacing under Brush Tip Shape or increase the Opacity and Flow Jitter under Other Dynamics).

1 *Select an area of an image.*

Fade decreases the attribute over the length of the stroke, using the number of steps you specify.

Pen Pressure, Pen Tilt, Stylus Wheel, and **Rotation** vary the attribute based on how the stylus is used.

Initial Direction sets the angle of an option based on the direction in which you first drag the brush.

Direction sets the angle of an option based on the direction the mouse is dragged.

TIP To temporarily turn off all the Brush Tip Shape options for the current preset, choose Clear Brush Controls from the Brushes palette menu. If you want to restore the default settings to a saved preset, reselect the preset.

TIP If you choose a Control pop-up menu option that isn't supported by any of the graphics tablet devices that you have connected, this warning icon will appear: ⚠️ If you think an option should be available, double-check that the tablet device is on the tablet and that its driver software is set up correctly.

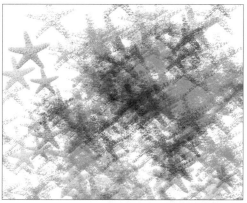

2 *After using the Brush tool to apply strokes with the newly **defined brush,** using a variety of Texture, Size Jitter, and Opacity Jitter settings*

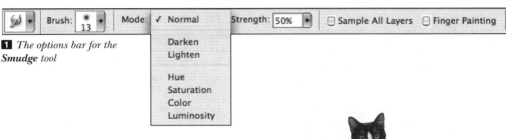

1 *The options bar for the* **Smudge** *tool*

Smudging colors

To smudge colors:

1. Click a layer or the Background.

2. Choose the **Smudge** tool (R or Shift-R).

3. On the options bar **1**, do the following:

   Click a **brush preset** on the Brush Preset picker or Brushes palette.

   Choose a blending **Mode:** Normal smudges all shades or colors; Darken pushes dark colors into lighter colors; Lighten pushes light colors into darker ones; Hue, Saturation, and Color smudge color attributes without changing light and dark values; and Luminosity smudges tonal values without changing colors.

   Choose a **Strength** percentage to control how forcefully the stroke smudges pixels.

   Check **Sample All Layers** to smudge colors found on all the currently visible layers and send the results to the active layer (uncheck Finger Painting if you use this option); or uncheck Sample All Layers to smudge colors from only the active layer.

   To start the smudge with the Foreground color, check **Finger Painting;** or leave Finger Painting unchecked to have the smudge start with the color under the pointer where the stroke begins.

   TIP Hold down Alt/Option to toggle the Finger Painting option on or off.

4. Drag across any area of the image **2**–**5**. Pause between strokes, if necessary, to let the screen redraw.

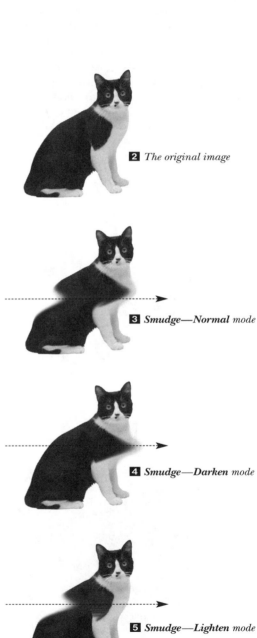

2 *The original image*

3 *Smudge—Normal* mode

4 *Smudge—Darken* mode

5 *Smudge—Lighten* mode

Smudge Tool

1 *The **Eraser** tool options bar*

2 *The original image*

3 *After erasing the tree branches from the top part of the CASTLE layer to reveal part of the CLOUDS layer underneath.*

Erasing

To use the Eraser tool:

1. Click a layer or the Background **2**.

   If Lock Transparent Pixels ▦ is on for the current layer or you clicked the Background instead of a layer, the erased area is going to fill with the current Background color; choose that color now.

   If Lock Transparent Pixels is off for the current layer, the erased area will fill with transparent pixels.

2. Choose the **Eraser** tool (E or Shift-E). 🖊

3. On the options bar **1**, do the following:

   Choose a **brush preset** from the Brush Preset picker or Brushes palette.

   Choose **Mode:** Brush, Pencil, or Block (square eraser).

   Choose an **Opacity** percentage.

   If you chose the Brush mode, you can choose a **Flow** percentage. The lower the Flow percentage, the rougher the erasure stroke.

   Click the **Airbrush** button 🖋 on or off.

4. Click on or drag across any area of the image **3**–**4**.

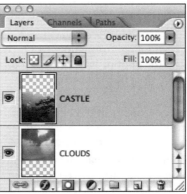

4 *The Layers palette for the final image*

Eraser Tool

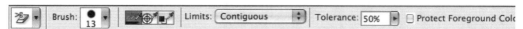

1 *The **Background Eraser** tool options bar*

The **Background Eraser** tool replaces colored pixels with either transparent pixels or the current Background color by dragging. This tool's strength is that you can control several criteria, such as whether the tool erases contiguous or noncontiguous pixels. And by choosing your tool settings carefully, you can control which colors are erased.

To use the Background Eraser tool:

1. Click a layer or the Background.

2. Choose the **Background Eraser** tool (it has a scissors icon)(E or Shift-E).

3. Click a **brush preset** on the Brush Preset picker or Brushes palette.

4. On the options bar **1**, click a **Sampling** button:

   NEW

   Continuous to replace all the colors you drag across with transparent pixels, within the current Tolerance range.

   Once to replace with transparent pixels only the pixels that closely match the first one you click on. To erase a flat, solid color, choose this option and make the Tolerance 1%.

   Background Swatch to erase only pixels that match the current Background color. Choose a Background color and a low Tolerance when using this option.

5. To control which pixels can be erased, click the Sampling: Contiguous or Once button on the options bar, then from the **Limits** pop-up menu, choose one of the following:

   Discontiguous to erase all pixels within the current Tolerance range, whether they're adjacent to one another or not.

   Contiguous to erase adjacent pixels only within the current Tolerance range that match the first pixel you click on.

2 *With **Find Edges** chosen from the **Limits** pop-up menu for the **Background Eraser** tool on the options bar, the tool successfully erased parts of the background area on this document.*

1 *The original image*

*Find Edges, Once,
Tolerance 18,
Brush size 45*

*Contiguous, Once,
Tolerance 40,
Brush size 65*

2 *After using the*
Background Eraser *tool with
various options bar settings*

*Contiguous, Once,
Tolerance 18,
Brush size 45*

Find Edges to erase some contiguous pixels while preserving object edges (high-contrast borders) (**2**, previous page).

6. Choose a **Tolerance** percentage to control how much the colors to be erased can differ from the first color you click.

7. *Optional:* To protect a solid, flat color from erasure, check Protect Foreground Color. In the document window, Alt-click/Option-click the color you want to protect, then press X to switch the current Foreground and Background colors.

   TIP For greater control, we recommend using Select > Color Range to select specific color areas.

8. Drag in the document window **1**–**2**.

TIP If you're using a pressure-sensitive tablet, you can set the brush size and tolerance to respond to pen pressure. Click the Brush Preset picker thumbnail, then set these options on the pop-up palette.

Background Eraser Tool

1 *The Magic Eraser tool options bar*

Magic Eraser Tool

With the **Magic Eraser,** you erase by clicking with the mouse—not by dragging. The tool erases pixels that are similar in color to the pixel you click on, within a user-defined Tolerance range. This tool also lets you make areas of a layer semitransparent.

To use the Magic Eraser tool:

1. Click a layer or the Background.

2. Choose the **Magic Eraser** tool (E or Shift-E).

3. On the options bar **1**, do the following:

   Choose a **Tolerance** value. The higher the Tolerance, the wider the range of colors that can be erased. Enter a low Tolerance if you want to erase only colors that are very similar to the color you click on; enter 0 to erase only one color.

   Check **Anti-alias** to soften the edges of the erased area.

   Check **Contiguous** to erase only pixels that are adjacent to one another, or uncheck this option to erase similarly colored pixels throughout the layer.

   Check **Sample All Layers** to erase colors found on all the currently visible layers; or uncheck this option to erase colors found on only the current layer.

   Choose an **Opacity** percentage. Enter 100% to replace colored pixels with transparent ones, or a lower opacity to replace with semitransparent pixels.

4. In the document window, click the area that you want to erase **2**–**4**. If the brush isn't a crosshair, press Caps Lock; it will be easier to position the pointer.

   If the erasure is too large or too small, undo, change the Tolerance value on the Magic Eraser tool options bar, then click again in the document window.

2 *The original image*

3 *Clicking the sky with the **Magic Eraser** tool, Tolerance of 30*

4 *Clicking the sky on the original image with the **Magic Eraser** tool, Tolerance of 10*

CAMERA RAW 15

New chapter!

Is my camera supported?

Of the many proprietary Raw file formats, some are unique to a particular manufacturer (e.g., Nikon, Canon) and some are unique to a particular camera model. To make sure you're using all the latest **interpreters** for the Raw formats that are supported by Camera Raw, periodically visit www.adobe.com and download any Camera Raw updates.

THE TOPICS COVERED IN THIS CHAPTER and the next four chapters will be of special interest to photographers: Importing images in Raw format, correcting photos for exposure and lighting deficiencies, retouching (e.g., removing noise and red-eye), creating vignettes, merging and framing images, and creating contact sheets.

In this chapter you'll learn how to open Raw digital photos via the Camera Raw dialog box. We'll try to break this big topic into digestible chunks.

Raw format photos

The digital cameras used by amateurs and consumers automatically store images in the JPEG format, whereas the cameras used by pros and advanced amateurs offer the option to save images in the **Raw** format, which has substantial advantages. (See our comparison of JPEG versus Raw on page 235.)

1 *The Camera Raw dialog box*

When a digital camera stores an image in a format other than Raw, it also performs processing operations, such as sharpening, white balance setting, and color adjustment. With Raw files, you get only the raw information that the lens captured onto its light sensors, so you have full control over subsequent image processing and correction. Photographs in the Raw format from most digital camera models can be processed through the Camera Raw dialog box **1**.

You can access the **Camera Raw** dialog box via Bridge or via Photoshop to open your Raw files, and, if desired, correct any deficiencies in your photos caused by unsatisfactory shooting conditions. Once opened in Photoshop, copies of your Raw files can be saved in any file format **2**; the original Raw files, like traditional film negatives, are left unchanged.

2 *After opening and saving the image in Photoshop*

(Continued on the following page)

Raw Format Photos

Via the Camera Raw dialog box, you can save your custom adjustment settings to a user-created file and apply those settings to subsequently opened photos (say, from the same shoot) that require the same corrections. In fact, a settings file can be applied to multiple images right in Bridge via batch processing (see page 235).

You can also make the current settings become the default settings used by Camera Raw for other photos that are captured by the same camera model.

The **rudimentary** steps for opening Raw files via the **Camera Raw** dialog box are outlined here.

NEW **To open a Raw file via the Camera Raw command:**

1. In Bridge, click a Raw image thumbnail. Note that different digital cameras attach different file extensions to Raw files, such as **.nef** for Nikon, **.crw** for Canon, and **.dcr** for Kodak. Raw files that have already been opened and edited in the Camera Raw dialog box will have this icon below the thumbnail ▓. Press Ctrl-R/Cmd-R to open the image.

2. The **Camera Raw** dialog box opens (**1**, next page). An alert symbol will display in the upper right of the preview window while the image data is being read in, and will disappear once all the data is read. In the title bar across the top of the dialog box, you'll see information about your photo, such as the camera model; the file name; and the camera metadata settings (ISO sensitivity, shutter speed, aperture setting, and focal length) that were used to capture the photograph.

NEW Wend your way through the five tabs and their corresponding panels on the right side of the dialog box (**Adjust,**

Getting to Camera Raw **NEW**

The Bridge Preferences dialog box controls whether the currently selected file opens in the Camera Raw dialog box from Bridge or Photoshop. In Bridge, choose Edit (Bridge, in Mac) > Preferences (Ctrl-K/ Cmd-K). Click Advanced on the left side, and note the status of the **Double-Click edits Camera Raw settings in Bridge** option. If this option is checked and you double-click a Raw file thumbnail in Bridge (or choose File > Open), the file will open into the Camera Raw dialog box from Bridge. With this option unchecked, you must press Ctrl-R/Cmd-R to open the selected file into Camera Raw from Bridge, or double-click the thumbnail to have the file open into Camera Raw in Photoshop.

Whether the preference option is on or off, **Ctrl-R/ Cmd-R** always opens the selected file into Camera Raw from Bridge, and in Photoshop, choosing File > Open and selecting a Raw photo file always opens the selected file into Camera Raw in Photoshop.

To learn about the Open a Copy option in the Camera Raw dialog box, see page 234.

Detail, Lens, Curve, and **Calibrate**), using the white balance, exposure, sharpening, color noise reduction, and other controls to correct your photo (see pages 228–233). The Camera Raw tools are discussed on pages 226–227.

The **Settings** pop-up menu lists predefined Camera Raw settings that can be applied to the Raw file (see page 234).

3. When you're satisfied with the way the image looks, click Open. Photoshop will process the image using your chosen settings and open it as a new file, leaving the original Raw file data untouched.

TIP Don't confuse the Photoshop Raw file format with the Raw format used by digital cameras.

When two or more Raw files are selected and **NEW** opened via Bridge or via the Open dialog box in Photoshop, the thumbnails display in the **filmstrip** panel on the left side of the Camera Raw dialog box. Click a thumbnail to work with that file.

1 *The **Camera Raw** dialog box, with the image preview and image attributes in the middle, and a histogram and controls on the right*

The labels on the Save and Open buttons change when more than one Raw file is opened.

To use the Camera Raw tools:

In the toolbox in the upper left corner of the dialog box, click the **Zoom** tool (Z), 🔍 then click the preview to zoom in or Alt-click/Option-click to zoom out.

Choose a preset zoom percentage (6–400%) or Fit in View from the **Zoom Level** pop-up menu below the image preview, or click the – or + zoom level button.

If the image preview is magnified, you can use the **Hand** tool (H) 🖐 to move the image in the preview window.

TIP Double-click the Zoom tool to change the zoom level to 100%, or double-click the Hand tool to change the zoom level to Fit in View.

For information about the **White Balance** tool see page 228.

NEW Choose the **Color Sampler** tool (S), 🖋 then click on the image preview to place up to four samplers. A breakdown of the RGB color components for pixels at that location will display below the tool area. The readouts will update to reflect new color breakdowns as color and tonal adjustments are made to the image. To reposition a sampler, choose the Color Sampler tool, position the tip of the eyedropper pointer over the sampler circle, then drag. To remove all samplers, click Clear Samplers.

TIP In the upper right of the dialog box is a breakdown of the **RGB** color components for the pixel directly under the cursor.

NEW To control which portion of the image will open in Photoshop, choose the **Crop** tool (C), 🔲 then drag a marquee on the preview image **1**. Pixels within the marquee will import; areas covered with the gray shield will not. To move the marquee, drag inside it; to resize the marquee, drag a handle.

TIP You can go back and readjust the crop marquee at any time, as it remains available even after you click Save, Done, or Open, and none of the Raw pixels are ever deleted. If you want to remove the crop marquee from the Raw file, with the Crop tool selected, press Esc.

Switcheroos

Hold down the following keys to change the function of buttons in the **Camera Raw** dialog box:

Alt/Option	Cancel becomes **Reset,** which restores the original dialog box settings
	Save... becomes **Save,** which bypasses the Save Options dialog box
Alt/Option	Changes the Hand tool to a temporary **zoom out** tool
Ctrl/Cmd	Changes the Hand tool to a temporary **zoom in** tool
Spacebar	Changes any tool into a temporary **Hand** tool

1 *Cropping* a photo in the preview window of the Camera Raw dialog box

Camera Raw Tools

1 *A marquee is drawn around part of a photograph with the **Straighten** tool in the Camera Raw dialog box*

To straighten out a crooked photo, choose **NEW** the **Straighten** tool (A), ✍ then drag horizontally or vertically across the preview **1**. A crop marquee will display, aligned to the angle you drew. When the Raw image is opened in Photoshop, the edges of the image will be aligned with the horizontal and vertical edges of the document window.

Click the ↺ button (L) to **rotate** the image 90° counterclockwise or the ↻ button (R) to rotate it 90° clockwise. The rotation will preview in the dialog box.

Check **Preview** (P) to preview the current color and tonal settings; uncheck it to see the original "as shot" image.

For the **Shadows** and **Highlights** options, **NEW** which indicate clipping, see page 229.

The **Workflow options** include color space, dimensions, bit depth, and resolution. They apply to the image that will be opened in Photoshop, not to the original Raw file.

To assign a color space, dimensions, bit depth, and resolution:

1. At the bottom of the Camera Raw dialog box, check **Show Workflow Options.**

2. From the **Space** pop-up menu, choose the color space profile to be used for the file in Photoshop: **Adobe RGB (1998), ColorMatch RGB, ProPhoto RGB,** or **sRGB IEC61966-1** (see page 45).

3. If you need to resize the image, from the **Size** pop-up menu, choose one of the five preset sizes (in megapixels) that match the proportions of your Raw image. (The default image size has no – or + after it.) Choosing a size larger than the original will cause resampling. If a crop marquee is present, the crop size will be the default size.

4. From the **Depth** pop-up menu, choose a color depth of 8 Bits/Channel or 16 Bits/Channel (see page 55). You need a fast system with a lot of RAM to work with 16 Bits/Channel files.

5. Specify a **Resolution.** This value affects only the print output size of the image.

Next, you'll adjust the preview image by choosing settings in the **Adjust, Detail, Lens,** and **Calibrate** panels of the Camera Raw dialog box. These adjustments are stored in a settings file and are applied to the image when it's opened in Photoshop.

Using the Adjust panel

As you choose settings in the **Adjust** panel, keep an eye on the **histogram** to monitor changes in the distribution of tonal values in your photo . The histogram is a graph of the red, green, and blue pixels, superimposed upon one another, with shadow pixels on the left side and highlights on the right. (For more about histograms, see pages 172–173.)

To make white balance and tonal adjustments to a Raw file:

1. Click the **Adjust** tab **2**, and choose the Fit in View zoom level for the preview.

2. To adjust the white balance, or color temperature, in the photo:

   On the **White Balance** pop-up menu, leave the setting of As Shot if you're satisfied with the white balance as recorded by the camera, or choose a preset setting that best describes the lighting conditions when the photo was taken: Auto, Daylight, Cloudy, Shade, Tungsten, Fluorescent, Flash, or Custom. *or*
   To adjust the color temperature of the lighting in the overall picture based on a sampled area, choose the **White Balance tool** (I), ✐ then click a neutral white area in the photo (an area that was neutral white in the original scene). If you can't figure out which area to click on (it's tricky), use the next method instead. *or*
   To correct the color temperature in a more straightforward way (and with greater control), move the **Temperature** slider to the left to add blue to cool the colors, or to the right to add yellow to warm them (values are shown in the

1 *The **histogram** in the Camera Raw dialog box charts the number of pixels at each tonal level in a photo for the red, green, and blue color components.*

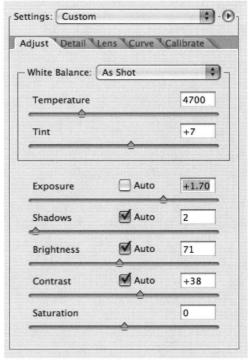

2 *Use the **Adjust** panel in the Camera Raw dialog box to apply color and tonal adjustments.*

3 *The **highlight clipping color** is evident in this image.*

1 *Alt-drag/Option-drag the **Exposure** slider until only a minimum of white shows.*

2 *Alt-drag/Option-drag the **Shadows** slider until only a minimum of black shows.*

Kelvin color temperature scale). Drag the **Tint** slider to the left (–) to add green or to the right (+) to add magenta.

3. For Exposure, Shadows, Brightness, and Contrast, you can check **Auto** to let Camera Raw determine the proper set-ting, or you can follow steps 4–7 to make the adjustments yourself. **NEW**

4. As you move the Exposure and Shadows sliders, your goal is to brighten or darken the image and to minimize clip-ping (see the sidebar on the next page). As you move the sliders, keep an eye on the histogram for any highlight or shadow pixels that are pushed to the extreme edge of the graph (clipped).

Just to get acquainted with the **Exposure** slider, move it to the right to lighten the image, or to the left to darken it.

Move the **Shadows** slider to the right to darken the darkest areas in the image.

5. To minimize pixel clipping, at the top of the dialog box, check **Shadows** (U) to turn on the Shadow clipping warning and check **Highlights** (O) to turn on the Highlight clipping warning **1**. Move the Exposure slider until only a trace remains of the red highlight warning color, and move the Shadows slider until only a trace remains of the blue shadow warning color. **NEW**
or
Alt-drag/Option-drag the **Exposure** slider and let go when tiny bits of white (representing pure white highlight val-ues) display in the black preview **2**; the color areas represent highlight pixels that are being clipped. Alt-drag/Option-drag the **Shadows** slider and let go when tiny bits of color (representing pure black shadow values) are left in the white preview **3**; the black areas represent shadow pixels that are being clipped.

TIP The Exposure slider in the Camera Raw dialog box works like the white Input slider in the Levels dialog box;

(Continued on the following page)

Adjust Panel

the Shadow slider works like the black Input slider in the Levels dialog box. These sliders control the amount of brightness in the highlights and shadows.

6. Move the **Brightness** slider to make the image brighter or darker overall.

7. Move the **Contrast** slider to the left to reduce contrast or to the right to increase it.

8. Move the **Saturation** slider. At +100 (far right), the Saturation slider will double the color saturation; at –100 (far left), it will convert the image to grayscale. Don't raise the Saturation levels too much, or you're likely to push the image colors beyond the gamut of your output device (see page 34), or produce onscreen colors that look unnatural.

Doing the lingo

The color temperature of a light source determines the amounts of red, green, and blue recorded in the image. A digital camera uses a technique called **white balance** to balance red, green, and blue in the image to create an accurate white. This initial in-camera adjustment becomes the basis for adjusting other colors in the image.

In the Camera Raw dialog box, we recommend using the White Balance controls to correct the overall color temperature and color tint in the photograph before making any other color adjustments. Unless you're aiming for a special effect, try to make the image look as natural as possible.

Clipping occurs when pixel values that are recorded by the camera extend beyond the range of tonal values (lights and darks) that can be displayed and printed. Pixels in these extended areas will be recorded as pure white and black, and detail from these areas will be lost (or "clipped").

Specular highlights are bright spots of light that appear on shiny, reflective surfaces. When using the Exposure slider to adjust brightness in the highlights, don't base the adjustment on specular highlights; they're meant to remain as pure white areas with no details.

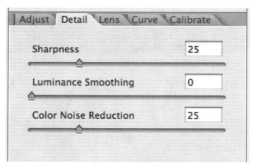

1 *Choose settings in the **Detail** panel of the Camera Raw dialog box.*

Using the Detail panel

Use options in the **Detail** panel to make sharpness, smoothing, and noise adjustments to an image.

To make detail adjustments to a Raw file:

1. Click the **Detail** tab **1**, and choose a zoom level of 100% for the preview.

2. Move the **Sharpness** slider to control edge definition in the image. If you plan to further edit the image in Photoshop, we recommend moving this slider to zero (no sharpening) and using a sharpening filter in Photoshop instead, such as our new favorite, Smart Sharpen.

3. All digital cameras produce some undesirable noise, such as visible artifacts and stray pixels. Low-quality cameras or high ISO (light sensitivity) settings produce the most noise, and it's most noticeable on solid-color surfaces. Noise should be removed before opening the file in Photoshop, as it can become accentuated by image editing. To reduce noise throughout all the tonal levels of the image, move the **Luminance Smoothing** slider slightly to the right.

   The more you sharpen the image, the more luminance smoothing is required.

4. Finally, move the **Color Noise Reduction** slider to the right to eliminate color artifacts from dark areas in the image.

   The effect of the Luminance Smoothing and Color Noise Reduction sliders tends to be more pronounced when the Sharpness value is increased.

TIP If you're not going to apply sharpening to your photos in Camera Raw but you do want to preview how sharpening would affect the image, choose Preferences on the Camera Raw plug-in menu, ⊙ and in the Camera Raw Preferences dialog box, choose "Apply sharpening to: Preview images only."

Detail Panel

Next, we'll discuss some advanced features: Lens optics correction, curve adjustments to tone, and hue/saturation calibration (some QuickStart, huh?).

Using the Lens panel

The **Lens** sliders help to correct for optical distortion caused by wide-angle or telephoto lenses. The Chromatic Aberration sliders resize specific color channels to remove fringes along the edges of high-contrast areas; the **Vignetting** sliders help to correct for over- or underexposure near the edges of a photograph.

To make lens adjustments to a Raw file:

1. Click the **Lens** tab, then do any of the following steps.

2. For **Chromatic Aberration** (that's a mouthful!):

NEW Move the **Fix Red/Cyan Fringe** slider to the left to remove a red fringe from high-contrast edges **1**–**2**, or to the right to remove a cyan fringe.

Move the **Fix Blue/Yellow Fringe** slider to the right to remove a blue fringe from high-contrast edges, or to the left to remove a yellow fringe.

We've found these sliders to be helpful for correcting landscape photos in which a light sky contrasts with trees and other foliage.

3. For **Vignetting:**

Move the **Amount** slider to the left to softly darken the outer border of the photo, or to the right to softly lighten it.

Move the **Midpoint** slider to the left to move the vignette effect inward toward the center of the photo, or to the right to move the effect outward to the edges.

NEW You can use the **Curve** panel to adjust lightness and contrast in a photograph. Choose a preset curve from the **Tone Curve** pop-up menu, or adjust the curve manually, employing the same techniques that you'd use in the Curves dialog box (see page 206).

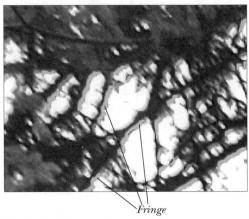

1 *The dark branches have a red fringe along the edges, which is visible against the light sky color.*

2 *Moving the Fix Red/Cyan Fringe slider in the Lens panel to the left made the red fringe disappear.*

Profile 2.4 or 3.0? NEW

The Camera Profile pop-up menu in the **Calibrate** panel lists the available Camera Raw (ARC) profile versions for the camera model that captured the photo. If the camera hasn't had a profile upgrade, only version **2.4** will be listed. If versions 2.4 and 3.0 are listed, you can choose 2.4 (say, if you've already created settings for that version) or the newer version, **3.0**.

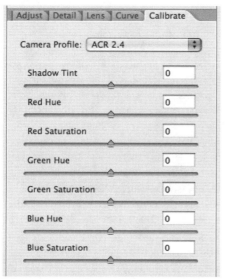

1 *Using the **Calibrate** panel in the Camera Raw dialog box, you can correct color casts.*

2 *The **Save Settings Subset** dialog box lets you specify which settings will be saved to a separate file.*

Correcting color casts

Sometimes discrepancies between the color profile used by a particular camera model and the built-in color profile that Camera Raw uses for that model may result in photos having a **color cast.** Color casts can be corrected via the hue and saturation sliders in the **Calibrate** tab panel.

To correct a color cast:

1. Click the **Calibrate** tab, and choose Fit in View as the zoom level **1**.

2. If the color cast is only in the shadow areas, move just the **Shadow Tint** slider to the left to add green to the shadow areas, or to the right to add magenta to those areas.

3. In small increments, move the **Saturation** sliders to the left to reduce saturation, or to the right to increase saturation; and/or move the **Hue** sliders to shift red, green, or blue to another hue.

Saving settings

Now that you've made custom adjustments to your photo, you can **save** your adjustments as a separate custom **settings** file. Then you'll be able to apply them to other photos via the Settings pop-up menu (say, to correct multiple images shot at the same scene).

To save Camera Raw settings:

1. With your corrected image open, choose **Save Settings** from the Camera Raw plug-in menu. ► Enter a name, leave the location as the Settings folder, then click Save.
   or
   To choose which settings are saved to the settings file, choose **Save Settings Subset** from the Camera Raw plug-in menu. In the Save Settings Subset dialog box **2**, check which settings you want saved, click Save, enter a name (leave the location as is), then click Save again.

2. *Optional:* To have the current settings become the default settings in Camera Raw for the currently listed camera model, choose Save New Camera Raw Defaults from the plug-in menu.

Opening the Camera Raw file

At last, the moment you've been waiting for.

To open a Camera Raw file:

Once you've chosen all the settings you're going to choose in the Camera Raw dialog box, click **Open** to open the corrected Raw file in Photoshop (or click **Done** to close the Raw file). Whether you click Open or Done, the current settings will be saved with the Raw file, either as part of the internal Camera Raw database in your system or as a hidden sidecar ".xmp" file in the same folder as the Raw file. To control where the settings file is saved, choose Preferences from the Camera Raw plug-in menu ⊙ (Ctrl-K/Cmd-K), then choose an option from the **Save image settings in** pop-up menu. This internal file is different from the user-created settings file that you created via the Save Settings command, accessed from the Camera Raw plug-in menu.

or

If you opened the Camera Raw dialog box from Photoshop, you can hold down **NEW** Alt/Option and click **Open a Copy.** This opens the Raw file in Photoshop with the current settings applied, without recording the settings in the Raw file's metadata. This way, the Raw file keeps its original Camera Raw settings, if any.

File conversion **NEW**

If you want to rename Raw files and convert them to the **DNG** (digital negative, or .dng), **JPEG, TIFF,** or **Photoshop** format without having to open them in Photoshop, in the Camera Raw dialog box, click Save; the **Save Options** dialog box opens.

DNG is an open-standard Raw format that preserves all the unprocessed pixel information as recorded by the camera. A wide range of hardware devices and software applications can read DNG files.

Return to Camera Raw

When you initially open a file in the Camera Raw dialog box, by default, the built-in profile created for the current camera model is used to adjust settings. To quickly assign a different collection of settings to a file, you can choose a preset from the **Settings** pop-up menu below the histogram:

➤ **Image Settings** to restore settings attached to the Raw file from either the initial photo shoot or a prior Camera Raw session.

➤ **Camera Raw Defaults** to remove any custom settings and reapply the built-in default settings for the current camera model.

➤ **Previous Conversion** to apply the settings from the last Raw image you adjusted.

➤ **Custom** to reapply any settings that you created during the current Camera Raw session.

➤ **User-created settings** to apply settings saved in a prior Camera Raw session to a group of photos that require the same type of correction.

Batch-processing files

The Settings presets (including any user-created settings) listed on the Settings pop-up menu in the Camera Raw dialog box are also accessible in **Bridge.**

To apply settings to multiple files: NEW

In Bridge, Shift-click or Ctrl-click/Cmd-click multiple Raw file thumbnails, then from the Edit > **Apply Camera Raw Settings** submenu, choose a preset settings file **1**. The settings will be attached to the selected files.
or
Click the thumbnail for a Raw file that contains the desired settings, choose Edit > Apply Camera Raw Settings > **Copy Camera Raw Settings,** click one or more Raw file thumbnails, then choose Edit > Apply Camera Raw Settings > **Paste Camera Raw Settings.**

1 *In* **Bridge,** *you can apply saved Camera Raw settings to* **multiple** *files simultaneously.*

JPEG versus Raw

JPEG pros

JPEG file sizes are smaller, so more of them can be stored in a digital camera.

JPEG files have shorter transfer speeds, so digital cameras create and store them faster than Raw files. This allows for faster shot sequencing (important for sports, nature, and other quick-motion photography).

Most software programs can read JPEG files.

JPEG cons

JPEG compression methods lower image quality; the greater the compression, the greater the loss. High compression levels produce pronounced side effects, such as artifacts, banding, and loss of detail, rendering photos unusable for high-end professional work.

Cameras that process and save photos as JPEG perform image-processing operations that alter the original pixel data. Although you can reprocess and readjust your photos in Photoshop, you can't retrieve the original pixel data.

Raw pros

Raw compression methods are lossless.

Raw files can be opened in 16-bit mode in Photoshop.

Raw files maintain a wider range of tonal levels even after being edited and adjusted.

Raw preserves the image's original pixel information.

You don't have to worry about the white point setting when shooting, as it can be adjusted in Camera Raw.

Raw con

Digital cameras create and store Raw files more slowly than JPEG files.

The bottom line

Although JPEG offers advantages in speed, we believe the reasons for using Raw are far more compelling.

NEW Raw photos as smart objects

What if you want to put a Raw camera file into a Photoshop document while preserving the ability to readjust it in the Camera Raw dialog box? No problem, just place the photo in your Photoshop document as a **smart object.**

To convert a Raw format file into a smart object:

1. Open a Photoshop document.

2. In Bridge, select a Raw photo thumbnail.

3. Choose File > Place > **In Photoshop.** The Camera Raw dialog box opens.

4. Make any adjustments to the photo, if desired, then click Open. It will appear on its own layer in the currently active Photoshop document **1**, within a transform box.

5. Make any desired transformations, then press Enter/Return or click the Commit transform checkmark ✔ on the options bar to accept the placed image; it's now a smart object layer.

   You can double-click the smart object layer image thumbnail at any time to reopen an embedded copy of the Raw file in the Camera Raw dialog box, make any desired adjustments, then click Done to apply your changes to the already placed file. The original Raw file is unaffected by settings changes you make to the embedded smart object. To learn more about smart objects, see pages 313–314.

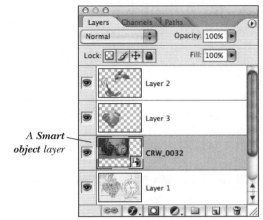

*A **Smart object** layer*

1 *When placed into a Photoshop document, a Raw format photo becomes a **smart object,** capable of being reedited in Camera Raw.*

EXPOSURE 16

New chapter!

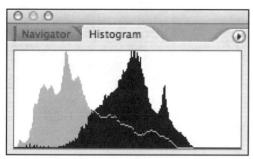

1 *As you make adjustments using the **Shadow/ Highlight** command, no gaps or spikes display on the Histogram palette—confirmation that all the existing tonal ranges in the image are preserved.*

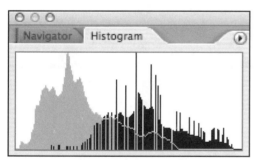

2 *As adjustments are made using the **Levels** command, gaps and spikes do appear on the Histogram palette—a sign that pixel data from those tonal ranges are being deleted.*

THE FIRST STEP AFTER OPENING A photograph in Photoshop is to take a few minutes to study it. Does it have any overall deficiencies or problems? Is it over- or underexposed? Does it have a color cast? (Does it look ghostly blue? Sickly green?) There are a number of commands that you can use to rectify these kinds of problems.

If you captured the photo in the Raw format, you were able to apply many critical corrections via the Camera Raw plug-in. For scanned images or photos captured in other formats, though, you may need to apply exposure corrections. In this chapter, you'll perform shadow and highlight corrections; modify the color temperature due to improper lighting; correct over- or underexposed photos by rebalancing light and dark values; remove noise from shadow areas; compensate for the failure to use a flash; achieve a wide dynamic range by merging multiple exposures of the same subject into one; and apply lighting effects.

Using the Shadow/Highlight command

The **Shadow/Highlight** command is a shining star in Photoshop's arsenal of adjustment tools because it's "smart." It recognizes the tonal boundaries of individual objects within an image when making calculations, and adjusts the luminance of each individual pixel depending on the darkness or lightness of neighboring pixels. It performs corrections in specified tonal ranges without unduly altering other areas of the image, and can prove to be invaluable, say, for increasing contrast in shadows and highlights or correcting overexposed and underexposed areas, such as subjects that may be in shadow as a result of strong side or backlighting.

(Continued on the following page)

Because **Shadow/Highlight** preserves the full range of tonal values, it's superior to the Levels and Curves commands, which discard pixel data. This can be verified by viewing the Histogram palette while using any one of the three commands (**1**–**2** previous page). And by letting you pinpoint the tonal ranges that need adjusting, Shadow/Highlight saves you from having to use layers or masks in conjunction with a command such as Curves or Levels.

The Shadow/Highlight command works with CMYK, RGB, LAB, Grayscale, and Duotone image files, and with 8-bit and 16-bit files, but not with Bitmap, Indexed Color, or Multichannel files. Also, it can't be applied via an adjustment layer. We tend not to fill our books with superlatives, but we can't praise this feature enough!

To apply the Shadow/Highlight command:

1. Click a layer or the Background **1**, and display the Histogram palette so you can monitor tonal adjustments.

2. Choose Image > Adjustments > **Shadow/Highlight.**

3. For the **Shadows 2**, choose an **Amount** percentage to control how much you want pixels to be lightened in the shadow areas. The default setting of 50% will compensate reasonably well for underexposure in the shadow areas of many images. Increase this value (but not to 100%) for stronger shadow correction, such as foreground subjects that are darkened by strong backlighting, and to extend those corrections into the midtone and highlight areas. A Shadow setting of 0%, like a straight line in the Curves dialog box, produces no change to the image.

4. For the **Highlights,** choose an **Amount** to establish how much you want the highlight areas of the image to be darkened (0% produces no darkening). Lowering the brightness of the highlights will allow the midtones to stand out more.

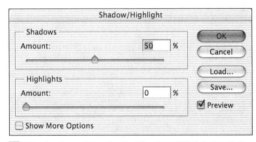

1 *The midtones and shadows in the bottom portion of this image are dark and murky; it's hard to see any details there.*

2 *The basic settings in the **Shadow/Highlight** dialog box*

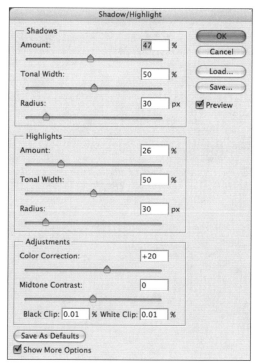

1 *The Shadow/Highlight dialog box with* **Show More Options** *checked offers—well, more options.*

2 *Shadow/Highlight corrections improved the tonal range in the overall image, preserved dark values (and contrast), and restored details to the midtones and shadows.*

5. Uncheck, then recheck Preview to compare the original to the adjusted image.

6. *Optional:* Check **Show More Options** **1**:

The higher the **Tonal Width** value, the wider the range of midtones (adjacent to the shadow or highlight areas) that will be affected.

The higher the **Radius** value (in pixels), the larger the area of neighboring pixels that will be compared to a specific pixel in a shadow or highlight area to produce the adjustment. Too high a value may actually reduce contrast because too many pixels will be compared, thus minimizing any adjustment.

TIP If too high a Tonal Width or Radius value is chosen, midtone areas may develop an unreal glow, or halos, around the edges.

If increasing the Shadows: Amount slider caused oversaturation, you can move the **Color Correction** slider to the left to reduce the saturation.

Move the **Midtone Contrast** slider to the right to increase contrast in the midtones, or to the left to decrease contrast in the midtones.

7. *Optional:* To save your Shadow/Highlight adjustment settings, click Save, enter a name (keep the .shh extension), choose a location, then click Save again. To load previously saved settings, click Load.

8. Click OK **2**.

TIP To restore the original settings in the dialog box while it's still open, hold down Alt/Option and click Reset.

Shadow/Highlight Command

Using the Photo Filter command

Photographers use colored lens filters to make a shot look warmer or cooler (change the color temperature). The **Photo Filter** command simulates the effect of using camera lens filters (cheaper than having to buy them!). You can choose one of the 18 preset filter tints or choose your own color via the Color Picker, and best of all, you can apply the command via an adjustment layer. When using this feature, go for subtle or extreme, but not in between.

To apply the Photo Filter command:

1. Click a layer or the Background.

2. Choose Image > Adjustments > **Photo Filter.**
   or
   From the New Fill/Adjustment Layer pop-up menu ⬤. at the bottom of the Layers palette, choose **Photo Filter.**

3. Make sure Preview is checked **1**.

4. Click **Filter,** then from the pop-up menu, choose a warming or cooling filter or a preset filter color. The color you choose will appear in the swatch.
   or
   Click the **Color** swatch to open the Color Picker, choose a color for the filter, then click OK.

5. Move the **Density** slider to choose an opacity percentage for the tint. Of course, if you're using an adjustment layer for this command, the layer opacity can also be adjusted after you click OK.

6. Check **Preserve Luminosity** to preserve the overall brightness and tonal range of the image. If you leave this option unchecked, the creditors will come knocking on your door.

7. Uncheck, then recheck Preview to compare the original to the adjusted image, then click OK.

TIP To restore the original settings in the dialog box while it's still open, hold down Alt/Option and click Reset.

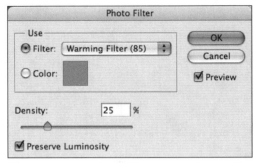

1 *You can use the **Photo Filter** command to simulate the effect of using a camera lens filter.*

1 *The original **over-exposed** image*

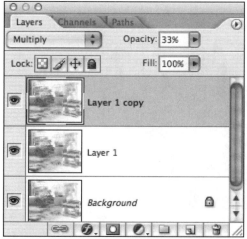

2 *The **Layers** palette with two duplicate layers, both set to **Multiply** blending mode. The topmost layer has an Opacity of 33%.*

3 *The exposure **corrected***

Correction via Layers palette

Here's an easy way to correct over- or under-exposed photos using only our old friend the **Layers palette.** It's not the most precise method in the world, but hey, if it works, it works (and if it makes your art director happy, maybe you can go home early).

To correct over- or underexposed images via the Layers palette:

1. Open an overexposed or underexposed photo **1**.

2. Drag the Background (or layer) over the New Layer button at the bottom of the Layers palette to duplicate the layer.
   or
   Click the Background (or layer), then press Ctrl-J/Cmd-J to duplicate it.

3. With the duplicate layer selected, choose a blending mode from the Layers palette, such as **Multiply** to darken an overexposed image or **Screen** to lighten an underexposed image.

4. If the image is still too light or dark, keep duplicating the topmost duplicate layer.

5. Eventually, you'll reach Nirvana—actually, you'll reach a point where you've overcorrected the image and you need to step back a bit. Lower the Opacity of the topmost layer **2** until the exposure is just where you need it to be.

6. Choose a merge or flatten command from the Layers palette menu to merge all the duplicate layers into the Background (or layer) **3**.

NEW Removing noise

Shooting photos with a digital camera at a high ISO setting produces noticeable "digital noise" in the shadows, but—good news—you can use the new **Reduce Noise** filter to remove it. JPEG photos can be improved with this command, too.

To remove digital noise from shadow areas:

1. *Optional:* To better judge the "noise level" in the image , make the zoom level 200%, then with the Hand tool, move the image around in the window and inspect the shadow areas for stray red, green, or blue dots.

1 *A detail of the original, very noisy image*

2. Choose Filter > Noise > **Reduce Noise** .

3. Make sure Preview is checked. You can click in the document window to make that area appear in the preview window.

4. Click **Basic,** and examine the result in the preview as you choose a **Strength** value (5 or 6), and **Preserve Details** and **Reduce Color Noise** values (around 60%).

5. Click **Advanced,** then click the **Per Channel** tab. Choose a channel from the **Channel** pop-up menu, then choose a **Strength** value of around 3 (leave the Preserve Details value at around 60%). Repeat for the other channels.

   TIP For a portrait photo, try these settings: Red Channel 3, Green 2, Blue 0.

2 *The **Reduce Noise** filter dialog box with the **Advanced** option chosen, and the **Overall** panel in front*

6. Click the **Overall** tab, then choose a **Sharpen Details** value of 10–15%. If you overdo the sharpening, the surface texture will become pixelated. If this happens, lower the Sharpen Details value.

7. *Optional:* To save the current Basic and Advanced settings, click the Save a Copy button, 💾 enter a name, then click OK. User-saved settings can be chosen from the Settings pop-up menu for any image.

8. Click OK **3**.

   TIP A flashing line appears below the zoom percentage level or the Preview checkbox while the dialog and document window previews, respectively, are rendering.

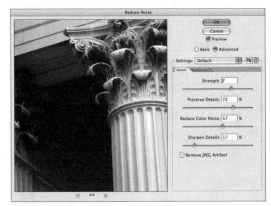

3 *After applying **Reduce Noise** corrections*

1 *The original image*

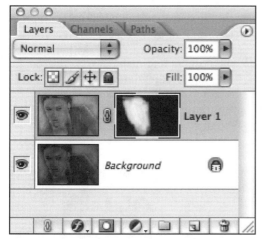

2 *Brush strokes are added to an adjustment layer to achieve dodge effects.*

©www.photospin.com

3 *The corrected image. Actually, she still looks like she's having a pretty bad day.*

Correcting for lack of flash

In these instructions, you'll **correct underexposed** areas in a photo **by hand** by adding soft, semitransparent brush strokes to an adjustment layer mask.

To correct for the lack of a flash:

1. Click the Background (or a layer), then press Ctrl-J/Cmd-J to duplicate it **1**.

2. With the duplicate layer selected, choose Image > Adjustments > **Levels.** Move the midtones slider to the left to lighten the midtones, move the white Input slider a bit to the left to lighten highlights, then click OK.

3. Alt-click/Option-click the **Add Layer Mask** button ▢ at the bottom of the Layers palette. The Levels effect is now fully masked from the image. Keep the Layer Mask thumbnail selected.

4. Make the Foreground color white (D).

5. Choose the **Brush** tool, ⁄ and on the options bar do the following:

   Click the **Brush** thumbnail, then choose a soft-edge brush, with a diameter of 100 pixels or wider.

   Choose a Mode of **Lighten** or **Normal.**

   Choose an **Opacity** of around 40–50%.

6. Drag the brush over the underexposed areas of the image. Where you drag, the layer mask will be removed and the Levels effect will be exposed **2**. Continue to paint until the desired correction is achieved **3**.

7. If you overlighten any areas, press X to switch the Foreground color to black, then paint over the same area to mask the Levels effect.

TIP Try changing the brush opacity to produce more subtle or more dramatic changes.

TIP Use a large, soft brush and a low opacity to lighten transition areas between properly exposed and underexposed areas.

Correct for Lack of Flash

NEW Merging multiple exposures

Both digital cameras and film-based cameras are limited in the brightness range they're capable of recording in a single shot. For example, in a scene consisting of a brightly lit background with shadow and light areas in the foreground and midground, most cameras can capture details in either the highlight areas or in the shadow areas, but not both.

Recording a wider brightness range requires taking multiple shots, using a tripod for consistent alignment, and changing only one parameter—the exposure time—from one shot to the next. You can then use the **Merge to HDR** command in Photoshop to combine all the image data into one 32 bits/channel image. Because the HDR (High Dynamic Range) image data contains the full brightness range from all of the exposures, the end result is a picture of remarkable dynamic range. After using the command, you can convert the resulting HDR 32-bit image down to a 16-bit image in Photoshop.

Before using this command, follow our suggestions for shooting multiple exposures:

➤ Shoot at least **5 exposures** to record the full brightness range of the scene; one to capture the shadows, one for the highlights, and several for the midtones.

➤ Use a **tripod** for consistent alignment.

➤ Keep the **lighting** consistent for all shots.

➤ Change the **exposure time** (TV) by two time values from one shot to the next (e.g., 1/50, 1/100, 1/200, 1/400). If the exposure times are too close together, the resulting HDR will lack contrast because the overall brightness range was too narrow; if they're too far apart, the final image will be posterized due to gaps in the brightness range.

➤ Don't change any other settings.

➤ Choose **Raw** as the format for recording data in the camera. Open the images in the Camera Raw dialog box, and set all the Adjust panel sliders (Exposure, Shadows, Brightness, Contrast, and Saturation) to zero. The Merge to HDR command will perform these adjustments instead.

With the above suggestions in mind, shoot a series of photos, then follow the instructions on the next page.

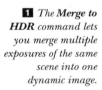

1 *The Merge to HDR command lets you merge multiple exposures of the same scene into one dynamic image.*

Merge to HDR Command

Jars 1.psd
Today, 2:21:56 PM
Adobe Photoshop CS2 Ma...

Jars 2.psd
Today, 2:23:11 PM
Adobe Photoshop CS2 Ma...

Jars 3.psd
Today, 2:24:03 PM
Adobe Photoshop CS2 Ma...

Jars 4.psd
Today, 2:24:51 PM
Adobe Photoshop CS2 Ma...

Jars 5.psd
Today, 2:25:41 PM
Adobe Photoshop CS2 Ma...

Jars 6.psd
Today, 2:27:16 PM
Adobe Photoshop CS2 Ma...

1 *The **Merge to HDR** command uses the underexposed photos to provide details for the highlight areas, and overexposed photos to provide details for the shadows.*

To create a multiexposure, HDR image:

1. In Bridge, make sure the multiple images to become the HDR image are aranged sequentially from their highest to lowest (or lowest to highest) exposure values, then Shift-select them all **1**.

2. Choose Tools > Photoshop > **Merge to HDR.** Stand by as the command opens the photos temporarily and performs its magic. The Merge to HDR dialog box opens (**1**, previous page). Set the zoom level to 100%.

Note: If the selected photos have an insufficient dynamic range to be processed by the command, an alert dialog box will appear.

3. *Optional:* To remove any of the source photos from the merged image data, uncheck the box next to its name on the left side of the dialog box, and pause to allow the preview to render. (Recheck the box to reinclude a photo.)

4. Move the **Set White Point Preview** slider to adjust which portion of the brightness range the preview displays. This option doesn't alter the brightness data stored in a 32-bits/channel image.

Don't use the Bit Depth menu to convert the image to 16 or 8 bits/channel; that conversion will be done later.

5. Click OK. A 32 bits/channel image will open in Photoshop. See the instructions on the following page for converting the 32 bits/channel image to 16 bits/channel.

TIP You can also open the source images directly into Photoshop, then open the Merge to HDR dialog box. To do this, you have to open the files in sequential order from their highest to lowest (or lowest to highest) exposure value before choosing File > Automate > Merge to HDR. In the first dialog box that opens, choose Use: Open Files, then click OK. Frankly, we think it's easier to use Bridge to arrange and select files, and to access the command.

Merge to HDR Command

32 bits/channel images are very large, slow to process, slow to render onscreen, and (at least for the moment) can be edited by using only a limited number of Photoshop commands. Better to **convert** them down to **16 bits/channel.**

To convert an HDR image to 16-bit:

1. With a merged HDR image open, choose Image > Mode > **16 Bits/Channel.**

2. Choose a compression method from the **Method** pop-up menu 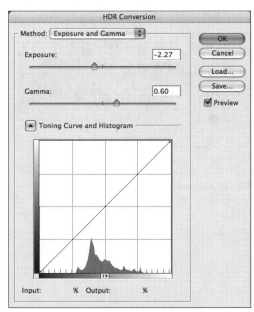:

   Highlight Compression or **Equalize Histogram** to see if these presets adjust the image preview to your satisfaction (see the sidebar at right). If you're satisfied with the results, your conversion is done; just click OK. Otherwise, try one of the remaining options.

   Exposure and Gamma, then move the Exposure slider slowly and gingerly to adjust brightness in the highlights and shadows, and move the Gamma slider to adjust brightness in the midtones. (These sliders offer similar controls to those in the Exposure dialog box.)

   Local Adaptation to access the toning curve and two related sliders. The **Radius** slider controls how many neighboring pixels will be analyzed when calculating a brightness adjustment. The higher the Radius value, the greater the number of neighboring pixels that will be factored in. Too low or high a setting will result in poor contrast. The **Threshold** slider controls which areas of contrast will be affected. At low Threshold settings, areas of high contrast are affected. As the Threshold increases, areas of lower contrast are also affected. You can reshape the **curve** to achieve additonal adjustments in specific brightness ranges. (Techniques used in the Curves dialog box can also be used here.)

3. Click OK. Your photo should now contain a dazzling range of brightness values.

(sidebar, left margin) **Convert HDR to 16 Bits/Channel**

Preset compression options

Highlight Compression shrinks an image's full 32-bit brightness range into a 16-bit range, sacrificing contrast, whereas **Equalize Histogram** shrinks the full 32-bit brightness range into a 16-bit range but may increase contrast.

HDR has limits

32 bits/channel HDR images have such a wide dynamic range and abundance of pixels that adjustment commands don't noticeably lower their quality. However, only a limited number of editing commands (e.g., Exposure, Lens Blur) are available for such images in Photoshop CS2, so in order to edit them beyond any initial adjustments, they have to be converted to 16 bits/channel.

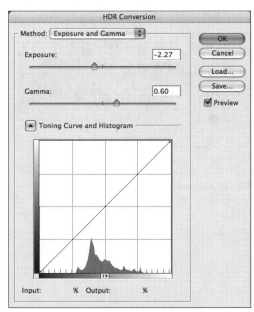

1 *In the **HDR Conversion** dialog box, the **Toning Curve** at the bottom affects image data only when Local Adaptation is chosen from the Method pop-up menu.*

1 *The original image*

Applying lighting effects

The **Lighting Effects** filter produces a tremendous variety of lighting effects. You can place up to 16 light sources in your image, and you can assign a different color, intensity, and angle to each source.

To cast a light on an image:

1. Click a layer in an RGB document **1**. *Optional:* Select an area on the layer to limit the filter's effect.

2. Choose Filter > Render > **Lighting Effects**. The Lighting Effects dialog box opens **2**.

3. From the **Style** pop-up menu, choose Default or a preset lighting effect.

4. For **Light Type:**

   Check **On** to access the Light Type options.

   From the **Light Type** pop-up menu, choose **Directional, Omni,** or **Spotlight.**

   Move the **Intensity** slider to adjust the brightness of the light.

   (Continued on the following page)

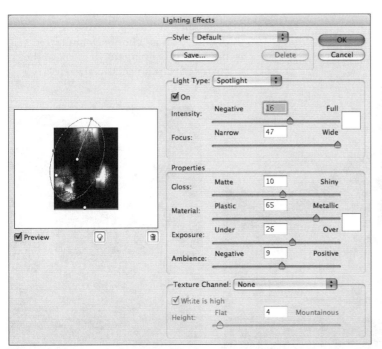

2 *In order to produce its effect, the **Lighting Effects** command darkens the whole layer; the only lighting comes from the filter.*

3 *Style: **Flood Light,** Light Type: **Spotlight,** after dragging a side point inward*

For the Spotlight Light Type, you can move the **Focus** slider to adjust the size of the beam that fills the ellipse.

To change the **color** of the light, click the color swatch, then choose a color from the Color Picker.

5. In the preview window, do any of the following :

To **move** the entire light, drag the center point.

To **rotate** the line without reshaping the ellipse, Ctrl-drag/Cmd-drag the end-point of an angle line.

To **intensify** the light, drag the endpoint of an angle line toward the center.

On an ellipse, drag either **side point** to change the direction of the light, or to widen or narrow it (**3**, prevous page).

6. Move the **Properties** sliders to adjust the surrounding light conditions on the current layer:

Gloss controls the amount of surface reflectance on the lighted surfaces.

Material adjusts the relative amount of color that emanates from either the light source (Plastic) or the image (Metallic).

Exposure lightens/darkens the whole layer **1**–**2**.

Ambience controls the balance between the light source and the overall light in the layer.

Click the Properties color swatch to choose a different **color** for the ambient light around the spotlight.

7. *Do any of these optional steps:*

To add the current configuration of settings to the Style pop-up menu so you can choose it again, click **Save,** enter a name, then click OK.

To **add** more light sources, drag the light bulb icon 💡 into the preview window **3**.

To **delete** a light source, drag its center point over the trash icon. 🗑 One light source must remain.

To **duplicate** a light source, Alt-drag/ Option-drag its center point.

8. Click OK. *Note:* The last-used settings of the Lighting Effects filter remain in the dialog box until you change them or exit/quit Photoshop. To restore the default settings, choose Default from the Style pop-up menu. To remove the current Style choice, click Delete.

1 *The original image*

2 *A Spotlight, with* **Exposure** *set to* **Over**

3 *An image after* **adding three spotlights**

REFOCUS 17

New chapter!

SOMETIMES PHOTOGRAPHERS deliberately "soft-focus" a shot to create an ethereal effect; at other times they might deliberately choose a wide depth of field (f-stop) to contrast an in-focus subject with a blurry background. Using Photoshop, you can apply special effects (blur an area that was previously in focus) or correct for photographic errors (sharpen an image that lacks focus). In this chapter, you'll do both: use the Lens Blur filter to create a focal point in your photo **1**–**2**; the Motion Blur filter to make objects appear as if they're in motion; the Lens Correction filter to correct for lens distortion; and the Smart Sharpen and Unsharp Mask filters to resharpen.

Lens Blur Filter

1 *The original image, entirely in focus*

2 *After using the **Lens Blur** filter to blur the pumpkins in the background*

Using the Lens Blur filter

When you photograph a subject, you know that whether you like it or not, some parts of your subject matter remain in focus and some don't. If your camera has dials that you can fiddle with (as opposed to a "point-and-shoot" type of camera), you can use an f-stop setting to control the "depth of field," or how much of the image is in focus. Objects that fall outside (are in front of or behind) the depth of field will look blurry. The appearance of the blurred area will vary depending on the individual camera lens and camera model being used to take the photo. For example, blurred white highlights, which photographers call "specular highlights," can vary in shape and brightness.

The **Lens Blur** filter in Photoshop attempts to replicate this type of blurring. What formerly required the use of multiple channels, gradients, and editing steps can now be accomplished via this single dialog box. All of this number crunching comes at a price, though: it can be slow when applied to large images.

1 The **Lens Blur** dialog box. We clicked the tip of the foreground pumpkin to make it the point in focus.

Lens Blur Filter

To apply the Lens Blur filter:

1. Open an image, then create an **alpha channel** (see page 334).
   or
   Click an image layer, then add a **layer mask** to the layer (see page 300).

2. Click the alpha channel or layer mask thumbnail, choose the **Gradient** tool, click the Gradient Picker arrowhead on the options bar, then click the "Black, White" preset. Drag across the document window to add a gradient.

   The gray areas of the gradient in the channel or mask will align with areas in the photo. Keep this in mind when you choose a Blur Focal Distance setting in step 5. (The white and black areas of the gradient can be switched from within the Lens Blur dialog box.)

3. Click the layer thumbnail, then choose Filter > Blur > **Lens Blur.** The Lens Blur dialog box opens (**1**, previous page).

4. At any time while you're making adjustments, you can uncheck, then recheck Preview to compare the original with the blurred image. Also click **Faster** or **More Accurate** for the preview speed.

   You can also change the zoom level for the preview by clicking the [+] or [-] zoom button in the lower left corner of the preview window or by choosing a preset zoom level from the pop-up menu. We recommend choosing Fit in View.

5. The grayscale values in a depth map control where the blur is applied, mimicking the depth of field in a camera. In the **Depth Map** area:

   From the **Source** pop-up menu, choose a source for the depth map. The change in grayscale values in the source will control what's in focus. Choosing **None,** or a source that has one overall value (such as a flat color background), will result in uniform blurring across the whole image.

   Move the **Blur Focal Distance** slider to specify which grayscale value (from 0, or black, to 255, or white) in your depth map is to remain fully in focus. Values lighter or darker than this value will become progressively more blurry and will look as though they're either in front of or behind the areas that are in focus. You'll see the change more readily after moving the other sliders.

   Alternately, in the preview, click the area that you want to keep in focus. Actually, what you're really doing is choosing a grayscale value that's located in that part of the chosen channel or mask (it's not visible, but it is aligned with the image) (**1**, next page).

   Optional: Check **Invert** to reverse what's in focus and what's not (swap the white and black areas in the depth map).

6. Use the settings in the **Iris** area to specify the size and shape of the camera lens iris, or aperture:

   From the **Shape** pop-up menu, choose the number of blades that create the lens opening.

   The **Radius** value controls the size of the iris opening and the intensity of the blur. It produces the most pronounced effect of any option in this dialog box.

   Choose a **Blade Curvature** value for the curvature on the blade shapes.

   Choose a **Rotation** value to rotate the iris opening.

   As the number of blades and the blade curvature increase, the shape of the iris becomes more circular and the shape effect becomes harder to discern. The shape will be most noticeable on specular highlights in the image.

   If these instructions seem overly complex, try experimenting with different settings until you achieve the look you want without analyzing how it works.

7. Blurring averages the values of neighboring pixels and tends to gray out white

(Continued on the following page)

Lens Blur Filter

specular highlights. In the **Specular Highlights** area, you can use the **Brightness** slider to brighten highlight areas that have become blurred, and use the **Threshold** slider to control the tonal range that the Brightness setting affects. At 255, only pure white pixels will be affected; at low settings, most of the pixels in the blurry areas will be brightened.

8. Blurring can also affect the film grain in an image, creating a nonuniform texture. To add **Noise** back to the blurred areas, do any of the following (move the sliders in small increments):

Move the **Noise:** Amount slider.

Click **Distribution:** Uniform or Gaussian.

Check **Monochromatic** to limit the noise to just grayscale pixels instead of color pixels.

9. Click OK.

TIP To create a vignette with an area of focus by using a layer mask and a blur filter, see page 278.

Blur focal distance

When you click the dialog box preview, you're actually choosing a grayscale value from the layer mask or alpha channel **1**, which becomes the **Blur Focal Distance** value. Image pixels at the location you click remain in focus; other image pixels become progressively more blurry, blurring at the same rate as the gray values transition toward black or white from the chosen value.

1 *When you click a spot in the preview window...*

...you're selecting a grayscale value located at that point in the chosen depth map channel or mask (the channel/mask isn't visible in the preview).

1 *Select an object.*

Using the Motion Blur filter

To create an illusion of motion, you'll select an object that is to remain stationary, copy it to a new layer, and then apply the **Motion Blur** filter to the original background.

To apply the Motion Blur filter to part of an image:

1. Select the imagery that is to remain stationary **1**.

2. Right-click/Control-click the selection and choose **Feather,** enter a value between 5 and 8 in the Feather Radius field, then click OK.

3. Press Ctrl-J/Cmd-J to copy the selected imagery to a new layer **2**.

4. Click the original layer that contains the background imagery.

5. Choose Filter > Blur > **Motion Blur.** The Motion Blur dialog box opens.

6. Enter an **Angle** value or move the dial (–360 to 360) **3**, choose a **Distance** (1–999) for the amount of blur, then click OK **4**.

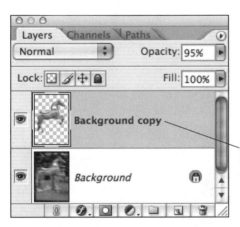

2 *Copy the selection to a new layer.*

3 *Choose an Angle in the Motion Blur dialog box.*

4 *The completed motion blur*

Motion Blur Filter

NEW Using the Lens Correction filter

The **Lens Correction** filter corrects for many types of lens distortion, such as the top of a tall building or column appearing to be smaller and tilting away from the camera (called "keystoning"); color fringes along shape edges (chromatic aberrations); under- or overexposure along the edges of a photo (vignetting); or horizontal or vertical perspective. The filter combines aspects of the Pinch filter and the Transform commands.

1 *In the original image, the columns are leaning toward the center of the image.*

To correct lens distortion:

1. Open an RGB image **1**, and click a layer.

2. Choose Filter > Distort > **Lens Correction 2**.

3. In the **Settings** area, do any of the following:

   Move the **Remove Distortion** slider to the left to spread the image out (e.g., widen the tops of buildings), or move it to the right to pinch the image inward.

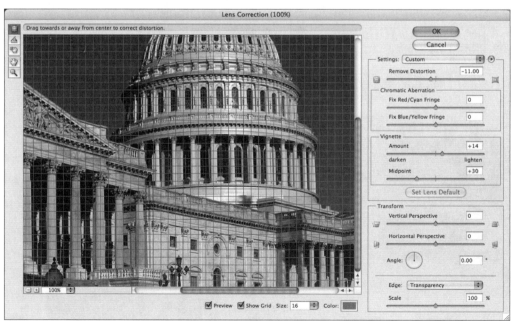

2 *The **Lens Correction** dialog box lets you correct various types of optical distortion.*

Lens Correction Filter

Use the **Chromatic Aberration** sliders to correct color fringes along high-contrast edges.

TIP If the grid is distracting, uncheck Show Grid below the preview window.

Use the **Vignette** sliders to help correct for under- or overexposure along the outer edges of an image (see page 232).

4. In the **Transform** area, do any of the following :

Move the **Vertical Perspective** slider to the left to widen the top of the image, or to the right to widen the bottom. The sliders apply perspective (like the Edit > Transform > Perspective command, except instead of moving handles, here you move sliders).

Move the **Horizontal Perspective** slider to the left to widen the left edge of the image, or to the right to widen the right edge of the image.

To rotate the image, drag the **Angle** dial or enter an Angle value.

5. If empty canvas areas result at the edges, from the **Edge** pop-up menu, choose whether those areas will fill with an **Edge Extension** (extension of the image), **Transparency,** or the current **Background Color.**

You can also enlarge or shrink the image by moving the **Scale** slider, or crop the image after exiting the dialog box.

6. Use any of the options below the preview window:

Click the **zoom in** [+] or **zoom out** [−] button or choose a preset zoom level from the pop-up menu.

Check/uncheck **Preview** to compare the original with the altered image.

Choose a grid size from the **Size** pop-up menu, or click the **Color** swatch to change the grid color.

7. *Optional:* To save the current settings, from the dialog box settings menu ⊙ choose Save Settings, enter a name (keep the .lcs extension), then click Save. Choose Load Settings to load in a saved setting. Presaved settings can be chosen from the Settings pop-up menu for any image.

8. Click OK **1**.

TIP To learn about any tool in the Lens Correction dialog box, rest the pointer on a tool, then read the usage description above the preview window.

TIP Hold down Alt/Option and click Reset to reset settings to their default values.

1 *To make the columns more vertical in this image, the **Remove Distortion** slider was moved to the left in the **Lens Correction** dialog box.*

Lens Correction Filter

Using sharpening filters

Blurring (as a result of resampling) may occur if you change a document's dimensions or resolution with Resample Image checked, convert the document to CMYK Color mode, or apply a transformation command. You can help correct blurring by using the **Smart Sharpen** filter or the **Unsharp Mask** filter (the latter, despite its name, has a focusing effect).

These filters can produce artifacts in an image, and therefore, with the following exceptions, should be applied at the end of the color correction cycle. If your image source is a scan or PhotoCD, we recommend applying some minimal sharpening before any editing and then again at the end of the correction cycle.

High-resolution print output also causes some minor blurring. You can anticipate and compensate for this by applying extra sharpening to the image—to the point where the image appears quite sharp onscreen. Experience will teach you how much sharpening is required.

Unsharp Mask vs. Smart Sharpen **NEW**

Although Unsharp Mask has been an industry standard for years and is a powerful sharpening tool, **Smart Sharpen** may very well replace it in your workflow because it offers many advantages:

Greater **control:** The Tonal Width sliders extend sharpening through a broader tonal range. Also, the ability to sharpen, then fade sharpening in the shadow and highlight areas separately, is far more powerful than the single, overall Threshold adjustment in Unsharp Mask.

More **power:** The More Accurate option automatically performs multiple sharpening passes on the image.

Fewer halos: Smart Sharpen's edge detection results in fewer color halos.

Flexibility: You have a choice of three algorithms for correction of Gaussian blur, lens blur, and motion blur; Unsharp Mask corrects only Gaussian blur.

Better **work flow:** The ability to save and reuse settings improves speed and consistency.

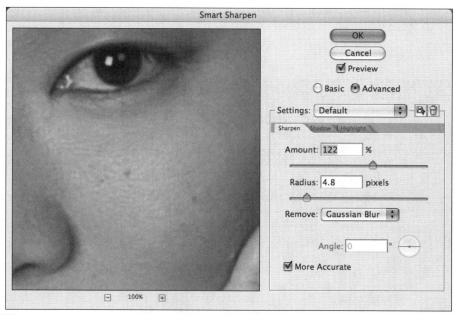

1 *The **Smart Sharpen** filter gives you a lot of control over how images are sharpened.*

1 *The original blurry image*

2 *This image is 2800 pixels wide. To achieve sharpening, we used the following values: In the Sharpen panel, Amount 130% and Radius 4 pixels; for the Advanced settings, in the Shadow and Highlight panels, the Fade Amount was determined "by eye," the Tonal Width value was 60%, and the Radius was 8.*

©www.photospin.com

Smart Sharpen (NEW)

Let's say you're starting off with a slightly blurry scan, or you tried to smooth skin irregularities or soften surface features in a photo by using the Gaussian Blur filter but you overdid it. **Smart Sharpen** can help resharpen the image.

To apply the Smart Sharpen filter:

1. Open a photo that needs sharpening **1**.

2. Choose Filter > Sharpen > **Smart Sharpen.** The Smart Sharpen dialog box opens (**1**, previous page). Leave the Zoom level at 100%.

3. Check **More Accurate** to produce a better sharpening effect via multiple passes of the filter. It takes longer, but it's worth it.

4. From the **Remove** pop-up menu, choose an algorithm for correction: **Gaussian Blur** is a good, all-purpose choice; **Lens Blur** sharpens details with fewer sharpening halos; and **Motion Blur** helps reduce blurring due to movement of the camera or subject. For Motion Blur, also choose an **Angle.**

5. Move the **Radius** slider to around 3–5 pixels, and move the **Amount** slider to slightly above 100%. The image should now look a bit oversharpened. That's OK. Now you'll fade the effect.

6. To control the amount of sharpening in shadow and highlight areas, click **Advanced.** Click the **Shadow** tab. Drag in the preview to display an area of the image that contains both shadows and midtones, then do the following:

   Move the **Radius** slider slightly to control how many neighboring pixels will be compared to a specific pixel. The higher the Radius, the larger the area of pixels that are compared.

   Move the **Tonal Width** slider to control the range of midtones that will be affected by the Fade Amount. The higher the width, the wider the range of midtones affected and the more

(Continued on the following page)

evenly the sharpening will fade into the shadows.

Move the **Fade Amount** slider until you see the desired reduction of oversharpening in the shadows. Too low a value for the Tonal Width slider will limit the effectiveness of this slider.

7. Click the **Highlight** tab **1**. Drag the image in the preview to display an area that contains both highlights and midtones. Move the Radius, Tonal Width, and Fade Amount sliders, as per the previous step.

8. The image should now have regained its sharpness. If the surface textures look too sharp, click the Sharpen tab and lower the Amount value a bit.

9. Click OK (**2**, previous page).

TIP To save the current settings, click the Save a Copy button, enter a name, then click OK. Presaved settings can be chosen from the Settings pop-up menu for any image.

TIP To restore all options to their default settings, hold down Alt/Option and click Reset; or if another settings preset is chosen, choose Default from the Settings pop-up menu.

TIP To have the Smart Sharpen filter affect only the tonal values (luminosity, not hue or saturation) in a document, after clicking OK, choose Edit > Fade Smart Sharpen. Choose Luminosity from the Mode pop-up menu, then click OK.

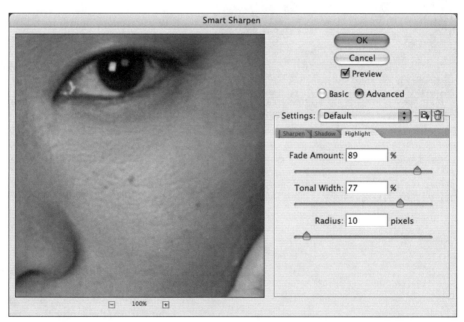

1 *In the **Smart Sharpen** dialog box, click **Advanced** to access the **Shadow** and **Highlight** panels.*

1 *The original 240 ppi image is a bit blurry.*

2 *When applying the **Unsharp Mask** filter, start off with conservative **Amount**, **Radius**, and **Threshold** settings.*

Suggested Unsharp Mask settings

Suggested values for a 2000 x 2000 pixel image:

➤ For **landscapes** and other soft-edged subjects: Amount about 100–150, Radius 1–1.5, Threshold 10–20.

➤ For **portrait** photos: Amount 100–120, Radius 2, Threshold 5–10, or to the point where skin areas start looking smoother.

➤ For **buildings** and **objects** in which contrast is a priority: Amount 150–200 or more, Radius 2, Threshold 1–5.

Unsharp Mask

The Unsharp Mask filter increases the contrast between adjacent pixels that already exhibit some contrast. You can specify the amount of contrast to be added (Amount), the number of surrounding pixels that will be modified around each pixel that requires more contrast (Radius), and determine which pixels the filter affects or ignores by specifying a minimum level of contrast between pixels (Threshold).

To apply the Unsharp Mask filter:

1. Choose a zoom level of 100% for your document. We recommend working on a duplicate layer **1**.

2. Choose Filter > Sharpen > **Unsharp Mask**. The Unsharp Mask dialog box opens **2**.

3. Choose an **Amount** value (1–500) for the percentage increase in contrast between pixels. Use a low setting (try 80–100) for figures or natural objects, a higher setting if the image contains sharp-edged objects. Too high a setting will produce noticeable halos around high-contrast areas (**1**, next page). The larger the image, the less sharpening may be required. For high-resolution images (say, 2000 x 3000 pixels and up), try an Amount of 130–200.

4. Choosing an appropriate **Radius** value is a bit trickier, as you need to factor in the final size, the total number of pixels, and the subject matter of the image. The Radius (0.1–250) controls the number of pixels surrounding high-contrast edges that will be modified (**2**, next page).

The more pixels the image contains, the higher the Radius value needed to achieve the desired result. Try a high Radius setting (around 2) for a low-contrast image containing large, simple objects and smooth transitions, and a lower Radius setting (around 1) for an intricate, high-contrast image with sharper transitions.

(Continued on the following page)

Unsharp Mask Filter

Note: The Amount and Radius settings are interdependent, meaning if you raise the Radius setting, you'll need to lower the Amount setting, and vice versa.

5. Choose a **Threshold** value (0–255) for the minimum amount of contrast an area must have before it will be sharpened ❸. At a Threshold of 0, the filter will be applied to the entire image. At a value of 10–30, sharpening will occur along already high-contrast edges but less so in low-contrast areas; at higher values, even fewer areas will be sharpened. When raising the Threshold value, you can also increase the Amount and Radius values to sharpen edges, without oversharpening areas that don't need it.

6. Click OK.

TIP With the Unsharp Mask dialog box open, you can click in the document window to have that area display in the preview window.

TIP For softer sharpening in an RGB image, try applying the Unsharp Mask filter to the Red and/or Green channels separately. If you sharpen both channels, use the same Radius value for both. The Blue channel contains the most noise but also the least amount of detail, so when sharpening individual channels, leave it be.

TIP Sharpening can produce color halos along edges within an image. To correct this, do the following: Perform the sharpening, then immediately choose Edit > Fade Unsharp Mask. Choose Luminosity from the Mode pop-up menu, then click OK. Now the sharpening is affecting only the luminosity in the image, not the hue or saturation.

❶ *After applying Unsharp Mask with a **high Amount** value (160), Radius 1.5, and Threshold 0: Note the halos around the edges and centers of the flowers.*

❷ *After applying Unsharp Mask with a **high Radius** value (6.0), Amount 130, and Threshold 0: The soft gradations have become choppy, and the image has developed an unnatural contrast and sharpness.*

❸ *After applying Unsharp Mask with a **higher Threshold** value (15), Amount 160, and Radius 1.5: Even using the same Amount setting as the top image, the soft gradations in the petals and the background are preserved.*

RETOUCH 18

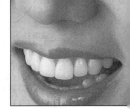

New chapter!

WE'RE DELIGHTED TO BE SEEING more and more middle-aged fashion models these days, but the pursuit of perfection continues. Even the most perfect portrait may need repair—perhaps the model has a birthmark or a slightly imperfect smile—horrors! On the opposite end of the spectrum are tears or stains in precious vintage photos that also could use a "magic" fix. Photoshop has a tool for every job.

In this chapter, you'll learn how to change product colors, whiten teeth, and perform other color changes by using the Match Color and the Replace Color commands; smooth skin and other textures by using the Surface Blur filter; change colors with the Color Replacement tool; smooth or remove wrinkles with the Healing Brush and Spot Healing Brush tools; repair tears, dust marks, and paper crinkles with the Patch tool **1**–**2**; and remove red-eye with the Red Eye tool.

(To dodge or burn areas of an image by using the Brush tool and a neutral gray layer, see page 179.)

1 *The original image has some crinkles.*

2 *The **Patch** tool magically repaired them.*

Using the Match Color command

Use the **Match Color** command to match the **overall** color and tonal values in one document with those in another document. Color matching comes in handy, say, if you have a series of product shots that exhibit inconsistent tonal values because they were shot in slightly different lighting conditions or using different camera settings. For the following steps, use one-layer documents.

To use the Match Color command:

1. Open an RGB document to be used as the source for the desired color and tone, and a second RGB document to be the target of the color match .

2. *Optional:* Show the Histogram palette to view a graph of the tonal changes.

3. With the target document active, on the Layers palette, drag the Background over the New Layer button. Leave the duplicate layer active.

4. Choose Image > Adjustments > **Match Color.** The Match Color dialog box opens. Make sure Preview is checked.

5. From the **Source** pop-up menu, choose the name of the source document that you opened in step 1 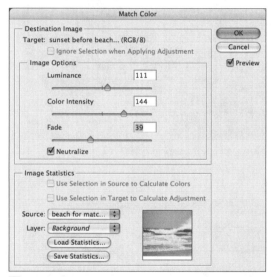. The target document will immediately adopt the color tones of the chosen source document.

6. In the **Image Options** area, do any of the following:

   Move the **Luminance** slider to adjust the overall brightness of the image.

   Move the **Color Intensity** slider to adjust the color saturation.

   Move the **Fade** slider to restore some of the original color to the image, blending the old and the new.

   Check **Neutralize** to remove any color casts from the target document. If this causes too great a color shift, you can try lessening the effect via the **Fade** slider.

7. Readjust any of the sliders as needed, then click OK .

1 *The original images: A sunset scene on the left and a daytime scene on the right*

2 *The **Match Color** dialog box, with an image chosen from the Source pop-up menu*

3 *The **Match Color** command caused the sunset image to adopt the lighter tones of the daytime image.*

Remove color cast

You can use **Match Color** to quickly remove a **color cast** from an image. Choose the Match Color command, but don't select a Source document. Check Neutralize, then adjust the Image Options sliders.

Save your settings

You can save your Match Color settings and apply them to any document. In the Image Statistics area of the dialog box, click **Save Statistics,** enter a name, then click Save. To reuse your saved settings, click Load Statistics, locate the saved settings file, then click Load.

1 *First, we loosely selected an area of an image.*

2 *Next, we carefully selected the wheelbarrow basin in another document.*

3 *Then we used the **Match Color** command to recolor the selection using the color from the source document.*

Match Color may also come in handy for matching a **single area** of color between two photos, such as an article of clothing or a product color for a catalog.

To match colors between two photos:

1. Open an RGB document to be used as the source for the desired color and tone, and create a rough selection that contains the desired color that you want to match **1**. Try to include both highlights and shadows in the selection.

2. Open a second RGB document to be the target of the color match.

3. In the target document, create a precise selection of the area to be adjusted **2**. With the selection still active, choose Layer > New > **Layer via Copy** (Ctrl-J/ Cmd-J) to duplicate the selection to a new layer.

4. Choose Image > Adjustments > **Match Color,** and make sure Preview is checked.

5. From the **Source** pop-up menu, choose the name of the source document you opened in step 1. Check **Use Selection in Source to Calculate Colors** to color-match using only the colors within the selection in the source photo (not the entire image).

6. Follow step 6 on the previous page to adjust the color match **3**.

7. Click OK. Merge the selection layer with the Background, if desired.

TIP If you hadn't chosen Layer via Copy (step 3), **Use Selection in Target to Calculate Adjustment** would be available. Uncheck this option to have only colors within the selection in the target document be used for calculating the adjustments (this helps to preserve light and dark values); or check it to have colors in the entire layer be used for the calculation.

TIP The Match Color command adjusts only the active layer in the target document. If you want to adjust the entire document instead, merge or flatten it before using the command.

Match Color Command

Using the Replace Color command

Using the **Replace Color** command, you can adjust the Hue, Saturation, or Lightness of colors in specific areas that you click on in the document window or in the dialog box —without using any selection tools. This powerful command works best for adjusting soft-edged areas, as in a landscape, that don't require a sharp-edged selection.

To use the Replace Color command:

1. *Optional:* For an RGB document, choose View > Proof Setup > Working CMYK to see a soft proof of the document and modifications to it in CMYK color.

   Once you've made a choice from the Proof Setup submenu, you can toggle the proof on and off while the Replace Color dialog box is open by pressing Ctrl-Y/Cmd-Y. Whether it's on or off, the Color and Result swatches in the Replace Color dialog box display in RGB.

2. Click a layer or the Background.

3. *Optional:* Create a selection to restrict color replacement to that area.

4. Choose Image > Adjustments > **Replace Color.**

5. Initially, the preview window will be solid black. In the preview window in the Replace Color dialog box or in the document window, click the color that you want to replace ■. That color will appear in the swatch at the top of the dialog box.

   Click **Selection** to preview the current selection in the preview window, or click **Image** to display the entire document. In Mac, you can press/release Control to toggle between the two display modes.

6. Move the **Fuzziness** slider to the right to add related colors to the selection, or to the left to shrink the selection.
   or
   To **add** other color areas to the selection, choose the first eyedropper, ✐ then

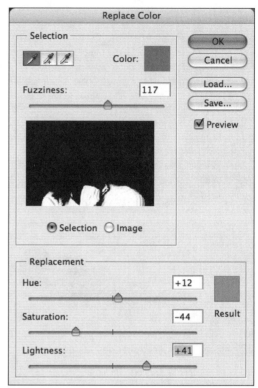

1 *The white areas in the preview window in the* ***Replace Color*** *dialog box represent the areas that will be modified (in this case, the woman's sweater).*

1 *The original image*

2 *After a Hue, Saturation and Lightness adjustment to the sweater by using the **Replace Color** command*

Shift-click in the preview window or document window.

(To start over, choose the eyedropper and click without holding down Shift.)

7. If you've added colors to the selection and you now want to **subtract** from it, with the first eyedropper, Alt-click/ Option-click in the preview window or document window. Or choose the eyedropper, then click without holding down Alt/Option.

8. Move the **Hue, Saturation,** or **Lightness** slider to modify the selected colors (only the Lightness slider will be available for a Grayscale document). The Result swatch will update as you move the sliders.
or
Click the **Result** swatch, choose a color from the Color Picker, then click OK. All three sliders will adjust to reflect the attributes of the new color.

Note: The Replacement sliders will stay in their current positions even if you click a different area of the image or add to or subtract from the selection.

9. Click OK **1**–**2**.

TIP The Result swatch color (Replace Color dialog box) also displays in the currently active square on the Color palette. If the gamut warning displays on the Color palette, it means the color is non-printable.

TIP The Replacement sliders won't change the amount of Black (K) in a color for a CMYK document; that component is set separately by the Black Generation feature in Photoshop.

TIP To restore the original dialog box settings, hold down Alt/Option and click Reset.

Replace Color Command

Here's another way to use the Replace Color command: To **whiten teeth** or the whites of the **eyes.** By selecting those areas in an image and then using the Replace Color command, you can quickly correct any discoloration.

To whiten teeth or eyes:

1. Choose the **Lasso** tool. Zoom in on the teeth or eye area.

2. Drag to create a tight selection of the teeth 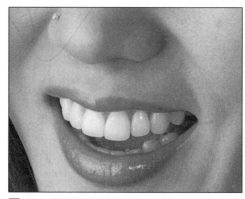 or of one side of the white area of an eye.

3. Choose Select > **Feather,** enter 1 or 2, then click OK.

4. Choose Image > Adjustments > **Replace Color**. The Replace Color dialog box opens 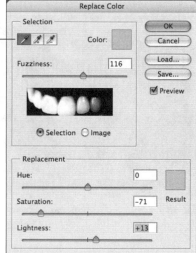.

5. Click the **Eyedropper** tool, then click the selection in the document window. Move the Fuzziness slider to add related shades of white to the selection.

6. Move the **Saturation** slider to the left to desaturate the selected area and remove the off-white tinge; and move the **Lightness** slider slightly to the right to brighten the selected area.

7. Click OK. Deselect the selection 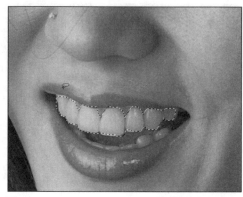.

8. If you're whitening the eyes, repeat the above steps for the remaining off-white areas.

TIP To select an area another way, put the image into QuickMask mode, zoom in, and using a brush, draw a mask over the area you want to retouch. Then, when you return to Standard mode, the mask will turn into a selection (see pages 339–340).

TIP Although we find it easier to select the desired color range by using the Replace Color command, with its Eyedropper tool and the Fuzziness slider, you could use Image > Adjustments > Hue/Saturation instead. Choose Yellows from the Edit pop-up menu, then use the Saturation and Lightness sliders as in step 6, above.

Whiten Teeth or Eyes

1 *Use the **Lasso** tool to select the teeth.*

2 *Use the Eyedropper tool in the **Replace Color** dialog box.*

3 *The **whitened teeth***

Smooth Skin; Restore Details

How smart is Smart Blur? NEW

You can also use the **Smart Blur** filter (on the Blur submenu) to smooth skin irregularities. It preserves sharpness and contrast in lips, eyes, eyebrows, and other details while blurring lower-contrast areas. Note that its Threshold and Radius sliders produce slightly different results than those in the Surface Blur dialog box. Moderate Threshold values can posterize skin tones. We recommend choosing High as the Quality setting. A quibble: The filter previews only in the small dialog box (not in the larger document window, as Surface Blur does).

1 *The original image has a too-prominent texture.*

2 *Surface Blur smooths skin textures while keeping facial details crisp.*

Using the Surface Blur filter

The **Surface Blur** filter makes an easy job of smoothing skin or other surfaces.

To smooth skin or other surfaces: NEW

1. Press Ctrl-J/Cmd-J to duplicate the Background.

2. Choose Filter > Blur > **Surface Blur.**

3. Choose a low **Threshold** value to maintain contrast and facial details. At a low Threshold value, only low-contrast areas will be blurred.

4. Move the **Radius** slider to around 5–10 to soften folds of skin, such as on the cheeks or forehead. A very low Radius value can make skin look blotchy. Increase the value enough to see a smoothing effect, but not so much as to posterize.

5. Readjust the Threshold to either increase or decrease the amount of blurring in low-contrast areas. Too much smoothing will make a face look artificial. But then again, this is all artifice anyway.

6. Click OK **1**–**2**. See the next set of instructions.

TIP Change the blending mode of the duplicate layer (try Darken to emphasize shadows or Lighten to emphasize highlights), and lower the layer opacity slightly to restore some surface details from the original image.

If the Surface Blur filter overdid it, you can restore details by using a mask and a brush.

To selectively restore details:

1. With the duplicate layer selected, click the **Add Layer Mask** button on the Layers palette.

2. Choose the **Brush** tool.

3. On the options bar, choose a small, soft-edged tip, and make the Opacity 50%.

4. Make the Foreground color black, then paint over the areas you want to restore sharpness to (e.g., lips, eyes, eyebrows, hair); or paint with white to restore the blur filter effect.

1 *Choose settings for the **Color Replacement** tool from the options bar.*

Using the Color Replacement tool

Like the Replace Color command, the **Color Replacement** tool lets you change color, hue, saturation, and luminosity values. But here, instead of using a dialog box, changes are applied manually using a brush. You can also specify sampling, limits, and tolerance parameters for the tool. And unlike the Brush tool, which applies flat colors, the Color Replacement tool tries to preserve the original texture as it changes colors. This tool, like the Replace Color and Match Color commands, is a boon for catalogue and ad designers.

To use the Color Replacement tool:

1. Open or convert a document to RGB, CMYK, or Lab Color mode.

2. Choose the **Color Replacement** tool.
NEW (B or Shift-B) (it's on the Brush pop-out menu).

3. Choose a Foreground color via the Color or Swatches palette, or Alt-click/Option-click with the tool to sample a color from the image (temporary Eyedropper).

4. From the options bar **1**, choose characteristics for the tool:

Click the **Brush Preset** picker arrowhead and choose brush attributes (diameter, hardness, spacing, etc.).

To control which color characteristics are applied, choose a blending **Mode:** Hue, Saturation, Color, or Luminosity. We recommend choosing Color.

Click the **Sampling: Continuous** button to apply the current Foreground color to all pixels the brush passes over; or **Sampling: Once** to sample the first pixel the brush crosshair clicks on and then apply the Foreground color only to pixels that match that initial sample (this option gives you the most control); or **Sampling: Background Swatch** to replace only colors that match or are similar to the current Background color.

Choose **Limits: Discontiguous** to recolor pixels that the pointer is over that fall within the Sampling parameters; or **Contiguous** to allow pixels that are adjacent to the pixel under the pointer to be recolored; or **Find Edges** to recolor pixels connected to color areas that match the sample color, while preserving distinct shape edges.

To control the range within which a color can differ from the sampled color and still be recolored, enter or choose a **Tolerance** value (1–100%). A high Tolerance value allows for a wider range of colors to be recolored; a low value limits recoloring to only those pixels that closely match the sample color.

Optional: Check Anti-alias to smooth the transitions between the existing colors and replacement colors.

Color Replacement Tool

5. Click a layer , then drag across the areas you want to recolor **2**. Only pixels that fall within the parameters of the Mode, Sampling, Limits, and Tolerance settings that you just established will be recolored. You can change the options bar settings between strokes to vary the results.

1 *We used the **Color Replacement** tool on the baby's shirt...*

2 *...to replace it with a brighter color.*

Choosing a healing tool

The three tools discussed on the next few pages sample a texture, apply it to the target area, then recolor the texture with the target area's color and brightness values, blending it seamlessly into the surrounding pixels. This makes it easy to fix imperfections, such as facial blemishes and paper crinkles.

With the **Healing Brush,** you Alt-click/ Option-click a pixel area for sampling, then stroke over, say, a blemish. The blemish pixels are replaced with the sampled pixels.

With the **Patch** tool, you select a blemish area first, then drag the selection marquee over a clean pixel area for sampling. Here again, blemish pixels are replaced with the sampled pixels.

And with the **Spot Healing Brush** tool, you simply stroke over blemishes without sampling. Pixels are magically replaced based on data from neighboring pixels.

1 *The options bar for the **Healing Brush** tool*

Healing Brush Tool

Using the Healing Brush tool
To use the Healing Brush tool:
1. Choose the **Healing Brush** tool (J or Shift-J).

2. On the options bar **1**, do all of the following:

   Click the Brush Preset picker arrowhead, make the brush **Diameter** slightly wider than the area you want to retouch, and choose a low **Hardness** value. (In Preferences > Display & Cursors, click Full Size Brush Tip and Show Crosshair in Brush Tip.)

   Choose **Mode:** Normal to preserve the grain, texture, and noise of the area surrounding the target; or choose a different mode if you don't need to preserve those attributes. Choose Screen for subtle retouching, or for wrinkles that are very close together to prevent them from cloning onto one another.

   Click Source: **Sampled.**

   Check **Aligned** to maintain the same distance between the source point (which will change) and the target area that you drag across; or uncheck Aligned to create repetitive strokes anywhere in the image, sampled from the same source point.

   To allow the brush to sample pixels from all layers below the pointer, check **Sample All Layers;** or uncheck Sample All Layers to allow the brush to sample pixels from only the current layer.

3. Click a layer **2**. If you're touching up the Background, press Ctrl-J/Cmd-J to duplicate it, then click the duplicate layer.
   or
   Create a new layer and check Sample All Layers, so you can apply retouching strokes to a new, blank layer **3**. This way,

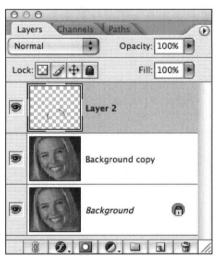

2 *The original image*

©www.photospin.com

3 *Use the **Sample All Layers** option to place strokes on a new layer.*

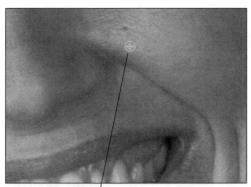

1 *With the **Healing Brush** tool, Alt-click/Option-click the area you want to use as **replacement** pixels...*

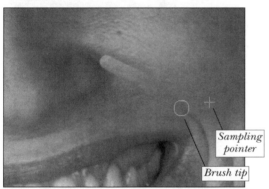

Sampling pointer

Brush tip

2 *...then drag across the area you want to **repair**; a brush tip and a sampling pointer appear onscreen.*

3 *The image after softening the smile lines with the **Healing Brush** tool*

rather than depending on the History palette to undo changes, you can simply erase the retouch strokes on the new layer. (When you're satisfied with the results, merge the layer down.)

4. Alt-click/Option-click the area to be used as the source texture **1**.

5. Drag across the area you want to repair **2**. When you release the mouse, the source texture will be applied to the target area and will be blended with its surrounding pixels. It will render in two stages, though: At first a full clone will appear, then the source color will disappear, leaving just the source texture **3**. Impressive tool!

   TIP Shift-drag to constrain your strokes to the horizontal or vertical axis.

6. *Optional:* To establish a new source point for further repairs, Alt-click/Option-click a different area, then continue on your way.

7. For more realistic results, if you're applying strokes to either a duplicate of the Background or a new layer, lower the layer opacity to blend it with the original photo.

TIP To confine the repair to a specific area and avoid picking up colors from surrounding areas, before using the Healing Brush tool, use the Lasso tool to select the area you want to repair.

TIP To selectively restore original pixels, create a layer mask for the duplicate layer; then, using the Brush tool, paint with black to mask out the retouched areas. Or if the Healing Brush strokes were placed on a new layer, simply erase individual strokes (you can hide the image layer to see the strokes more easily).

TIP Just for the sake of comparison, the Clone Stamp tool simply copies a source color to a target area, whereas the Healing Brush, Spot Healing Brush, and Patch tools blend a texture into a target area's color and brightness values.

Healing Brush Tool

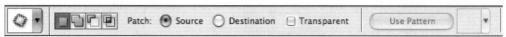

1 *The options bar for the **Patch** tool*

Using the Patch tool

The **Patch** tool is a good choice for repairing tears, stains, and dust marks in vintage photos. With this tool, you create a selection before applying the repair.

To use the Patch tool:

1. Choose the **Patch** tool (J or Shift-J).

2. On the options bar, click **Patch: Source 1**.

3. Drag a marquee around the area you want to **repair 2** (the Destination). You can Alt-click/Option-click to create a straight-edged selection.

4. *Optional:* Add to (Shift-drag) or subtract from (Alt-drag/Option-drag) the selection as needed, or use any Select menu commands to feather or otherwise modify the selection.

5. Drag from inside the selection to the area you want to sample **3**. When you release the mouse **4**, imagery from the sampled area will appear within the original selection. Deselect.

TIP You could also click Destination instead of Source for step 2, above, select the area you want to sample from, then drag from inside the selection to the area you want to repair (the Destination).

TIP To patch (fill) the selection with a pattern (in this case, a texture that you've defined as a pattern), with the Patch tool chosen, on the options bar, click a pattern on the Pattern Preset picker, click Use Pattern, and also check Transparent if you want the fill to be semitransparent.

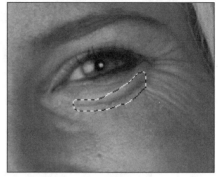

2 *Using the **Patch** tool, select the area you want to repair.*

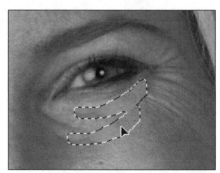

3 *Drag from the selected area to the area that you want to **sample** pixels **from**.*

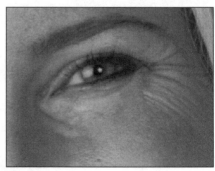

4 *The patch is applied to the **selection**.*

1 *The original image*

2 *An area is selected for repair with the **Patch** tool.*

3 *The selection is dragged over an area to be **sampled**.*

Removing dust and scratches
You can also use Filter > Noise > **Dust & Scratches** to repair imperfections in old photos.

4 *After using the **Patch** tool several times to repair the damaged area on the left side*

Patch Tool

1 *The options bar for the **Spot Healing Brush** tool*

NEW Using the Spot Healing Brush tool

The **Spot Healing Brush** tool is an effective wrinkle remover, and it's cheaper than Botox. Skin folds have both light and dark areas, making it difficult to pick a sample area; this tool lets you make corrections without sampling.

To use the Spot Healing Brush tool:

1. Press Ctrl-J/Cmd-J to duplicate the Background, and keep the duplicate selected.

or

Create a new, blank layer to apply the correction strokes to, and keep it selected.

2. Choose the **Spot Healing Brush** tool, then set the zoom level to 100%.

3. On the options bar **1**, do the following:

Choose a brush **tip** size that's slightly wider than the area to be retouched. (In Preferences > Display & Cursors, click Full Size Brush Tip and Show Crosshair in Brush Tip.)

Choose a **Mode.** For preserving skin tones, we find that Normal or Screen works best with Proximity Match. With Replace Mode, the tool may pick up other facial details in the stroke, such as hair or eyelashes.

Click **Type: Proximity Match** to correct large or long facial lines; it helps preserve tonal values in the skin tones. Or if you're going to retouch a small facial area with a small brush tip, click Type: **Create Texture**; it evens out the tonal values. The latter option may produce an unnatural texture if the tool is used with a large brush tip or if multiple strokes are made in the same area.

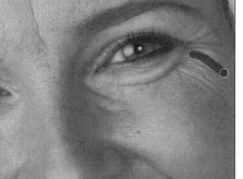

1 *Drag the **Spot Healing Brush** tool along an area to be retouched.*

To allow the brush to sample pixels from all layers below the pointer, check **Sample All Layers;** or uncheck Sample All Layers to allow the brush to sample pixels from only the current layer. If you created a new, blank layer for step 1, be sure to check Sample All Layers.

4. Drag across areas to be repaired **1**–**2**.

5. To produce more naturalistic results, lower the opacity of the duplicate or new layer to blend it with the original photo. For even more naturalistic results, don't retouch anything in the first place!

If you applied strokes to a new layer, you can erase the strokes from the layer to remove them. When you're done making corrections, merge the layer down.

2 *The result*

NEW Using the Red Eye tool

Red-eye (literally, red eyes) in portrait photographs results from using a camera-mounted or built-in electronic flash. Some cameras have a built-in red-eye controls. For photos taken without such controls, you can **remove red-eye** with a click of the Red Eye tool.

To remove red-eye from a portrait:

1. Open a portrait file. Zoom in to 200%–300% view on the eye area.

2. Choose the **Red Eye** tool 🖳 (J or Shift-J).

3. On the options bar **1**, do the following:

Choose a **Pupil Size** to control how large the recolored pupil shape will be; try 60–80%. You don't want the tool to increase the size of the existing pupil.

Choose a **Darken Amount** to control how dark the resulting pupil color will be. The proper setting depends on the eye color; light eyes need a lower setting. Try a value around 30–40%. Too high a setting will produce overly dark pupils.

4. Click the red area on each pupil. The tool will remove all traces of red **2**–**3**.

TIP If you find the pupil size produced by the tool to be too large, undo the initial click, lower the Pupil Size value, then click again. Similarly, if you want to experiment with lighter Darken Amount values, undo the initial click first.

TIP You don't need to drag over the eye with the Red Eye tool; the tool is smart enough to find the area of the pupil within an "eye" shape automatically when you click on it!

Fixing the iris

If the Red Eye tool fails to remove red traces from the iris of the eyes (the area around the pupils), do the following: Zoom in on an eye (200%–300%), then choose the **Color Replacement** tool. 🖉 On the options bar, choose a very small brush tip, Mode: Color, Sampling: Once 🖉, Limits: Contiguous, and a Tolerance of 30%. Alt-click/Option-click to sample an iris color to replace the red, then draw strokes to paint out the remaining traces of red.

1 *The **Red Eye** tool options bar*

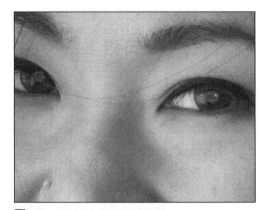

2 *The original image, with red-eye*

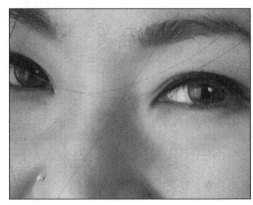

3 *Click once on each eye—bye-bye red-eye!*

New chapter!

1 *The original image (Peter's relatives—no joke)*

2 *The vignette*

3 *For this image, we applied the Glass filter after step 5.*

THE COMMANDS AND TECHNIQUES discussed in this chapter range from putting finishing touches on images to the presentation of multiple versions of the same image. You'll learn how to frame your subject matter as a vignette; create a hand-printed look; embed a copyright mark into an image; organize images into a contact sheet or picture package; create a Web gallery or PDF presentation; and create and use layer comps for presenting multiple versions of documents to clients.

Creating vignettes

A **vignette** has the effect of visually guiding the viewer's attention to a particular area of a photo (usually the center). We offer three methods for creating vignettes.

To create a vignette:

1. In a multilayer document, click an image layer, and make sure Lock Transparent Pixels is off to allow the vignette to look as if it's fading into the underlying layers.

   For a file containing just a Background **1**, choose a Background color (see pages 181–184) to be used for the area around the vignette.

2. Choose the **Rectangular Marquee** or **Elliptical Marquee** tool (M or Shift-M), or the **Lasso** tool (L or Shift-L).

3. Enter a **Feather** value on the options bar (the more pixels the image contains, the higher the Feather value needed).

4. Select the part of the image that you want to keep, then right-click/Control-click in the document window and choose **Select Inverse.**

5. Press Backspace/Delete.

6. Right-click/Control-click the image and choose **Deselect 2**–**3**.

Next you'll create a **vignette** in which you'll create an area of **focus.**

To create a vignette with an area of focus:

1. Open an image in which you want to emphasize the center .

2. On the Layers palette, click the Background, then press Ctrl-J/Cmd-J twice to make two duplicates.

3. Click the topmost duplicate layer, then **select** the area of the image that you want to emphasize (remain in focus). For example, you could use the Elliptical Marquee tool (M or Shift-M), then Alt-drag/Option-drag to create an oval, or use the Lasso to create an irregular selection (as we did).

4. Click the **Add Layer Mask** button ⬜ on the Layers palette. The selection has now become a mask 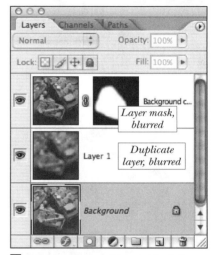. Keep the layer mask thumbnail selected.

5. Choose Filter > Blur > **Gaussian Blur.** The Gaussian Blur dialog box opens. Lower the zoom level in the dialog box by clicking the zoom out (–) button so you can see the mask in the preview window, move the **Radius** slider to soften the edge of the mask, then click OK.

6. Click the first duplicate layer.

7. Choose Filter > Blur > **Box Blur** or ⬤NEW **Gaussian Blur.** Gaussian Blur produces a smooth blur; Box Blur produces a blur with a subtle geometric pattern.

8. Move the **Radius** slider to blur the layer by the desired amount, then click OK .

TIP For even softer feathering in the vignette, click the layer mask thumbnail, then reapply the Box or Gaussian Blur filter, moving the Radius slider to soften the edge more.

TIP See also "To move the vignette area" on the next page.

1 *The original image, all in focus*

2 *A Background and two duplicate layers.*

3 *The "focus" vignette*

1 *After darkening Layer 1 via the Levels command*

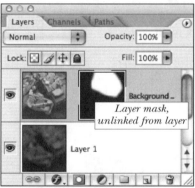

2 *The mask is moved to the upper right.*

Layer mask, unlinked from layer

3 *After unlinking the layer and layer mask, then moving the mask to the upper right*

Another way to create (or enhance) a **vignette** is via lighting, in this case by using the **Levels** command.

To create a vignette via Levels:

1. Open an image in which you want to emphasize the center.

2. Follow steps 2–6 on the previous page.

3. Choose **Levels** from the New Fill/ Adjustment Layer pop-up menu at the bottom of the Layers palette.

4. Move the white **Output** slider to the left to darken the image.

5. Click OK **1**.

In the previous two sets of instructions, you used a layer mask to control where the vignette is positioned on an image. If you're not happy with the placement, no problem—you can change where the **vignette** is **located** by moving the layer mask.

To move the vignette area:

1. On the Layers palette, click the layer mask thumbnail that's being used to create the vignette.

2. Click the **Link Layer Mask** icon 🔗 to unlink the mask from the layer image.

3. Choose the **Move** tool (V) and then, in the document window, drag the mask shape to a new location **2**–**3**.

4. Click again between the layer mask thumbnail and the layer thumbnail to relink them (the link icon will reappear).

Creating a hand-printed look

To add distinction to an image, you can create a **hand-painted frame,** paint the image on a layer mask, or apply a texture via a filter.

To create a hand-printed look:

1. Open an image.

2. To create room for a frame, choose Image > **Canvas Size** (Ctrl-Alt-C/Cmd-Option-C), choose **percent** from the Width and Height pop-up menus, and enter 130 in both fields. Choose Canvas extension color: White, leave the gray Anchor square in the center of the resize grid where it is, then click OK.

3. Click the **New Layer** button ▣ on the Layers palette to create a new layer.

4. Choose the **Brush** tool (B or Shift-B). ✎

5. On the options bar:

Click the **Brush Preset** picker thumbnail, then choose Large List from the picker menu to display the presets by name. Locate and click the Oil Pastel Large preset, then move the Master Diameter

slider to a setting that's appropriate for your document (we chose 300 px as our setting; our document is 3000 pixels wide).

Choose Mode: **Normal.**

Set the **Opacity** to 100% and the **Flow** to 60%.

6. Press **D** to reset the Foreground and Background colors, press **X** to reverse them, then drag across the outer edge of the image, covering some of the image **1** (and **1**, next page) Don't worry if your strokes aren't straight; you want it to look handmade.

or

Choose Edit > **Fill,** choose Use: White, then click OK. Click the Add Layer Mask button ▣ on the Layers palette, click the layer mask thumbnail, then draw

1 *After applying white brush strokes to the edge of an image using the **Oil Pastel Large** brush preset*

strokes in the document window to "paint" in the image **2**.

7. *Optional:* Try applying a texture filter to the layer mask or brush stroke layer, and also to the image layer.

TIP Experiment with other brush presets—the rougher, the better **3**.

TIP "Prefab" frames are available from third-party suppliers, such as the PhotoFrame collection from Extensis **4**.

1 *The image on the previous page after choosing* ***Overlay*** *mode for the layer containing the brush strokes*

4 *An edge from* ***PhotoFrame***

2 *After* ***painting*** *the image on a* ***layer mask***

3 *After painting black strokes with the* ***Hard Pastel on Canvas*** *brush preset (Shift held down to get straight lines), and some white lines with a smaller brush diameter*

Adding copyright marks

If you're planning to display any of your images online, such as via Photoshop's Web Photo Gallery or PDF Presentation command, you can help protect them from unauthorized usage by embedding a **copyright mark** into them. To do this, you'll create a copyright shape with the Custom Shape tool, then save the shape as a tool preset for use in any document.

To embed a copyright mark into a file:

1. Choose the **Custom Shape** tool (U).

2. On the options bar, do the following:

   Click the **Shape layers** button.

   Click the **Shape** picker thumbnail, then click the copyright symbol © (it's in the default custom shape preset library) **1**.

   Click the **Style** picker thumbnail, then click Default Style (None).

   Click the **Color** swatch. In the Color Picker, choose white as the Foreground color, then click OK.

3. Shift-drag with the tool in the document window until it's the size you want the symbol to be. A shape layer appears on the Layers palette.

4. On the Layers palette, make the shape layer **Fill** value 0%.

5. Double-click next to the layer name to open the Layer Style dialog box, then click **Bevel and Emboss** (don't check Contour). Choose Style: Inner Bevel, Technique: Smooth, Depth around 60–90%, Size around 5–25, Soften around 6–10; then click OK **2**.

6. You can use the Move tool to reposition the shape. To better view the copyright symbol **3**, click another layer.

7. *Optional:* To save the shape style to the Styles palette (recommended!), click the shape layer for the copyright mark on the Layers palette. On the Styles palette, click the New Style button, enter a name, then click OK.

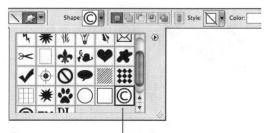

1 *Click the **Copyright symbol** on the **Custom Shape** picker*

2 *The **shape** layer for the © symbol on the Layers palette*

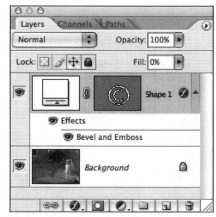

3 *The final **copyright** symbol*

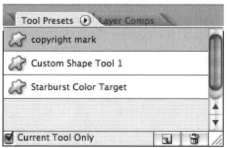

1 *Text converted to a custom shape and styled as a* ***copyright mark***

2 *The **Custom Shape** tool options bar with our designated Shape, Style, and Color options chosen*

3 *Our new tool preset appears on the **Tool Presets** palette (shown here, in the Dock).*

You can also create a **copyright mark** by using the Type tool.

To create a copyright mark using text:

1. Choose the Type tool, enter some text on the image, then scale and style it.

2. Choose Layer > Type > **Convert to Shape.**

3. Choose Edit > **Define Custom Shape,** enter a name, then click OK.

4. Delete the shape layer. Follow the steps on the previous page, except in step 2, choose your new custom shape from the Custom Shape picker **1**.

For the quickest and easiest reapplication, we recommend going one step beyond step 7 on the previous page: Save your copyright mark as a Shape tool **preset.**

To save a copyright shape and style as a tool preset:

1. After following step 7 on the previous page, choose the **Custom Shape** tool.

2. On the options bar **2**, make sure the copyright symbol or your custom text shape is showing in the **Shape** thumbnail.

3. Click the **Style** thumbnail on the options bar. In the Style picker, click your custom copyright style.

4. Click the **Tool Preset** picker thumbnail at the far left side of the options bar, or click the **Tool Presets** tab in the Dock.

   On the picker or the palette, click the **New Tool Preset** button, enter a name (leave Include Color unchecked), then click OK **3**.

5. To place the mark in any photo, click your tool preset on the Tool Preset picker or the Tool Presets palette, then Shift-drag in the document window. *Note:* If Show Current Tool Presets is checked on the picker or palette menu, you'll have to choose the Custom Shape tool to make the preset appear as a listing.

Creating picture packages

You can use the four commands discussed next—Contact Sheet II, Picture Package, Web Photo Gallery, and PDF Presentation—to organize and display your images. Although they're accessible from Photoshop and Bridge, we use Bridge, as it lets us select and organize our image thumbnails first.

A **contact sheet** is an arrangement of image thumbnails on a page, with or without captions—sort of like thumbnails "on paper."

To create a contact sheet:

1. Depending on which source option you're going to choose (see step 3), you can either go to Bridge and select all the files that you want placed on the contact sheet, or you can put all the files in a folder. The command can locate files in a folder as well as in any nested subdirectories/subfolders in the folder.

Also make sure that all the files you want on the contact sheet are saved in a format that Photoshop can read (Raw format photos are readable).

2. In Bridge, choose Tools > Photoshop > **Contact Sheet II,** or in Photoshop, choose File > Automate > Contact Sheet II.

3. The Contact Sheet II dialog box opens (**1**, next page). For the **Source Images,** choose **Use: Current open documents, Folder,** or **Selected Images from Bridge.** If you chose Folder, click Browse/Choose, click the folder that contains the files for the contact sheet, then click Choose.

Optional: Check Include All Subdirectories/Subfolders to have the command process files in the designated folder as well as in any subdirectories/subfolders in the folder.

4. In the **Document** area:

Choose a measurement unit from the **Units** pop-up menu, then enter overall **Width** and **Height** values for the sheet.

Choose a **Resolution** and **Mode** for the contact sheet.

Optional: Check Flatten All Layers to have all images (and optional captions) appear on a single layer, or uncheck this option to have each image/caption appear on a separate layer.

5. In the **Thumbnails** area:

Choose a **Place** option for the direction in which the images are to be arranged.

Enter the desired number of **Columns** and **Rows** for the contact sheet.

Check **Use Auto-Spacing** to have Photoshop automatically calculate the spacing between thumbnails, or uncheck this option and enter the desired spacing between thumbnails in the Vertical and Horizontal fields.

Optional: Check Rotate for Best Fit to have Photoshop automatically orient each thumbnail to fit on the sheet.

The contact sheet layout will preview on the right side of the dialog box, and the current page, number of images, and thumbnail size will also be listed.

6. *Optional:* Check Use Filename As Caption to have a caption with the file name appear under each thumbnail. If you choose this option, also choose a Font and Font Size for the captions.

7. Click OK. Pause while the command creates a new file, then save it (**2**, next page). (To cancel the command in progress, press Esc.)

(Contact Sheet — side tab)

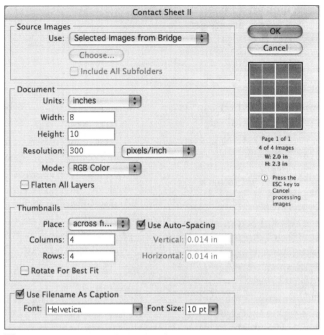

1 In the **Contact Sheet II** *dialog box, locate the images you want on the contact sheet and choose layout options for the sheet.*

2 *A* **contact sheet** *with* **filename captions**

The **Picture Package** command arranges multiples of the same image in various sizes on one sheet, like the layouts produced by traditional photo studios. You can use preset or custom sizes and configurations.

To create a picture package:

 1. In **Bridge** (our preferred method), select the photo you're going to use, then choose Tools > Photoshop > **Picture Package.** The Picture Package dialog box opens (**1**, next page). For Source Images, choose Use: **Selected Images from Bridge.**

   or

   In **Photoshop,** choose File > Automate > **Picture Package,** then for Source Images, choose Use: **File,** click Browse/Choose, locate an image, then click Open; or **Folder,** click Browse/Choose, locate a folder, then click Open to create a Picture Package for each image in that folder; or **Frontmost Document** to use the currently open, active document.

2. In the **Document** area, do the following:

   Choose a **Page Size** for the overall picture package.

   Choose a **Layout** option (in inches) for the page; note the preview in the Layout area.

   Choose a **Resolution** and a document **Mode.**

   Optional: Check Flatten All Layers to have all images (and optional labels) appear on one layer. Uncheck this option to have each image/label appear on a separate layer.

3. In the **Label** area (optional):

   If you want each file to be labeled, choose a **Content** type. If you chose Custom Text, enter the desired label in the Custom Text field. Labels for other Content types will be extracted, if available, from the file's metadata info.

   Choose a **Font, Font Size, Color,** and **Opacity** for the text.

Choose a **Position** for each label, relative to the image.

Choose a **Rotate** option or leave it on the default setting of None.

4. *Optional:* To customize the layout, click **Edit Layout** on the right side of the dialog box. The Picture Package Edit Layout dialog box opens (**2**, next page). Do any of the following:

   Enter a **Name** for the new layout.

   Choose a preset size from the **Page Size** pop-up menu, or enter custom **Width** and **Height** settings in the currently chosen Units.

   Click **Add Zone** to add a new thumbnail or placeholder box.

   Click a thumbnail or placeholder box and drag a handle to **resize** it, or drag inside it to **reposition** it.

   Click **Delete Zone** to delete a selected thumbnail or placeholder box.

   To exit the dialog box, click **Save,** enter a file name, then click Save again. (Or click Cancel, then click No to cancel any Edit Layout changes you've made.)

   For other options, see Photoshop Help.

5. Click OK. Sit by idly while the command does its work. (Press Esc, if need be, to stop the command during processing.)

6. Save the new picture package file in a format of your choosing.

TIP You can also drag pictures into a layout from Windows Explorer/Finder.

TIP To use more than one file in a picture package, in the Layout area, click a thumbnail. The Select an Image File dialog box opens. Locate a file, then click Open. The replacement image will display in the selected box.

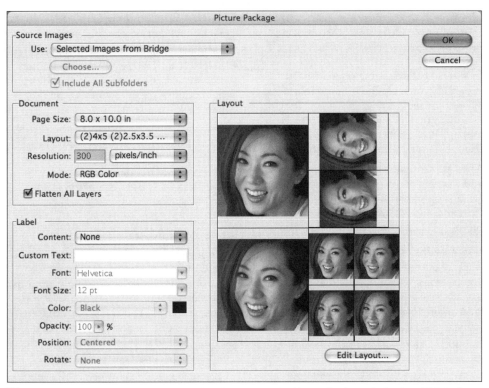

1 *Choose Source Images, Document, and Label options in the **Picture Package** dialog box. This is the (2) 4 x 5 & (2) 2.5 x 3.5 & (4) 2 x 2.5 layout.*

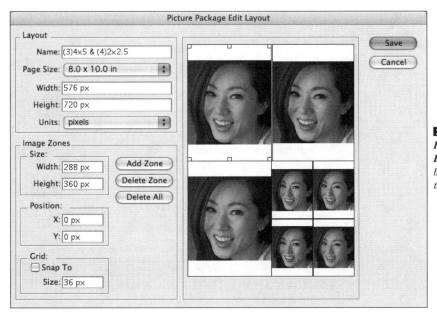

2 *You can use the **Picture Package Edit Layout** dialog box to further customize any layout.*

Using the **Web Photo Gallery** command, you can export multiple files directly as a website for viewing by friends or clients. When you use this command, Photoshop produces the following: a gallery home page with its index.htm file, which can be opened in any Web browser for previewing; individual JPEG file pages in an images subfolder; HTML page files in a pages subfolder; and JPEG thumbnail images in a thumbnails subfolder.

Note: When you're ready to upload your Web gallery to a server, ask your Internet service provider (ISP), domain host, or Webmaster which file- and folder-naming conventions to use, and for uploading instructions.

To create a Web photo gallery:

1. Make sure all the files you want to use for the website are selected in Bridge (don't select a folder in Bridge), or are contained in one folder.

2. In Bridge, choose Tools > Photoshop > **Web Photo Gallery,** or in Photoshop, choose File > Automate > Web Photo Gallery. The Web Photo Gallery dialog box opens **1**.

3. From the **Styles** pop-up menu, choose a layout style for the website. The styles preview on the right.

4. *Optional:* Enter an **Email** address to serve as a contact address for the gallery.

5. For **Source Images,** choose Use: **Selected Images from Bridge.** Or choose **Folder,** click Browse/Choose, locate the folder that contains the files you want to use, then click Choose.

Optional: Check Include All Subdirectories/Subfolders to have the command process files in any subdirectories/subfolders inside the designated folder, in addition to any files on the top level.

6. Click **Destination,** locate the folder that you want to save the resulting files in, then click Choose.

7. When you choose different categories on the **Options** pop-up menu, the dialog box options change accordingly; options also vary depending on which style you chose in step 3. You can go through the categories one by one to specify such settings as file size, resolution, font, file naming, and link colors.

Choose **General** to choose HTML options for your website: Choose an **Extension** for the HTML files; check Use UTF 8 Encoding for URL to include Unicode™ file names; check Add Width and Height

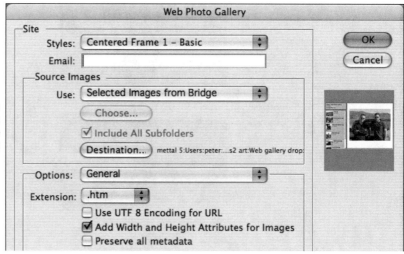

1 *The Web Photo Gallery dialog box (with General chosen on the Options pop-up menu)*

1 *With* ***Banner*** *chosen on the Options pop-up menu in the* ***Web Photo Gallery*** *dialog box*

2 *With* ***Large Images*** *chosen on the Options pop-up menu in the* ***Web Photo Gallery*** *dialog box*

3 *With* ***Thumbnails*** *chosen on the Options pop-up menu in the* ***Web Photo Gallery*** *dialog box*

4 *With* ***Custom Colors*** *chosen on the Options pop-up menu in the* ***Web Photo Gallery*** *dialog box*

Attributes for Images to display file sizes; check Preserve All Metadata to keep file metadata information.

Choose **Banner** **1**, then enter information to appear on every gallery page, such as the Site Name, Photographer, Contact Info, and Date. Choose a Font and Font Size for the banner text, if available for the chosen Style.

Choose **Large Images** **2** to choose options for the large image previews used on gallery pages. *Optional:* Check Add Numeric Links to include a number sequence to aid in navigating between previews; check Resize Images to enable options for changing the size of the previews; choose a preset size from the pop-up menu or enter a size in pixels. Choose a Constrain option to resize the file width, height, or both. Choose a preset JPEG Quality, then enter a value (0–12) or move the File Size slider; the higher the JPEG Quality, the larger the file size. Enter a Border Size in pixels (0–99). If available, check any Titles Use options (to be extracted from File > File Info), and finally (Phew!) choose Font and Font Size settings for the titles text.

Choose **Thumbnails** **3** to choose options for the small images on the pages of the gallery. Choose a thumbnail image Size, and choose any of the available thumbnail layout settings (Columns, Rows, and Border Size). If available, check Titles Use options (to be extracted from the File > File Info dialog box), and choose Font and Font Size settings.

Choose **Custom Colors** **4** to choose colors for the Background, Banner, Text, and Links spaces. Click a color swatch to change it via the Color Picker. This isn't available for all the Styles.

Choose **Security** (**1**, next page) to display text over your images as an antitheft measure. Choose a type of Content. For Custom Text, type the desired text in the field. The other options are extracted

(Continued on the following page)

Web Photo Gallery

automatically, if available, from File > File Info. Choose a Font, Font Size (the default is 36 pt), Color (Web-safe colors, if possible), and an Opacity (lower this value to create transparent text). Choose a Position for the text relative to the image, and a Rotate option (or None for no rotation).

8. Click OK. Photoshop will create the following files: at least one home page, named "index"; HTML files for the other pages of the site bearing the extension chosen in Options: General; and JPEG files for the images and thumbnails.

The gallery will display in your default Web browser. If you click a thumbnail or caption in the Web browser, an enlarged view of that image will appear **2–3**. There may also be navigation arrows to let the viewer navigate to the previous or next picture or to the home page.

Note: To preserve the links, store all the gallery files and folders in the same folder.

TIP Extra gallery templates are found in the Goodies/Web Photo Gallery Template folder on the Photoshop CS2 Installation CD. To make them accessible on the Styles pop-up menu in the Web Photo Gallery dialog box, drag any or all of the template folders from the CD into the Photoshop CS2/Presets/Web Photoshop Gallery folder.

TIP For more information about this feature, type "web photo" in the Search field in the Adobe Help Center (Photoshop Help).

TIP Web Photo Gallery templates can be restrictive as far as the choice of colors, fonts, and, in particular, large file size options. Note that when many image files are used, navigating between previews can be time-consuming. Try running tests with a few moderately sized files and simple font and color schemes.

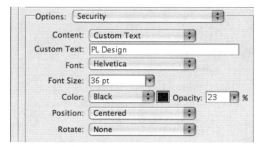

1 *With **Security** chosen on the Options pop-up menu in the **Web Photo Gallery** dialog box*

2 *This is a finished **Web Photo Gallery** page (Centered Frame 1–Basic style). When a thumbnail is clicked, an enlargement displays on the right.*

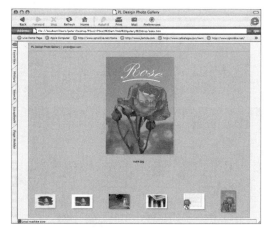

3 *This finished **Web Photo Gallery** page uses the Simple Horizontal thumbnails style.*

1 *The **PDF Presentation** dialog box, with Presentation chosen as the Output Option*

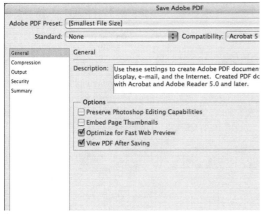

2 *The **Save Adobe PDF** dialog box, with the General panel displayed*

Another way to package and send your files to a client is via a **PDF Presentation.** You can make the finished presentation file size small enough that it can be included as an e-mail attachment.

To create a PDF presentation:

1. In Bridge, click the files to be included in the presentation. Try to limit the selection to 10 image files or fewer.

2. Choose Tools > Photoshop > **PDF Presentation** **1**. The PDF Presentation dialog box opens.

3. *Optional:* Click Browse to locate and include other files. Click Remove to delete a selected filename from the Source Files list.

4. Under Output Options, click **Multi-Page Document** to create one multipage PDF file; or click **Presentation** to create a multipage PDF file plus a slide show, and choose Presentation Options for the show.

5. Click **Save,** enter a filename, choose a location, then click **Save.** The Save Adobe PDF dialog box opens **2**.

6. Do the following:

   In the **General** panel, choose Adobe PDF Preset: **[Smallest File Size]** and check **View PDF After Saving.**

   In the **Compression** panel, for Options, try using the Bicubic Downsampling To option with a value of 100 or 150 pixels/ inch; leave Compression as JPEG; and set the Image Quality to Medium or Medium Low. You will need to experiment with these settings to produce a small file size while preserving image quality. Leave all other options at their default settings. (For more about the PDF format, see pages 493–496.)

7. Click **Save PDF**. Photoshop will output the files to a PDF file and open Adobe Acrobat or Adobe Reader. If the Presentation option was chosen, a slide show will commence. Press Esc at any time to stop the slide show.

Creating and using layer comps

A **layer comp** (short for "composition") is a set of layer characteristics, including the current state of image pixels, as well as visibility, position, and appearance (applied layer effects). Via the Layer Comps palette, you can store multiple versions of the same image in one file, for easy presentation to clients. To display a layer comp, you simply click a button on the palette.

To create a layer comp:

1. Create all the layers to be used in an image, including any fill or adjustment layers, masks, smart object layers, or type layers, and image-edit them to create a document version (apply filters, choose layer blending modes, layer opacity, etc.).

2. Choose visibility (hide/show), position (location in the image), and appearance (layer effects) settings for each layer.

3. Click the **New Layer Comp** button at the bottom of the Layer Comps palette **1**. The Layer Comp Options dialog box opens **2**.

4. Enter a **Name** for the comp, then check the layer settings you want saved in the comp: **Visibility, Position,** and/or **Appearance.**

5. *Optional:* Enter information in the Comment field to display on the palette when the layer comp list is expanded **3**.

6. Click OK. To create more layer comps, repeat steps 2–5.

TIP To bypass the Layer Comp Options dialog box when creating a comp, Alt-click/Option-click the New Layer Comp button.

TIP To change which characteristics a layer comp applies at any time, double-click the comp on the Layer Comps palette, then check or uncheck any Apply To Layers options. To rename a comp, it's faster to double-click the comp name on the palette.

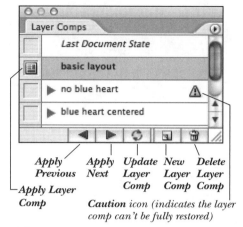

1 *Use the **Layer Comps** palette to create, store, apply, update, and delete layer comps.*

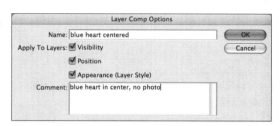

2 *In the **Layer Comp Options** dialog box, name the layer comp, decide which characteristics you want saved in the comp, and enter comments, if desired.*

3 *Comp lists expanded to reveal comments*

Start with a comp

To preserve the original state of a document, create a **layer comp** from the **original** image before making any edits. Yes, snapshots on the History palette serve a similar purpose, but they don't save with the file, whereas layer comps do.

1 *The **Layer Comps** palette for the images shown on this page and the next*

2 *Layer Comp 1 (white background, original objects)*

To display a layer comp:

On the Layer Comps palette, click in the left column for a comp; the **Apply Layer Comp** icon ▤ will appear.
or
To cycle through comps on the palette, click the **Apply Next** ▶ or **Apply Previous** ◀ button at the bottom of the palette **1**–**2** (and **1**–**2**, next page).

Let's say you edit your document, then cycle through some layer comps. Here's how you can get back to the last **working state** of the document.

To restore the last document state:

On the Layer Comps palette, click the **Apply Layer Comp** button ▤ next to Last Document State.
or
Right-click/Control-click a layer comp and choose **Restore Last Document State.**

You can **update** any existing layer comp to incorporate new modifications made to the document.

To update a layer comp:

1. Edit or change the visibility, position, or layer style of any layers in a document.

2. On the Layer Comps palette, click the name of the layer comp you want to update, then click the **Update Layer Comp** button ○ at the bottom of the palette.

TIP If you change the number of layers in a document that are recorded in a layer comp (e.g., delete or merge layers), an alert icon ⚠ will appear next to the comp name(s). When this occurs, to apply the change to the comps, click the alert icon, then click Clear; or click the Update Layer Comp button; or right-click/Control-click the alert icon and choose Clear Layer Comp Warning or Clear All Layer Comp Warnings.

Deleting a **layer comp** has no effect on a document's appearance.

To delete a layer comp:

1. On the Layer Comps palette, click the layer comp you want to delete.

2. Click the **Delete Layer Comp** button 🗑 at the bottom of the palette.

You can use an automate command to produce a **multipage PDF** slide show of layer comps in a Photoshop file.

To create a PDF slide show of layer comps:

1. Open a Photoshop file that contains layer comps.

2. Choose File > Scripts > **Layer Comps to PDF.**

3. Click **Browse,** enter a file name, choose a location, then click **Save.**

4. Choose **Slideshow Options** to control how the comp displays sequentially onscreen in the PDF viewing application.

5. Click **Run.** The script will output the images to an Adobe Acrobat file. Click OK when the alert dialog box appears onscreen, then open the presentation file in Adobe Acrobat or Adobe Reader to view the slide show. (Press Esc at any time to stop the presentation.)

TIP Two other related scripts, found on the File > Scripts submenu, are Layer Comps To Files, which creates a flattened file for each comp, and Layer Comps To WPG, which creates a Web photo gallery page containing images of individual comps.

Duplicate comp

If you don't want to create a new layer comp from scratch, you can start from a **duplicate.** Drag a layer comp name over the **New Layer Comp** button. 🔲

1 *Layer Comp 2 (layer effects applied to two of the layers)*

2 *Layer Comp 5 (two additional layers visible; the butterfly layer in a new position)*

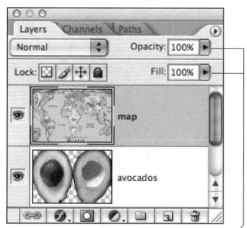

1 *Each layer can have a different **Opacity** and/or **Fill** percentage.*

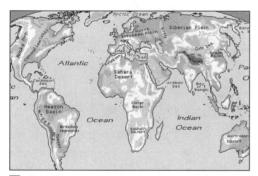

2 *The map layer, 100% Opacity, on top of the avocados layer*

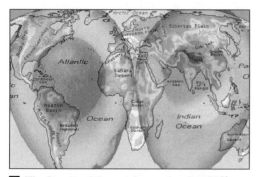

3 *The Opacity of the map layer reduced to 50%*

BY THIS POINT, HOPEFULLY YOU'RE comfortable with using the Layers palette and basic layer features, and are ready to explore this "power" palette further. We'll show you how to blend pixels between layers; create and use layer masks; create and use clipping masks; link layers; align and distribute layers; transform layers; and create and edit smart object layers. (Adjustment layers are discussed on pages 166–168, shape layers on pages 382–383.)

Changing layer opacity and fill

The **Opacity** setting on the Layers palette controls the opacity of layer imagery plus any applied layer effects, whereas the **Fill** setting controls only the opacity of layer imagery (not of layer effects). Both settings can be applied to image, type, adjustment, smart object, and shape layers.

To change the opacity or fill percentage of a layer:

Choose an **Opacity** or **Fill** percentage from the Layers palette (drag across the word, enter a value, or use the slider) **1**. The lower the Opacity or Fill, the more pixels from the layer below will show through the active layer **2**–**3**. You can't change the Opacity or Fill of the Background.
or
Choose a tool other than a painting tool, then press 1 on the **keyboard** to change the Opacity of the active layer to 10%, 2 to change the **Opacity** to 20%, and so on. Or type both digits quickly (e.g., 15, for 15%). Hold down **Shift** using this method to change the **Fill** of the active layer.

TIP Press 0 to restore the Opacity to 100%; press Shift-0 to restore the Fill to 100%.

Blending layers

To choose a layer blending mode:

The layer blending mode you choose for a layer affects how that layer's pixels blend with pixels in the layer directly below it. Blending modes can be applied to any type of layer (e.g., image, type, smart object). Some modes produce subtle effects (e.g., Soft Light), whereas others produce dramatic color shifts (e.g., Difference). Normal is the default mode. The blending modes are discussed in detail and illustrated on pages 190–194.

There are three ways to choose a blending mode for a layer:

➤ From the mode pop-up menu in the top left corner of the Layers palette **1**–**3**.

➤ By pressing Shift-+ (plus) or Shift--- (minus). This shortcut cycles through the modes for the currently active layer (don't have a painting or editing tool selected when you do this, or you'll change the mode for the tool).

➤ By double-clicking the layer, then in the Layer Style dialog box, choosing a Blend Mode under General Blending.

1 *The original image (two layers)*

2 *Blending modes on the pop-up menu on the Layers palette*

3 *After choosing **Overlay** mode for the pine cone layer*

Behind and Clear

You can choose **Behind** mode for tools (e.g., Brush, Paint Bucket, Pencil, History Brush, Clone Stamp, Pattern Stamp, or Gradient) from the options bar, but not for a layer. In Behind mode, it will appear as if you're painting on the back of the current layer.

For the Paint Bucket or Brush tool, or for any shape tool with the Fill Pixels button ▢ clicked on the options bar, you can choose **Clear** mode, which works like an eraser.

To access Behind and Clear modes, make sure neither the Lock Image Pixels button ✎ nor the Lock Transparent Pixels button ▨ is selected on the Layers palette.

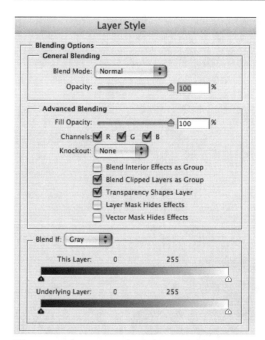

Layer Style

Blending Options
General Blending
Blend Mode: Normal
Opacity: 100 %

Advanced Blending
Fill Opacity: 100 %
Channels: ☑ R ☑ G ☑ B
Knockout: None
☐ Blend Interior Effects as Group
☑ Blend Clipped Layers as Group
☑ Transparency Shapes Layer
☐ Layer Mask Hides Effects
☐ Vector Mask Hides Effects

Blend If: Gray
This Layer: 0 255
Underlying Layer: 0 255

1 *The **Blending Options** settings in the **Layer Style** dialog box*

2 *Blend Interior Effects as Group unchecked:*
Linear Dodge was chosen as the blend mode for the Inner Glow effect, and Difference was chosen as the blend mode for the Gradient Overlay effect. Both of these layer effects are more visible than the layer's blending mode (Difference).

3 *Blend Interior Effect as Group checked: The Inner Glow and Gradient Overlay effects have the same blend modes as in the previous figure, but those modes are less obvious because the layer blend mode (Difference) now controls the overall blending with underlying layers.*

The **Blending Options** in the Layer Styles dialog box offer, in addition to the blending mode, opacity, and fill controls we've already discussed, a number of advanced settings for controlling how a layer and layer effects blend with underlying layers.

To choose blending options for a layer:

1. Double-click a layer on the Layers palette, then click **Blending Options** at the top left side of the dialog box.

2. *Optional:* In the General Blending area, change the Blend Mode or Opacity **1**.

3. Check Preview on the right side of the dialog box.

4. In the **Advanced Blending** section, do any of the following:

   To control the opacity of image or shape pixels but not of layer effects, adjust the **Fill Opacity** (this has the same function as the Fill option on the Layers palette).

5. The two "Blend…" options control how single layers or layers in a clipping mask blend with underlying layers (read more about clipping masks on pages 305–306).

   If **Blend Interior Effects as Group** is unchecked (the default setting) for a layer that has a blending mode other than Normal, the layer's interior effects (e.g., Inner Glow, Satin, Color Overlay, Pattern Overlay, or Gradient Overlay) will be used to blend the layer with the underlying layers, and the layer's overall blending mode will be less evident.

   With Blend Interior Effects as Group checked, the layer's interior effects will blend first with the layer's own blending mode, then the whole blended collection of layers will blend with the underlying layers, thus diminishing the visual impact of the interior effects **2**–**3**.

   For the Blend Clipped Layers as Group option, see Photoshop Help.

   (Continued on the following page)

Blending Options for Layer

6. *Check any of these options:*

Transparency Shapes Layer (default setting is on) to limit some layer effects (e.g., Satin, Overlay) to opaque parts of the layer; or uncheck this option to permit effects to cover the whole layer, including any transparent areas. (Layer effects are discussed in the next chapter.)

Layer Mask Hides Effects to hide any portions of layer effects that fall outside a layer mask shape.

Vector Mask Hides Effects to hide any portions of layer effects that fall outside a vector mask shape.

7. Using the **Blend If** sliders, you can control which pixels in the current layer stay visible and which pixels from the underlying layer show through the current layer:

Move the leftmost This Layer slider to the right to remove shadow areas from the active layer.

Move the rightmost This Layer slider to the left to remove highlights from the active layer.

Move the leftmost Underlying Layer slider to the right to restore shadow areas from the layer directly below the active layer.

Move the rightmost Underlying Layer slider to the left to restore highlights from the layer directly below the active layer.

8. Click OK **1**–**2**.

TIP To set the blending range separately for each channel, choose a channel from the Blend If pop-up menu in the Layer Style dialog box; to work on all the channels at once, leave Gray as the choice. To adjust the midtones independently, Alt-drag/Option-drag either slider (it will divide in two).

1 *In this image, a photo layer was duplicated, then the Find Edges filter was applied to the duplicate.*

2 *To allow some of the light and dark tones in the photo to peek through the duplicate layer, we divided and moved the white **This Layer** slider and the black **Underlying Layer** slider in the **Blending Options** panel of the Layer Style dialog box.*

1 *The original image*

2 *After applying the Mezzotint filter to the duplicate layer, then lowering the opacity of the duplicate layer*

3 *Blended layers, with the Grain filter applied*

In these instructions, a filter is applied to a duplicate layer and then the original and duplicate layers are blended using Layers palette **opacity** and **blending mode** controls. You can use this technique to soften the effect of an image-editing command, such as a filter, or to experiment with various blending modes. You can also use a layer mask to limit the area affected. And if you don't like the results, you can just trash the duplicate layer and start over.

To blend a modified layer with the original layer:

1. Click a layer **1**, then press Ctrl-J/Cmd-J to duplicate it.

2. Modify the duplicate layer by applying image-editing commands, such as filters, or adjustment commands.

3. On the Layers palette, adjust the Opacity to achieve the desired degree of transparency between the original layer and the modified, duplicate layer **2** and/or choose a different blending mode.

4. *Optional:* Create a layer mask from a feathered selection on the duplicate layer to partially hide pixels (see the next page). Another way to gradually fade the blend effect is by applying a gradient to the layer mask.

TIP To create a beautiful textural effect, duplicate an image layer in a color file, click the new layer, and choose Image > Adjustments > Desaturate (Ctrl-Shift-U/ Cmd-Shift-U) to make it grayscale. Next, apply the Artistic > Film Grain, Noise > Add Noise, or Texture > Grain filter **3**. Finally, lower the opacity of, and try out different blending modes for, the new layer via the Layers palette.

Blend Modified Layer

Using layer masks

A **layer mask** is an 8-bit grayscale channel that lets you hide all or some of the pixels on a layer. By default, white areas in a layer mask permit pixels to be seen, black areas hide pixels, and gray areas partially mask pixels. Via the layer mask thumbnail, you can edit, move, invert, or deactivate the mask, or even copy it to other layers. When you're done working with the mask, you can either apply it to make the effect permanent or discard it to completely undo its effect.

To create a layer mask:

Method 1 (no selection)

1. Click a layer or layer group **1**.

2. To create a white mask in which all the layer pixels are **visible,** click the Add Layer Mask button **▢** at the bottom of the Layers palette (or choose Layer > Layer Mask > Reveal All) **2**–**3**.
   or
   To create a black mask in which all the layer pixels are **hidden,** Alt-click/Option-click the Add Layer Mask button on the Layers palette (or choose Layer > Layer Mask > Hide All).

Method 2 (using a selection)

1. Create a selection on a layer.

2. To **reveal** layer pixels within the **selection,** click the Add Layer Mask button **▢** on the Layers palette (or choose Layer > Layer Mask > Reveal Selection).
   or
   To **hide** layer pixels within the **selection,** Alt-click/Option-click the Add Layer Mask button on the Layers palette (or choose Layer > Add Layer Mask > Hide Selection).

TIP A layer mask will be listed on the Channels palette when its layer is active.

TIP You can also mask image layer pixels by creating a vector mask using a pen tool or shape tool (see page 378).

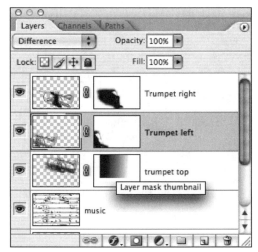

1 *The original image*

2 *Each of the three "Trumpet" layers in this image has its own **mask**.*

3 *The topmost trumpet fades out due to a gradient in its layer mask; portions of the middle and bottom trumpets are also hidden via a black-and-white layer mask.*

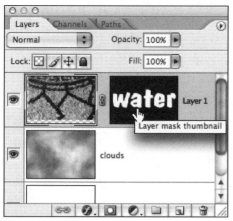

1 *Layer 1 pixels are revealed through the white areas in the **layer mask**.*

To use type shapes as a layer mask:

1. Create an editable type layer.

2. Ctrl-click/Cmd-click the type layer thumbnail. A selection will display in the document window.

3. Hide the type layer by clicking the eye icon. The selection marquee will still be visible.

4. Click the layer that you want to add the mask to. *Optional:* Choose a selection tool and reposition the type selection, if necessary. (Don't use the Move tool to move the selection—that would remove image pixels from the current layer.)

5. To **reveal** layer pixels within the selection, click the Add Layer Mask button ▣ on the Layers palette.
   or
   To **hide** layer pixels within the selection, Alt-click/Option-click the Add Layer Mask button ▣ on the Layers palette.

   The type will display as white or black areas in the layer mask thumbnail **1**–**2**.

TIP To toggle the mask function between hide and reveal, click the layer mask thumbnail, then press Ctrl-I/Cmd-I.

TIP To reposition the type shape area within the layer mask, you need to unlink the layer mask from the layer (see page 303).

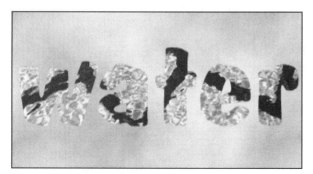

2 *In this image, the water layer is visible only through the letter shapes of the **layer mask**.*

Type Shapes as Layer Mask

To reshape a layer mask:

1. Choose the **Brush** tool (B or Shift-B). ✐
(You could also use the Eraser, Paint Bucket, or Gradient tool.)

2. On the options bar, click a brush on the Brush Preset picker, choose Mode: Normal, and choose 100% Opacity (or a lower opacity to partially hide layer pixels).

3. To display the layer mask with the image, click the layer mask thumbnail (on the right) on the Layers palette **1**.
or
To display the mask by itself in the document window, Alt-click/Option-click the layer mask thumbnail. (Alt-click/Option-click the layer mask thumbnail to redisplay the mask on the image.)
or
Alt-Shift-click/Option-Shift-click the layer mask thumbnail to display the mask as a colored overlay. (Repeat the shortcut to restore the normal display.)

4. Do any of the following:

   Paint on the image with **black** as the Foreground color to **enlarge** the mask and hide pixels on the layer.

   Paint with **white** as the Foreground color to **reduce** the mask and restore pixels on the layer.

   Lower the **opacity** for the current tool to make the layer look semitransparent.

5. When you're finished modifying the layer mask, click the layer thumbnail **2**–**3**.

TIP To invert the effect of a layer mask, click the layer mask thumbnail, then press Ctrl-I/Cmd-I. Hidden areas will be revealed, and formerly visible areas will be hidden.

TIP You can use a shape tool to create a shape on a layer mask (see page 384).

1 *Click the* **layer mask thumbnail**

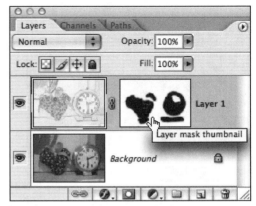

2 *The original top layer*

3 *The* **layer mask** *allows the heart sachet and clock face from the underlying image to be visible.*

1 *Click the **link** icon to disengage a layer from its layer mask.*

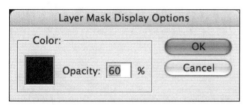

2 *Use the **Layer Mask Display Options** dialog box to change the layer mask overlay **Color** and **Opacity**.*

By default, a layer and its layer mask are linked and, when moved, move in unison. If you want to move each component separately, you have to **unlink** them first.

To move the layer image or mask independently:

1. On the Layers palette, click the link icon 🔗 between the layer thumbnail and the layer mask thumbnail **1**. The icon will disappear.

2. Click either the layer thumbnail or the layer mask thumbnail, depending on what you want to move.

3. Choose the **Move** tool (V). 🖐️

4. Drag in the document window.

5. Click again between the layer and layer mask thumbnails to restore the link.

To move or duplicate a layer mask: NEW

To **move** a mask, drag a layer mask thumbnail onto another layer (not the Background).
or
To **duplicate** a mask, Alt-drag/Option-drag a layer mask thumbnail onto another layer.

On the previous page, we showed you how to display the mask as a colored overlay (Alt-Shift-click/Option-Shift-click the layer mask thumbnail). If you like, you can change the the **overlay** color or **opacity** (say, if the image has a lot of red in it and it's hard to see the overlay).

To choose layer mask display options:

1. Double-click a layer mask thumbnail. The Layer Mask Display Options dialog box opens.

2. Click the **Color** square, then choose a different overlay color, and/or change the **Opacity** percentage **2**.

3. Click OK.

To deactivate a layer mask temporarily:

Shift-click the **layer mask thumbnail** on the Layers palette (the thumbnail won't become selected). A red X will appear over the thumbnail and the entire layer will be visible **1**. (Shift-click the layer mask thumbnail again to remove the X and restore the mask effect.)

One disadvantage of using layer masks is that they take up storage space, so when you're done using them, you should **apply** the ones you like to make their effects permanent and **delete** any that you don't need. *Note:* Before applying or deleting any masks, you may want to copy the file using Save As and keep the original with layer masks in reserve for future editing.

To apply or delete a layer mask:

Right-click/Control-click a layer mask thumbnail and choose **Delete Layer Mask** or **Apply Layer Mask.**
or
Click the layer mask thumbnail, then click the **Delete Layer** button. An alert dialog box will appear. To make the mask effect permanent, click **Apply 2**, or to remove the mask and undo its effect, click **Delete.**

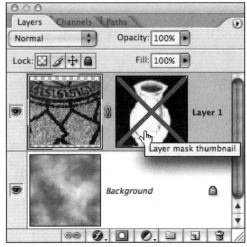

1 *Shift-click the* **layer mask thumbnail** *to deactivate/ activate a layer mask.*

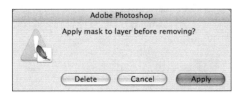

2 *Click* **Apply** *to make the mask effect permanent.*

1 *After you Alt-click/Option-click between two layers to create a **clipping mask**, the clipped layers will be indented and the base layer name will be underlined.*

2 *The map of India is **clipping** (limiting) the view of the puppets.*

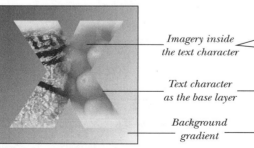

Imagery inside the text character

Text character as the base layer

Background gradient

3 *You can also use a clipping mask to fill type with imagery.*

Using clipping masks

When layers are formed into a **clipping mask,** the bottommost (base) layer clips (limits) the display of pixels on, and also controls the mode and opacity of, the layers above it. The base layer can be a type, image, smart object, or shape layer.

To create a clipping mask:

1. Alt-click/Option-click the line between two layers (the pointer will turn into two overlapping circles) **1**–**3**, or right-click/Control-click a layer and choose **Create Clipping Mask.**
   or
   Or click the layer to be clipped, then **NEW** press Ctrl-Alt-G/Cmd-Option-G.

   Notes: The layers used in a clipping mask must be listed consecutively on the palette. When clipping layers in a group, all the layers must reside within the group.

   The base layer name will be underlined; the thumbnails for the clipped layers will have a downward-pointing arrow and will be indented.

2. *Optional:* Repeat the previous step to add more contiguous layers to the mask.

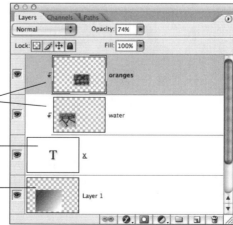

Create Clipping Mask

305

When you **release** a layer from a clipping mask, any masked layers above the one you're releasing are also released.

To release a layer from a clipping mask:

Alt-click/Option-click the line below the layer that you want to release **1**–**2**.

or

NEW Right-click/Control-click a layer to be released and choose **Release Clipping Mask.**

or

Click the layer you want to release and press

NEW Ctrl-Alt-G/Cmd-Option-G.

To release an entire clipping mask:

1. Click the base layer in the group.

2. Choose Layer > **Release Clipping Mask**

NEW or press Ctrl-Alt-G/Cmd-Option-G.

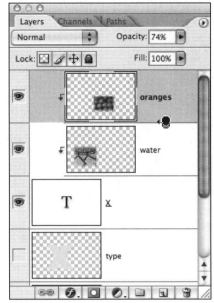

1 *Alt-click/Option-click below a layer to* **release** *it from a* **clipping mask**.

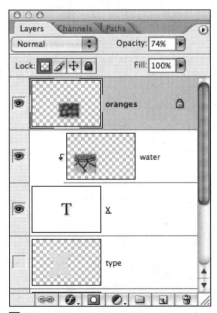

2 *The top layer is* **released** *from the mask.*

Linking layers

Linked layers move as a unit in the document window and drag-and-drop as a unit to other files. If you align, distribute, or transform (e.g., scale or rotate) a linked layer, the edit will also apply to all the layers it's linked to.

To link layers: **NEW**

1. On the Layers palette, select two or more consecutive or nonconsecutive layers **1** (Ctrl-click/Cmd-click to select nonconsecutive ones).

2. Click the **Link** button 🔗 at the bottom of the Layers palette. Now if you click any one of the linked layers, a link icon will appear for all the linked layers **2**.

TIP To unlink a layer, click the layer, then click the Link button. The link icon will disappear.

TIP To align or distribute linked layers, see the instructions on the following page. To move linked layers, choose the Move tool (V), click one of the linked layers, then drag in the document window.

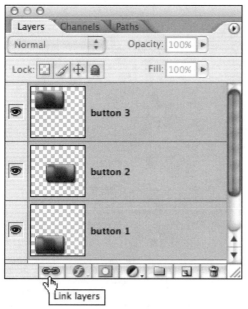

1 *Select all the layers to be linked, then click the **Link** button at the bottom of the palette.*

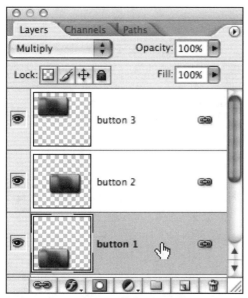

2 *When you click a **linked** layer, link icons appear.*

NEW Aligning and distributing layers

The **Align** buttons align multi-selected or linked layers by their opaque pixel edges. You can use these commands on all types of layers (say, to align button shapes for a Web page).

To align two or more layers:

1. Select two or more layers **1**, or click a layer that one or more other layers are linked to. For linked layers, the layer you click will be the reference position that the other linked layers will align to.

2. Choose the **Move** tool (V), then click an **Align** button on the options bar **2**–**3**.

TIP To align layers to a selection, create the selection before step 1 in the instructions above.

TIP You can also choose alignment options from the Layer > Align (or Align Layers To Selection) submenu.

TIP If a layer being aligned contains pixels outside the live canvas area, an align command could shift other layers outside the canvas area.

Like the Align buttons, the **Distribute** buttons redistribute selected or linked layers by their opaque pixel edges.

To distribute layers:

1. Select three or more layers or linked layers (not the Background).

2. Choose the **Move** tool (V), then click a **Distribute** button on the options bar **4**. The layers will be redistributed evenly between the two layers that are farthest apart **5**.

TIP If you don't like the results and you want to click a different align or distribute button, undo the last command before applying a new one. Otherwise, you'll be even farther from your goal.

TIP You can also choose distribute options from the Layer > Distribute submenu.

1 *The original image*

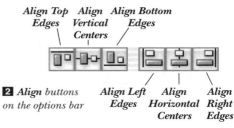

Align Top Edges   Align Vertical Centers   Align Bottom Edges

2 *Align buttons on the options bar*   *Align Left Edges   Align Horizontal Centers   Align Right Edges*

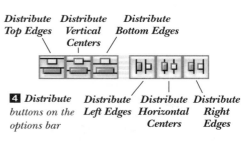

3 *After clicking* **Align Bottom Edges**

Distribute Top Edges   Distribute Vertical Centers   Distribute Bottom Edges

4 *Distribute buttons on the options bar*   *Distribute Left Edges   Distribute Horizontal Centers   Distribute Right Edges*

5 *After clicking* **Distribute Horizontal Centers**

Align, Distribute Layers

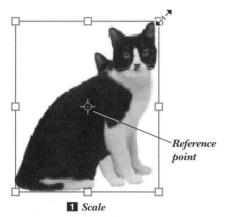

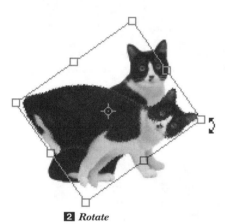

Reference point

1 *Scale*

2 *Rotate*

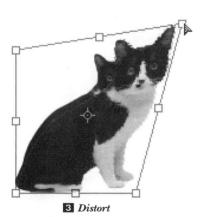

3 *Distort*

Transforming layers

In this section, you'll learn how to **scale, rotate, skew, distort,** and apply **perspective** to a layer, layer group, selection, or linked layers. First we'll show you how to use the individual **Transform** commands; after that you'll learn how to use the Free Transform command or Move tool to perform multiple transformations (our favorite); and finally you'll learn how to apply transformations by entering values on the options bar.

To transform a layer or group using a command:

1. On the Layers palette, click a layer or group, or select multiple layers. You can scale, rotate, or skew editable type layers. Linked layers transform together.

   Optional: For an image layer (not a group), create a selection to limit the transformation to those layer pixels.

2. Choose Edit > Transform > **Scale, Rotate, Skew, Distort,** or **Perspective.** A transform box will appear around the opaque part of the layer or selection.

3. *Optional:* To transform the layer or selection from a point other than its center, move the reference point (you can move it outside the transform box) **1**.

4. *Note:* If you're going to perform multiple transformations, to save time and preserve image quality, after performing one transform command, choose and then perform additional commands— then accept them all at once (step 5). Similarly, transforming multiple layers all at once helps to preserve image quality, as resampling occurs just once rather than for each individual layer.

   To **Scale** the layer horizontally and vertically, drag a corner handle **1**. To scale only the horizontal or vertical dimension, drag a side handle. Shift-drag to scale proportionately; Alt-drag/Option-drag to scale from the reference point.

   For **Rotate 2**, position the pointer near a transform box handle, either just

(Continued on the following page)

Transform Commands

inside or just outside the box (the pointer will become a curved, double-headed arrow), then drag in a circular direction. Shift-drag to constrain the rotation to a multiple of 15°.

For **Skew,** drag along an edge of the transform box to skew along the horizontal or vertical axis **1**–**2**. Alt-drag/Option-drag to skew symmetrically from the reference point.

For **Distort,** drag a corner handle to freely reposition just that handle (**3**, previous page), or drag a side handle to distort the side of the transform box along the horizontal and/or vertical axis. Alt-drag/Option-drag to distort symmetrically from the center of the layer. Distort tends to be more drastic than Skew.

For **Perspective,** drag a corner handle along the horizontal or vertical axis to create one-point perspective along that axis. The adjacent corner will move in unison. Or drag a side handle to skew along the current horizontal or vertical axis.

5. To accept the transformation, double-click inside the transform box or click the ✔ on the options bar (Enter/Return). To cancel the transformation, click the ⊘ (Esc).

TIP To undo the last handle modification, choose Edit > Undo.

TIP To move the entire layer (or selection), drag inside the transform box.

TIP To rotate a layer along an angle that you define, choose the Measure tool (I or Shift-I), drag in the document window to define an angle, then with the Measure tool still selected, choose Edit > Transform > Rotate.

TIP To transform a vector mask containing a path, click the mask thumbnail, choose a command from the Edit > Transform Path submenu, then follow the instructions on the previous page, starting with step 3.

1 *The original image (rasterized type)*

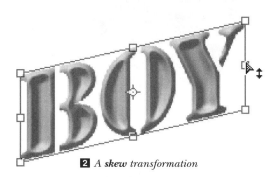

2 *A skew transformation*

What's left?

If you transform an image **layer** (or a selection on an image layer), any empty space remaining as a result of the transformation will become **transparent.**

If you transform the **Background,** any empty space remaining as a result of the transformation will be filled with the current **Background color.**

What else?

In addition to transforming an image layer, you can also transform a **type** layer, **shape** layer, **smart object** layer, **alpha channel, selection marquee, path, vector mask,** or unlinked, active **layer mask.**

To transform a selection marquee, right-click/Control-click in the document window and choose **Transform Selection,** then follow the instructions at right. To transform a path, choose the Path Selection tool, click a path name, then right-click/Control-click and choose **Free Transform Path.**

1 *The original image*

2 *After **scaling** and **distorting** the butterfly layer*

Once you're acquainted with the individual Transform commands, you'll probably want to start using either the **Free Transform** command or the **Move** tool transform controls because they let you perform multiple transformations without having to choose individual commands from a menu. What's more, image data is resampled only once, when you accept the changes.

To transform using the Free Transform command or Move tool:

1. Click a layer, multiple layers, or a group **1**. Any layers that are linked to a selected layer will also be transformed. You can also transform editable type layers. To transform the Background, you must create a selection.

2. Choose Edit > **Free Transform** (Ctrl-T/Cmd-T).
   or
   Choose the **Move** tool (V), check **Show Transform Controls** on the options bar, then click a handle. **NEW**

3. Follow step 4, starting on page 309, with the following exceptions:

   To **Skew,** Ctrl-Shift-drag/Cmd-Shift-drag.

   To **Distort 2**, Ctrl-drag/Cmd-drag.

   To apply **Perspective**, Ctrl-Alt-Shift-drag/Cmd-Option-Shift-drag a corner handle.

   At this point, you can also use the **options bar** to apply numerous transform settings, including changing the reference point from which the transformation occurs (**1**, next page).

4. To accept the transformation, double-click inside the bounding box or click the ✔ on the options bar (Enter/Return). To cancel the transformation, click the ⊘ (Esc). You must either accept or cancel to return to normal editing.

TIP As you transform a layer or a selection, note how the readouts change on either the options bar or the Info palette.

Free Transform/Move Tool Transform

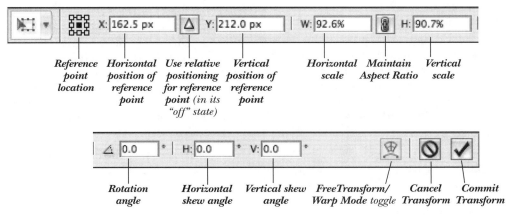

Reference point location — Horizontal position of reference point — Use relative positioning for reference point *(in its "off" state)* — Vertical position of reference point — Horizontal scale — Maintain Aspect Ratio — Vertical scale

Rotation angle — Horizontal skew angle — Vertical skew angle — FreeTransform/ Warp Mode *toggle* — Cancel Transform — Commit Transform

1 *The left and right sides of the options bar when a **Transform** command is chosen*

The **Warp** command on the Edit > Transform submenu distorts an entire layer by using an editable grid. You can choose preset warp shapes, an orientation, and other controls for the warp via the options bar.

NEW **To warp a layer:**

1. Click a layer on the Layers palette **2**–**3**.

2. Choose Edit > Transform > **Warp.** A grid with handles will display over the layer image.

3. To distort the layer image "by hand," on the options bar, choose **Warp: Custom,** then drag any of the grid squares, points, or direction lines.
   or
   To apply distortion via options bar controls (**1**, next page), choose a preset style from the **Warp** pop-up menu; then, if desired, click the **Warp Orientation** button 🔛 to toggle between horizontal and vertical distortion; or drag across **Bend, H** (horizontal distortion), or **V** (vertical distortion) to choose positive or negative values for those attributes **4**.

4. To accept the warp, press Enter/Return or click ✔ on the options bar (**2**, next page) (To cancel it, press Esc or click ⊘ on the options bar.) To remove an applied warp, use the History palette.

2 *The original label layer*

3 *A 3D object, placed from Illustrator*

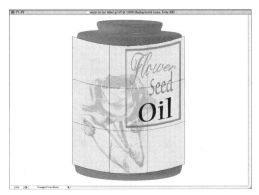

4 *We applied the **Arch** warp preset to the label layer and adjusted the **Bend** value to make the label fit the 3D object.*

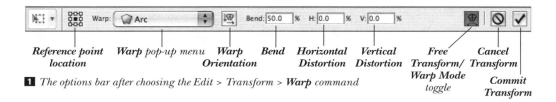

Reference point Warp *pop-up menu* Warp Bend Horizontal Vertical Free Cancel
location   Orientation   Distortion Distortion Transform/ Transform
                                                                              Warp Mode   Commit
1 *The options bar after choosing the Edit > Transform > **Warp** command*   toggle   Transform

Preset Warp commands

Arc	Curves a layer onto a flat circle
Arch, Bulge	A positive value curves a layer onto the back of a cylinder; a negative value curves a layer onto the front of a cylinder
Shell Lower	Fans out the bottom of a layer
Shell Upper	Fans out the top of a layer
Flag, Wave, Fish, Rise	Curves a layer onto a ribbon or banner
Inflate	Curves a layer onto the outside of a curved object
Squeeze	Curves a layer onto the inside of a curved object

2 *We **warped** a **layer** around a **3D** object using the Arch style and a negative Bend value, and resized the label layer to fit. A layer mask on the label layer was used to lower the opacity of the label on the left side to blend it in with the shading on the 3D object.*

Smart warp

When the **Warp** command is applied to a **smart object** layer, it remains live and can be reedited at any time by rechoosing the command. After converting multiple layers into a smart object, you can warp them in one pass. Just keep in mind that smart objects can't be converted back to separate layers (nothing's perfect!).

Creating smart object layers NEW

A **smart object** layer can contain either the contents of one or more layers in the current Photoshop document, or the contents of a file from another application (such as Adobe Illustrator, Acrobat, or Camera Raw) that you import into a Photoshop document.

When you edit the contents of a smart object from another application, you're escorted to the application in which it was created. When you edit a smart object made from Photoshop layers, a separate document opens containing the separate layers. In either case, when you edit, save, and close the file, the Photoshop document updates to reflect your edits (that's the "smart" part).

(Continued on the following page)

Smart Object Layers

Create, Edit, Rasterize, Convert Smart Object Layer

NEW To create a smart object:

Select one or more layers (e.g., image, type, adjustment, or shape) on the Layers palette, then choose **Group into New Smart Object** from the Layers palette menu.

or

Via File > **Place** in Photoshop or Bridge, import a Raw photo file, another Photoshop file, or a file from another application into the current document **1**. The smart object is now embedded in the document.

NEW To edit a smart object:

1. On the Layers palette, double-click the smart object layer thumbnail. Click OK when the prompt appears.

2. Either a separate document will open in Photoshop, displaying the original individual layers, or the creation application will launch and open the document. Edit the document as you wish.

3. Save and close the file, but don't change the file name or the location. You'll go back automatically to the Photoshop document, and the smart object layer will update to reflect your edits.

TIP Apply raster edits, such as filters, to the contents of a smart object (double-click the smart object thumbnail)—not to the smart layer!

TIP After editing a vector smart object in Illustrator, you may have to rescale the smart object layer in Photoshop to match how it looked in Illustrator.

Don't **rasterize** a smart object or **convert** it **to a layer** until you're done editing the image, because once you do so you won't be able to access the contents of the embedded file.

NEW To rasterize or convert a smart object layer:

To **rasterize** the layer, click the layer, then choose Layer > Rasterize > **Smart Object.**

or

To **convert** a smart object back into an image layer, click the layer, then choose Layer > Smart Objects > **Convert to Layer.**

Don't merge—be smart!

When you're contemplating whether to merge or flatten layers, consider grouping them into a **smart object layer** instead. You will achieve the same reduction of layers, plus you'll gain the ability to reedit the original separate layers by double-clicking the smart object layer thumbnail.

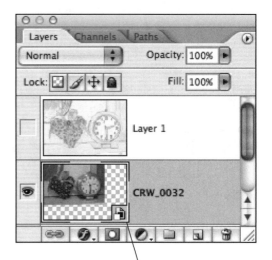

1 Smart object layers *have this boring icon. This smart object contains the contents of a Camera Raw file.*

Editing smart object layers

When applied to smart object layers, **Layers** palette edits, such as opacity, blending modes, masks, and effects, affect the layer appearance, not the original embedded smart object file.

Replacing smart object contents

To replace the contents of a smart object with another file, click the smart object layer, choose Layer > Smart Objects > **Replace Contents,** locate a replacement file, then click Place. If you edit the original file a smart object is based on (not the embedded file), you can also use this command to update the smart object in your Photoshop file.

LAYER EFFECTS 21

1 *The **Drop Shadow** effect: Drop shadows can help to anchor objects to a surface or, as in this case, make them appear to float in mid-air.*

AS A PHOTOSHOP USER, YOU'RE IN the business of creating illusions, and layer effects let you do it in short, easy steps. The layer effects that you can apply solo or in combination include Drop Shadow **1**, Inner Shadow, Outer Glow, Inner Glow, Bevel and Emboss, Satin, Color Overlay, Gradient Overlay, Pattern Overlay, and Stroke. Once applied (via the Layer Style dialog box **2**), layer effects can be edited, hidden, or removed at any time. And best of all, when you edit layer pixels, the effect(s) update accordingly (they should be called "smart effects"). First we'll give you generic instructions for applying layer effects, then instructions for applying individual effects and for saving applied effects as styles to the Styles palette.

Click any effect name to switch to that panel so you can choose custom settings (the box will become checked automatically).

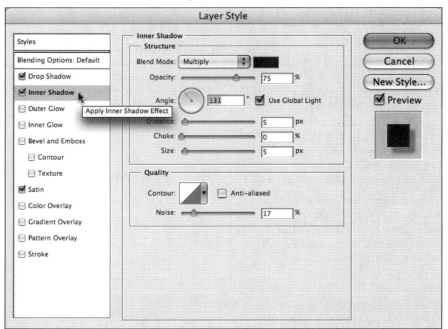

2 *Use the **Layer Style** dialog box to apply or change the settings for **layer effects.***

Applying layer effects

Layer effects can be applied to any layer, even to editable type, and individual effects can be turned on or off for a layer at any time via the eye icon. Layer effects affect all the visible pixels on a layer and will **update** instantly if pixels are added, modified, or deleted from the layer.

TIP A **style** is a combination of one or more layer effects (see pages 331–332).

All the layer effects are applied and edited via the **Layer Style** dialog box, and they're listed on the Layers palette below the name of the layer to which they're applied. They can't be applied to the Background of an image. Before we get into the individual effects, here are some general pointers:

➤ To **apply** an effect to a layer, double-click the layer (or for an image layer—not a type or smart object layer—you can double-click the layer thumbnail). The Layer Style dialog box opens. Click an effect **name** on the left side (**2**, previous page), then choose settings; click other effect names to apply additional effects to the same layer. Be sure to check **Preview** to preview the effect in the image.

You can also apply an effect by choosing a layer and then choosing an effect from the **Add Layer Style** pop-up menu 🖉 at the bottom of the Layers palette **1**.

➤ On the Layers palette, any layer to which a layer effect is currently applied will have a 🖉 icon. Click the arrowhead next to the icon to expand/collapse the list of effects applied to that layer.

➤ To **edit** an existing layer effect (or add another one), double-click the 🖉; or double-click the effect name nested under the layer name; or click a layer and then choose an effect from the Add Layer Style pop-up menu at the bottom of the Layers palette.

➤ To **hide** one layer effect, expand the effects list for the layer in question, then click the eye icon for the effect you want

The "f" icon indicates that one or more layer effects are applied to that layer.

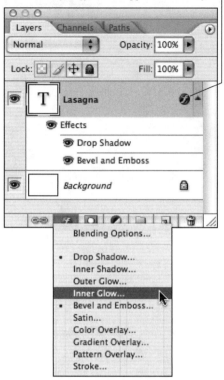

1 *Choose an effect from the **Add Layer Style** pop-up menu. A check mark/bullet signifies that that effect is already applied to the active layer. Effects can also be applied via **Layer > Layer Style**.*

What kind of imagery should I use?

We recommend applying the layer effects that work inward or outward from edges—**Drop Shadow, Inner Shadow, Outer Glow, Inner Glow, Bevel and Emboss,** and **Stroke**—to a text layer, a shape layer, or any layer imagery that has transparent pixels around it. You can use the Extract command to isolate subject matter from its background before applying a layer effect (see pages 134–136).

The **Satin, Color Overlay, Gradient Overlay,** and **Pattern Overlay** effects can be used effectively on layers that are fully opaque or on layers that contain transparency.

Don't bother creating a selection before applying a layer effect—the selection will be ignored.

to hide **1**. (Click there again at any time to redisplay the effect.) To hide all the effects on a layer, click the eye icon for the Effects bar.

➤ If you **move** layer pixels, the effect will move along with it.

➤ Alt-click/Option-click **Reset** in the Layer Style dialog box to restore the last-used settings in all panels in the dialog box.

➤ Once you become familiar with the individual effects, check out the helpful tips in the **"Layer effects plus!"** sidebar on page 321.

➤ After applying an effect, edit some layer pixels and watch the "smart" effect **update!**

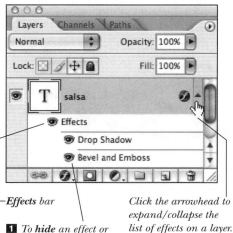

—***Effects*** *bar*

1 *To **hide** an effect or effects from view, click the **eye** icon.*

Click the arrowhead to expand/collapse the list of effects on a layer.

Applying Layer Effects

You can create **drop shadows** and **inner shadows** with a few clicks of the mouse.

To apply the Drop Shadow or Inner Shadow effect:

1. Double-click a layer.

2. Click **Drop Shadow** or **Inner Shadow.**

3. Change any of the following settings **1**:

Choose a **Blend Mode** from the pop-up menu.

To choose a different **shadow color,** click the color swatch, choose a color from the Color Picker (the new color will preview immediately), then click OK.

Choose an **Opacity** percentage for the transparency of the shadow.

Choose an **Angle** for the angle of the shadow relative to the original layer shapes. Check **Use Global Light** to use the current angle setting from the Layer > Layer Style > Global Light dialog box, or uncheck this option to use a unique angle setting for this particular effect. *Note:* If you readjust the Angle for an individual effect while Use Global Angle is checked, all effects that utilize the Global Angle option will also be modified! This option unifies the lighting across multiple layer effects.

Choose a **Distance** for the distance (in pixels) of a drop shadow from the original layer shapes **2**, or for the width of an inner shadow **3**–**4**.

TIP You can drag the shadow in the document window while the dialog box is open, but be aware that this will also move all other effects that utilize the Global Light option.

Choose a **Spread** or **Choke** percentage to control the point at which the shadow starts to fade.

Choose an overall **Size** for the shadow, in pixels.

In the Quality area, click the arrowhead, then choose a preset **Contour** from the

1 *Choose settings in the **Drop Shadow** or **Inner Shadow** panel of the **Layer Style** dialog box.*

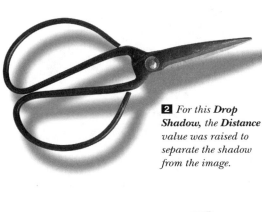

2 *For this **Drop Shadow**, the **Distance** value was raised to separate the shadow from the image.*

3 *The original image*

4 *Inner Shadow*

1 *The original layer with a **Drop Shadow***

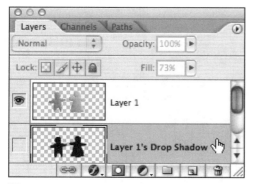

2 *Choosing the new **Drop Shadow** layer*

3 ***Distorting** the drop shadow*

4 *The final image*

Contour Preset picker for the edge profile of the shadow (see also page 324). The profiles can change a shadow dramatically.

Check **Anti-aliased** to soften the jagged edges between the shadow and other parts of the image.

Adjust the **Noise** level. Noise (speckling) helps to prevent banding on print output.

For a drop shadow, check **Layer Knocks Out Drop Shadow** to prevent the shadow from showing through layer pixels that have a low Fill opacity.

4. Click OK. If you're not satisfied with the resulting shadow shape, see the next set of instructions.

TIP When we apply the Drop Shadow effect, we usually raise the Distance, Spread, and Size values, and lower the Opacity a bit.

Depending on the time of day and the angle of the sun or other light source, shadows can be short or elongated. You can **reshape** a **drop shadow** via the **Distort** command.

To transform a Drop Shadow effect:

1. Apply the Drop Shadow effect (see the previous instructions) **1**, and keep the layer selected.

2. Choose Layer > Layer Style > **Create Layer(s),** then click OK. This transfers the shadow effect to its own layer.

3. Click the new shadow layer **2**.

4. Choose Edit > Transform > **Distort,** drag the handles of the transform box to achieve the desired shape, then press Enter/Return **3**–**4**. (If you don't see all the handles, press Ctrl-0 (zero)/Cmd-0 to enlarge the document window.)

5. *Optional:* Change the luminosity of the shadow by choosing a different blending mode or opacity. Turn on the Lock Transparent Pixels option ⬚ on the Layers palette to limit any painting or fill changes to just the shadow shape.

TIP Link the shadow layer and its original object layer to move them in unison.

Transform Drop Shadow

The **Outer Glow**  and **Inner Glow** ❷ effects add a soft, airbrushed accent to object edges.

To apply an Outer or Inner Glow effect:

1. Display the Swatches palette.
2. Double-click a layer.
3. Click **Outer Glow** or **Inner Glow.**
4. Choose **Structure** settings ❸:

   Choose a **Blend Mode.**

   Choose an **Opacity** for the transparency level of the glow.

   Adjust the **Noise** level. Noise (speckling) helps to prevent banding on print output.

   To change the glow **color,** click the color square in the Structure area, choose a color from the Color Picker (or, while the picker is open, from the Swatches palette). Choose a color that contrasts with the background color. It might be hard to see a light Outer Glow color against a light background color. The new color will preview in the image. Click OK.
   or
   To create a glow using a **gradient,** click the arrowhead to choose a gradient from the Gradient Preset picker; or click the gradient thumbnail to edit one of the presets or create a new gradient (see pages 411–413).

5. Choose **Elements** settings:

   Choose Softer or Precise from the **Technique** pop-up menu to control how closely the mask follows the contours of areas that contain pixels.

   For an Inner Glow, click Source: **Center** to create a glow that spreads outward from the center of the layer pixels. (Suggestion: Try this on type.) Or click **Edge** to create a glow that spreads inward from the inside edges of the layer pixels.

   Choose a **Spread** or **Choke** percentage to control where the glow starts to fade.

   Choose an overall **Size** for the glow.

❶ *Inner Glow (Center, with a Drop Shadow, too)*

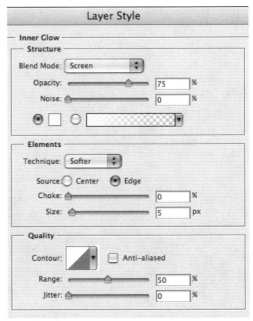

❷ *Outer Glow (in this document, the solid gray background is on a separate layer)*

❸ *Choose Structure, Elements, and Quality settings for an **Inner Glow** effect in the **Layer Style** dialog box.*

Outer or Inner Glow

320

Layer effects plus!

➤ When choosing which effect or effects to use, think first of the **surface texture** you're trying to create. Stone? Metal? Paper? Embossed text that looks as if it's embedded into porous paper, or satin text that looks as if it's cast in metal?

➤ Except for the Drop Shadow and Overlay effects, you may need to apply effects in **combination** in order to achieve a convincing or pleasing result **1**–**2**.

➤ Click **Blending Options** in the upper left side of the Layer Style dialog box, and change any of the settings (see pages 297–298). You can change the layer **blending mode** and/or **Fill** opacity on the Layers palette or in the Layer Style dialog box.

➤ Layer effects (or combinations thereof) can be saved as **styles** on the Styles palette in Image-Ready or Photoshop (see pages 331–332). This is a great timesaver!

➤ Lower the **opacity** of the layer that contains the effect(s) so you can see through to the layer below it, then change the **color** of the underlying layer or apply a **filter** (e.g., a Texture filter) to it.

6. Choose **Quality** settings:

Click the arrowhead to choose a preset **Contour** from the Contour Preset picker for the edge profile of the glow (see page 324).

Choose a **Range** to control the placement of the contour along the width of the glow.

If the glow contains a gradient, choose a **Jitter** value to control how randomly colors are distributed in the gradient.

7. Click OK.

TIP To apply a layer effect to type, make the type large, and don't apply negative tracking.

1 *To produce this image, we applied the **Drop Shadow, Outer Glow,** and **Bevel and Emboss** layer effects. The layer blending mode is Multiply, the layer Opacity is 85%, and the layer Fill opacity is 34%.*

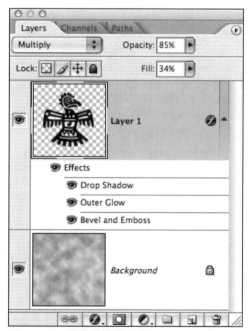

2 *This is the **Layers** palette for the image shown at left. The soft Background imagery was created by using Filter > Render > Clouds.*

The **Bevel and Emboss** command creates an illusion of depth by adding a highlight and shadow to layer shapes. The results can range from a chiseled bevel that looks factory-made to a pillowy emboss that looks as if it's been stamped onto porous paper. For variety, take advantage of the Contour options.

1 *The original image (on two layers)*

To apply the Bevel or Emboss effect:

1. Display the Swatches palette.

2. Double-click a layer on the Layers palette **1**. It can be a type layer.

3. Click **Bevel and Emboss.**

4. Choose **Structure** settings **2**:

    Choose a **Style: Outer Bevel 3, Inner Bevel 4, Emboss, Pillow Emboss** (**1**–**2** next page), or **Stroke Emboss.**

    From the **Technique** pop-up menu, choose Smooth, Chisel Hard, or Chisel Soft.

    Choose a **Depth** for the amount the highlight and shadow are offset from the layer shapes.

    Click the **Up** or **Down** button to switch the highlight and shadow positions.

    Choose a **Size** for the bevel or emboss effect.

    Raise the **Soften** value to soften the shadows and highlights along the edge.

5. Choose **Shading** settings:

    Choose an **Angle** and an **Altitude** to change the location of the light source. These settings will in turn affect the highlight and shadow. Check Use Global Light to use the current Angle and Altitude settings from the Layer > Layer Style > Global Light dialog box. Or uncheck this option to use a unique setting for this particular style. *Beware!* If you readjust an individual style's Angle or Altitude while Use Global Light is checked, all other styles that utilize the Global Light option will update, too.

    Click the **Gloss Contour** arrowhead, then choose from the Contour Preset picker (see page 324).

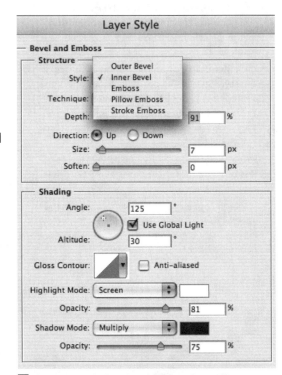

2 *Options for the **Bevel and Emboss** layer effect*

3 ***Outer Bevel*** *(plus a Drop Shadow)*

4 ***Inner Bevel*** *(plus a Drop Shadow)*

Bevel or Emboss

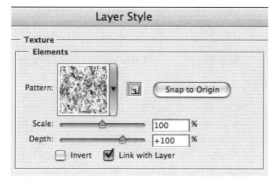

1 *Emboss*

2 *Pillow Emboss*

Choose a **Highlight Mode** and **Opacity** and a **Shadow Mode** and **Opacity** for image highlight and shadow areas.

To change the highlight or shadow **color,** click either color swatch, then choose a color from the Color Picker (or, while the picker is open, choose from the Swatches palette). The color will preview on the image. Click OK.

6. To add a **Contour** to the edges of the bevel or emboss, click Contour at the left side of the dialog box, below Bevel and Emboss. Click the Contour arrowhead, then click a preset contour in the picker (see page 324). This can dramatically change the appearance of the effect.

    Check **Anti-aliased** to soften the hard edges between adjoining areas.

    Set the **Range** to control the placement of the contour along the width of the glow. The Range option affects only the Bevel style options.

3 *Texture options for the Bevel and Emboss layer effect*

7. To add a texture to a bevel or emboss, click **Texture** at the left side of the dialog box, click the Texture arrowhead, choose a pattern from the picker, then do any of the following **3**–**4**:

    Adjust the **Scale** of the pattern.

    Change the **Depth** to adjust the contrast of shadows and highlights in the pattern.

    Check **Invert** to flip the shadows and highlights. This has the same effect as changing the Depth percentage from negative to positive, or vice versa.

    Check **Link with Layer** to ensure that the texture and the layer move in unison.

    Drag in the document window to reposition the texture within the effect. Click **Snap to Origin** to realign the pattern to the upper left corner of the image.

    If you've changed settings for the current pattern, click the New Preset button ⬚ to add it as a new preset.

8. Click OK.

4 *To produce this image, we applied two layer effects: **Outer Glow** and **Bevel and Emboss** (with the **Texture** option). The blending mode for the layer is Overlay, and the layer Opacity percentage is 40%.*

For all the layer effects except the Stroke effect and the Overlay effects, you can choose a different contour (edge style) or create a **custom contour.** The contours influence such elements as the fade on a drop shadow and the highlight on a bevel. You can produce dramatic changes in the appearance of an effect by changing the contour.

To change the profile of a contour:

1. Double-click a layer or an effect name to open the Layer Style dialog box. For the Bevel and Emboss effect only, also click Contour at the left side of the dialog box.

2. Click the **Contour** thumbnail (not the arrowhead). The Contour Editor opens **1**.

3. *Optional:* From the **Preset** pop-up menu, choose a preset contour to use as a starting point.

4. When you do any of the following, the name "Custom" automatically appears on the Preset pop-up menu:

   Click on the graph to **add** points.

   Drag points to adjust the graph.

   To **delete** a point, drag it off the graph.

   To convert the currently selected point into a **corner** point, check Corner.

5. To save the custom graph as a contour preset, click **New,** enter a name, then click OK. The custom contour will appear on the Contour Preset picker.

6. *Optional:* To save the custom graph as a file for reuse, click Save, enter a file name, then click Save again. Click Load to retrieve any saved contour file.

7. Click OK to close the Contour Editor (**1**, next page).

TIP To delete a contour, open the Contour Preset picker, Alt-click/Option-click the contour you want to delete, then close the picker. *Note:* The contour will be deleted only from the current picker—not from the actual preset library.

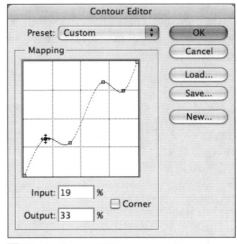

1 *Use the **Contour Editor** to customize a contour.*

Pick from the picker

The profile thumbnails in the **Contour Preset** picker illustrate different edge styles **2**. The gray areas in the profile represent opaque pixels; the white areas represent transparency. To close the picker, double-click a contour; or click the Contour arrowhead; or click somewhere outside the picker in the Layer Style dialog box.

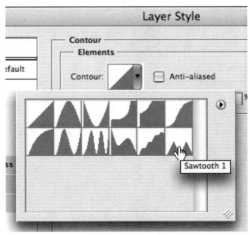

2 *You can use tool tips to learn the **names** of the contours in the **Contour Preset** picker.*

Contour Editor

1 *The Bevel and Emboss effect with an edited variation of the Cone **Contour** option: The letters look carved or molded.*

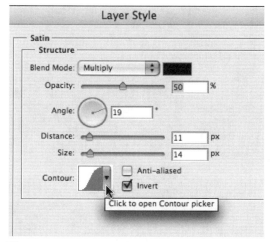

2 *Options for the **Satin** layer effect*

3 *The Bevel and Emboss and **Satin** layer effects combined: The Satin effect makes the surface of the letters look more **reflective**.*

TIP To restore the default contour library, open the Contour Preset picker, choose Reset Contours from the Contour Preset picker menu, then click OK. If an alert dialog box appears and you want to save the current contour changes to a new library, click Yes/Save, enter a name, then click Save again. To open a different library, choose a library name from the bottom of the Contour Preset picker menu (click Append, or click OK to replace).

Use the **Satin** layer effect to make the surfaces of objects look reflective or metallic.

To apply the Satin effect :

1. Double-click a layer on the Layers palette. The default Blend Mode for this effect, Multiply, deepens some tonal values and heightens contrast, so start with imagery that has a good range of tonal values.

2. Click **Satin.**

3. Do any of the following **2**:

   Change the **Blend Mode.**

   To change the overlay **color,** click the color swatch, then choose a color from the Color Picker.

   Adjust the **Opacity** of the effect.

   Change the **Angle** of the effect. This angle is independent of the Global Light settings.

   Set the **Distance** and the **Size** of the effect. You can also drag in the document window to adjust the distance.

   Click the **Contour** arrowhead, then choose from the Contour Preset picker for the edge profile of the effect.

   Check **Anti-aliased** to soften the hard boundary between the effect and the underlying shape.

   Check **Invert** to swap the shadows and highlights.

4. Click OK **3**.

Satin

The three overlay effects, **Color Overlay,** **Gradient Overlay,** and **Pattern Overlay,** can be applied to partial layers, whole layers, shape layers, text layers, or a selection.

To apply the Color Overlay effect :

1. Double-click a layer on the Layers palette or create a selection.

2. Click **Color Overlay.**

3. Do any of the following 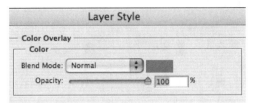:

Choose a **Blend Mode.**

Click the color swatch, then choose a different **color** for the overlay.

Adjust the **Opacity** of the overlay.

4. Click OK.

To apply the Gradient Overlay effect:

1. Double-click a layer on the Layers palette 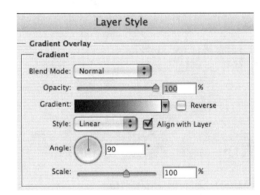.

2. Click **Gradient Overlay.**

3. Do any of the following :

Choose a **Blend Mode.**

Adjust the **Opacity** of the overlay.

Click the **Gradient** arrowhead, then choose a preset gradient from the Gradient Preset picker.

Choose a **Style: Linear, Radial, Angle, Reflected,** or **Diamond** .

Check **Reverse** to change the direction of the gradient .

Check **Align with Layer** to align the gradient with visible pixels in the layer. If this option is off, the gradient will align with the full canvas.

Set the **Angle** of the gradient.

Choose a **Scale** percentage for the placement of the midpoint of the gradient.

You can also drag in the document window to reposition the gradient.

4. Click OK. Read more about creating and editing gradients in Chapter 26.

1 *Options for the **Color Overlay** layer effect*

2 *The Bevel and Emboss effect*

3 *Options for the **Gradient Overlay** layer effect*

4 *The **Gradient Overlay** layer effect (Style: Reflected) applied to the image shown above*

5 *Gradient Overlay layer effect, **Reverse** checked*

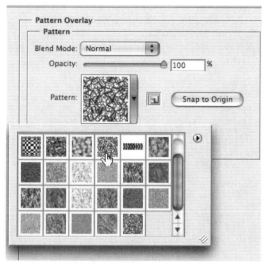

1 *Options for the **Pattern Overlay** layer effect*

2 *The **Pattern Overlay** effect applied to a shape layer object*

3 *The **Pattern Overlay** effect (35% Opacity) applied to an entire layer*

Remember, when you think "pattern": **Patterns** can have obvious repeats, as in polka dots or stripes, or can have an overall texture, as in gritty sandpaper, woven fabric, or variegated stone.

To apply the Pattern Overlay effect:

1. Double-click a layer on the Layers palette.

2. Click **Pattern Overlay.**

3. Do any of the following **1**:

   Choose a **Blend Mode.**

   Adjust the **Opacity** of the overlay.

   Click the **Pattern** arrowhead, then choose a pattern preset in the picker. To load patterns from other libraries, choose from the picker menu.

   Click **Snap to Origin** to align the pattern with the upper left corner of the image. You can also drag in the document window to reposition the pattern.

   Choose a **Scale** percentage for the size of the pattern.

   Check **Link with Layer** to link the pattern to the layer.

   If you've changed settings for the current pattern, click the New Preset button **🔳** to add it as a new preset.

4. Click OK **2**–**4**.

4 *This combination of the **Pattern Overlay**, **Bevel and Emboss**, and **Satin** layer effects creates the appearance of polished granite.*

Pattern Overlay

To apply a Stroke effect:

1. Double-click a layer on the Layers palette.

2. Click **Stroke.**

3. Do any of the following 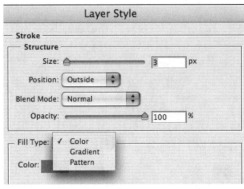:

Choose a **Size** (width) for the stroke.

From the **Position** pop-up menu, choose whether you want the stroke to be **Outside, Inside,** or **Centered** on the edges of shapes in the layer.

Choose a **Blend Mode.**

Choose an **Opacity** percentage.

Choose **Fill Type: Color, Gradient,** or **Pattern,** and choose options using the controls that become available. See the Color Overlay and Gradient Overlay information on page 326, or the Pattern Overlay information on the previous page.

4. Click OK .

■ *Options for the **Stroke** layer effect*

Other effects commands

The effects commands that are discussed in this section can be accessed by right-clicking/Control-clicking an existing effects icon 🗃 for a layer on the Layers palette (■, next page). Most commands are also available on the Layer > Layer Style submenu.

NEW **Disable Layer Effects** hides (turns the eye icon off for) all effects in the layer. Choose Enable Layer Effects to redisplay them.

Global Light establishes a common Angle and Altitude for all current and future effects for which the Use Global Light option is on. A dialog box will open from which you can choose settings (■, next page). And conversely, if you change the Angle or Altitude of any individual layer effect when Use Global Light is on, all the other effects that have a Global Light option will update, as will the Angle and Altitude in the Global Light dialog box. Using a Global Light helps to unify the lighting across multiple effects.

2 *The **Stroke** effect, Fill Type: **Color** (also the Drop Shadow, Inner Shadow, and Bevel and Emboss effects) applied to a shape layer object*

3 *The **Stroke** and **Bevel and Emboss** layer effects*

Stroke; Other Effects Commands

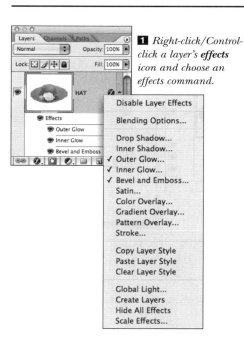

1 *Right-click/Control-click a layer's **effects** icon and choose an effects command.*

If more than one effect has been applied to a layer and you choose **Create Layer(s),** each effect will be placed on its own layer. The image won't look substantially different after this command is chosen, but the effects will no longer be editable via the Layer Style dialog box, and will no longer be associated with the layer to which they were originally applied. You may get a warning that effects may not completely carry over to the layers. You don't have much choice, though, if you want to proceed.

After you apply the Create Layer(s) command, any layer effect that's inside a shape (e.g., an inner glow, or a highlight or a shadow for a bevel or an inner emboss) will be placed on a new, separate layer. It will also be united with the original layer in a clipping mask; the original layer will be the base layer of the mask. Any effect that's outside a shape (e.g., a drop shadow, an outer glow, or a shadow for a bevel or an outer emboss) will be converted into separate layers below the original layer.

TIP After Effects 5 and later can import a layered Photoshop file, with the option of preserving individual layers, layer masks, and layer effects. Use Create Layer(s) before exporting a layered file to a multimedia program that can't import Photoshop layer effects.

Hide All Effects temporarily hides layer effects for all the layers in the document. To redisplay them, choose Show All Effects.

Scale Effects opens a dialog box **3** that allows you to increase or decrease the size of all the effects currently applied to the selected layer (not the layer imagery). Only parameters defined in pixels (not those defined by a percentage) are affected.

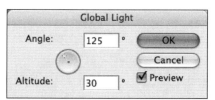

2 *In the **Global Light** dialog box, choose an **Angle** and **Altitude** to be applied to all effects for which the Use Global Light option is on.*

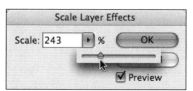

3 *Using the **Scale Layer Effects** dialog box, you can scale all the effects on the currently selected layer in one fell swoop.*

Other Effects Commands

329

To move effects from one layer to another:

To **move one** effect at a time, drag any individual effect **name** from one layer to another.

or

To **replace** any existing effects on a layer with **all** the effects on another layer, drag the **Effects bar** from one layer to another.

When you use either of these two methods to **copy** effects from one layer to another, the new effects **replace** any existing effects on the target layer.

To copy effects between layers:

Alt-drag/Option-drag one effect or the Effects bar to another layer.

or

Right-click/Control-click the layer that contains the effect(s) you want to copy and choose **Copy Layer Style.** Next, click another layer, then right-click/Control-click and choose **Paste Layer Style.**

Clicking the eye icon for a layer effect, or unchecking the box for an effect in the Layer Style dialog box, doesn't remove the effect—it merely hides it from view. Follow these instructions to **remove effects** from a layer.

To remove layer effects:

Drag an individual effect name over the **Delete Layer** button 🗑 at the bottom of the Layers palette. Or drag the Effects bar over the Delete Layer button to remove all effects from the layer.

or

To remove all styles from a layer, right-click/Control-click an effects icon 🔘 for a layer and choose **Clear Layer Style.**

TIP If you turn off an effect and then turn it back on again via the check box, or reapply an effect that was dragged singly to the Delete Layer button, the last-used options for that effect will redisplay.

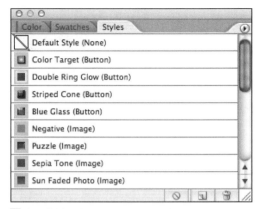

1 *Small List* display mode on the *Styles* palette

2 *Click a layer, then click a thumbnail or style name on the* **Styles** *palette (this is* **Large Thumbnail** *display mode).*

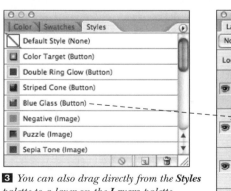

3 *You can also drag directly from the* **Styles** *palette to a layer on the* **Layers** *palette.*

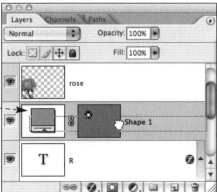

Applying styles

You can conveniently store settings for a layer, including layer effects, opacity, blending mode, fill opacity, etc., collectively as a style on the Styles palette. Once stored, styles can be applied to any layer with a click of the mouse. The same styles are available in both ImageReady and Photoshop (they're stored in Adobe Photoshop CS2 > Presets > Styles). You can choose a display mode for the Styles palette from the palette menu: Small List **1**, Large List, Small Thumbnail or Large Thumbnail.

To apply a style to a layer:

Click a **layer** (not the Background), then click a style on the **Styles** palette **2**.
or
Drag a style name or thumbnail from the **Styles** palette over any selected or unselected layer on the **Layers** palette **3**.
or
Double-click a layer to open the **Layer Style** dialog box, click **Styles,** click a style thumbnail (**1**, next page), then click OK.

TIP Normally, when you apply a style, it replaces any existing effects on a layer, but you can Shift-click or Shift-drag a style to add its effects to the existing ones. *Note:* Whether you hold down Shift or not, if two effects have the same name, the effect in the style will replace the effect in the layer.

Apply StyleS

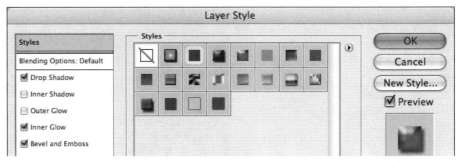

1 *Styles can also be applied from within the **Layer Style** dialog box. Click **Styles** at the top left of the dialog box, then click a style thumbnail to apply that style to the currently selected layer.*

When you **save** settings for the current layer as a **style,** you can include any currently applied layer effects and/or Blending Options settings (e.g., layer opacity, blending mode, and fill opacity) in the style.

To save a style to the Styles palette:

1. On the **Layers** palette, click a layer **2**, then on the **Styles** palette, click the blank area **3** or click the **New Style** button.
   or
   Double-click a layer to open the **Layer Style** dialog box, then click the **New Style** button.

2. Enter a **Name** for the new style, check whether you want to **Include Layer Effects** and/or **Include Layer Blending Options** in the style, then click OK.

TIP You can load styles from other libraries via the Styles palette menu. To create a style library, see pages 463–464.

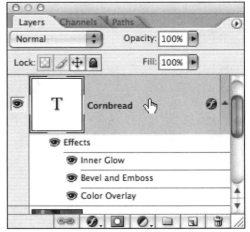

2 *On the **Layers** palette, click a layer that contains layer effects…*

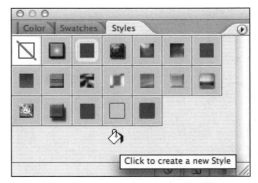

3 *…then on the **Styles** palette, click either the blank area or the New Style button.*

MASKS 22

ONE TRADEMARK CHARACTERISTIC of Photoshop pros is that they use the minimum number of steps to accomplish their tasks, without redoubling their efforts. Among the most tedious of tasks, even considering the large number of tools and commands at your disposal, is selecting specific areas of an image. A "saving" grace is that once you've created a selection, it can be saved as an **alpha channel** **1**, then loaded onto the image at any time or even copied to other documents. Any selection that would be time-consuming to recreate is a logical candidate for this procedure.

In Chapter 8, you learned how to save and load alpha channel selections. In this chapter, we'll delve further into this topic by showing you how to choose options for alpha channels as you create and load them, delete and duplicate alpha channels, and reshape alpha channel masks "by hand."

One drawback to using alpha channels is that they increase the file size, so try to create and keep only the ones you need. (To create vector masks as an alternative to alpha channels in order to conserve storage space, see page 378.)

Another way to create selections is by putting your document into **Quick Mask** mode and then painting a mask **2**. You can also use this mode to reshape a selection "by hand." The Quick Mask itself can't be saved, but when you put the document back into Standard (non-Quick Mask) mode, the mask turns into a selection, which can be saved either as an alpha channel or as a layer mask.

(In addition to the masking techniques discussed in this chapter, you can explore adjustment layer masks on page 178, layer masks on pages 300–304, using type shapes in a layer mask on pages 301 and 406, and clipping masks on pages 305–306.)

*The **composite color channel***

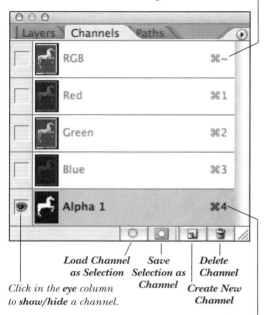

Load Channel as Selection *Save Selection as Channel* *Delete Channel* *Create New Channel*

*Click in the **eye** column to **show/hide** a channel.*

1 *Noncolor channels are called **alpha channels**.*

2 *The active (selected) area is clear, the **Quick Mask** is semitransparent.*

333

Using alpha channels

A **selection** that's saved in an **alpha channel** can be loaded into any image when needed.

To save a selection to a channel using the current options settings:

1. Create a selection **1**.

2. Click the **Save Selection as Channel** button  at the bottom of the Channels palette **2**.

TIP To convert an alpha channel into a spot color channel, see page 479.

To choose options as you save a selection to a channel:

1. Create a selection. *Optional:* Also click a layer if you want to create a layer mask for it.

2. Right-click/Control-click in the document window and choose **Save Selection**, (or choose Select > Save Selection). The Save Selection dialog box opens **3**.

3. Do the following:

    Leave the **Document** setting as the current file, or choose Document: **New** to save the selection to an alpha channel in a new, separate document.

    Optional: Choose Channel: [layer name] Mask to turn the selection into a layer mask for the current layer. Pixels will be visible only within the former selection area.

    Type a **Name** for the selection.

    Optional: Choose an Operation option to combine the current selection with an existing alpha channel that you choose from the Channel pop-up menu. (The Operation options are illustrated on page 336.)

4. Click OK. The selection will remain active. *Note:* You can save alpha channels with a document in most formats, such as Photoshop, Large Document, BMP, PICT, TIFF, and Photoshop PDF. Or to save a copy of a file without alpha channels, uncheck Alpha Channels in File > Save As.

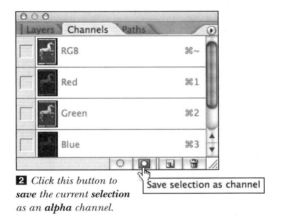

PHOTO: CARA WOOD

1 *Select an area of a layer.*

2 *Click this button to* **save** *the current* **selection** *as an* **alpha** *channel.*

3 *In the* **Save Selection** *dialog box, choose* **Document** *and* **Channel** *options and give the channel a* **Name**.

Save Selection to Channel

1 *Click an* **alpha channel** *on the* **Channels** *palette.*

2 *An* **alpha channel** *in the document window: The* **selected** *area is* **white***, the* **protected** *area is* **black***.*

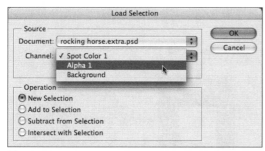

3 *Choose from the* **Channel** *pop-up menu in the* **Load Selection** *dialog box.*

You can **display** an alpha channel without loading it onto the image as a selection, just to see what it looks like.

To display a channel selection:

1. Click an alpha channel name on the **Channels** palette **1**. The selected area will be white, the protected area black **2**.

2. To restore the normal document display, click the top (composite) channel name on the palette (Ctrl-~/Cmd-~)—not the eye icon.

TIP If a selection saved as an alpha channel had a Feather radius above zero, the feathered area will be gray, and will be only partially affected by editing.

TIP To rename an alpha channel, double-click the channel name on the palette.

To load a channel selection onto an image using the current options:

On the Channels palette, Ctrl-click/Cmd-click the **name** of the alpha channel that you want to load.

To choose options as you load a channel selection onto an image:

1. If the composite image isn't displayed, click the top channel name on the Channels palette. *Optional:* Create a selection in the document to combine with the channel selection.

2. Choose Select > **Load Selection.**
   or
   If you didn't create a selection, right-click/Control-click in the document window and choose **Load Selection.**

3. The Load Selection dialog box opens **3**. Choose an alpha channel name from the **Channel** pop-up menu.

4. To combine the channel with an active selection in the image, click an **Operation** option (see the next page).

5. *Optional:* Check Invert to switch the selected and unselected areas in the loaded selection.

6. Click OK.

Save Selection Operations

When saving a selection, you can choose from these **Operation** options in the **Save Selection** dialog box:

Channel and selection to be saved

Resulting channel

ADD

New Channel saves the current selection in a new channel.

Shortcut: Click the Save Selection as Channel button on the Channels palette.

Add to Channel adds the new selection to the channel.

Channel and selection to be saved

Resulting channel

SUBTRACT

Channel and selection to be saved

Resulting channel

INTERSECT

Subtract from Channel removes white or gray areas that overlap the new selection.

Intersect with Channel preserves only white or gray areas that overlap the new selection.

Load Selection Operations

If a channel is loaded while an area of a layer is selected, you can choose from these **Operation** options in the **Load Selection** dialog box:

Selection and channel to be loaded

Resulting selection

ADD

New Selection: The channel becomes the current selection.

Shortcut: Ctrl-click/Cmd-click the channel name or drag the channel name over the Load Channel as Selection button.

Add to Selection adds the channel selection to the current selection.

Shortcut: Ctrl-Shift-click/Cmd-Shift-click the channel name.

Selection and channel to be loaded

Resulting selection

SUBTRACT

Selection and channel to be loaded

Resulting selection

INTERSECT

Subtract from Selection removes areas of the current selection that overlap the channel selection.

Shortcut: Ctrl-Alt-click/Cmd-Option-click the channel name.

Intersect with Selection preserves only areas of the current selection that overlap the channel selection.

Shortcut: Ctrl-Alt-Shift-click/Cmd-Option-Shift-click the channel name.

Save and Load Selection Operations

1 *Choose **Duplicate Channel** from the context menu.*

2 *The horse is the selected area in this alpha channel.*

3 *After applying the **Invert** command to the channel, the background is the selected area.*

To delete an alpha channel:

Right-click/Control-click a channel name, then choose **Delete Channel.**
or
On the Channels palette, click the channel you want to delete, then drag it over the **Delete Channel** button. 🗑

You can **duplicate** an alpha channel in the same file, or drag and drop an alpha channel from the Channels palette to another document (a copy will appear on the palette in the target document).

To duplicate an alpha channel:

Drag the name of the channel you want to duplicate over the **New Channel** button 📑 or into another document window.
or
Right-click/Control-click an alpha channel name, choose **Duplicate Channel** from the context menu, change the name in the Duplicate Channel dialog box, if desired, then click OK **1**.

TIP To quickly reverse the masked and unmasked areas in an alpha channel, click an alpha channel on the Channels palette, then press Ctrl-I/Cmd-I (Image > Adjustments > Invert) **2**–**3**.

Delete, Duplicate Channel

You can superimpose an alpha channel selection as a colored mask (or rubylith, for folks with traditional design training) over an image, and then **reshape** the mask.

To reshape an alpha channel mask:

1. Make sure nothing is selected in your document.

2. Click an alpha channel on the Channels palette; an eye icon will appear.

3. Click in the left column at the top of the palette; an eye icon will appear there, too **1**. A colored mask will cover the whole image except for where the white areas in the alpha channel are. Keep the alpha channel highlighted.

4. Choose the **Pencil** ✏ or **Brush** tool ✐ (B or Shift-B).

5. On the options bar, do the following:

   Click the **Brush Preset** picker arrowhead, then click a brush in the picker.

   Choose Mode: **Normal.**

   Choose 100% **Opacity** and 100% **Flow** to create a full mask or a lower Opacity and/or Flow to create a partial mask.

6. Press D to reset the Foreground and Background colors. To enlarge the **masked** (protected) area, draw brush strokes with **black 2**.
   and/or
   Press X to swap the Foreground and Background colors, then enlarge the **unmasked** area by applying **white** brush strokes **3**.

7. To hide the mask, click the eye icon for the alpha channel. To edit the image (not the alpha channel), click a layer on the Layers palette.

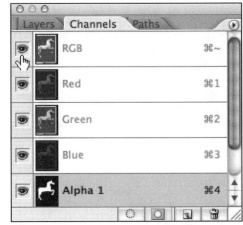

1 *On the **Channels** palette, click the **eye** column for an **alpha** channel, then for the **composite** channel.*

2 *Paint with **black** to **enlarge** the **masked** area.*

3 *Paint with **white** to **enlarge** the **unmasked** area.*

1 *Select an area of a layer.*

Standard — mode

Edit in Quick Mask Mode (Q)

2

3 *The unselected area is covered with a mask.*

Using Quick Masks

If you put your document into **Quick Mask** mode, you'll then be able to "paint" a mask onto your image where you need it, and also remove areas of the mask where necessary. If you create a selection first, the mask will cover just the unselected areas. In either case, by default, the mask is semitransparent red, as in a traditional rubylith.

To reshape a selection by using a Quick Mask:

1. Select an area of a layer **1**.

2. Click the **Quick Mask Mode** button on the Toolbox (Q) **2**. A mask will cover the unselected areas of the image **3**. (If it doesn't, double-click the Quick Mask Mode button, click Color Indicates: Masked Areas, then click OK.) Also, "Quick Mask" will become a listing on the Channels palette and in the document window title bar.

3. Choose the **Pencil** or **Brush** tool.

4. On the options bar, do the following:

   Click the Brush Preset picker arrowhead, then click a **brush** on the picker.

   Choose Mode: **Normal.**

   Set the **Opacity** and **Flow** to 100%.

5. Draw strokes with black as the Foreground color to enlarge the **masked** (protected) area.
   or
   Stroke on the mask with white as the Foreground color to enlarge the **unmasked** area. (Press X to swap the Foreground/Background colors.)
   or
   Stroke with a brush **Opacity** below 100% (options bar) to create a partial mask. When you edit the layer, that area will be partially affected by modifications.

6. Click the **Standard Mode** button on the Toolbox (or press Q) when you're done working in Quick Mask mode. The unmasked areas will turn into a selection. *Note:* If you want to preserve the selection, save it as an alpha channel.

In these instructions, you'll **paint** the **mask** directly in the document window without first creating a selection. You can use this technique to select areas for retouching, such as eyes or teeth in a portrait photo.

To paint a Quick Mask:

1. Choose the **Pencil** or **Brush** tool, and choose options for the tool as per step 4 on the previous page.

2. Double-click the **Quick Mask Mode** button ⬤ on the Toolbox.

3. Click Color Indicates: **Selected Areas**, then click OK.

4. Paint with black in the document window **1**. The mask you're creating will become the selection when you return to Standard mode. Paint with white if you need to remove any areas of the mask.

5. Press Q to put the document back into Standard mode.

Using the **Quick Mask Options** dialog box, you can control whether the mask covers the protected or unprotected areas, as well as the color and opacity of the mask.

To choose Quick Mask options:

1. Double-click the **Quick Mask Mode** button ⬤ on the Toolbox. The Quick Mask Options dialog box opens.

2. Do any of the following **2**:

   Choose whether **Color Indicates: Masked Areas** or **Selected Areas.**

   Click the **Color** swatch, then choose a new color for the Quick Mask.

   Change the **Opacity** of the mask color.

3. Click OK.

> ### Quick switch
> To switch the mask color between the **selected** and **masked** areas without opening the Quick Mask Options dialog box, Alt-click/Option-click the **Quick Mask Mode** button on the Toolbox.

1 *Painting a mask on an image in* **Quick Mask** *mode*

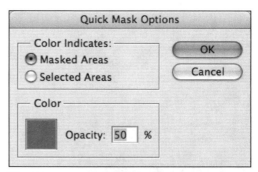

2 *In the* **Quick Mask Options** *dialog box, you can choose whether* **Color Indicates: Masked Areas** *or* **Selected Areas,** *or click the* **Color** *swatch to change the mask color.*

FILTERS 23

1 *The original image*

2 *After applying the **Photox** filter to smooth the wrinkles on the doggy's forehead, etc.*

YOU PROBABLY USED A FILTER OR two in an earlier chapter. Here they are star players. Depending on which filters you use (and which settings you choose), the results can range from barely noticeable to a complete morph. You can make an image look hand painted, silkscreened, or sketched; apply distortion; create patterns or textures; make an image look like a mosaic —the possibilities are infinite. This chapter has four sections: techniques for applying filters, an illustrated compendium of all the filters, instructions for using filters to make a photo look like a drawing or painting, and instructions for using the Pattern Maker and Vanishing Point filters.

Filter basics
How filters are applied

Filters can be applied to a whole layer or to a selection on a layer. For a soft transition between filtered and nonfiltered areas, feather the selection before applying them.

Some filters are applied in one step, without using a dialog box. Other filters are applied either via the Filter Gallery or via the filter's own dialog box. Choose Filter > **Last Filter** [last filter name] **(Ctrl-F/Cmd-F)** to reapply the last-used filter using the same settings. To open the dialog box or Filter Gallery for the last-used filter, with its last-used settings displayed, press **Ctrl-Alt-F/Cmd-Option-F.** To reapply a filter using different settings, choose it from the Filter menu or Filter Gallery.

Filter availability varies depending on the document color mode and bit depth: All are available for RGB files; most, but not all, for Grayscale, Multichannel, and Lab Color files; even fewer for CMYK Color and 16-bits/channel files; still fewer for 32-bits/ channel files; and none for Bitmap and Indexed Color files.

(Continued on the following page)

Applying Filters

The **Filter Gallery** dialog box (**1**, next page) houses most of the Photoshop filters under one roof. Here you can preview dozens of filters; show and hide each filter effect that you've previewed; and also change the sequence in which they're applied— all before exiting the dialog box or making permanent changes to your document. By using the Filter Gallery, you also avoid making multiple trips to the Filter menu.

To use the Filter Gallery:

1. With a document open, choose Filter > **Filter Gallery.** *Note:* If a filter is included in the Filter Gallery, the Filter Gallery dialog box opens automatically when that filter is chosen from the Filter menu.

2. To change the **zoom** level for the preview, click the Zoom Out or Zoom In button in the lower left corner of the dialog box or choose a zoom level from the pop-up menu. You can drag a magnified preview in the window, or use the scroll bar(s) or arrows.

3. In the middle panel, click an arrowhead to expand one of the six filter categories, then click a filter **thumbnail.**
or
After clicking one filter, you can choose any other filter **name** from the pop-up menu below the Cancel button.

4. Choose **settings** for the filter from the panel on the right side. The filter name you've chosen will display in the scroll list below.

5. *Do any of the following optional steps:*

To apply an additional filter effect, click the **New Effect Layer** button, click another filter thumbnail in the same category or another category, then choose settings.

To **replace** one filter effect with another, leave the existing filter effect name selected in the scroll list (don't click the New Effect Layer button), click a new thumbnail, then choose settings. The most recently applied effect will be at the top of the list.

To **hide** a filter effect, click the eye (visibility) icon in the scroll list; click again to redisplay it.

To change the **stacking position** of a filter effect in the sequence to produce a different effect in the image, drag it upward or downward on the list.

To remove the currently selected filter effect from the list, click the **Delete Effect Layer** button.

6. When you're satisfied with the filter(s) and settings you've chosen, click OK.

TIP Alt-click/Option-click the eye icon to hide/show all the previews but the one you click on.

TIP In addition to the filters that ship with Photoshop, there are also filters from third-party suppliers to explore.

Click this button to hide the thumbnail panel and expand the preview window to two panels wide; click it again to redisplay the thumbnail panel.

Zoom | Zoom | Zoom level | | Hide/show *filter effect preview* | Drag to **resize**
Out | In | *pop-up menu* | | | *the dialog box.*

1 The **Filter Gallery** *dialog box has three panels: a preview on the left; filter categories with thumbnails in the middle; and on the right, filter settings and a list of the filter effects you've previewed so far.*

Using individual filter dialog boxes

Some individual filter dialog boxes have a **preview** window **2**. You can drag in the preview window to move the image inside it.

With some filter dialog boxes open (e.g., Add Noise), you can click with the square pointer in the document window to make that area of the image appear in the preview window.

Check Preview if you want to preview the effect in the dialog box and the document window.

Click the + button to zoom in on the image in the preview window, or click the – button to zoom out **3**. We usually find we need to zoom out to gauge the effect. A line will blink on and off below the preview percentage while the preview is rendering.

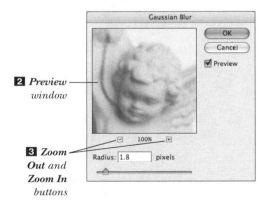

2 *Preview window*

3 *Zoom Out and Zoom In buttons*

Lessening a filter's effect

The Fade command lets you modulate the effect of the last filter, adjustment command, or paint, eraser, or other editing tool stroke. Choose Edit > **Fade** (Ctrl-Shift-F/ Cmd-Shift-F). The Fade dialog box opens. Change the Opacity and/or blending Mode, then click OK **1**–**3**.

A more flexible approach is to **duplicate** an image layer, apply filters to the duplicate, then lower the Opacity or Fill percentage of, or choose a different blending mode for, the new layer (**1**–**2**, next page). You can also create a layer mask for the duplicate layer to hide portions of the filter effect, merge the duplicate layer with the original layer, or discard the filter layer.

Another way to modulate a filter's effect is by applying it to an individual color channel instead of the composite channel. Click a layer, click a **channel** color name on the Channels palette, apply a filter (Add Noise and Gaussian Blur are good ones to experiment with), then click the top channel on the palette (Ctrl-~/Cmd-~) to redisplay the composite image.

And finally, you can selectively reduce a filter effect by hand with the **History Brush** tool. ✎ Set the History Brush icon to a prior state on the History palette, then draw strokes on the image (**3**, next page).

To have a filter affect multiple layers, Shift-select those layers, then hold down **Alt/ Option** and choose **Merge Layers** from the Layers palette menu. This creates a new merged layer (called "Stamp Layers" on the History palette) and preserves the selected layers. Apply the filter to the new layer.

1 *Filter > Texture > **Mosaic Tiles** applied to an image*

2 *You can use the **Fade** command to lessen the effect of the most recent edit.*

3 *After using the **Fade** command in **Overlay** mode to lessen the filter effect on the overall image*

1 *The original image*

2 *After applying the **Find Edges** filter to a dupli-cate of the original layer, lowering the Opacity of the duplicate layer, and choosing Mode: Hard Light (also try Overlay, Color Dodge, or Difference)*

3 *After applying the **Poster Edges** filter to an image and then using the **History Brush** tool to restore the angel's face and tummy to their original state*

Controlling the impact of filters

Before applying a filter, create a **selection** on a layer; the filter will affect pixels only within the selection. To create a soft-edged transi-tion between the filtered and nonfiltered areas, **feather** the selection before applying the filter.

Another option is to duplicate a layer, then apply both a filter and a **layer mask** to the duplicate. Click the layer mask thumbnail, and paint with black over areas that you want to remove the filter effect from. The edge between the white and black areas on the mask can be soft, hard, or painterly, depending on the type of brush strokes you use. Paint with a low opacity to create a partial mask.

To fade a filter effect gradually across an image, apply a black-to-white **gradient** to a layer mask, then apply filters with the layer thumbnail (not the mask thumbnail) selected. The filter will apply fully to the

(Continued on the following page)

Controlling the Impact of Filters

image where the mask is white and fade to nil in areas where the mask is black **1**–**3**.

Making filter effects look less artificial

Use the Filter Gallery to apply **multiple** filters—the effect will look less "canned." Try concocting your own formulas. If you come up with a sequence that you think you might like to reuse, you can save it in an action. If you get carried away and apply too many filters, you can revert to an earlier state or snapshot via the History palette.

Maximizing a filter's effect

Pumping up a layer's **brightness** and **contrast** values before applying a filter can help intensify a filter's effect (choose Image > Adjustments > Levels, move the black Input slider to the right and the white Input slider slightly to the left, then click OK).

Texture mapping using a filter

And finally, in lieu of choosing a preset pattern in filter dialog boxes that offer a pattern option (e.g., Conté Crayon, Glass, Rough Pastels, and Texturizer) for the filter to apply as a texture, you can load in another image for the filter to use. Lights and darks from the image you load in will be used to create peaks and valleys in the texture (this is called "texture mapping"). The image you load in must be saved in the Photoshop file format. If the filter dialog box has a Texture pop-up menu, click the ⊙ and choose **Load Texture,** locate a color or grayscale 8-bits/channel image file in the Photoshop (.psd) format, then click Load.

TIP The Sketch filters (with the exception of Water Paper) reduce a layer's colors to just white and the current Foreground color, so choose a Foreground color before applying them.

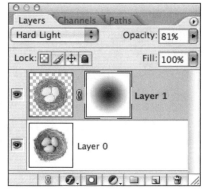

1 *A radial gradient in the layer mask...*

2 *...is diminishing the Stamp filter effect in the center of the nest.*

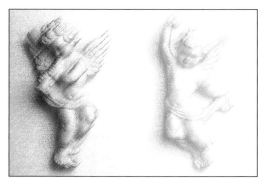

3 *The Rough Pastels filter is applied to the whole layer, but a linear gradient in the **layer mask** is diminishing the filter's impact on the right side.*

Filters illustrated

Artistic filters

Original image

Colored Pencil

Cutout

Dry Brush

Film Grain

Fresco

Neon Glow

Paint Daubs

Palette Knife

Artistic Filters

Artistic filters

Original image

Plastic Wrap

Poster Edges

Rough Pastels

Smudge Stick

Sponge

Underpainting

Watercolor

Blur filters

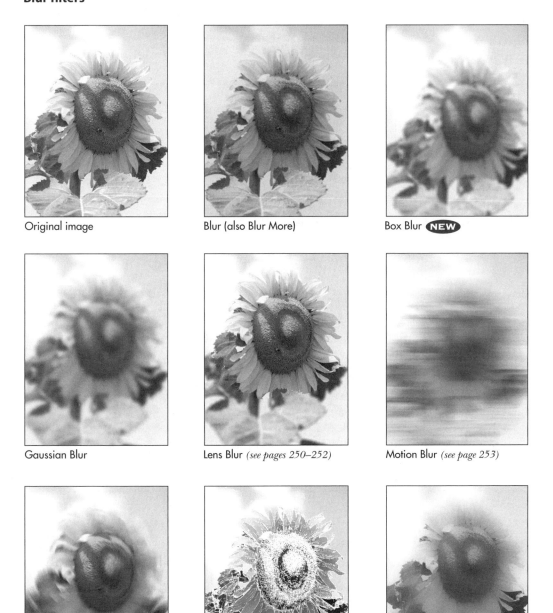

Original image

Blur (also Blur More)

Box Blur **NEW**

Gaussian Blur

Lens Blur *(see pages 250–252)*

Motion Blur *(see page 253)*

Radial Blur

Smart Blur (Overlay Edge)

Surface Blur **NEW** *(see page 267)*

*Not illustrated: The **Average** filter finds the average color in the image or selection and uses it to fill the image or selection with a solid color; the **Shape Blur** filter **NEW** blurs an image based on a shape that you select in the dialog box.*

Blur Filters

349

Brush Strokes filters

Original image

Accented Edges

Angled Strokes

Crosshatch

Dark Strokes

Ink Outlines

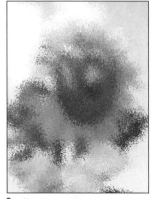

Spatter

Sprayed Strokes

Sumi-e

Brush Strokes Filters

Distort filters

Original image

Diffuse Glow

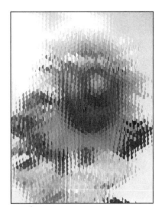

Displace

Glass

Lens Correction **NEW**
(see pages 254–255)

Ocean Ripple

Pinch

Polar Coordinates

Ripple

Distort Filters

Distort filters

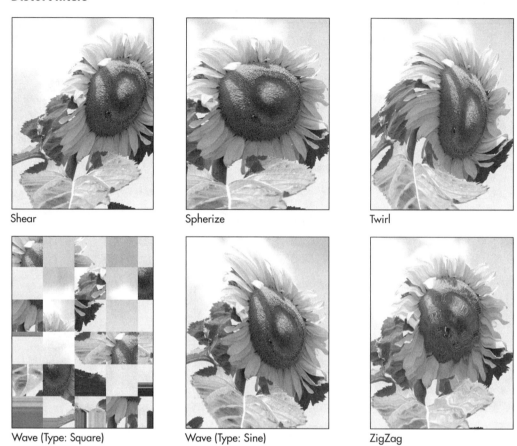

Shear

Spherize

Twirl

Wave (Type: Square)

Wave (Type: Sine)

ZigZag

Distort Filters; Noise Filters

Noise filters *Not illustrated:* **Despeckle** *and* **Dust & Scratches** *filters; for the* **Reduce Noise** *filter, see page 242*

Original image

Add Noise

Median

Pixelate filters

Original image

Color Halftone

Crystallize

Facet

Fragment

Mezzotint (Short Strokes)

Mezzotint (Medium Dots)

Mosaic

Pointillize

Render filters   *For the **Lighting Effects** filter, see pages 247–248.*

Original image

Clouds *(try using as a background for a portrait photo)*

Difference Clouds

Fibers

Lens Flare

Sharpen filters   *For the **Smart Sharpen** filter, see pages 257–258.* **NEW**

Sharpen Edges

Sharpen More

Unsharp Mask

Sketch filters

Original image

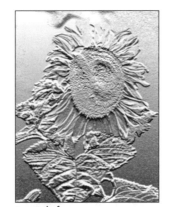

Bas Relief

Chalk & Charcoal

Charcoal

Chrome

Conté Crayon

Graphic Pen

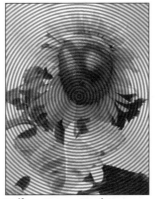

Halftone Pattern (Circle)

Halftone Pattern (Dot)

Sketch Filters

Sketch filters

Sketch Filters

Original image

Note Paper

Photocopy

Plaster

Reticulation

Stamp

Torn Edges

Water Paper

Stylize filters

Original image

Diffuse

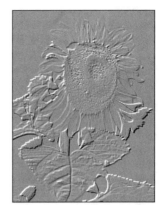

Emboss

Extrude

Find Edges

Glowing Edges

Solarize

Tiles

Tiles, then Fade (Overlay mode)

Stylize filters

Original image

Trace Contour

Wind

Texture filters

Craquelure

Grain (Horizontal)

Mosaic Tiles

Patchwork

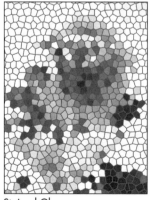

Stained Glass

Texturizer

Stylize Filters; Texture Filters

1 *The original image*

2 *The final image*

3 *The original image*

Photos into drawings/paintings

In the instructions on this page and the next, you'll learn how to apply multiple filters to the same image, and use such features as masks, layer opacity, and blending modes to modify the result. These instructions are just here for inspiration. See if you can come up with your own formulas!

To turn a photograph into a drawing:

1. Open an image, duplicate an image layer, and keep the duplicate selected.

2. Choose Filter > Stylize > **Find Edges.**

3. With the duplicate layer still active, click the **Add Layer Mask** button 🔘 at the bottom of the Layers palette.

4. Choose the **Brush** tool and paint with black at below 100% opacity (Normal mode) on the layer mask to reveal parts of the underlying layer **1**–**2**.

5. *Optional:* Lower the opacity of the duplicate layer.

   Or for a dramatic "scratchboard" effect —colors on a dark background—click the layer thumbnail, then choose Image > Adjustments > Invert (Ctrl-I/Cmd-I).

TIP To produce a magic marker drawing, in lieu of step 2 above, apply Filter > Stylize > Trace Contour, then apply Filter > Other > Minimum (Radius 1 or 2).

To turn a photo into an oil painting:

1. Open an image, duplicate an image layer, and keep the duplicate selected **3**. We suggest using an image that's fairly light in tone.

2. Choose Filter > **Filter Gallery,** then:

   Click Artistic > **Dry Brush,** and choose these settings: Brush Size 2, Brush Detail 8, and Texture 1.

   Click the **New Effect Layer** button. 🔳 Click the lower filter effect name on the list, then click Sketch > **Chrome.** In the settings panel, set the Detail to 1–2, and the Smoothness to 6–8.

(Continued on the following page)

On the filter effects list, Dry Brush should now be listed above Chrome. Click OK.

3. Change the blending mode of the filter layer; try Luminosity, Overlay, Darken, or Hard Light .

4. *Optional:* Create a layer mask for the filter layer, then paint with black to restore details from the original image layer.

In these instructions, you'll turn a photograph into a **watercolor** by using the Median Noise and Minimum filters. Compare it to Photoshop's Watercolor filter. This is but one of the infinite ways you can apply multiple filters to the same image.

To create a watercolor:

1. Duplicate the layer you want to turn into a watercolor **2**.

2. With the duplicate layer active, choose Filter > Noise > **Median.**

3. Move the **Radius** slider to between 2 and 8, then click OK.

4. Choose Filter > Other > **Minimum.**

5. Move the **Radius** slider to 1, 2, or 3, then click OK.

6. Choose Filter > Sharpen > **Smart Sharpen,** click Basic, choose high Amount and Radius values (fiddle with the sliders until you're happy with the results), then click OK **3**–**4**.

1 *The finished "oil painting" (we used Overlay mode)*

2 *The original image*

3 *The Photoshop* **Watercolor** *filter*

4 *Our own watercolor*

1 *The original imagery*

2 *Used as a pattern*

3 *The original imagery*

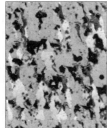

4 *Used as a pattern*

5 *The original imagery*

6 *Used as a pattern*

7 *The original imagery*

8 *Used as a pattern*

Using the Pattern Maker filter

The **Pattern Maker** filter allows you to generate multiple patterns from imagery on a layer or imagery that has been copied to the Clipboard. Instead of utilizing the imagery exactly, though, Photoshop jumbles the pixels slightly in order to create an assortment of different pattern tiles **1**–**8**. You can use this feature simply to fill a layer with a pattern once, or you can save your favorite pattern tiles as a pattern preset to use with any tool or command that uses pattern presets, such as Pattern Overlay in Layer Style, the Healing Brush tool, the Pattern Stamp tool, or the Fill command.

The sample you use for a tile can range from an area just a few pixels square to a whole layer. If the tile is smaller than the layer it's generated from, it will be repeated in a grid formation to fill up the layer. If the tile is the same size as the current layer, just a single tile will fill the whole layer.

Note: The Pattern Maker filter can be used only on 8-bit images in RGB Color, CMYK Color, Lab Color, and Grayscale modes.

To generate a pattern:

1. Click the layer that contains the imagery you want to use for the pattern. This layer will be replaced by the pattern, so we suggest that you duplicate it and leave the duplicate layer selected.

2. Choose Filter > **Pattern Maker** (Ctrl-Alt-Shift-X/Cmd-Option-Shift-X). If the dialog box is gobbling up your whole screen, you can resize it by dragging the lower right corner.

3. To generate a pattern in the current layer, choose the **Rectangular Marquee** tool in the dialog box, then marquee an area to become a tile (**1** next page).

4. To specify the dimensions of tiles in the generated pattern:

   Click **Use Image Size** to have the tile size match the current image size.
   or
   Choose **Width** and **Height** values.

(Continued on the following page)

5. From the **Offset** pop-up menu, choose whether you want the tiles to be offset from one another (**None, Horizontal,** or **Vertical**). For either of the latter two options, choose an offset **Amount** (0–99%); the tiles will be offset from one another by that percentage of the tile dimensions in the chosen direction.

6. Click **Generate** (Ctrl-G/Cmd-G). The tiled pattern will display in the preview area.

> **TIP** If the tile takes time to process, a progress bar will appear. You can press Esc to cancel the generation.

7. Click **Generate Again** to generate additional randomized patterns using the same options, or change any of the options, such as the Width and/or Height, then click Generate Again.

> **TIP** To use a different part of the image for the pattern, choose Show: Original

in the Preview area, redraw the marquee, then click Generate Again.

8. Next, you'll delete any tiles that you don't want and save the tiles that you may want to use later. In the **Tile History** area, **navigate** through the patterns that have been generated:

Click the **First Tile, Previous Tile, Next Tile,** or **Last Tile** button (**1**, next page).
or
Highlight the current tile number, **type** the number of the tile you want to view, then press Enter/Return.

To delete a pattern tile, use the navigation buttons to locate the tile you want to delete, then click the **Delete Tile from History** button. 🗑 When you delete a tile from the Tile History, its preview is discarded, too; this can't be undone.

9. To save a tile, use the navigation buttons to locate the tile you want to save, click

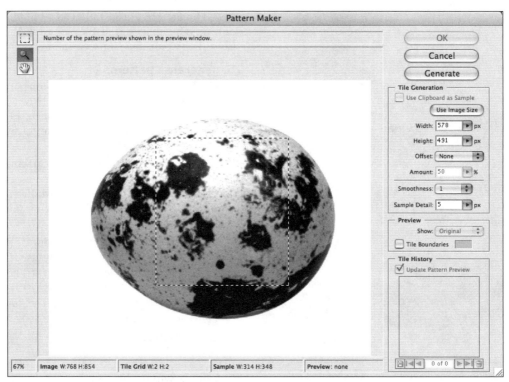

1 *In the* ***Pattern Maker*** *dialog box, with the* ***Rectangular Marquee*** *tool, marquee an area to be used as a tile.*

Using the preview

In the **Pattern Maker** dialog box:

➤ To magnify the preview, choose the **Zoom** tool (Z) 🔍 in the dialog box, then click the preview image; Alt-click/Option-click to zoom out. The current zoom level is listed in the lower left corner of the dialog box.

➤ If the zoom level is above 100%, you can move the pattern in the preview window with the **Hand** tool (H) 🖐 (or with the Spacebar held down if another tool is chosen).

➤ To see where the nonprinting tile boundaries are, check Preview: **Tile Boundaries.** To choose a different color for the boundaries to make them contrast better with the imagery, click the color swatch, then choose a color from the Color Picker.

➤ To switch between the original image and the generated pattern, choose **Show: Original** or **Generated.**

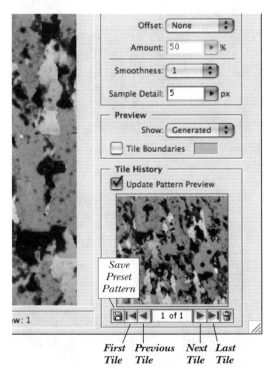

Offset: None

Amount: 50 ▶ %

Smoothness: 1

Sample Detail: 5 ▶ px

Preview

Show: Generated

☐ Tile Boundaries

Tile History

☑ Update Pattern Preview

Save Preset Pattern

w: 1   🖫 ◀ ◀ 1 of 1 ▶ ▶ 🗑

*First   Previous   Next   Last
Tile   Tile   Tile   Tile*

1 *Use the **Tile History** buttons to **navigate** through tile variations.*

---

the **Save Preset Pattern** button, 🖫 type a Name for the preset, then click OK.

Once a tile has been **saved** as a **preset** pattern, it becomes a swatch on the Pattern Preset picker and is available for any command or tool that the picker is normally used with. Only the single tile will be saved, not the full, generated pattern. To create and manage preset libraries, use the Preset Manager (see pages 462–464).

Click OK to exit the Pattern Maker dialog box.

TIP If the current layer's transparent pixels are locked, the pattern will replace only nontransparent pixels.

Using the Vanishing Point filter NEW

The **Vanishing Point** filter helps make sure your edits are parallel with the perspective planes of your image. You can align brush strokes with, or paste copied imagery into, the sides of buildings, billboards, boxes—any image that has obvious perspective planes.

To place imagery in perspective:

1. With a selection tool, select the imagery that will be pasted in perspective onto another image. It can contain layer effects. For text, Ctrl-click/Cmd-click the T icon on the Layers palette. Press Ctrl-C/Cmd-C to copy the selection.

2. Open a document that contains an image in perspective (**2**, next page). Create a new layer, and leave it selected.

3. Choose Filter > **Vanishing Point** (Ctrl-Alt-V/Cmd-Option-V). The Vanishing Point dialog box opens (**3**, next page).

4. Choose the **Create Plane** tool (C) 🔲 in the dialog box, then do the following:

   Click on the preview to place the first corner point for the perspective grid, then click another area of the image to create the second point for the grid.

   Optional: Press X to zoom in temporarily, click to place a point, then release X.

(Continued on the following page)

Vanishing Point Filter

Place two more points to complete the four-sided blue grid 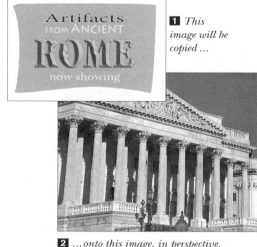. The Edit Plane tool becomes selected automatically.

5. *Optional:* Choose the **Edit Plane** tool (V), ▶ then drag any midpoint on the edge of the grid to lengthen or shorten it, or drag the whole grid to reposition it.

   The grid color must be blue (signifying it's a valid plane). If it's not, drag a corner point until it becomes blue.

6. Press Ctrl-V/Cmd-V to paste in the copied image. Don't deselect it! The Marquee tool □ becomes selected automatically. Drag the pasted image into the outline of the plane grid. The pasted image will align to the perspective of the grid .

   Optional: To blend the pasted image with the background, try choosing Luminance or On from the Heal pop-up menu.

7. Choose the **Transform** tool (T), ▦ then drag any handle on the pasted image to scale it to the desired size and/or drag to reposition it.

8. Check/uncheck **Show Edges** to hide/show the grid and selection, make any adjustments, then click OK.

9. Use opacity, layer effects, or blending modes to blend the "vanishing point" layer into its new surroundings 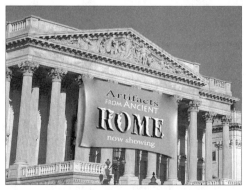. For type, try changing the fill color for the layer (Lock Transparent Pixels).

TIP Read the helpful tool hints in the Vanishing Point dialog box.

1 *This image will be copied …*

2 *…onto this image, in perspective.*

3 *Place four corner points using the **Create Plane** tool to create a blue grid.*

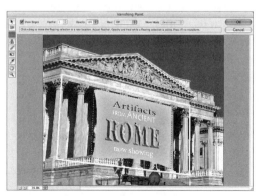

4 *Drag the pasted image into the grid outline.*

5 *We applied layer effects to the vanishing point layer to integrate it with the building layer.*

IT GIVES US GREAT PLEASURE to present the fresh, juicy bumper crop of images that you see in these color pages.

The work is, as they say in the art world, painterly. Even artists who had intially been leery of (or downright resistant to) anything digital have found a way to produce sensuous textures, soft brushstrokes, and realistic shadows using Photoshop. In exchange for giving up the tactile quality of traditional media, they've gained access to an ever expanding range of image-editing commands and features, such as transparency, blending modes, filters, feathering, defringing, cloning, transforming, adjusting, gradients, masking, layer effects, patterns, paths, shapes, type, distortion—not to mention brushes and pens. If you're new to Photoshop, skim through our table of contents (Egads!). Artists are developing their own methods, employing the features and commands that suit them. Some create montages from scanned imagery, some work entirely from memory or imagination, some pin a photograph to their copystand and reinterpret it "by eye."

Don't get us wrong. We love—and will always love—oil painting, drawing, printmaking, paper collage, and other traditional media, not to mention crafts and anything homey and handmade. But having the ability to transfer files almost instantaneously to clients, prepare images for print or web output, and output duplicates on archival paper isn't just an added incentive for artists to use Photoshop—nowadays it's often a requirement. Like it or not, folks, this is the digital age.

Using Photoshop, artists also enjoy being able to undo or partially undo edits, using the Undo and Fade commands, the History palette, and tools such as the Eraser and the History Brush. These features are the electronic equivalent of scrubbing down a canvas with a turpentine-soaked rag, minus the smell. As one artist said, working in Photoshop has enabled him to take more artistic "chances" with his work, and he's delighted with the results.

Artists are a solitary and idiosyncratic lot, but they don't work in a vacuum. They've always inspired and learned from one another—and always will. We're grateful to the artists who contributed to this collection of images. We hope you'll enjoy looking at it as much as we enjoyed gathering it together.

Bert Monroy

©*Bert Monroy*

All of Bert Monroy's digital paintings were created entirely in Adobe Illustrator and Photoshop without the use of scans.

Bert Monroy

Bert Monroy

Bert Monroy

Bert Monroy

©Bert Monroy

Clifford Alejandro

Clifford Alejandro

Clifford Alejandro

Clifford Alejandro

august   20(
october 20(
january 20(

William Low

William Low

William Low

William Low

Marty Blake

Marty Blake

Marty Blake

Marty Blake

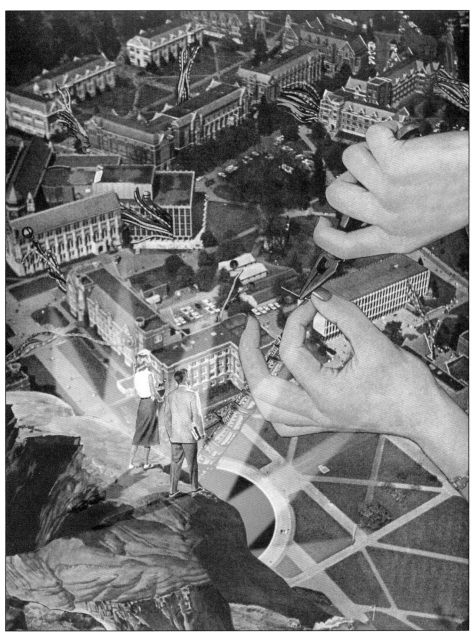

Mick Wiggins

Mick Wiggins

©Mick Wiggins

Mick Wiggins

Mick Wiggins

John Kachik

John Kachik

©John Kachik

©John Kachik

©John Kachik

John Kachik

Keri Smith

the New Shape

Keri Smith

Keri Smith

Keri Smith

Paul Mirocha

Paul Mirocha

©Paul Mirocha

©Paul Mirocha

Paul Mirocha

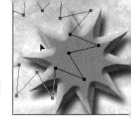

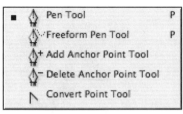

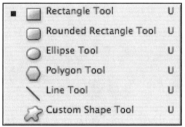

1 *Pen tools and path reshaping tools*

2 *Shape tools*

ECTOR OUTLINES, OR PATHS, CAN BE
Vcreated with either a **pen** tool **1** or a **shape** tool **2**. Before drawing a path, you'll click either the first button on the options bar ▢ for your chosen tool to create a **shape layer** or click the second button ▣ to create a **Work Path.** Both types of paths have anchor points that are connected by curved or straight-line segments, and can be reshaped and filled **3**. They're also resolution-independent, meaning they'll look sharp and precise whether scaled, output on a PostScript printer, or saved in PDF format.

Paths are created by a pen or shape tool or by converting a selection, and are displayed, activated, deactivated, restacked, saved, and deleted via the Paths palette **4**.

Shape layers have a vector mask that controls which part of the layer is visible and which areas are hidden. When a shape layer is selected, a shape mask listing also appears on the Paths palette.

Vector masks work like layer masks, except they can be used on any layer; have sharp, precise path edges; and take up less storage space than layer masks or channels.

Paths and Shapes

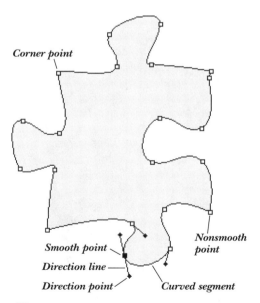

Corner point

Smooth point

Direction line

Direction point

Nonsmooth point

Curved segment

3 *To reshape a **path** or **shape,** you can drag, add, or delete a point or move a segment. You can also reshape a curved line segment by adjusting its direction lines.*

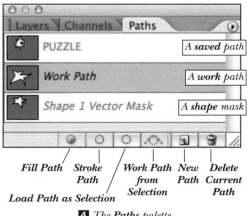

Fill Path *Stroke Path* *Work Path from Selection* *New Path* *Delete Current Path*

Load Path as Selection

4 *The **Paths** palette*

Converting selections into paths

Before delving into the pen tools, we'll show you how to create a **path** using a **selection** as a starting point. Once a selection has been converted into a path, you can precisely reshape it and use it either as a standard path or as a vector mask. You can also convert it back into a selection, if need be.

To convert a selection into a path:

1. Select an area of an image, and show the Paths palette **1**.

2. To choose a Tolerance setting as you convert the selection into a path, Alt-click/Option-click the **Work Path from Selection** button ⌖ at the bottom of the Paths palette (or choose Make Work Path from the Paths palette menu). In the Make Work Path dialog box **2**, enter a **Tolerance** value (0.5–10; try 4–5), then click OK **3**–**4**. A low Tolerance produces a path with many anchor points that closely matches the selection marquee (a path with too many points may cause a printing error, though). A high Tolerance value produces a smoother path (with fewer anchor points) that matches the selection less precisely.
   or
   To convert the selection into a path using the current Tolerance setting, click the **Work Path from Selection** button ⌖ at the bottom of the Paths palette.

3. A new **Work Path** listing will appear on the Paths palette. Don't leave it as a temporary work path! Save it by double-clicking the path name, entering a name in the Save Path dialog box, then clicking OK.

TIP You can copy Photoshop paths to Adobe Illustrator, then use them as fully functional paths in that program (see page 377).

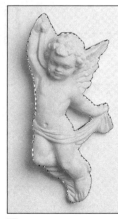

1 *The original selection*

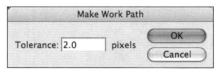

2 *In the **Make Work Path** dialog box, enter a **Tolerance** value to control the number of points on the resulting path.*

3 *The selection converted into a **path: Tolerance 2**. (This shows our path after we clicked on it with the Path Selection tool.)*

4 *The selection converted into a **path: Tolerance 6** (fewer points resulted)*

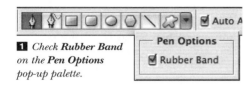

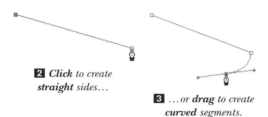

1 *Check **Rubber Band** on the **Pen Options** pop-up palette.*

2 *Click to create straight sides...*

3 *...or drag to create curved segments.*

4 *Drag in the direction you want the curve to follow. Try to place anchor points at the **ends** of a curve, not at the peak of a curve. For graceful curves, use as few anchor points as possible.*

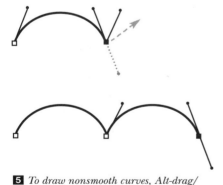

5 *To draw nonsmooth curves, Alt-drag/ Option-drag from the last anchor point in the direction you want the next curve to follow. Both direction lines will be on the same side of the curve segment.*

Using the Pen tool

To draw a path with the Pen tool:

1. Choose the **Pen** tool (P or Shift-P).

2. Click the **New Path** button on the Paths palette, or to add the new path to an existing path, click that name on the palette.

3. On the options bar:

   Click the **Paths** button.

   To preview the line segments as you draw them, click the Geometry options arrowhead, then check **Rubber Band 1**.

4. Click in the document window, move the mouse, then click again to create a straight segment (Shift-click to draw the line at a multiple of 45°) **2**.
   or
   Drag to create a curved segment. Direction lines will appear **3**–**4**.
   or
   To create a nonsmooth point, starting from on top of the last anchor point, Alt-drag/Option-drag in the direction you want the next curve to follow, release Alt/Option and the mouse, then drag in the direction of the new curve **5**.

5. Repeat the previous step as many times as necessary to complete the shape.

   TIP As you draw, press Esc once to erase the last created anchor point, or twice to delete the entire path.

6. To end the path but leave it **open,** Ctrl-click/Cmd-click outside the path or click any tool.
   or
   To **close** the path, click the starting point (a small circle appears in the pointer).

7. Deselect the path or the path name if you don't want the next path you draw to share that name. To reshape the path, see pages 374–375.

   TIP You can use the Convert Point tool to convert smooth points into nonsmooth points later—so don't fret about drawing an exact path now (see page 375).

Pen Tool

367

Using the Freeform Pen tool

To create a path with the **Freeform Pen** tool when Magnetic is unchecked on the options bar, you draw a path by dragging the mouse (the tool creates the anchor points for you). To end a freeform path, as with the Pen tool, Ctrl-click/Cmd-click outside it or click the starting point.

For tracing image elements, you should use the **Freeform Pen** tool with the Magnetic option checked. The tool will snap a path to high-contrast edges that it detects in an image, creating anchor points as you move or drag the mouse.

To draw a magnetic Freeform Pen path:

1. Open an image, and hide any layers that you don't want to trace.

2. Choose the **Freeform Pen** tool (P or Shift-P).

3. Deselect all paths on the Paths palette.

4. On the options bar, click the **Paths** button and check **Magnetic.** To choose other options, see the following page.

5. Click to begin the path, then slowly move the mouse—with or without pressing the mouse button—along the edge of the shape you want to trace **1**. As you move or drag, the path will snap to the edge of the shape. Don't move the mouse too quickly—the tool might not keep pace with you.

6. If the path snaps to any shapes that you don't want included, get the tool back on track by clicking the edge of a shape (an anchor point will be created), then continue to move or drag the mouse. You can reshape the path later.

7. To **close** the path **2**, double-click anywhere over the shape to close with magnetic segments; or Alt-double-click/Option-double-click to close with a straight segment; or click the starting point (a small circle appears next to the tool pointer).
   or

Drawing straight lines

To draw **straight** segments with a temporary Pen tool while the **Freeform Pen** is being used, Alt-click/Option-click, and continue clicking. Release Alt/Option (but keep the mouse button down) to return to normal Freeform Pen behavior.

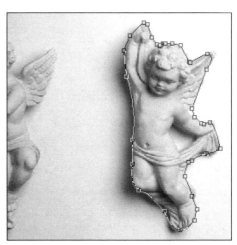

1 *When using the **Freeform Pen** tool with the **Magnetic** option, click to start the path, then move the mouse around the object you want to trace.*

2 *The completed path*

Geometry options

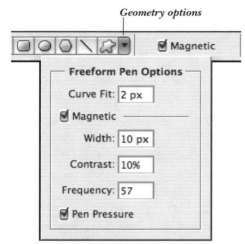

1 *Options for the Freeform Pen tool (with Magnetic checked on the options bar)*

To end the path but leave it **open,** press Enter/Return.

TIP Press Esc to delete an incomplete path.

TIP You can also create a Work Path by using a shape tool. See page 383.

To choose options for the Freeform Pen tool:

Click the "Geometry options" arrowhead on the options bar to open the Freeform Pen Options palette **1**.

Curve Fit (0.5–10 pixels) controls how closely the Freeform Pen path matches the movement of your mouse. The higher the Curve Fit, the fewer the points, and thus the smoother the shape.

If Magnetic is checked on the options bar, you can also choose these settings:

The **Width** (1–256 pixels) is the width of the area under the pointer that the tool considers when creating points. Use a wide Width for a high-contrast image that has clear delineations between shapes, or a narrow Width for more exact line placement in a low-contrast image that contains subtle gradations or closely spaced shapes.

TIP To decrease the Width incrementally while creating a path, press [; or to increase the Width, press].

Contrast (0–100%) is the degree of contrast needed between shapes for the tool to discern an edge. At a low Contrast setting, edges between even low-contrast areas are considered.

Frequency (0–100) controls the speed at which points are placed as you draw a path. The lower the Frequency, the more points are created.

Check **Pen Pressure** if you have a stylus tablet and want to control the width using stylus pressure. As you apply more pressure, the width decreases.

Freeform Pen Options

Working with paths

In this section, you will learn how to save, move, duplicate, rename, display/hide, and deselect paths.

When you draw a new path, it's labeled "Work Path." Although it will save with your document, you should think of it as temporary, because it will be replaced by the very next work path you create! To **save** a **Work Path** permanently, follow these instructions. Once a path is saved, Photoshop resaves it automatically each time you modify it.

To save a Work Path:

On the Paths palette, double-click the **Work Path** listing, enter a name 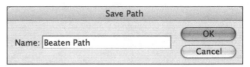, then click OK.
or
Drag the Work Path over the **New Path** button.

To move a path:

1. On the Paths palette, click a path name.
2. Choose the **Path Selection** tool (A or Shift-A).
3. In the document window, drag inside the path **2**.

To duplicate a saved path:

Drag the path name over the **New Path** button at the bottom of the Paths palette **3**.

TIP To change the stacking position of a path, drag the path name up or down on the Paths palette. The Work Path always remains at the bottom.

To rename a path:

Double-click a path name, type a new name right on the palette, then press Enter/Return.

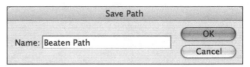

1 *Type a name in the **Save Path** dialog box.*

2 *A path is **moved** with the **Path Selection** tool.*

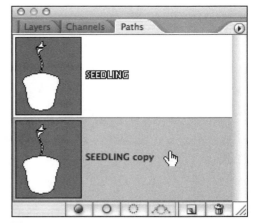

3 *After a path name is dragged over the **New Path** button, a duplicate appears on the palette.*

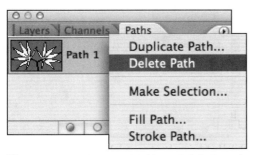

1 *To delete a path, right-click/Control-click the path name, then choose **Delete Path** from the context menu.*

Later you'll learn how to display and select individual anchor points on a path. In these instructions, you'll simply learn how to **show** the overall path shape in the document window.

To show a path:

Click the path **name** or **thumbnail** on the Paths palette.

TIP To change the size of the palette thumbnails, right-click/Control-click the gray area below the path listings and choose None, Small, Medium, or Large.

To hide a path:

On the Paths palette, Shift-click the path **name** or click **below** all the path names.

To **delete** a Work Path, simply draw a new path with the Pen tool; a new Work Path will take its place. To delete a non-Work Path, follow these instructions.

To delete a path:

1. On the Paths palette, click the path you want to delete.

2. Right-click/Control-click the path name and choose **Delete Path** **1**.
   or
   Click the **Delete Path** button, 🗑 then click Yes; or to bypass the prompt, drag the path name over the button.

Show, Hide, Delete Path

371

Reshaping paths

Not even the best Pen tool artists can draw a perfect path from scratch. In this section, you'll learn how to add segments to a path; transform a path; select points on a path; and, finally, reshape a path by adding, deleting, converting, or manipulating its anchor points.

To add segments to an existing, open path:

1. Choose the **Freeform Pen** tool 🖋 or **Pen** tool ✒ (P or Shift-P).

2. On the Paths palette, click the name of a path that contains at least one open (not closed) path.

3. Drag from either endpoint of the path **1**–**2**. To close the path, drag over the other endpoint, or to keep it open, click the tool again.

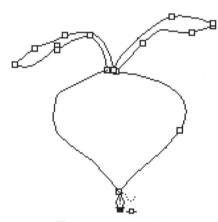

1 *To* **add** *to a path, drag from an* **endpoint** *with the* **Pen** *or* **Freeform Pen** *tool.*

To transform an entire path:

1. Choose the **Path Selection** tool (A or Shift-A). ▸

2. Click a path name on the Paths palette. If multiple paths were saved under one path name, they'll all be transformed.

3. Choose Edit > Transform Path > **Scale, Rotate, Skew, Distort,** or **Perspective;** or right-click/Control-click in the document window and choose **Free Transform Path** (Ctrl-T/Cmd-T).
   or
   Click inside a path in the document window, check **Show Bounding Box** on the options bar, then transform the path using the bounding box handles, as you would use the handles on the Free Transform box.

4. Follow the instructions on pages 309–311 to perform the transformation **3**.

TIP To repeat the last transformation, choose Edit > Transform Path > Again (Ctrl-Shift-T/Cmd-Shift-T).

TIP To learn about the Free Transform/ Warp Mode button 🔲 on the options bar, see pages 312–313.

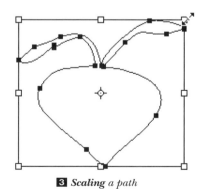

2 *Completing the addition*

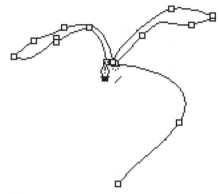

3 *Scaling a path*

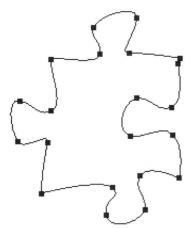

1 *Click with the **Path Selection** tool to select **all** the points on a path.*

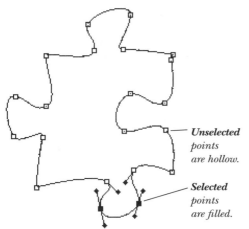

Unselected
points
are hollow.

Selected
points
are filled.

2 *Click with the **Direct Selection** tool to select **individual** points on a path.*

Before you can manipulate individual anchor points on a path, you have to make them **visible.**

To select anchor points on a path:
Method 1

1. Click a path name on the Paths palette.

2. Choose the **Path Selection** tool (A or Shift-A).

3. Click the path in the document window. All the anchor points on the path will become selected **1**.

Method 2

1. Click a path name on the Paths palette.

2. Choose the **Direct Selection** tool (A or Shift-A).

3. Click the path, then click an anchor point **2**. Shift-click, or drag a marquee around, additional anchor points. Direction lines will be visible. (Shift-click to deselect points.)
or
To select all the anchor points on the path, Alt-click/Option-click the path or draw a marquee around it. (The direction lines won't be visible.) An entire path can be moved when all its points are selected.

TIP To turn any pen tool except the Freeform Pen into a temporary Direct Selection tool, press Ctrl/Cmd.

To deselect a path:

1. Choose the **Direct Selection** tool or the **Path Selection** tool (A or Shift-A).

2. Click outside the path in the document window. The path will still be visible in the document window, but its anchor points and direction lines will now be hidden.

To **reshape** a path, you can move, add, or delete an anchor point; move a segment; or convert points from smooth to corner and vice versa. To modify the shape of a curved line segment, you can move a direction line toward or away from its anchor point or rotate it around its anchor point.

To reshape a path:

1. On the Paths palette, click the name of the path you want to reshape.

2. Choose the **Direct Selection** tool (A or Shift-A).🔧 Or to turn another pen tool into a temporary Direct Selection tool, press Ctrl/Cmd.

3. Click the path in the document window.

4. Do any of the following:

   Drag an anchor **point** 🔳.

   Select a segment by Shift-clicking both of its endpoints, then **drag** the **segment.**

   Drag or **rotate** a **direction line** 🔳. If you move a direction line on a smooth point, the two segments that are connected to that point will reshape accordingly. If you move a direction line on a nonsmooth point, only one curve segment will move.

5. Choose the **Pen** tool,🖋 then do any of the following:

   To **add** an anchor **point,** check Auto Add/Delete on the options bar, then click a line segment (the pointer will have a plus sign when it's over a segment) 🔳–🔳.

   To **delete** an anchor **point,** check Auto Add/Delete on the options bar, then click the anchor point (the pointer will have a minus sign when it's over a point)(🔳, next page).

   TIP To turn off the Add/Delete function of the Pen tool temporarily, hold down Shift. If this option is off, you can use the Add Anchor Point tool 🖋 or Delete Anchor Point tool 🖋 to add or delete points, respectively.

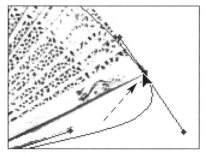

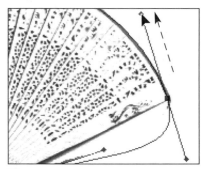

🔳 *Dragging an anchor point*

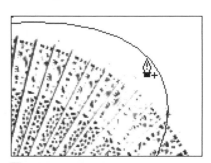

🔳 *Pulling a direction line*

🔳 *Adding an anchor point*

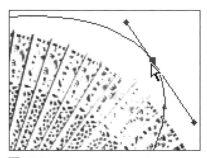

🔳 *Clicking the new anchor point*

Fill or stroke

To fill or apply a stroke to a path using the current Foreground color and the default dialog box settings, click the path name, then click the **Fill Path Color** button ⬤ or **Stroke Path** button ○ at the bottom of the Paths palette.

To change the default fill settings, Alt-click/Option-click the **Fill Path Color** button. To change the default stroke settings, choose Edit > **Stroke.**

To apply a stroke to a shape layer, apply the **Stroke** effect (Layer Style dialog box); or for a fill, apply one of the **Overlay** effects.

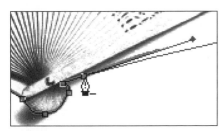

1 *Deleting an anchor point*

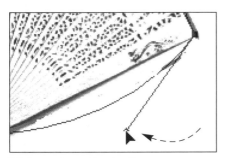

2 *Converting a direction line*

To convert a **smooth** point into a **corner** point, choose the **Convert Point** tool ⌐ (or hold down Ctrl-Alt/Cmd-Option if the Direct Selection tool is chosen or Alt/Option if a pen tool is chosen), then click the anchor point (deselect the Convert Point tool by choosing another tool). To convert a corner point into a smooth point, use the same tool to drag away from the anchor point.

You can also use the Convert Point tool to **rotate** one direction line in a pair independently of the other **2**. Once this tool has been used on part of a direction line, you can use either the Convert Point tool or the Direct Selection tool to move its partner.

6. Click outside the path to deselect it.

TIP Another strategy is to start by drawing an initial path as all smooth points, then if you need to manipulate any direction lines independently, use the Convert Point tool to convert smooth points to nonsmooth points.

Reshape Path

Converting paths to selections

To convert a path to a selection:

1. *Optional:* Create a selection to add, delete, or intersect the new path selection with.

2. On the Paths palette, Ctrl-click/Cmd-click the **path** that you want to convert into a selection.

or

On the Paths palette, click the path that you want to convert to a selection, then click the **Load Path as Selection** button 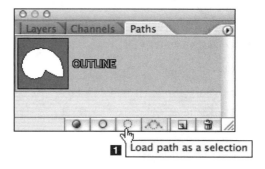 **1** on the palette. The last used Make Selection settings will apply.

or

To choose options as you load a path as a selection, right-click/Control-click the path name and choose **Make Selection** from the context menu **2**. The Make Selection dialog box opens. You can apply a **Feather Radius** to the selection; but if you check Anti-aliased, make the Feather Radius 0. You can also add, subtract, or intersect the path with an existing selection on the image by clicking an **Operation** option (see also the Operation shortcuts in the sidebar). Click OK.

3. On the Layers palette, click the layer you created the selection for.

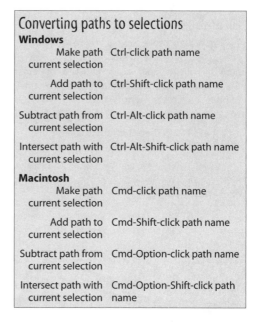

Converting paths to selections	
Windows	
Make path current selection	Ctrl-click path name
Add path to current selection	Ctrl-Shift-click path name
Subtract path from current selection	Ctrl-Alt-click path name
Intersect path with current selection	Ctrl-Alt-Shift-click path name
Macintosh	
Make path current selection	Cmd-click path name
Add path to current selection	Cmd-Shift-click path name
Subtract path from current selection	Cmd-Option-click path name
Intersect path with current selection	Cmd-Option-Shift-click path name

1 Load path as a selection

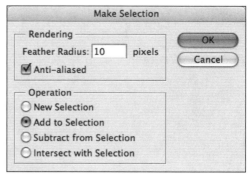

2 *Choose options for a selection in the* **Make Selection** *dialog box.*

Plan B

As an alternative to creating paths and text in Photoshop, you can use the File > Place command in **Adobe Illustrator** to import your Photoshop image. Then in Illustrator, create vector paths or text on top of your imported image.

Copying paths to other files

Although you can use File > Export > Paths to Illustrator to export your Photoshop paths to Illustrator, there are easier methods, such as drag–and-drop or copy-and-paste, as per the following instructions.

To copy a path to an Adobe Illustrator file or another Photoshop file:

1. With your Photoshop document open, open an Illustrator or Photoshop document, position them so you can see them both, then click in the source document window.

2. Click a path name on the Paths palette. Choose the **Path Selection** tool, ▶ then drag the path from the source document window into the target document window **1**.

   or

   Click a path name on the Paths palette, choose Edit > **Copy** (Ctrl-C/Cmd-C), click in the target document window, then choose Edit > **Paste** (Ctrl-V/Cmd-V). In Illustrator, the Paste Options dialog box opens. Click Paste As: **Compound Shape (fully editable),** then click OK.

   TIP When the Photoshop path arrives in Illustrator, it won't have a stroke or fill.

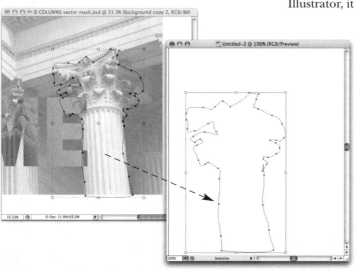

1 *Drag a path from a **Photoshop** document window into an **Illustrator** document window.*

Creating vector masks

A **vector mask** works like a layer mask in that it hides pixels on a layer, except in this case a clean, sharp-edged path shape delineates the visible and masked areas in the current layer.

The path that will be used for the mask can be created using the Pen tool, Freeform Pen tool, or a shape tool, or it can be created from a selection that you convert into a path. You can reshape the path being used for the mask or discard the mask at any time.

A vector mask displays as a gray thumbnail on the Layers palette, and also on the Paths palette when the layer that contains the mask is selected. As with layer masks, each vector mask is associated with only one layer.

To create a vector mask:
Method 1
1. On the Layers palette, click the layer that you want to add a vector mask to **1**.

2. To create a mask that reveals all the layer pixels, choose Layer > Vector Mask > **Reveal All,** or Ctrl-click/Cmd-click the **Add Vector Mask** button ⬜ on the Layers palette.
   or
   To create a mask that hides the layer pixels, choose Layer > Vector Mask > **Hide All,** or Ctrl-Alt-click/Cmd-Option-click the **Add Vector Mask** button ⬜ on the Layers palette.

3. Choose the **Pen** tool, **Freeform Pen** tool, or a **shape** tool (Rectangle, Rounded Rectangle, Ellipse, Polygon, or Custom Shape), then create a clipping path in the desired shape **2**–**3**.

Method 2
1. On the Layers palette, click the layer that you want to add a vector mask to.

2. To reveal only layer pixels within a selected, existing path, click a path on the Paths palette, then choose Layer > Vector Mask > **Current Path.**

Create Vector Mask

1 *The original layer*

2 *A **vector mask** is added using the **Hide All** option, and the Pen tool is used to reshape it.*

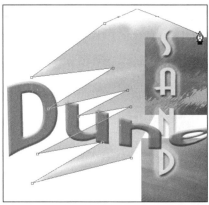

3 *The **vector mask** is hiding part of the brush strokes on the layer.*

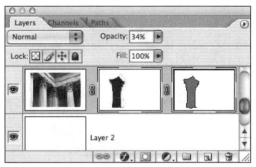

1 *The selection made from a **layer mask** becomes the path for a **vector mask**.*

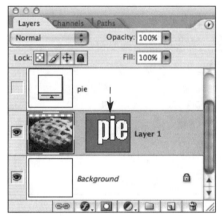

2 *A type layer was converted into a **shape** layer, then the **vector mask thumbnail** was dragged to Layer 1.*

3 *The image is visible only within the confines of the **mask shapes**.*

Should you decide that you want a hard-edged mask to define an image layer, you can **convert** a layer mask into a vector mask.

To convert a layer mask into a vector mask:

1. Ctrl-click/Cmd-click a layer mask thumbnail on the Layers palette.

2. On the Paths palette, click the **Make Work Path from Selection** button.

3. Keep the path selected, and choose Layer > Vector Mask > **Current Path** **1**.

4. *Optional:* To remove the layer mask, right-click/Control-click the layer mask thumbnail and choose Delete Layer Mask. The vector mask will remain.

You can also fill **type** shapes with imagery by using a vector mask.

To create a vector mask from type:

1. Create a type layer, then duplicate it to keep an editable copy available. Hide the duplicate, then click the original type layer.

2. Right-click/Control-click the layer (not the thumbnail) and choose **Convert to Shape** (or choose Layer > Type > Convert to Shape).

3. Drag the vector mask thumbnail that you just created over another layer. The vector mask will move to that layer **2**–**3**. (Layer effects can be moved from one layer to another the same way.)

4. Delete the (former) type shape layer.

TIP Marquee the mask shapes with the Path Selection tool, then reposition the vector mask within the layer (see the next page) or reverse what's revealed and what's hidden on the layer (see page 381).

Create Vector Mask

Working with vector masks

A vector mask can be **moved** independently of its layer pixels at any time. It will stay on its designated layer.

To reposition a vector mask:

1. Choose the **Path Selection** tool (A or Shift-A).

2. On the Layers palette, click a vector mask thumbnail.

3. If the mask consists of multiple paths (such as type shapes), marquee them. Drag the vector mask in the document window. A different part of the image will now be visible inside the path **1**.

If you **reshape** a vector mask, the masking effect in the image will change accordingly.

To reshape a vector mask:

1. Choose the **Direct Selection** tool (A or Shift-A).

2. Click a vector mask thumbnail on the Layers palette. The vector mask should now be visible in the document window.

3. Click the edge of the vector mask to make its anchor points visible.

4. Follow any of the steps on pages 372–375 to reshape the path.

NEW To copy a vector mask to another layer:

Alt-drag/Option-drag a vector mask thumbnail to another layer **2**–**3**. A duplicate of the vector mask will appear.

TIP To move (not copy) a vector mask to another layer, drag it without holding down Alt/Option.

TIP To combine two vector masks by using a pathfinder button, see page 386.

To deactivate a vector mask:

Shift-click the vector mask thumbnail on the Layers palette. A red X will appear over the thumbnail, and the entire layer will now be visible **4** (this doesn't select the vector mask thumbnail). You can Shift-click the vector mask thumbnail again at any time to remove the X and restore the masking effect.

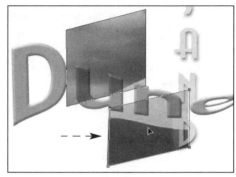

1 *The vector mask is **moved**, and now a different part of the image is visible within it.*

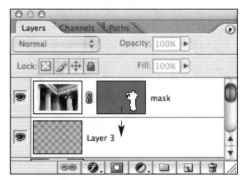

2 *Alt-drag/Option-drag the vector mask thumbnail to another layer.*

3 *A **copy** of the vector mask appears on the target layer (in this case, Layer 3).*

4 *The vector mask is **deactivated**, as indicated by the big X.*

EPS clipping paths

If a file that contains a vector mask is saved in the Photoshop EPS format for import into another program (e.g., InDesign or QuarkXPress), check **Include Vector Data** in the EPS Options dialog box if you want the vector mask to remain in effect.

Note: To import a Photoshop file that contains a vector mask into Adobe Illustrator CS2, use the Place command (Link option unchecked) or the Open command in Illustrator, and choose the option that converts layers to objects.

To reverse the visible and hidden areas in a vector mask:

1. Choose the **Path Selection** tool (A or Shift-A).

2. On the Layers palette, click a vector mask thumbnail. The vector mask will be visible in the document window.

3. Click the vector mask in the document window. Its anchor points and segments will become selected 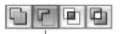.

4. Click the **Subtract from Shape Area** (second) button on the options bar **2**–**3**, or press – (minus key).

   To switch the revealed and hidden areas again, click the **Add to Shape Area** (first) button on the options bar, or press + (plus key).

You can **delete** any vector masks that you no longer need, though you won't recoup any file storage space by doing so.

To discard a vector mask:

On the Layers palette, click the thumbnail for the vector mask that you want to remove, click the **Delete Layer** button, then click OK, or to bypass the prompt, Alt-click/Option-click the button.

or

Right-click/Control-click a vector mask, choose **Delete Vector Mask,** then click OK.

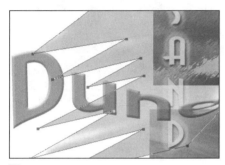

1 *Select a vector mask.*

2 *Click the Subtract from Shape Area button.*

3 *The hidden and visible areas are reversed.*

Using the shape tools

In this section, you'll learn the three basic functions of all the shape tools: to create a shape layer, to create a Work Path, and to define an area of pixels. First, shape layers.

A **shape layer** is a precise geometric or custom-shaped clipping path that reveals a solid-color, gradient, or pattern fill within its contour **1**. At any time, shapes can be repositioned, transformed, or reshaped; their fill content can be modified or changed to a different type; and the usual Layers palette settings (e.g., layer effects, blending modes, opacity and fill settings) can be applied to them. Creating a shape layer involves creating a vector path, but Photoshop makes it easy for you by supplying ready-made shapes—and of course you can also create your own custom shapes.

To create a shape layer:

1. Click a layer on the Layers palette. The new shape layer will be created above the current layer.

2. Choose a Foreground color for the shape's fill. (To fill a shape with a gradient or pattern, see page 387.)

3. Choose one of the **shape** tools on the Toolbox (U or Shift-U) **2**. Once a shape tool is selected, you can switch to any other shape tool by clicking one of the six shape tool buttons on the options bar **4**.

4. On the options bar:

   Click the **Shape Layers** button! ▢ **3**

   For the Rounded Rectangle tool, choose a **Radius** value; for the Polygon tool, choose a number of **Sides;** for the Line tool, choose a **Weight;** or for the Custom Shape tool, choose a shape from the **Custom Shape Preset** picker **5**.

Special effects

Apply **layer effects** (e.g., Inner Glow, Bevel) to a shape layer or to a layer that has a vector mask to enhance edges, add a shadow, etc.—you'll be able to modify them at any time.

1 *A star **shape** with a solid-color fill*

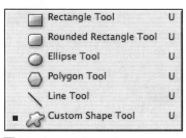

2 *The **shape** tools*

5 *Custom Shape Preset picker (for the Custom Shape tool only)*

3 *Shape Layers   Paths   Fill Pixels*

4 *Shape tool buttons*

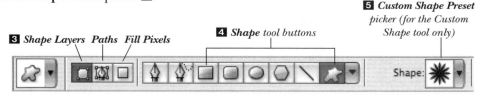

Shape:

Create Shape Layer

1 *A* **shape** *created using the* **Custom Shape** *tool*

Adjustment layer *thumbnail*   *Thumbnail for a* **vector mask** *(created via a shape tool)*

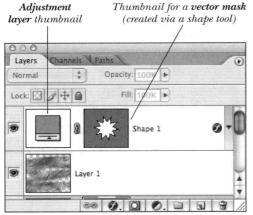

2 *The* **shape** *layer appears on the Layers palette.*

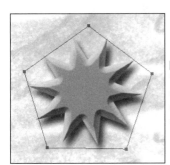

3 *Click the* **Paths** *button on the options bar.*

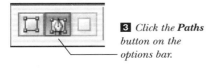

4 *A pentagonal* **Work Path** *created with a shape tool (drawn on top of a shape layer)*

5. Drag in the document window to create the shape **1**. While dragging, you can hold down Alt/Option to draw from the shape's center or Shift-drag to maintain the shape's proportions. *Note:* In Windows, to draw from the center, the procedure is to click, hold down Alt, then drag.

A new Shape 1 layer will be listed on the Layers palette **2**. It will have an adjustment layer thumbnail that controls its fill content and a vector mask thumbnail that controls its contour and location. You can choose layer style, blending mode, opacity, and fill settings for this new layer.

TIP When the Custom Shape tool is selected, you can right-click/Control-click the image to open an "on-the-fly" shape picker.

TIP To append other libraries to the Custom Shape preset picker, choose a library name from the bottom of the Custom Shape picker menu, then click Append.

TIP To choose options for the individual shape tools, click the Geometry Options arrowhead on the options bar (see below). For example, we like to keep the Defined Proportions option on for our Custom Shape tool so we don't have to hold down the Shift key.

Any of the shape tools can also be used to create a temporary **Work Path** (which, of course, can be saved as a permanent path).

To create a Work Path using a shape tool:

1. Choose a **shape** tool, then click the **Paths** button on the options bar **3**.

2. Drag in the document window to create the path shape **4**. A new Work Path listing will appear on the Paths palette. To save it as a permanent path, double-click it, then click OK. To learn more about work paths, see page 370.

Last but not least, using the **Fill Pixels** function of any shape tool, you can create an area of pixels on a standard layer in any predefined shape—without having to use a selection marquee or draw a path.

To create a shape-defined area of pixels:

1. On the Layers palette, create a new layer, and keep it selected.

2. Choose a Foreground color.

3. Choose a **shape** tool (U or Shift-U). You can click a different shape tool button on the options bar.

4. On the options bar, do the following:

Click the **Fill Pixels** button 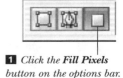 **1**.

If you're using the Rounded Rectangle tool, choose a **Radius** value; for the Polygon tool, choose a number of **Sides;** for the Line tool, choose a **Weight;** or for the Custom Shape tool, choose a shape from the **Custom Shape Preset** picker.

Choose **Mode** and **Opacity** settings.

5. Drag across the document window to create the shape (or Shift-drag to preserve its proportions). A filled area of pixels will be created **2**.

Use brushes, editing tools, filters—whatever—to modify the pixels, or change the Layers palette settings (e.g., apply layer effects). It's just a regular ol' layer.

TIP To add a shape to a layer mask, click a layer mask thumbnail on the Layers palette, choose a shape tool, click the Fill Pixels button on the options bar, choose black or white as the Foreground color, then drag or Shift-drag in the document window **3**.

1 *Click the* **Fill Pixels** *button on the options bar.*

2 *The cat image, created by using the* **Custom Shape** *tool with the* **Fill Pixels** *button clicked, is a normal, standard, regular ol' layer.*

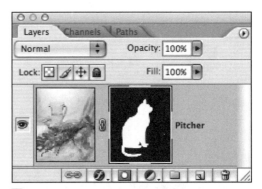

3 *You can also use a shape tool with the* **Fill Pixels** *button clicked to redefine an existing* **layer mask.** *(We created a "hide all" layer mask, made the Foreground color white, then dragged with the Custom Shape tool.)*

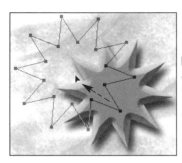

1 *Use the* ***Path Selection*** *tool to drag the* ***mask*** *in the document window.*

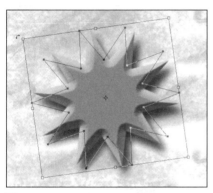

2 *Use the* ***Path Selection*** *tool with the* ***Show Bounding Box*** *option checked to display the bounding box handles on a shape layer's vector mask, then drag a handle to transform it.*

3 *Use the* ***Direct Selection*** *tool to drag an anchor point on the shape layer vector mask.*

Using shape layer masks

You can **modify** a shape layer mask using the same methods as for a path.

To modify a shape layer mask:

1. Choose the **Path Selection** tool (A or Shift-A).

2. Click a shape in the document window.
   or
   Click a shape layer on the Layers palette.

3. Do any of the following:

   To **move** the vector mask, drag it in the document window **1**.

   To **transform** the mask, click the high-lighted shape to display its anchor points (and its bounding box, too, if Show Bounding Box is checked on the options bar) **2**. Follow the instructions on pages 309–311 to transform the shape.

   To **reshape** the mask, click the edge of the shape to display its anchor points **3**, then follow the instructions on pages 372–375 to reshape it.

You **deactivate** a shape **layer mask** the same way you deactivate any other type of layer mask.

To deactivate a shape layer's vector mask:

Shift-click the vector mask thumbnail for the shape layer on the Layers palette. An X will appear over the thumbnail, and the entire layer's fill contents will display. (To restore the masking effect, Shift-click the vector mask thumbnail again to remove the X.)

Shape layers from Illustrator

To paste a path from Illustrator to Photoshop as a shape layer:

1. In Adobe Illustrator, copy a vector object.

2. In Photoshop, choose Edit > **Paste.** In the Paste dialog box, click Paste As: **Shape Layer,** then click OK 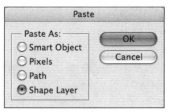. The shape layer will be filled with the current Foreground color, but it won't have a stroke. You have just pasted the vector mask outline for the shape layer.

1 *Click Paste As:* **Shape Layer** *in the* **Paste** *dialog box.*

Combining shapes

To add to or subtract from a shape:

1. Create a shape layer, and keep the shape layer's vector mask thumbnail selected.

2. Make sure a shape tool is chosen and the **Shape Layers** button ⬜ is selected on the options bar.

3. Click a **pathfinder** button on the options bar **2**.

4. Drag partially across the existing shape. A new shape path will be created that either extends or subtracts from the existing shape, depending on which pathfinder button you clicked **3**.

TIP To reverse what a vector mask shape clips and reveals, click the shape with the Path Selection tool; then, on the options bar, click the Subtract from Shape Area button **4**. Click the Add to Shape Area button **5** to restore the original setup.

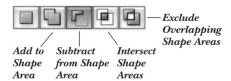

Add to Shape Area *Subtract from Shape Area* *Intersect Shape Areas* — *Exclude Overlapping Shape Areas*

2 *Click a* **pathfinder** *button on the options bar. (We chose Subtract from Shape Area.)*

3 *The new shape path* **subtracts** *(cuts out) from the existing shape area.*

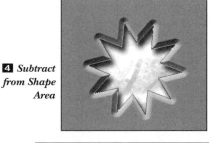

4 *Subtract from Shape Area*

5 *Add to Shape Area*

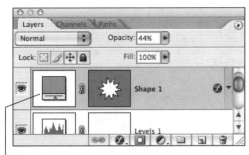

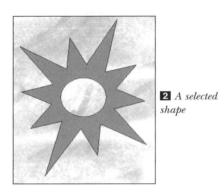

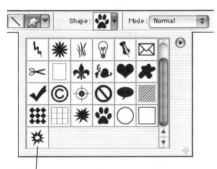

1 *Shape layer thumbnail*

2 *A selected shape*

3 *The new shape appears on the* **Custom Shape Preset** *picker.*

Change layer content

To create an adjustment layer that uses a vector mask, create a shape layer (see pages 382–383), choose a command from the Layer > **Change Layer Content** submenu, make the desired adjustments in the dialog box, then click OK.

Recoloring shape layers

To recolor a shape layer:

To apply a new **solid** color, double-click the shape layer thumbnail on the Layers palette **1** (or click a shape layer, then choose Layer > Layer Content Options), choose a color from the Color Picker, then click OK.
or
To change the contents of a shape layer to a gradient or pattern, click the shape layer, then from the Layer > **Change Layer Content** submenu, choose **Gradient** or **Pattern.**

TIP To change the style or color of the currently active shape layer, make sure the link icon 🔗 is selected (visible in Windows/dark in Mac), choose the Custom Shape tool, then, on the options bar, choose a style from the Style Preset picker or click the Color swatch and choose a color from the Color Picker.

Saving shapes

If you've altered the contour of a preset shape, pasted in a shape from Adobe Illustrator, or drawn your own custom shape, you can save it to the **Custom Shape Preset** picker so you can use it again.

To save a shape as a preset:

1. On the Layers palette, click the vector mask thumbnail on a shape layer that you created or customized in Photoshop or pasted from Adobe Illustrator. The shape will become selected in the document window **2**.

2. Choose Edit > **Define Custom Shape,** enter a Name in the Shape Name dialog box, then click OK. The new shape will appear at the bottom of the Custom Shape Preset picker **3** and is now available for any document.

    If you load in another shape library, to ensure that the new shape isn't deleted, click Append (not Replace); or if you do click Replace, in the alert dialog box, click Save to save the current library as a file; the new library name will appear on the Custom Shape picker menu.

Rasterizing shape layers

Before you can perform pixel edits on a shape layer (e.g., apply brush strokes or a filter) or convert a layer vector mask into a layer (pixel) mask, the layer must be **rasterized.** (*Note:* If you used a shape tool to create a pixel area instead of creating a shape layer, it's already rasterized, so this step is unnecessary.)

To rasterize a shape layer:

1. Click a shape layer on the Layers palette ■.

2. From the Layer > **Rasterize** submenu, choose:

   Shape to convert the shape layer into a filled pixel shape on a transparent layer, without a vector mask. You can now paint or edit the layer ■.

   Fill Content to convert the shape layer's fill content into a pixel area clipped by the existing vector mask. You can now paint or edit the layer ■.

   Vector Mask to convert the vector mask into a pixel-based layer mask in the same shape and position as the vector mask. The fill content is still an editable solid-color fill. The layer mask can be repositioned within the layer ■.

   Layer converts a shape layer into a filled pixel shape (or converts a vector mask into a layer mask) ■.

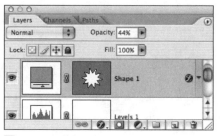

■ *The original shape layer on the Layers palette*

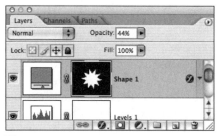

■ *Layer > Rasterize > **Shape** removed the vector mask and the adjustable fill.*

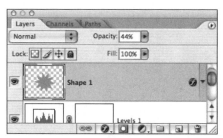

■ *Layer > Rasterize > **Fill Content** converted the adjustable fill into a normal pixel area.*

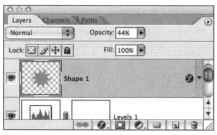

■ *Layer > Rasterize > **Vector Mask** converted the vector mask into a layer mask.*

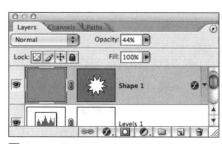

■ *Layer > Rasterize > **Layer** produced the same results as in figure ■, above.*

Rasterize Shape Layer

VECTOR

1 *This is **editable** vector type.*

PIXELS

2 *This is type was **rasterized**, and then the Sponge and Diffuse Glow filters were applied to it.*

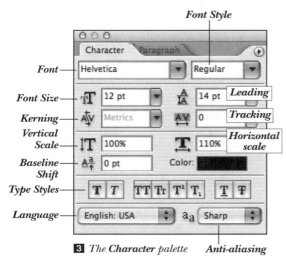

Font Style

Font — Helvetica / Regular

Font Size — 12 pt / 14 pt — *Leading*

Kerning — Metrics / 0 — *Tracking*

Vertical Scale — 100% / 110% — *Horizontal scale*

Baseline Shift — 0 pt / Color:

Type Styles — T T TT Tr T¹ T₁ T T

Language — English: USA / Sharp

3 *The **Character** palette*   Anti-aliasing

WE'VE NEVER HEARD THE PHRASE "A word is worth a thousand pictures," but in Photoshop, where you can do such artful things with type, the line between pictures and words is blurred (sometimes literally!). In this chapter, you'll start by learning how to create and select editable type and apply a host of character and paragraph attributes. After mastering those basics, you'll learn how to transform, warp, and rasterize type; fill it with imagery; fade type by using a layer mask; screen back an image behind type; screen back type; create a type mask; and create type in a spot color channel.

Editable versus rasterized type

A new layer is created each time you use the **Horizontal Type** tool or **Vertical Type** tool, and fully **editable** type appears instantly in the document window **1**. You can change its attributes (e.g., font, style, point size, color, kerning, tracking, leading, alignment, and baseline shift), transform it, apply layer effects to it, change its blending mode, and change its opacity. Photoshop uses a typeface's vector outlines when resizing editable type, when saving to the PDF and EPS formats, and when outputting to PostScript printers. Editable type outputs crisply at the printer resolution, not at the file resolution.

Not all Photoshop commands can be applied to editable type layers, however. For example, you can't apply filters or brush strokes to them or fill them with a gradient or a pattern. In order to apply those kinds of edits, you have to **rasterize** the type layer **2**. But you can't have your cake and eat it, too. Once type is rasterized, its typographic attributes (e.g., font, style) can't be altered.

Attributes are chosen for type by using the **Character** palette **3**, the **Paragraph** palette, and the options bar (shown on the next page).

Creating editable type

Because **editable type** automatically appears on its own layer, it can be edited, moved, transformed, restacked, or otherwise modified without affecting any other layers. You can be very casual about where you position editable type initially and about which typographic attributes you choose for it, too, because it's so easy to edit afterward.

Note: Type that's created in a Bitmap, Indexed Color, or Multichannel image will appear on the Background, not on a layer, and can't be edited.

To create an editable type layer:

1. Choose the **Horizontal Type** tool or **Vertical Type** tool (T or Shift-T) **1**.

2. To create **point** type, click to define an insertion point (see the sidebar).
   or
   To create **paragraph** type, drag a marquee to define the boundaries of the bounding box for the text to fit into.

3. On the options bar, do the following:

   Choose a **font family 2**. A sample of each font displays on the right side of the menu. **NEW**

   Choose a **font style.**

   Choose or enter a **font size** (.10 to 1296 pt). You can drag left or right over the font size icon to choose a size.

   Choose an **anti-aliasing** method: Sharp (sharpest), **Crisp** (somewhat sharp), **Strong** (heavier), or **Smooth** (smoothest). Photoshop will smooth the edges of the type by introducing partially transparent pixels along its edges. With anti-aliasing off (None), type will have jagged edges (**1**–**4**, next page).

Point or paragraph?

Point type is created when you click in the document window with the Horizontal Type tool or Vertical Type tool and then type some characters. This kind of type keeps on going, disappearing off the edge of the image, until you press Enter/Return. Use this method if you want to control hyphenation and line breaks manually in just a few lines of text.

Paragraph type is created when you drag in the document window with the Horizontal or Vertical Type tool to define an area for the type to fit into before typing any characters. It's better suited for larger text blocks. From the Paragraph palette menu, you can choose between two algorithms for paragraph type—**Adobe Single-line Composer** and **Adobe Every-line Composer**—that control how Photoshop flows type to the next line when the type reaches the edge of the text bounding box (the differences between the two are subtle).

Click an **alignment** button to align point type relative to its original insertion point, or to align paragraph type to the left edge, right edge, or center of its bounding box (**5**, next page).

Choose a **color** for the type by clicking the type color swatch, then choosing a color from the Color Picker (or from the Swatches palette or Color palette, if the palette you want to use is already open).

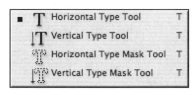

1 *The first two type tools create **editable** type; the second two create type **selections**.*

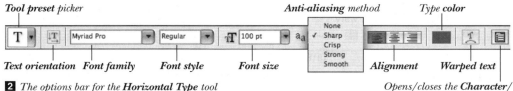

Tool preset picker   *Anti-aliasing* method   *Type **color***

Text orientation   *Font family*   *Font style*   *Font size*   *Alignment*   *Warped text*

2 *The options bar for the **Horizontal Type** tool*

*Opens/closes the **Character/
Paragraph** palette group*

1 *No anti-aliasing*

2 *Crisp anti-aliasing*

3 *Strong anti-aliasing*

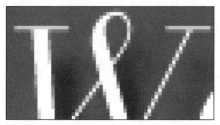

4 *Smooth anti-aliasing*

Align left
　　　Align Right
　　Center

5 *The **Alignment** buttons control where paragraph type is positioned relative to its bounding box (or where point type is positioned relative to the insertion point).*

You can also click the Toggle Palette button 🗐 to open the Character/Paragraph palette group and adjust settings on either palette (you'll learn about them throughout this chapter).

4. Type text in the document window.

5. Press Enter on the keypad or click the ✔ button on the options bar to accept the new text. (To cancel it, press Esc or click the ⊘ button.)

TIP Each time type is created using the Horizontal or Vertical Type tool, a new layer is created **6**. If your type layers start to overpopulate, you can periodically delete any that you don't need and gather the ones you want to keep into layer groups.

TIP See page 73 for an explanation of the missing fonts alert icon. ⚠

TIP You can right-click/Control-click an editable type layer name and choose an anti-aliasing method from the context menu.

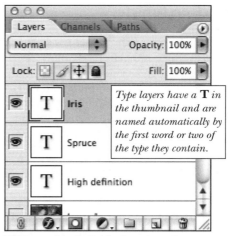

6 *If you place individual words or characters on separate layers, you'll be able to move them around or apply effects to them independently.*

To add type on or inside a path:

1. Create a path, as per the instructions on pages 366–369. The path can be open or closed.

2. Click the path on the Paths palette.

3. Choose the **Horizontal Type** tool T or **Vertical Type** tool T (T or Shift-T).

4. Click the outside or inside of the path, then start typing **1**. You could also copy type from another object and paste it onto or into the path.

   If you placed type on the edge of a path, with the Path Selection tool (A or Shift-A), you can drag it along the path or to the other side of the path.

TIP To shift type upward or downward from the edge of a path, select the type you want to shift (see the instructions below), then drag left or right over the baseline shift icon 🄰 on the Character palette.

TIP If you want to draw standard paragraph or point text, and the pointer is near a path, you can disable the path type feature by Shift-clicking.

Selecting type

If you want to edit a whole type layer, simply double-click the layer thumbnail; if you want to correct typing mistakes or change the type attributes of a partial layer, you need to select the characters you want to edit. Once **type** is **selected,** you can edit the characters as you would in a word processing program, or change attributes via the options bar, Character palette, or Paragraph palette.

To select type for editing or style changes:

1. To highlight type **characters** for editing, click a type layer, choose the **Horizontal Type** tool T or **Vertical Type** tool T (T or Shift-T), click in the type to create an insertion point, then drag across one or more characters or words to select them **2**.

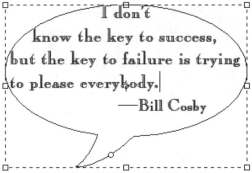

1 *This type was entered **inside** a **path** using the Horizontal Type tool.*

You can select whole paragraphs or just a handful of characters, depending on what you want to edit.

2 *Drag across the characters you want to **select**.*

Selecting type with a type tool

Select consecutive characters or words	Drag across them. Or click at the beginning of a text string, then Shift-click at the end.
Select **word**	Double-click
Select **line**	Triple-click
Select **paragraph**	Quadruple-click
Select **all**	Double-click the thumbnail on the Layers palette; or click in the text, then press Ctrl-A/Cmd-A

(sidebar) Type on or in a Path; Select Type

Smart type **NEW**

If you create type in Adobe Illustrator CS or CS2 and then import it into Photoshop by using either of the two methods outlined below, it becomes a **smart object layer** in Photoshop. Its contents can be edited at any time.

AI format

In Illustrator, make sure the type is on its own layer, then save the file in the **Illustrator Document (.ai)** format. Open a file in Photoshop, then use File > **Place** in Photoshop or Bridge to import the type file. A new smart object layer will appear on the Layers palette. If you double-click the smart object layer thumbnail, the file will reopen in Illustrator. If you edit it and then save and close the document, the type will update in the Photoshop document.

PSD format

To create a smart object layer that can be edited as a separate Photoshop file, in Illustrator, choose File > **Export,** choose Format: **Photoshop (.psd),** click Write Layers, check Preserve Text Editability, Maximum Editability, and Anti-alias, then click OK. Open a Photoshop file, then use File > **Place** in Photoshop or Bridge to place the type file. If you double-click the new smart object layer thumbnail, a separate Photoshop file will appear onscreen, with the editable type in a layer group. If you edit the file and then save and close it, the type will update in the original Photoshop document.

(To learn more about smart object layers, see pages 313–314.)

Or double-click a word to select the whole word; or double-click a word, then drag to select multiple words; or drag downward to select multiple lines (see also the sidebar on the previous page).
or
To select **all** the type on the layer, with any tool selected, double-click the T icon on the Layers palette. All the text on that layer will become selected, and the appropriate type tool will become selected automatically.

2. After performing your text edits, to take the text tool out of edit mode and commit to the editing changes, click the ✔ on the options bar, or press Enter on the keypad, or click any other tool, or click a different layer.

   (To cancel your editing changes before committing to them, click the ◎ on the options bar or press Esc.)

TIP If you want to see the bounding box for a block of text, choose the Move tool (V), click the type layer on the Layers palette, and check Show Transform Controls on **NEW** the options bar. To move a type layer, follow the instructions on page 113.

Converting type

To convert paragraph type to point type:

On the Layers palette, right-click/Control- **NEW** click a type layer name and choose **Convert To Point Text.** A return will be added to the end of every line of type except the last. *Note:* If the type object contains hidden (overflow) text, an alert dialog box will warn you that the hidden text will be deleted.

TIP We don't know of a command in Photoshop that reveals hidden characters (paragraph returns and the like).

To convert point type to paragraph type:

On the Layers palette, right-click/Control- **NEW** click a type layer name and choose **Convert To Paragraph Text.** To reshape the resulting bounding box, see page 404. Be sure to delete any unwanted hyphens that may have been added.

Convert Point/Paragraph Type

Styling type

To scale characters uniformly by number, change the **point size** on the options bar or the Character palette.

To scale type by choosing a value:

1. On the Layers palette, double-click a T icon, then select the characters or words you want to scale.
   or
   To scale all the characters in a layer, click the layer, but don't select anything.

2. Choose the **Horizontal Type** or **Vertical Type** tool; then, on the options bar, drag left or right over the **font size** icon ⁀T (Alt-drag/Option-drag for finer increments) **1**, or enter a value, or choose from the pop-up menu **2**. You can also change point sizes via the Character palette **3**.

Type can also be **scaled interactively.**

To scale type interactively:

1. On the Layers palette, click a type layer.

2. Choose the **Move** tool (V) and check **NEW** **Show Transform Controls** on the options bar.

3. Do any of the following:

   To scale just the **height** or **width,** click a corner handle, then drag it.

   To scale **both** the height and width, click and drag a side handle.

   To preserve the **proportions** of the type as you scale it, Shift-drag a corner handle **4**.

4. To commit to the scale change, click the ✔ on the options bar or double-click the text block. (To cancel the scale change before committing to it, click the ⊘ on the options bar or press Esc.)

TIP To change the Vertical Scale or Horizontal Scale via the Character palette, see the sidebar on page 397.

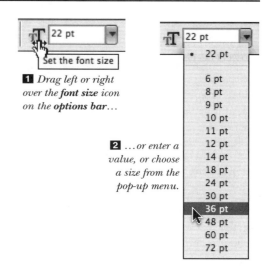

1 *Drag left or right over the font size icon on the options bar…*

2 *…or enter a value, or choose a size from the pop-up menu.*

3 *You can also change point sizes via the font size icon, field, or pop-up menu on the Character palette.*

Type can be resized interactively. That way, you can see how it's going to look immediately on your screen.

4 *Shift-drag a corner handle to resize type interactively while preserving its proportions.*

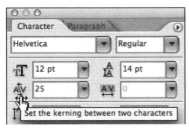

1 *The kerning icon, field, and pop-up menu on the Character palette*

Kern
Kern

2 *Use a negative **kerning** value (–100, in this case) to tighten the spacing **between** characters.*

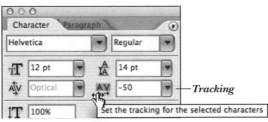

3 *The **Character** palette has some features that aren't found on the options bar.*

TRACKING TIPS

Tracking can help or hinder readability, depending on how high the tracking values are. Try not to overdo it!

4 *Occasionally we'll spread out **little bits** of text, as in the headline in this illustration—but never whole paragraphs.*

Kerning affects the spacing between pairs of text characters.

To apply kerning:
Method 1
1. On the Layers palette, double-click a T icon.

2. Click to create an insertion point between any two characters.

3. Display the Character palette (see the sidebar).

4. Choose Metrics from the **Kerning** pop-up menu on the Character palette to apply the font's built-in kerning, or choose Optical to have Photoshop control the kerning.
   or
   Drag left or right over the **kerning** icon ＡＶ **1**, or enter a value (–1000 to 1000), or choose a value from the pop-up menu. A negative value moves characters closer together **2**, a positive value spreads them apart. (For kerning and tracking shortcuts, see page 560.)

Method 2
With a type tool chosen and the cursor inserted between two characters, press Alt/Option and the left or right arrow key.

Tracking is like kerning, only it affects multiple characters instead of just pairs.

To apply tracking:
1. On the Layers palette, double-click a T icon, then select the characters or words you want to apply tracking to.
   or
   To apply tracking to a whole layer, click the layer, but don't select anything.

2. On the Character palette, drag left or right over the **tracking** icon ＡＶ **3**; or enter a value in the field (–1000 to 1000); or choose a value from the pop-up menu. A negative value moves characters closer together, a positive value spreads them apart **4**.
   or
   If type is selected, you can press Alt/Option and the left or right arrow key.

Leading is the space that separates one line of text from the next. Each character can have its own leading value; the highest value in a line controls that line. Consequently, if you apply different leading values to different lines of paragraph text and then edit the text so as to cause it to reflow, the spacing between lines may change as a result.

Note: If you need to create large blocks of text, we recommend creating the visuals in Photoshop and the text in a layout or Web page creation program.

To adjust leading in horizontal type:

1. On the Layers palette, double-click a T icon.

2. *Optional:* For point type (not paragraph type), you can highlight a line or lines of text, or even individual characters; or to change the leading for all the type on the layer, don't highlight anything.

   Note: Leading doesn't affect the first line in a paragraph. To change the space before a paragraph, see page 401.

3. Drag left or right over the **leading** icon **1**–**2** (Alt-drag/Option-drag for finer increments), or enter a value in the field (.01 to 5000 pt.), or choose a value from the pop-up menu.

TIP Auto leading is calculated as a percentage of the font size. The ratio is set in the Justification dialog box, which is opened from the Paragraph palette menu. The default value is 120% of the font size. The Auto leading amount for 30-point type, for example, would be 36 points.

TIP To adjust the vertical spacing between characters in vertical type, highlight the characters you want to adjust, then change the Tracking value on the Character palette.

1 *The **leading** area on the **Character** palette*

Never worry about numbers. Help one person at a time, and always start with the person nearest you.

Mother Teresa

~

Never worry about numbers.

Help one person at a time,

and always start with the

person nearest you.

Mother Teresa

~

2 *Same size type, with different **leading**: 13-point leading on top, 19-point leading on the bottom*

Create a preset!

After styling your type, click the type layer, then click the Tool Preset picker thumbnail or arrowhead T ▾ on the left side of the options bar. Click the **New Tool Preset** button, ⬛ then click OK. You can now choose this tool preset from either the **Tool Preset picker** or the **Tool Presets palette** any time you create type. It's sort of like having a style sheet, because all your carefully chosen attributes are saved in the preset—except in this case you pick the preset before creating the type. You can create different presets for print and Web graphics.

Stretchhhh!

Use the **Horizontal Scale** or **Vertical Scale** option to make characters wider or narrower ▮. Double-click the layer, then select the characters you want to scale; or to scale all the characters in the layer, click the layer but don't select anything. Next, drag over the vertical scale ⟨T or horizontal scale ⟨T⟩ icon on the Character palette to the left or right (0–1000%). Personally, we'd rather use an extended or condensed font (it looks better).

stretch *Horizontal scale 50%*

stretch *Horizontal scale 100% (normal)*

stretch *Horizontal scale 200%*

stretch *Vertical scale 300%*

1 *Type can be **scaled** horizontally, vertically, or uniformly (both).*

You can change the **orientation** of existing horizontal type to vertical, or vice versa.

To change type orientation:

On the Layers palette, right-click/Control-click a type layer name and choose **Horizontal** or **Vertical** (the opposite of the current orientation). **〈NEW〉**

or

Choose the **Horizontal Type** or **Vertical Type** tool. On the Layers palette, click a type layer **2**; then, on the options bar, click the **Change Text Orientation** button ▥ **3**.

You may need to reposition, or change the tracking value for, the type after changing its orientation.

TIP To rotate vertical type a different way, double-click its layer thumbnail (and highlight the characters you want to rotate, if you don't want to rotate them all), then choose Standard Roman Vertical Alignment from the Character palette menu to uncheck the command **4**. This command isn't available for horizontal type.

Change Type Orientation

2 *The original **vertical** type*

3 *The same type after clicking the **Change Text Orientation** button on the options bar*

4 *The original vertical type after unchecking **Standard Roman Vertical Alignment** on the Character palette menu*

To apply Character palette menu commands:

1. To modify a whole type layer, click the layer; or double-click a T icon, then select the type to be modified.

2. Click any **style** button on the Character palette **1** (use tool tips to identify them), or choose any of these styles from the Character palette menu **2**:

If the chosen font isn't available, **Faux Bold** simulates the bold style, and **Faux Italic** simulates the italic style. Faux Bold isn't available for warped text.

All Caps converts all letters to uppercase.

Small Caps converts lowercase characters to small caps.

Superscript shrinks type and raises it above the baseline; **Subscript** shrinks type and lowers it below the baseline.

Underline produces underlines in horizontal and vertical type.

Strikethrough produces a horizontal line through horizontal type or a vertical line through vertical type.

Fractional Widths allows Photoshop to use fractions of pixels for type spacing for optimal appearance (it applies to the entire layer). Uncheck this option only for small type to be output online.

System Layout allows you to preview text as it would appear in the current operating system. Use this for designing interfaces, such as dialog boxes or menus.

No Break forces the currently selected words to stay on the same line (e.g., to keep the words "Mr. Smith" together).

Reset Character resets the selected characters (or all the type on the layer) to the default Character palette settings.

3. For type set in an OpenType or other font that contains the desired characters, choose from the **OpenType** submenu: **NEW**

Standard Ligatures are combinations of the characters fi, fl, ff, ffi, and ffl, which are joined together (they look better!) **3**.

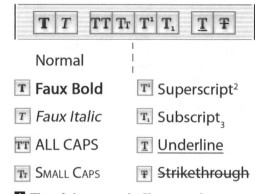

Normal

T **Faux Bold**	**T¹** Superscript²
T *Faux Italic*	**T₁** Subscript₃
TT ALL CAPS	**T** <u>Underline</u>
Tʀ Sᴍᴀʟʟ Cᴀᴘs	**F** ~~Strikethrough~~

1 *The **style** buttons on the Character palette*

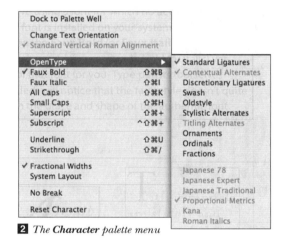

2 *The **Character** palette menu*

1 *A* swash glyph **1**

1 2 3 4 5 6 7 8 9

2 *Old-style numerals (Adobe Garamond Pro font) are beautiful.*

1 2 3 4 5 6 7 8 9

3 *Standard numerals (Adobe Garamond font)*

Titling capitals are stately and sophisticated.

4 *A **titling** capital*

5 *Some **ornaments** in the Minion Pro font*

6 *Baseline shift area, Character palette*

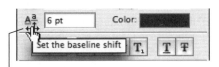

+20 pts

0 pts

Normal baseline

–20 pts

7 *A positive **baseline shift** value raises characters upward; a negative value moves them downward.*

Contextual Alternates are glyphs that provide better character joining for some letter pairs.

Discretionary Ligatures substitutes specialty characters for some letter pairs, such as "ct," "st," and "ft."

Swash 1 substitutes swash glyphs, which are stylized characters with extended strokes.

Oldstyle numerals **2** are shorter than standard numerals **3**. Some old-style numerals descend below the baseline.

Stylistic Alternates substitutes ornate characters for some letters.

Titling Alternates 4 substitutes special capital letters.

Ornaments 5 are decorative symbols (use for borders or paragraph dividers).

Ordinals substitutes specially formatted superscript characters (e.g., 8th, 3rd).

Fractions substitutes preformatted fraction characters. Type in the numerator, a slash, and the denominator, select them all, then choose this command—presto!

TIP The Change Text Orientation and Standard Vertical Roman Alignment commands are discussed on page 397.

Use the **baseline shift** feature to shift a character or two, or to shift type on a path.

To shift characters from the normal baseline:

1. On the Layers palette, double-click a T icon, then select the characters or words you want to shift.

2. On the Character palette, drag left or right over the **baseline shift** icon (Alt-drag/Option-drag for finer increments), or enter a baseline shift value **6**. A positive value raises characters above the normal baseline **7**; a negative value moves them below the baseline.

TIP To shift whole lines of type, use leading —not baseline shift. To shift a whole layer, drag it with the Move tool!

Applying paragraph settings

For paragraph type, Photoshop offers a range of formatting options. You forego the manual control you have with point text, but gain sophisticated layout tools. The Paragraph palette lets you choose settings for justification, alignment, indents, and paragraph spacing, and the palette menu allows you to fine-tune those options.

To set paragraph alignment and justification for horizontal type:

1. On the Layers palette, double-click a T icon, then click in a paragraph or select a series of paragraphs.
   or
   To modify all the type in a layer, click the layer, but don't select anything.

2. If the Paragraph palette isn't open, click the 🗐 button on the options bar, then click the Paragraph tab.

3. Click an alignment and/or justification button at the top of the palette **1**:

   The buttons in the first group—**Left-Align Text, Center Text,** and **Right-Align Text**—align type to an edge or the center of the text bounding box **2**. (These options can also be used on point type.)

   The buttons in the second group—**Justify Last Left, Justify Last Centered,** and **Justify Last Right**—justify the type, forcing all but the last line to fill the space between the margins **3**.

   The last button, **Justify All,** forces all the lines to fill the space, even the last line.

4. Check **Hyphenate** at the bottom of the palette to enable automatic hyphenation. Be sure to check this option for justified text to help minimize gaps between words.

TIP To change the alignment and/or justification for vertical type, the procedure is the same as outlined above, except the buttons have different labels.

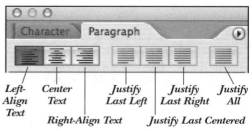

Left-Align Text **Center Text** **Justify Last Left** **Justify Last Right** **Justify All**

Right-Align Text **Justify Last Centered**

1 The **alignment** and **justification** buttons at the top of the **Paragraph** palette, for horizontal type

---

Left Align Text

The reward for conformity was that everyone liked you except yourself.

Center Text

The reward for conformity was that everyone liked you except yourself.

Right Align Text

The reward for conformity was that everyone liked you except yourself.

—*Rita Mae Brown*

2 Paragraph **alignment** options

Justify Last Left

Civilization is the encouragement of differences. Civilization thus becomes a synonym of democracy.

Justify Last Centered

Civilization is the encouragement of differences. Civilization thus becomes a synonym of democracy.

Justify Last Right

Civilization is the encouragement of differences. Civilization thus becomes a synonym of democracy.

Justify All

Civilization is the encouragement of differences. Civilization thus becomes a   synonym   of   democracy.

— *Mohandas Gandhi*

3 Paragraph **justification** options

The paragraph **indent** and **spacing-between-paragraph** controls let you shape your paragraphs for improved readability.

To adjust paragraph indents and spacing for horizontal type:

1. On the Layers palette, double-click a T icon, then click in a paragraph or select a series of paragraphs.
or
To modify all the type in a layer, click the layer, but don't select anything.

2. On the Paragraph palette, change the **Indent Left Margin, Indent Right Margin,** or **Indent First Line** value **1**–**2**. Please don't apply an Indent First Line value above zero and also add space between paragraphs (bad typesetting!).
and/or
Change the **Add Space Before Paragraph 3** or **Add Space After Paragraph** value.

TIP To change the alignment and/or justification for vertical type, the procedure is the same as above, except the fields have different labels.

1

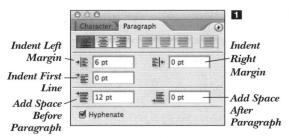

Indent Left Margin → 6 pt
Indent Right Margin ← 0 pt
Indent First Line → 0 pt
Add Space Before Paragraph → 12 pt
Add Space After Paragraph ← 0 pt
☑ Hyphenate

The best way to get most husbands to do something is to suggest that perhaps they're too old to do it.

    The best way to get most husbands to do something is to suggest that perhaps they're too old to do it.

    The best way to get most husbands to do something is to suggest that perhaps they're too old to do it.
— *Shirley MacLaine*

Indents of 0 (zero)

Indent left and right, 2 px

Indent first line, 16 pt

2 *Indent values*

Civilization is the encouragement of differences.

Civilization thus becomes a synonym of democracy.

Force, violence, pressure, or compulsion with a view to conformity, is both uncivilized and undemocratic.
— *Mohandas Gandhi*

3 *Add Space Before Paragraph, 7 pt*

These are some of the **paragraph settings** that can make the difference between okay-looking type and professional-looking type.

To fine-tune paragraph settings:

1. On the Layers palette, double-click a T icon, then click in a paragraph or select a series of paragraphs. Or to modify all the type in a layer, click the layer, but don't select anything.

2. From the **Paragraph** palette menu, choose any of the following:

   Roman Hanging Punctuation to have Photoshop nudge punctuation marks that fall at the beginning and end of lines outside the type bounding box.

   Justification and **Hyphenation** to specify the limits within which the Photoshop algorithms can operate as they adjust text to optimize its appearance **1**–**2**. (In the Justification dialog box, you can also set the Auto Leading value as a percentage of the type size.)

   Adobe Single-line Composer or **Adobe Every-line Composer** for the method Photoshop will use to evaluate potential word breaks (hyphenation) in a paragraph, factoring in letter and word spacing values in an attempt to minimize hyphenation. The Adobe Single-line Composer does this line by line; the Adobe Every-line Composer does it by evaluating the appearance of the paragraph as a whole. Every-line Composer (our preferred method) can change the word breaks at the beginning of a paragraph in order to create more visually appealing word breaks toward the end of the paragraph.

   Reset Paragraph to reset all the selected paragraphs to their factory default settings.

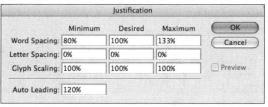

1 *In the **Justification** dialog box, choose Minimum, Desired, and Maximum values for Photoshop to adhere to when adjusting line widths in justified text.*

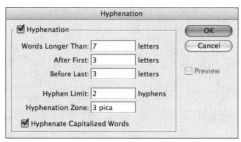

2 *In the **Hyphenation** dialog box, choose settings for word breaks created in paragraph type.*

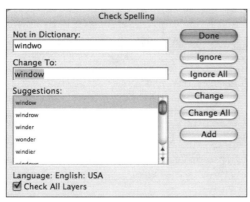

1 *The **Check Spelling** dialog box*

Check spelling in Spanish?

Use the **Language** pop-up menu **2** on the Character palette to choose which dictionary Photoshop will use when checking spelling.

2 *Language options for the dictionary*

Checking spelling

The **Check Spelling** command checks spelling on a single type layer or in an entire document, using a built-in dictionary to which you can add entries. As far as we know, you can't edit the dictionary, though.

To check spelling:

1. Choose Edit > **Check Spelling.**
   or
   Choose the **Horizontal Type** or **Vertical Type** tool (T or Shift-T), then right-click/Control-click in the document window and choose **Check Spelling.** (You don't have to select a type layer.)

   The first word the dictionary doesn't recognize will appear in the **Not in Dictionary** field **1**. The dictionary's best guess for a replacement word will appear in the **Change To** field, and other possible replacements will be listed in the **Suggestions** window.

2. *Optional:* Check **Check All Layers** to have Photoshop search through every type layer in the document, not just the current layer.

3. For each word that appears, do one of the following:

   If the Change To word is incorrect but the correct word appears on the **Suggestions** list, click the correct word to make it appear in the **Change To** field. If the correct word doesn't appear on the Suggestions list, type it in the Change To field yourself. Next, click **Change** to change only the current instance of the word, or click **Change All** to change all instances of the word.

   Click **Ignore** to skip over only this instance of the word, or click Ignore All to skip over all instances of the word.

   Click **Add** to add the unrecognized word, as is, to the dictionary and leave it unchanged in the image.

4. Click Done at any time to end the spelling check; or if a summary of the spelling check appears onscreen, click OK.

Transforming the bounding box

Follow these instructions to **scale, rotate,** or **move** the **bounding box** that holds paragraph type without distorting the characters. The characters will reflow to fit the new shape.

To transform a type bounding box:

1. On the Layers palette, double-click the type layer thumbnail for paragraph type.

2. Position the cursor over a handle, pause, then drag to scale the bounding box **1**. (Shift-drag to preserve the proportions of the box.) The type will reflow **2**.
   or
   Position the cursor outside one of the corners of the box (curved, double-arrow pointer), then drag to rotate the box.
   or
   Ctrl-drag/Cmd-drag in the box to move the whole type block (this is a temporary Move tool).

3. To accept the transformation, press Enter on the keypad or click the ✔ on the options bar. (To cancel it, press Esc or click the ⃠ on the options bar.)

TIP **NEW** To align multiple type layers, select them, then choose from the Layer > Align submenu. With three or more layers active, you can also choose from the Layer > Distribute submenu. See page 308.

> ### Transforming type
>
> The **transform commands,** discussed on pages 309–311, reshape both type and its bounding box and affect the whole type layer. You can move, scale, rotate, and skew editable and rasterized type, and also apply distortion and perspective to rasterized type. If you want to transform individual characters, put them on separate layers.
>
> You can also use the **Move tool** (with **Show Transform Controls** checked on the options bar) to transform point type.

An immense stretch of flat country, a bird's eye view of it seen from the top of a hill — vineyards

1 *Drag a handle to* **scale** *the* **bounding box.**

An immense stretch of flat country, a bird's eye view of it seen from the top of a hill — vineyards and fields of newly reaped wheat. All this multiplied in endless repetitions.
— Vincent Van Gogh

2 *The type* **reflows** *into the new shape.*

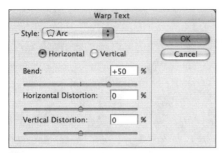

1 *The **Warp Text** dialog box*

2 *Arc*

3 *Bulge*

4 *Flag* **5** *Rise*

Warping type

The **Warp Text** command, with its various style choices (arc, flag, arch, shell, wave, fish, etc.), transforms the bounding box that holds the type and distorts the type accordingly. Warped type remains fully editable.

To warp editable type:

1. On the Layers palette, double-click a T icon, then click the **Warp Text** button ⌁ on the options bar.
   or
   Right-click/Control-click an editable type layer name and choose **Warp Text.** NEW
   The Warp Text dialog box opens **1**.

2. Choose a transform option from the **Style** pop-up menu.

3. Click **Horizontal** or **Vertical** as the overall orientation for the distortion.

4. Watch the warp preview in the document window as you move the **Bend, Horizontal Distortion,** and **Vertical Distortion** sliders.

5. Click OK **2**–**5**. The warp text icon will appear in the layer thumbnail.⌁ You can reopen the Warp Text dialog box at any time (repeat step 1 above) and choose a different style or adjust the sliders, or undo the warp by choosing Style: None.

TIP To scale or reshape warped type to make it fit into a specific area of a composition, click the warped type layer, choose the Move tool (V), check Show Transform Controls on the options bar, then reshape the bounding box. To learn about the Free Transform/Warp Mode button on the options bar, see pages 311–313.

Filling type with imagery

To fill type with imagery:

Do any of the following:

➤ Use an editable type layer as the base layer in a **clipping mask** to clip the image layers above it **1**. You can edit, apply filters to, or reposition the image layers without affecting the type. (See also page 305.)

➤ Use a type selection in a **layer mask 2**. Stack a group of image layers directly over a type layer, Ctrl-click/Cmd-click the type layer thumbnail to create a type selection, then hide the type layer. Position the selection where desired, click the group on the Layers palette, then click the Add Layer Mask button. The type shape(s) will mask the imagery. (See also page 301.)

➤ Convert an editable type layer into a **vector mask,** see page 379.

➤ Use the Rectangular Marquee tool to select part of an image for a pattern tile, choose Edit > **Define Pattern,** then apply the **Pattern Overlay** effect to an editable type layer using your new pattern. You can scale or reposition the pattern within the type area. (See also page 327.)

Rasterizing type

Before you can rework type shapes using a filter, a tool (such as Brush, Eraser, or Smudge), or the Transform > Distort or Perspective command, you must **rasterize** it (convert it into pixels). Once type is rasterized, however, you can't change its typographic attributes.

To rasterize type into pixels:

1. *Optional:* If you want to preserve the editable type layer, duplicate it and keep the duplicate selected.

2. Right-click/Control-click an editable
NEW type layer name and choose **Rasterize Type.** The layer thumbnail will update.

The ways in which rasterized type can be dressed up are limitless! **3**–**4**

1 *The type is the base layer in a* **clipping mask.** *The other layers in the mask contain image layers (altered using filters).*

2 *A type selection, converted into a* **layer mask,** *is masking a group of image layers.*

3 *This type was* **rasterized,** *filled with a* **pattern,** *and distorted using* **filters.**

4 *After applying the Drop Shadow, Inner Glow, and Bevel and Emboss layer effects to a type layer, it was* **rasterized** *and the* **Smudge** *tool was used to rough up the edges of the shapes.*

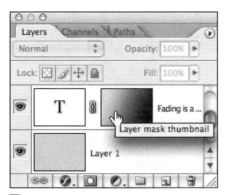

1 *Layer mask* thumbnail

2 *Fading* type

Don't forget layer effects!

Layer effects 3 can be applied to both editable and rasterized type layers. To apply effects, double-click the layer. Browse through Chapter 21—it contains numerous examples of effects applied to type.

3 *Layer effects* applied to *type*

Fading type

In these instructions, you'll create an illusion of type fading away by applying a **gradient** to a **layer mask.**

To create fading type:

1. Click an editable or rasterized type layer.

2. Click the **Add Layer Mask** button ▣ at the bottom of the Layers palette. A layer mask thumbnail will appear next to the layer name.

3. Choose the **Gradient** tool (G or Shift-G). ▬

4. On the options bar:

    Click the **Gradient Preset** picker arrowhead, then click the Foreground to Background swatch in the picker.

    Click the **Linear** gradient button.

    Choose **Mode: Normal.**

    Choose an **Opacity** of 100%.

5. In the document window, drag from top to bottom or from left to right, at least halfway across the type. The type layer mask will fill with a white-to-black gradient **1**. Type will be hidden where black is present in the layer mask **2**.

TIP Click the type layer thumbnail or next to the layer name to modify the type or the layer; click the layer mask thumbnail to modify the layer mask. Read more about layer masks in Chapter 20.

Fading Type

Screening back imagery and type

Printing dark **text** on top of a **picture** can be tricky. The picture has to be light enough to allow the text to be readable, yet visible enough to be interpreted as an image.

To screen back an image behind type:

1. In a document that contains both a type layer and an image layer, click the image layer.

2. From the New Fill/Adjustment Layer pop-up menu ⬤, at the bottom of the Layers palette, choose **Levels.**

3. Check Preview.

4. Move the gray Input slider to the left and the black Output slider to the right.

5. Click OK .

   To produce **2**, we went a step further. To mask the Levels effect in the upper right corner in order to restore contrast to the image in that area, we clicked the adjustment layer mask thumbnail, then filled the adjustment layer with a black-to-white gradient by dragging the Gradient tool from the middle of the document window to the upper right corner.

TIP To have the adjustment layer affect only the layer immediately below it, Alt-click/ Option-click the line between the two layers on the Layers palette. This creates a clipping mask.

1 *The background image was lightened via the* **Levels** *command on an adjustment layer.*

2 *The impact of the Levels command was then lessened on the right side by applying a* **gradient** *to the* **adjustment layer mask.**

1 *The original image*

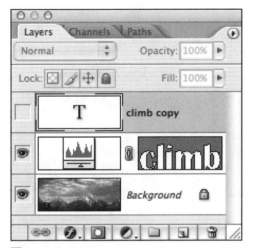

2 *A Levels **adjustment layer** with a **vector mask***

3 *Screened-back type*

4 *A screened-back image with **darkened type***

In these instructions, instead of screening back the image, as in the instructions on the previous page, you'll be **screening** back the **type,** thus allowing the image to be visible inside it.

To screen back type:

1. Create a type layer above an image layer **1**.

2. Duplicate the type layer by dragging it over the **New Layer** button **⬛** at the bottom of the Layers palette. Hide the original type layer by clicking its eye icon (keep it for future type edits).

3. With the duplicate layer chosen, choose Layer > Type > **Convert to Shape.** The type layer will be converted into a shape layer with a vector mask. The original type shapes will be preserved, but their typographic attributes will no longer be editable.

4. Choose Layer > **Change Layer Content** > **Levels** **2**. The clipping effect won't be visible until you perform the next step.

5. Move the gray **Input** (midtones) slider to the left to lighten the midtones in the type. You can also move the Input highlights slider.
   and
   Move the **Output** shadows slider to the right to reduce the contrast in the type.

6. Click OK. Click the image layer **3**.

TIP Change the blending mode for the adjustment layer to restore some of the color to the background (try Overlay, Color Burn, or Hard Light mode). Lower the layer's opacity to lessen the Levels effect. You can also apply layer effects to the adjustment layer.

TIP To produce the effect shown in **4**, follow steps 1–4 above. In step 5, adjust the sliders to darken the type, remove any opacity or blending mode changes, then follow the instructions on the previous page to lighten the imagery below the type layer.

Screen Back Type

Using type selections

Instead of using the Type Mask tools to create a **selection** in the shape of **type** characters, we prefer the following method.

To create a type mask in an adjustment layer:

1. Create editable type. On the Layers palette, Ctrl-click/Cmd-click the T icon.

2. Hide the type layer.

3. Click the layer you want the new adjustment layer to affect (use a selection tool to reposition the selection, if you wish). From the New Fill/Adjustment Layer pop-up menu, ⊘. choose an adjustment command **1**, choose options, then click OK. The change will affect only pixels below the type shapes in the mask **2**.

TIP To swap the black and white areas in the mask, click the adjustment layer mask thumbnail, then choose Image > Adjustments > Invert (Ctrl-I/Cmd-I).

TIP Use the Move tool to reposition a mask on a selected adjustment layer.

To create type in a spot channel:

1. Create editable type. Ctrl-click/Cmd-click the T icon to select the type shapes.

2. Hide the type layer (click the eye icon).

3. Follow the instructions on page 478 to create a new spot channel.

4. On the Channels palette, click the new spot color channel.

5. Choose Edit > **Fill,** choose Use: Black, Normal mode, choose an Opacity value that matches the tint (density) value of the spot color ink to be used on press, then click OK. The selection will fill with the spot channel color.

6. Deselect (Ctrl-D/Cmd-D) **3**.

TIP Use the Move tool to reposition the type shapes in the spot color channel.

TIP You can't edit type in a spot channel—you have to redo it. Fill the channel with White, 100% Opacity, edit the original type layer, then redo the steps above.

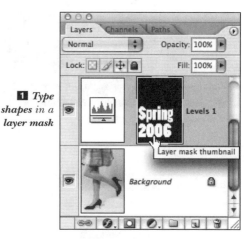

1 *Type shapes in a layer mask*

2 *Only pixels below the character shapes are affected by the adjustment layer.*

3 *Type shapes in a spot channel*

GRADIENTS 26

How to apply a gradient

➤ By dragging the **Gradient tool** on an image layer, layer mask, fill layer, or adjustment layer

➤ Via an editable **Gradient Fill layer**

➤ Via an editable **Gradient Overlay effect**

➤ Via an editable **Gradient Map adjustment layer**

➤ Via Edit > **Fill**

1 *In the* **Gradient Fill** *dialog box, click the gradient arrowhead, then choose from the* **Gradient Preset** *picker…*

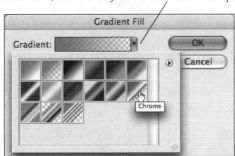

2 *…and also choose a gradient* **Style, Angle,** *and a* **Scale** *percentage.*

A **GRADIENT IS A GRADUAL BLEND** between two or more colors, and in Photoshop, there are many ways to apply and use them.

Creating a gradient fill layer

A gradient applied via a **gradient fill layer** appears in its own layer, complete with a layer mask that can be used to mask the gradient layer pixels. This type of gradient is easier to edit than a gradient applied directly to a layer.

To apply a gradient as a fill layer:

1. Click a layer.

2. *Optional:* Select an area of a layer (see the sidebar on the next page). If you don't create a selection, the gradient will fill the entire layer.

3. Choose **Gradient** from the New Fill/ Adjustment Layer pop-up menu ⬤. at the bottom of the Layers palette. The Gradient Fill dialog box opens **1**.

4. Click the gradient arrowhead at the top of the dialog box, click a gradient preset on the picker, then click back in the dialog box. (To access other gradients, choose a library from the bottom of the picker menu; see page 465.)

5. Do all of the following:

   Choose a gradient **Style: Linear, Radial, Angular, Reflected,** or **Diamond** **2**–**3**.

   Choose an **Angle** by moving the dial or entering a value.

   (Continued on the following page)

Gradient Fill Layer

Linear *gradient*   **Radial** *gradient*   **Reflected** *gradient*   **Angle** *gradient*   **Diamond** *gradient*

3 *The five basic gradient* **styles**

Use the **Scale** slider or enter a value to scale the gradient relative to the layer. The higher the scale value, the more gradual the transition between gradient colors.

6. *Optional:* Drag in the document window (with the dialog box still open) to reposition the gradient. Cool!

7. Do any of the following optional steps:

    Check/uncheck **Reverse** to reverse the order of colors in the gradient.

    Check **Dither** to minimize banding (stripes) in the gradient on output.

    Check **Align with layer** to have the length of the gradient fill be calculated based on the location of either visible pixels or a current selection on the layer. With this option off, the gradient will stretch across the whole layer, even if the layer contains transparent pixels or a selection is present.

8. Click OK **1**–**3**.

9. Do any of the following optional steps:

    Click the gradient fill layer, then change its **opacity** or **blending mode.** You can get some beautiful effects this way.

    Double-click to the right of the gradient fill layer name (not either of the thumbnails) to open the **Layer Style** dialog box, and apply a layer style. A style that spreads outward from the edge of a layer will be visible only if the gradient doesn't cover the entire layer.

    Double-click the gradient fill layer thumbnail. The **Gradient Fill** dialog box reopens. Adjust any of the settings. This is what we meant when we said that this type of gradient is easy to edit.

TIP To hide a gradient fill layer, click the eye icon for the layer. To delete a gradient fill layer, drag the layer thumbnail or the layer name (not the layer mask thumbnail) over the Delete Layer button. 🗑 Easy come, easy go.

Mask a gradient fill

If you create a **selection** before creating a gradient fill layer, the gradient will be limited to the selection area. The former selection will be displayed as a white area within the gradient fill layer mask thumbnail on the Layers palette.

To reshape a gradient fill mask any time after creating the fill layer, click the **layer mask** thumbnail, then paint with white to enlarge the white area, black to enlarge the black area, or lower the opacity of the tool to create a partial mask. You could also drag with the **Gradient tool** to apply a black-to-white gradient to the layer mask.

1 *The original image*

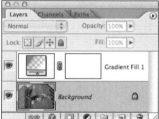

2 *The **radial** gradient on the **Gradient Fill** layer contains a white ending color stop and transparency at the center.*

3 *The final image*

Using the Gradient tool

Use the **Gradient tool** if you want to apply a gradient by dragging. Each time you drag with this tool, an additional gradient is applied. Any additional gradient that you create at less than 100% opacity will only partially cover over the existing one(s). Unlike a gradient fill layer, once this type of gradient is applied, it can't be edited (only undone).

To apply a gradient using the Gradient tool:

1. Click a layer or create a new layer.

2. If the layer already contains pixels, turn on Lock Transparent Pixels if you want to recolor only existing pixels, or turn this option off to have the gradient fill the entire layer. You could also select an area on the layer.

3. Choose the **Gradient** tool (it's on the Paint Bucket tool pop-out menu) (G or Shift-G).

4. On the options bar **1**:

   Click the **Gradient Preset** picker arrowhead, then click a preset on the picker.

   Click a gradient **style** button: **Linear, Radial, Angle, Reflected,** or **Diamond.**

Choose a blending **Mode.**

Choose an **Opacity.**

5. *Do any of these optional steps:*

   Check **Reverse** to reverse the order of colors in the gradient.

   Check **Dither** to minimize banding (stripes) in the gradient on output.

   Check **Transparency** to enable any transparency that was edited into the gradient (see page 413). With Transparency off, the gradient will be fully opaque.

6. For a Linear gradient, drag from one **side** or **corner** of the image (or selection) to the other. For any other gradient style, drag from a **center point** outward. Shift-drag to constrain the gradient to a multiple of 45°. Drag a long distance to produce a subtle transition area, or drag a short distance to produce an abrupt transition **2**–**4**. This works like the Scale slider in the Gradient Fill dialog box.

   To delete a Gradient tool fill, remove its state from the History palette.

TIP To apply a gradient to a layer mask to fade the layer imagery, click the mask thumbnail, then drag across the Gradient tool in the document window.

1 *The options bar for the **Gradient** tool*

2 *After dragging the Gradient tool from one edge to the other to apply a linear gradient*

3 *After dragging the Gradient tool a **short** distance in the middle to create more abrupt color transitions between the same colors.*

4 *The **Gradient** tool was used in two different directions to fill a rasterized type layer (with Lock Transparent Pixels on).*

Gradient Tool

413

Creating gradient presets

When you edit or delete a **preset** swatch, the actual gradient in the current gradient library doesn't change; you'll automatically be editing or deleting a **copy** of the preset.

To create or edit a gradient preset:

1. *Optional:* Open the Swatches or Color palette if you're going to use it to choose colors for the gradient, and move it to the corner of your screen. Weirdly enough, you won't be able to move them around once the Gradient Editor is open.

2. Choose the **Gradient** tool (G or Shift-G),  then click the Gradient thumbnail **1** on the options bar to open the Gradient Editor.
or
Double-click an existing **Gradient Fill layer thumbnail** on the Layers palette, then click the gradient thumbnail at the top of the Gradient Fill dialog box.

3. In the Gradient Editor **2**, click the **preset** swatch that you want to create a variation of. (As you start to edit the gradient, the Name will change to "Custom" automatically to ensure that you'll be working on a copy instead of the original.)

1 *Click the* **Gradient thumbnail** *on the options bar to open the* **Gradient Editor.**

or

To create a gradient that uses the current Foreground and Background colors at the time the gradient is applied, click the **Foreground to Background** preset. (If you opened the Gradient Editor from the options bar, a color stop that uses the Foreground color will have this checkerboard pattern: , and a stop that uses the Background color looks like this: .)

4. For any gradient except Foreground to Background, click the starting (left) or ending (right) color **stop** under the gradient bar, then:

Click a color on the **Swatches** palette that you conveniently stuck in a corner, or on the spectrum bar at the bottom of the Color palette, or in any open document window.
or

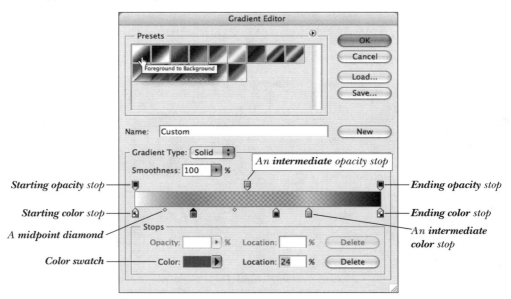

2 *Use the* **Gradient Editor** *to create or edit a gradient preset.*

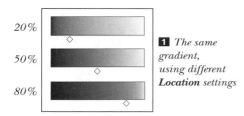

20%

50%

80%

1 *The same gradient, using different Location settings*

Make noise!

For a more serendipitous approach, in the Gradient Editor, choose Gradient Type: **Noise** **2**. Next, raise the **Roughness** to add colors to the gradient with abrupt transitions, or lower the Roughness to reduce colors in the gradient and produce smoother transitions. To define a color range for the gradient, choose a **Color Model,** then move the sliders. For Options, you can click **Restrict Colors** to remove oversaturated colors from the gradient, and click **Add Transparency** to have transparent areas added to the gradient. The gradient will be composed of randomly chosen colors within the parameters you've specified. You can click, and keep clicking, **Randomize** to cycle through some further options within those parameters. Fun!

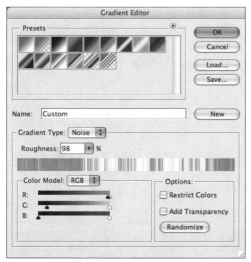

2 *The Gradient Editor with **Noise** chosen as the Gradient Type*

Click the **Color** swatch at the bottom of the **Gradient Editor,** choose a color from the Color Picker, then click OK.

5. To change the opacity of any opacity stop, click the stop above the bar, then change the **Opacity** percentage.

6. *Do any of these optional steps:*

To **add** an intermediate **color** to the gradient, click below the gradient bar to produce a new stop, then choose a color for the new stop, as per step 4 on the previous page.

To **add** an **opacity** stop, click above the gradient bar, then choose or enter an Opacity percentage.

Move any color or opacity stop by dragging it or by changing its Location percentage (you can drag to the left or right over the word "Location").

To control the **abruptness** of a color transition, click a color or opacity stop, then drag a midpoint diamond on either side of it; or click the diamond, then change the Location percentage. The diamond marks the point where the two colors it's situated between are evenly blended (50% of each color) **1**. 0% is for the far left, 100% is for the far right.

To **delete** a color or opacity stop, drag it downward off the bar.

Use Ctrl-Z/Cmd-Z to undo the previous operation (if it's undoable).

7. Don't click OK yet! To create a preset from your custom gradient, enter a name in the Name field, then click New.

8. Now you can click OK. The new gradient preset is now available for use on the Gradient Preset picker.

Note: To save the current gradient presets to a file, see page 463–464. To load alternate gradient preset libraries or restore the default library, see page 465.

TIP To rename a gradient preset, double-click the swatch in the Gradient Editor (the Gradient Name dialog box opens), change the Name, then click OK.

Create or Edit Gradient Preset

Layering gradients

These steps describe how to use multiple gradient fill layers to apply a **multicolor wash.**

To layer multiple gradients:

1. Click a layer.

2. *Optional:* Select an area of the layer .

3. Choose **Gradient** from the New Fill/ Adjustment Layer pop-up menu 🖋▾ at the bottom of the Layers palette.

4. In the **Gradient Fill** dialog box, click the gradient thumbnail to open the Gradient Editor.

5. In the Gradient Editor, either choose an existing gradient preset that fades to (finishes with) transparency or create a new gradient that fades to transparency (0% Opacity), then click OK.

6. In the Gradient Fill dialog box, choose a Style, Angle, and Scale for the gradient fill layer, then click OK.

7. Create another gradient fill layer, then repeat steps 4–6. Try out different Style, Angle, and Scale settings, or drag with the Gradient tool in the document window 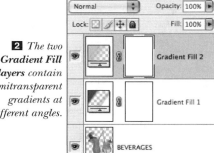.

8. *Optional:* Using the Layers palette, change the opacity or blending mode for, or restack, the gradient fill layers.

1 *The original image*

2 *The two Gradient Fill layers contain semitransparent gradients at different angles.*

3 *The final image*

Layer Multiple Gradients

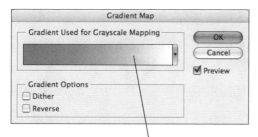

1 *Click the gradient **thumbnail** in the **Gradient Map** dialog box.*

Creating a gradient map layer

The **Gradient Map** command applies (maps) a gradient based on luminosity levels (lights and darks) in the layer below it. You can use this command to colorize a grayscale image or to re-render a color image in new tonalities, with the result being anything from subtle to Day-Glo. If you apply the gradient map via an adjustment layer, it will be fully re-editable.

The starting (left) color of the selected gradient is applied to the shadow areas of the layer. The ending (right) color of the gradient is applied to the highlight areas of the layer. Any color stops that are added to the gradient are applied to the midtone areas of the layer. The number of color transitions in the resulting layer will be based on the number of color stops in the selected gradient.

To create a gradient map layer:

1. Click a layer.

2. Choose **Gradient Map** (not Gradient) from the New Fill/Adjustment Layer pop-up menu ⬤. at the bottom of the Layers palette.

    Note: You can also apply a gradient map directly to a layer via Image > Adjustments > Gradient Map, but a gradient map applied in this way can't be edited or removed the way an adjustment layer can, and so is less flexible.

3. Click the arrowhead to open the **Gradient Preset** picker, then click a preset.

4. Click the gradient thumbnail **1** to open the **Gradient Editor.**

5. *Do any of the following optional steps:*

    Change the starting and/or ending stop **colors**.

    Add more color stops to the middle of the gradient ramp to add colors to the midtone areas of the image. As an example, if a gradient contains four color stops, the layer will contain four major color transition areas.

    (Continued on the following page)

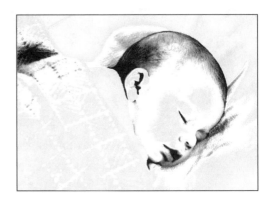

Move any of the color stops to change the distribution of colors within the layer's tonal range.

6. Click OK.

7. *Optional:* Check **Dither** to have random noise be added to color transitions in the layer to help prevent color banding on print output.

8. *Optional:* Check **Reverse** to reverse the direction of the gradient colors.

9. Click OK **1**. To reedit a gradient map at any time, double-click the gradient map layer thumbnail on the Layers palette (the thumbnail on the left).

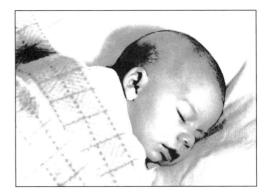

TIP To create a silkscreen effect by heightening contrast between colors applied via a gradient map adjustment layer, create a Posterize adjustment layer, enter 4, 5, or 6 for the number of Levels, then restack the posterize adjustment layer between the image layer and the gradient map layer.

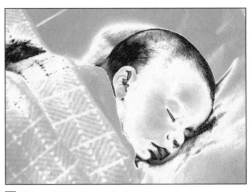

1 *Three different gradient map effects*

LIQUIFY **27**

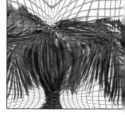

1 *The original image*

THE LIQUIFY FILTER LETS YOU TWIST, warp, stretch, and otherwise distort all or part of an image layer, with a full-size preview right in the dialog box **1**–**2**. You can apply the distortion (or reconstruction) with an assortment of **Liquify** tools, use a brush to freeze parts of the image to protect them from distortion, and undo the havoc you have wrought, partially or completely, with the **Reconstruct** tool. The edits are applied to the image when you click OK.

Liquify Filter

2 *The **Liquify** dialog box, after using the **Twirl Clockwise** tool in the preview area*

Applying the Liquify filter

The instructions for using the **Liquify** filter below are long-winded, but you don't have to follow them to the letter—you can choose among the various options.

This filter works on 8-bit and 16-bit images in the following document color modes: RGB Color, CMYK Color, Lab Color, Grayscale, and Duotone. It can't be applied to editable type or shape layers.

To apply the Liquify filter:

1. Click a layer, then press Ctrl-J/Cmd-J to duplicate it. *Optional:* You'll have the option in the Liquify dialog box to base a mask on a nonrectangular selection, layer mask, layer transparency, or alpha channel that you create now.

2. Choose Filter > **Liquify** (Ctrl-Shift-X/ Cmd-Shift-X). The dialog box is resizable. If you created a rectangular selection, only the selected portion will appear in the dialog box. If the selection is nonrectangular or is feathered and View Options: **Show Mask** is checked in this dialog box, the unselected part of the layer will be masked. This is akin to using the Freeze Mask tool (see step 6).

3. The settings you choose in the **Tool Options** area (except for Brush Rate and Turbulent Jitter) will apply to all the Liquify tools:

Enter or choose a **Brush Size** (1–600 pixels) for the brush width; a **Brush Density** (0–100%) to control edge feathering (similar to brush hardness on the Brushes palette); and a **Brush Pressure** (1–100%) to control how quickly distortion is applied when a tool is dragged.

For the Reconstruct, Twirl, Pucker, Bloat, or Turbulence tool, choose a **Brush Rate** (0–100%) to control how much distortion is applied when you click rather than drag with the tool.

If you're using a graphics tablet, check **Stylus Pressure** to control the brush pressure using your stylus.

1 *The tools in the **Liquify** dialog box*

— *Forward Warp (W)*
— *Reconstruct (R)*
— *Twirl Clockwise (C)*
— *Pucker (S)*
— *Bloat (B)*
— *Push Left (O)*
— *Mirror (M)*
— *Turbulence (T)*
— *Freeze Mask (F)*
— *Thaw Mask (D)*
— *Hand (H)*
— *Zoom (Z)*

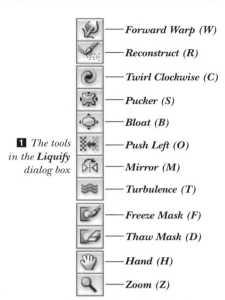

2 *The original image*

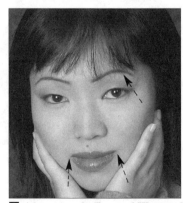

3 *After using the **Forward Warp** tool in the directions shown by the arrows*

1 *After holding the **Pucker** tool stationary at the top of the tree*

2 *After dragging the **Push Left** tool in the directions shown by the arrows*

3 *After holding the **Turbulence** tool stationary at the top of the tree*

4. Choose any of the following Liquify **tools** (press a tool shortcut to select that tool) (**1**, previous page), then drag across areas of the image in the preview window:

The **Forward Warp** tool (W) 🖌 pushes pixels in the direction the brush is dragged (**2**–**3**, previous page).

The **Reconstruct** tool (R) 🖌 restores distorted pixels to their undistorted state. Choices on the Tool Options: Reconstruct Mode pop-up menu control how the reconstruct effect is applied (see page 424).

The **Twirl Clockwise** (C) 🌀 tool rotates pixels for as long as you hold down the mouse button or drag. Alt-click/Option-click to rotate pixels counterclockwise. The higher the Brush Pressure, the faster the rotation.

The **Pucker** (S) 🖌 **1** and **Bloat** (B) ⬭ tools push pixels toward or away from the center of the brush for as long as you hold down the mouse button or drag. The higher the Brush Pressure when you drag with either tool, the faster pixels will move.

The **Push Left** tool (O) 🖌 moves pixels at right angles to the direction the brush is moved **2**. Alt-drag/Option-drag to move pixels to the opposite side of the brush direction. Use a low brush density and pressure to preserve edge patterns.

The **Mirror** tool (M) 🖌 copies pixels from the area to the right of your brush and applies a mirror image of them to the area the brush passes over. The tool picks up pixels on the right side of an upward stroke or on the left side of a downward stroke. Alt-drag/Option-drag to copy pixels from the opposite side of the brush.

TIP Before using the Mirror tool, freeze any areas that you don't want to distort (see step 6).

The **Turbulence** tool (T) 〰 jumbles pixels, creating a crumbly effect **3**.

(Continued on the following page)

Adjust the Tool Options: **Turbulence Jitter** value (0–100%) to control the tightness of the effect.

5. To move a magnified image in the preview window, drag with the **Hand** tool (H). Or to access this tool without selecting it, Spacebar-drag.

   To change the **Zoom** level of the preview image, you can use the Zoom tool (Z), but it's faster to use the same shortcuts that you'd use in the document window: Ctrl-click/Cmd-click or Ctrl-Alt-click/Cmd-Option-click. You can also click the ⊟ or ⊞ button in the bottom left corner of the dialog box, or choose a preset zoom level from the pop-up menu. Double-click the Zoom tool to reset the preview to 100%.

   TIP You can invoke the Undo/Redo commands (Ctrl-Z/Cmd-Z) and the Step Backward/Step Forward commands (Ctrl-Alt-Z/Cmd-Option-Z) while using any Liquify tool or reconstruction controls.

6. *Optional:* To paint a mask to protect areas of the image from distortion (or to add to an existing mask), choose the **Freeze Mask** tool (F), choose tool options, then paint on the preview image. The higher the Brush Pressure, the stronger the freeze effect. If the Brush Pressure is below 100%, you can drag again across the same spot to intensify the effect.

   To remove protection from frozen areas, choose the **Thaw Mask** tool (D), choose Tool Options, then paint on the preview image.

   Optional: To create a mask based on an existing nonrectangular selection, layer transparency, layer mask, or alpha channel in the original image (**1**, next page), choose from one of the Mask Options pop-up menus **1**: **Replace Selection** to use the selection, transparency, layer mask, or alpha channel as a mask; **Add to Selection** or **Subtract from Selection** to add to or subtract from the mask shape;

Intersect with Selection to intersect the current mask shape with your menu choice; or **Invert Selection** to invert the mask.

7. *Optional:* Use the Mask Options buttons to make additional changes to the mask. To unmask the entire image (make all pixels editable again), click **None.** To mask the entire image, click **Mask All.** To reverse what's masked and what isn't, click **Invert All.**

   To hide (but not disable) the mask, uncheck View Options: **Show Mask.** Choose a different overlay color for the frozen area from the **Mask Color** pop-up menu.

8. Although the Liquify filter modifies only the currently active layer in your image, other visible layers can be viewed as a "Backdrop," either one at a time or all together as a composite image. To have only the active layer display in the preview window, uncheck View Options: **Show Backdrop.** Or to display the active layer along with the Backdrop, check Show Backdrop and, from the Use pop-up menu, choose All Layers for the composite, or choose any individual layer.

   Make a choice from the **Mode** pop-up menu to control how the Backdrop interacts with the active layer: **In Front** places the Backdrop in front of the active layer; **Behind** places it behind the active layer; **Blend** lets you combine the two.

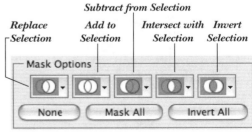

1 *The Mask Options pop-up menus and buttons*

1 *At left is the original image, with a selection that was saved as an **alpha channel**. At right is the image after applying the Liquify filter using the alpha channel as a mask. Only the unmasked area was altered.*

2 *Both the **image** and the **mesh** are visible.*

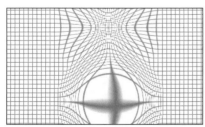

3 *The **mesh** is visible, but the image is not (Show Image is unchecked).*

Set the **Opacity** slider from 0–100% to reveal more or less of the layer chosen on the Use pop-up menu.

TIP When working on a copy of a layer, check Show Backdrop, choose the original layer from the Use pop-up menu, then compare your changes to the original as you move the Opacity slider (0–100%).

9. Don't click OK yet! To partially or completely undo the Liquify changes, read about the Reconstruct Options on the following page. Then, when you're done using the Liquify dialog box, click OK.

To help gauge the extent of your Liquify filter edits, you can superimpose a **mesh** over the image that maps the pattern of distortion. Using the mesh is helpful if your document lacks contrast or detail and you're finding it hard to see the shape or extent of the Liquify changes. You can adjust the mesh color and size.

To display the Liquify mesh:

1. In the Liquify dialog box, check View Options: **Show Mesh.** A regularly spaced set of gridlines displays **2**.

2. *Do any of the following optional steps:*

Choose a size from the **Mesh Size** pop-up menu.

Choose a color from the **Mesh Color** pop-up menu.

To hide the image and show only the mesh, uncheck View Options: **Show Image 3**. Now distortion patterns in the mesh will be more evident.

TIP If you can't see the mesh, try lowering the Opacity for Show Backdrop.

TIP You can save a mesh and then apply it to another layer or another document. Click Save Mesh at the top of the dialog box, type a name for the mesh (keep the .msh extension), choose a location for it, then click Save. To load in a mesh, click Load Mesh.

Reversing Liquify changes

If you've kept the dialog box open, you can use the **Reconstruct Options** and/or **Reconstruct tool** to undo some or all of the distortion.

To remove all distortion:

In the Reconstruct Options area of the Liquify dialog box, click **Restore All.** The entire preview image will return to the state it was in when you originally opened the Liquify dialog box.

or

Alt-click/Option-click Cancel to **reset** the preview to its unaltered state and also reset all tools and options to their default settings.

To restore unfrozen areas using a command:

1. Using the Freeze Mask tool, freeze any areas you don't want to restore. In the Reconstruct Options area of the Liquify dialog box, choose **Mode: Revert, Rigid, Stiff, Smooth,** or **Loose** (see the sidebar). Revert, the default mode, reverses all changes without introducing additional distortion.

2. Click the **Reconstruct** button several times. Unfrozen parts of the preview will revert incrementally to the state they were in when you opened the dialog box. The number of reverse steps depends on which Reconstruct mode you chose.

   or

   From the palette menu in the Reconstruct Options area, choose a **Reconstruct mode.** In the dialog box that opens, use the slider to specify the amount of reconstruction, then click OK.

To restore unfrozen areas using a tool:

1. In the Liquify dialog box, choose **Reconstruct Mode: Revert** from the pop-up menu in the Tool Options area.

2. Choose the **Reconstruct** tool (R), then drag across areas that you want to restore. Restoration occurs more quickly at the center of the brush cursor.

The Reconstruct modes

You can choose the **Revert, Rigid, Stiff, Smooth,** or **Loose** mode for the Reconstruct tool or as a Reconstruct option. Each mode reverses the distortion in its own fashion. Some modes extend distortion from frozen areas into unfrozen areas, with the result being part restoration and part distortion. Rigid and Stiff both produce sharp transitions between the frozen and nonfrozen areas; both Smooth and Loose produce additional distortion, with a more gradual transition between the frozen and nonfrozen areas; and Revert reverses all changes without introducing additional distortion.

For an explanation of the Displace, Amplitwist, and Affine modes, which can be chosen for the Reconstruct tool in the Tool Options area, see Photoshop Help ("Reconstruct tool modes").

AUTOMATE **28**

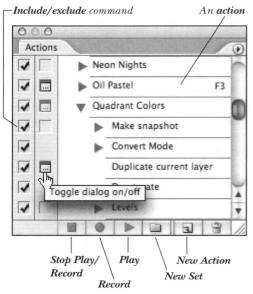

Include/exclude command

*An **action***

Stop Play/
Record

Play

Record

New Action

New Set

1 *With the **Actions** palette in **List** (edit) mode, you can toggle a dialog box pause on/off; add, exclude, delete, rerecord, or change the order of commands; or save actions and/or sets to an actions file.*

2 *With the **Actions** palette in **Button** mode, button colors and function keys assigned via the Action Options dialog box are displayed.*

AN ACTION IS A RECORDED SEQUENCE of menu commands, tool operations, or other image-editing functions that can be played back on a single file, a handful of files, or a folder full (batch) of files. Actions can execute anything from one simple editing step to a complex sequence of commands that trigger still other actions. And they can be used to accomplish multiple tasks, such as to convert files to a different format or color mode, apply a series of adjustment commands or filters, or perform a sequence of "preflight" steps to prepare files for print output. Actions can help you achieve consistent editing results on multiple files, and they can save you seconds or hours of work time, depending on how they're used.

Photoshop ships with dozens of ready-made actions—some of which you may find useful. In this chapter, we'll teach you how to create, edit, and play your own actions. Start by recording a few simple ones; you'll be programming more complex processes and boosting your productivity in no time.

The **Actions** palette is used to record, play back, edit, delete, save, store, and load actions. It can be displayed in **List** (edit) mode **1** or **Button** mode **2**. When **Button Mode** is unchecked on the Actions palette menu, the palette is in List mode.

Actions can be triggered via the **Play** button on the Actions palette, via an assigned keyboard **shortcut,** by dragging a file or folder full of files onto a **droplet** icon (a mini-application created from an action), or via the **Batch** command.

Actions

Recording actions

As you **create** an action, the commands you use are recorded. When you're finished recording, the commands will appear as a list in indented format below the action name on the Actions palette.

To record an action:

1. Actions are saved in **sets** on the Actions palette, and provide a convenient way of organizing task-related actions. To save the new action into a new set (instead of an existing set), click the **New Set** button at the bottom of the Actions palette, type a Name, then click OK.

2. Open a document or create a new one. Just to be on the safe side, copy the document using File > Save As.

3. Click the **New Action** button at the bottom of the Actions palette (or choose New Action from the Actions palette menu). The New Action dialog box opens.

4. Enter a Name for the action **1**, and from the Set pop-up menu, choose the set you created in step 1.

5. *Optional:* Assign a keyboard shortcut Function Key and/or display Color to the action. These options display on the palette only when it's in Button mode.

6. Click **Record.**

7. Execute the commands that you want to record as you would normally apply them to any image. When you enter values in a dialog box and click OK, those settings will be recorded (unless you click Cancel). See the list of recordable commands on the following page.

> ### It's all relative
>
> Position-related operations (e.g., using a selection tool or the Gradient, Magic Wand, Path, Slice, or Notes tool) are recorded based on the current ruler units. The units can be **actual** (e.g., inches or picas) or **relative** (percentages). An action that's recorded when an actual measurement unit is chosen can be played back on a file that's smaller than the one in which the action was recorded, provided there's enough canvas area to execute the action. An action that's recorded when a relative unit is chosen will work in any other relative space and on a file of any dimensions. To change units, in Preferences (Ctrl-K/Cmd-K) > Units & Rulers, from the Units: Rulers pop-up menu, choose a unit or choose "percent."

8. When you're done recording, click the **Stop** button or press Esc.

9. The action will now be listed on the Actions palette. With the palette in List mode, you can click the arrowhead next to the new action name to expand/collapse the list of commands.

To play the action (or any other action), see the following page.

TIP To rename an action, double-click its name.

TIP Use caution when recording the Save As command in an action. Be especially careful not to enter specific file names that could be written over when the action is played. We suggest you add a modal control to make the action pause at the Save As command (see page 432).

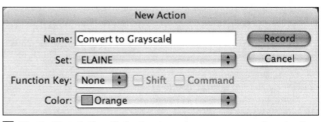

1 *Use the **New Action** dialog box to assign a name, set, function key, or color to your action, and to start recording.*

Playback options

To choose playback options, with the palette in List mode, choose **Playback Options** from the Actions palette menu, then choose any of the following:

Accelerated: The fastest playback option.

Step by Step: The action's list expands on the Actions palette, and each command or edit name becomes highlighted on the list as it's executed.

Pause for [   ] seconds: This option works like Step by Step, plus a user-defined pause is inserted at each step.

Pause for Audio Annotation: The playback pauses until an audio annotation, if included, has completed.

Playing actions

To play an action on an image:

1. Open an image.

2. Put the Actions palette into List mode.

3. Click an action name on the palette.

4. Click the **Play** button ▶ on the palette.

TIP You can also drag a file onto a droplet icon that you've created for the action (page 435), or run it on multiple files via the Batch command (pages 436–437).

TIP Make a snapshot of your image before running an action on it. That way, you can quickly restore its pre-action state.

TIP To play an action starting from a specific command in the action, click the command name before clicking Play. To play just one command in an action, click the command name, then Ctrl-click/Cmd-click the Play button; or Ctrl-double-click/Cmd-double-click the command.

TIP To load actions from other sets onto the palette, see page 438.

What can (or can't) be recorded in an action

TOOLS			MENU COMMANDS			PALETTES		
Selection tools	YES		File commands	MOST		Actions	SOME	
Slice tools	YES		Edit commands	MOST		Brushes		NO
Retouching tools		*	Image commands	MOST		Channels	YES	
Painting and Stamp tools		*	Layer commands	MOST		Character	YES	
Erasers		*	Select commands	MOST		Color	YES	
Gradient	YES		Filter commands	MOST		Histogram		NO
Paint Bucket	YES		View > Proof setup	YES		History	YES	
Editing tools		*	View commands		NO	Info		NO
Path Selection tools		*	Window commands	SOME		Layer Comps	YES	
Type tools	YES		Help commands		NO	Layers	YES	
Pen tools		*				Navigator		NO
Shape tools	YES					Options		SOME
Notes	YES		*Some tool edits can't be recorded in an			Paragraph	YES	
Audio Annotation	YES		action, such as strokes made with, and			Paths	YES	
Eyedropper	YES		options bar settings chosen for, the painting			Styles	YES	
Color Sampler	YES		tools, stamp tools, and tonal editing tools			Swatches	YES	
Measure		NO	(Blur, Sharpen, Dodge, Burn, etc.). To use			Tool Presets	YES	
Hand		NO	these tools effectively in an action, record			Tools		NO
Zoom		NO	the selection of the tool, then insert a Stop					
Quick Mask Mode		*	into the action, with a message for the user					
Screen Mode		NO	as to which settings to choose for the tool					
			and how to use it.					

Editing actions

You can insert a variety of commands into an action. For example, you can **insert** a **stop** into an **action** that will interrupt the playback, at which point the user can manually perform a nonrecordable operation, such as using the Brush or Clone Stamp tool. When the manual operation is finished, the user resumes the playback by clicking the Play button again. A stop can also be used to allow an informative alert message to display at a designated pause.

To insert a stop in an action:

1. As you're creating an action, pause at the point at which you want the stop to appear. For an existing action, on the Actions palette, click the command name after which you want the stop to appear.

2. Choose **Insert Stop** from the Actions palette menu. The Record Stop dialog box opens.

3. Type an instructional or alert message for users to read as they replay the action . It's a good idea to spell out in the message that after performing a manual step, the user should click the Play button on the Actions palette to resume the playback. (If the Actions palette is in Button mode, the Play button isn't accessible; instead, the user will need to click the action name, displayed in red, to resume the playback.)

4. *Optional:* Check **Allow Continue** to include a Continue button in the alert dialog box 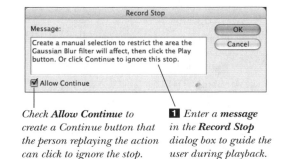. This gives the user the option to continue the action without performing any manual tasks. If Allow Continue isn't checked, the user will still be able to click Stop at that point in the action playback and then click the Play button on the palette to resume playing back the action.

5. Click OK. The Stop will appear below the command you clicked in step 1 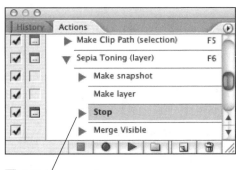.

*Check **Allow Continue** to create a Continue button that the person replaying the action can click to ignore the stop.*

1 *Enter a message in the **Record Stop** dialog box to guide the user during playback.*

2 *The **Continue** button lets the user continue an action without performing any manual tasks.*

3 *A **Stop** command*

The **Insert Menu Item** command allows you to add nonrecordable menu commands to an action. No values for the command are recorded, but during playback, the dialog box for the command opens onscreen, allowing the user to choose custom settings.

To insert a menu item in an action:

1. In an existing action, click the command name after which you want the new menu command to be inserted.

2. Choose **Insert Menu Item** from the Actions palette menu. The Insert Menu Item dialog box opens.

3. From the Photoshop menu bar, choose the command that you want to add to the action. The command name will be listed in the Insert Menu Item dialog box **1**.

4. Click OK. The menu command you chose is now added to the action **2**. The ability to toggle the dialog box open or closed (called "modal control") is disabled for inserted commands (see page 432).

TIP To change the settings for an inserted command, see page 433.

TIP With the Actions palette in List mode, Alt-click/Option-click a right-pointing triangle next to an action name to expand/collapse all the steps in the action.

Insert Menu Item in Action

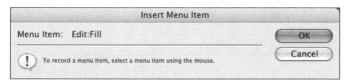

1 *When we chose the Fill command from the Photoshop menu bar, the command name appeared in the dialog box.*

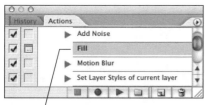

2 *The **menu item** that we inserted*

A **path** can also be **inserted** into an **action,** just as if you copied and pasted it from another document or application. Because the path is saved in the action, you can place it in as many files as you want. What's more, after the path is placed, you can have your action transform and/or manipulate it.

Note: Adding paths to actions requires significant memory. If you need to increase the memory allocated to Photoshop, see page 458.

To insert a path in an action:

1. With the **Pen** or **Freeform Pen** tool, create the path that you want to use in an action (see pages 367–369), and leave Work Path selected on the Paths palette.

2. Click the **Record** button ● to start recording a new action, and pause at the point in your action at which you want the path to be inserted.
or
To insert the path into an existing action, click the command name after which you want the path to be inserted, then click the **Record** button.

3. Choose **Insert Path** from the Actions palette menu. The command Set Work Path will be added to the action ▮.

4. Choose **Save Path** from the Paths palette menu, then click OK to accept the default name.

5. Finish recording your action, including any transformations of the path, then click the **Stop** button.▮

TIP If "percent" is the current ruler unit when the Insert Path command is recorded, the action will draw the path in proportion to the size of the document it's played back on. For example, if you create a path, insert that path into an action in an 8.5"x11" document, and then play the action back in a document half that size, the path will be drawn at half its original size.

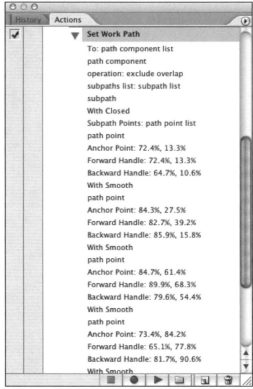

▮ *Set Work Path* appears on the Actions palette. If you expand it, you'll see a list of the path's anchor points and related attributes. More information than you ever wanted!

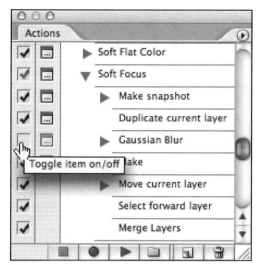

1 *The Gaussian Blur step is unchecked in this action to exclude it from playback.*

To exclude a command from playback:

1. Put the Actions palette into List mode (in Button mode, you can't edit any actions).

2. Expand the list for the action you want to edit.

3. Click in the leftmost column to remove the check mark for the command you want to exclude from playback **1**.

   (You can click in the same spot again at any time to restore the check mark and include the command.)

   Beware! If you click the check mark for an entire action or actions set, any commands that you've painstakingly checked will become unchecked. (An alert dialog box will appear.)

If you want to experiment with an action or add to it without messing around with the original, work on a **duplicate.**

To duplicate an action:

Click an action, then choose **Duplicate** from the Actions palette menu.
or
Drag an action over the **New Action** button ⬛ at the bottom of the Actions palette.

A **modal control,** or pause in an action, can be toggled on or off for any command that uses a dialog box or any tool that requires pressing Enter/Return in order to be executed. If users encounter a modal control upon playing an action, they can either enter different settings in the dialog box or just click OK to proceed with the settings that were originally recorded for the action.

To add a modal control to an action:

1. Make sure the Actions palette is in List mode, and expand the list for the action you want to add a modal control to.

2. Click in the second column from the left; a dialog box icon will appear **1**. When the action is played and the modal control is encountered, the action will pause and the dialog box for that command will appear onscreen. The user can then enter new values, accept the existing values (click OK), or click Cancel. The playback will resume after the dialog box is closed.

A red dialog box icon for an action signifies that some modal controls in that action were turned off and some are still on.

To remove a modal control, click the dialog box icon.

Beware! If you click the dialog box icon next to an action name, it will turn on/off all the modal controls in that action.

Keep in mind that if you change the **order** of **commands** in an action, the revised action may produce different results from the original.

To change the order of commands:

1. Work on a duplicate action, or at least save the set before proceeding (see page 438).

2. On the Actions palette, expand the list for an action, if it's not already expanded.

3. Drag a command upward or downward on the list **2**. It's as simple as that.

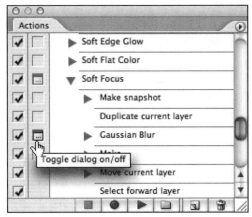

1 *The **dialog box** icon lets you turn individual commands (or whole actions) **on** and **off**.*

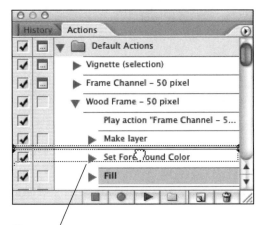

2 *The Fill command is **moved upward** on the list.*

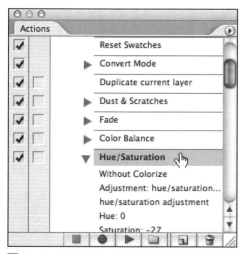

1 *Double-click the command you want to rerecord.*

To rerecord an action using different dialog box settings:

1. Click the name of the action you want to edit.

2. Choose **Record Again** from the Actions palette menu. The action will play back, stopping at any command that uses a dialog box.

3. When each dialog box opens in succession, enter new settings, if desired, then click OK. When a dialog box is closed, the rerecording continues.

4. To stop the rerecording, click **Cancel** in a dialog box or click the **Stop** button ■ at the bottom of the Actions palette.

To change the settings for a command in an action:

1. On the Actions palette, double-click a command that uses a dialog box (or alert dialog box) that you want to rerecord **1**.

2. Enter new settings.

3. Click OK. (Click Cancel to have any revisions be disregarded.)

TIP To duplicate a command in an action, drag the command over the New Action button ▣ at the bottom of the palette.

To delete an action:

1. Click the action you want to delete.

2. Click the **Delete** button 🗑 at the bottom of the Actions palette, then click OK, or to bypass the prompt, Alt-click/Option-click the Delete button.

Rerecord Action, Command; Delete Action

To add commands to an action:

1. On the Actions palette, expand the list for the action you want to add a command to, then click the command name after which you want the new command to appear.

2. Click the **Record** button.⬤

3. Perform the steps required to record the command(s) that you want to add. *Note:* A command that's available only under certain conditions (e.g., the Feather command, which requires an active selection) can't be added to an action unless the creation of those conditions is also included as steps in the action.

4. Click the **Stop** button ▪ to stop recording.

TIP To copy a command from one action to another, expand both action lists, then Alt-drag/Option-drag the command you want to copy from one list to the other. If you don't hold down Alt/Option while dragging, you'll cut the command from the original action. Be careful if you copy any Save commands—they may contain information that's specific to the original action.

You can **delete** individual **commands** from an action. *Note:* To save the current list of actions as a set for later use, before deleting any commands (or actions), follow the instructions on page 438.

To delete a command from an action:

1. Click the name of the command you want to delete. Ctrl-click/Cmd-click to highlight additional commands, if desired.

2. Click the **Delete** button 🗑 at the bottom of the Actions palette, then click OK.
or
To bypass the prompt, drag the command to the Delete button.

Creating droplets

An action can be turned into its own little mini-application, called a **droplet,** that sits out on the Desktop or in a folder, waiting to be triggered. If you drag a file or a folder full of files onto a droplet icon, Photoshop CS2 will launch, if it's not already open, and the action that the droplet represents will be applied to those files. Droplets can be given to other users and used on other computers.

To create a droplet for an action:

1. Choose File > Automate > **Create Droplet.** The Create Droplet dialog box opens **1**.

2. Click **Choose.** A Save dialog box opens. Enter a name in the Save As field, choose a location for the droplet, then click Save.

3. Back in the Create Droplet dialog box, choose a set from the **Set** pop-up menu, then choose the action you want saved as a droplet from the **Action** pop-up menu.

Back and forth

To make a droplet that was created in Windows usable in Macintosh (Mac OS-ready), drag the Windows droplet onto the Macintosh Photoshop CS2 **application** icon.

To make a Mac-made droplet usable in Windows, add the extension **.exe** at the end of the droplet name. *Note:* References to file names and paths within an action aren't supported between operating systems.

---

4. Check any **Play** options you want included in the droplet (see the next page) and choose **Destination** and **Errors** options for the processed files (see steps 6–7 on the next page).

5. Click OK. The droplet **2** will appear in the designated location.

TIP In ImageReady, you can create a droplet by dragging an action to the Desktop.

Wood frame
2 *A **droplet** icon*

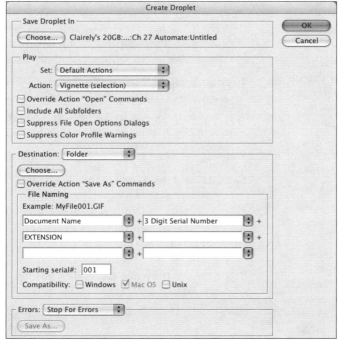

1 *Use the **Create Droplet** dialog box to choose a location for the droplet.*

Batch processing

The ability to play an action on multiple files using the **Batch** command is one of the most powerful features of actions. You can drag a folder onto a droplet, or use the Batch command if you need to choose options.

To play an action on a batch of images:

1. Make sure all the files to be batch-processed are located in the same folder. Or for ease and simplicity, select multiple files in Bridge.

2. In Bridge, choose Tools > Photoshop > **Batch,** or in Photoshop, choose File > Automate > **Batch.**

3. Choose a set from the **Set** pop-up menu, and choose an action from the **Action** pop-up menu (**1**, next page).

4. For **Source,** choose Folder, click Browse/Choose, and locate the folder that contains the files to be processed; or if files were selected in Bridge, simply choose Bridge.

If **Override Action "Open" Commands** is checked, the action must contain an open command in order for the batch command to open any files.

5. Check **Suppress File Open Options Dialogs** and/or **Suppress Color Profile Warnings** to have the Batch command bypass alerts or dialog boxes that may appear onscreen as source files are opened.

6. From the **Destination** pop-up menu, choose one of the following options:

None to have the files stay open after processing.

Save and Close to have the files save over their originals and then close.

Folder to have the files save to a new folder. Click Browse/Choose, then choose a destination folder. If **Override Action "Save As" Commands** is checked, the action must contain a Save As command in order for the batch command to save any files.

7. *Optional:* By default, Photoshop ends a batch process if it encounters an error message. To have the batch play through instead and keep track of the error messages in a text file, choose Log Errors to File from the Errors pop-up menu, click Save As, type a name, choose a location, then click Save. Now, if errors are encountered, you'll be alerted via a prompt that errors were logged into the designated error log file.

8. Click OK. The batch processing begins.

When Folder is chosen as the Destination for batch files, many options are available for **naming** the resulting files. For example, the files can be named sequentially using serial numbers or letters so they don't replace each other in the new folder. There are also options for ensuring that file names are compatible with other operating systems.

To choose file naming options:

1. Follow steps 1 and 2, above.

2. Choose options from the pop-up menus in the **File Naming** area, or simply type in any text you want included in the name.

3. Make sure the **Example** name exhibits the naming convention that you chose.

4. If you chose a naming option that uses sequential (serial) numbers, enter up to a four-digit starting number in the **Starting serial#** field.

5. Check any file name **Compatibility** boxes: Windows, Mac OS, or Unix.

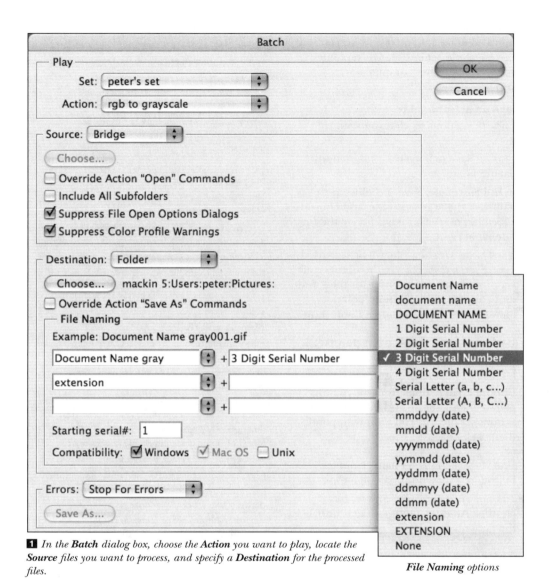

1 *In the **Batch** dialog box, choose the **Action** you want to play, locate the **Source** files you want to process, and specify a **Destination** for the processed files.*

File Naming options

Saving and loading actions sets

Each time you create a new action, you have to choose a set for it to be stored in. You can also save a whole actions set to a **separate file** for use on another computer or as a backup for safekeeping.

To save an actions set to a file:

1. Click the actions set that you want to save.

2. Choose **Save Actions** from the Actions palette menu.

3. In the **File name**/**Save As** field, type a name for the actions set file, and choose a location in which to save it (see the first sidebar at right).

4. Click Save. The new file will be regarded as one set, irrespective of the number of actions it contains. In order for the saved set to appear on the Actions palette menu, you need to relaunch Photoshop.

To load a set onto the Actions palette:

1. Click the set name that you want the loaded set to appear below.

2. Choose **Load Actions** from the Actions palette menu, locate and highlight the actions set file that you want to append, then click **Load.**
   or
   Choose an actions **set name** from the bottom of the Actions palette menu.

TIP To copy an action from one set to another, Alt-drag/Option-drag it into the target set.

To replace the current actions set with a different set:

1. Choose **Replace Actions** from the Actions palette menu.

2. Locate and click the actions set file that you want to replace the existing sets with.

3. Click **Load.**

TIP To restore the default actions set, choose Reset Actions from the palette menu.

Where are actions stored?

In Mac, the actions that are visible on the Actions palette list when Photoshop is launched are stored in the **Actions Palette** file in Users/[UserName]/Library/Preferences/Adobe Photoshop CS2 Settings. They'll live there until they're replaced or the file is trashed. To keep a set from being inadvertently deleted, save it as a separate file! In Windows, the storage location of the action files isn't visible to the user.

For easy access, save your actions sets in Presets > **Photoshop Actions** inside the application folder. The sets you save will be listed at the bottom of the Actions palette menu.

To save a **text** version of all the actions sets currently listed on the palette, hold down Ctrl-Alt/Cmd-Option while choosing Save Actions from the Actions palette menu. This file can't be imported back into Photoshop.

Actions and AppleScript

Although Photoshop actions can be real time-savers because they let you record and play back a series of commands, they do have some limitations. They can't use **conditional logic,** meaning you can't tell an action to perform one command if one situation exists and another command when it doesn't. (ImageReady actions can use limited conditional logic.) Also, you can control only Photoshop files with an action, not files in other programs.

Fortunately, you can get around these limitations by controlling Photoshop with scripts written in any of these widely known languages: AppleScript on the Mac platform, Visual Basic on Windows, and JavaScript for cross-platform use.

We don't cover scripting in this book, but in the Adobe Photoshop CS2 > **Scripting Guide** folder, you'll find sample scripts, the Photoshop Scripting Guide, and substantial guides to the scripting languages.

ANIMATION 29

Animation lingo

Looping: The number of times an animation plays back without stopping.

Tweening: The addition of in-between frames between a designated starting and ending frame.

Propogate: The duplication of a change onto all frames.

Delay: The duration of time a frame stays visible onscreen.

THERE'S SOMETHING SO SATISFYING about making a static image or graphic move across a screen. Both Photoshop **NEW** and ImageReady (formerly only Image-Ready) give you the tools to choreograph animations in which a series of image frames play back in sequence. Animation effects that you can create for a Web page include type or images that move, fade in or out, or undergo other changes. In this chapter, you'll learn how to move an object across the screen; fade an object in or out; morph normal type into warped type; edit, preview, save, and optimize your animations; and save animation frames as layers.

Creating animations

To produce an animation, you'll create starting and ending frames via the Animation palette **1**, use the Tween button to add in-between frames, then modify individual frames by changing Layers palette settings (e.g., blending mode, opacity, fill opacity, and layer effects). When your animation is completed, you'll play it back to see how it's working, then save the sequence of frames as a single GIF file, prepped for online viewing.

Animations

Currently selected frame

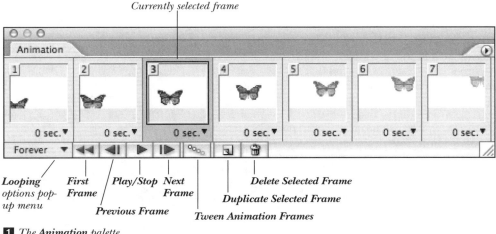

Looping options pop-up menu *First Frame* *Play/Stop* *Next Frame* *Delete Selected Frame*

Previous Frame *Duplicate Selected Frame*

Tween Animation Frames

1 *The **Animation** palette*

To move layer imagery across an image via animation:

1. Open or create an image that contains imagery silhouetted on transparency and a Background or solid-color layer behind it ◼. The canvas size needs to be large enough to provide room for the object to move.

2. Show the **Animation** palette.

NEW 3. Click a layer (not the Background) on the Layers palette, and uncheck **Propagate Frame 1** on the Layers palette.

4. Choose the **Move** tool (V), then drag the layer image to one side (or corner) of the document window ◼. The Frame 1 thumbnail on the Animation palette will update to reflect this new position.

5. Click the **Duplicate Selected Frame** button ◼ at the bottom of the Animation palette. Both the duplicate frame and the layer chosen for step 3 should now be selected.

6. With the Move tool, drag the layer element to the opposite side (or corner) of the document window ◼. The current thumbnail on the Animation palette will update to reflect this change ◼. Leave this layer selected!

7. Click the **Tween** button 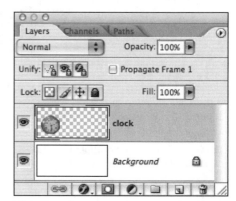 on the Animation palette. (Tweening adds in-between frames.) The Tween dialog box opens (◼, next page).

8. Do all of the following:

   From the **Tween With** pop-up menu, choose to add the in-between frames between the currently selected frame and the **Previous Frame.** (*Note:* If you select two or more frames before opening the Tween dialog box, only the Selection option will be available on this pop-up menu.)

   In the **Frames to Add** field, specify how many frames are to be added in total
NEW (1–999). The greater the number of frames, the smoother (less choppy) the

◼ *A file with an image layer and a Background*

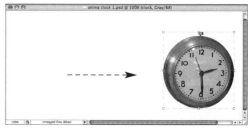

◼ *Drag the layer image to one side of the document window.*

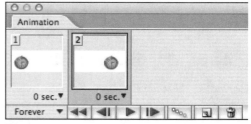

◼ *Drag the same layer image to the opposite side of the document window for the duplicate animation frame.*

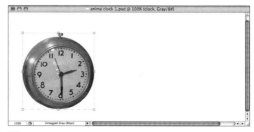

◼ *The **original** (start) and **duplicate** (end) frames*

More animation options

➤ Drag one frame or a selected range of frames to a different **position** on the palette. (Click, then Shift-click, to select a range of frames.)

➤ To convert all the frames to layers, choose **Flatten Frames into Layers** from the Animation palette menu. Any preexisting layers will remain but will become hidden.

➤ To reverse the frame sequence, choose **Reverse Frames** from the Animation palette menu. This is equivalent to playing the animation backward.

➤ To redo a tween, modify the start or end frames, Shift-click to select all the frames that were added by the tween, then click the **Tween** button; the selected frames will update. You could also delete all the tweened frames and use the Tween dialog box to add new ones.

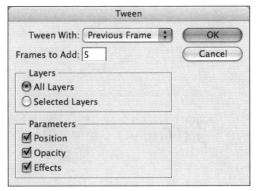

1 *Use the **Tween** dialog box to add in-between frames to an animation.*

animation, but also the larger the file size and the longer its download time.

Click Layers: **All Layers** to copy pixels from all layers to the new frames—even layers that weren't modified. Or click **Selected Layer** to copy pixels from only the currently selected layer to the new frames. All other layers (including the Background) will be hidden in the added frames.

Check which of these layer **Parameters** the in-between frames will modify: Position, Opacity, and/or Effects (layer effects).

9. Click OK **2**. Save your file. Click the **Play** button ▶ to preview the animation; then click the **Stop** button. ■

TIP You can use editable and rasterized type layers for animations. You can make type fade in or out (see the following page) or move across the image, or use it in any other layer animation effect.

TIP If you want your animations to download and play back quickly, keep them small (approximately 300 x 200 pixels or less).

TIP With the All Layers option checked in the Tween dialog box, changes occurring on all layers are recorded in the in-between frames, meaning you can add complexity to your animation by modifying objects on multiple layers.

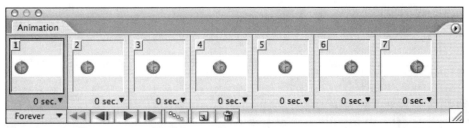

2 *The Animation palette after **tweening**. When the animation is played back, the layer element moves smoothly from one side of the document window to the other.*

To add something that fades in:

1. Open an animation file, such as the one you created in the previous instructions.

2. On the Animation palette, click the frame where you want the added animation effect to start, and uncheck **New Layers Visible in All Frames** on the palette menu.

3. Create a type or image layer.

4. Move the type or image to a starting position in the document window, and lower the layer Opacity to around 5% 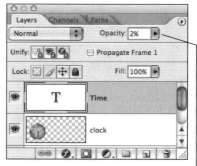.

5. Click the frame in which the type or image animation will end, make the layer visible on the Layers palette, then move the type or image to its ending location. Change the layer Opacity to 100%.

6. If the new animation runs from the first to the last frame, choose Select All Frames from the Animation palette menu; otherwise, click, then Shift-click to select the necessary frames.

7. Click the Tween button ⁰⁰°ₒ to add incremental transitions to the selected frames. Click the Play button ▶ to preview the animation **2**–**3**. Save your file.

1 *The Opacity setting for the type layer for the first animation frame*

2 *After tweening, the clock still moves to the right and the word "Time" moves up and fades in.*

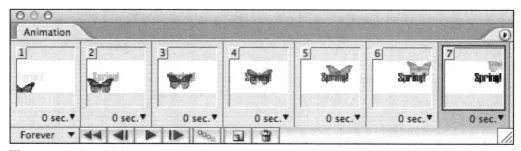

3 *In this animation, the type fades in as it moves horizontally across the screen.*

What you can tween

An animation can involve a change in an image or type layer's **position** or **opacity,** or a transition from one layer **effect** to another. Or you can simply tween between a layer effect that's turned **on** and then **off.** These types of modifications are created via Layers palette options and don't modify layer pixels, whereas the animation effect discussed on page 445 does involve modifying layer pixels.

Previewing animations

The **looping** option that you choose for an animation controls how many times the animation repeats itself without stopping. The **delay** time you choose for each frame controls how long you see that frame onscreen during playback. These settings save with the file and control how the animation plays back when the page is viewed in a browser.

To choose playback options:

From the **Looping** pop-up menu in the lower left corner of the Animation palette, choose **Once** or **Forever**; or choose **Other** and enter a specific value, then click OK. Endlessly looping animations (Forever) can be tedious to watch—a turnoff for viewers.

From the **Delay Time** pop-up menu below a frame **1**, choose a delay value. The "No delay" option equals 0 seconds. You can also choose Other, enter a custom delay time (0–240 seconds), and click OK. Repeat for any other frames.

To preview an animation in your browser:

With the animation open in Photoshop, choose File > **Save for Web** (Ctrl-Alt-Shift-S/ NEW Cmd-Option-Shift-S. Click the Preview in [default browser] button (or another icon) at the bottom of the dialog box. (If the animation Looping is set to Once, you can click the Refresh button in the browser to replay the animation.) When you're done previewing, exit/quit the browser. Click back in Photoshop, then click Cancel to close the Save for Web dialog box.

1 *You can choose a delay time for individual frames in an animation from the pop-up menu below each frame. The default **delay time** is No delay (0 seconds).*

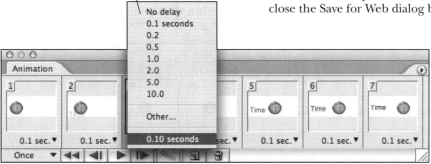

Completing the loop

In these instructions, you'll expand an animation by adding all or part of the same animation in reverse. During playback, the animation will play forward and then backward in one smooth **loop.**

To cycle back to the first frame:

1. Click the last frame on the Animation palette.
2. Click the **Tween** button. The Tween dialog box opens.
3. Choose Tween With: **First Frame;** enter the desired number of **Frames to Add;** click Layers: **All Layers;** check all the **Parameters,** then click OK.

Removing frames

To remove frames from an animation:

To remove one frame from an animation, click the frame, then drag it over the **Delete Current Frame** button.

or

To delete all the frames except the first one, choose **Delete Animation** from the Animation palette menu.

Editing frames

If the first frame is selected in an animation and **Propagate Frame 1** is checked on the Layers palette, any changes made to frame 1 via the Layers palette will automatically copy to all the other frames. With this option unchecked, Layers palette changes, such as position, visibility (show/hide), and layer style (effects, opacity, blending mode) will affect only the first frame. Regardless of the Propagate Frame 1 setting, painting and editing changes made to existing layers are applied automatically to all frames.

By default, the contents of newly added layers are added to all animation frames. To prevent this, uncheck **New Layers Visible in All Frames** on the Animation palette menu.

Unify with caution NEW

Changes to a layer's **position, visibility,** or **style** (effects, blending mode, and opacity) affect just the currently selected frame. If you want to apply these types of changes to all your existing animation frames, use the **Unify** buttons on the Layers palette **1**–**3**. Click the frame and the layer that contains the position, visibility, or style you want to copy, then click the desired Unify button. Warning: Any position, visibility, or style changes that were applied manually or via tweening will be **wiped out** when you click a Unify button! If you can't afford to lose such changes, make changes frame by frame instead of via the Unify buttons (that is, click a frame, change Layers palette settings for that frame, and so on).

Unify   Unify   Unify
Layer   Layer   Layer
Position   Visibility   Style

1 *The* **Unify** *buttons on the Layers palette let you apply changes quickly to **all** your animation frames.*

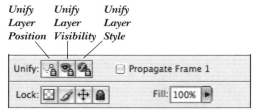

2 *A layer style is applied to the "phone base" layer for the first frame.*

3 *The* **Unify Layer Style** *button copied the layer style of the selected layer to **all** the frames.*

Create a Loop; Delete, Edit Frames

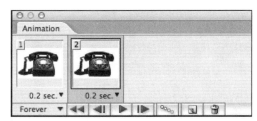

1 *We duplicated the first frame*

2 *The "receiver left tilt" layer (duplicate of "receiver") is visible and the "receiver" layer is hidden.*

In this image, the handle is tilting to the left.

3 *Now the "receiver" layer is visible and the "receiver left tilt" layer is hidden.*

In this image, the handle is level.

Because many edits aren't "tweenable," a lot of animation editing has to be done frame by frame. In these instructions, you'll **make an object rock** by alternately showing and hiding layers.

To create a rocking motion:

1. Open or create an image that contains a Background (a solid color or imagery), plus a layer that contains a silhouetted image surrounded by transparent pixels.

   For our animation, we divided the telephone image into two layers: The base layer will remain static and the receiver layer will tilt. In Frame 1, both layers are visible, so it looks like a complete telephone.

2. To create the animation frames, click the **Duplicate Selected Frame** button ◪ at the bottom of the Animation palette. Keep the duplicate frame selected **1**.

3. Click the **Tween** button, °o°o click Layers: All Layers, enter the total number of Frames to Add to complete the animation, then click OK.

4. Click the animation frame where you want the modification to start, and make sure New Layers Visible in All Frames is unchecked on the palette menu.

5. On the Layers palette, uncheck Propagate Frame 1, and duplicate the layer that you want to be in motion.

6. Rotate or move the duplicate layer slightly **2**. Hide the original layer so you can see the change in the selected frame on the Animation palette.

7. Click the next animation frame. Show the original layer and hide the duplicate, modified layer **3**.

8. Click the next consecutive frame. Show the duplicate, modified layer and hide the original, unmodified layer.

9. Continue to alternately hide then show the two layers for the remaining frames in the animation (and don't forget to save the file!).

Rotated and applied
the Motion Blur filter

Scaled down,
rotated, and moved

Scaled, moved
and lowered the opacity

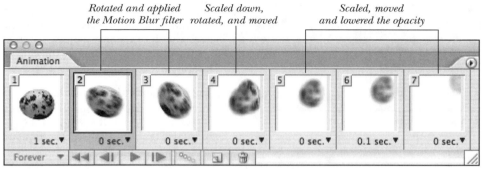

1 *You can create an animation using simple objects (here, a speckled egg). We created a separate layer for each frame and applied filters and/or transform commands to individual layers.*

Warping text in an animation

Here you'll create a type animation by using the **Warp Text** feature, which lets you apply up to 15 different types of distortion.

To create a warped type animation:

1. Open or create an image that contains a Background and an editable type layer, then click the type layer.

2. On the Animation palette, click the first frame, then click the **Duplicate Selected Frame** button.

3. With the Type tool still selected, click the **Warp Text** button on the options bar. The Warp Text dialog box opens.

4. Watch the type change in the document window as you do any of the following: Choose a warp style from the **Style** pop-up menu; click **Horizontal** or **Vertical** to control the direction of the warp; use the **Bend, Horizontal Distortion,** and **Vertical Distortion** sliders or fields to achieve the desired degree of "warpage." Click OK.

5. The current frame in the Animation palette will update to display the warp. With the second frame still selected, click the **Tween** button on the Animation palette. Enter the desired number of **Frames to Add,** click Layers: **All Layers,** check all **Parameters,** then click OK **2**.

Frame by frame

Remember that when you edit animation frames manually, you need to make **incremental** changes. For example, you could change the layer opacity by small increments, rotate or move an object gradually, apply brush strokes one by one, or apply a filter or color adjustment in increasing values **1**.

6. Choose a delay value for the frames, if desired, and click the Play button on the Animation palette to run the animation.

TIP To adjust warped type, double-click the warped type layer thumbnail, click the Warp Text button on the options bar, then change any of the settings. (To remove the warp, choose Style: None.) Reselect all frames that contain the warp effect, then Ctrl-click/Cmd-click the Tween button to update the other frames.

smile

smile

smile

2 *The finished **warped type animation***

Photoshop format

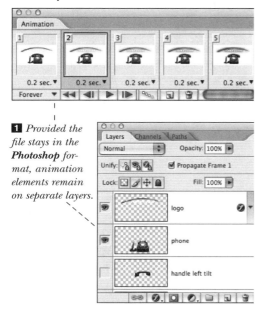

*Provided the file stays in the **Photoshop** format, animation elements remain on separate layers.*

GIF format

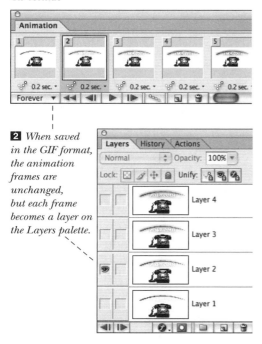

When saved in the GIF format, the animation frames are unchanged, but each frame becomes a layer on the Layers palette.

Outputting your animation

In this section, first we'll show you how to choose optional settings for your animation from the **Optimize Animation** dialog box. After that, you'll be ready to save your file as a GIF for online output.

To choose preoptimization settings:

1. Choose **Optimize Animation** from the Animation palette menu. The Optimize Animation dialog box opens.

2. Check either or both **Optimize By** options:

   Bounding Box to save the initial frame plus any areas that are modified from one frame to the next. This helps to reduce the file size, but it also may prevent the file from being edited in some GIF-editor applications.

   Check **Redundant Pixel Removal** to make transparent any pixels in an object or a background that don't undergo a change, and thus don't need to be reloaded for each frame. This also helps to reduce the file size.

3. Click OK.

As you work on your animation, you'll use the plain old File > **Save** command to save it as a Photoshop (.psd) file; this format keeps layers and frames intact. This is the file to keep in reserve for future editing ■.

Once you've previewed your animation in a browser and made your final edits, the last step is to save it in the **GIF** format so it can be output online.

To save an animation as a GIF:

Choose File > **Save for Web,** choose settings in the Optimize panel as per our instructions on page 506, then click Save. When saved in this format, each frame in the animation becomes a layer on the Layers palette ■ (the original layers are replaced).

Once saved as a GIF file, in Bridge, you can use File > Open With to open the animation

(Continued on the following page)

Optimize Animation

in ImageReady and display the animation frames. (The animation frames won't display in Photoshop.) Note the change on the Layers palette when you reopen a GIF file in ImageReady.

The speed at which an animation plays back in a browser is determined by several factors, such as the speed of the Web viewer's CPU, the browser version, and the amount of RAM currently allocated to the browser. The smaller the file size, the faster the download time. One way to reduce the file size is by making the canvas size of the animation file as small as possible; another is to reduce the number of colors in the color table of the GIF file.

TIP .avi files and QuickTime .mov files can also be opened in ImageReady.

TIP In ImageReady, you can create a rollover that triggers an animation (see pages 532–541).

If you want to use your animation frames as images in another project, the **Animation Frames as Files** command in ImageReady comes in handy. It creates a separate file for each frame in an animation.

To save animation frames as layers:

1. In ImageReady, open a file that contains an animation.

2. Choose File > Export > **Animation Frames as Files.**

3. In the **File Options** area, enter a Base Name for the files, click Choose, locate a destination folder, then click OK/Choose.

4. In the **Format Options** area, choose a preset (if you've created one for the Optimize palette), or enter optimization options in the Format area.

5. Click OK.

TIP If you want to export some, but not all, of the frames in your animation, select the desired frame(s), then in File > Export > Animation Frames as Files, check Selected Frames Only.

Mr. Softy

Layer effects, which also produce soft outer edges, don't always optimize well, even in files that are optimized in the GIF format. Bear this in mind as you create animations, and always remember to preview them via the Preview in [default browser] button (or other) in the Save for Web dialog box.

PREFERENCES/PRESETS 30

PREFERENCES ARE SETTINGS THAT apply to the application as a whole, such as which ruler units are used, or whether tool tips display onscreen. Most preference changes take effect immediately; a few take effect only upon relaunching (we've noted those exceptions). All preference changes are saved when you exit/quit Photoshop. In this chapter, you'll also learn how to save and load brush, gradient, and other **presets.**

To open the **Preferences** dialog box in Photoshop or Bridge, press **Ctrl-K/Cmd-K** or choose Edit (Photoshop, in Mac) > Preferences. In Photoshop **1**, you can cycle through the various panels by using the shortcuts listed on the pop-up menu or by clicking Prev or Next; in Bridge, click a panel name on the left side of the dialog box.

Open Preferences Dialog Box

Preferences

✓ General	⌘1
File Handling	⌘2
Display & Cursors	⌘3
Transparency & Gamut	⌘4
Units & Rulers	⌘5
Guides, Grid & Slices	⌘6
Plug-Ins & Scratch Disks	⌘7
Memory & Image Cache	⌘8
Type	⌘9

OK
Cancel
Prev
Next

Changes will take effect the next time you start Photoshop.

☑ Export Clipboard   ☑ Beep When Done
☑ Show Tool Tips   ☑ Dynamic Color Sliders
☑ Zoom Resizes Windows   ☑ Save Palette Locations
☐ Auto–Update Open Documents ☑ Use Shift Key for Tool Switch
☑ Show Menu Colors   ☐ Automatically Launch Bridge
☑ Resize Image During Paste/Place ☐ Zoom with Scroll Wheel

☑ History Log
Save Log Items To: ● Metadata
                   ○ Text File   Choose...
                   ○ Both
Edit Log Items: Sessions Only ⬍

Reset All Warning Dialogs

1 The **Preferences** dialog box in Photoshop has 9 panels.

Photoshop Preferences

General Preferences

Choose the Adobe or Apple **Color Picker.**

Choose an **Image Interpolation** option for commands that involve resampling or transforming: Nearest Neighbor (Faster) is the fastest but least precise (use for hard-edged graphics); Bilinear is medium quality; Bicubic is the highest quality (creates the smoothest gradations) but also the slowest; Bicubic Smoother is appropriate for enlarging documents; and Bicubic Sharper is appropriate for reducing documents but may cause oversharpening.

NEW From the **UI Font Size** pop-up menu, choose Small, Medium, or Large as the font size for the Photoshop user interface (menus, palettes, tool tips, options bar, etc.). Small is the default. The change will take effect upon relaunch.

Enter the maximum number of **History States** that can be listed on the History palette at a time (1–1000).

Options

Check **Export Clipboard** to have the current Clipboard contents stay on the Clipboard when you exit/quit Photoshop.

Check **Show Tool Tips** to permit the function and name of whichever tool, button, or palette feature the pointer is currently over (mouse button up) to pop up onscreen.

Uncheck **Zoom Resizes Windows** to prevent the document window from resizing when the view size is changed via the Ctrl/Cmd- + (plus) or Ctrl/Cmd- - (minus) shortcut.

Check **Auto-Update Open Documents** to have documents save automatically when jumping between Photoshop and ImageReady. Documents always update after jumping, whether this option is on or off.

NEW Check **Show Menu Colors** to enable any colors assigned to menus via Edit > Menus.

NEW Check **Resize Image During Paste/Place** to have images scale to fit the current canvas area automatically when the Edit > Paste and File > Place commands are used.

Check **Beep When Done** to have a beep sound when any command that takes time to process (has a progress bar) is finished processing.

With **Dynamic Color Sliders** checked, colors above the sliders on the Color palette will update as the sliders are moved. Turn this option off to speed performance.

With **Save Palette Locations** checked, palettes that are open when you exit/quit Photoshop will reopen in the same locations when you relaunch the application.

With **Use Shift Key for Tool Switch** checked, in order to access tools that share the same pop-out menu, you must press Shift plus the assigned letter (e.g., press Shift-R to cycle through the Blur, Sharpen, and Smudge tools). With this option unchecked, you can press the letter without holding down Shift.

NEW Check **Automatically Launch Bridge** to have Bridge launch whenever Photoshop is launched.

NEW If your mouse has a scroll wheel and you check **Zoom with Scroll Wheel,** you can scroll the wheel to change the zoom level.

History Log

Check **History Log** to choose where the log of document edits is saved: to the Metadata section of a file, to a separate Text File, or to Both. From the Edit Log Items pop-up menu, choose Sessions Only to log when Photoshop was launched and exited/quit and which files were opened; or Concise to log Sessions information plus a list of edits, as displayed on the History palette; or Detailed, which is like Concise, except that it also logs the options and parameters used in each editing step.

Click **Reset All Warning Dialogs** to reenable all alert dialog boxes that were disabled by checking Don't Show Again.

General Preferences

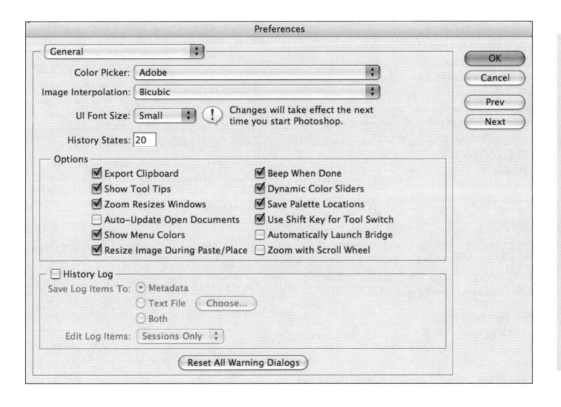

File Handling Preferences

File Saving Options

Choose **Image Previews**: Never Save to save files without a thumbnail preview for the desktop; or choose Always Save to have an updated preview save with files whenever they're saved; or choose Ask When Saving to decide whether to include a preview on a case-by-case basis when files are saved for the first time.

In Mac, check Icon to have a thumbnail of an image display as its file icon on the Desktop and in the Open dialog box. Check Full Size to include a 72-ppi PICT preview for applications that require this option when importing non-EPS files. Check Macintosh Thumbnail and/or Windows Thumbnail to have a thumbnail of an image display when its name is highlighted in the Open dialog box.

In Mac, choose **Append File Extension:** Always or Ask When Saving to include a three-letter abbreviation of the file format (e.g., .tif for TIFF) when Macintosh files are saved. This is helpful when converting files for Windows, and essential when saving files for the Web. Check **Use Lower Case** to have file extensions appear in lowercase characters rather than uppercase characters.

In Windows, choose **File Extension: Use Lower Case** or **Use Upper Case.**

File Compatibility

Check **Ignore EXIF profile tag** to have Photoshop ignore EXIF metadata color space information when opening files.

Check **Ask Before Saving Layered TIFF Files** to have an alert dialog box appear when a file is saved as a TIFF, giving you the option to proceed with the save or not.

Check **Enable Large Document Format (.psb)** to enable the Large Document Format option in the Save As dialog box.

Choose a **Maximize PSD and PSB File Compability** option (Never, Always, or Ask) to maximize file compatibility with previous

versions of Photoshop and other programs (e.g., to include a flattened vesion of the file so all programs can read it). We recommend choosing Ask to force an alert dialog box to open when you save a file, at which point you can check or ignore the option. Including a flattened version with a file produces a larger file size.

Version Cue

Check **Enable Version Cue Workgroup File Management** when you need to share and manage files among Adobe CS2 applications. When checked, you can click the Use Adobe Dialog button in the Open or Save dialog box in Photoshop to see a list of all the currently available CS and CS2 documents. See the Photoshop Help file for more information about this feature.

In the **Recent file list contains [ ] files** field, enter the maximum number of files that can be listed at a time on the File > Open Recent submenu (0–30).

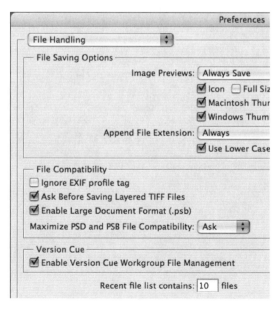

File Handling Preferences

Display & Cursors Preferences

Display

Check **Color Channels in Color** to have individual RGB or CMYK channels display in color on the Channels palette and in the document window. With this option off, channels will display as grayscale.

Check **Use Pixel Doubling** to have a low-resolution preview display onscreen temporarily when moving layer imagery.

Painting Cursors NEW

For the **Painting Cursors** (Spot Healing Brush, Healing Brush, Brush, Color Replacement, Clone Stamp, Pattern Stamp, History Brush, Art History Brush, Eraser, Background Eraser, Blur, Sharpen, Smudge, Dodge, Burn, and Sponge tools), click the type of cursor you want displayed onscreen as you use the tool: **Standard** for the tool

icon; **Precise** for a crosshair; **Normal Brush Tip** for a half-size circle; or **Full Size Brush Tip** for a circle the full size of the brush tip. For either of the latter two options, you can also check **Show Crosshair in Brush Tip** to have a crosshair appear within the circle.

Other Cursors

For the **Other Cursors** (all those not listed under "Painting Cursors," at left), click **Standard** to have the tool icon display onscreen as you use the tool, or click **Precise** to have a crosshair display onscreen instead.

TIP Press Caps Lock to turn nonprecise cursors into Precise cursors (crosshairs) or, if Precise is the current Preferences setting, to turn the cursor into a Full Size Brush Tip.

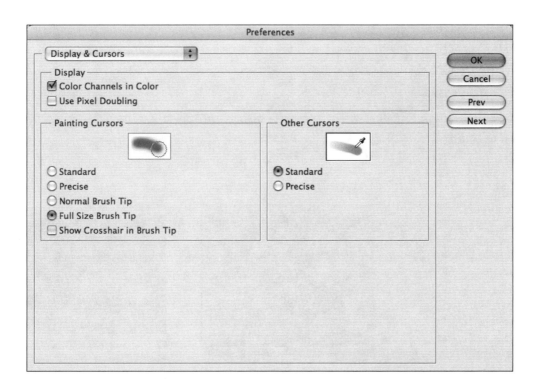

Transparency & Gamut Preferences

Transparency Settings

Photoshop uses a checkerboard grid to represent transparent areas on a layer. You can choose a different **Grid Size.**

Change the **Grid Colors** for the transparency checkerboard by choosing Light, Medium, Dark, Red, Orange, Green, Blue, or Purple. Or choose Custom, then choose a color from the Color Picker **1**.

Check **Use video alpha (requires hardware support)** if you use a 32-bit video card that allows chroma keying for video editing. This will let you preview transparency in the video image.

Gamut Warning

To change the color used to mark out-of-gamut colors in a document when View > **Gamut Warning** is on, click the **Color** square, then choose a color from the Color Picker. You can also lower the **Opacity** of the Gamut Warning color to make it easier to see image colors behind it.

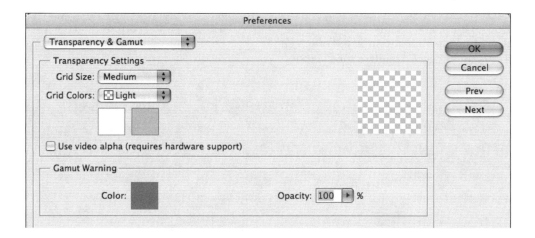

1 *Grid Size: Large; Grid Colors: Medium*

Units & Rulers Preferences

Units

Choose a unit of measure from the **Rulers** pop-up menu for the horizontal and vertical rulers that display in the document window. (Choose View > Rulers to show/hide the rulers.)

Choose a unit for **Type** (as shown on the Character and Control palettes).

Note: If you change the measurement units for the Info palette **1**, the ruler units will also change in this Preferences dialog box, and vice versa.

TIP To change ruler units quickly, right-click/Control-click either ruler in the document window and choose a unit from the context menu. Or to open the Preferences dialog box and get right to the Units & Rulers panel, double-click either ruler.

Column Size

Enter **Width** and **Gutter** values to allow the Image Size and Crop commands to fit images for a specific column width in a target layout program.

New Document Preset Resolutions

Values entered in the **Print Resolution** and **Screen Resolution** fields will display in the New dialog box when a preset print or screen size is chosen. The default settings are 300 ppi for print output and 72 ppi for onscreen display.

Point/Pica Size

Click **PostScript** (the default) to have Photoshop use the PostScript value for calculating the points-to-inch ratio, or click **Traditional** to use the ancient, pre-desktop publishing value.

1 *The Info palette*

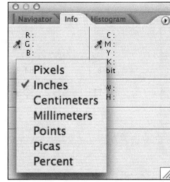

Unit symbols used in entry fields

Pixels	**px**
Inches	**in** or **"**
Centimeters	**cm**
Millimeters	**mm**
Points	**pt**
Picas	**p**
Percent	**%**

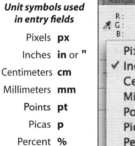

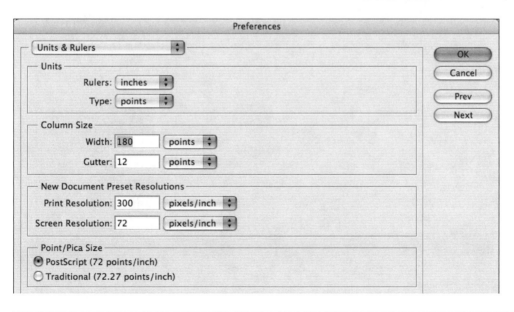

Guides, Grid & Slices Preferences

Note: Changes in this dialog box preview immediately in the document window.

Guides

Choose a **Color** for the removable ruler guides. Choose Lines or Dashed Lines for the guides **Style** **1**.

NEW Smart Guides

Choose a **Color** for smart guides, the temporary lines that display onscreen as you move layers or selections.

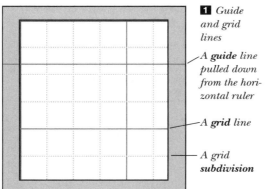

1 *Guide and grid lines*

—A ***guide*** *line pulled down from the horizontal ruler*

—A ***grid*** *line*

— A ***grid subdivision***

Grid

Choose a color for the nonprinting grid from the **Color** pop-up menu. For the grid **Style,** choose Lines, Dashed Lines, or Dots.

To have gridlines appear at specific unit-of-measure intervals, choose the desired unit from the pop-up menu, then enter a **Gridline every** value. If you choose "percent" from the drop-down menu, gridlines will appear at those percentage intervals of the overall document, starting from the left edge. For the thinner gridlines between the main gridlines, enter a **Subdivisions** value.

TIP For the Guides, Smart Guides, and Grid color, you can choose Custom from the pop-up menu, then choose a color from the Color Picker or Color Libraries dialog box.

Slices

Choose a **Line Color** for the lines that mark slices. Check **Show Slice Numbers** to have a slice number display in the upper left corner of every slice.

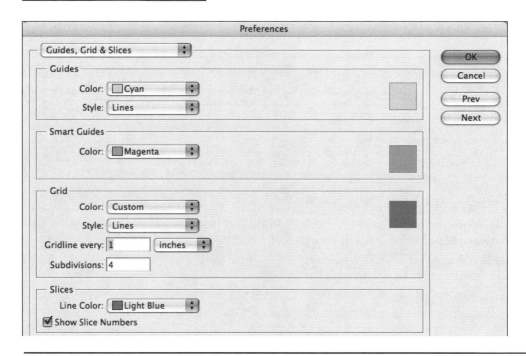

Guides, Grid & Slices Preferences

Plug-ins & Scratch Disks Preferences

Note: For changes made in this dialog box to take effect, you must relaunch Photoshop.

Plug-Ins

To make a plug-ins folder available to Photoshop, check **Additional Plug-Ins Folder,** locate the desired folder, then click Choose. Photoshop needs to know where to find this folder in order to access third-party plug-ins. *Note:* Don't move the Photoshop internal Plug-Ins module out of the Photoshop folder unless you have a specific reason for doing so. Moving it could inhibit access to filters, the Import, Export, and Effects commands, and some file formats under the save commands.

Some third-party plug-ins that are installed for earlier versions of Photoshop may require the pre-CS version serial number in order to run properly. Enter this number in the **Legacy Photoshop Serial Number** field.

Scratch Disks

The **First** (and optional Second, Third, or Fourth) scratch disk is used when available RAM is insufficient for processing or storing image data. Choose an available hard drive from the First pop-up menu. Startup is the default.

As an optional step, choose an alternative **Second, Third,** or **Fourth** hard drive to be used as extra work space when necessary. If you have only one hard drive, of course, you'll have only one scratch disk.

TIP If you hold down Ctrl-Alt/Cmd-Option when launching Photoshop, the Scratch Disk Preferences dialog box will open (this is a different dialog box from the Preferences dialog box shown below).

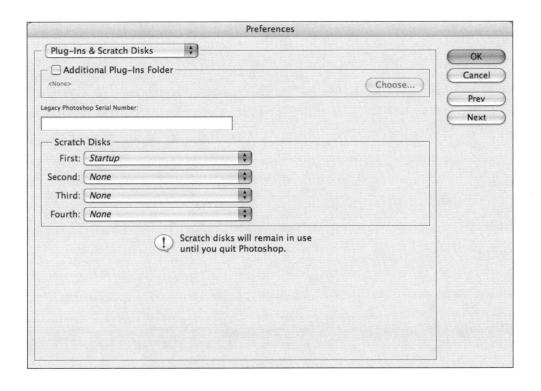

Plug-ins & Scratch Disks Preferences

Memory & Image Cache Preferences

Note: For changes made in this dialog box to take effect, you must relaunch Photoshop.

Cache Settings

The image cache is designed to help speed up screen redraw when you're editing high-resolution files. Low-resolution versions of the file are saved in individual cache buffers and are used for updating the document onscreen. The higher the **Cache Levels** value (1–8), the more buffers are used and the speedier the redraw but the more RAM is used. The Histogram palette also uses the current Cache Levels value to calculate pixel values based on cached data rather than actual data.

Memory Usage

In the **Maximum Used by Photoshop** field, specify the maximum percentage of your machine's RAM that Photoshop can use, or leave it at the default setting of 55%/70%.

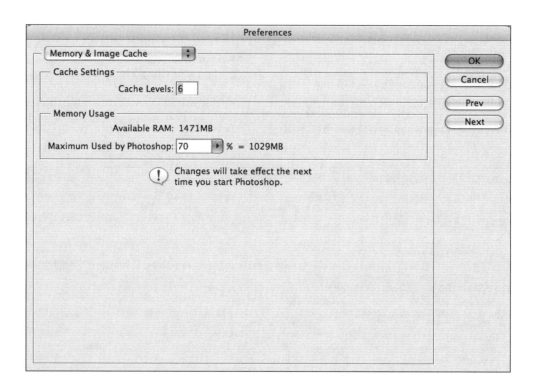

Type Preferences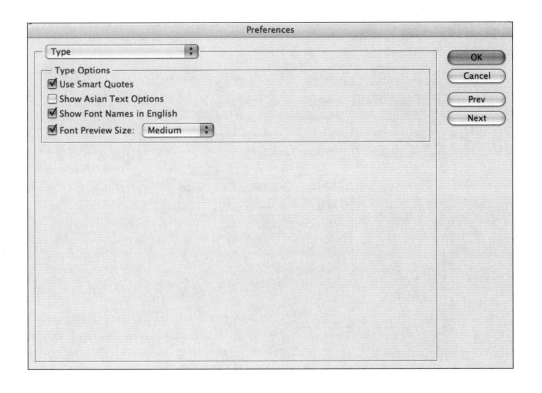

Type Options

Be sure to check **Use Smart Quotes** to have typographically correct curly quotation marks inserted automatically when text is created, instead of straight (foot and inch) marks.

Check **Show Asian Text Options** to display and choose options for Chinese, Japanese, and Korean type on the Character and Paragraph palettes.

Check **Show Font Names in English** to have non-Roman font names on the Font pop-up menus display in English.

Check **Font Preview Size,** then choose Small, Medium, or Large for the preview size on the font menu on the options bar and Character palette. We find the large previews to be helpful when choosing fonts.

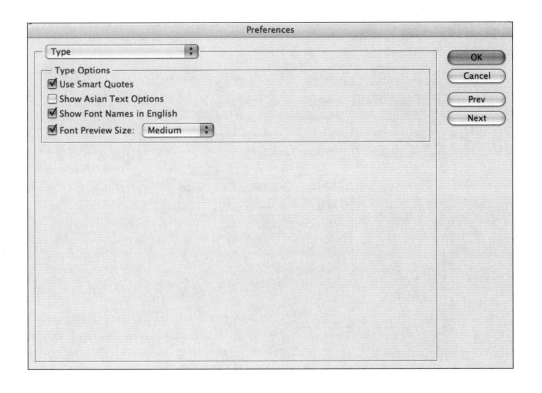

Bridge Preferences NEW

General Preferences

Thumbnails

Choose a value between Black and White for the **Background** area of the Browser panel.

Check **Show Tooltips** to allow tool tips to display for image thumbnails in the Browser panel.

For **Additional Lines of Thumbnail Metadata,** choose what file information you want listed below the image thumbnails.

Favorites Items

Check which items and folders you want listed in the **Favorites** panel.

Metadata Preferences

Check the metadata categories you want displayed in the Metadata panel.

Labels Preferences

Check whether to **Require the Command Key to Apply Labels and Ratings** to selected file thumbnails. You can also change the label names, but not the colors.

File Type Associations Preferences

These settings tell Bridge which application to use to open each file type. Don't change these unless you know what you're doing!

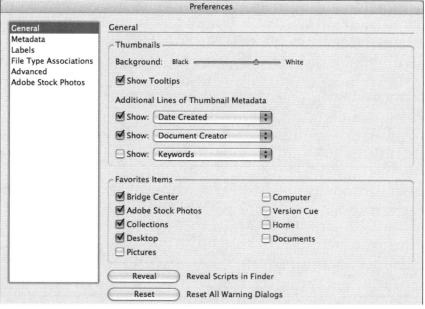

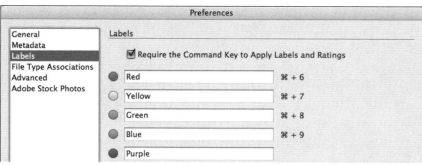

Advanced Preferences

Miscellaneous

For **Do Not Process Files Larger than,** enter the maximum file size (0–2047 MB; default is 200 MB) that you will permit Bridge to process. Large files process slowly.

For **Number of Recently Visited Folders to Display in the Look In Popup,** enter the maximum number of folders (0–30) that can be listed at a time on the Look In popup menu at the top of the Bridge window.

The **Double-click edits Camera Raw settings in Bridge** option controls whether the Camera Raw plug-in is opened via Bridge or via Photoshop. To learn the difference between the two pathways, see page 224.

Choose a **Language** for Bridge.

Cache

For **When Saving the Cache,** choose whether you want Photoshop to **Use a Centralized Cache File** or **Use Distributed Cache Files When Possible.**

We recommend leaving the **Centralized Cache Location** as is.

Adobe Stock Photos Preferences

Choose options for purchasing and downloading **Adobe Stock Photos.**

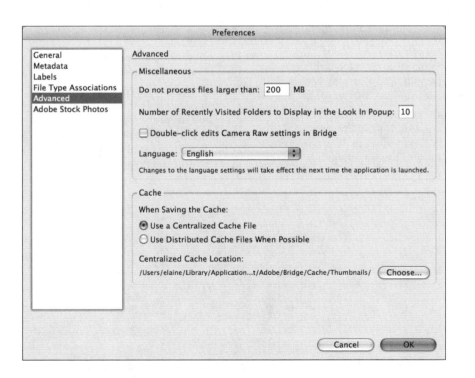

Bridge Preferences

Using the Preset Manager

No doubt you've already become acquainted with many of the preset pickers in Photoshop, such as the Brush and Gradient Preset pickers. The Swatches palette also functions as a preset picker. Each picker item is called a **preset,** and each collection of presets is called a **library.** You can use the **Preset Manager** to organize, append, replace, and reset which items are loaded onto each of the preset pickers at startup, or you can make those changes in any of the individual preset pickers. Changes made in an individual preset picker will be reflected in the Preset Manager, and vice versa.

To use the Preset Manager:

1. Choose Edit > **Preset Manager.**
   or
   With any palette or preset picker pop-up palette open (e.g., the Brush Preset picker or Gradient Preset picker), choose **Preset Manager** from the palette menu.

   The Preset Manager dialog box opens.

2. Choose a category of presets from the **Preset Type** pop-up menu (or use one of the shortcuts listed on the menu) **1**.

3. *Optional:* From the pop-up menu, ◉ choose a view option for the Preset Manager (e.g., Text Only, Small Thumbnail, Large Thumbnail, Small

List, or Large List). For Brushes, you can also choose Stroke Thumbnail to see a sample of the brush stroke alongside each brush thumbnail.

4. Do any of the following:

   From the bottom of the pop-up menu, ◉ choose a **library** name. Click Append to add that library to the current library, or click OK to replace the current library with the new one.

   Click **Load,** locate a library that's not already on the menu to append to the current presets, then click Load again.

   Click a preset you want to **delete** (or click, then Shift-click a series of them or Ctrl-click/Cmd-click nonconsecutive presets), then click Delete. The default presets can be deleted, and they can also be restored at any time (see the next page and page 465).

5. Click Done. The edited picker will update.

TIP Preset libraries can be shared among Photoshop users. Nice to know.

TIP Each preset library type has its own file extension and default folder, which is located in Adobe Photoshop CS2/ Presets. The default preset libraries aren't listed on any of the preset picker menus or on the Preset Manager menu.

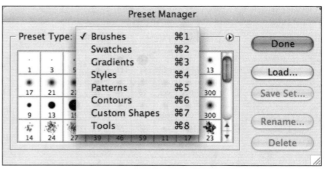

1 *Choose a category from the **Preset Type** pop-up menu in the **Preset Manager.***

Preset Manager

A preset by any other name

To rename a preset when the Preset Manager is in a Thumbnail view, double-click the **thumbnail,** then change the name in the dialog box that opens.

If the Preset Manager is in Text Only view or a List view, double-click the preset **name,** then change it right there.

You can also select multiple presets and then click **Rename.** In this case, the naming dialog boxes will open one by one in succession.

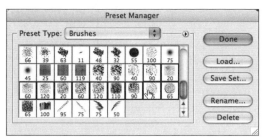

1 *Shift-click the presets you want saved in a* **set.**

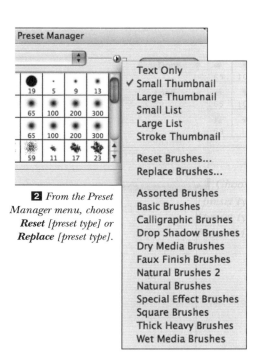

2 *From the Preset Manager menu, choose* **Reset** *[preset type] or* **Replace** *[preset type].*

Via the Preset Manager, you can save a selected group of presets into a **library** for quick access and safekeeping.

To save selected presets to a new library:

1. Choose Edit > **Preset Manager** or choose Preset Manager from any picker or palette menu.

2. From the **Preset Type** pop-up menu, choose the category of presets for which you want to create a set.

3. Shift-click or Ctrl-click/Cmd-click the presets that you want saved in a set **1**.

4. Click **Save Set,** leave the location as is (the default preset folder), then enter a name for the new library.

5. Click **Save,** then click Done to close the Preset Manager dialog box.

To reset or replace presets:

1. Choose Edit > **Preset Manager** or choose Preset Manager from any preset picker or palette menu.

2. From the **Preset Type** pop-up menu, choose the category of presets that you want to reset or replace.

3. *Optional:* Any unsaved presets on the list will be deleted, so we recommend saving the current library before proceeding (see the previous set of instructions).

4. From the **Preset Manager** menu **2**:

Choose **Reset** [preset type] to restore the default library for the chosen type, then click Append to append the default presets to the current library, or click OK to replace the current library with the default presets (click Cancel if you change your mind).
or
Choose **Replace** [preset type], locate the library that you want to replace the current library with, then click Load.

Managing presets via pickers/ palettes

A new preset will appear on the corresponding preset picker if you define a new pattern or custom shape via the Edit menu, add a new swatch to the Swatches palette, add a new style to the Styles palette, create a new gradient in the Gradient Editor dialog box, create a new contour in any Contour picker, or create a new brush or tool preset. It will also display when its Preset Type is chosen in the Preset Manager.

New presets are saved in the Adobe Photoshop Preferences file temporarily and will display in the appropriate preset picker even after you relaunch Photoshop—that is, provided you don't open another library in the same category (e.g., another brush library), or reset the individual preset picker, or reset the preset picker category via the Preset Manager. If you do any of the above, the new item will be discarded! Luckily, there's a way to preserve all your hard work.

The following method **saves all** the **presets** in the current picker without using the Preset Manager, whereas in the instructions on the previous page, using the Preset Manager, you could pick and choose.

To save the presets in the current picker to a new library:

1. Customize the individual presets you want to customize (as described in the first paragraph above), then from the menu on whichever preset palette or picker you're using, choose **Save** [preset type].

2. Enter a name, leave the default extension and location as is, then click **Save**.

   Note: In order for the newly created library to appear on the palette or preset picker menu and on the Preset Manager menu 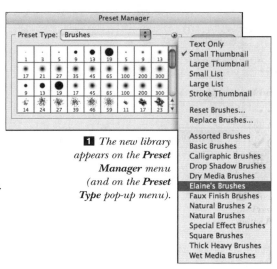, you have to relaunch Photoshop.

TIP To create tool presets, see page 466. To create document presets, see page 63.

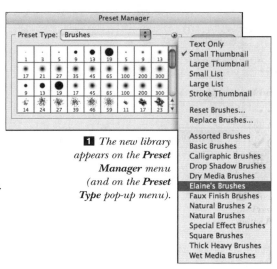

1 *The new library appears on the* **Preset Manager** *menu (and on the* **Preset Type** *pop-up menu).*

How are presets made?

A **new preset** is created when you:

Customize a **brush** via the Brushes palette or Brush Preset picker, then click the New Preset button ⬚ on the palette or picker.

Add a **swatch** to the Swatches palette.

Create a **gradient** by clicking New in the Gradient Editor.

Create a **style** by clicking the New Style button on the Styles palette or by clicking New Style in the Layer Style dialog box.

Create a **pattern** via Edit > Define Pattern or Filter > Pattern Maker.

Create a **contour** by choosing New Contour from the Contour preset picker in the Layer Style dialog box.

Create a **custom shape** via Edit > Define Custom Shape.

Create a **tool** preset (see the next page) by clicking the New Tool Preset button in the Tool Preset Picker or Tool Presets palette.

In addition to the default presets, Photoshop supplies specialty **preset libraries** that can be **loaded** onto the appropriate palette at any time. The libraries are listed on and accessed from the lower portion of the palette or picker menu when a tool that uses that palette or picker is selected (e.g., from the Brush Preset picker when the Blur or Dodge tool is selected).

To load a preset library:

1. From the bottom portion of the palette or the picker menu, choose a library name.

2. When the alert dialog box appears, click **Append** to add the additional presets to the palette/picker, or click **OK** to replace the current presets on the palette/picker with those in the library.

   Note: If changes were made to the current palette, another alert dialog box appears. Click **Save** to save your changes.

TIP If you need to access a library that isn't listed on the menu, choose Load [preset name] from the palette or picker menu, locate the desired library, then click Load.

The presets that are on a palette or picker when you exit/quit Photoshop will still be there when you relaunch the application. Follow these instructions when you need to restore the **default library.**

To restore default presets:

1. Choose **Reset** [preset name] from the palette or picker menu.

2. When the alert dialog box appears, click OK to **replace** the existing presets on the palette/picker with the default presets. See also the *Note* above.

Deleting a preset doesn't alter existing strokes in an image or delete anything from a library.

To delete a preset from a palette/picker:

On a preset picker or palette, Alt-click/ Option-click a **preset.**
or
Right-click/Control-click a preset and choose **Delete** [preset name]. If an alert dialog box appears, click OK.

Creating tool presets

If you're looking for a worthwhile method for streamlining your workflow, create **tool presets!** For any tool, you can choose a preset, customize the preset, choose options bar settings, and choose a Foreground color (if applicable), then save all those settings together as a tool preset. Thereafter, your saved tool preset can be chosen from the **Tool Preset picker** on the options bar or from the **Tool Presets palette** for that tool at any time. It's worth your while to create tool presets even for seemingly minor variations, as it saves time in the long run.

If you check **Current Tool Only** on the Tool Presets palette or on the Tool Preset picker, only those tool presets that were created for the currently chosen tool will display on the palette and picker. If you uncheck Current Tool Only, the tool presets for all tools will display; if you click a tool preset, the tool that uses that preset becomes selected.

To create a tool preset:

1. Choose and customize any tool (e.g., customize the Brush tool via the Brush Preset picker and/or options bar).

2. *Optional:* Choose a Foreground color to be saved with the preset, if applicable.

3. On the options bar, click the **Tool Preset picker** thumbnail or arrowhead **1**.
   or
   Click the **Tool Presets** tab in the palette well **2**.

4. Click the **New Tool Preset** button on the picker or palette. The New Tool Preset dialog box opens.

5. *Optional:* Change the tool preset name, if desired. Check Include Color, if available, to save the current Foreground color with the preset.

6. Click OK. The new tool preset will appear on, and can be chosen from, the Tool Preset picker and Tool Presets palette.

7. To preserve your tool presets for future use in any document, you should go the extra step and save them to a tool presets library by choosing **Save Tool Presets** from the picker or palette menu. Saved preset libraries can be **loaded** via the Tool Preset picker menu or the Tool Presets palette menu.

Brush: 27   Mode: Normal

Click to open the Tool Preset picker

1 *Click the thumbnail or arrowhead to open the* **Tool Preset** *picker.*

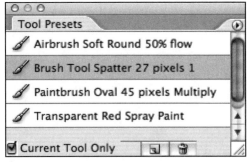

Tool Presets

Airbrush Soft Round 50% flow
Brush Tool Spatter 27 pixels 1
Paintbrush Oval 45 pixels Multiply
Transparent Red Spray Paint
Current Tool Only

2 *The* **Tool Presets** *palette has the same function as the Tool Preset picker.*

Create Tool Preset

PRINT **31**

So many options!?

Page Setup **Ctrl-Shift-P/Cmd-Shift-P**
Specify paper size

Print with Preview **Ctrl-Alt-P/Cmd-Option-P**
Choose scale, registration
marks, color profiles, etc., with
a preview

Print **Ctrl-P/Cmd-P**
Choose printer options and
send the image to be printed

Print One Copy **Ctrl-Alt-Shift-P/
Cmd-Option-Shift-P**
Print a single copy based on
current Print dialog box settings

Color Settings **Ctrl-Shift-K/Cmd-Shift-K**
Choose settings for the current
working space and for RGB-to-
CMYK conversion

1 *Press and hold on the **status bar** in the lower left corner of the application/document window to display a thumbnail **preview** of the image relative to the current **paper size.** Alt-press/Option-press and hold on the status bar to display file information.*

WHEN YOUR PHOTOSHOP IMAGE IS done, it can be output on a laser printer, color printer (e.g., inkjet, dye sublimation), or imagesetter. This chapter contains instructions for choosing print options in Photoshop, applying trapping, preparing a file for imagesetting, creating and printing spot color channels, producing duotones, and choosing color settings for offset printing.

(To export your file to other applications, see Chapter 32; to optimize a file for online viewing, see Chapter 33.)

Printing from Photoshop

Getting a good print of an image, especially a color image, is both an art and a science. It's not accomplished simply by twiddling Photoshop's dials and knobs. It requires a thorough understanding of the color management software that's built into your computer's operating system, as well as the settings available on your printing device. Here, we can provide only the basics for printing from Photoshop. You'll also need to refer to Photoshop Help, which contains a wealth of specialized technical information, as well as the documentation for your specific printer. If you're preparing images for an output service provider, be sure to consult the experts there about specific settings and formats before setting up your image for printing.

Print

The first step for any kind of print job is to tell Photoshop what type of **printer** and **paper size** you're using. Your printer drivers and operating system determine which print options are available.

To choose a paper size and orientation:

1. Choose File > **Page Setup** (Ctrl-Shift-P/ Cmd-Shift-P) **1**.

2. From the **Paper Size** pop-up menu, choose the paper size you want the file to print on.

3. *Windows:* From the **Source** pop-up menu, choose the tray that holds the paper you want to print on; and click the Printer button to choose printer-specific options.

4. *Mac:* From the **Format** for pop-up menu, choose the desired printer, then use the **Settings** menu to switch to other panels for printer-specific options.

Leave the Scale value at 100%. If you need to change the scale, it's better to do so in File > Print with Preview, where you can preview the results.

5. Click an **Orientation** button to have Photoshop print the image parallel to the length or width of the paper.

6. Click OK. Now you're ready to use one of the print commands.

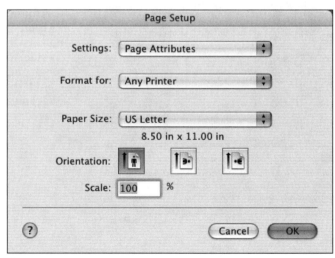

1 *The **Page Setup** dialog box in **Mac***

In Photoshop CS2, the simple **Print** command takes you directly to the Print dialog box that's specified in your printer driver, bypassing all Photoshop-specific options.

To print using the basic Print command:

1. Choose File > **Print** (Ctrl-P/Cmd-P). The default Print dialog box for your printer opens ◼.

2. If available, choose the number of copies to be printed.

3. Choose the printer-specific options that are appropriate for your document.

4. Click OK/Print.

TIP Only the currently visible layers and channels will print.

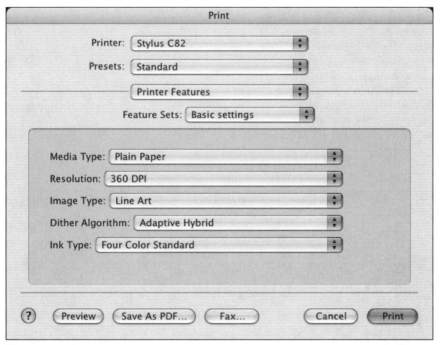

◼ *The* ***Print*** *dialog box for a* ***color,*** *non-PostScript, inkjet printer in* ***Mac***

Print Command

The **Print with Preview** command lets you
see a preview of the image on the printed
page, along with other options for adjusting
position, print size, color management, and
output settings. We prefer to use this command for printing.

To print using the Print with Preview command:

1. Choose File > **Print with Preview** (Ctrl-
Alt-P/Cmd-Option-P). The Print with
Preview dialog box opens ■. Study the
preview for a minute.

2. Check **Center Image** to position the
image in the center of the page, or
uncheck this option and enter new **Top**
and **Left** values to move the image on
the page.

3. Do any of the following optional steps to
scale the print size:

   Change the Scaled Print Size: **Scale** percentage or enter specific **Height** and
Width values in any of the available measurement units to reduce or enlarge the
image for printing purposes only. The
Scale, Height, and Width options are
interdependent; changing any one
option will cause the other two to change.
or

Print one

If you're in a hurry, and if you've already configured your print options to your liking, you can skip all print-related dialog boxes and print your file by choosing File > **Print One Copy** (Ctrl-Alt-Shift-P/ Cmd-Option-Shift-P).

To print an individual **layer** or **channel,** make it the sole visible layer or channel before choosing File > Print or File > Print with Preview.

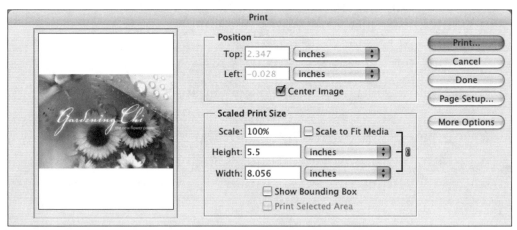

■ *The **Print (with Preview)** dialog box, showing a print preview of the file*

The hidden buttons

In the **Print with Preview** dialog box, pressing **Alt/Option** changes the functions of these buttons:

Print becomes **Print One.** One copy of the document will print immediately, without the printer's Print dialog box opening.

Done becomes **Remember.** Your custom settings will be saved for the current document, and the dialog box will stay open.

Cancel becomes **Reset.** All settings in the dialog box will be restored to their default values.

Resolution of output devices

PostScript b&w laser	600 *or* 1200 dpi
Color inkjet	2880 x 1440 dpi
IRIS	300 to 600 dpi (perceived resolution of 1500–2400 dpi)
Color laser	600 x 2400 dpi
Photo inkjet	4800 x 1200 *or* 4800 x 2400 dpi
Large format inkjet	600 x 1200 *or* 1440 x 2880 dpi
Imagesetter	1200–4000 dpi

Check **Scale to Fit Media** to have the image fit automatically to the paper size chosen in File > Page Setup.

Check **Show Bounding Box** to display the image boundary in the preview window. Pull a handle or side of the box to scale your image (for printing purposes only). If Center Image isn't checked, you can drag the whole bounding box to change the position of the image on the printed page. *Note:* Show Bounding Box won't print a border around an image; to print a border, see the next page.

If a rectangular selection is currently active in the image, check **Print Selected Area** to print only that selected portion (the selection won't preview).

4. Click **More Options** to display and **NEW** choose Color Management and Output settings (see the next page).

5. If you haven't yet chosen page setup settings, click **Page Setup.** When you're done, click OK in the Page Setup dialog box to get back to Print with Preview.

6. When you're done choosing the above-mentioned options, click **Print** to access your printer's Print dialog box (see page 469), then click **Print.**
or
Press Alt-click/Option-click and click **Print One.** One copy of the document will print immediately, without the printer's Print dialog box opening.

You can also click **Done** to close the dialog box without printing; your custom settings will be saved with the document. *Note:* If you click Cancel to close the dialog box, you'll lose all your custom settings—Ouch!

Print with Preview Command

To print using color management:

1. Choose File > **Print with Preview** (Ctrl-Alt-P/Cmd-Option-P).

2. Click **More Options** and choose **Color Management** from the pop-up menu (**1**, next page):

3. In the **Print** area, we recommend clicking **Document,** which uses the current document color profile listed next to the option (see page 50). **Proof** will convert the document profile to the proofing profile chosen via View > Proof Setup > Custom; choose this option when you need to print a **soft proof** of your image (see page 51).

4. From the **Color Handling** pop-up menu in the **Options** area, choose one of the following:

    Let Printer Determine Colors to let the chosen output printer device handle color conversion. All of the file's color information will be sent along with the document profile to the printer, and the printer, not Photoshop, will manage the color conversion. Make sure to turn on color management options in the printer driver.

    Let Photoshop Determine Colors to let Photoshop handle color conversion. This is our preferred choice. Use this option when you have a profile for a specific printer, ink, and paper combination. You also need to choose your printer profile from the Printer Profile pop-up menu. Make sure to turn off any color management options in the printer driver.

    Separations if your file is in CMYK mode and you want to print separations.

    No color management to prevent color values from being converted.

5. If you're letting your printer or Photoshop determine colors, choose an intent from the **Rendering Intent** pop-up menu to determine how the color conversion will render (see pages 48–49).

6. If you're letting Photoshop determine colors, check **Black Point Compensation** if you're printing the image in RGB mode, but consult with your print shop before checking it for a CMYK image that will be printed on a device that uses a non-CMYK profile. This option preserves shadow details by mapping the full dynamic range of the source profile to the full range of the output profile.

7. *Optional:* If you clicked Proof (in step 3), the current Proof Setup preset will be listed on the Proof Setup Preset pop-up menu. If you want to proof the file by using another Proof Setup preset, choose that preset from this menu.

8. Choose **Output** from the pop-up menu (**1**, page 474), then:

    To print a colored background around the image, click **Background,** then choose a color.

    To print a black border around the image, click **Border,** choose a measurement unit, then enter a Width (0–10 pt.).

    Click **Bleed** to specify a Width (distance) inward from the edge of the canvas area for the placement of crop marks (0–9.01 pt.).

    Click the **Screen** button to open the Halftone Screens dialog box, where you can change the halftone screen settings. Consult with your print shop before changing these settings.

    The **Transfer** option requires a knowledge of high-end printing. Again, consult with your press shop before changing these settings.

    Check any of the following options:

    Interpolation reduces jaggies when outputting to some PostScript Level 2 (or higher) printers.

    Calibration Bars creates a grayscale and/or color calibration strip outside the image area.

    (Instructions continue on page 474)

Desktop printers

When printing to a desktop printer, leave your image in **RGB** mode. Even though such printers print using CMYK inks (with some using six or more process ink colors), their drivers expect to receive RGB data and then perform the conversion to printer ink colors internally. Usually, the printer driver installation program installs a set of profiles for the printer to output on different kinds of paper.

When the time comes to print, choose File > **Print with Preview** (Ctrl-Alt-P/ Cmd-Option-P), click More Options, then choose Color Management from the pop-up menu. In the Options area, choose Color Handling: Let Photoshop Determine Colors, and choose an intent from the Rendering Intent pop-up menu.

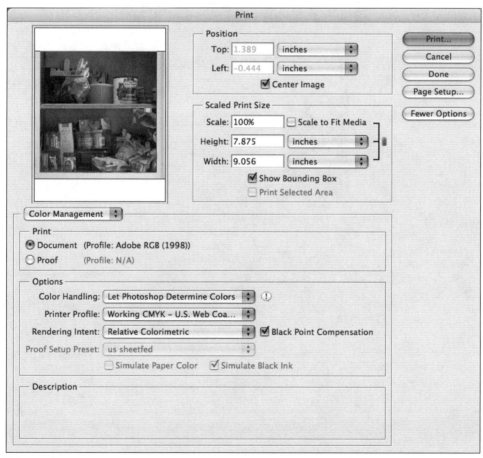

1 *The* **Print** *dialog box with* **More Options** *clicked and the* **Color Management** *panel showing*

Registration Marks creates marks that a print shop uses to align color separations.

Corner Crop Marks and **Center Crop Marks** create short little lines that a print shop uses to trim the final printed page.

Description (formerly called Caption) prints, outside the image area, whatever information is listed in the Description heading of File > File Info.

Labels prints the file name, document color mode, and current channel name on each page, outside the image area.

For film output, ask your print shop whether you should check **Emulsion Down** and/or **Negative.**

Check **Include Vector Data** to have the edges of any vector objects (e.g., type or shapes) print at the printer resolution, not at the document resolution.

Choose an **Encoding** method from the pop-up menu if you're using a PostScript printer. Binary is the default method. JPEG encoding (available only on PostScript Level 2 or higher printers) compresses image files and speeds up the transfer of data to the printer but results in a lower image quality. If you run into problems with your print spooler or printer driver, use ASCII85 encoding (a newer, more compact ASCII method). Both ASCII options double the size of print files, slowing down the printing process accordingly.

9. Click Print (**1**, next page).

Print Using Color Management

1 *The* ***Print*** *dialog box with* ***More Options*** *clicked and the* ***Output*** *panel showing*

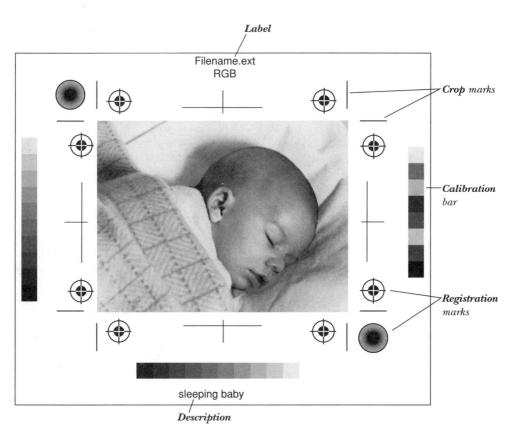

Label

Filename.ext
RGB

Crop *marks*

Calibration
bar

Registration
marks

sleeping baby

Description

1 *A printout showing various **Output** options*

Photoshop's **Trap** command slightly overlaps solid-color areas in an image to help compensate for gaps that may occur due to plate misregistration or paper shift. Trapping is necessary only when two distinct, adjacent color areas share less than two of the four process colors, and is unnecessary for photographs and other continuous-tone images.

Unlike applications that use both the spread and choke methods for trapping, Photoshop uses only the spread method. Photoshop's Trap command also flattens all layers.

Consult with your press shop before using this command. If you do decide to use it, apply it to a copy of your image, and store your original image without trap settings.

To apply trapping:

1. Open the image that you want to apply trapping to **1**, and make sure it's in CMYK Color mode.

2. Choose Image > **Trap.** If a prompt appears regarding flattening layers, click OK. The Trap dialog box opens.

3. Enter the **Width** (in Trap Units) that your press shop recommends **2**–**3**.

4. Click OK.

1 *Open the image to which you want to apply trapping.*

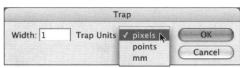

2 *Choose a **Trap Width.***

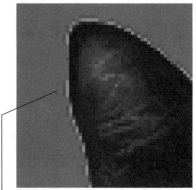

3 *This detail of the kitty's ear shows that the command added extra pixels along edges where trapping was needed.*

Printing Color Separations

Convert the image to CMYK Color mode, then choose File > **Print with Preview.** Click **More Options,** then choose Color Management from the pop-up menu. Under Print, click Document. The CMYK Working Space option you've chosen in the Color Settings dialog box should be listed. Under Options, choose Separations from the Color Handling pop-up menu, click Print, then click OK/Print.

Also, you can check any of the options in the **Output** panel of the Print with Preview dialog box, such as Calibration Bars, Registration Marks, Corner Crop Marks, Center Crop Marks, or Labels. Some of these options aren't available on non-PostScript printers.

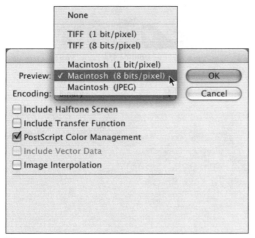

1 *Preview options in the **EPS Options** dialog box*

Preparing files for imagesetting

When printing to an **imagesetter,** convert your file to CMYK Color and follow the instructions on this page. (When printing to any other type of printer, leave your file in RGB Color and let Photoshop or the print device do the conversion.)

To prepare a file for an imagesetter:

1. Before printing your file, save it at the resolution that your output service provider says is appropriate for the color printer or imagesetter you're going to use.

2. Choose Image > Mode > CMYK Color, if the document isn't already in that mode.

3. Choose File > **Save As** (Ctrl-Shift-S/ Cmd-Option-S).

4. Check As a Copy, choose Format: Photoshop EPS, choose a location in which to save the file, then click Save. The EPS Options dialog box opens.

5. Choose a **Preview** option **1**, and choose **Encoding: Binary.**

6. If you changed the screen settings in the Halftone Screen dialog box (as per your output service provider's instructions, of course), check **Include Halftone Screen.**

7. Click OK.

Screens

For PostScript Level 2 (or higher) printers, in the Print with Preview dialog box, click Screen, uncheck Use Printer's Default Screens, and check Use Accurate Screens **2** (don't change the Ink angles). The Halftone Screen options will take effect if you print directly from Photoshop to a PostScript printer, or if you save the file in the Photoshop EPS or Photoshop DCS 2.0 format and print to a PostScript printer from another application.

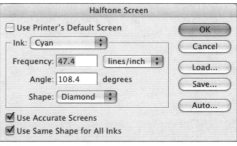

2 *The **Halftone Screen** dialog box*

Creating spot color channels

A spot color can be placed in its own separate channel. When the image is color-separated, the **spot color channel** will appear on its own plate.

To create a spot color channel:

1. Display the Channels palette, and drag it away from the Layers palette so you can see both palettes at once.

2. Choose **New Spot Channel** from the Channels palette menu.

3. Click the **Color** swatch **1**, and if necessary, click Color Libraries to open the Color Libraries dialog box.

4. Choose a PANTONE or other spot color matching system name from the **Book** pop-up menu, choose a color, then click OK.

5. *Optional:* To change the way color in the spot channel is simulated onscreen, change the Ink Characteristics: Solidity percentage. At 100%, it will display as a solid color; at a lower percentage, it will look more transparent.

6. Click OK. The new spot color channel will appear on the Channels palette, with the color you chose as its name **2**. Any brush strokes that are applied or imagery that's created while the spot color channel is active will appear in that color (see the following page). The spot color won't appear as a new layer on the Layers palette.

TIP To change the spot color in a channel, double-click the channel thumbnail, then follow steps 3–6, above. The channel will be renamed automatically for the new color.

Copy to a spot color channel

➤ To copy an **image shape** to a spot color channel, first make a selection on a layer. With the selection active, create a new spot color channel using the Channels palette, or choose an existing spot color channel and fill the selection with black.

➤ To copy an image's **light** and **dark values** to a spot color channel as shades of a spot color, create a selection, copy it to the Clipboard, create or choose a spot color channel, then paste onto that channel.

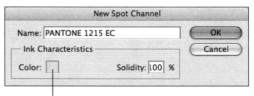

1 *Click the* **Color** *swatch in the* **New Spot Channel** *dialog box.*

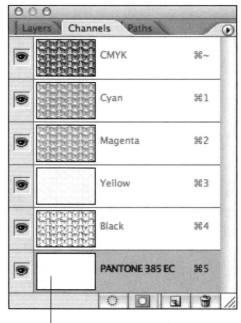

2 *The* **spot channel** *appears on the palette.*

Lighten/darken a spot channel tint

Click a spot channel on the Channels palette, then choose Image > Adjustments > **Levels.** To darken the tint, move the black Input slider to the right; to lighten the tint, move the black Output slider to the right. Position the pointer over the image so you can get an opacity readout on the Info palette (choose Actual Color mode for the readout). Readjust either slider, if needed.

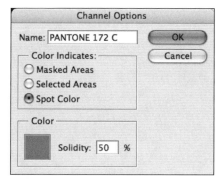

1 *Click Color Indicates: Spot Color in the* ***Channel Options*** *dialog box.*

To paint on a spot color channel:

1. Create a spot color channel (instructions are on the previous page).

2. Double-click the spot color channel, enter 90 as the **Solidity** value, then click OK.

3. Choose the **Brush** tool. (The Color palette will display in Grayscale mode while the spot color channel is active.) Choose black as the Foreground color.

4. On the options bar, choose Mode: Normal, and choose an Opacity percentage to be used as the tint percentage for the spot color ink on the spot color plate.

5. Make sure the spot color channel is still active, then paint on the image.

TIP The color that displays in a spot color channel merely simulates how that color will appear in print, so don't concern yourself with how it looks onscreen—just create and apply the colors where you want them to appear on the channel.

Another way to create a spot color channel is by converting an **alpha channel.**

To convert an alpha channel to a spot color channel:

1. Click an alpha channel on the Channels palette, then press Ctrl-I/Cmd-I to invert it.

2. Double-click the alpha channel thumbnail.

3. Choose Color Indicates: **Spot Color 1**.

4. Click the **Color** swatch. If the Color Libraries dialog box doesn't open, click Color Libraries. Choose a spot color, then click OK.

5. Click OK. Black or gray areas in the channel will now display in the chosen spot color.

Paint on Spot Color Channel; Convert Alpha

More about spot color channels

To display a spot color channel along with all the main image channels, make sure an **eye** icon is present for both the spot color channel and the topmost (composite) channel on the Channels palette. Or to display the spot color channel by itself, hide the composite channel by clicking its eye icon.

If you need to know the **opacity** percentage of a spot color area, click the spot color channel, choose Actual Color mode for the readout on the Info palette, move the pointer over the image, and then note the K value on the Info palette.

While a spot color channel is active on the Channels palette, only that spot channel can be edited—not any layers. To resume editing the most recently active layer, click the topmost (composite) channel.

To add **type** to a spot color channel, see page 410.

To **tint** an entire image with a spot color, convert the image to Duotone mode and specify the desired spot color as the mono-tone color (see pages 482–483). Then convert the duotone to Multichannel mode by choosing Image > Mode > Multichannel.

To **export** a document that contains spot color channels, save it in the DCS 2.0 format, making sure Spot Colors is checked in the Options panel. Each spot color channel will be preserved as a separate file, along with the composite DCS file. Let Photoshop assign the proper spot color channel name for you so other applications will recognize it as a spot color. The Photoshop PDF and TIFF formats also support spot colors, but DCS is the most reliable format for export-ing and printing spot colors. A PSD file con-taining spot channels that's placed directly into Adobe InDesign will color-separate correctly from that program.

Printing spot color channels

Spot color channel colors **overprint** all other image colors, and the stacking order of spot color channels on the Channels palette controls the order in which spot colors overprint each other. If you need to prevent a spot color from overprinting, you must manually knock out (delete) any areas from other channels that fall beneath these spot color shapes (read more about this in Photoshop Help). Talk with your print shop before doing so, though, to see if this step is necessary.

The **Merge Spot Channel** command on the Channels palette menu merges any spot colors into the existing color channels and flattens all layers, allowing a composite (single-page) proof to be printed on a color printer. If you don't merge spot channels, they'll print as separate pages. Merging a spot color channel into the other color channels changes the way colors look when printed, because CMYK inks can't exactly replicate spot color inks. When a spot color channel is merged into other color channels, its Solidity value determines the tint percentage of the merged spot color; the lower the Solidity, the more transparent the newly merged color.

TIP Use the Solidity option in the Spot Channel Options dialog box to produce an onscreen simulation of the ink opacity for the spot color plate. For an opaque ink, such as a metallic ink, use a Solidity value of 90%. For a transparent, clear varnish, use a Solidity value of 0%. This value doesn't affect output unless you merge the spot color channels.

Custom colors that are applied to image or shape layers will be converted to process colors on output. Only color areas on spot color channels will separate to spot color plates.

Print Spot Color Channels

Producing duotones

To give an image added depth and richness and extend its tonal range in the midtones or highlights, commercial printers can print a grayscale image with extra printing plates and ink colors. Via the **Duotone Options** dialog box in Photoshop, you can set up a duotone (two plates), tritone (three plates), or quadtone (four plates). This dialog box les you control not only the colors used, but also how those colors are distributed in the tonal ranges of the image.

To produce a duotone:

1. Choose Image > Mode > **Grayscale.** An image with medium to high contrast will work better than an image with low contrast.

2. Choose Image > Mode > **Duotone.** The Duotone Options dialog box opens **1**. Check Preview to see a live preview of your curve changes in the document window.

3. Choose Type: **Duotone.**

4. Leave the Ink 1 color as Black. Click the **Ink 2 color square.** The Color Libraries dialog box opens.

5. Ink 1 needs to be the darker of the two ink colors.

   To choose a matching system color, such as PANTONE color, choose from the **Book** pop-up menu, then type a color number or click a swatch. Subtle colors tend to look better in a duotone than bright ones.
   or
   To choose a process color, click **Picker,** then enter C, M, Y, and K percentages.

6. Click OK.

7. For a process color, enter a name next to the color square. For a custom color, leave the name as is.

8. Click the **Ink 2 curve.** The Duotone Curve dialog box opens.

It's not easy

Printing a **tritone** (three inks) or a **quadtone** (four inks) requires specifying the order in which the inks will print on press, so be sure to ask your commercial printer for advice. Only a press proof offers reliable feedback for duotone effects—they can't be proofed on a PostScript color printer.

If you're a novice at producing duotones, try using one of the duotone, tritone, or quadtone curve presets that Photoshop supplies. You can load them in to use as is or adapt them for your own needs. Go to Image > Mode > Duotone, click Load, click a preset in **Adobe Photoshop CS/Presets/Duotones,** then click Open.

*Click a **curve**   Click a **color square**
—to modify it.   to choose a color.*

1 *In the **Duotone Options** dialog box, choose Type: **Duotone,** then click the **Ink 2** color square.*

Nice curves!

When you reshape the duotone curve for an ink color, you're **redistributing** that color among an image's **highlights, midtones,** and **shadows.** Using the curve shape shown in the figure on the previous page, Ink 2 will tint the image's midtones. To produce a pleasing duotone, try to distribute Ink 1 and Ink 2 into different tonal ranges.

Here's an example. Use black as Ink 1 in the shadow areas, somewhat in the midtones, and a little bit in the highlights 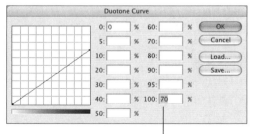. Then use an Ink 2 color in the remaining tonal ranges—more in the midtones and light areas than in the darks.

Image highlights   *Image midtones*   *Image shadows*

Highlights   *Shadows*

1 *A sample* ***duotone curve***

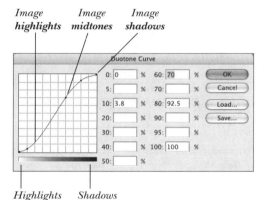

2 *This is the* ***Duotone Curve*** *dialog box for a monotone print. The 100% value has been lowered to the desired PANTONE tint percentage.*

Click to create data points, or drag existing points in the graph **1**. To produce a pleasing duotone, the Ink 1 curve should be different from the Ink 2 curve. Click OK.

Click the **Ink 1 curve,** then reshape the graph.

9. Click OK to close the dialog box, then save the file in the Photoshop EPS format (see pages 489–490).

TIP Click Save in the Duotone Options dialog box to save the current settings for use with other images.

TIP To reduce black ink in the highlights, for the black ink (Ink 1) curve, enter 0 in the 10% field. To reduce color in the shadows, for the color ink (Ink 2) curve, enter 85 in the 100% field.

TIP If you change the duotone Type and then decide you want to restore the last-used settings, hold down Alt/Option and click Reset.

Here's a low-budget—but effective—way to add a color tint to a grayscale print. It will print as a **monotone** (from one plate).

To print a grayscale image using a spot color tint:

1. Open a grayscale image.

2. Choose Image > Mode > **Duotone.**

3. Choose Type: **Monotone.**

4. Click the **Ink 1 color square,** click Custom, choose a spot (non-process) color, such as a PANTONE color, then click OK.

5. In the Duotone Options dialog box, click the **Ink 1 curve.**

6. In the 100% field, enter the desired tint percentage value **2**. Leave the 0% field at 0 and all the other fields blank, then click OK.

7. Click OK to close the dialog box, then use File > Save As to save the file in the Photoshop EPS format.

Preparing files for offset printing

A computer monitor displays additive colors by projecting red, green, and blue (RGB) light, whereas an offset press prints subtractive colors using CMYK and/or spot color inks. Obtaining good CMYK color reproduction from an offset press is an art. Before you create or start editing an image, you need to carefully calibrate your monitor so the onscreen image closely resembles what will come off the press (see pages 40–43).

When you're ready to have your file color separated, you need to change settings in the Color Settings dialog box in Photoshop to control the conversion of images from RGB to CMYK mode. You can either choose a predefined profile or create a custom preset or profile.

To choose a predefined CMYK profile:

1. Choose Edit (Photoshop, in Mac) > **Color Settings** (Ctrl-Shift-K/Cmd-Shift-K).

2. From the **Working Spaces: CMYK** pop-up menu, choose one of the predefined U.S. prepress profiles that matches your chosen press and paper type (that is, unless the file will be printed in Japan or Europe).

3. Click OK.

To create a custom CMYK preset or profile:

1. Choose Edit (Photoshop, in Mac) > **Color Settings** (Ctrl-Shift-K/Cmd-Shift-K).

2. In the Working Spaces area, from the CMYK pop-up menu, choose **Custom CMYK.** Enter a **Name** for the setting. The Custom CMYK dialog box opens **1**.

3. Ask your commercial printer which settings to choose or enter in the **Ink Options** and **Separation Options** areas, as these settings are particular to each press. In brief:

   The **Separation Type** tells Photoshop whether the press uses the GCR (gray component replacement) or UCR (undercolor removal) method.

What to ask your commercial printer

Asking your print shop the following questions will help you choose the right settings in the Custom CMYK dialog box:

What lines-per-inch setting is going to be used on the press for my job? Knowing this value will help you choose the appropriate scanning resolution.

What is the dot gain for my choice of paper stock on the press? Allowances for dot gain can be made by using the Custom CMYK dialog box.

Which printing method will be used on the press—UCR or GCR? GCR produces better color printing and is the default choice in the Custom CMYK dialog box. (UCR stands for undercolor removal; GCR stands for gray component replacement.)

What is the total ink limit and the black ink limit for the press? These values can also be adjusted in the Custom CMYK dialog box.

Note: Change the dot gain, GCR or UCR method, and ink limits before you convert your image from RGB Color mode to CMYK Color mode. If you change any of these values after the conversion, you must convert the image back to RGB, then reconvert it to CMYK.

In which file format should the file be saved? Save the image in the requested format.

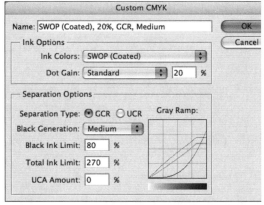

1 *In this screen shot of the **Custom CMYK** dialog box, the **Black Ink Limit** and the **Total Ink Limit** values have been changed as per a commercial printer's recommendation. The graph maps the current ink limits.*

Total readout

To display total ink coverage percentages on the Info palette for the pixels currently under the pointer, click the eyedropper on the palette and choose **Total Ink 1**. This readout is based on the current CMYK Separation Options settings.

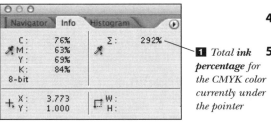

1 *Total ink percentage for the CMYK color currently under the pointer*

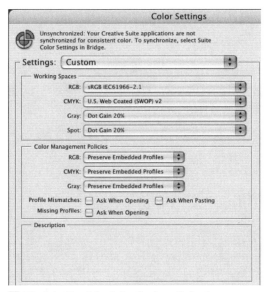

2 *The left side of the **Color Settings** dialog box*

The **Black Generation** amount controls how much black ink is substituted for a percentage of the CMY inks to prevent dark areas of the image from becoming muddy.

Ask your commercial printer about the **Total Ink Limit** setting, too. Each printer uses its own amount of ink coverage on individual separation plates; some use less than 100% coverage for each plate.

4. Click OK to return to the Color Settings dialog box.

5. By saving your custom CMYK and other choices as a profile or preset, you won't have to reenter them each time you need to convert files from RGB to CMYK.

To create a **profile,** in the Working Spaces area of the Color Settings dialog box, from the **CMYK** pop-up menu, choose **Save CMYK.** Leave the name, extension, and file location as is, then click Save. (When you're ready to output a file to that particular press situation, choose the profile from the lower part of the CMYK pop-up menu.)

or

To create a **preset,** choose other **Working Spaces** and **Color Management Policies** options **2**, click **Save,** name the file, leave the default location (the Settings folder) as is, then click **Save** again. In the **Description** area of the Color Settings Comment dialog box, enter a description of the settings, then click OK. When you're ready to output to that particular press situation, open the Color Settings dialog box and choose your preset from the Settings pop-up menu.

6. Click OK to exit the Color Settings dialog box. *Note:* These settings apply only when converting files from RGB to CMYK. If you subsequently readjust any settings in the Custom CMYK dialog box, you'll have to reconvert your image from RGB to CMYK again to apply the new settings. Moral: Always reserve a copy of your RGB image for possible reconversion!

CMYK Preset or Profile

The color correction workflow

As complex a process as color correction is beyond the scope of this QuickStart Guide. Just by way of introduction, these are the basic steps in the process:

➤ Calibrate your monitor.

➤ Open an image in Photoshop from a Photo CD, digital camera, or scanner.

➤ Use the printer profile (Color Settings) that best describes the press, ink, and paper type to be used. Photoshop will convert the color and tonal range of the image to the color space and gamut of that profile.

➤ Adjust the color to correct any undesirable color cast in the image. You can correct either the overall color balance or the neutral gray component of the image.

➤ Use a sharpen filter, such as Smart Sharpen or Unsharp Mask, to resharpen the image.

➤ Print a CMYK proof, and then analyze the proof with color-reading instruments to determine the exact color characteristics of the output.

➤ Readjust the Photoshop image, then print and analyze another proof.

If you're working with a CMYK scan, do all your correction in CMYK Color mode. For an image that's going to be color-separated, Adobe recommends editing in RGB Color mode and then converting the document to CMYK Color mode using the appropriate printer profile. To output to a desktop printer, though, keep the image mode as RGB Color.

Check your preferences

If you want to open a Photoshop (.psd) file in another application, find out if the target application requires File Compatibility: **Maximize PSD Compatibility** to be checked in Preferences > File Handling. This option saves a composite preview with the layered version for applications that don't support layers, and saves a rasterized copy of any vector art for those applications that don't support vector data. Checking this option will result in lengthier saving times and larger file sizes.

Some applications also require the Image Previews options to be checked. For Web output, however, uncheck **Image Previews** to save a few extra bytes of storage size and speed up the transfer time.

Keeping background transparency

To preserve transparency in a Photoshop image, before placing it into a drawing or page layout application, save it with a **vector mask** (see pages 378–379).

Photoshop to CorelDRAW 12

Save the file in the PSD (Photoshop) or PDF format, and in RGB Color or CMYK Color image mode, then place it into a CorelDRAW file. Alternatively, you could drag and drop a layer or copy and paste a layer or selection from Photoshop into a CorelDRAW window. Note, however, that all vector data, such as shapes and type, will be converted into bitmaps. CorelDRAW 12 can read a layered Photoshop image; each layer will become a separate object. You can also use the Export Paths to Illustrator command to export a Photoshop path to a file, and then open that file in CorelDRAW.

Once imported into CorelDRAW, a bitmap image can be moved around; you can perform some bitmap edits on it; you can apply filters to it; you can convert it to a different color mode or change its color depth; and you can resample it by changing its image size and/or resolution.

WHEN YOU'RE READY TO EXPORT your Photoshop image, you need to save it in the proper format for the program you're going to import it into, whether it's a drawing program, such as FreeHand or Illustrator; a layout program, such as QuarkXPress or Adobe InDesign; or a multimedia program, such as Adobe After Effects. This chapter contains general guidelines for preparing an image for other programs and specific instructions for saving files in the EPS, DCS, TIFF, and PDF formats. (To optimize a file for online viewing, see the next chapter.)

Preparing files for other applications

Photoshop to QuarkXPress

To color-separate a Photoshop image in QuarkXPress, you can convert it to CMYK Color mode before importing it into Quark-XPress; or you can let QuarkXPress read the embedded profiles and convert your RGB TIFF into a CMYK TIFF. Ask your output service provider which program to use for the conversion. QuarkXPress 6.5 (with the PSD Import XTension installed) can also import a PSD file and lets you make simple modifications to the layers, channels, and paths.

Photoshop to Adobe InDesign

InDesign can separate Photoshop PDFs (RGB or CMYK), and it can import PSD files directly. Layer comps can be viewed; alpha channels and layer masks are preserved. The program can also read any ICC profile that's embedded in a Photoshop file. InDesign, being part of the Creative Suite, also uses Bridge for file management.

Photoshop to Adobe Illustrator

Not surprisingly, Photoshop CS2 and Adobe Illustrator CS2 files are compatible in many

(Continued on the following page)

respects. For example, if you drag and drop a Photoshop selection or layer into Illustrator, the imagery will appear on the Layers palette in Illustrator as a group containing both a generic clipping path layer and an image layer. Custom opacity and blending mode settings are reset to 100% and Normal, respectively, and any layer or vector mask will be applied to its layer.

You can also use the Path Selection tool to drag and drop a selected path for a vector shape or a path for a vector mask from a Photoshop document window into an Illustrator window. Or you can select a path, then copy and paste it into an Illustrator file. In either case, the path will become an editable vector object in Illustrator, but with its fill and stroke colors removed.

If you copy and paste a layer from Photoshop into Illustrator, any layer masks and vector masks will be discarded.

You can place a whole Photoshop image into Illustrator, or just a single layer comp. **NEW** If you place a Photoshop image using the File > Place command in Illustrator with the Link option checked, the image will appear on the Layers palette on a single image layer, and any masks will be applied.

If you embed a Photoshop image as you place it into Illustrator (uncheck Link in the Place dialog box), or open it via File > Open in Illustrator, you can choose whether layers will be converted into objects or flattened into one layer. If you opt to convert Photoshop layers into objects, each layer will appear as an object on its own editable nested layer within a group, and the Background (if any) will also be a separate, opaque layer. All transparency values and blending modes will be preserved and will be listed as editable appearances in Illustrator.

Layer masks will become opacity masks, vector masks will become clipping paths, and shape layers will become editable vector objects. Any clipping paths that were saved to the Paths palette in the Photoshop file will remain in effect.

The presence of any adjustment layers or layer effects in a Photoshop image will prevent Photoshop layers from becoming individual layers in Illustrator. Merge any adjustment layers down and delete the layer effects before opening/placing the image in Illustrator, and use Illustrator effects to produce similar results.

If you opt to flatten Photoshop layers into one layer, all transparency, blending modes, and layer mask effects will be preserved visually, but they won't be editable in Illustrator. Any clipping paths from the Paths palette in the Photoshop file, on the other hand, will remain in effect.

The resolution of any Photoshop TIFF, EPS, or PSD image that's opened or placed in Illustrator will stay the same, but the Photoshop image will adopt the color mode of the Illustrator file. Illustrator raster filters, raster effects, and some vector effects can be applied to the imported image.

And finally, if you place a Photoshop file that contains slices into Illustrator CS2 with the Link option unchecked, a slice group will show up on the Layers palette in Illustrator.

Photoshop to Adobe After Effects

You can import a layered Photoshop image into Adobe After Effects 6 and later, and position it in the Time Layout window to create animated effects over time for video or QuickTime output. After Effects preserves image and adjustment layers, layer effects, layer masks, vector masks, blending modes, editable type, and alpha channels. A Photoshop clipping mask will import into After Effects as a composition, and as such, can be placed and manipulated as a unit.

Photoshop to Adobe GoLive

Layered Photoshop files are imported into GoLive as separate GoLive layers. A Photoshop image containing slices can be imported into GoLive using GoLive Smart Photoshop objects; the slices are automatically placed into a table.

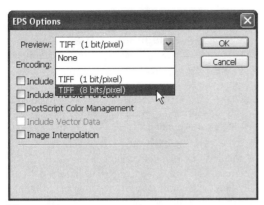

1 *In the **EPS Options** dialog box in Windows, choose a Preview option.*

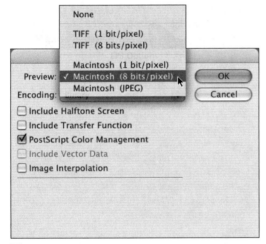

2 *In the **EPS Options** dialog box in Macintosh, choose a Preview option.*

Saving files in the EPS format

The **EPS** format is a good choice for importing Photoshop images into illustration or page layout programs that can't import PSD or PDF files. When you save a file in the EPS format, layers are flattened, and any alpha channels and spot channels are discarded. The EPS format is available for files in any color mode except Multichannel; and only for 8-bits/channel images. Printing an EPS file requires a PostScript or PostScript-emulation printer.

To save a file in the EPS format:

1. If the image is going to be color-separated by another application, choose Image > Mode > CMYK Color to view how the mode conversion will affect the image.

2. Choose File > **Save As** (Ctrl-Shift-S/Cmd-Shift-S). The Save As dialog box opens. Do the following:

Enter a **file name.**

Choose Format: **Photoshop EPS.**

Choose a **location** in which to save the file.

Optional: Check ICC Profile/Embed Color Profile to have Photoshop embed the document color profile or the current working color space. Check Use Proof Setup to include a soft proof with your file (an onscreen preview of how your image will look when output on a specific type of printer). For more about color management, see pages 44–52.

Click **Save.** Note that any layers will be flattened. The EPS Options dialog box opens **1**–**2**.

3. From the **Preview** pop-up menu, choose TIFF (1 bit/pixel) to save the file with a black-and-white preview, or TIFF (8 bits/pixel) to save the file with a grayscale or color preview. Mac users, choose one of the "Macintosh" previews only if you're sure you won't be opening the file on another platform.

(Continued on the following page)

4. On a Mac, choose **Encoding: Binary,** the default method used by PostScript printers. Binary-encoded files are smaller and process more quickly than ASCII files. In Windows, and for some applications, PostScript printers, or printing utilities that can't handle binary files, you'll have to choose **ASCII** or **ASCII85.** JPEG is the fastest encoding method, but it causes some data loss. A JPEG file can print only on a PostScript Level 2 or higher printer.

5. If you've changed the frequency, angle, or dot shape settings in the Halftone Screen dialog box, check **Include Halftone Screen.** (In case you're wondering, to get to the Halftone Screen dialog box, you choose File > Print with Preview, click More Options, choose Output from the pop-up menu, then click Screen.)

6. The **PostScript Color Management Option** converts the file's color data to the printer's color space. Don't choose this option if you're going to import the file into another color-managed application, as unpredictable color shifts may occur.

7. If your page contains vector elements, such as shapes or type, check **Include Vector Data.** Saved vector data in EPS files is available to other applications, but, as a warning will tell you when you reopen the file in Photoshop, the vector data will be rasterized.

8. Check **Image Interpolation** to enable other applications to resample image pixels in an effort to reduce jagged edges on low-resolution printouts.

9. Click OK.

Multichannel

You can save a **Multichannel** mode document in the Photoshop DCS 2.0 format as a single file or as multiple files, with or without grayscale or color composites. If you check the Spot Colors option, the DCS 2.0 format will preserve channels. A Multichannel image can't be saved as a Photoshop EPS for composite (single-page) printing.

When an RGB or CMYK image is converted to Multichannel mode, all layers are flattened, the channels are converted to cyan, magenta, and yellow (with no composite channel), and the black channel and any spot color channels (if present) are preserved.

Big squeeze

To reduce the storage size of an image, use a compression program such as **WinZip** or **PKZip** (Win)/ **Stuffit** (Mac). Mac OS X users can also Control-click a file name and choose **Create Archive from [file name]** to create a ZIP file. This kind of compression is non-lossy, meaning it doesn't cause data loss.

If you don't have compression software, choose File > Save As, and choose **TIFF** from the Format pop-up menu. If you want to save the file without alpha channels, also uncheck Alpha Channels. Click Save. Check the LZW or ZIP Compression option in the TIFF Options dialog box. *Note:* LZW and ZIP compression are non-lossy, but not all programs can import files in these formats, and some programs will import an LZW or ZIP TIFF only if it doesn't contain any alpha channels.

JPEG compresses files more compactly than LZW or ZIP TIFF but causes additional image data loss with each compression. The data loss may not be noticeable onscreen, but will be very noticeable in high-resolution print output, so this format is more suitable for Web output than for print output.

Saving files in the DCS format

The DCS (Desktop Color Separation) formats are relatives of the EPS format. The DCS 1.0 format preseparates the image and produces five related files, one for each CMYK channel and one for the combined, composite CMYK channel. The newer **DCS 2.0** format preserves color channels and any spot color channels, and also offers the option to save the combined channels into one file or as multiple files. A DCS file can be printed only on a PostScript printer.

To save a file in the DCS 2.0 format:

1. Choose Image > Mode > **CMYK Color** (to preview the mode change). Choose File > **Save As,** enter a name, choose Format: **Photoshop DCS 2.0,** then choose a location in which to save the file.

   Optional: Check Use Proof Setup or ICC Profile/Embed Color Profile (see step 2 on page 489).

2. Click Save. The DCS 2.0 Format dialog box opens **1**–**2**.

3. From the **Preview** pop-up menu, in Windows, choose any TIFF preview. In Mac, choose a 1 bit/pixel option (for a black-and-white preview) or choose an 8 bits/pixel option (for a grayscale or color preview).

4. Choose a **DCS** option: **Single File** (all the separations together in one file) or

Multiple File (one file for each separation), with **No Composite,** a **Grayscale Composite,** or a **Color Composite** preview.

5. Choose **Encoding: Binary, ASCII, ASCII85,** or a **JPEG** option (see page 490).

6. Leave both Include Halftone Screen and Include Transfer Function unchecked. Let your output service provider choose settings for these options.

7. Check **Include Vector Data** if the file contains vector graphics (e.g., type).

8. Check **Image Interpolation** to enable other applications to resample image pixels in an effort to reduce jagged edges on low-resolution printouts.

9. Click OK.

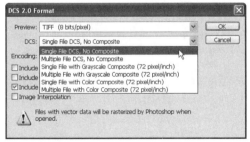

1 *Choose a **DCS** option in the **DCS 2.0 Format** dialog box (Windows).*

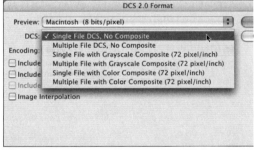

2 *Choose a **DCS** option in the **DCS 2.0 Format** dialog box (Mac).*

Saving files in the TIFF format

TIFF files can be imported by most applications, including QuarkXPress and Adobe InDesign. Color profiles are recognized by, and color management options are available for, this format. QuarkXPress and InDesign can color-separate CMYK TIFFs.

To save a file in the TIFF format:

1. Choose Image > Mode > **CMYK Color** (to preview the mode change), choose File > Save As, then enter a name. Choose Format: **TIFF,** and choose a location for the file.

2. You can check **Layers** to preserve any layers in your file, but note that few image or layout programs can work with a layered TIFF, and those that don't will flatten a TIFF upon import. You can also choose to save any spot color channels, alpha channels, or annotations.

3. *Optional:* Check ICC Profile/Embed Color Profile to include the currently embedded color profile with the file. For more about color management, see pages 44–52.

4. Click Save. The TIFF Options dialog box opens 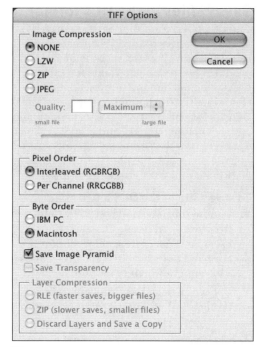.

5. Choose an **Image Compression** method to reduce the file's storage size. Some programs can't open a TIFF that's saved with JPEG or ZIP compression. LZW is a non-lossy method. For files that are going to be color-separated, output service providers recommend clicking None (no compression). For a layered TIFF, click a **Layer Compression** method at the bottom of the dialog box.

Leave the Pixel Order on the default setting of **Interleaved (RGBRGB).**

1 *The **TIFF Options** dialog box in **Macintosh***

6. For **Byte Order,** click IBM PC or Macintosh for the platform the file will be exported to.

7. Check **Save Image Pyramid** to create a file that contains multiple resolutions of the image. Photoshop doesn't currently offer options for opening image pyramids; Adobe InDesign does.

If your file contains transparency that you want to preserve, check **Save Transparency.** To access this option, the bottommost layer in the file must be a layer—not the Background.

8. Click OK.

Saving files in the PDF format

PDF (Portable Document Format) files can be opened in both Windows and Mac applications, and in Adobe Reader and Acrobat 6 (or later). This versatile format is a good choice for transferring files to other applications or platforms, as it preserves the image, font, and vector data from a Photoshop file. An image in any color mode except Multichannel can be saved as a PDF.

To save a file in the Adobe PDF format: NEW

1. Choose File > **Save As,** type a name in the File Name/Save As field, choose a location in which to save the file, choose Save as Type/Format: **Photoshop PDF,** then click Save. If an alert dialog box appears, click OK. The Save Adobe PDF Options dialog box opens **1**.

2. *Optional:* From the **Adobe PDF Preset** pop-up menu, choose one of these predefined settings, depending on how the file will be used (press, Internet, etc.):

High Quality Print (the default preset) creates PDF files for desktop printers and proofers. Files can be opened with Acrobat 5.0 and later.

PDFX1a and **PDFX3** create PDF files that will be checked for compliance with specific printing standards, thus helping to eliminate printing problems. The resulting file is Acrobat 4-compatible. However, editing capabilities for Photoshop data aren't preserved,

meaning that PDF/X files can't be reopened or reedited in Photoshop, and transparency isn't preserved.

Press Quality is for high-quality prepress output. The files are compatible with Adobe Acrobat 5 and later, all fonts are automatically embedded, compression is JPEG, the quality is Maximum, and custom color and high-end image options are preserved. To accommodate all this data, the resulting file size is large.

Smallest File Size creates compact PDF files for output to the Web, e-mail, or onscreen viewing; fonts aren't embedded.

Note: Information about the presets can be found in the Description window.

If you're satisfied with the preset you've chosen, click OK, or if you want to customize the preset, proceed with any or all of the remaining steps.

3. Choose a PDF/X standard from the **Standard** pop-up menu. See Photoshop Help or the Acrobat User Guide for more info.
or
Choose Standard: **None,** then choose from the **Compatibility** pop-up menu: Acrobat 4, Acrobat 5, Acrobat 6, or Acrobat 7. Acrobat 6 and 7 preserve layers. Acrobat 5, 6, and 7 preserve transparency. (Not all applications can read Acrobat 6 or 7 files yet.)

(Continued on the following page)

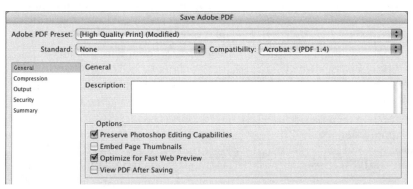

1 *In the **Save Adobe PDF** dialog box, choose settings from the first four panels listed on the left side.*

If you've changed any settings from the preset defaults, the Adobe PDF Preset pop-up menu will say "[Chosen Preset] (Modified)."

If you want to further alter the preset, click a category at the left of the dialog box to display that panel.

4. The **Compression** panel (**1**, next page) lets you control how imagery will be compressed in the PDF, which in turn will affect the overall file size. Downsampling an image performs the same function as checking Resize Image in the File > Image Size dialog box (see page 94); it reduces the total number of pixels in the image. For print output, you shouldn't downsample images; for online output, downsampling is recommended because it decreases the file size.

Choose an interpolation method from the pop-up menu:

Do Not Downsample keeps the image at the size it was created.

Average Downsampling To divides the image into sample areas, averages the pixels in each area, and substitutes the average values for the original values.

Subsampling To replaces a specified area with pixel data from the middle of that area, producing smaller but not necessarily accurate files.

Bicubic Downsampling To replaces the specified area with a weighted average, and often is more accurate than average downsampling.

If you choose an interpolation method, enter a resolution to downsample to, and a resolution threshold above which images will be downsampled.

Other options in the Compression panel:

The Compression pop-up menu lets you choose a type of compression: **None, ZIP, JPEG,** or **JPEG2000. ZIP** and **JPEG2000** can be lossy or lossless; **JPEG** is lossy. Options on the Image Quality pop-up menu depend on which compression type you choose. For JPEG200, you also

Create your own

Once you've chosen General and Compression settings, you can save them in your own user-created preset by clicking **Save Preset** at the bottom left of the Save Adobe PDF dialog box. The resulting file can be saved anywhere, but we suggest you choose the default location; it will have a ".joboptions" extension. Your newly saved settings will be listed on the Adobe PDF Preset pop-up menu and can be chosen as a preset when saving other files as PDF.

In the Edit > Adobe PDF Presets dialog box, your user-created preset will be listed on the Presets scroll list. To create a new preset, choose a preset, then click **New.** To edit a selected user-created preset, click **Edit.**

can choose a Tile Size. Finally, check Convert 16 Bit/Channel Image to 8 Bits/Channel if you want to make that conversion.

5. The **Output** panel (**2**, next page) lets you control color conversion and profile inclusion in the PDF file. The panel contains two areas:

The **Color** area is where you specify color conversions. From the Color Conversion pop-up menu, choose **No Conversion** or **Convert to Destination,** depending on whether you want Photoshop or the output device to convert colors to a destination profile. If you opt for conversion, choose a destination profile from the Destination pop-up menu. For no Conversion, include the destination profile by choosing it from the Profile Inclusion Policy pop-up menu.

The **PDF/X** options are available if you've chosen a PDF/X Standard:

Output Intent Profile Name lets you choose a profile to embed from the pop-up menu.

Output Condition lets you type your own Description, which is saved with the PDF.

Output Condition Identifier is a pointer to more information about that profile. **Registry Name** lists the Web site for

(Instructions continue on page 496)

Ready to convert?

Choices made in the **Output** panel of the **Save Adobe PDF** dialog box control whether the output device or Photoshop converts colors in the file.

➤ To have the **output device** (not Photoshop) convert colors to the profile you include in the PDF file, choose Output settings of Color Conversion: No Conversion, and Profile Inclusion Policy: Include Destination Profile.

➤ To have **Photoshop** convert the colors to the destination (output) profile and save the converted colors in the pdf file, choose Output settings of Color Conversion: Convert to Destination, Destination: [the profile for your output device], and Profile Inclusion Policy: Don't Include Profile.

➤ If you're in doubt, leave the **default** PDF presets settings as is. To learn about an option, rest the pointer on it and read the Description below.

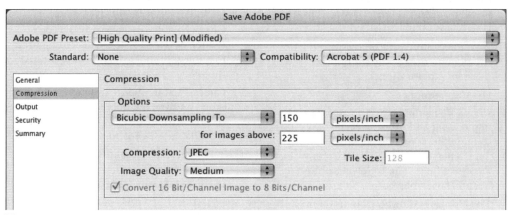

1 *The **Compression** panel of the **Save Adobe PDF** dialog box*

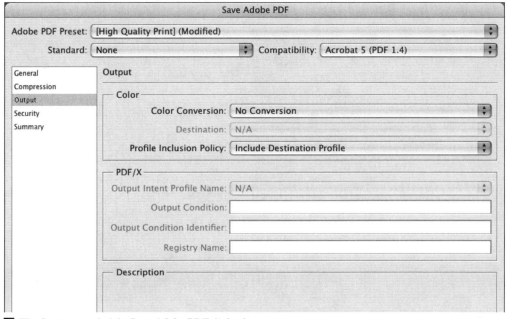

2 *The **Output** panel of the **Save Adobe PDF** dialog box*

Save File in PDF Format

more information about that registry. For some profiles, both of these will be filled in. If not, you can enter the information yourself.

6. The **Security** panel 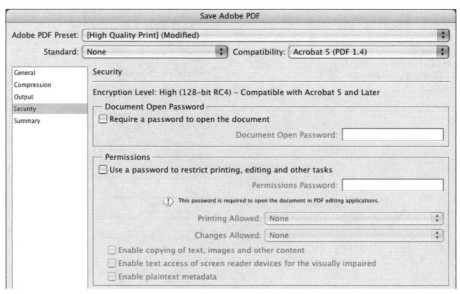 lets you restrict user access to the PDF. The following options are available to only non-PDF/X-compliant files:

For **Document Open Password:**

Check **Require a password to open the document** if you want the file to be password protected. Type a password in the Document Open Password field.

Note: Passwords can't be recovered from the document, so they should be saved in a separate location.

For **Permissions:**

Check **Use a password to restrict printing, editing and other tasks** if you want to maintain control over these options. Type a password in the Permissions Password field. The following options become available:

The **Printing Allowed** pop-up menu lets you restrict whether the user can print the file. Options are None, Low Resolution (150 dpi) and High

Resolution. (*Note:* Low Resolution isn't available for Acrobat 4 documents.)

The **Changes Allowed** pop-up menu lets you precisely specify what the user can and cannot alter. Options are None; Inserting, deleting, and rotating of pages; Filling in form fields, and signing; Commenting, filling in form fields, and signing; Any except extraction of pages.

Check **Enable copying of text, images and other content** if you want the user to be able to alter text or images.

Check **Enable text access of screen reader devices for the visually impaired** to allow screen readers to view and read the file.

7. Check **Enable plaintext metadata** if you want the file metadata to be searchable by other applications. (*Note:* This option is available only for Acrobat 6 and 7.)

The Summary panel lists the settings you've chosen for each category, for your perusing pleasure. Expand any category to view its settings.

8. Click OK, then reward yourself with a fattening snack.

1 *The Security panel of the Save Adobe PDF dialog box*

WEB/IMAGEREADY 33

*The Peachpit Press website: **www.peachpit.com***

Using ImageReady

When preparing graphics to be viewed online (as opposed to print), issues of file size and transmission of data come into play. The process of saving a file within format, storage size, and color parameters for online viewing is called **optimization.** The overall goal is to compress images enough that they download quickly on the Web while preserving image quality.

Although you can optimize your images using Photoshop's File > **Save for Web** command (a one-stop optimize dialog box), we like having the ability to choose optimization features via separate palettes, as in ImageReady. Among the palettes you can use in the latter program are **Color Table, Image Map, Optimize, Slice, Table,** and **Web Content.**

Before plunging into ImageReady, though, you need to familiarize yourself with the basic optimization choices, such as **file formats, image compression,** and **color depth**—all of which will affect how successfully your images download. After that, you can follow our step-by-step instructions for optimizing files.

ImageReady features

You can optimize a file in either Photoshop or ImageReady, but here's a list of other tasks that you can perform only in **ImageReady:**

➤ Create **rollovers**

➤ Create **image maps**

➤ Choose settings on the **Slice, Table,** and **Image Map** palettes

➤ Display slices and image maps via the **Web Content** palette

➤ Adjust the **gamma** of an image

➤ **Preview rollovers**

To switch from Photoshop to ImageReady:

You'll be jumping back and forth between ImageReady and Photoshop for the instructions in this chapter. If Photoshop is already launched, and you want to go to ImageReady (or go back to Photoshop from ImageReady), click the **Edit in** button at the bottom of the Toolbox **1** or press **Ctrl-Shift-M/Cmd-Shift-M**.

The Optimize palette in ImageReady is illustrated below, with two different file formats chosen **2**–**3**.

<aside>

Why not use Photoshop?

Most of ImageReady's file optimization features have counterparts in Photoshop's File > **Save for Web** dialog box (e.g., Original, Optimized, 2-Up, and 4-Up preview tabs at the top of the main window; a Color Table palette; and format, matte, quality, and other options). Photoshop also has a Preview menu and a Preview in [default browser] button. Once you learn how to use ImageReady, you can either stick with that program (as we do), or you can use the Save for Web dialog box, which is illustrated on page 544.

</aside>

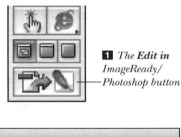

1 *The **Edit in** ImageReady/ Photoshop button*

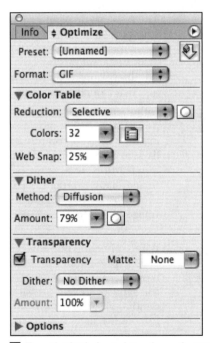

2 *From the **Optimize** palette, choose the GIF format for images that contain sharp-edged elements (e.g., flat-color shapes, line art, text). The PNG-8 format is similar to GIF and has the same Optimize palette options, except it doesn't have a "Lossy" option.*

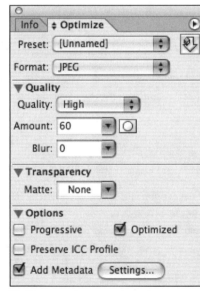

3 *The **JPEG** format is a good choice for continuous-tone, photographic images.*

Optimize Palette

Tip for Web output

➤ Let the content of the image—whether it be flat colors or continuous tones—determine which file **format** you choose.

➤ For flat-color images, choose colors using the Web color sliders and the **Web Safe** color ramp on the Color palette, and Web-shift any existing flat-color areas.

➤ When optimizing files in the GIF format, try to **reduce** the number of colors in the color table.

➤ View your Web image through a Web **browser** on computers other than your own, so you can see how quickly it actually downloads and how good (or bad) it looks.

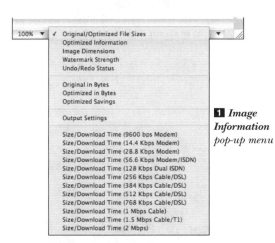

1 *Image Information pop-up menu*

2 *We chose **Original/Optimized File Sizes** from the **Image Information** pop-up menu on the right so we could view the size readouts for our optimized file.*

Making optimization choices

The basic formula for outputting an image for online viewing may seem straightforward: Design the image in Photoshop (RGB Color mode, of course), save it, click the **Edit in** button [icon] on the Toolbox, then optimize the file for Web output. But how do you know if you've been successful? If the image downloads quickly in the browser and looks okay, you've chosen the right optimization settings for it. If the image looks overly dithered (grainy), was subject to unexpected color substitutions, or takes too long to view on the Web page, it's not outputting well.

Next, we'll discuss issues you'll need to address when optimizing files: The image size, compression, file format (GIF, JPEG, or PNG), dithering, and anti-aliasing.

Image size

Your first task is to calculate the appropriate image size, and it's not hard to figure out. Normally, you'll be designing images for an 800 x 600-pixel viewing area, the most common browser window size, and for a 56 Kbps modem (although a majority of users now have faster broadband access). Your maximum image size will occupy only a portion of the browser window—about 10 inches wide (740 pixels) by 7.5 inches high (550 pixels). The image resolution need only be a mere 72 ppi.

To find out the optimized file size for an image, don't rely on the Document Sizes readout on the document window status bar in Photoshop. Instead, go to ImageReady, click the Optimized tab, make sure **Original/ Optimized File Sizes** is chosen from either of the two Image Information pop-up menus at the bottom of the document window **1**, and note the file size information **2**. Saving your file in the GIF, JPEG, or PNG file format will reduce its storage size significantly, as these formats have built-in compression schemes. We'll discuss them in depth shortly.

Compression

If you know the exact file size of a compressed image, you can calculate how long it will take to transmit over the Web. Even better, in ImageReady, choose a **Size/Download Time** from the Image Information pop-up menu at the bottom of the document window for various modem speeds, and look at the readouts . Just by way of example, a 70K file traveling on a 56 Kbps modem will take about 14 seconds to download.

Some images are more compressible than others. A document with a solid background color and a few solid-color shapes will compress a great deal, whereas a large document (say, over 100K) with many color areas, textures, or patterns won't compress nearly as much.

When saved in the GIF format, continuous-tone (photographic) images may compress less than flat-color images. If you reduce the color table of a continuous-tone image down to around 8 to 16 colors, the resulting GIF file size will be similar to that of a flat-color image, but you will have lost continuous color transitions in the bargain **2**–**3**. That leaves JPEG as the best format choice for continuous-tone images.

Both the GIF and JPEG formats cause a small reduction in image quality as they compress files, but the resulting smaller file sizes download more quickly on the Web, so it's worth it. They also offer a weighted optimization option, which helps finesse that trade-off by letting you selectively compress different areas of an image (see page 510).

To summarize, large images (say, 500 x 400 pixels or larger) should ideally contain only a handful of large, flat-color shapes, and images with intricate shapes and colors should be restricted in size to only a portion of the Web browser window. One more option worth considering is to divide your image into slices. Each slice can be optimized separately using different settings (more about that later!).

Browser window layer

Take a **screen shot** of your browser window, open the file in Photoshop, and paste it into a document as your bottommost layer. Now you can design your layout for the dimensions of that browser window.

1 *Choose a Size/Download Time option from either of the Image Information pop-up menus.*

2 *A continuous-tone image, saved as a 120K GIF...*

3 *...as compared with the same image saved with a reduced color table, which shrank the file size to 20K*

Compression

1 *GIF is a suitable optimization format for this image because it contains only a few flat colors.*

Color depth

Number of Colors	Bit Depth
256	8
128	7
64	6
32	5
16	4
8	3
4	2
2	1

GIF (pronounced "giff" or "jiff")

GIF is an 8-bit file format, meaning it can include up to 256 colors. It's appropriate for images that contain flat-color areas or shapes with well-defined edges (e.g., type) where color fidelity is important **1**. These types of images contain fewer colors to begin with than continuous-tone images, so a color restriction won't have a negative impact.

To save an image in the GIF format and to see how it will actually look when viewed via a browser, you can either use File > Save for Web in Photoshop or optimize and save it in ImageReady (see pages 506–507).

Your color choices for a GIF image should be based on the equipment your Web viewers are using. 8-bit monitors can display a maxiumum of 256 colors, whereas 16-bit monitors can display thousands. Colors that a monitor doesn't display are simulated by dithering (see page 503). To prevent unexpected dithering, you can use the Web Snap option in ImageReady to shift a portion of an image's colors to the Web-safe palette, or you can Web-shift flat-color areas manually.

By lowering the color depth of a GIF file in Photoshop or ImageReady, you reduce the number of colors it contains. The result is a smaller file size that downloads faster on the Web. Color reduction may produce dithered (grainy) edges and duller colors, but you'll achieve the desired reduction in file size.

You can reduce the number of colors in an 8-bit image from its original 256 colors by using the Save for Web dialog box in Photoshop or the Optimize palette in ImageReady. Both features provide options for previewing how your image will look with fewer available colors. To evaluate the color quality, preview your image at a zoom level of 100%.

JPEG (pronounced "jay-peg")

The JPEG format will do a better job of preserving color fidelity than GIF if your image is continuous-tone (contains gradations of color or is photographic) and will be viewed on 24-bit monitors, which can display millions of colors **1**–**3**. Another advantage of JPEG is its compression power: It can shrink an image significantly without lowering its quality.

The JPEG format does have some shortcomings. Unlike GIF files, JPEG files are decompressed as they're downloaded for viewing on a Web page, which takes time. Second, the JPEG compression methods tend to produce artifacts along well-defined edges of flat-color images and type, so it's not a good format choice for those types of images.

JPEG format files can also be optimized as **Progressive JPEG,** which displays in increasing detail as it downloads onto a Web page. Some older browsers don't support progressive JPEGs.

If you choose JPEG as your output format, you can experiment in ImageReady or in Photoshop's Save for Web dialog box by optimizing an image and then using the 4–Up option to preview versions of it in varying degrees of compression. Decide which degree of compression is acceptable by weighing the file size versus diminished image quality. In ImageReady or Photoshop, you can save the optimized file separately, leaving the original file intact for potential future revision.

Each time an image is optimized in the JPEG format, some image data is lost; the greater the compression, the greater the loss. To prevent data loss, edit and save your image in Photoshop, then optimize the file in the JPEG format. Don't panic—we'll break it down into steps for you later!

1 *JPEG is a suitable optimization choice for this **continuous-tone** image.*

2 *JPEG isn't a great choice for optimizing **sharp-edged** imagery. Note the artifacts around the type.*

3 *The sharp-edged type looks crisper in this **GIF**.*

1 *A closeup of an image with a **small** amount of* **dithering**

2 *Same image, a lotta **dithering***

PNG-8 and PNG-24 (pronounced "ping")
There are two PNG formats, PNG-8 and
PNG-24. PNG-24 can save semitransparent
pixels, such as soft, feathered edges. Each
pixel can have one of 256 levels of opacity,
ranging from totally transparent to totally
opaque. It allows for millions of colors in
the optimized image, and is similar to JPEG.
The PNG-8 format supports only one level of
transparency, can contain a maximum of
only 256 colors, and is more similar to GIF.
The compression method used by both PNG
formats is lossless, meaning it doesn't cause
data loss. PNG is supported by most major
Web browsers.

Any drawbacks to PNG? You can't save animations in the PNG format (whereas you
can in GIF), and PNG-24 produces larger file
sizes (compresses less) than JPEG.

Dithering

Dithering is the juxtaposition of two or
more palette colors to create the impression
of a third color. Images that contain a limited number of colors (256 or fewer) benefit
from dithering, which makes it appear as if
they contain a wider range of colors and
shades. This technique is usually applied to
continuous-tone images to increase their
tonal range, but unfortunately, it can also
make them look grainy **1**–**2**.

Continuous-tone imagery, because it contains a wide mixture of colors, looks okay
on both 8-bit and 24-bit displays. However,
if you reduce the number of colors on the
color table of a continuous-tone image, you'll
increase the likelihood of banding. Banding
can be prevented by applying dithering (we
recommend using a low value). You can
choose a dither method and amount on the
Optimize palette in ImageReady or in the
Save for Web dialog box in Photoshop.

Keep in mind that the higher the dither
value, the more seamless the color transitions, but the more grainy the image texture.
Also, dithering adds noise and additional
colors to a file, so compression is less effective with dithering on than with it off.

(Continued on the following page)

PNG-8, PNG-24 Formats; Dithering

Anti-aliasing

Anti-aliasing blends the edges of an object with its background by adding pixels with progressively less opacity along the edges. This feature helps to smooth the transitions between shapes when imagery is composited or montaged in Photoshop. With anti-aliasing off, the edges of an object will look sharp because edge pixels won't be blended with the background color.

One potential problem to bear in mind is that if you create a selection using a tool with anti-aliasing on, it may pick up a fringe, or halo, of pixels from the background of the image. If you copy and paste this type of shape onto a flat-color background, the fringe may become painfully visible **2**. To prevent this from happening, before creating your selection, uncheck Anti-aliased on the options bar for your marquee, lasso, or Magic Wand tool.

You can also use the Matte option on the Optimize palette in ImageReady to control how semitransparent pixels (the kind of pixels that anti-aliasing creates) are treated in GIFs and JPEGs. Both Photoshop and ImageReady also provide options for controlling the amount of anti-aliasing on type. These options can be chosen in, and will transfer correctly between, the two programs. The matting and anti-aliasing controls both help to eliminate halos.

Halos nobody wants

When copying an image to a Web page layout, to prevent halos, Ctrl-click/Cmd-click a layer name in Photoshop to select an object on its layer without its anti-aliased edge, then zoom in to a level of 200% or higher so you can see the object's edge clearly. Use Select > Modify > **Contract** to contract the selection by 1 or 2 pixels in order to remove the anti-aliased edge **1**, copy the selected object, then paste it into your Web page.

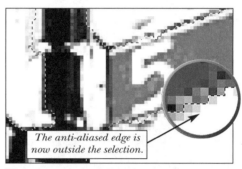

The anti-aliased edge is now outside the selection.

1 *After using the Magic Wand tool to select the white background around the signpost and then inverting the selection, some of the original anti-aliased edge remained. Select > Modify > **Contract** was then used to shrink the selection inward by 1 pixel.*

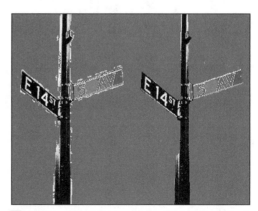

2 *These two signposts were pasted into a flat color in a Web page layout program. The one on the left was copied without contracting the selection in Photoshop, whereas the one on the right was copied after contracting the selection in Photoshop so as to remove its halo.*

The ImageReady toolbox

Now let's go to ImageReady. In Photoshop, click the **Edit in ImageReady** button at the bottom of the Toolbox, or press **Ctrl-Shift-M/ Cmd-Shift-M.**

The ImageReady toolbox **1** is similar to the toolbox in Photoshop, but it also contains Web-related tools for creating image maps, viewing image maps, viewing slices, previewing rollovers and animation effects, and switching to a Web browser.

Features on the options bar in ImageReady, like the options bar in Photoshop, change depending on which tool is selected **2**–**3**. You can drag the left edge of the bar to move it anywhere on the desktop.

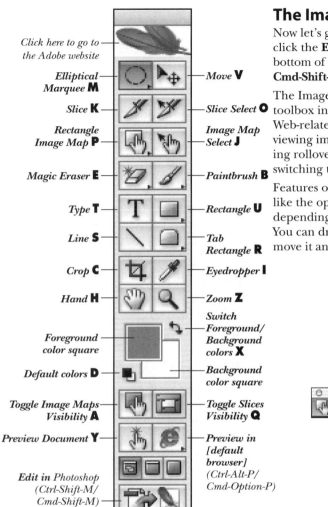

Click here to go to the Adobe website

Elliptical Marquee **M**

Slice **K**

Rectangle Image Map **P**

Magic Eraser **E**

Type **T**

Line **S**

Crop **C**

Hand **H**

Foreground color square

Default colors **D**

Toggle Image Maps Visibility **A**

Preview Document **Y**

Edit in Photoshop (Ctrl-Shift-M/ Cmd-Shift-M)

Move **V**

Slice Select **O**

Image Map Select **J**

Paintbrush **B**

Rectangle **U**

Tab Rectangle **R**

Eyedropper **I**

Zoom **Z**

Switch Foreground/ Background colors **X**

Background color square

Toggle Slices Visibility **Q**

Preview in [default browser] (Ctrl-Alt-P/ Cmd-Option-P)

1 *The ImageReady Toolbox*

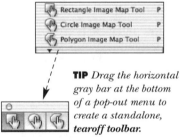

TIP *Drag the horizontal gray bar at the bottom of a pop-out menu to create a standalone, tearoff toolbar.*

2 *The options bar with the **Rectangle** tool chosen*

3 *The options bar with the **Type** tool chosen*

ImageReady Toolbox

Optimizing in the GIF or PNG-8 format

To optimize a file in the GIF or PNG-8 format:

1. If you're working in Photoshop, save your file, then click the **Edit in** button at the bottom of the Toolbox (Ctrl-Shift-M/Cmd-Shift-M). ImageReady will launch, if it isn't already open, and the image will open in that application.
or
In ImageReady, choose File > **Open,** locate an image, then click Open.

2. Click the **2-Up** tab at the top of the document window to display both the original and optimized previews of the image simultaneously 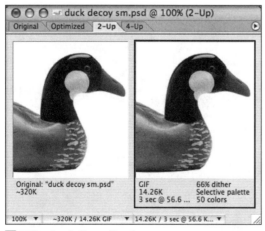.

3. Display the **Optimize** palette (Window > Optimize) 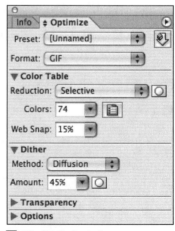.

4. Choose a named, preset combination of optimization settings from the **Settings** pop-up menu. Leave the preset as is, and save your file.
or
Follow the remaining steps to choose custom optimization settings.

5. From the **Format** pop-up menu, choose **GIF** or **PNG-8.**

6. From the **Reduction** pop-up menu in the **Color Table** panel, choose a color reduction method (see the sidebar).

Color reduction methods

Note: ImageReady's tool tip calls the Reduction pop-up menu "color reduction algorithm" (huh?).

Perceptual
Generates a color table based on the colors currently in the document, with a bias toward how people actually perceive colors.

Selective
Generates a color table based on the colors currently in the image, with a bias toward preserving flat colors, Web-safe colors, and overall color integrity.

Adaptive
Generates a color table based on the part of the color spectrum that represents most of the colors in the document. This choice produces a slightly larger optimized file.

TIP If you switch among the Perceptual, Selective, and Adaptive options, most of the Web-safe colors that are currently on the Color Table palette will be preserved.

Restrictive (Web)
Generates a color table by shifting image colors to colors that are available in the standard Web-safe palette. (The Web-safe palette contains only the 216 colors that the Windows and Mac OS browser palettes have in common.) This choice produces the least number of colors and the smallest file size but not necessarily the best image quality.

1 *2-Up view in* **ImageReady**

2 *The* **Optimize** *palette*

Optimize in GIF or PNG-8 Format

1 *The **Selective** palette produces **smoother** optimization.*

2 *The **Web** palette produces **dithered** optimization.*

3 *The **Selective** palette with a **high Dither** value*

4 *The **Web** palette with a **high Dither** value produces, as one would expect, a lot of **dithering**.*

Perceptual, Selective 1, and **Adaptive** render the optimized image using colors from the original image.

Restrictive (Web) shifts all the image colors to Web-safe colors **2**.

Custom optimizes image colors based on a palette you have previously saved in Photoshop or ImageReady.

Mac OS and **Windows** optimize image color based on the Standard palette for the respective operating system.

7. Choose the maximum number of **Colors** to be generated in the color table by choosing a standard setting from the pop-up menu or by entering an exact number in the field. Auto (available for the Restrictive [Web] reduction method only) sets the number of colors in the color table automatically to either the number of colors used in the image or to 216, whichever number is lower.

8. Choose or enter a **Web Snap** percentage to establish the range of colors that will automatically snap to their Web-safe equivalents. The higher the Web Snap, the fewer the colors in the image and the smaller the file size, but also the more dithered or posterized the image will become.

9. In the **Dither** panel, choose a dither method from the **Method** pop-up menu: No Dither, Diffusion, Pattern, or Noise. Dithering simulates image colors for 8-bit display (you won't be able to see this on the palette), and it increases the file size. Diffusion produces the most subtle results, with the least increase in file size.

   Also choose the **Amount** of dither **3–4**. A high dither amount will produce more color simulation and a larger file size. (To modify dithering via a channel, see page 510.)

10. In the Transparency panel, check **Transparency** to have ImageReady preserve any transparent pixels in the

(Continued on the following page)

Optimize in GIF or PNG-8 Format

image. Neither GIF nor PNG-8 allow for semitransparent pixels. The Transparency option allows for the creation of nonrectangular image borders. With Transparency unchecked, transparent pixels will be filled with the current Matte color.

11. To control how semitransparent pixels along the edge of an image blend with the background of a Web page (as on the edges of anti-aliased elements), choose a **Matte** option. Set the Matte color to the color of the Web page background (if you happen to know what that color is) **1**. Any soft-edged effect (such as a Drop Shadow) on top of transparent areas will fill with the current Matte color. If the backgound color is unknown, set Matte to None; this will create a hard, jagged edge **2**.

Another option is to choose **Matte: None** and then, in the Transparency panel, check Transparency and choose one of three options from the **Dither** pop-up menu **3**. These effects will look the same on any background. **Diffusion** applies a random pattern to semitransparent pixels and diffuses it across adjacent pixels. This is often the least noticeable of the three dither patterns, and the only one that lets you set the dithering amount. **Pattern** applies a halftone pattern to the semitransparent pixels. **Noise** applies a pattern similar to Diffusion, but it doesn't affect adjacent pixels. All three Dither options eliminate halo effects along the edge of an image when it's displayed on the Web.

12. In the **Options** panel, check **Interlaced** to have the GIF or PNG image display in successively greater detail as it downloads on the Web page. This option causes a slight increase in file size.

13. *Optional:* For a GIF only, you can adjust the **Lossy** value to further reduce the file size of the optimized image. As the name "Lossy" implies, some image

Fading away redux

Another way to fade your GIF or JPEG image into a flat-color background is by creating two layers in your Photoshop or ImageReady document: A lower layer filled with a **flat,** Web-safe color to be used as an area on the Web page, and a layer above it containing **imagery** with a soft edge or an effect such as Drop Shadow or Outer Glow.

1 *A GIF image with **Transparency** checked and **Matte** set to **a color,** resulting in a thin line of that color along the edge of each shape*

2 *A GIF image with **Transparency** checked and **Matte** set to **None**. There's a hard edge along each shape.*

3 *To apply transparency dithering, check **Transparency,** then choose from the **Transparency Dither** pop-up menu.*

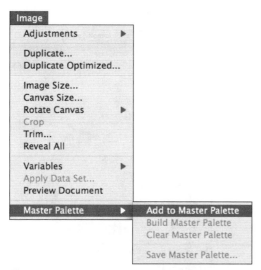

1 *Choose Image > Master Palette > **Add to Master Palette** to add the colors from the currently open document to a master palette.*

data will be discarded, but the slight reduction in image quality may be justified by the savings in file size. (To modify lossiness by using a channel, see the following page.)

14. Save the file (see pages 518–519).

TIP To save a current (Unnamed) set of palette options, choose Save Settings from the palette menu. Enter a name (in Windows, use the .irs extension), locate and open the Adobe Photoshop CS2 > Presets > Optimized Settings folder (the default location), then click Save. Your saved set will display on the Preset pop-up menu on the Optimize palette in ImageReady and in the Save for Web dialog box in Photoshop.

Creating a master palette

By creating and applying a **master palette,** you can ensure that every image in a series or group of optimized GIF files has an identical color palette.

To create a master palette for optimized images in ImageReady:

1. In ImageReady, choose Image > Master Palette > **Clear Master Palette,** if a master palette already exists.

2. Open an image whose colors you want to use in building a master palette.

3. Choose Image > Master Palette > **Add to Master Palette** **1**.

4. Repeat steps 2–3 to add the colors of the other images to the master palette.

5. Once you've added colors from all the desired images, choose Image > Master Palette > **Build Master Palette.**

6. Finally, choose Image > Master Palette > **Save Master Palette.**

7. Type a name for the palette (in Windows, use the .act extension), then click Save. The palette can now be applied to other images (see the next page).

Master Palette

To apply a master palette to an image:

1. Open an image within ImageReady.

2. For the GIF or PNG-8 format, from the **Reduction** pop-up menu in the Color Table panel on the Optimize palette, choose the master palette you've saved.

Using weighted optimization

Using a technique called **weighted optimization,** you can apply different optimization settings to different areas of an image. First, you'll create an alpha channel, then you'll apply maximum-quality optimization settings to pixels that fall within the channel's white areas and minimum-quality settings to pixels that fall within the black areas. You can choose limits for color reduction, dithering, lossiness, and overall quality.

To use weighted optimization:

1. Create an alpha channel mask by selecting an area in the image and choosing Select > **Save Selection.**

2. Leave the Channel pop-up menu choice as New, enter a name in the Name field, then click OK.

3. On the Optimize palette, click a channel button **1** next to the **Reduction** pop-up menu, or next to the **Lossy** field for a GIF, the **Amount** field for a GIF or PNG, or the **Quality** field for a JPEG. A Modify… Settings dialog box opens.

4. Text and vector shapes automatically have masks. Check **Use: All Text Layers** and/or **All Vector Shape Layers 2** to use those masks to control where optimization settings are applied. For all other areas, choose your new channel mask from the **Channel** pop-up menu.

If available, you can move the white slider to control the level of optimization to be applied to white areas of a mask, and the black slider to control optimization for the black areas of a mask.

5. Click OK.

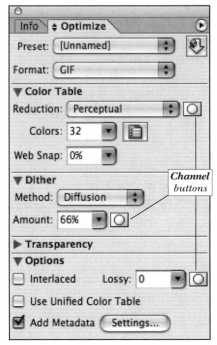

Channel buttons

1 *The **Channel** buttons for a GIF*

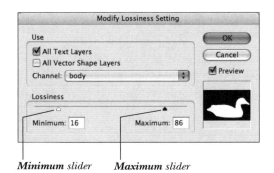

Minimum slider   *Maximum slider*

2 *Use a text or vector shape mask or an alpha channel to control where optimization is applied.*

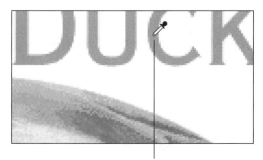

1 *Click a flat-color area with the Eyedropper tool.*

A diamond with a diagonal line signifies that the swatch was made Web-safe via the Shift Selected Colors to Web Palette button. *A small square signifies that a swatch is locked.*

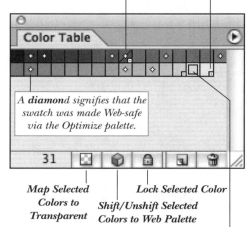

A diamond signifies that the swatch was made Web-safe via the Optimize palette.

Map Selected Colors to Transparent   Lock Selected Color

Shift/Unshift Selected Colors to Web Palette

2 *The color you click will become the highlighted swatch on the Color Table palette in ImageReady.*

Making flat colors Web-safe

Let's say you've got an image that you're going to optimize in the GIF format by using the Perceptual, Selective, or Adaptive palette, but it contains flat-color areas that aren't **Web-safe.** Before outputting it online, you can make the flat-color areas Web-safe.

To make flat-color areas Web-safe:

1. Open the image in ImageReady and optimize it in the GIF format.

2. Choose the **Eyedropper** tool (I).

3. Click a flat-color area **1**.

4. On the Optimize palette, click the **Show Color Table Palette** button 🗒 to open the Color Table palette. The color you just clicked will be the highlighted swatch **2**.

5. Click the **Shift Selected Colors to Web Palette** button 🔲 at the bottom of the palette. A diamond with a diagonal line will appear on the selected swatch, signifying that the color was shifted to its Web-safe equivalent. The swatch will also become locked (see the next step).

6. *Optional:* To lock any unlocked color to ensure that it will be preserved even if the number of colors in the GIF palette is subsequently reduced, click the swatch, then click the **Lock Selected Color** button 🔒 on the palette.

TIP Shift-click with the Eyedropper tool on other areas in the image to select more than one color, then shift all the selected colors to the Web palette at once. Or use the Magic Wand tool or a lasso or marquee tool to create a selection or selections in the image, choose Select All From Selection on the Color Table palette menu, then click the Shift Selected Colors to Web Palette button 🔲 at the bottom of the Color Table palette.

TIP To assign transparency to a color in the Color Table, click the swatch, then click the Map Selected Colors to Transparent button. 🔲 To unassign a selected swatch, click the button again.

Optimizing in the JPEG format

JPEG is the format of choice for optimizing continuous-tone imagery (photographs, paintings, gradients, or blends). If you optimize to this format, the file's 24-bit color depth will be preserved, and its colors will be seen and enjoyed by any viewer whose display is set to thousands or millions of colors. Two drawbacks to JPEG are that its compression method eliminates image data, and that it doesn't preserve transparency.

(To learn about optimization options for the PNG-24 format, see Photoshop Help. PNG-24 produces larger file sizes than JPEG.)

To optimize an image in the JPEG format:

1. If you're working in Photoshop, save your file, then click the **Edit in** button 🖼️ at the bottom of the Toolbox. ImageReady will launch, if it isn't already open.
   or
   In ImageReady, choose File > **Open,** locate the image, then click Open.

2. Click the **2-Up** tab at the top of the document window to display the original and optimized previews of the image simultaneously.

3. Display the **Optimize** palette (Window > Optimize) **1**.

4. From the **Preset** pop-up menu, choose **JPEG High 2**, **JPEG Low,** or **JPEG Medium.** Leave this preset setting as is, then save your file.
   or
   Follow the remaining steps to choose custom settings.

5. From the **Quality** pop-up menu in the Quality panel, choose **Low, Medium, High,** or **Maximum** as the resulting quality level for the optimized image (**1–2**, next page).
   or
   Move the **Amount** pop-up slider to an exact level of compression. Watch the adjacent Quality pop-up menu setting change as you change the Amount value.

JPEGs and Web-safe colors

Although **JPEG** compression adds compression artifacts to an image and renders Web-safe colors un-Web-safe, it's usually the format of choice for optimizing **continuous-tone** images in which browser dither isn't objectionable. Don't try to match a color area in a JPEG file to a color area in a GIF file or to the background of a Web page, though, because JPEG compression will cause the color to shift.

1 *The **Optimize** palette in ImageReady, with **JPEG** chosen as the **Format***

2 *A **JPEG** optimized with **High** Quality*

Optimize in JPEG Format

Check your profiles

An embedded **ICC profile** will slightly increase a file's size. As of this writing, Safari and Internet Explorer for Mac support profiles. On the Mac, **ColorSync** makes sure the browser and the operating system know the viewer's display profile; this helps to ensure consistent color between the display and JPEG files. An alternative is to convert the image to the **sRGB** profile, the color space most browsers expect the image to be in (see pages 44–45).

1 *A JPEG optimized with* **Medium** *Quality*

2 *A JPEG optimized with* **Low** *Quality. Note how pixelated the image has become.*

(To vary the compression by using an alpha channel, see page 510.)

Always remember, the lower the compression, the higher the image quality —and the larger the file size.

6. Increase the **Blur** value to lessen the visibility of JPEG artifacts that arise from the JPEG compression method and reduce the file size. Be careful not to overblur the image, though, or the details will soften too much. The Blur setting can be lowered later to reclaim some of the diminished sharpness.

7. In the Transparency panel, choose a **Matte** color to be substituted for areas of transparency in the original image. If you choose None, transparent areas will appear as white.

   Note: The JPEG format doesn't support transparency. To have the Matte color simulate transparency, make it the same solid color as the background of the Web page (if that color is known).

8. In the Options panel, check **Progressive** to have the optimized image render on the Web page in successively greater detail.

9. *Optional:* Check Preserve ICC Profile to embed an ICC Profile in the optimized image. To utilize this option, the original image must have had a profile embedded into it in Photoshop. See the sidebar on this page.

10. *Optional:* Check Optimized to produce the smallest file size. Check Add Metadata if you imported the file from a digital camera and want camera settings, caption, and keyword information to be saved with the file.

11. Save the file (see pages 518–519).

TIP To save the current settings as a named preset, see page 509.

Quick optimization

Why not let ImageReady make all the decisions **for you?** All you need to decide is how large you want the optimized image to be.

To quick-optimize:

1. *Optional:* Click a slice (see pages 521–525) to optimize just that area of the image.

2. Choose **Optimize to File Size** from the Optimize palette menu.

3. Enter the **Desired File Size** for the final optimized file **1**.

4. Click Start With: **Current Settings** to use the current settings on the palette.
   or
   Click **Auto Select GIF/JPEG** to let ImageReady pick the optimize method.

5. Click Use: **Current Slice,** or click **Each Slice** or **Total of All Slices,** if available.

6. Click OK. Presto—ImageReady will choose all the Optimize palette settings for you and generate an optimized file based on your desired file size.

Creating droplets

A **droplet** is a tiny but powerful application that remembers the Optimize palette settings that are in effect when it's created. When you drag a file over a droplet, Image-Ready launches automatically and optimizes the file based on the instructions contained in the droplet.

To create and apply a droplet:

1. Choose Optimize palette settings.

2. **Click** the **Droplet** button on the Optimize palette **2**, choose a location in which to save it, then click Save.
   or
   Drag the **Droplet** button from the Optimize palette to the Desktop.

3. To optimize a file or a whole folder of files using the droplet and its settings, drag the file or folder icon over the droplet icon on the Desktop **3**–**4**. An optimized version of the file(s) will be saved in the same location as the originals.

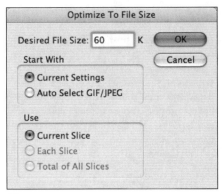

1 *Using the* **Optimize To File Size** *dialog box, you can let ImageReady make optimization calculations for you.*

2 *To create a droplet, click the* **Droplet** *button on the* **Optimize** *palette or drag it to the Desktop.*

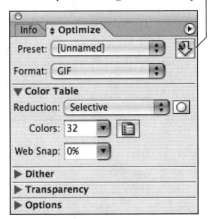

3 *A* **droplet** *icon on a Windows Desktop*

Make PNG-8.exe

4 *A* **droplet** *icon on a Mac Desktop*

Make JPEG (quality60)

Revert is a state

The **Revert** command records as a **state** on the History palette in Photoshop and ImageReady, and won't wipe out any existing states. This means you can undo a Revert.

Calling all auto-updates!

Whether **Auto-update open documents** in Preferences > General is checked or unchecked in ImageReady or Photoshop, files update automatically when you switch between the two programs.

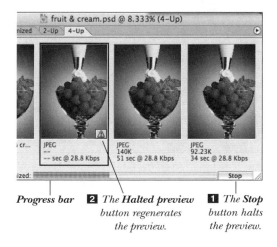

Progress bar   **2** *The **Halted preview** button regenerates the preview.*   **1** *The **Stop** button halts the preview.*

Previewing optimized files

To use the ImageReady previews:

Click the **4-Up** tab in the document window to see the original view and three previews simultaneously. ImageReady will use the current Optimize palette settings to generate the first preview (to the right of the original), and then automatically generate (autopopulate) the two other previews as variations on the current optimization settings. You can click any preview and change the Optimize palette settings for just that preview.

With **Auto Regenerate** checked on the Optimize palette menu, the Optimized preview(s) will update every time a value or setting is changed on the Optimize palette.

If you need to stop the preview from updating, click the **Stop** button in the lower right corner of the document window **1** (or uncheck the Auto Regenerate command). A **halted preview** button **2** will display in the lower right corner of any halted preview. If you click this button or change any settings on the Optimize palette, the preview will update automatically.

To switch between Photoshop and ImageReady:

Leave both Photoshop and ImageReady open so you can quickly make changes to your file in either program. To go back and forth, click the **Edit in** button 🖻🔳 on the Toolbox. The two programs will automatically close, open, and update your file when you switch between them.

If you start working on an image in Image-Ready, go to Photoshop to perform some edits, then go back to ImageReady, the Photoshop edits will be identified on the History palette in ImageReady as a single history state named **Update From Photoshop.** Similarly, Photoshop's History palette will list an **Update From ImageReady** history state when a change is made in ImageReady. Here's the good part: You can click an earlier state at any time to undo an edit made in the other program.

Because the Windows operating system uses a higher gamma value than the Macintosh operating system, the same image will appear darker in Windows than on a Mac. When creating Web graphics for cross-platform use, it's important to **preview** your image in, and adjust it for, **both platforms.**

To preview Windows and Mac gamma values:

With an optimized preview showing in ImageReady, choose View > Preview > **Standard Macintosh Color** to simulate the Mac gamma value, or **Standard Windows Color** to simulate the Windows gamma value.

Choose View > Preview > **Uncompensated Color** to preview the image without gamma compensation, or **Use Embedded Color Profile** to match the ImageReady preview (based on the display RGB) with the profile assigned to, or embedded in, the file in Photoshop. This option will be dimmed if the file lacks a profile.

You can compensate for differences in **gamma** between operating systems for an individual file.

To change the gamma for an optimized file:

1. With an optimized preview showing for an image in ImageReady, choose Image > Adjustments > **Gamma.**

2. Click **Windows to Macintosh** to change the gamma to the Mac gamma value. The image will look darker on a Mac **1**–**2**.
   or
   Click **Macintosh to Windows** to change the gamma to the Windows gamma value. The image will look lighter on a Mac **3**.

3. Click OK.

TIP You can also use the Gamma slider to make the current gamma value lighter or darker. This setting is relative, though, meaning it displays only the degree to which you're changing the gamma—not the actual setting.

1 *Click either of these buttons in the **Gamma** dialog box to preview the other platform's gamma values.*

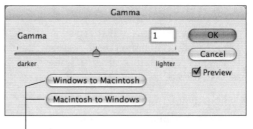

2 *An image after clicking the **Windows to Macintosh** button: The lower gamma value makes the image look darker.*

3 *After clicking the **Macintosh to Windows** button, the same image looks lighter.*

Preview Gamma; Change Gamma

Keep the code

To copy the HTML source code from ImageReady into an HTML-editing program, choose Edit > **Copy HTML Code** > **For All Slices** for the current file, then paste the source code into an HTML-editing or Web page layout program. (The source code is displayed at the bottom of the browser window **3**.)

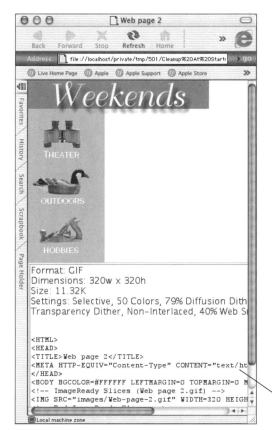

1 *Click this button to **preview** your optimized image in the default **browser**.*

2 *An image being viewed in Microsoft **Internet Explorer***

For a more definitive simulation of online viewing for an optimized image, use ImageReady's **Preview in [default browser]** feature. You can choose from any of the browsers that are currently installed in your system.

Note: This preview feature won't test the actual download time for an image over an actual Web connection, and it will display a preview for your display type only—not for any other display type. Nevertheless, it's still very useful.

To preview an optimized image in a browser on your system:

1. With an optimized image opened in ImageReady, click the **Preview in [default browser]** button on the Toolbox (Ctrl-Alt-P/Cmd-Option-P) **1**, or press and hold the button and choose a browser from the submenu.

2. The browser will launch, and the image will load into the browser window **2**. You can preview any GIF animations or rollovers that you created in ImageReady.

3. Exit/quit the browser, if desired, then click in any ImageReady palette or window to switch back to ImageReady.

   Note: Be sure to preview your final files by actually uploading them to the Web so you can see how they look on both computer platforms and, ideally, on a spectrum of display types.

TIP If your display's color depth setting is higher than 8 bits and you want to see how an image will look in an 8-bit browser, set your system to 256 colors before launching your browser. We've noted only minor differences between this method and choosing View > Preview > Browser Dither (in ImageReady).

3 *The **HTML source code** from ImageReady*

Saving files in ImageReady

To save a file in ImageReady:

Most likely the file you're working with in ImageReady will have originated in Photoshop. To save the current changes, choose File > **Save** (Ctrl-S/Cmd-S). Optimization settings will be saved, but not applied to the image.

Follow these instructions to save a file as an **optimized** file based on the current settings on the Optimize palette.

To save an optimized file in ImageReady:

1. Choose File > **Save Optimized As** (Ctrl-Alt-Shift-S/Cmd-Option-Shift-S).

2. To control how the file will be saved, choose one of the following from the **Save as Type/Format** pop-up menu :

HTML and Images to create an HTML file and save the image slices in a separate folder of files.

Images Only to save just the image slices.

HTML Only to create an HTML file without saving the optimized image files. It will have the .htm or .html extension and will be saved in the location you'll choose in step 6.

3. *Optional:* To choose additional options, choose Other from the Settings pop-up menu. The **Output Settings** dialog box opens.

To choose HTML preferences for formatting and coding, choose **HTML** from the second pop-up menu 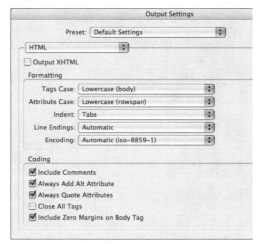. Use these options to establish consistency between the HTML generated by ImageReady and an HTML-editing application.

Click OK now, or follow the next step before clicking OK.

4. Choose **Saving Files** from the second pop-up menu, then do the following:

1 *Choose a format in the **Save Optimized As** dialog box.*

2 *The **Output Settings** dialog box, with custom settings chosen in the **HTML** panel*

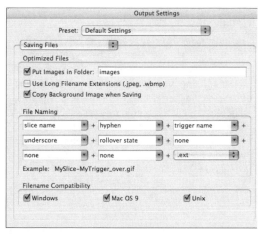

1 *Choose options for saving files in the* ***Saving Files*** *panel of the* ***Output Settings*** *dialog box.*

Metadata for a Web page

You can use the File > **File Info** dialog box **2** to modify the page title for the browser window and embed metadata and copyright information into the optimized HTML file. You can also categorize your page by using keywords (metadata) and a description (file name) to make it easier for viewers to locate it when using a Web search engine.

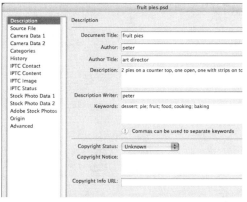

2 *Use the* ***File Info*** *dialog box to embed metadata into your Photoshop or ImageReady files.*

Check any **Optimized Files** options **1**. Enter the name of the folder you want to save the autogenerated optimized files in.

Choose **File Naming** conventions for any autogenerated files, such as slices or rollover frames, to be saved with the optimized file and used in the HTML page. Consult with your HTML specialist before making changes in these fields. If the naming convention seems confusing, leave the default settings as is.

Check any platform **Filename Compatibility** options.

5. Click OK to exit the Output Settings dialog box.

6. Type a file name, choose a location, then click Save.

TIP Use the Save As or Save Optimized As command to save a version of a file under a different name.

TIP To attach a URL or an Alt tag to an image, use the Slice palette (see pages 524 and 531).

TIP You can also open the Output Settings dialog box by choosing any option from the File > Output Settings submenu.

To update an HTML file:

If you have modified an optimized file and you want to update the HTML file that's associated with it, choose File > **Update HTML,** locate the HTML file for that image, then click Open. If an alert box appears, click Replace. Click OK when the update is finished. Any HTML code generated for the optimized file will be updated, even if the code was already copied and pasted into a larger HTML file, and even if that larger file contains tables from other image files.

Creating type

Type is created and styled in **ImageReady** using the same methods as in Photoshop, and it remains editable even after layer effects and styles are applied to it. When your file is optimized in ImageReady, the type becomes bitmapped, along with the rest of the image.

Note: Editable type in a file that's exported to the Flash (SWF) format will remain as vector shapes unless it contains any layer effects with soft outer edges, such as a Drop Shadow, Outer Glow, or Emboss.

Creating display type for Web pages

➤ All type layer attributes and anti-aliasing options are **preserved** for editable and rasterized type, whether you use Photoshop or ImageReady to edit the file.

➤ **Anti-aliasing** can be applied to type in Photoshop or ImageReady. Opinions are divided on whether anti-aliasing should be applied to small type for onscreen output; we think it looks better **without** it. Use ImageReady's preview features to decide for yourself.

➤ For type that's smaller than 18 points, **uncheck Fractional Widths** on the Character palette menu.

➤ To help make online type more legible, choose a **slightly larger** point size than you would normally use for print output.

Note: The same type size on a Web page will look as if it's a different size on a Macintosh screen than on a Windows screen due to the difference in monitor resolution between the two platforms (e.g., 72 ppi for the former, 96 ppi for the latter). Be sure to test your page(s) on both platforms.

➤ Remember to make your type colors **Web-safe** to prevent dithering. To make a color Web-safe in ImageReady, choose the Eyedropper tool (I), click a type character in an optimized preview, then shift the color to the Web palette by using the Color Table palette (see page 511).

Mixed optimization

Hybrid images that contain both continuous-tone imagery and flat-color areas (such as type) pose a special optimization challenge **1**. One solution is to use the **slicing** feature in Photoshop or ImageReady to frame off different areas of the image and apply different optimization settings to each slice (use GIF for the type slices and JPEG for the continuous-tone areas). To facilitate slicing for mixed optimization, whenever possible position the type so it doesn't overlap any continuous-tone areas. (Read more about slicing in the next section.)

1 *This image would be considered a hybrid because it contains both continuous-tone imagery and flat-color areas (type).*

1 *All three types of slices can be used in one image. Every document starts out with a default auto slice that's the size of the entire image, which has a light gray label and is numbered "01."*

Slicing

Slicing is a process by which an image is divided into distinct zones. A group of small slices downloads more quickly than a whole, large image, and each slice can be optimized using settings that are most appropriate for its contents. The browser assembles the slices into the overall image in sequence by using HTML tables and frames.

There are three types of slices, and each has its own icon **1**:

➤ Slices that are created manually by using the Slice tool are called **user slices.** These are discussed next.

➤ **Layer-based slices** (page 522) resize automatically to include all the visible pixels within the currently selected layer.

➤ Whatever's left of the image after you've created user slices and/or layer-based slices is divided automatically into **auto slices** (lighter gray label).

Although **Slices** can be created, selected, edited, and displayed in Photoshop, we prefer to use ImageReady for these tasks because it offers more options. To show the **Slice** palette in ImageReady, choose Window > **Slice** or choose the **Slice Select** tool, then click the **Bring Slice Palette Forward** button on the options bar. Or in Photoshop, choose the Slice Select tool, then click the **Set Options for Current Slice** button on the options bar to open the Slice Options dialog box.

With the **Slice tool,** you can control the slice divisions manually. And unlike auto slices, the user slices that this tool creates can be resized, repositioned, restacked, and, most important, optimized separately.

To slice an image manually:

1. Choose the **Slice** tool (K).

2. Drag diagonally across part of the image to define the first slice (**1**–**2**, next page). A label with a number will appear in the upper left corner of the slice

(Continued on the following page)

zone, and a thin highlight (frame) with resizing handles will appear around the new slice. The program will divide the rest of the image into auto slices.

3. *Optional:* Draw additional user slices with the Slice tool. Each new slice will be assigned a label and a number, and the program will continue to redivide and renumber the rest of the image into auto slices as it sees fit.

4. *Optional:* To divide a slice into smaller user slices, choose the Slice Select tool (O), 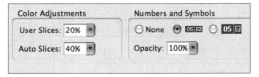 click a user slice or auto slice, choose Slices > Divide Slice, enter values, then click OK. Each new slice will be assigned a number.

TIP Selected slices display normally; unselected slices are dimmed. To control how dimmed they get, in ImageReady, go to Edit (ImageReady, in Mac) > Preferences > Slices, and in the Color Adjustments area, choose or enter User Slices and/or Auto Slices percentages .

1 *With the **Slice tool**, drag to create a slice.*

2 *A **new slice** is created.*

The borders around a **layer-based** slice automatically update whenever you transform, move, or add layer effects to a layer. Layer-based slices are especially useful when creating rollovers using effects that might enlarge a layer, such as a Drop Shadow.

To create a layer-based slice:

Click a layer on the Layers palette, then choose Layer > New **Layer Based Slice.** Mission accomplished.

3 *A portion of the **Slices** panel in the **Preferences** dialog box*

To convert an auto slice or a layer-based slice into a user slice:

1. Choose the **Slice Select** tool (O).

2. Click the slice you want to convert.

3. Choose Slices > **Promote to User Slice.**

TIP To convert an auto slice, you can also right-click/Control-click and choose Promote to User Slice.

Hide/show slice borders and labels

In ImageReady, click the **Toggle Slices Visibility** button on the Toolbox (or press Q) to hide/show slices.

Or in ImageReady or Photoshop, you can hide or show slices by choosing View > **Show** > **Slices.**

 The Toggle Slices Visibility button on the Toolbox

2 *To resize a user slice, drag a handle with the Slice Select tool.*

3 *The auto slices around the resized slice will reconfigure automatically.*

To delete slices:

1. Choose the **Slice Select** tool (O).

2. To delete one slice, click on it; to delete multiple slices, Shift-click all the slices you want to delete. Then choose **Delete Slice(s)** from the Slices menu or the Slice palette menu, or press Backspace/ Delete.
or
To delete all the slices in an image, choose Slices > **Delete All.**

If you **enlarge** a slice, it may obscure other slices behind it. The hidden slices can be removed manually, or you can ignore them for now because any overlapping or hidden slice frames (or table cells) will be eliminated automatically when you optimize the file. To see what's hidden behind a slice, you can resize or move it.

To resize user slices:

1. Choose the **Slice Select** tool (O). Slice borders will display onscreen.

2. Click the user slice you want to resize.

3. Drag a side handle to resize the slice along one axis, or drag a corner handle to resize along two axes **2**–**3**.

Delete Slices; Resize User Slices

If you attach a URL **link** to a slice on a Web page, when viewers click that slice, they'll be taken automatically to that URL address (Web page). Slices with links are usually created on prominent or conspicuous graphic elements (buttons, words, or icons) so viewers can identify them easily. In ImageReady, you can create multiple **slices** in a single image, and you can assign a different **URL** address to each slice.

To slice an image into multiple links:

1. Open or create a document that contains imagery that you want to use as links, such as buttons, thumbnails, or icons **1**. A series of links arranged in a column or row is called a navigation bar.

2. Choose the **Slice** tool (K). ✐

3. Drag diagonally to create a slice over each individual portion of the image that you want to use as a link **2**.

4. Choose the **Slice Select** tool (O). ✐

5. Click a slice. Information about the selected slice will display on the Slice palette.

6. In the **URL** field, enter the destination Web address **3**.

7. *Optional:* The **Target** field becomes available when information is entered into the URL field. Target info tells the browser which HTML frame to load the link contents into and which existing HTML frames to preserve. Press Tab to move to this area of the palette, then choose one of the following from the pop-up menu: **_blank** to have a new browser window open for the link contents; **_self** to have the new link contents load into the HTML frame for the current slice; **_parent** to have the new link contents replace the current HTML frames; or **_top** to have the new link contents load into the entire browser window (this is similar to the _parent option).

8. Repeat steps 5–7 for any other slices you want to designate as links.

Join forces

To combine multiple auto slices or user slices into one larger slice, select two or more slices, then choose Slices > **Combine Slices.** The resulting single user slice will be the size of the smallest rectangle that could surround all the selected slices.

1 *These elements will become* **links.**

2 *A* **slice** *is created for each element that is to become a* **link.**

3 *Enter the destination address (Web page) in the* **URL** *field.*

TIP If the image has only one slice (the default auto slice for the image), you can attach a link address to the entire image via the URL field on the Slice palette.

To align user slices along a common edge:

1. Choose the **Slice Select** tool (O), 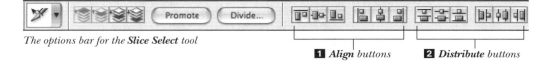 then Shift-click two or more slices.

2. Click one of the six **align** buttons on the options bar **1**. The slices will align, but not the imagery inside them.

To evenly distribute user slices along a common axis:

1. Choose the **Slice Select** tool (O), then Shift-click three or more slices.

2. Click one of the six **distribute** buttons on the options bar **2**.

*The options bar for the **Slice Select** tool*

1 *Align buttons*   **2** *Distribute buttons*

Creating image maps

An **image map** is an image that contains designated hotspots, each with its own URL link **3**. When a viewer clicks a hotspot, the browser displays the linked page. Use this method if you want to create nonrectangular hotspots, or if you'd rather export a single image file than slice and export it as multiple files.

ImageReady lets you create layer-based or tool-based image maps. **Layer-based** maps include all nontransparent pixel areas in a layer and are automatically updated when the layer is edited.

Tool-based maps are created with one of three image map tools or by converting a layer-based image map, and can be aligned to a common edge or distributed along a common axis. Also, you can duplicate the dimensions and settings of tool-based maps.

(Continued on the following page)

3 *This image, because its elements are close together, is a good candidate for encoding as an **image map**.*

To create a layer-based image map:

1. On the Layers palette, click a layer that contains transparent areas.

2. Choose Layer > **New Layer Based Image Map Area.** A rectangular image map will surround the layer's nontransparent areas.

3. On the **Image Map** palette **1**, do the following:

   Enter a **URL** address (include the "http://" prefix). A hand icon will appear to the right of the layer name on the Layers palette **2**.

   Optional: The Target field becomes available once a URL is entered. The Target info tells which HTML frame to load the link contents into and which existing HTML frames to preserve (see page 524).

   Optional: In the Alt field, enter the word or words you want displayed if the user's Web browser doesn't display images (see page 531).

   In the **Layer Based Settings** area, from the **Shape** pop-up menu, choose a shape for the hotspot (Rectangle, Circle, or Polygon).

4. *Optional:* Repeat steps 1–3 for any other layers.

TIP You can change the shape of a layer-based image map by choosing the Image Map Select tool (J), clicking the image map, then choosing from the Shape pop-up menu on the Image Map palette.

TIP When using a Polygon shape, you can adjust how tightly the image map follows the outline of the imagery via the Quality field or slider. To generate smaller HTML files, try to limit the complexity of any polygonal image maps you use.

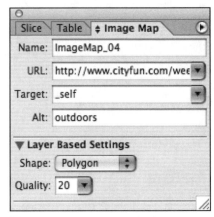

1 *On the **Image Map** palette, enter the **URL** address, and under Layer Based Settings, choose a **Shape.***

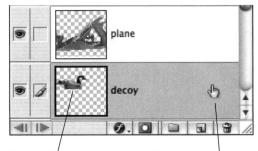

*Only visible (nontransparent) pixel areas can become **hotspots** for an image map.*

2 *Layer-based* image maps have a **hand** icon near the layer name.

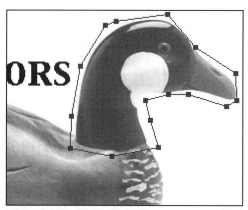

1 *Double-click to have an image map shape close automatically.*

2 *On the options bar, you can enter exact dimensions for an* **image map.**

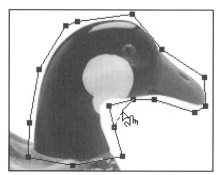

3 *You can* **resize** *a tool-based image map* **manually** *by dragging a handle.*

To create a tool-based image map:

1. Choose the **Rectangle Image Map** or **Circle Image Map** tool (P or Shift-P), then draw a rectangle or circle over an area of the image. (Shift-drag to create a square. Alt-drag/Option-drag to draw the shape from its center.)
   or
   Choose the **Polygon Image Map** tool, click a starting point, then click for each subsequent corner until you surround the desired area. Double-click anywhere, and the shape will close automatically **1**.

2. Enter a **URL** address (including the "http://" prefix) on the Image Map palette.

3. *Optional:* The Target field becomes available when you enter a URL. The Target info tells which HTML frame to load the link contents into and which existing HTML frames to preserve (see page 524).

4. *Optional:* In the Alt field, enter the word or words you want displayed if the user's Web browser doesn't display images.

5. Repeat steps 1–4 for any other image maps you want to create.

TIP To specify the exact dimensions of a rectangular or circular image map before drawing it, check Fixed Size on the options bar, then enter Width and Height or Radius values **2**.

TIP To resize a tool-based image map, click on it with the Image Map Select tool, then drag a handle **3**.

To change an image map from layer-based to tool-based:

1. Choose the **Image Map Select** tool (J), then click the layer-based image map you want to convert.

2. From the Image Map palette menu, choose **Promote Layer Based Image Map Area.**

To hide/show image maps:

To toggle between the hide and show settings for all image maps in the document, click the **Image Maps Visibility** button 👆 on the Toolbox, or press A.

or

Choose View > Show > **Image Maps.**

TIP You can change the display characteristics for image maps (such as whether the line and/or the bounding box are visible) in Edit (ImageReady, in Mac) > Preferences > Image Maps **1**.

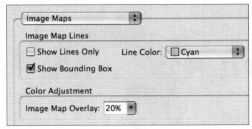

1 *The **Image Maps** panel in the Preferences dialog box in ImageReady*

To select an image map:

1. Make sure the image maps are visible, and choose the **Image Map Select** tool (J). 👆

2. Click an image map in the document window (or Shift-click to select multiple image maps).

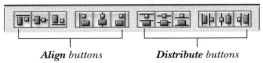

Align buttons   *Distribute buttons*

2 *Select multiple image maps, choose the **Image Map Select** tool, then click an **align** or **distribute** button on the options bar.*

To delete an image map:

1. Select an image map.

2. Press Backspace/Delete.

   or

   From the Image Map palette menu, choose **Delete Image Map Area.**

To align tool-based image maps:

1. Choose the **Image Map Select** tool (J), 👆 then Shift-click the image maps you want to align.

2. Click one of the six **align** buttons on the options bar **2**.

To distribute tool-based image maps:

1. Choose the **Image Map Select** tool, 👆 then Shift-click three or more image maps.

2. Click one of the six **distribute** buttons on the options bar **2**.

Hide/Show, Select, Delete, Align Image Maps

1 *The continuous-tone element (the plane) in this hybrid image should be optimized as a JPEG; the vector element (lightbulb) should be optimized as a GIF.*

Optimizing and linking slices

If the image you're working with is a hybrid, meaning it contains both sharp-edged elements (e.g., type or linework) and continuous-tone areas, you can draw a separate slice around each of those areas, then **optimize** each **slice** separately using a format and settings that are appropriate for its contents **1**.

To optimize an individual slice:

1. Choose the **Slice Select** tool (O).

2. Click a slice.

3. Choose **Optimize** palette settings. Use the **GIF** format to optimize sharp-edged areas, and **JPEG** for continuous-tone areas.

TIP If you select two or more slices that have different Optimize palette settings, the palette will display only the settings that the selected slices have in common. If you change any of the available settings, however, the new settings will apply to all the currently selected slices.

TIP If you later decide you want to optimize all the slices in the same way, choose the Slice Select tool, choose Select > All Slices, then choose settings on the Optimize palette. (If you choose Select > Deselect Slices, the Optimize palette will go blank.)

This technique for **copying optimization** settings is speedy and efficient.

To copy optimization settings from one slice to another:

1. Choose the **Slice Select** tool (O).

2. Click a slice that has the desired optimization settings.

3. Drag the **Droplet** button from the Optimize palette over any unselected slice. The current palette settings will be applied to that slice **2**.

2 *Drag the **Droplet** button from the **Optimize** palette onto any unselected **slice**.*

Linked slices share the same optimization settings. When optimized in the GIF format, linked slices also share the same color table and dither pattern, which helps to disguise any edge seams between slice areas.

To link slices:

1. Choose the **Slice Select** tool (O).

2. Click a slice, then Shift-click one or more additional slices **1**.

3. Right-click/Control-click and choose **Link Slices for Optimization.**
   or
   Choose Slices > **Link Slices for Optimization.**

   The linked slices will now be assigned a link icon with a unique group color **2**, which will display next to the other labels in the image and on the Web Content palette.

TIP To add a slice to a group of already linked slices, click one of the slices already in the group, Shift-click the slice you want to add, then choose Slices > Link Slices for Optimization.

To unlink slices:

To unlink one slice, click on it with the **Slice Select** tool (O), then right-click/Control-click and choose **Unlink Slice,** or choose Slices > Unlink Slice.
or
To unlink a whole group of slices, click one of the linked slices with the **Slice Select** tool, then right-click/Control-click and choose **Unlink Shared Links,** or choose Slices > Unlink Shared Links.
or
To unlink all the slices in the image, right-click/Control-click and choose **Unlink All,** or choose Slices > Unlink All.

Note: Auto slices that are created by ImageReady are already linked. If you unlink an auto slice, it becomes a user slice.

1 *Three slices are **selected**.*

2 *Linked slices have a link icon of the same color.*

Slice Sets

In ImageReady CS2, you can create **slice sets** that contain slicing for a particular layout in your image. If you create a different layout (say, when creating layer comps), you can hide the first slice set, create slices that fit the new layout, then gather the new slices into a new set. When you optimize the file, only the currently visible slice set(s) will be saved to the HTML file. To create a slice set, Shift-select existing slices on the **Web Content** palette, then click the **New Slice Set** button ⬜ on the palette **1**.

Older, nongraphic Web browsers (or any browser for which a "show pictures" preference is turned off) display only text, not graphics. In order to display an image as a generic icon with text for browsers that can't or won't display graphics, Web designers attach a unique HTML Alt tag to each graphic. Then, if the image displays in the browser only as the Alt tag text, the viewer will still be able to get to the designated site via the URL attached to the slice. Alt tags also help visually impaired people use text browsers that "speak" the link, a legal requirement for some websites in order to meet accessibility standards (see www.section508.gov for more information). Follow these instructions to attach an **Alt tag** to a **slice.**

To attach an Alt tag to a slice or to an entire image:

1. Show the **Slice** palette.

2. *Optional:* Click a slice using the Slice Select tool (O). 🔪

3. In the **Alt** field on the Slice palette, enter the word or words to be substituted for the image **2**.

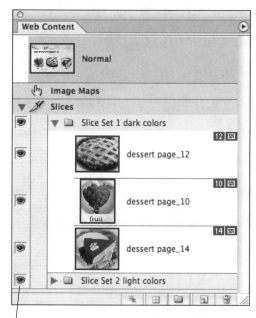

1 *Show/hide a set by clicking the Slice Visibility button.*

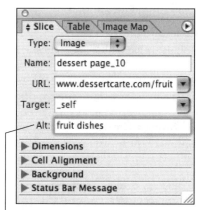

2 *In the Alt field on the Slice palette, enter the word or words to be substituted for the image, when necessary.*

Creating rollovers

Now that you understand something about slices, you're ready to create another kind of hotspot: a **rollover.** A rollover is a built-in screen event (change) that occurs when a user's mouse moves over or clicks on an area of a Web page. Rollovers are like the dynamic voice of a Web page, and are entertaining for viewers to use. Three basic types of rollovers can be created:

➤ A **change** in an image area (e.g., a color changes, a layer effect appears, an animation is triggered) **1**

➤ One image is **substituted** for another **2**

➤ Text or a **remote** graphic appears in another area of the browser window when the mouse is over a button, keyword, or icon **3**

To create a **rollover,** the first step is to divide the image into **slices.** (So go back and read the section on slices first—no cheating!) In ImageReady, rollovers are created by using the **Web Content** palette and by displaying and hiding layers on the **Layers** palette. When ImageReady previews a rollover, it turns different layers on or off, as per your built-in instructions, and onscreen, one image is substituted for another.

To create a rollover for a slice:

1. Choose the **Slice** tool (K), ✐ click a layer on the Layers palette, then marquee an area to be used for the rollover.

2. If the imagery you want to use for the rollover isn't already on its own layer, choose Select > **Create Selection from Slice,** then choose Layer > New > **Layer via Copy** (Ctrl-J/Cmd-J).
   or
   If the imagery contained in the slice is already on its own layer, press Ctrl-J/Cmd-J to **duplicate** that layer.

3. Leave both the new layer and its associated slice selected.

Three basic rollovers

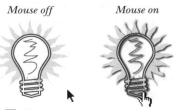

Mouse off   *Mouse on*

1 *The **image changes** (in this case, a Drop Shadow layer effect appears).*

Mouse off

Mouse on

2 *A **new image** is substituted for the current one.*

Mouse off

Mouse on

3 *Remote text (or an image) appears in another part of the browser window.*

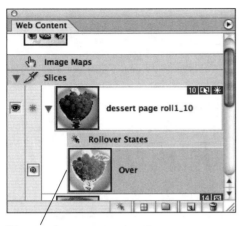

1 *A thumbnail for the new* **rollover** *appears on the palette. To change a rollover state, double-click its thumbnail...*

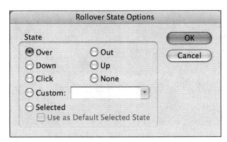

2 *...then click a* **State** *in the* **Rollover State Options** *dialog box.*

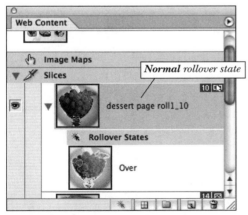

3 *We applied a filter to a duplicate layer in the same image for the* **Over** *rollover state.*

4. Display the **Web Content** palette. The currently selected slice will appear as a thumbnail on the palette.

5. Click the **Create Rollover State** button ▣ at the bottom of the palette. A rollover state will appear as a new nested thumbnail on the palette **1**.

6. *Optional:* ImageReady automatically assigns a rollover state to thumbnails in this default sequence: Over, Down, Click. If you want to override this default sequence, double-click the new rollover thumbnail. The Rollover State Options dialog box opens. Click a mouse **State** to be the trigger for the rollover that you'll create in the remaining steps **2**:

For **Over,** the user's mouse must be over the slice area but not pressed down.

For **Down,** the mouse button must be down when it's over the slice. Some Web designers like to have a special graphic appear when the button is down.

For **Click,** the mouse must be clicked (button pressed and released) when it's over the slice. When the slice is clicked, the browser tries to link to any URL that's attached to it.

Click OK.

7. **Modify** the imagery on the separate or duplicate layer (created in step 2) to make it look different from the original layer. A few suggestions: Invert the layer's color or luminosity (Image > Adjustments > Invert); apply a texture or filter to the layer **3**; change the layer's hue or saturation; or paste in new imagery (see also page 537). This won't change the imagery on the original layer.

8. On the **Web Content** palette, click the slice that contains the nested rollover state. On the Layers palette, hide the duplicate layer, and show the original layer. Next, select the rollover state on the Web Content palette, show the duplicate layer, and hide the original layer, if

(Continued on the following page)

necessary, from which the duplicate was created .

9. On the **Web Content** palette, click back and forth between the original slice thumbnail and the rollover thumbnail, and compare them in the document window. This palette tracks which layers are visible or hidden, as well as other changes on the Layers palette, as each rollover thumbnail is selected. Make sure the correct layers are visible or hidden for each rollover state.

For a more realistic preview, click the **Preview in [default browser]** button (or other icon) on the Toolbox. Or try using the preview function in Image-Ready (see page 538). Roll the mouse over or click the rollover area to see the effect.

Beware! Always take note of which thumbnail is currently selected on the Web Content palette as you modify a layer. Each thumbnail should look different from the rest. Rollover effects created by applying brush strokes, filters, transformations, or image substitutions require a separate layer for each state. To create different rollover states, you'll need to hide or show the different layers.

TIP To create a rollover using a layer effect, see page 535. To create a remote rollover, see pages 539–540.

TIP To choose a different Thumbnail Size for the Web Content palette, choose Palette Options from the palette menu.

TIP To create a rollover in which supplemental imagery is added to an existing image, create new imagery on a new layer, making sure to match the size and location of the imagery on the original layer 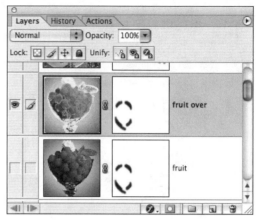–. In this case, the original layer should always remain visible.

TIP To add a third state to the selected slice, click the Create Rollover State button again on the Web Content palette.

1 *When the Over thumbnail is clicked on the Web Content palette, the layer that we applied a filter to becomes **visible** and the normal layer is **hidden**.*

2 *An image in the **Normal** rollover state*

3 *In the **Over** rollover state, a layer with a hand-drawn glow effect becomes visible below the bulb layer.*

1 *The image in the **Normal** rollover state*

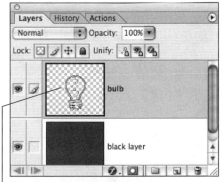

2 *Click a layer that contains some **transparent** areas.*

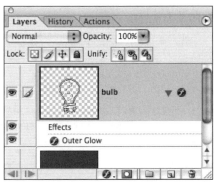

3 *When the image is in the **Over** rollover state, an Outer Glow **effect** that was added to the layer becomes visible both on the Layers palette...*

4 *...and in the image.*

A great advantage to using **layer effects** for producing **rollovers** is that because different layer effects can be applied to (or turned off for) the same layer for each rollover state, you don't have to duplicate a whole layer to achieve a visible change between states.

To create a rollover using a layer effect:

1. Choose the **Slice Select** tool, ✂ then click a slice.

2. Click the **Create Rollover State** button 🔲 at the bottom of the Web Content palette. An Over state will be created.

3. *Optional:* Double-click the new rollover thumbnail if you want to choose a different rollover state.

4. Click a layer that contains transparent areas **1**–**2**.

5. Via the Add Layer Style pop-up menu *ƒ* at the bottom of the Layers palette, choose and apply one or more effects, such as Inner Shadow to recolor the inner edges of the layer image, or Outer Glow to recolor the area behind it.

   To intensify an effect, in the Layer Style dialog box, increase the Size, Spread, Distance, Depth, Opacity, or similar setting. If you're using the Bevel and Emboss effect to make a button look convex, you could click the opposite Direction (e.g., Up or Down) to reverse the lighting direction and make the rollover version look concave. To make a button look more concave, try applying a tint at a low opacity via the Color Overlay effect.

   You can also apply effects via the Styles palette (see page 331).

6. Click OK. The layer effect will be visible on the Layers palette **3** and in the image **4** only when the rollover state thumbnail that it's assigned to is selected on the Web Content palette.

7. Preview the rollover (see page 538).

Rollover Using Layer Effect

The **Create Layer-based Rollover** button automatically makes the current layer a layer-based slice and creates a new rollover state based on that slice. *Note:* When using this method to create a rollover, the only way you can produce changes between rollover states is by adding layer effects to each rollover state.

To create a layer-based rollover:

1. Click a layer (not the Background).

2. Click the **Create Layer-based Rollover** button ![] at the bottom of the Web Content palette. A star icon ![] and an icon indicating that the slice is layer-based ![] will display next to the slice name on the Web Content palette, and an icon indicating that the layer contains a layer-based slice ![] will appear for the layer on the Layers palette.

Normally, changes made to the currently active layer affect only the current rollover state. The **Unify** buttons in ImageReady let you apply the active layer's position, visibility, style, or a combination thereof to all the states, thus unifying those attributes in an entire rollover.

Beware! Any preexisting layer style effects are deleted when you click a Unify button!

To unify layer attributes in a rollover:

1. On the Layers palette, click the layer you want to change **1**, then click one, two, or all three **Unify** buttons **2**.

2. Depending on your choice, an alert box will appear **3**, asking if you want to match the current layer's position, visibility, style, or a combination thereof with the other rollover states. Click **Match** to unify those states with any current and future changes to the selected layer (**1**, next page).

TIP To turn off a Unify command, click the layer, then click the highlighted Unify button.

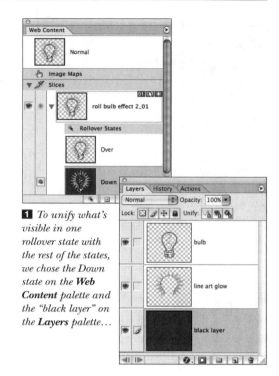

1 *To unify what's visible in one rollover state with the rest of the states, we chose the Down state on the* **Web Content** *palette and the "black layer" on the* **Layers** *palette...*

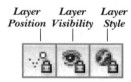

Layer Position Layer Visibility Layer Style

2 *...then we clicked a* **Unify** *button on the* **Layers** *palette.*

3 *When you click a* **Unify** *button, this alert dialog box appears.*

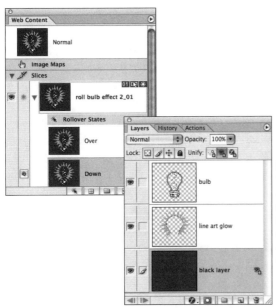

1 *Clicking the **Layer Visibility** button for the selected "black layer" on the Layers palette and then clicking Match in the alert dialog box causes that layer to become visible in all the rollover states.*

2 *The **original** button*

3 *After applying the **Radial Blur** filter*

More ideas for rollovers

The following suggestions for creating visually effective rollovers require creating a layer for the Normal state and a duplicate layer for the Over state:

To produce a rollover in which imagery enlarges and contracts, scale the duplicate layer up a bit using Edit > Transform > **Scale**, or use Filter > Blur > **Radial Blur** to stretch the shape **2**–**3**, or use Filter > Distort > **Pinch** (with a negative Amount) to bulge it out **4**.

To make a button or image area look like it's flipping, use Edit > Transform > **Flip Horizontal** or **Flip Vertical** (see the ducky on page 532).

4 *After applying the **Pinch** filter to the original image, using a negative Amount value*

(This button changes sizes for a rollover, making it a good choice for a layer-based slice. The slice will resize based on the largest area of imagery on the layer.)

Unify

You can **preview** a **rollover** within ImageReady or, if you prefer, stick with the tried-and-true Web browser-based preview. Take yer pick.

To preview a rollover in ImageReady:

1. Click the **Preview Document** button 👆 on the Toolbox (Y).

2. In the document window, roll the mouse **over** (Over), press the mouse **down** on (Down), or **click** on (Click) the area of the image that contains the rollover to see it in action. Press the mouse button down to preview a Down state. To stop the preview, click the Preview Document button again.

To preview a rollover in a Web browser:

1. Save your ImageReady file.

2. Choose a currently installed browser from the File > **Preview in** submenu.
or
Click the **Preview in [default browser]** button on the Toolbox (Ctrl-Alt-P/ Cmd-Option-P).

3. In the browser, roll the mouse **over** (Over), press the mouse **down** on (Down), or **click** on (Click) the area of the image that contains the rollover to see it in action.

Note: You won't be able to preview the Down state in any pre-4.0 browser version of Navigator or Explorer. In these earlier browsers, the mouse action opens a browser context menu instead.

1 *For this layout, we arranged small images in a column, then drew a **slice** around each image.*

2 *A **larger** version of each of the small images was imported and moved to the right side of the Web page, then a slice was drawn around that area.*

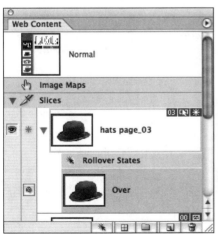

In a **remote rollover,** as the viewer moves the mouse over a keyword, image, or button, supplementary text or imagery appears onscreen; and when the mouse is moved away, the supplementary info disappears. Remote rollovers help to reduce visual clutter by reducing what the viewer initially sees on a Web page.

To create a remote rollover:

1. Create a new layer, then create supplementary image or text on that layer to become the remote image. For example, to have a larger version of an existing small photo image become the remote image, import a larger version of the photo.

2. Choose the **Move** tool (V), then drag the new remote layer imagery to the location in the image where you want it to appear.

3. Choose the **Slice** tool (K), 📏 then draw a slice around the remote layer image **1**–**2**. The slice will appear as a new thumbnail on the Web Content palette. Hide that image layer on the Layers palette.

4. On the Web Content palette, click the slice that will trigger the remote rollover, then click the **Create Rollover State** button 🔲 at the bottom of the palette. A rollover state for the "triggering" slice will appear as a nested thumbnail on the palette **3**.

5. With the new Over state on the Web Content palette still selected, drag the remote targeting icon 🔘 from the palette onto the slice containing the area

(Continued on the following page)

3 *A new **Over** state is created for the selected slice that will trigger a remote rollover. In our example, the small bowler hat triggers the rollover.*

for the hidden remote imagery; the slice border will become highlighted **1**. Make the remote image layer visible on the Layers palette. The targeted slice now has a target icon ⊕ on the Web Content palette (next to the eye icon) and in its label, and the slice that triggers the rollover has an "affects remote" icon. ⤴

6. Click the slice thumbnail the rollover state is nested below. The new remote image layer should be hidden when this slice thumbnail is clicked, and visible when the Over state slice is clicked **2**–**3**.

Be careful not to hide the layer containing the image that triggers the rollover; it should be visible for all the states.

1 *When you drag the **remote targeting** icon over the slice to be designated as a remote rollover, the slice border becomes highlighted.*

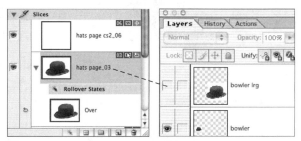

2 *When we click the **slice** that contains the nested Over state on the Web Content palette, the "bowler lrg" layer is **hidden**...*

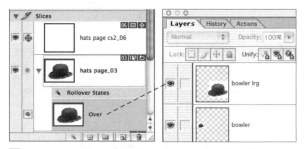

3 *...and when we click the Over state for that slice, the "bowler lrg" layer becomes visible.*

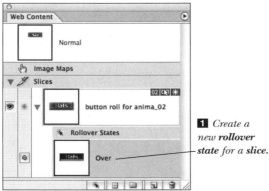

1 *Create a new **rollover** state for a **slice**.*

2 *With the rollover state selected, **add frames** to the animation via the **Animation** palette.*

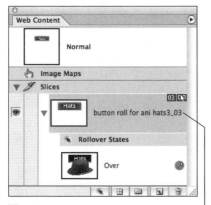

3 *When you click the original slice name…*

*…all the frames but the first one temporarily disappear from the **Animation** palette.*

4

It's easy to program a rollover state so it triggers an **animation** sequence—and it makes for a lively and entertaining Web page. To achieve this effect, you'll use your newly acquired rollover and animation skills.

To make a rollover trigger an animation:

1. In ImageReady, on the **Web Content** palette, create a new rollover state for a selected slice in an image, preferably using the Over state (see pages 532–534) **1**.

2. With the new nested rollover state selected on the Web Content palette (not the slice thumbnail), click on the **Animation** palette and create frames and events for the animation (see pages 439–442) **2**.
   or
   Copy and paste frames from another animation file by using the **Copy Frame** and **Paste Frame** commands on the Animation palette menu.

   Imagery for the animation must be positioned within the slice area for the selected slice (make sure slices are visible as you do this). Don't enlarge the slice too much—remember, the rollover is triggered when a viewer's pointer is over the slice area.

3. On the **Web Content** palette, click the name of the original slice that contains the nested rollover **3**. All the animation frames will temporarily disappear from the Animation palette **4**.

4. Save the file, and preview it via the Preview Document button or Preview in [default browser] button (see page 538).

TIP To display animation frames as nested thumbnails for a state on the Web Content palette, choose Palette Options from the palette menu, check Include Animation Frames, then click OK.

Animation Triggered by Rollover

To create a button for a Web page:

1. Click the **Normal** state on the Web Content palette.

2. Choose a shape tool: **Rectangle** ▣, **Rounded Rectangle** ▣, **Ellipse** ◯ (U or Shift-U), **Tab** ▭ (R), or **Pill** ◯ (R).

3. On the shape tool options bar, click the **Create New Shape Layer** button.▢

4. Choose a Foreground color, then drag diagonally to draw a shape **1**. The shape will appear on its own layer. Add a text layer, if desired.

1 *The new shape*

To add rollover states to a button:

To quickly apply a predefined rollover effect to a button, display the **Styles** palette, choose the **Rollover Buttons** library from the Styles palette menu, then click Replace when asked via an alert dialog box if you want to replace the current styles. Click a shape layer, then click any of the style thumbnails or names listed. The Web Content palette will display the button state for that style and will generate a layer-based slice for the shape automatically **2**. You can also drag a style name or swatch from the **Styles** palette over a shape in the document window.

TIP To add a rollover state to a button another way, choose the **Slice** tool, ✄ then draw a slice around the new button for the normal rollover state. The new slice will appear as a thumbnail on the Web Content palette. Follow steps 2–9, starting on page 532, to create a rollover state for the button.

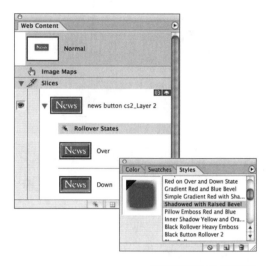

A preset style is used for the Over state

2 *We created designs for the button's **Normal**, **Over**, and **Down** states by using a preset rollover button style from the **Styles** palette (the Shadowed with Raised Bevel style from the Rollover Buttons style library).*

Rollover states can be **stored** in a **style**, along with layer effects.

To store rollover states in a style:

1. Create a **layer-based slice** for an ImageReady layer, then create a **rollover** for that layer.

2. Click the layer on the Layers palette, then click the **New Style** button ▣ on the Styles palette. The Style Options dialog box opens.

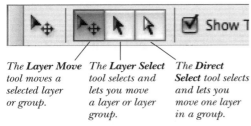

*The **Layer Move** tool moves a selected layer or group.* *The **Layer Select** tool selects and lets you move a layer or layer group.* *The **Direct Select** tool selects and lets you move one layer in a group.*

1 *Choices on the options bar when the* ***Move*** *tool is selected*

3. Enter a name and check Include Rollover States (and any other options that apply to the style you're using), then click OK.

You can drag any rollover style thumbnail (designated by the black triangle in the upper left corner) from the Styles palette over a layer name or layer shape in the document window to apply that rollover, or click the style thumbnail to apply it to the currently active layer.

Using the Move tool options

Using the three tools on the **Move** tool options bar, you can select and/or move layers in an ImageReady document window, like objects in a drawing program. As you drag a layer, blue smart guides display, which you can use to help you align objects by their edges or centers.

To use the Move tool modifiers:

1. Choose the **Move** tool (V).

2. Do any of the following:

Click the **Layer Select** tool ▸ on the options bar **1**, then click an area of the image. The layer that contains the pixels you clicked will become selected on the Layers palette.

Shift-click or drag-select multiple layer objects in the document window, then align them via the align buttons on the options bar.

NEW To create a layer group that can be moved as a unit, click the Layer Select tool, select multiple layer objects in the document (or select two or more layers on the Layers palette), then choose Layer > **Group Layers** (Ctrl-G/Cmd-G).

Move Tool Modifiers

Using Save for Web in Photoshop

The **Save for Web** dialog box in Photoshop offers most of the same optimizing features as ImageReady. If you want to learn more about the features in this dialog box, use the page numbers in the callouts in the illustration below to direct yourself to the equivalent information in this chapter about ImageReady.

To open the Save for Web dialog box in Photoshop, press **Ctrl-Alt-Shift-S/Cmd-Option-Shift-S** or choose File > Save for Web.

TIP In the Save for Web dialog box, choose Edit Output Settings from the Optimize menu to change the HTML and image output settings (see page 518).

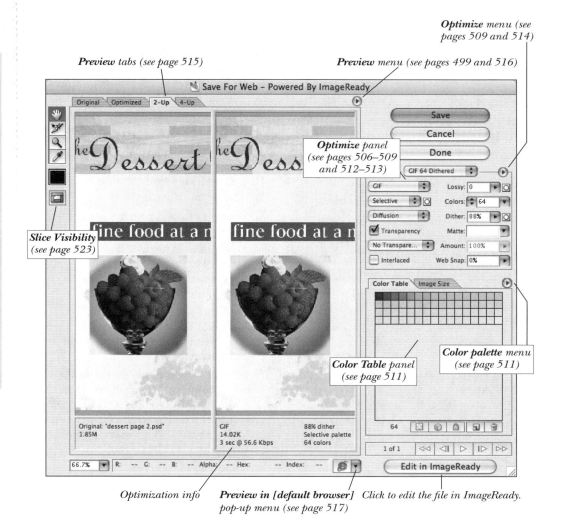

Optimize menu (see pages 509 and 514)

Preview tabs (see page 515)

Preview menu (see pages 499 and 516)

Optimize panel (see pages 506–509 and 512–513)

Slice Visibility (see page 523)

Color Table panel (see page 511)

Color palette menu (see page 511)

Optimization info

Preview in [default browser] pop-up menu (see page 517)

Click to edit the file in ImageReady.

Save for Web Dialog Box in Photoshop

SHORTCUTS A

	Windows	**Mac**
CREATING AND OPENING FILES		
New	Ctrl + N	Cmd + N
Open	Ctrl + O	Cmd + O
Browse (Go to Bridge)	Ctrl + Shift + O	Cmd + Option + O
File Info	Ctrl + Alt + Shift + I	Cmd + Option + Shift + I
Color Settings	Ctrl + Shift + K	Cmd + Shift + K
Edit in ImageReady	Ctrl + Shift + M	Cmd + Shift + M
Open As	Ctrl + Alt + O	NA
SAVING FILES		
Save	Ctrl + S	Cmd + S
Save As	Ctrl + Shift + S	Cmd + Shift + S
Save a Copy	Ctrl + Alt + S	Cmd + Option + S
Save for Web	Ctrl + Alt + Shift + S	Cmd + Option + Shift + S
Revert	F12	F12
IMAGE MENU		
Image Size	Ctrl + Alt + I	Cmd + Option + I
Canvas Size	Ctrl + Alt + C	Cmd + Option + C
CLOSING AND QUITTING		
Minimize document window	NA	Cmd + Control + M
Close	Ctrl + W	Cmd + W
Close All	Ctrl + Alt + W	Cmd + Option + W
Go to Bridge, close current document	Ctrl + Shift + W	Cmd + Shift + W
Hide Photoshop		Cmd + Control + H
Hide Others		Cmd + Option + H
Exit/Quit	Ctrl + Q or Alt + F4	Cmd + Q
GENERAL SHORTCUTS		
Accept crop, transform, or any dialog box	Enter	Return or Enter
Toggle Cancel to Reset in dialog box	Alt	Option
Cancel crop, transform, or any dialog box	Esc	Esc or Cmd + . (period)
Cancel out of pop-up slider (mouse button up)	Esc	Esc

	Windows	**Mac**
Commit edit in pop-up slider (mouse button up)	Enter	Return or Enter
Activate button in alert dialog box	First letter of button (e.g., N = No)	First letter of button (e.g., C = Cancel)
Increase value in highlighted field by 1 or .1 (or .01, in Rotate Canvas)	Up Arrow	Up Arrow
Increase value in highlighted field by 10 or 1 (or .1, in Rotate Canvas)	Shift + Up Arrow	Shift + Up Arrow
Decrease value in highlighted field by 1 (or .01, in Rotate Canvas)	Down Arrow	Down Arrow
Decrease value in highlighted field by 10 (or .1, in Rotate Canvas)	Shift + Down Arrow	Shift + Down Arrow
Adjust angle in 15° increments	Shift + drag in angle wheel	Shift + drag in angle wheel
Adjust roundness in 10% increments (brush and tool shapes)	Shift + drag points on angle wheel	Shift + drag points on angle wheel
Help	F1	Help or Cmd + /
Adobe Online	Click identifier icon on Toolbox	Click identifier icon on Toolbox

PALETTES

	Windows	**Mac**
Show/hide all palettes, Toolbox, and options bar	Tab	Tab
Show/hide all palettes	Shift + Tab	Shift + Tab
Show/hide Brushes	F5	F5
Show/hide Color	F6	F6
Show/hide Layers	F7	F7
Show/hide Info	F8	F8
Show/hide Actions	F9	Option + F9
Show options bar (if hidden)	Double-click tool, or press Enter if tool is selected	Double-click tool, or press Return or Enter if tool is selected

UNDO

	Windows	**Mac**
Undo	Ctrl + Z	Cmd + Z
Step Forward	Ctrl + Shift + Z	Cmd + Shift + Z
Step Backward	Ctrl + Alt + Z	Cmd + Option + Z
Fade	Ctrl + Shift + F	Cmd + Shift + F

CHOOSING TOOLS
Choose a tool

To cycle through tools on the same pop-out menu when Use Shift Key for Tool Switch is checked in Preferences > General, press **Shift** *plus the shortcut listed below. If this preference is off, omit Shift.*

	Windows	**Mac**
Rectangular Marquee, Elliptical Marquee (not Single Row Marquee or Single Column Marquee)	M	M
Move	V	V

	Windows	Mac
Lasso, Polygonal Lasso, Magnetic Lasso	L	L
Magic Wand	W	W
Crop	C	C
Slice, Slice Select	K	K
Spot Healing Brush, Healing Brush, Patch, Red Eye	J	J
Brush, Pencil, Color Replacement	B	B
Clone Stamp, Pattern Stamp	S	S
History Brush, Art History Brush	Y	Y
Eraser, Background Eraser, Magic Eraser	E	E
Gradient, Paint Bucket	G	G
Blur, Sharpen, Smudge	R	R
Dodge, Burn, Sponge	O	O
Path Selection, Direct Selection	A	A
Horizontal Type, Vertical Type, Horizontal Type Mask, Vertical Type Mask	T	T
Pen, Freeform Pen (not Add Anchor Point, Delete Anchor Point, or Convert Point)	P	P
Rectangle, Rounded Rectangle, Ellipse, Polygon, Line, Custom Shape	U	U
Notes, Audio Annotation	N	N
Eyedropper, Color Sampler, Measure	I	I
Hand	H	H
Zoom	Z	Z

Except for the Rectangular Marquee and Pen tools, the shortcut selects whichever tool on the pop-out menu was used last.

Toggle tools

Move tool	Ctrl	Cmd
Precise cursors	Caps Lock	Caps Lock
Brush or Pencil to Eyedropper	Alt	Option
Shapes or Line to Eyedropper	Alt	Option
Gradient or Paint Bucket to Eyedropper	Alt	Option
Blur to Sharpen; Sharpen to Blur	Alt	Option
Dodge to Burn; Burn to Dodge	Alt	Option
Hand tool	Spacebar	Spacebar
Zoom Out	Ctrl + - (minus)	Cmd + - (minus)
Zoom In	Ctrl + + (plus)	Cmd + + (plus)

	Windows	Mac
TOOL BEHAVIOR		
Tool opacity		
Change tool opacity, exposure, strength, or flow in 10% increments	Number keys (2 = 20%, 3 = 30%)	Number keys (2 = 20%, 3 = 30%)
Change tool opacity, exposure, strength, or flow in 1% increments	Number keys (2 + 3 = 23%)	Number keys (2 + 3 = 23%)
Constrain tools		
Constrain to horizontal or vertical axis (Eraser, Brush, Pencil, Blur, Sharpen, Smudge, Dodge, or Burn tool)	Shift + drag	Shift + drag
Draw, erase, etc. in straight lines (Eraser, Brush, Pencil, Blur, Sharpen, Smudge, Dodge, or Burn tool)	Shift + click	Shift + click
Constrain to 45° axis (Line, Gradients, (or Convert Point tool)	Shift + drag	Shift + drag
Move tool (V)		
Move constrained to 45°	Shift + drag	Shift + drag
Copy selection or layer	Alt + drag	Option + drag
Select topmost visible layer	Ctrl + Alt + click	Control + Option + click
Nudge layer or selection 1 pixel	Arrow keys	Arrow keys
Nudge layer or selection 10 pixels	Shift + arrow keys	Shift + arrow keys
Lasso tool (L)		
Add to selection	Shift + click, then draw	Shift + click, then draw
Delete from selection	Alt + click, then draw	Option + click, then draw
Intersect with selection	Alt + Shift + click, then draw	Option + Shift + click, then draw
Temporary Polygonal Lasso	With mouse button down, hold down Alt, then click	With mouse button down, hold down Option, then click
Polygonal Lasso tool (L)		
Add to selection	Shift + click, then draw	Shift + click, then draw
Delete from selection	Alt + click, then draw	Option + click, then draw
Intersect with selection	Alt + Shift + click, then draw	Option + Shift + click, then draw
Temporary Lasso	Alt + drag	Option + drag
Constrain to 45° while drawing	Shift + drag	Shift + drag
Magnetic Lasso tool (L)		
Add to selection	Shift + click, then draw	Shift + click, then draw
Delete from selection	Alt + click, then draw	Option + click, then draw
Intersect with selection	Alt + Shift + click, then draw	Option + Shift + click, then draw
Add point	Single click	Single click

	Windows	Mac
Remove last point	Backspace or Delete	Delete key
Close path	Double-click or Enter	Double-click or Return or Enter
Close path using straight line segment	Alt + double-click	Option + double-click
Cancel operation	Esc	Esc or Cmd + . (Period)
Temporary Lasso	Alt + drag	Option + drag
Temporary Polygonal Lasso	Alt + click	Option + click
Increase width option	] (close bracket)	] (close bracket)
Decrease width option	[(open bracket)	[(open bracket)

Crop tool (C)

Rotate crop marquee	Drag outside crop marquee	Drag outside crop marquee
Move crop marquee	Drag inside crop marquee	Drag inside crop marquee
Resize crop marquee	Drag crop handle	Drag crop handle
Maintain aspect ratio of crop box	Shift + drag handle	Shift + drag handle
Resize crop from center	Alt + drag handle	Option + drag handle
Constrain crop from center	Alt + Shift + drag handle	Option + Shift + drag handle
Apply crop	Enter	Return or Enter
Discard crop without applying	Esc	Esc

Slice tool (K)

Toggle between Slice and Slice Select tool	Ctrl	Cmd
Draw square slice	Shift + drag	Shift + drag
Draw from center outward	Alt + drag	Option + drag
Draw square slice from center outward	Alt + Shift + drag	Option + Shift + drag
Reposition slice while drawing it	Spacebar + drag	Spacebar + drag

Eraser tool (E)

Temporary Erase to History	Alt + drag	Option + drag

Smudge tool (R)

Smudge using Foreground color	Alt	Option

Burn and Dodge tools (O)

Set Range for Burn or Dodge to Shadows	Alt + Shift + S	Option + Shift + S
Set Range for Burn or Dodge to Midtones	Alt + Shift + M	Option + Shift + M
Set Range for Burn or Dodge to Highlights	Alt + Shift + H	Option + Shift + H

Sponge tool (O)

Desaturate setting	Alt + Shift + D	Option + Shift + D
Saturate setting	Alt + Shift + S	Option + Shift + S

	Windows	**Mac**
Path Selection tool (A) or Direct Selection tool (A)		
Duplicate path	Alt + drag	Option + drag
Toggle Path Selection tool	Ctrl + click	Cmd + click
Pen tool (P)		
Temporary Convert Anchor Point tool	Alt key (over anchor point)	Option key (over anchor point)
Temporary Direct Selection tool	Ctrl	Cmd
Freeform Pen tool (P) *(with Magnetic enabled on options bar)*		
Add point	Single click	Single click
Remove last point	Backspace or Delete	Delete
Close path	Double-click	Double-click
Cancel operation	Esc	Esc
Disable magnetic function temporarily	Alt + click	Option + click
Increase magnetic width	] (close bracket)	] (close bracket)
Decrease magnetic width	[(open bracket)	[(open bracket)
Eyedropper tool		
Choose Background color	Alt + click	Option + click
Toggle to Color Sampler tool	Shift	Shift
Delete sampler	Alt + Shift + click sampler	Option + Shift + click sampler
Color Sampler tool		
Delete sampler	Alt + click sampler	Option + click sampler
Measure tool		
Measure constrained to 45° axis	Shift + drag	Shift + drag
Create protractor	Alt + click end point + drag	Option + click end point + drag
Hand tool		
Temporary Zoom tool (zoom in)	Ctrl	Cmd
Toggle to zoom out	Alt	Option
Fit image on screen	Double-click Hand tool	Double-click Hand tool
Zoom tool		
Zoom out	Alt + click	Option + click
Actual pixels (100% view)	Double-click Zoom tool	Double-click Zoom tool
DISPLAY		
Change zoom levels		
Zoom in	Ctrl + Spacebar + click or drag or Ctrl + + (plus)	Cmd + Spacebar + click or drag or Cmd + + (plus)
Zoom out	Ctrl + Alt + Spacebar + click or Ctrl + - (minus)	Cmd + Option + Spacebar + click or Cmd + - (minus)
Fit on screen	Ctrl + 0	Cmd + 0

	Windows	Mac
Actual pixels	Ctrl + Alt + 0	Cmd + Option + 0
Zoom in without changing window size	Ctrl + Alt + + (plus)	Cmd + Option + + (plus)
Zoom out without changing window size	Ctrl + Alt + - (minus)	Cmd + Option + - (minus)
Keep Zoom field highlighted after changing zoom percentage	Shift + Enter	Shift + Return

Switch screen modes

Toggle Standard/Full Screen with Menu Bar/Full Screen modes	F	F
Toggle Menu Bar when in Full Screen mode with Menu Bar	Shift + F	Shift + F

Show/hide

Show/Hide Extras	Ctrl + H	Cmd + H
Show/Hide Target Path	Ctrl + Shift + H	Cmd + Shift + H
Show/Hide Rulers	Ctrl + R	Cmd + R
Show/Hide Guides	Ctrl + ; (semicolon)	Cmd + ; (semicolon)
Show/Hide Grid	Ctrl + ' (quote)	Cmd + ' (quote)

Grid and guides

Toggle Snap on/off	Ctrl + Shift + ; (semicolon)	Cmd + Shift + ; (semicolon)
Lock/Unlock Guides	Ctrl + Alt + ; (semicolon)	Option + Cmd + ; (semicolon)
Snap guide to ruler increment (View > Snap on); or to the grid (View > Show > Grid and View > Snap To > Grid on)	Shift + drag guide	Shift + drag guide
Toggle H/V orientation of guide as you create it	Alt + drag guide	Option + drag guide

NAVIGATING
Move image in window

Scroll up one screen	Page up	Page up
Scroll up 10 pixels	Shift + page up	Shift + page up
Scroll down one screen	Page down	Page down
Scroll down 10 pixels	Shift + page down	Shift + page down
Scroll left one screen	Ctrl + page up	Cmd + page up
Scroll left 10 pixels	Ctrl + Shift + page up	Cmd + Shift + page up
Scroll right one screen	Ctrl + page down	Cmd + page down
Scroll right 10 pixels	Ctrl + Shift + page down	Cmd + Shift + page down
Move view to upper left corner	Home key	Home key
Move view to lower right corner	End key	End key

	Windows	**Mac**
Navigator palette		
Scroll viewable area of image	Drag view box	Drag view box
Move view to new portion of image	Click in preview area	Click in preview area
View new portion of image	Ctrl + drag in preview area	Cmd + drag in preview area
Keep Zoom field highlighted after changing Zoom percentage	Shift + Enter	Shift + Return
SELECTIONS		
All	Ctrl + A	Cmd + A
Deselect	Ctrl + D	Cmd + D
Reselect	Ctrl + Shift + D	Cmd + Shift + D
Inverse	Ctrl + Shift + I or Shift + F7	Cmd + Shift + I or Shift + F7
Feather	Ctrl + Alt + D	Shift + F6
Nudge selection marquee 1 pixel	Arrow keys	Arrow keys
Nudge selection marquee 10 pixels	Shift + arrow keys	Shift + arrow keys
CLIPBOARD		
Cut	Ctrl + X	Cmd + X
Copy	Ctrl + C	Cmd + C
Copy Merged	Ctrl + Shift + C	Cmd + Shift + C
Paste	Ctrl + V	Cmd + V
Paste Into	Ctrl + Shift + V	Cmd + Shift + V
LAYERS		
Create a layer		
New layer	Ctrl + Shift + N	Cmd + Shift + N
New layer without dialog box	Ctrl + Alt + Shift + N	Cmd + Option + Shift + N
Layer via Copy	Ctrl + J	Cmd + J
Layer via Cut	Ctrl + Shift + J	Cmd + Shift + J
Layers palette		
Show/hide layer	Click in eye column	Click in eye column
Toggle show all layers/show just this layer	Alt + click in eye column	Option + click in eye column
Show/hide multiple layers	Click + drag thru eye column	Click + drag thru eye column
Select all layers (but not Background)	Ctrl + Alt + A	Cmd + Option + A
Link selected layers	Click Link Layers button	Click Link Layers button
Create new, empty layer	Click New Layer button	Click New Layer button
Create new, empty layer with Layer Options dialog box	Alt + click New Layer button	Option + click New Layer button
Duplicate layer(s)	Drag layer(s) to New Layer button	Drag layer(s) to New Layer button

	Windows	Mac
Delete layer using warning alert	Click Delete Layer button	Click Delete Layer button
Delete layer, bypass warning alert	Alt + click Delete Layer button	Option + click Delete Layer button
Change layer opacity in 10% increments	Number keys (2 = 20%, 3 = 30%)	Number keys (2 = 20%, 3 = 30%)
Change layer opacity in 1% increments	Number keys (2 + 3 = 23%)	Number keys (2 + 3 = 23%)
Toggle last chosen Lock button for selected layer on/off	/ (forward slash)	/ (forward slash)
Load layer pixels as selection	Ctrl + click layer thumbnail	Cmd + click layer thumbnail
Add layer pixels to selection	Ctrl + Shift + click layer thumbnail	Cmd + Shift + click layer thumbnail
Subtract layer pixels from selection	Ctrl + Alt + click layer thumbnail	Cmd + Option + click layer thumbnail
Intersect layer pixels with selection	Ctrl + Alt + Shift + click layer thumbnail	Cmd + Option + Shift + click layer thumbnail
Select top layer	Alt + . (period)	Option + . (period)
Select next layer (up)	Alt +]	Option+]
Select previous layer (down)	Alt + [	Option + [
Select bottom layer	Alt + , (comma)	Option + , (comma)
Edit layer style	Double-click layer	Double-click layer

Merge layers

	Windows	Mac
Merge selected layer(s) or Merge Down one layer	Ctrl + E	Cmd + E
Merge Visible	Ctrl + Shift + E	Cmd + Shift + E
Merge a copy of pixels in current layer into layer below	Ctrl + Alt + E	Cmd + Option + E
Merge a copy of all visible layers into a new layer	Ctrl + Alt + Shift + E	Cmd + Option + Shift + E
Merge a copy of current layer into layer below	Ctrl + Alt + E	Cmd + Option + E

Arrange layers

	Windows	Mac
Bring to Front	Ctrl + Shift +]	Cmd + Shift +]
Bring Forward	Ctrl +]	Cmd +]
Send to Back	Ctrl + Shift + [	Cmd + Shift + [
Send Backward	Ctrl + [	Cmd + [
Group layers	Ctrl + G	Cmd + G
Ungroup layers	Ctrl + Shift + G	Cmd + Shift + G

Clipping masks

	Windows	Mac
Create/Release Clipping Mask	Ctrl + Alt + G	Cmd + Option + G

	Windows	**Mac**
BLENDING MODES		
Blending modes for layers, and for tools that have a Mode pop-up menu		
Set layer to next blend mode on menu	Shift + + (plus)	Shift + + (plus)
Set layer to previous blend mode on menu	Shift + - (minus)	Shift + - (minus)
Normal	Alt + Shift + N	Option + Shift + N
Dissolve	Alt + Shift + I	Option + Shift + I
Darken	Alt + Shift + K	Option + Shift + K
Multiply	Alt + Shift + M	Option + Shift + M
Color Burn	Alt + Shift + B	Option + Shift + B
Linear Burn	Alt + Shift + A	Option + Shift + A
Lighten	Alt + Shift + G	Option + Shift + G
Screen	Alt + Shift + S	Option + Shift + S
Color Dodge	Alt + Shift + D	Option + Shift + D
Linear Dodge	Alt + Shift + W	Option + Shift + W
Overlay	Alt + Shift + O	Option + Shift + O
Soft Light	Alt + Shift + F	Option + Shift + F
Hard Light	Alt + Shift + H	Option + Shift + H
Vivid Light	Alt + Shift + V	Option + Shift + V
Linear Light	Alt + Shift + J	Option + Shift + J
Pin Light	Alt + Shift + Z	Option + Shift + Z
Hard Mix	Alt + Shift + L	Option + Shift + L
Difference	Alt + Shift + E	Option + Shift + E
Exclusion	Alt + Shift + X	Option + Shift + X
Hue	Alt + Shift + U	Option + Shift + U
Saturation	Alt + Shift + T	Option + Shift + T
Color	Alt + Shift + C	Option + Shift + C
Luminosity	Alt + Shift + Y	Option + Shift + Y
Behind (Brush tool only)	Alt + Shift + Q	Option + Shift + Q
HISTORY		
History palette		
Step forward	Shift + Ctrl + Z	Cmd + Shift + Z
Step backward	Alt + Ctrl + Z	Cmd + Option + Z
Duplicate history state (other than current)	Alt + click state	Option + click state

	Windows	Mac
ADJUSTMENT COMMANDS		
Levels	Ctrl + L	Cmd + L
Auto Levels	Ctrl + Shift + L	Cmd + Shift + L
Auto Contrast	Ctrl + Alt + Shift + L	Cmd + Option + Shift + L
Auto Color	Ctrl + Shift + B	Cmd + Shift + B
Color Balance	Ctrl + B	Cmd + B
Desaturate	Ctrl + Shift + U	Cmd + Shift + U
Invert	Ctrl + I	Cmd + I
Reopen dialog box		
Levels, with last settings	Ctrl + Alt + L	Cmd + Option + L
Curves, with last settings	Ctrl + Alt + M	Cmd + Option + M
Color Balance, with last settings	Ctrl + Alt + B	Cmd + Option + B
Hue/Saturation, with last settings	Ctrl + Alt + U	Cmd + Option + U
Hue/Saturation dialog box		
Hue/Saturation	Ctrl + U	Cmd + U
Move color range to new location	Click in image	Click in image
Add to range	Shift + click/drag in image	Shift + click/drag in image
Subtract from range	Alt + click/drag in image	Option + click/drag in image
Edit individual colors	Ctrl + 1–6	Cmd + 1–6
Edit master	Ctrl + ~ (tilde)	Cmd + ~ (tilde)
Slide color spectrum	Ctrl + drag on ramp	Cmd + drag on ramp
Curves dialog box		
Curves	Ctrl + M	Cmd + M
Add a new point on the curve	Ctrl + click in image	Cmd + click in image
Add a new point on each individual color curve	Ctrl + Shift + click	Cmd + Shift + click
Move curve point	Arrow keys	Arrow keys
Move curve point by larger increment	Shift + Arrow keys	Shift + Arrow keys
Add point	Click in grid	Click in grid
Delete point	Ctrl + click point	Cmd + click point
Deselect all points	Ctrl + D	Cmd + D
Toggle grid between fine and coarse	Alt + click grid	Option + click grid
Select next control point	Ctrl + Tab	Ctrl + Tab
Select previous control point	Ctrl + Shift + Tab	Ctrl + Shift + Tab
Select multiple control points	Shift + click	Shift + click

	Windows	Mac
COLORS		
Color buttons on Toolbox		
Swap Foreground/Background colors	x	x
Reset to default colors	D	D
Proofing colors		
Proof Colors	Ctrl + Y	Cmd + Y
Gamut Warning	Ctrl + Shift + Y	Cmd + Shift + Y
Fill		
Open Fill dialog box	Shift + F5 or Shift + Backspace	Shift + F5 or Shift + Delete
Fill with Foreground color	Alt + Backspace/Delete	Option + Delete
Fill with Foreground color, Preserve Transparency on	Shift + Alt + Backspace/Delete	Shift + Option + Delete
Fill with Background color	Ctrl + Backspace/Delete	Cmd + Delete
Fill with Background color, Preserve Transparency on	Shift + Ctrl + Backspace/Delete	Shift + Cmd + Delete
Fill from previous history state	Ctrl + Alt + Backspace	Cmd + Option + Delete
Color palette		
Cycle through color bars	Shift + click color bar	Shift + click color bar
Swatches palette		
Add Foreground color as a new swatch	Click blank area	Click blank area
Choose swatch as Foreground color	Click swatch	Click swatch
Choose swatch as Background color	Ctrl + click swatch	Cmd + click swatch
Delete swatch	Alt + click swatch	Option + click swatch
BRUSHES		
Select first brush	Shift + , (comma)	Shift + , (comma)
Select previous brush	, (comma)	, (comma)
Select next brush	. (period)	. (period)
Select last brush	Shift + . (period)	Shift + . (period)
Increase brush size	]	]
Decrease brush size	[	[
Increase brush hardness	Shift +]	Shift +]
Decrease brush hardness	Shift + [	Shift + [
Delete brush preset	Alt + click	Option + click
Rename brush preset	Double-click stroke thumbnail	Double-click stroke thumbnail
Constrain to horizontal or vertical axis	Shift + drag	Shift + drag
Paint straight lines	Shift + click	Shift + click

	Windows	Mac
QUICK MASK		
Toggle Quick Mask mode on/off	Q	Q
Invert Quick Mask	Alt + click Quick Mask button	Option + click Quick Mask button
Open Quick Mask Options dialog box	Double-click Quick Mask button	Double-click Quick Mask button
LAYER MASKS		
Create layer mask with Reveal All/ Reveal Selection	Click Add Layer Mask button	Click Add Layer Mask button
Create layer mask with Hide All/ Hide Selection	Alt + click Add Layer Mask button	Option + click Add Layer Mask button
Link/unlink layer and layer mask	Click Link Layer Mask icon	Click Link Layer Mask icon
Open Layer Mask Display Options dialog box	Double-click layer mask thumbnail (on the right)	Double-click layer mask thumbnail (on the right)
Toggle layer mask on/off	Shift + click layer mask thumbnail (on the right)	Shift + click layer mask thumbnail (on the right)
Toggle rubylith mode on/off	\	\
Toggle viewing layer mask/composite	Alt + click layer mask thumbnail	Option + click layer mask thumbnail
Toggle create clipping mask on/off	Alt + click line between layers	Option + click line between layers
CHANNELS PALETTE		
Target individual channels	Ctrl + 1–9	Cmd + 1–9
Target composite channel	Ctrl + ~ (tilde)	Cmd + ~ (tilde)
Show or hide channel	Click in eye column	Click in eye column
Create new channel	Click New Channel button	Click New Channel button
Create new channel via New Channel dialog box	Alt + click New Channel button	Option + click New Channel button
Duplicate channel	Drag channel to New Channel button	Drag channel to New Channel button
Delete channel using warning alert	Click Delete Channel button	Click Delete Channel button
Delete channel, bypassing warning alert	Alt + click Delete Channel button	Option + click Delete Channel button
Create new spot color channel	Ctrl + click New Channel button	Cmd + click New Channel button
Create new channel from selection	Click Save Selection as Channel button	Click Save Selection as Channel button
Create new channel from selection, with New Channel dialog box	Alt + click Save Selection as Channel button	Option + click Save Selection as Channel button
Load channel as selection	Click Load Channel as Selection button or Ctrl + click channel thumbnail	Click Load Channel as Selection button or Cmd + click channel thumbnail

	Windows	**Mac**
Add channel to selection	Shift + click Load Channel as Selection button or Ctrl + Shift + click channel thumbnail	Shift + click Load Channel as Selection button or Cmd + Shift + click channel thumbnail
Subtract channel from selection	Alt + click Load Channel as Selection button or Ctrl + Alt + click channel thumbnail	Option + click Load Channel as Selection button or Cmd + Option + click channel thumbnail
Intersect channel with selection	Alt + Shift + click Load Channel as Selection button or Ctrl + Alt + Shift + click thumbnail	Option + Shift + click Load Channel as Selection button or Cmd + Option + Shift + click thumbnail

LAYER EFFECTS

Toggle show/hide effect	Show/hide layer effect eye icon	Show/hide layer effect eye icon
Edit layer effect options	Double-click layer effect name	Double-click layer effect name

In Layer Style dialog box

Drop Shadow	Ctrl + 1	Cmd + 1
Inner Shadow	Ctrl + 2	Cmd + 2
Outer Glow	Ctrl + 3	Cmd + 3
Inner Glow	Ctrl + 4	Cmd + 4
Bevel and Emboss	Ctrl + 5	Cmd + 5
Satin	Ctrl + 6	Cmd + 6
Color Overlay	Ctrl + 7	Cmd + 7
Gradient Overlay	Ctrl + 8	Cmd + 8
Pattern Overlay	Ctrl + 9	Cmd + 9
Stroke	Ctrl + 0	Cmd + 0

PATHS

Paths palette

Create new path	Click New Path button	Click New Path button
Create new path, with New Path dialog box	Alt + click New Path button	Option + click New Path button
Duplicate path	Drag path to New Path button	Drag path to New Path button
Delete selected path using warning alert	Click Delete Path button	Click Delete Path button
Delete selected path, bypass warning alert	Alt + click Delete Path button or Alt + drag path to Delete Path button	Option + click Delete Path button or Option + drag path to Delete Path button
Save work path into path item	Drag Work Path onto New Path button	Drag Work Path onto New Path button

Paths and selections

Convert selection into work path	Click Make Work Path button	Click Make Work Path button
Convert selection into work path, with Make Work Path dialog box	Alt + click Make Work Path button	Option + click Make Work Path button

	Windows	**Mac**
Convert path into selection	Click Load Path as Selection button	Click Load Path as Selection button
Convert path into selection, with Make Selection dialog box	Alt + click Load Path as Selection button	Option + click Load Path as Selection button
Load path as selection	Ctrl + click path thumbnail	Cmd + click path thumbnail
Add path to selection	Ctrl + Shift + click path thumbnail	Cmd + Shift + click path thumbnail
Subtract path from selection	Ctrl + Alt + click path thumbnail	Cmd + Option + click path thumbnail
Intersect path with selection	Ctrl + Alt + Shift + click thumbnail	Cmd + Option + Shift + click thumbnail

Stroke/fill path

	Windows	**Mac**
Stroke path with Foreground color	Click Stroke Path with Brush button	Click Stroke Path with Brush button
Stroke path with Stroke Path dialog box	Alt + click Stroke Path button	Option + click Stroke Path button
Fill path with Foreground color	Click Fill Path with Foreground Color button	Click Fill Path with Foreground Color button
Fill path using Fill Path dialog box	Alt + click Fill Path with Foreground Color button	Option + click Fill Path with Foreground Color button

TRANSFORM

	Windows	**Mac**
Transform Again	Ctrl + Shift + T	Cmd + Shift + T
Transform Again, with duplication	Ctrl + Alt + Shift + T	Cmd + Option + Shift + T

Free Transform

	Windows	**Mac**
Free Transform	Ctrl + T	Cmd + T
Free Transform, with duplication	Ctrl + Alt + T	Cmd + Option + T
Transform, constrain proportions	Shift + drag handle	Shift + drag handle
Transform from center	Alt + drag handle	Option + drag handle
Transform from center, constrain proportions	Alt + Shift + drag handle	Option + Shift + drag handle
Constrain rotation of a selection to 15° increments	Shift + drag	Shift + drag
Distort	Ctrl + drag handle	Cmd + drag handle
Skew	Ctrl + Shift + drag side handle	Cmd + Shift + drag side handle

TYPE
Type tools

	Windows	**Mac**
Designate type origin	Click or click + drag	Click or click + drag
Set paragraph text box size via a dialog box	Alt + click with a type tool	Option + click with a type tool
Re-edit existing type	Click type in image or double-click type thumbnail	Click type in image or double-click type thumbnail

559

SHORTCUTS

	Windows	**Mac**
Reposition type while typing	Ctrl + drag type in image	Cmd + drag type in image
Bold	Ctrl + Shift + B	Cmd + Shift + B
Italic	Ctrl + Shift + I	Cmd + Shift + I
All Caps	Ctrl + Shift + K	Cmd + Shift + K
Small Caps	Ctrl + Shift + H	Cmd + Shift + H
Superscript	Ctrl + Shift + + (plus)	Cmd + Shift + + (plus)
Subscript	Ctrl + Shift + Alt + + (plus)	Cmd + Shift + Control + + (plus)
Underline	Ctrl + Shift + U	Cmd + Shift + U
Strikethrough	Ctrl + Shift + /	Cmd + Shift + /

Alignment

Left (or Top for vertical type)	Ctrl + Shift + L	Cmd + Shift + L
Center	Ctrl + Shift + C	Cmd + Shift + C
Right (or Bottom for vertical type)	Ctrl + Shift + R	Cmd + Shift + R

Size

Increase point size by 2 pts.	Ctrl + Shift + >	Cmd + Shift + >
Decrease point size by 2 pts.	Ctrl + Shift + <	Cmd + Shift + <
100% Horizontal or Vertical Scale	Ctrl + Shift + X	Cmd + Shift + X

Leading

Increase leading by 2 pts.	Alt + Down Arrow	Option + Down Arrow
Increase leading by 10 pts.	Ctrl + Alt + Down Arrow	Cmd + Option + Down Arrow
Decrease leading by 2 pts.	Alt + Up Arrow	Option + Up Arrow
Decrease leading by 10 pts.	Ctrl + Alt + Up Arrow	Cmd + Option + Up Arrow

Justification

Justify paragraph, left-align last line	Ctrl + Shift + J	Cmd + Shift + J
Justify paragraph, force last line	Ctrl + Shift + F	Cmd + Shift + F

Hyphenation

Toggle paragraph hyphenation on/off	Ctrl + Alt + Shift + H	Cmd + Option + Shift + H
Toggle single/every-line composer	Ctrl + Alt + Shift + T	Cmd + Option + Shift + T

Kerning/tracking

Increase kern/track 20/1000 em space	Alt + Right Arrow	Option + Right Arrow
Increase kern/track 100/1000 em space	Ctrl + Alt + Right Arrow	Cmd + Option + Right Arrow
Decrease kern/track 20/1000 em space	Alt + Left Arrow	Option + Left Arrow
Decrease kern/track 100/1000 em space	Ctrl + Alt + Left Arrow	Cmd + Option + Left Arrow
Set tracking to 0	Ctrl + Shift + Q	Cmd + Control + Shift + Q

	Windows	Mac
Baseline shift		
Increase baseline shift by 2 pts.	Alt + Shift + Up Arrow	Option + Shift + Up Arrow
Increase baseline shift by 10 pts.	Ctrl + Alt + Shift + Up Arrow	Cmd + Option + Shift + Up Arrow
Decrease baseline shift by 2 pts.	Alt + Shift + Down Arrow	Option + Shift + Down Arrow
Decrease baseline shift by 10 pts.	Ctrl + Alt + Shift + Down Arrow	Cmd + Option + Shift + Down Arrow
Move insertion point		
Move to the right one character	Right Arrow	Right Arrow
Move to the left one character	Left Arrow	Left Arrow
Move up one line	Up Arrow	Up Arrow
Move down one line	Down Arrow	Down Arrow
Move to the right one word	Ctrl + Right Arrow	Cmd + Right Arrow
Move to the left one word	Ctrl + Left Arrow	Cmd + Left Arrow
Select		
Select word	Double-click	Double-click
Select one character to the right	Shift + Right Arrow	Shift + Right Arrow
Select one character to the left	Shift + Left Arrow	Shift + Left Arrow
Select one word to the right	Ctrl + Shift + Right Arrow	Cmd + Shift + Right Arrow
Select one word to the left	Ctrl + Shift + Left Arrow	Cmd + Shift + Left Arrow
Select one line	Triple-click	Triple-click
Select one line above	Shift + Up Arrow	Shift + Up Arrow
Select one line below	Shift + Down Arrow	Shift + Down Arrow
Select one paragraph	Quadruple-click	Quadruple-click
Select all characters	Ctrl + A	Cmd + A
Select characters from insertion point	Shift + click	Shift + click
Horizontal Type Mask and Vertical Type Mask tools		
Add to selection	Shift + click, then draw	Shift + click, then draw
Designate type origin	Click + drag	Click + drag
FILTERS		
Reapply last filter using same settings	Ctrl + F	Cmd + F
Open last filter dialog box	Ctrl + Alt + F	Cmd + Option + F
Extract	Ctrl + Alt + X	Cmd + Option + X
Liquify	Ctrl + Shift + X	Cmd + Shift + X
Pattern Maker	Ctrl + Alt + Shift + X	Cmd + Option + Shift + X
Vanishing Point	Ctrl + Alt + V	Cmd + Option + V

	Windows	Mac
Render > Lighting Effects dialog box		
Clone light in preview area	Alt + drag light	Option + drag light
Adjust light footprint without changing angle	Shift + drag handle	Shift + drag handle
Adjust light angle without changing footprint	Ctrl + drag handle	Cmd + drag handle
PRINTING FILES		
Page Setup	Ctrl + Shift + P	Cmd + Shift + P
Print with Preview	Ctrl + Alt + P	Cmd + Option + P
Print	Ctrl + P	Cmd + P
Print One Copy	Ctrl + Alt + Shift + P	Cmd + Option + Shift + P
PREFERENCES		
General	Ctrl + K	Cmd + K
In Preferences dialog box		
File Handling	Ctrl + 2	Cmd + 2
Display & Cursors	Ctrl + 3	Cmd + 3
Transparency & Gamut	Ctrl + 4	Cmd + 4
Units & Rulers	Ctrl + 5	Cmd + 5
Guides, Grid & Slices	Ctrl + 6	Cmd + 6
Plug-Ins & Scratch Disks	Ctrl + 7	Cmd + 7
Memory & Image Cache	Ctrl + 8	Cmd + 8
Type	Ctrl + 9	Cmd + 9
KEYBOARD SHORTCUTS		
Keyboard Shortcuts dialog box	Ctrl + Alt + Shift + K	Cmd + Option + Shift + K
Menus Shortcuts dialog box	Ctrl + Alt + Shift + M	Cmd + Option + Shift + M
BRIDGE		
Browse (Go to Bridge, from Photoshop)	Ctrl + Shift + O	Cmd + Option + O
Go to Bridge, close current document	Ctrl + Shift + W	Cmd + Shift + W
New window	Ctrl + N	Cmd + N
New folder	Ctrl + Shift + N	Cmd + Shift + N
Open	Ctrl + O	Cmd + O
Open in Camera Raw	Ctrl + R	Cmd + R
Eject	NA	Cmd + E
Close window	Ctrl + W	Cmd + W
Move to Recycle Bin/Trash	Ctrl + Delete	Cmd + Delete
Return to Photoshop, from Bridge	Ctrl + Alt + O	Cmd + Option + O

	Windows	Mac
File Info	Ctrl + Alt + Shift + I	Cmd + Option + Shift + I
Versions	Ctrl + Alt + Shift + V	Cmd + Option + Shift + V
Select All	Ctrl + A	Cmd + A
Select Labeled	Ctrl + Alt + L	Cmd + Option + L
Select Unlabeled	Ctrl + Alt + Shift + L	Cmd + Option + Shift + L
Invert selection	Ctrl + Shift + I	Cmd + Shift + I
Deselect All	Ctrl + Shift + A	Cmd + Shift + A
Find	Ctrl + F	Cmd + F
Copy Camera Raw Settings	Ctrl + Alt + C	Cmd + Option + C
Paste Camera Raw Settings	Ctrl + Alt + V	Cmd + Option + V
Rotate 90° CW	Ctrl +]	Cmd +]
Rotate 90° CCW	Ctrl + [	Cmd + [
Batch Rename	Ctrl + Shift + R	Cmd + Shift + R
Toggle between Compact and Full modes	Ctrl + Enter	Cmd + Return
Show Thumbnail only	Ctrl + T	Cmd + T
Refresh	F5	F5
Reset to default workspace	Ctrl + F1	Cmd + F1
Lightbox	Ctrl + F2	Cmd + F2
File Navigator	Ctrl + F3	Cmd + F3
Metadata Focus	Ctrl + F4	Cmd + F4
Filmstrip Focus	Ctrl + F5	Cmd + F5

Bridge slideshow

	Windows	Mac
Slide Show	Ctrl + L	Cmd + L
Show/Hide Slideshow Commands	H	H
Exit Slideshow	Esc	Esc
Play/Pause	Spacebar	Spacebar
Loop on/off	L	L
Window mode on/off	W	W
Change caption mode	C	C
Change display mode	D	D
Increase/decrease slide duration	S or Shift + S	S or Shift + S
Previous page	Left Arrow	Left Arrow
Next page	Right Arrow	Right Arrow
Previous document	Ctrl + Left Arrow	Cmd + Left Arrow

	Windows	Mac
Next document	Ctrl + Right Arrow	Cmd + Right Arrow
Rotate 90° CCW	[	[
Rotate 90° CW	]	]
Set rating	1–5	1–5
Set label	6–9	6–9
Decrease rating	, (comma)	, (comma)
Increase rating	. (period)	. (period)
Clear rating	0	0
Toggle rating	' (apostrophe)	' (apostrophe)

Bridge Version Cue

Synchronize	Ctrl + Shift + B	Cmd + Shift + B
Mark in Use	Ctrl + Shift + M	Cmd + Shift + M
Save a Version	Ctrl + Shift + V	Cmd + Shift + V
Make Alternates	Ctrl + Shift + G	Cmd + Shift + G

Bridge labels

No Rating	Ctrl + 0	Cmd + 0
Rating * (one star)	Ctrl + 1	Cmd + 1
Rating ** (two stars)	Ctrl + 2	Cmd + 2
Rating *** (three stars)	Ctrl + 3	Cmd + 3
Rating **** (four stars)	Ctrl + 4	Cmd + 4
Rating ***** (five stars)	Ctrl + 5	Cmd + 5
Decrease rating	Ctrl + , (comma)	Cmd + , (comma)
Increase rating	Ctrl + . (period)	Cmd + . (period)
Label Red	Ctrl + 6	Cmd + 6
Label Yellow	Ctrl + 7	Cmd + 7
Label Green	Ctrl + 8	Cmd + 8
Label Blue	Ctrl + 9	Cmd + 9

Index

Index

Index

Index